# True Names

# True Names

## Vergil and the Alexandrian Tradition of Etymological Wordplay

James J. O'Hara

New and Expanded Edition

*Ann Arbor*
The University of Michigan Press

First paperback edition 2017

Published in the United States of America by
The University of Michigan Press
Manufactured in the United States of America
♾ Printed on acid-free paper

2020 2019 2018 2017 4 3 2

*A CIP catalog record for this book is available from the British Library.*



Library of Congress Cataloging-in-Publication Data

O'Hara, James J., 1959–
True names : Vergil and the Alexandrian tradition of etymological wordplay / James J. O'Hara.
p. cm.
Includes bibliographical references and index.
ISBN 0-472-10660-0 (hardcover : alk. paper)
1. Virgil—Style. 2. Greek poetry, Hellenistic—Egypt—Alexandria—History and criticism. 3. Virgil—Knowledge—Language and languages. 4. Alexandria (Egypt)—Intellectual life. 5. Latin poetry—Greek influences. 6. Latin language—Etymology. 7. Names in literature. 8. Rome—In literature. 9. Rhetoric, Ancient. 10. Play on words. I. Title.
PA6932.04 1996
873'.01—dc20 96-4240
CIP

ISBN 978-0-472-03687-5 (pbk.)

# Preface

Scholars ancient and modern have long noted Vergil's poetic use of etymological wordplay: the different ways in which his texts refer to, allude to, or exploit for poetic reasons the origins or etymological connotations of Latin words. In recent years, interest in such wordplay in Greek and Roman poetry has grown rapidly, and lies near the heart of contemporary scholarship's growing concern with the learned aspects of Vergilian poetry and its relationship to the poetics of third-century B.C. Alexandria. Recognizing and understanding etymological wordplay has considerable consequences for the study of Vergil's style, his place in the literary traditions of ancient Greece and Rome, and for the interpretation of numerous passages in the *Aeneid, Eclogues,* and *Georgics.* This book offers a richly annotated, reasonably comprehensive collection of examples of etymological wordplay in Vergil, prefaced by an extensive introduction on both pre-Vergilian and Vergilian etymologizing. I'd like to think it will have a place on the bookshelf of anyone trying to read, teach, or write about Vergil, and that it may be of some use to anyone interested in Greek and Latin literature, because the phenomenon of etymological wordplay is so extensive and important in so many ancient authors.

The goal of the introduction is to familiarize all readers, both specialists and those who have never considered the topic before, with ancient etymological wordplay, and with Vergil's particular and extensive use of it. Three sections of the introduction cover etymological thinking and wordplay before Vergil, typical features of Vergilian etymological wordplay, and the poetic function of Vergilian etymologizing. The first discusses Homer and other archaic poets, Greek tragedy and philosophy (including the pre-Socratics, Plato's *Cratylus,* and the Stoics), the influential and sometimes neglected Alexandrian scholar-poets, and scholars and poets at Rome (including Ennius, Lucretius, Cicero, and Varro). As my subtitle indicates, Alexandrian poetry will be a special focus of attention, and I believe my introduction offers the most extensive survey of Alexandrian etymological wordplay now available, in part because earlier surveys of Greek etymologizing tended to be scornful of the Alexandrians. The second part of the introduction analyzes the form and style of Vergilian wordplay, with extensive examples and convenient "features lists" of such things as "suppression" of one of the words involved in etymologizing; wordplay that frames lines or that comes at the start or finish of successive lines; "signposts" that call attention to wordplay; glosses of names of gods, mortals, or places; and wordplay that alludes to etymologizing in earlier poets. The third section of the introduction discusses how etymologizing serves Vergil's poetic goals, in effect explaining the role of origins of words in Vergil's poems about the origins and essential characteristics of the Roman people. A fourth brief section of the introduction describes the catalogue.

Brief description of the catalogue, which in my view is the more important and more useful part of the book, may also be useful here. The catalogue quotes each Vergilian passage, then explains the wordplay or possible wordplay, weighing the factors that should go into the difficult task of distinguishing genuine from doubtful instances of etymologizing. For uncertain examples a question mark appears at the start of the entry. (For additional examples of names that are glossed, the catalogue contains asterisks that refer you to the appendix.) I then quote passages from ancient grammarians and poets who mention or allude to the same or similar etymologies; these are crucial both for understanding whether Vergil is etymologizing, and how his wordplay fits into what I call the Alexandrian tradition. Bibliographical references (available in such quantities on this topic nowhere else) are provided for most examples, but many entries in the catalogue describe examples of learned wordplay not noticed before. To make consultation easy, extensive cross-references direct the reader to other sections of the book relevant for understanding each example: both other catalogue entries and the numbered sections of the introduction. At all times, I have given the information in the form that I myself would have found most useful; I have tried to make the book "user-friendly."

One goal of the book is to present in a convenient format a large amount of information useful for understanding Vergil, but I have also tried to offer extensive analysis of the data I provide. The goal of both the introduction's discussion of ancient and Vergilian theory and practice, and each entry in the catalogue, is to help modern readers see more of what ancient readers did, or to increase readers' "competence" in recognizing and appreciating Vergilian etymologizing. Some may read the book only in chunks or by consulting specific entries in the catalogue while reading, teaching, or writing, but those who read the catalogue straight through should be able to perceive a running argument about what is and is not characteristic of Vergilian etymologizing. We can never read exactly as the ancients did and should not be embarrassed about bringing modern perspectives and tastes to any ancient text, but what can be recovered about ancient traditions of poetic etymological wordplay should lead to greater enjoyment, understanding, and appreciation of Vergil's accomplishment and significance. I particularly hope that *True Names* will be useful to those trying to write books narrowly focused on questions of interpretation, like my earlier *Death and the Optimistic Prophecy in Vergil's Aeneid* (Princeton, 1990). I have written this book partly because it would have been extremely helpful to me if such a book as this had existed when I was working on that study. In addition to the interpretive material I frequently offer here, I hope and expect that others will use *True Names* to open up new ways of looking at the passages I treat, many of which will never have occurred to me.

In putting the final touches on the manuscript I am aware of its inadequacies and limitations, and of how an ideal book on the topic "would require an ideal author, with a range of competence beyond anything to which the present author may lay claim" (to borrow from the preface of a recent book I admire). This has turned out to be a larger and longer project than I envisioned when I first began working on this topic a little over a decade ago, but it is easy now to think of ways the project could have been larger and its gestation period longer: a more compulsively thorough search for Greek sources, and for more suggestions in Medieval, Renaissance, or early modern authors; more detailed and elaborate description of the flow of influence from earlier authors, particularly the Alexandrians, through Vergil, and then into the authors after Vergil (about whose "commentary" on Vergilian etymologizing I have only made brief suggestions); a more exhaustive search for modern bibliography; and finally more extensive tracing and holistic analysis of the interpretive consequences of what I have learned about this poet's etymological wordplay. But it has seemed best not to have exaggerated ideas about what one scholar and one study can accomplish, and so to stop here and make what contribution I can.

Warmest thanks go to those who have read a daunting manuscript and made invaluable comments: Robert Maltby, Jim McKeown, and Mark Petrini, each of whom read two drafts with great care, patience, and insight and discussed etymologizing with me at great length; Garth Tissol, who made valuable comments about both Alexandrian poetry and early modern Vergilian scholarship; John Miller, who offered exacting and learned comments about the whole manuscript; my colleague Michael Roberts, for helpful comments both on my introduction and in response to numerous queries; and David Ross, who made his usual concise and incisive comments on a draft of my manuscript, but whose greatest contribution to this project was in teaching me about Vergil and Vergilian etymological wordplay over a decade ago.

For helpful comments or criticism, oral or written, on drafts of articles, on grant applications related to this project, or simply in conversations or correspondence about etymological wordplay (which not all of them may remember), I thank Joe Farrell, Jim Zetzel, Ward Briggs, Nicholas Horsfall, Richard Hunter, David Konstan, Stephen Wheeler, Peter Bing, Stephen Hinds, Richard Thomas, and Cliff Weber.

For dependable work in checking the numerous quotations, and with the other duties of a research assistant, I thank Wesleyan students Curtis Nelson '95, Marissa Damon '92, and Lisa Taylor '94.

For grants to aid in my research, I thank both Wesleyan University and the Department of Classical Studies.

For allowing me to be a visiting fellow and to have access to computing and library facilities during the spring 1990 sabbatical most crucial to my work on this project, I thank Elaine Fantham and the Department of Classics at Princeton University. Thanks also go to the members of Professor Fantham's *Georgics* seminar for helpful comments on a paper I delivered to them.

For an invitation to give my first paper on etymologizing and for letting me call it "Carl Yastrzemski and the Study of Etymological Wordplay in Vergil," I thank Joe Farrell.

For the kind of prompt and professional service that made it possible to carry out a project like this at a "little university," I thank the late Steve Lebergott and the staff of Interlibrary Loan at Wesleyan. For access to the one book no one would send me, I thank Harvard University's Houghton Rare Book Room.

For deft handling of a difficult manuscript and for helpful comments drawing on her skills as both editor and classicist, I thank Ellen Bauerle of the University of Michigan Press. Thanks too to Nancy Vlahakis for overseeing the copyediting and final revisions of the manuscript.

For unflagging support during all the phases and moods of this long project, I thank Diane Juffras.

# Contents

# Key to Abbreviations, and Dates of Sources

The following list should make clear all abbreviations, including those that specify editions. I also give the date of the author by century. Citations by author's name alone refer to the first work listed; e.g. Isid. = Isidore *Etymologiae*.

A.: see Vergil
Accius (ii–i B.C.)
Aelius Stilo (ii–i B.C.)
Aeschylus (vi–v B.C.)
  *Ag.: Agamemnon*
  *PV: Prometheus Vinctus*
  *Sept.: Septem contra Thebas*
  *Suppl.: Supplices*
Ammianus Marcellinus (iv A.D.)
  *Res Gestae*
*Anth. Pal.: Anthologia Palatina*
Apollodorus of Athens (ii B.C.)
Apollodorus mythographus (i A.D.?)
  *Bibliotheca*
Apollonius of Rhodes (iii B.C.)
  *Arg.: Argonautica*
Apuleius (ii A.D.)
  *Met.: Metamorphoses*
  *Mund.: de Mundo*
Aratus (iv–iii B.C.)
  *Phaen.: Phaenomena*
  *Progn.: Prognostica*
Aristaenetus (v A.D.)
  *Ep.: Epistulae*
Aristophanes (v–iv B.C.)
  *Ach.: Acharnenses*
Aristotle (iv B.C.)
  *Gen. An.: de Generatione Animalium*
  *Poet.: Poetica*
  *Pol.: Politica*
  *Rhet.: Rhetorica*
  *Top.: Topica*
[Aristotle]
  *Mund.: De Mundo*
Athenaeus (ii–iii A.D.)
  *Deipnosophistae*
Augustine (iv–v A.D.)
  *Civ.: de Civitate Dei*
  *Dialect.: de Dialectica*
Aulus Gellius (ii A.D.)
  *Noctes Atticae*
[Aurelius Victor, Sextus] (v–vi A.D.?)
  *Orig.: Origo Gentis Romanae*
Beda (vii–viii A.D.) (cited from *Gramm. Lat.*)
  *de Orthographia*
Brev. Exp.: *Brevis Expositio Vergilii Georgicorum*
*CIL: Corpus Inscriptionum Latinarum*
Caesar, C. Iulius (i B.C.)
  *Civ.: Bellum Civile*
Callimachus (iii B.C.) (Pfeiffer except where Hollis or *SH* specified)
  *Aet.: Aetia*
  *Epig.: Epigrammata*
  *Hec.: Hecale*
  *Hymn* 1 = *Hymnus in Jovem*
  *Hymn* 2 = *Hymnus in Apollinem*

*Hymn* 3 = *Hymnus in Dianam*
*Hymn* 4 = *Hymnus in Delum*
*Hymn* 5 = *Lavacrum Palladis*
*Iam.*: *Iambi*
Cassiodorus (vi A.D.)
*in Psalm.*: *Expositio in Psalmos*
Cato (iii–ii B.C.)
*Agr.*: *de Agri Cultura*
*Orig.*: *Origines*
Catullus (i B.C.)
Charisius (iv A.D.)
*Gram.*: *Ars Grammatica*
Chrysippus (iii B.C.)
Cicero (i B.C.)
*Acad.*: *Academicae Quaestiones*
*ad Att.*: *Epistulae ad Atticum*
*ad Fam.*: *Epistulae ad Familiares*
*Amic.*: *de Amicitia*
*Arat.*: *Aratea* (Soubiran)
*Balb.*: *Pro Balbo*
*Cat.*: *In Catilinam*
*Cluent.*: *Pro Cluentio*
*de Orat.*: *de Oratore*
*Div.*: *de Divinatione*
*Fin.*: *de Finibus*
*Hort.*: *Hortensius*
*Leg.*: *de Legibus*
*ND*: *de Natura Deorum*
*Off.*: *de Officiis*
*Progn.*: *Prognostica* (Soubiran)
*Rep.*: *de Republica*
*Sen.*: *de Senectute*
*Tusc.*: *Tusculanae Disputationes*
Cinna (i B.C.)
Claudian (iv–v A.D.)
*de Rapt. Pros.*: *de Raptu Proserpinae*
Columella (i A.D.)
*de Re Rustica*
Comment. Luc.: *Lucani Commenta Bernensia*
Cornutus (i A.D.)
*de Natura Deorum*
Curtius Rufus, Quintus (i A.D.)
*Historiae Alexandri Magni*
D.H.: Dionysius of Halicarnassus (i B.C.)
*Antiquitates Romanae*
Diodorus Siculus (i B.C.)
*Bibliotheca Historica*
Diogenes Laertius (iii A.D.)
*Vitae Philosophorum*
Diomedes (iv A.D.) (cited from *Gramm. Lat.*)
*Ars Grammatica*
Donatus, Aelius (iv A.D.)
on Ter. *Andr.*: *Commentum Terenti Andriae*
E.: see Vergil
Empedocles (Diels–Kranz) (v B.C.)
Ennius (iii–ii B.C.)
*Alex.*: *Alexander*
*Ann.*: *Annales* (Skutsch)
*Trag.*: *Tragedies* (Jocelyn; cf. too *SRP*)
*Var.*: *Varia* (Vahlen)
Epicurus (iv–iii B.C.)
Eratosthenes (Powell) (iii B.C.)
*Etym. Gen.*: *Etymologicum Genuinum* (ix A.D.?)
*Etym. Gud.*: *Etymologicum Gudianum* (xi–xii A.D.?)
*Etym. Mag.*: *Etymologicum Magnum* (xii A.D.?)
Euphorion (iii B.C.) (Powell)
Euripides (v B.C.)
*Alc.*: *Alcestis*
*And.*: *Andromache*
*Bacch.*: *Bacchae*
*Hel.*: *Helena*
*IT*: *Iphigenia Taurica*
*Phoen.*: *Phoenissae*
*Tro.*: *Troades*
Eustathius (xii A.D.)
*Commentarii ad Homeri Iliadem*
*EV*: *Enciclopedia Virgiliana* (Della Corte)
Festus, Sextus Pompeius (ii A.D.) (Lindsay)
*de Verborum Significatione*
*Epitoma Verri Flacci*
*FGrH*: *Fragmente der griechischen Historiker* (Jacoby)
fr.: fragment
Fulgentius (v–vi A.D.)

*Myth.*: *Mythologiae*
G.: see Vergil
Gloss. (Goetz): *Corpus Glossarium Latinorum* (Goetz)
*Gramm. Lat.*: *Grammatici Latini* (Keil)
*GRF*: *Grammaticae Romanae Fragmenta* (Funaioli)
Hesiod (viii B.C.?)
*Cat.*: *Catalogue of Women* (Merkelbach–West)
*Op.*: *Opera et Dies*
*Th.*: *Theogonia*
Hieronymus (Jerome) (iv–v A.D.)
*ad Galat.*: *Commentarius in epistulam Paulinam ad Galatas*
*Vulg. Gen.*: *Vulgate Genesis*
Homer (viii B.C.?)
*Il.*: *Iliad*
*Od.*: *Odyssey*
*Hom. Hymn*: *Homeric Hymn* (most viii–vi B.C.?)
*Hom. Hymn Ap.*: *Homeric Hymn to Apollo*
*Hom. Hymn Aphr.*: *Homeric Hymn to Aphrodite*
Horace (i B.C.)
*Ars.*: *Ars Poetica*
*C.*: *Carmina*
*Epist.*: *Epistulae*
*HRR*: *Historicorum Romanorum Reliquiae* (Peter)
Hyginus (ii A.D.?)
*Astr.*: *Astronomica*
*Fab.*: *Fabulae*
*Il.*: see Homer
Isidorus (vii A.D.)
*Etymologiae* = *Origines*
*Diff.*: *Differentiae*
*in Deut.*: *Quaestiones in Deuteronomium*
Iustinus (iii A.D.?)
*Epitoma Historiarum Philippicarum Pompei Trogi*
Juvenal (i–ii A.D.)
L&S: Lewis & Short, *A Latin Dictionary*
Lactantius (iii–iv A.D.)
*Inst.*: *Divinae Institutiones*
*Opif.*: *de Opificio Dei*
Leonidas (i A.D.)
Livius Andronicus (iii B.C.)
Livy (i B.C.– i A.D.)
*Ab Urbe Condita*
*Fragmenta* (Weissenborn–Müller)
*Periochae*
Longus (ii–iii A.D.?)
*Daphnis and Chloe*
LSJ: Liddell/Scott/Jones, *A Greek-English Lexicon*
Lucan (i A.D.)
*Bellum Civile* or *Pharsalia*
Lucretius (i B.C.)
*de Rerum Natura*
Lycophron (iii B.C.?)
*Alex.*: *Alexandra*
Lydus, Ioannes (vi A.D.)
*Mens.*: *de Mensibus*
*Mag.*: *de Magistratibus Populi Romani*
Macrobius (iv A.D.)
*Saturnalia*
Marius Victorinus (iv A.D.) (cited from *Gramm. Lat.*)
*Ars Grammatica*
Martial (i A.D.)
*Epigrammata*
Menander Rhetor (iii A.D.)
Menophilus Damascenus (B.C.?)
Milton, John (xvii A.D.)
*PL*: *Paradise Lost*
Moschus (ii B.C.)
*Eur.*: *Europa*
Naevius (iii B.C.)
Nepos, Cornelius (i B.C.)
*Att.*: *Atticus*
Nicander (ii B.C.) (Gow–Scholfield)
*Alex.*: *Alexipharmaca*
*Geo.*: *Georgica*
*Ther.*: *Theriaca*
Nigidius Figulus (i B.C.)
Non.: Nonius Marcellus (iv A.D.)
*de Compendiosa Doctrina* (Lindsay)
Nonnus (iv–v A.D.?)

*Dionysiaca*
OCD: *Oxford Classical Dictionary*
*Od.*: see Homer
OLD: *Oxford Latin Dictionary*
*Origen (ii–iii* A.D.)
*Contra Cels.: Contra Celsum*
Ovid (i B.C.– 1 A.D.)
*Am.: Amores*
*Ars: Ars Amatoria*
*F.: Fasti*
*Her.: Heroides*
*Med. Fac.: Medicamina Faciei*
*Met.: Metamorphoses*
*Pont.: Epistulae ex Ponto*
*Tr.: Tristia*
Pacuvius (ii B.C.)
*Paraphrasis Dionysii Periegetou* (?; Dion. = ii A.D.)
Paul.-Fest.= Paulus, *Epitoma Festi* (viii A.D.) (Lindsay)
Pausanias (ii A.D.)
*Graeciae Descriptio*
Persius (i A.D.)
*Satirae*
Petronius (i A.D.)
*BC: Bellum Civile*
*Sat.: Satyricon*
Pindar (v B.C.) (Snell-Mahler)
*I.: Isthmian Odes; fragments*
*O.: Olympian Odes*
*P.: Pythian Odes*
Plato (v–iv B.C.)
*Crat.: Cratylus*
*Gorg.: Gorgias*
*Phaedr.: Phaedrus*
*Rep.: Respublica*
*Symp.: Symposium*
Plautus (iii–ii B.C.)
*Amph.: Amphitruo*
*Bacch.: Bacchides*
*Cist.: Cistellaria*
*Curc.: Curculio*
*Men.: Menaechmi*
*Pers.: Persa*
*Pseud.: Pseudolus*
*Stich.: Stichus*
*Trin.: Trinummus*
*Truc.: Truculentus*
Pliny (i A.D.)
*NH: Naturalis Historia*
Plutarch (i–ii A.D.)
*Rom.: Romulus*
[Plutarch] (?; Plut. = i–ii A.D.)
*de Fluv.: de Fluviis*
Pollianus (ii A.D.?)
Pomponius Mela (i A.D.)
*de Chorographia*
Porphyry (iii A.D.)
Priscian (vi A.D.) (cited from *Gramm. Lat.*)
*Institutio de Arte Grammatica*
[Prob.] E., G.: *Probi qui dicitur commentarius in Vergilii bucolica et georgica*
Propertius (i B.C.)
*Elegiae*
Prudentius (iv A.D.)
*Peristeph.: Peristephanon*
Quadrigarius, Q. Claudius (i B.C.)
Quintilian (i A.D.)
*Institutio Oratoria*
Rabirius (i B.C.–i A.D.)
*RE:* Pauly–Wissowa–Kroll, *Real-Encyclopädie der classischen Altertumswissenschaft*
*Rhet. Her.:* [Cic.] *Rhetorica ad Herennium* (i B.C.)
Rhianus (iii B.C.) (Powell)
Sallust (i B.C.)
*Cat.: Bellum Catilinae* or *de Catilinae Coniuratione*
*Hist.: Historiae*
*Iug.: Bellum Iugurthinum*
Schol.: Scholiast or scholia
Schol. Bern.: *Scholia Bernensia ad Vergili Bucolica atque Georgica*
Schol. Germ. Bas.: *Scholia Basileensia ad Germanici Caesaris Aratea*
Schol. Veron.: *Scholia Veronensia in Vergilii Bucolica Georgica Aeneiden*
Seneca (i A.D.)
*Med.: Medea*
*NQ: Naturales Quaestiones*

Servius (iv–v A.D.)
Servius Auctus = Servius Danielus
*SH*: *Supplementum Hellenisticum* (Lloyd-Jones/Parsons)
Silius Italicus (i A.D.)
*Punica*
Simmias of Rhodes (Powell) (iii B.C.)
Sinnius Capito (i B.C.)
Solinus (ii–iii A.D.)
*Collectanea Rerum Memorabilium*
Sophocles (v B.C.)
*Aj.*: *Ajax*
*OC*: *Oedipus Coloneus*
*OT*: *Oedipus Tyrannus*
*Phil.*: *Philoctetes*
*SRP*: *Scaenica Romanorum poiesis fragmenta* (Ribbeck)
Statius (i A.D.)
*Ach.*: *Achilleis*
*Theb.*: *Thebais*
Stephanus Byzantinus (v A.D.?)
Stobaeus, Ioannes (v A.D.)
*Eclog.*: *Eclogae*
Strabo (i B.C.)
*Geographica*
Suetonius (i–ii A.D.)
*Aug.*: *Divus Augustus*
*de Poet.*: *de Poetis*
*Gramm.*: *de Grammaticis*
*Iul.*: *Divus Iulius*
*Lus. Puer.*: *de Lusibus Puerorum*
*Vita Verg.*: *Vita Vergili*
*Suida* (x A.D.)
*Lexicon*
*SVF*: H. von Arnim *Stoicorum Veterum Fragmenta*
*TGF*: *Tragicorum Graecorum Fragmenta* (Nauck)
*TLL*: *Thesaurus Linguae Latinae*
Terence (ii B.C.)
*Andr.*: *Andria*
*Eun.*: *Eunuchus*
*Hec.*: *Hecyra*
test.: fragment consisting solely of *testimonium*
Theocritus (iii B.C.)
*Idylls*
Thucydides (v B.C.)
*Historiae*
Tibullus (i B.C.)
*Elegiae*
Timaeus (iv–iii B.C.)
Tzetzes, Johannes (xii A.D.)
Valerius Aedituus (ii–i B.C.)
Valerius Flaccus (i A.D.)
*Argonautica*
Varro (i B.C.)
*Gen. Pop. Rom.*: *de Gente Populi Romani*
*LL*: *de Lingua Latina*
*RR*: *de Re Rustica*
Varro Atacinus (i B.C.)
*Arg.*: *Argonautae*
Velleius Paterculus (i A.D.)
*Historiae*
Vergil (i B.C.)
A.: *Aeneid*
E.: *Eclogues*
G.: *Georgics*
[Vergil] (i A.D.?)
*Mor.*: *Moretum*
Verrius Flaccus (i B.C.–i A.D.)
*de Significatu Verborum*
*Vulg. Gen.*: see Hieronymus
Xenophon (iv B.C.)
*Symp.*: *Symposium*

# Introduction to the New and Expanded Edition

This new introduction[1] reflects on the wide scholarly response to the first edition of the book. There are new examples and bibliographic entries in this edition; the remaining pages are the same as they were in 1996.

This introduction will mainly be about the work of others, but first things first: I think I've figured out one example of etymological wordplay that I could not understand twenty years ago. In the first edition I spent over a page talking about *Aen.* 6.441 *Lugentes campi; sic illos nomine dicunt*, which I described as "a puzzle I cannot quite solve, but I can outline the interesting problem." The key is that "*nomine dicunt* looks like an etymological signpost," which is to say the kind of naming construction that often points to etymological wordplay in Vergil and other Greek and Roman authors.[2] At that time it was "not clear exactly what kind of etymologizing might be involved." But I think I have it now: the name *Lugentes campi* and the etymological signpost point to the genre of love elegy (and related erotic poetry), through the common etymology that connects Greek and Latin words for elegy with mourning, as if from Greek ἒ ἒ λέγειν ("to say ah, ah") or ἔλεος ("pity"). It is possible that not everyone will believe this suggestion right away; I will discuss this example in more detail in an article soon, but I present much of the evidence here. Explicit references to the etymology come from either a little later (Ovid *Amores* 3.9.3–4) or from much later,[3] but the sheer number of these, and other pieces of evidence, have led scholars to assume widespread knowledge of the derivation,[4] probably dating back to fifth-century Athens.[5] Vergil is not referring narrowly to the poetry of Gallus, Propertius, and Tibullus, for the particular women in the *Lugentes campi* do not figure prominently in their texts. Rather he alludes more broadly to erotic poetry and its tensions with epic, since in the Augustan period elegy often is representative of all poetry about love.[6] The etymology helps set up the introduction to Dido's appearance in the underworld, which both stresses the threat that erotic concerns pose for the epic mission and calls back to the reader's mind the generic tensions of book 4.[7]

The rest of this new introduction, as noted above, will be mainly about the work of others in the years since *True Names* appeared. Much good work was already being done in the years leading up to 1996, so the book did not cause, but helped promote and facilitate, interest in the study of etymological wordplay in Vergil and related authors. The last two parts of this introduction will offer a spare list of new suggestions or information about etymologizing in Vergil, and then new bibliographical items. The bibliography will no doubt be incomplete, but it does offer some value. I tried especially hard to find new work on Vergil, even going so far as to e-mail my preliminary bibliography to some two dozen scholars, to ask what I had missed, and I received a number of helpful replies. I also offer some citations on authors other than Vergil, but these are likely to be extremely incomplete.

In the '90s I put considerable effort into trying to figure out whether my idea, or someone else's, about etymological wordplay in a particular passage reflected something that was really there, that readers would have been able and likely to notice, or instead something that we were imagining, and "foisting" on the poet. Many writing soon after me pushed the envelope for creative engagement further than I had, some in ways that I like (especially Hinds 2006), some in ways that still make me skeptical. I used asterisks to mark examples where I was doubtful, and to see commentators like Nicholas Horsfall or others like Shelton (2013) questioning any particular asterisk—questioning my hesitation—is perfectly fine with me. My other work, especially O'Hara (2007), has grown friendlier to indeterminacy and uncertainty.

Some of the most interesting work in fact has focused on the interpretive implications of presenting multiple names, etymologies, or aetiologies. Bleisch (1998), for example, says that "Vergil's etymological wordplay" on the *Arae* "in *Aeneid* 1.108–10 reveals the relationship between words and their meanings to be shifting and unstable." By giving or alluding to both Italian and Greek names in this passage, "Vergil deliberately destabilizes the focalization and the national identity of both narrator and audience; odd, to say the least, at this juncture in the Roman national epic."[8] In both O'Hara (1996a) and below at pp. 101–2, 209–10, I noted that Ovid in the *Fasti* calls attention to Vergil's two incompatible explanations for the name Lupercal, one dating to Evander's time, one to the Romulus and Remus story. What I did not point out then (but am doing now in some work in progress on *Aeneid* 8) is how the conflicting explanations call into question the truth of each, and point to the contingent and unreliable nature of stories of early Roman history.[9]

Still, I think that my asking, for any particular example, whether "I am not simply foisting etymologies on the helpless poet" (p. 6) was and remains valuable. With new suggestions, I sometimes find myself skeptical, generally when I think the poet is not being asked to do enough work. It is good that more and more scholars have called attention to the likelihood that Roman readers actively looked for wordplay. But I still like to have the poet put ink on the page that calls attention to the etymologizing. I am particularly skeptical of claims that the poet is etymologizing when only one word is involved in the supposed wordplay: I like to see the word being etymologized either used or alluded to (in suppressed wordplay, pp. 79–82), and then at least one other element calling attention to the wordplay. One-word wordplay seems implausible, like the sound of one hand clapping.

I did not originate the idea, but gave credence to the claim that differences in the quantity of the vowels in the key syllables of two words do not prevent etymological wordplay between them (pp. 61–62). But the claim sometimes made that quantity is irrelevant I think goes too far: my position is still that quantity is one of several factors that can make words look similar or different. Differences in quantity are only a minor factor, but they are a factor.

One of the most useful parts of the book has apparently been my listing of "typical features" of etymological wordplay (pp. 57–102), which others have often used in finding or describing new examples. Francis Cairns made similar suggestions in an article about Tibullus in 1996, all compatible, I think, with mine: where I say "signpost," he says "marker." Michalopoulos' monograph on Ovid's *Metamorphoses* (2001, 1–12) also discusses "classification," "markers," and "features" of etymological wordplay, and Grewing (1998) on Martial is also strong on the typical features of etymologizing.[10]

As my book was appearing, I had the pleasure of speaking on etymologizing at Cairns' Leeds Latin Seminar. My paper, on Callimachus and Vergil, became O'Hara (2001); among the other papers were Günther (1998) and Hinds (2006). My complementary paper on Ovid became O'Hara (1996a), and has been reprinted in a collection. Among general discussions of etymologizing some of the most valuable have been Cairns (1996), Hinds (2006), Bleisch (1998a), Peraki-Kyriakidou (2002), Nifadopoulos (2003a), Shelton (2014), Bishop (2016), and several sections of Horsfall (2016), and, on wordplay and play more broadly, Katz (2009) and Katz (2013), and Habinek (2009). Several volumes of essays on etymologizing or wordplay have appeared, usually following conferences: Nifadopulos (2003), Booth and Maltby (2006), which I reviewed, and Kwapisz, Petrain, and Szymański (2013).

Etymological wordplay has always been mentioned in Vergilian commentaries, and this continues in those written after *True Names*: Horsfall's several commentaries, Tarrant (2012), and the Focus-Hackett school commentaries being produced by a team that includes me: cf. Ganiban (2012),

O'Hara (2011). The same is true of commentaries on other poets, especially Ovid, Horace, and Tibullus; I generally do not list these in the new bibliography unless they are especially noteworthy for etymologizing, since anyone reading this book will be able to find commentaries easily enough. The commentaries of Horsfall on *Aeneid* 2, 3, 6, 7, and 11 are too rich in their discussions of etymologizing for me to cite all his relevant notes; he often provides further information on examples I discuss, and occasionally says that I am wrong, or on the other hand was wrong to be hesitant. I do mention below several times where Horsfall has material I missed.

Two works must be mentioned that have too many examples for me to include them in my new list below. Paschalis (1997) offers a book-length study of etymologizing with respect to names in the *Aeneid*, using a more creative method than mine, and offering so many examples that I cannot list them here, though his study has, alas, no index. In the bibliography I list reviewers of both his book and mine after the entries for our books. Ahl's (2007) translation of the *Aeneid* has over a hundred pages of notes, and many of them deal with etymologizing, other types of punning, and even anagrams, and he tries to reproduce some of the punning in his translation. Someone who wants to know what has been suggested for any passage should check my original text, my new list, Horsfall's commentaries, and Paschalis and Ahl.

Mention should be made of the superior tools now available for the study of etymological wordplay. Everyone knows that searching texts online or on a device has become much easier. I did have the advantage of Robert Maltby's 1991 *Lexicon of Ancient Latin Etymologies*, as well as the indices to Hartmut Erbse's *Iliad* scholia (1966–88, still not fully exploited, I think). Claudio Marangoni and then Neil Adkin in a series of articles have offered supplements to Maltby, each including more source authors. There have been books on Isidore and two ambitious full translations. Robert Kaster's great new Loeb of Macrobius has three columns in the index s.v. "etymology." A new edition of Fulgentius (whose etymologies I snarkily dismissed in my second footnote, but they have been used with profit by some scholars) is forthcoming. Juan Luis De la Cerda's invaluable early-seventeenth-commentary is still difficult to access, but less so than before, as Joseph Farrell has made a PDF available at upenn.edu. Casali (2008a) discusses both de la Cerda in general and some etymologizing in his commentary that I missed (I did look for them, but not thoroughly enough).[11]

There have been numerous books and articles on etymologizing in Greek authors, only a few of which I can even mention. I think there is still no collection, however, that goes beyond what I did in a few pages, and I'd be happy to see one—though anyone interested should, I think, attempt this not as a dissertation but as a later publication.[12] One good development in the study of Greek poetry that is relevant to etymologizing is that, increasingly, scholars working on Alexandrian or Hellenistic poetry have moved away from thinking of their poets as writing "poetry for poetry's sake," without regard for thematic or ideological concerns, in keeping with the broader move toward new historicism.[13]

There has been a great deal of work on Plautus, Ennius, Lucretius, Catullus, Varro, Caesar, Propertius, Tibullus, and especially Ovid (Michalopoulos' monograph, which I reviewed, deserves special mention), including Ovidian comment on Vergil.[14]

*True Names* treats acrostics only at G. 1.427–35. There has been a great deal of work on acrostics lately, much (but not all) of it convincing; some of this work has good discussions of how the poet calls attention to things like wordplay and acrostics.[15]

Some reviewers noted or even complained that I had too few examples from the *Eclogues*. I list a few more now.

One early footnote needs updating. In a startling development, the photograph of baseball player Carl Yastrzemski in a pose strikingly similar to that of the Augustus of Prima Porta statue, discussed at p. 6n7 in the context of the possible "role of chance in producing some phrases that might merely look like etymological wordplay," has inspired a statue of Yastrzemski, erected outside Boston's Fenway Park in 2013. This can hardly be due to chance.

## Notes

1. My thanks for help with this new introduction to my research assistants Zack Rider and Tedd Wimperis, and for help finding recent bibliography by themselves or by others to Neil Adkin, Caroline Bishop, Peter Bing, Barbara Weiden Boyd, Francis Cairns, Sergio Casali, Robert Cowan, Raymond Cormier, Jennifer Ferriss-Hill, Michael Fontaine, Stephen Harrison, Julia Hejduk, Stephen Heyworth, Stephen Hinds, Robert Maltby, Kevin Muse, Chris Nappa, David Petrain, and Jay Reed. I am grateful to have been able to work on this reprint, as with the first printing, with Ellen Bauerle of the Press, who was as insightful and helpful as always.

2. Cf. O'Hara (1996), 75–82; Maltby (1993), 257–75; Cairns (1996), 24–59, and (2003), 239–42; Michalopoulos (2001), 4–6, esp. 4n9. On the line, cf. most recently Horsfall (2016), 117.

3. Sources gathered from Maltby (1991); Janko (2011), 490; Kannicht (1969), 73; and online searches: Ovid *Amores* 3.9.3–4: *flebilis indignos, Elegia, solve capillos! / a, nimis ex vero nunc tibi nomen erit*! Horace seems to allude to the deriva-

tion at *Odes* 1.33.1–4 *Albi . . . . miserabilos . . . elegos*, 2.9.9 (to Valgius) *flebilibus modis*, *AP* 75 *versibus inpariter iunctis querimonia primum*. Cf. Porph. Hor. *Carm.* 1.33.2–3 *nomen ipsum elegiorum* παρὰ τὸ ἒ ἒ, *quae vox est lamentium, dictum putant*; Diom. gramm. I 484–85 (citing Horace) *elegia dicta sive* παρὰ τὸ εὖ λέγειν τοὺς τεθνεῶτας . . . , *sive* ἀπὸ τοῦ ἐλέου, *id est miseratione*; Isid. *Orig.* 1.39.14 *elegiacus . . . dictus eo, quod modulatio eiusdem carminis conveniat miseris*, Sacerd. Gramm. VI 509.31; Mar. Victorin. Gramm. VI 110.17; Schol. Ar. *Av.* 217 ; Etym. Magnum 326, 47; Suda 774 Adler; Schol. Dion Thr. 21, 1 Hilg.

4. Nisbet and Hibbard (1970) on Hor. *Carm.* 1.33.2 ("The ancients frequently derived the name of elegy from ἔλεος and took lament to be its primary function"), Nagle (1980), 22–23, on Ovid *Tristia* 5.1.5 *flebile carmen* and 48 *tibia funeribus convenit ista meis*, Hinds (1987), 103, and (1992), 105–7 (sees allusion to the etymology at Ovid *Fasti* 3.213–14 and elsewhere in elegy), Rudd (1989) on Hor. *Ars Poetica* 75–76, Keith (1992), 334–35, and (2011), 2; Knox (1995) on *Epistula Sappho* 7 = ([Ovid] *Her.* 15.7) *flendus amor meus est—elegiae flebile carmen.*

5. Bowie (1986, 25) points to a unique cluster of fifth-century uses of the Greek word "in the seven or eight years following 415 BC" and suggests that one of Euripides' contemporaries with an interest in etymology and the history of music came up with the derivation. Cf. also Kannicht (1969) on Eurip. *Helen* 185.

6. Already in discussing A. 6.450–54 I suggested that the etymological background of *Dido/errabat* means that "the connection between Dido and wandering suggests elegy, or more broadly speaking the nonepic love poetry of the few decades preceding the *Aeneid*" (below, p. 111).

7. Feldherr 1999; Myers 2013. For epic's tendency to view women and love as in tension with epic despite the importance of both in epic from the *Odyssey* onward, see Hinds 2000, 223: "The role of the female in actual epics never becomes canonized within stereotyped descriptions of the genre, but a case can be made that surprise at the role of the female in actual epics does become so canonized: woman never becomes theorized into epic as an essential element of the genre, but woman does achieve a kind of essentialized theoretical status as an ambusher of the purity of epic."

8. Cf. Bleisch 1998a, her review of *True Names*: "I take issue with O'Hara because he does not discuss how etymologies work to destabilize the inquiry into truth." On Greek and Roman names, see also Bishop (2016).

9. I discuss how multiple conflicting aetiologies "can serve to undercut the authority of a speaker" in Ovid in O'Hara (2007), 123–27. Differently and challengingly, Hinds (2006), after noting how "the name of Venus seems variously to be linked in ancient etymologizing contexts with *vincire*, *vincere*, *vis*, *venire* and *vendere*, as well as with its true cognates *venia*, *venerari* and *venenum*," argues for "a view of the proliferation of etymologies as symptomatic of a kind of totalizing grammar, a grammar which finds in the negotiations between *Venus*, *vincire*, *vincere*, etc. not a movement towards infinite deferral and unfixity of meaning, but a movement towards plenitude and perfection of meaning."

10. O'Hara (2004) is my review of Michalopoulos. From my 1996 bibliography, Maltby (1993) is still important.

11. Supplements to Maltby's *Lexicon*: Marangoni (2007); Adkin: 2006a, 2006b, 2008, 2008a, 2009, 2009a, 2009b, 2009d, 2010b, 2010c. For Isidore, cf. the trans-

lations of Throop (2006) and the more scholarly Barney et al. (2006), as well as Henderson (2007), Fear and Woods (2015). For Macrobius, see Kaster (2011); for Fulgentius, Hays (n.d.) and (using Fulgentius for Vergil) McGowan (2002). For de la Cerda, see http://ccat.sas.upenn.edu/~jfarrell, and Casali (2008a).

12. Skutsch (1987), Pendergraft (1995), Kraus (1998), Gee (2000), Cairns (2002), Tsitsiou-Chelidoni (2003), Broggiato (2003), Schironi (2003), Tsitsibakou–Vasalos (2003), Tsitsibakou-Vasalos (2007), Skempis (2008), Skempis and Ziogas (2009), Kanavou (2011), Canevaro (2015), Bishop (2016). The forthcoming Levaniouk, entitled *A Concise Inventory of Greek Etymologies*, is described as "an ongoing publication that will be expanded and revised as time goes on."

13. Cf. e.g. Stephens (2002), Mori (2008).

14. A far from complete list: Plautus: Papaioannou (2008–09), Fontaine (2010), Heil (2012), Cowan (2014a); Ennius: Fisher (2014), Goldschmidt (2013); Lucretius: O'Hara (1998), Gale (2001), Possanza (2001), Maltby (2005), Maltby (2014), Victor et al. (2014); Caesar: Cairns (2012a); Cicero, Dyck (2003), Uría (2006), Katz (2009), Bishop (2016); Catullus: Michalopoulos (1996), Cairns (2012), esp. 89–92 but see also index; Varro: Korenjak (1999), Hinds (2006), Krostenko (2013), Shelton (2014), Nelsesteuen (2015); Horace: Cowan (2006), Cowan (2012a), Cowan (2014), Paschalis (1995), Paschalis (2003), Katz (2008), Adkin (2009h), Adkin (2010d), Cairns (2012), Roche (2013), Shelton (2014), Sullivan (2016); Propertius: Hendry (1997), Günther (1998), Michalopoulos (1998), Petrain (2000), Yardley (2001), Hinds (2006), Booth (2006), Cairns (2006a), Cairns (2007); Tibullus: Cairns (1996), Maltby (1999), Maltby (2002), Putnam (2005), Shelton (2014), Henkel (2014); Sulpicia: Hinds (2006); Ovid: Schawaller (1987), O'Hara (1996a), Tissol (1997), Wheeler (1997), P. Hardie (1999), Gee (2000), Boyd (2000), Boyd, (2001), Boyd (2006), Cairns (2003), Cairns (2007), Michalopoulos (2001), Michalopoulos (2003), Michalopoulos (2006), Pavlock (2003), Hinds (2006), Cairns (2007), Cowan (2011), Ziogas (2013), Shelton (2013), (2014), Curtis (2015), Adkin (2011f); Flavians: Keith (2008), Cowan (2009), Mulligan (2011); Martial: Grewing (1998), Maltby (2006), Vallat (2006), Cowan (2015).

15. Just a sampling of references on acrostics, all with further references: Feeney and Nelis (2005), Grishin (2008), Katz (2008a), Katz (2013), Somerville (2010) on G. 1.429–33, Adkin (2012a), Adkin (2014), Adkin (2015), Adkin (2015a), Adkin (2015b), Adkin (forthcoming), and the substantial Hejduk (forthcoming).

# List of New Examples

This list is much more spare than that of the original catalogue, and seldom provides either the relevant ancient evidence or a discussion as to whether I find the suggested etymology convincing; this list therefore requires that the reader do more follow-up work than does my original catalogue. As noted above, this list does not include examples discussed by Paschalis (1997) or Ahl (2007). It includes some examples from Horsfall's commentaries, but not all of the many times he discusses my original entries.

A. 1.7: Reed (2007) discusses *altae . . . Romae* in the light of Phoenician/Punic *rom-*, "high."

A. 1.8: A. Hardie (2007) discusses the connection between Muses and memory here and elsewhere. Sharrock (1997) is critical of my hesitation in seeing etymologizing here, or in 1.71–73 between *Iuno* (suppressed; see pp. 79–82) and *iungere*. See below on 1.252.

A. 1.9–10: A. Hardie (2007) suggests a link between Juno's *ira* and *–ire* in *tot adire labores*, and a link between *causas* and *casus*.

A. 1.22, 27: Adkin (2009e) argues that *excidio Libyae* at 22 plays on an etymology of Libya from λεπ[ι]υία in Varro, and that in 27 Vergil alludes to the shared etymology of *iudicium* and *iniuria* from *ius* (*iudicium Paridis spretaeque iniuria formae*).

A. 1.108–12: Bleisch (1998, quoted above) pushes much further my observations on the *Arae* (see my original entry); see too Fletcher (2014).

A. 1.71–3: See above on A. 1.8 on Sharrock (1997).

A. 1.164–65: Maltby (2003) discusses examples where I worried that an etymologist was deriving an etymology from Vergil rather than Vergil alluding to a known etymology, but he thinks that the derivation was known before Vergil: A. 1.164–65 *scaena*, 6.160 *sermo serebant*, 6.204 *auri aura*, 8.641 *caesa . . . foedera porca*.

A. 1.195–201: Adkin (2000) sees wordplay between *Acestes* in 195 and *accestis* in 201.

A. 1.252: A. Hardie (2007) suggests allusion to *Iuno* < *iungere* in *Italis longe disiungimur oris* (see above and entry on 1.73 and below 7.57).

A. 1.263–96: Booth (2006) discusses Quirinus and κοίρανος ("king"); in O'Hara (2008) I explain my skepticism.

A. 1.379: See Foster (1996) on the association of Aeneas' name with the adjective αἰνός "dread, terrible" as perhaps at A. 12.947 *terribilis* (see entry), but also perhaps with the noun αἶνος, "tale, story, > praise," in A. 1.379 *fama super aethera notus*.

A. 1.441: Shelton (2013) argues that words in 437–45 make the passage invite "an etymologizing interpretation," and that my hesitation in seeing κατ' ἀντίφρασιν (see p. 66) wordplay between *lucus* and *umbrae* is unwarranted.
A. 1.500–501: Adkin (2006) sees a link between *pharetram* and *fert*; see entry on A. 1.336–38.
A. 1.640–42: Hannah (2004) sees reference to the connection of *ingens* with *gens* (see entry on G. 2.131) in *ingens argentum . . . gentis*, of Dido's silverware carved with family exploits, as at Turnus' shield in A. 7.791.
A. 1.720: Michalopoulos (2001) is on Ovid, but has information relevant to my entry on *Erycina*.
A. 1.742: Bishop (2016) has a great deal more information on Greek and Ciceronian etymologies for the Hyades; see also below on 3.516.
A. 2.13–32: Adkin (2011f) sees here and later in book 2 allusions to a derivation of *abies* from *abire*.
A. 2.50–53: Adkin (2012a) sees in *hastam . . . stetit illa* allusion to a derivation of *hasta* from *stare* (see below on A. 12.722).
A. 2.81–104: Adkin (2011d) sees etymologizing here involving *fari/fama/falsus/infandum*, *remeo/me*, *insons*, and *verbum*.
A. 2.116–21: Adkin (2011c) argues that in Sinon's speech *ventus* is linked to *venio* and both *animus* and *anima* to ἄνεμος (see entry on A. 1.56–57), with further etymologizing of *litus* and other words.
A. 2.263–64: Adkin (2009c) suggests that the delayed *primusque Machaon/et Menelaus* evokes the etymology of Menelaus' name as μένει λαός or "the audience waits."
A. 2.374: Casali (2008a) discusses possible wordplay (suggested by de la Cerda, but I missed it) with *segnities* and *incensa*, as well as on *ignes* and *segnius* at 12.521–28 (see entry).
A. 2.413–15: Adkin (2006) argues for a connection between *gemitu* and *gemini*.
A. 2.470–73: Kyriakidou (2003) discusses the names Pyrrhus and Neoptolemus; see entry.
A. 2.682-704: Pandey (2013) discusses etymology, the flames in Iulus' hair, and the Sidus Iulium; see entry.
A. 3.2–3: Heyworth and Morwood (forthcoming) see wordplay involving *superis . . . superbum . . . humo*.
A. 3.45–46: Gowers (2011) sees in *Polydorus . . . telorum seges* a Greek etymology of the name not as "man of many gifts" but "man of many spears."
A. 3.129–31: Heyworth and Morwood (forthcoming), after Heyworth (1993), see an "etymological link between Crete and Curetes"; see also Horsfall (2006).
A. 3.210: Casali (2007) adds more information, and Ovidian commentary, on the Strophades; see entry.
A. 3.211–15: Casali (2007) sees glosses of both words in the phrase *dira Celaeno*, the first from *ira deum* (see entry on A. 12.845), the second as "black." Harrison (1985) had already made the connection for *dira*.
A. 3.414–17: Horsfall (2006) notes, citing Henry (1873–92) and others, a Greek etymology of the (suppressed) name Rhegium < ῥήγνυμι as where Sicily was "broken" off from the mainland.

A. 3.516: Bishop (2016) has a great deal more information on Greek and Ciceronian etymologies for the Hyades.

A. 3.544: Heyworth and Morwood (forthcoming) see a single-adjective gloss in *Palladis armisonae.*

A. 3.553: Heyworth and Morwood (forthcoming) see a single-adjective gloss in *navifragum Scylaceum.*

A. 3.586: Heyworth and Morwood (forthcoming) see an etymology from *celare* in *obscuro sed nubila caelo.*

A. 3.589: Heyworth and Morwood (forthcoming) see a single-adjective gloss in *umentem . . . umbram* and 4.351 *umentibus umbris.*

A. 3.614: Heyworth and Morwood (forthcoming) link the name Achaemenides also to ἄχος (see my p. 8).

A. 3.63: Casali (2007) sees wordplay with *manare* in *stant Manibus arae.*

A. 3.660: Heyworth and Morwood (forthcoming) add information on the wordplay *sola . . . solamen*; see entry.

A. 3.692–708: Goldschmidt (2013) suggests that "early Roman epic" may have been a source for some of the etymologizing here (see entry).

A. 4.254: Dyson (1997) suggests wordplay between *avus* "grandfather" and *avis* "bird" (see below on 7.412).

A. 4.271: Casali (2008a) discusses de la Cerda's note on *teris otia terris* (see entry). Muse (2005) suggests a model in the Homeric wordplay at *Od.* 15.10 on the Tel- (= "far") in Telemachus.

A. 4.351: See above, Heyworth and Morwood (forthcoming) on 3.589.

A. 4.359: Michalopoulos (2001) has information relevant to *auribus hausi*; see entry.

A. 4.402–407: Katz (2008a) sees more wordplay than I did in the ant simile, provides more information, and discusses acrostics and anagrams.

A. 4.492–93: Konstan (2000) shows that *cara* here, adapted from Cat. 66.40, itself a translation of Callimachus frag. 110.40, echoes the sound of Callimachus' κάρην, "head," which is then translated by *caput* in 493.

A. 4.569: Reed (2016) explores *Aeneid* passages (e.g., *rumpe moras* here) where *mora*, through wordplay with *amor* and *Roma* (see entry on A. 4.347), "meaningfully interacts with ideas of desire and national foundation."

A. 4.705: Peraki-Kyriakidou (2002) sees wordplay in *in ventos vita recessit* involving *ventus*, *anima*, and ἄνεμος; see above on A. 2.116–21.

A. 5.362–484: McGowan (2002) sees etymologizing of Dares from δέρω, "flay, beat," as found in Homeric scholia and in Fulgentius.

A. 5.746: Adkin (2000) sees wordplay between the last two words, *accersit Acestes.*

A. 5.835: Sansone (1996) sees in *Nox umida metam* allusion to an etymology of Greek grammarians connecting νύσσα (=*meta*) with the verb νύσσω, and with νύξ.

A. 6.42: See on A. 6.625–27.

A. 6.160, 204: See above on A. 1.164–65 for Maltby (2003) on A. 6.160 *sermo serebant* and 6.204 *auri aura.*

A. 6.232–35: Fletcher (2014) discusses the naming of Cape Misenus after Aeneas' trumpeter, and other "Trojan eponyms in Italy"; see entry.

A. 6.285–87: Adkin (2006) sees a link between *Centauri* and *centumgeminus* found in Fulgentius.

A. 6.378–83: Fletcher (2014) discusses the naming of Cape Palinurus after Aeneas' helmsman; see entry.

A. 6.432–33: Adkin (2002) sees a link between *consilium* and *silentium*.

A. 6.441: As noted in my first paragraph above, my original entry suspected etymological wordplay here; I now think *Lugentes campi* alludes to the etymology linking "elegy" with mourning, as if from ἒ ἒ λέγειν or ἔλεος.

A. 6.450–51: Complementing the idea that in these lines *Dido/errabat* alludes to an etymology connecting Dido's name with a word meaning "wanderer" (see entry), Reed (2007, 141) cites a suggestion that Dido in Semitic means "beloved," which would also link Dido's name to that of Amata (see A. 7.56–7 both below and in entry).

A. 6.458–60: Reed (2008) builds on and complements Konstan (2000) on 4.492–93 (see above); *per sidera iuro* in 6.458, before *invitus, regina* in 460, suggests σίδηρος, which must have been in the Callimachean original where Catullus 66 has *ferro*.

A. 6.494–547: Bleisch (1999) discusses the name Deiphobus; see also Horsfall (2013).

A. 6.625–27: Gowers (2005) says that when Sibyl uses the topos "not if I had a hundred tongues/mouths," *centum* evokes the etymology of Hecate (see entry on 4.510), and that, earlier, the reference at 6.42 to the *centum ostia* of her cave also evokes the topos, due to a link of *ostia* and *ora*.

A. 6.684–86: Adkin (2012) suggests that Vergil plays on the linked etymology of *alacris* and *lacrimae*.

A. 6.803, 805: Adkin (2012b) sees in *arcu* and *tigris* at line-end in 803 and 805 allusion to Varro's derivation of *tigris* from an Armenian word for arrow, as also in A. 10.166–69 and 11.573–77.

A. 7: Ferriss-Hill (2011) discusses several Sabellic glosses from *A.* 7, providing new or better detail on *mensa* at 116, *Tibur superbum* at 360, *Nar* at 517, *Hernica* at 684, *Rosea rura* at 712, *Tetrica* at 713, and *maliferae Abellae* at 740; see also Horsfall on 3.701–2 on Gela and the Oscan language. See my pp. 91–92.

A. 7.1–4: Fletcher (2014) discusses the naming of Caieta after Aeneas' nurse (see entry).

A. 7.37: A. Hardie (2007) suggests that the name Erato is associated not only with Eros but also with the names Hera and Amata (see entry). On Erato and especially the other muses, see now also A. Hardie (2009).

A. 7.56–7: Wills (1997) questions my hesitation in seeing suppressed wordplay between *regia coniunx* [=*Amata*] and *amore* at the ends of consecutive lines.

A. 7.57: A. Hardie (2007) suggests allusion to *Iuno* < *iungere* in *adiungi generum*.

A. 7.118–19: Gowers (2011), citing Paschalis (1997), suggests that *eripuit pater* alludes to the connection Harpy/*diripiunt* in A. 3.227—the scene that Aeneas in 7 forgets/ignores in attributing the "eat your tables" prophecy to Anchises.

A. 7.191: Horsfall (2000) on *fecit avem*: "there just might be an etymological play here, between Circe and κίρκος" (see Harrison on my p. 291).

A. 7.399: Horsfall (2000) sees possible etymologizing in *torquens . . . torvumque*.

A. 7.412: Dyson (1997) discusses *avus/avis*, *Ardea/ardeam*, as at A. 4.254.

A. 7.648: Rivero García and Librán Moreno (2011) point to impious characters in Aesch. *Septem* and suggest an etymology of Mezentius in A. 7.648 *contemptor divum* and elsewhere as "not-Zeus-honoring," μὴ Ζῆν τίων.

A. 7.791: Horsfall (2000), Hannah (2004), and Adkin (2011) see paronomasia of *argumentum/Argus* and the (suppressed) *Argos*, and well as the etymological connection of *ingens* with *gens* in this reference to Turnus' genealogy.

A. 8.91: Adkin (2011e) sees in *uncta vadis abies* allusion to a derivation of *abies* from *abire*.

A. 8.98–100: *Romana potentia* is likely an allusion to an etymology of *Roma* < ῥώμη; see Maltby (1991) s.v. "Roma," Watson (2003) on Hor. *Epod.* 16.2, O'Hara (forthcoming, *Vergil*) ad loc.

A. 8.203–4: In his description of Hercules' cattle, Vergil probably alludes to the etymology of the name of the Forum Boarium. See O'Hara (forthcoming, *Vergil*) ad loc.

A. 8.361: Feeney (2007, 164) notes allusion in *mugire* to the name of the nearby Porta Mugonia ("Moo-Gate").

A. 8.641: See above on A. 1.164–65 for Maltby on *caesa . . . foedera porca.*

A. 8.660: For *virgatis . . . sagulis*, Reed (2007, 56) calls attention to Servius' claim that Vergil alludes to the fact that *virga* = *purpura* in Gaulic; Ovid *Ars* 3.269 may allude to Vergil.

A. 8.696: Chaudhuri (2012) sees in *regina . . . patrio vocat . . . sistro* allusion to the etymology of Cleopatra; the name is suppressed in 688 and 696.

A. 9.69: Adkin (2003) sees a link between *lateri* and *latebat.*

A. 9.373–75: Jolivet (2004) sees allusion to an etymology of the adverb *temere* from a noun meaning "obscurity," "darkness."

A. 9.387–88: Bleisch (2001) argues that here, where I suspected but could not find the etymological wordplay, "*stabula* is an etymological pun on the toponym *Bovillae*," a word "glossed in ancient glossaries as *boustasia*."

A. 9.428: Casali (2004) notes that Euryalus' use of the word *fraus* alludes to the connection of the name Dolon with trickery, δόλος.

A. 9.570: Butterfield (2011) adds further notes on *Lucetius*; see entry.

A. 9.576: Adkin (2010e) argues for etymologizing the name of the town Privernum (*A.* 11.540) and the warrior Privernus (*A.* 9.576) from *primus* and *vis.*

A. 9.684: Thomas (2003–04) discusses the names *Quercens* and *Aquiculus.*

A. 10.166, 169: Adkin (2012b) sees in *Tigri* and *arcus* at line-end in 166 and 169 Varro's derivation of *tigris* from Armenian "arrow"; see above on A. 6.803, 805.

A. 10.737: P. Hardie (1999) suggests Ovid *Met.* 8.526 *iacet alta Calydon* as a parallel for or comment on Vergil's *iacet altus Orodes.*

A. 10.747–48: Cucchiarelli (2001) sees etymological wordplay alluding to violation of virginity in the names Parthenius and Rapo.

A. 10.822: Fontaine (2016) sees, when Aeneas sees Lausus' face growing pale (*pallentia*), a reminder of the name Pallas.

A. 11.30–31: Horsfall (2003), modifying Paschalis (1997), sees in *Acoetes/servabat* a Greek etymology of Acoetes who "watches unsleeping" over the body of Pallas.

A. 11.540: Adkin (2010e) argues for etymologizing the name of the town Privernum (*A.* 11.540) and the warrior Privernus (*A.* 9.576) from *primus* and *vis.*

A. 11.577: Adkin (2012b) sees in *tigridis exuviae* further allusion to *tigris* = Armenian "arrow"; see above on A. 6.803, 805.

A. 11.686–89: Daly (2016) discusses how the derivation of the name Ornytus from ὀρνύναι is glossed by the phrase *feras agitare*, and further play on the name in 686–89.

A. 11.721: Kyriakidou (2003) discusses *accipiter*; see entry. P. Hardie (1999) cites Isidore and adds a suggestion of etymologizing in *ales ab alto*.
A. 11.768: Horsfall (2003) notes that *croceam chlamydem* in 775 may gloss the suggestion in the name Chloreus of effeminate paleness (cf. χλωρός).
A. 12.391–92: Jacobson (2001) adds that the final syllable of the physician Iapyx's name suggests healing, since *pyxis* = "medicine-box."
A. 12.521–28: Casali (2008a) and Adkin (2007) discuss wordplay on *ignes* and *segnius* (see entry; see also Putnam [2005] on Tibullus).
A. 12.722: In *hasta . . . stabat*, Tarrant (2012) notes etymologizing found in Varro and noted by de la Cerda that I missed; see above Adkin on A. 2.50–53.
A. 12.75: Casali (2000) discusses the etymology of the name Idmon as "knowing."
A. 12.845: Michalopoulos (2001) has information relevant to *Dirae* here; see also above on A. 3.211–15.
E. (throughout): Davis (2012) discusses the names Tityrus, Amaryllis, Corydon, Gryne, Lycidas, Bianor. On Corydon, see also Lipka (2001) and Lipka (2002); the latter also discusses *fagus* (see entry on E. 1.1).
E. 1: Paschalis (2008) suggests that in E. 1 Tityrus and Galatea form a "significant" pair of pastoral names, suggesting "cheese" and "milk."
E. 1.1–2: Cairns (1999) argues for an implied etymology linking Tityrus to the word *avena*; Van Sickle (2004) rejects parts of Cairns' argument, but also links Tityrus and *avena*.
E. 1.8: Du Quesnay (1981, 109) sees in *tener . . . agnus* allusion to a derivation of *agnus* from ἁγνός, "pure."
E. 1.43: Du Quesnay (1981, 109) sees in *altaria fumant* allusion to a derivation of *altaria* from *adolesco* or *altus*, or both.
E. 1.11–15: Adkin (2011a) suggests allusion to etymologies involving *ager* and *aeger* drawn from Varro.
E. 1.34: Cairns (2015) argues that Vergil etymologizes *caseus* from *cogo* by juxtaposing it with *premeretur*, cf. too *pressi copia lactis* (*E*. 1.81).
E. 1.42: Bing (2016) cites the idea of Du Quesnay (1981) that *iuvenis* plays on an etymology of *iuvenis* from *iuvare*, as at G. 1.500 (see entry), and connects it to Epicurus as ἐπίκουρος, "helper" or "ally."
E. 1.53–55, 59: Adkin (2010a) see several etymologies in E. 1: in 1.59 *cervi . . . leves* a derivation of ἔλαφος, "deer," from ἐλαφρός, "light," and in 53–55 a link between *saepes* and *saepe*, and further wordplay involving *saepes*.
E. 1.57–58: Adkin (2010) sees allusion to etymologies involving "repetition" for both *gemere* and *turtur*, complementing the avian soundplay here.
E. 1.64–66: Du Quesnay (1981, 137) reports a suggestion of J. McKeown that the reference to exile in Scythia alludes to *parthi* as the Scythian word for "exiles."
E. 3.40–42: See Katz (2008) on *arator* and the name Aratus (see entry), and also Prioux (2005). Kubiak (2009) shows that Germanicus made wordplay on Aratus' name similar to that seen here.
E. 3.84–88, 100: Savage (1958), in a comment I overlooked before, pointed out how in E. 3 Vergil is probably punning on the name of Pollio (*polleo*) in 84–88 and on the name of Aemilius Macer in 100 *quam . . . macer est mihi taurus*.
E. 3.95: Adkin (2009f) argues that the description of a ram as wet in *ipse aries etiam nunc vellera siccat* plays on the etymology of *aries* from *ares* ("you are dry") as in Varro; see also G. 3.387–90 and 3.445–47.

E. 6: Peirano (2009) discusses the name Scylla in E. 6.

E. 6.41–3: Paschalis (2001) sees etymologizing involving Pyrrha and Caucasia and Greek words for fire (πῦρ) or lighting a fire (καίω), and on *Saturnia* and *iactos* (cf. *sero*).

E. 7: Petrovitz (2003) discusses etymologizing with names in *E.* 7.

E. 7.66: Adkin (2011e) sees an allusion to a derivation of *abies* from *abire*.

E. 10.21–23: Cowan (2012) finds in various learned poets more examples of the *cura*/ κούρη/*amica* wordplay I discuss in the entry here.

G. 1.1–2: Katz (2008) sees *terram*/*vertere* (= *arare*) in 1–2 as a complicated allusion both to Aratus' name and to Aratus' allusion to his name at *Phaen.* 1–2 (*vertere* also = "translate").

G. 1.17: Peraki-Kyriakidou (2006) suggests that the name Pan in 17 is glossed by the mention in 20 of *dique deaeque omnes*; I express skepticism in O'Hara (2008).

G. 1.338: Bishop (2016) has a great deal more information on Greek and Ciceronian etymologies for the Pleiades and Hyades.

G. 1.173–74: Cairns (2013) argues for etymologizing and translation by homonym in the description of the use of lime-wood (*tilia*) for a yoke, as well as discussing Vergil's treatment of *fagus* (see entry on E. 1.1).

G. 1.460–64: P. Hardie (1999) questions my hesitation in seeing *umidus* as a κατ' ἀντίφρασιν gloss on *Auster*, since the passage "is already charged with word-play" and concerns "the interpretation of (weather-)signs"; he suggests further word-play on *serus* and *serenus*.

G. 1.491–92, 2.484–88: Hendry (1997), Nappa (2002), and Nelis (2010) discuss *Emathia*, *Haemi*, and *sanguine* (see entry on G. 1.491–92).

G. 3.28–29: Schork (1998) sees reference in *magnumque fluentem*/*Nilum* to an Egyptian term for the Nile meaning "the Great River."

G. 3.387–90, 445–47: Adkin (2009f) argues that references here as in E. 3.95 to wet rams play on the etymology of *aries* from *ares*.

G. 3.515–16: Adkin (2006) sees a link between *vomer* ("plough") and *vomo*.

G. 4.291: Schork (1998) sees reference in *viridem Aegyptum nigra fecundat harena* to the notion of Egypt as Kemet, "the Black Land."

G. 4.310: P. Hardie (1999) suggests Ovid *Met.* 15.383–84 *melliferarum apium sine membris corpora nasci / et serosque pedes . . . adsumere* "renders more probable" Vergil's play on *apes* and *trunca pedum*, "with perhaps a further translingual pun on μέλι μέλος in *melli-ferarum—membris*."

# New Bibliography


Adkin, N. 2000. "Vergilian Etymologizing: The Case of Acestes." *AC* 69:205–7.

Adkin, N. 2002. "Further Vergilian Etymologizing: *Aeneid* 6,432–3." *AC* 71:149–50.

Adkin, N. 2002–03. "Etimologizing in Horace *Epistles* 1,2,62–63." *ACD* 38–39:239–40.

Adkin, N. 2003. "Vergil, *Aeneid* 9,69: A Jingle?" *AC* 72:231.

Adkin, N. 2005. "Some Additions to Maltby's *Lexicon of Ancient Latin Etymologies*." In *SLLRH* 12, ed. C. Deroux, 74–96. Brussels.

Adkin, N. 2006. "More Yukky Virgil: *Aeneid* 2,410–15." *Hermes* 134.4: 398–406.

Adkin, N. 2006a. "Further Vergilian Etymologizing: *Georg.* 3, 515–6; *Aen.* 1, 500–1; *Aen.* 6, 285–7." *AC* 75:171–75.

Adkin, N. 2006b. "Further Additions to Maltby's *Lexicon of Ancient Latin Etymologies*: Priscian." In *SLLRH* 13, ed. C. Deroux, 462–78. Brussels.

Adkin, N. 2007. "The Etymology of *segnis* in Vergil." *AC* 76:171–76.

Adkin, N. 2008. "Supplements to Marangoni's *Supplementum Etymologicum*: The Commentators on Terence." *Eos* 95:183–200.

Adkin, N. 2008a. "Further Supplements to Marangoni's *Supplementum Etymologicum*: The Commentators on Horace." *Invigilata Lucernis* 30:261–77.

Adkin, N. 2009. "More Additions to Maltby's *Lexicon of Ancient Latin Etymologies* and Marangoni's *Supplementum Etymologicum*: The Scholia to Statius." *ACD* 45:45–56.

Adkin, N. 2009a. "Further Supplements to Marangoni's *Supplementum Etymologicum*: The Scholia to Persius and Juvenal." *BStudLat* 39:173–82.

Adkin, N. 2009b. "Further Supplements to Marangoni's *Supplementum Etymologicum*: The Collections of 'Differentiae' Published by Beck and Brugnoli." *Euphrosyne*, n.s., 37:407–14.

Adkin, N. 2009c. "Exiting Virgil's Trojan Horse: *Primusque Machaon*." *L'Antiquité Classique* 78:195–96.

Adkin, N. 2009d. "More Additions to Maltby's *Lexicon of Ancient Latin Etymologies* and Marangoni's *Supplementum Etymologicum*: Isidore of Seville on Grammar, Rhetoric and Dialectic (*Etym.* 1–2)." *Habis* 40:17–25.

Adkin, N. 2009e. "The Mind of Juno: Etymologizing in the Exordium of the *Aeneid*." *Latomus* 68:170–71.

Adkin, N. 2009f. "Wet Rams: The Etymology of *aries* in Virgil." *Wiener Studien* 122:121–24.

Adkin, N. 2009g. Review of Marangoni 2007. *Latomus* 68:497–99.

Adkin, N. 2009h. "Horace's Weak Sheep: Etymologizing in *Epode* 2,16." *Invigilata Lucernis* 31:7–8.

Adkin, N. 2010. "'Acoustic' Etymologizing in Virgil, *Eclogue* 1,57–58." *Bollettino di Studi Latini* 40:523–26.

Adkin, N. 2010a. "Harts and Hedges: Further Etymologizing in Virgil's First 'Eclogue'." *Arctos* 44:9–23.

Adkin, N. 2010b. "More Additions to Maltby's *Lexicon of Ancient Latin Etymologies* and Marangoni's *Supplementum Etymologicum*: The Scholia to Lucan." *C&C* 5.1: 31–76.

Adkin, N. 2010c. "Further Supplements to Marangoni's *Supplementum Etymologicum*: Servius and Servius Auctus on Virgil." In *SLLRH* 15, ed. C. Deroux, 473–91. Brussels.

Adkin, N. 2010d. "The Etymology of *amnis* in Horace's 'Ars Poetica'." *Acta Classica* 53:207–9.

Adkin, N. 2010e. "Further Virgilian Etymologizing: Privernum and Privernus." *Invigilata Lucernis* 32:7–11.

Adkin, N. 2011. "Etymology and the Shield of Turnus." *Latomus* 70:1118–19.

Adkin, N. 2011a. "Etymologizing in Virgil, *Eclogue* 1,11–15." *L'Antiquité Classique* 80:163–166.

Adkin, N. 2011b. "Two Etymological Clusters in Apuleius." *Eos* 98:87–92.

Adkin, N. 2011c. "Virgil, *Aeneid* 2,116–121: An Etymological 'Cluster'." *Bollettino di Studi Latini* 41:594–600.

Adkin, N. 2011d. "Sinon on His 'Pal' Palamedes (Virgil, *Aeneid* 2,81–104)." *ACD* 47:155–69.

Adkin, N. 2011e. "Virgil's Wooden Horse: Which Wood?" *Arctos* 45:11–26.

Adkin, N. 2011f. "What Did Pan Say to Syrinx? Etymology in Ovid, *Metamorphoses* 1,698-712." *Eirene* 47:144–49.

Adkin, N. 2012. "*Anchises alacris* (Virgil, *Aeneid* 6,684–686)." *Latomus* 71:845–46.

Adkin, N. 2012a. "Laocoon's Shot: A Note on *Aeneid* 2,50–53." *Maia* 64:424–28.

Adkin, N. 2012b. "Virgil and the Etymology of 'Tiger'." In *SLLRH* 16, ed. C. Deroux, 211–19. Brussels.

Adkin, N. 2014. "'Read the Edge': Acrostics in Virgil's Sinon Episode." *ACD* 50:45–72.

Adkin, N. 2015. "A Virgilian Onomastic (*Ecl.* 10,5–9)." *Bollettino di Studi Latini 45:433–55.*

Adkin, N. 2015a. "On A New Virgil Acrostic: *Aen.* 6,77–84." *Mnemosyne n.s. 68:118–19.*

Adkin, N. 2015b. "*Quis est nam ludus in undis?* (Virgil, *Ecl.* 9,39–43)." *ACD 51:43–58.*

Adkin, N. Forthcoming. "A Political Acrostic in Virgil *Ecl.* 6,14–24." *Museum Helveticum.*

Ahl, Frederick, trans. 2007. *Virgil:* Aeneid. Oxford.

Barney, S. A., W. J. Lewis, J. A. Beach, and O. Berghof. 2006. *The Etymologies of Isidore of Seville.* With the collaboration of Muriel Hall. Cambridge.

Bing, P. 2016. "Epicurus and the *iuvenis* at Vergil's *Eclogue* 1.42." *CQ* 66.1: 172–79.

Bishop, C. 2016. "Naming the Roman Stars: Constellation Etymologies in Cicero's *Aratea* and *De Natura Deorum.*" *CQ* 66.1: 155–71.

Bleisch, P. 1998. "Altars Altered: The Alexandrian Tradition of Etymological Wordplay in *Aeneid* 1.108–12." *AJP* 119.4: 599–606.

Bleisch, P. 1998a. Review of O'Hara 1996. *AJP* 119.2: 300–303.
Bleisch, P. 1999. "The Empty Tomb at Rhoeteum: Deiphobus and the Problem of the Past in *Aeneid* 6.494–547." *CA* 18.2: 187–226.
Bleisch, P. 2001. "Nisus' Choice: *Bovillae* at *Aeneid* 9.387–8." *CQ* 51.1: 183–89.
Booth, J. 2006. "Naming Names—or Not: Some Significant Choices and Suppressions in Latin Poetry." In Booth and Maltby 2006, 49–63.
Booth, J., and R. Maltby, eds. 2006. *What's in a Name? The Significance of Proper Names in Classical Latin Literature*. Swansea.
Bowie, E. L. 1986. "Early Greek Elegy, Symposium and Public Festival." *JHS* 106:13–35.
Boyd, B. W. 2000. "*Celeus rusticus*: A Note on Ovidian Wordplay in *Fasti* 4." *CP* 95:190–93.
Boyd, B. W. 2001. "Arms and the Man: Wordplay and the Catasterism of Chiron in Ovid *Fasti* 5." *AJPh* 122.1: 67–80.
Boyd, B. W. 2006. "Two Rivers and the Reader in Ovid, *Metamorphoses* 8." *TAPA* 136.1: 171–206.
Broggiato, M. 2003. "The Use of Etymology as an Exegetical Tool in Alexandria and Pergamum: Some Examples from the Homeric Scholia." In Nifadopoulos 2003, 65–70.
Butterfield, D. 2011. "Two Notes on Virgil's *Aeneis* (8.503 and 9.570)." *REL* 11:33–38.
Cairns, F. 1996. "Ancient 'Etymology' and Tibullus: On the Classification of 'Etymologies' and on 'Etymological Markers'." *PCPS* 42:24–59; repr. in Cairns 2007.
Cairns, F. 1999. "Virgil *Eclogue* 1.1–2: A Literary Programme?" *HSCP* 99:289–93.
Cairns, F. 2002. "Acontius and his οὔνομα κουρίδιον: Callimachus *Aetia* fr. 67.1–4 Pf." *CQ* 52.2: 471–47.
Cairns, F. 2003. "The 'Etymology' in Ovid *Heroides* 20.21–32." *CJ* 98.3: 239–42.
Cairns, F. 2006. "The Nomenclature of the Tiber in Virgil's *Aeneid*." In Booth and Maltby 2006, 65–82.
Cairns, F. 2006a. *Sextus Propertius: The Augustan Elegist*. Cambridge.
Cairns, F. 2007. *Papers on Roman Elegy 1969–2003: Eikasmos*. Quaderni Bolognesi di Filologia Classica, Studi 16. Bologna.
Cairns, F. 2012. *Roman Lyric: Collected Papers on Catullus and Horace*. Beiträge zur Altertumskunde 301. Berlin.
Cairns, F. 2012a. "Caesar fr. 1 Courtney: The Etymologies." *Paideia* 67:371–77.
Cairns, F. 2013. "Virgil's Lime-wood Yoke (*Georgics* 1.173–4)." *CQ* 63.1: 434–38.
Cairns, F. 2015. "Fat Victim and Fat Cheese (Vergil *Eclogue* 1.33–5)." In *Virgilian Studies: A Miscellany Dedicated to the Memory of Mario Geymonat*, ed. H-C Günther, Studia Classica et Mediaevalia 10, 27–38. Nordhausen.
Canevaro, L. G. 2015. *Hesiod's* Works and Days*: How to Teach Self-Sufficiency*. Oxford.
Carter, M. A. S. 2002. "*Vergilium vestigare: Aeneid* 12,587–588." *CQ* 52:615–17.
Casali, S. 2000. "The Messenger Idmon and Turnus' Foreknowledge of His Death: A Note on the Poetics of Names in the *Aeneid*." *Vergilius* 46:114–24.
Casali, S. 2004. "Nisus and Euryalus: Exploiting the Contradictions in Virgil's *Doloneia*." *HSCP* 102:319–54.
Casali, S. 2007. "Correcting Aeneas's Voyage: Ovid's Commentary on *Aeneid* 3." *TAPA* 137.1: 181–210.

Casali, S. 2008. "The King of Pain: Aeneas, Achates and ἄχος in *Aeneid* 1." *CQ* 58.1: 181–89.

Casali, S. 2008a. "Agudezas virgiliane nel commento di La Cerda all'*Eneide*." In *Esegesi dimenticate di autori classici*, ed. C. Santini and F. Stok, 233–62. Pisa.

Chaudhuri, P. 2012. "Naming *nefas*: Cleopatra on the Shield of Aeneas." *CQ* 62.1: 223–26.

Cowan, R. W. 2006. "The Land of King Mane: A Pun at Horace, *Odes* 1.22.15." *CQ* 56.1: 322–24.

Cowan, R. W. 2009. "Thrasymennus' Wanton Wedding: Etymology, Genre, and *virtus* in Silius Italicus *Punica*." *CQ* 59.1: 226–37.

Cowan, R. W. 2011. "Passing Over Cephisos' Grandson: Literal *praeteritio* and the Rhetoric of Obscurity in Ovid *Met.* 7.350–93." *Ramus* 40.2: 146–67.

Cowan, R.W. 2012. "Valerius Cato, Callimachus and the Very Large Girl (Ticida fr. 103 *FRP*)." In *SLLRH* 16, ed. C. Deroux, 94–100. Brussels.

Cowan, R. W. 2012a. "Alas, Poor Io! Bilingual Wordplay in Horace *Epode* 11." *Mnemosyne* 65:753–63.

Cowan, R. W. 2014. "Tall, Pale and Noble: Beauty, Rank and Wordplay at Horace *Satires* 1.2.123–126." *Latomus* 73.4: 1012–28.

Cowan, R.W. 2014a. "Purchasing Priam: Bilingual Wordplay at Plautus *Bacchides* 976–7." *Classical Quarterly* 64.2: 844–47.

Cowan, R.W. 2015. "How's Your Father? A Recurrent Bilingual Wordplay in Martial." *CQ* 65:336–46.

Cucchiarelli, A. 2001. "Vergil on Killing Parthenius (*Aen.* 10.748)." *CJ* 97:51–54.

Curtis, L. 2015. "Explaining Exile: The Aetiological Poetics of Ovid, Tristia 3." *TAPA* 145.2: 411–44.

Daly, A. 2016. "Camilla and the Name and Fame of Ornytus the Beast-Rouser at *Aeneid* 11.686–689." Paper delivered at annual meeting of the Society for Classical Studies, San Francisco, January 6–9.

Danielewicz, J. 2005. "Further Hellenistic Acrostics: Aratus and Others." *Mnemosyne* 58.3: 321–34.

Davis, G. 2012. *Parthenope, The Interplay of Ideas in Vergilian Bucolic.* Leiden.

Del Bello, D. 2007. *Forgotten Paths: Etymology and the Allegorical Mindset.* Washington, DC.

Du Quesnay, I. M. Le M. 1981. "*Vergil's First* Eclogue." *PLLS* 3:29–182.

Dyck, A. R. 2003. "Etymologising the Gods: Cicero's Experiments at N.D. 2.63–69." In Nifadopoulos 2003, 55–64.

Dyson, J. T. 1997. "Birds, Grandfathers, and Neoteric Sorcery in *Aeneid* 4.254 and 7.412." *CQ* 47.1: 314–15.

Erbse, H., ed. 1969–88. *Scholia Graeca in Homeri Iliadem.* 7 vols. Berlin.

Fear, A., and J. Wood, eds. 2015. *Isidore of Seville and His Reception in the Early Middle Ages: Transmitting and Transforming Knowledge.* Amsterdam.

Feeney, D. 2007. *Caesar's Calendar: Ancient Time and the Beginnings of History.* Berkeley.

Feeney, D., and D. Nelis. 2005. "Two Virgilian Acrostics: Certissima Signa?" *CQ* 55.2: 644–46.

Feldherr, A. 1999. "Putting Dido on the Map: Genre and Geography in Vergil's Underworld." *Arethusa* 32.1: 85–122.

Ferriss-Hill, J. L. 2011. "Virgil's Program of Sabellic Etymologizing and the Construction of Italic Identity." *TAPA* 141.2: 265–84.

Fisher, J. 2014. *The* Annals *of Quintus Ennius and the Italic Tradition*. Baltimore.

Fletcher, K. 2014. *Finding Italy: Travel, Colonization, and Nation in Vergil's* Aeneid. Ann Arbor.

Fontaine, M. 2010. *Funny Words in Plautine Comedy*. Oxford.

Fontaine, M. 2013. "Puns." In *The Virgil Encyclopedia*, ed. R. Thomas and J. Ziolkowski, 1054–55. Chichester; Malden, MA.

Fontaine, M. 2016. "Freudian Bulls-eyes in Classical Perspective—the Psycholinguistics of Guilt in Virgil's *Aeneid*." In *Wordplay and Powerplay in Latin Poetry*, ed. P. Mitsis and I. Ziogas, Festschrift for Frederick M. Ahl. Berlin.

Foster, J. 1996. "Some Interactive Instances of the Hero's Name in the *Aeneid*." *PVS* 22:101–5.

Gale, M. 2001. "Etymological Wordplay and Poetic Succession in Lucretius." *CP* 96.2: 168–72.

Ganiban, R., ed. 2012. *Vergil,* Aeneid, *Books 1–6*. Contributing editors C. Perkell, J. O'Hara, J. Farrell, P. Johnston. Newburyport, MA: Focus Press.

Gee, E. 2000. *Ovid, Aratus, and Augustus: Astronomy in Ovid's* Fasti. Cambridge.

Goldschmidt, N. 2013. *Shaggy Crowns: Ennius'* Annales *and Virgil's* Aeneid. Oxford.

Gowers, E. 2005. "Virgil's Sibyl and the 'Many Mouths' Cliché (Aen. 6.625–7)." *CQ* 55.1: 170–82.

Gowers, E. 2011. "Trees and Family Trees in the *Aeneid*." *CA* 30.1: 87–118.

Grewing, F. 1998. "Etymologie und etymologische Wortspiele in den Epigrammen Martials." In *Toto notus in orbe: Perspektiven der Martial-Interpretation*, ed. Grewing, 315–56. Stuttgart.

Grishin, A. A. 2008. "*Ludus in undis*: An Acrostic in *Eclogue* 9." *HSCP* 104:237–40.

Günther, H.-C. 1998. "Word Play in Propertius." *Eikasmos* 9:243–57.

Habinek, T. 2009. "Situating Literacy at Rome." In *Ancient Literacies: The Culture of Reading in Greece and Rome*, ed. W. A. Johnson and H. N. Parker, 114–40. New York.

Hannah, B. 2004. "Manufacturing Descent: Virgil's Genealogical Engineering." *Arethusa* 37.2: 141–64.

Hardie, A. 2007. "Juno, Hercules, and the Muses at Rome." *AJPh* 128.4: 551–92.

Hardie, A. 2009. "Etymologising the Muse." *MD* 62:9–57.

Hardie, P. 1999. Review of O'Hara 1996. *IJCT* 6:284–86.

Harrison, E. L. 1985. "Foundation Prodigies in the *Aeneid*." *PLLS* 5:131–64.

Hays, B. G. Forthcoming. *Fulgentius the Mythographer*. Oxford.

Heil, A. 2012. "*Hector Ilius*: Ein obzönes Wortspiel in Plautus, *Casina* 994–5." *Mnemosyne* 65.3: 480–87.

Hejduk, J. Forthcoming. "Voices on the Edge: Acrostic Conversations in Latin Epic."

Henderson, J. 2007. *The Medieval World of Isidore of Seville: Truth from Words*. Cambridge.

Hendry, M. 1997. "Three Propertian Puns." *CQ* 47.2: 599–603.

Henkel, J. 2014. "Metrical Feet on the Road of Poetry: Foot Puns and Literary Polemic in Tibullus." *CW* 107.4: 451–75.

Henry, J. 1873–92. *Aeneidea, or Critical, Exegetical, and Aesthetical Remarks on the* Aeneid. 5 vols. Dublin.
Heyworth, S. J. 1993. "Deceitful Crete: *Aeneid* 3.84. and the Hymns of Callimachus." *CQ* 43.1: 255–57.
Heyworth, S. J., and J. H. W. Morwood. Forthcoming. *A Commentary on Vergil,* Aeneid *3*. Oxford.
Hinds, S. E. 1987. *The Metamorphosis of Persephone: Ovid and the Self-Conscious Muse*. Cambridge.
Hinds, S. E. 1992. "*Arma* in Ovid's *Fasti* Part 1: Genre and Mannerism." *Arethusa* 25:81–112.
Hinds, S. E. 2000. "Essential Epic: Genre and Gender from Macer to Statius." In *Matrices of Genre: Authors, Canons, and Society*, ed. M. Depew and D. Obbink, 221–44. Cambridge, Mass.
Hinds, S. E. 2006. "Venus, Varro and the *vates*: Toward the Limits of Etymologizing Interpretation." *Dictynna* 3:175–210.
Horsfall, N. 2000. Aeneid *7: A commentary*. Leiden.
Horsfall, N. 2003. Aeneid *11: A commentary*. Leiden.
Horsfall, N. 2006. Aeneid *3: A commentary*. Leiden.
Horsfall, N. 2008. Aeneid *2: A commentary*. Leiden.
Horsfall, N. 2013. Aeneid *6: A commentary*. Berlin.
Horsfall, N. 2016. *The Epic Distilled: Studies in the Composition of the* Aeneid. Oxford.
Jacobson, H. 2001. "*Aeneid* 12.391–2: *Iamque aderat Phoebo ante alios dilectus Iapyx/Iasides*." *CQ* 51.1: 308–09.
Janko, R. 2011. *Philodemus On Poems Books 3–4: With the Fragments of Aristotle On Poets*. Oxford.
Jolivet, J. C. 2004. "*Nyctegresiae Romanae*: Exégèse homérique et *retractatio* de la Dolonie chez Virgile et Ovide." *Dictynna* 1:181–212.
Kanavou, N. 2011. *Aristophanes' Comedy of Names: A Study of Speaking Names in Aristophanes*. Berlin.
Kannicht, R. 1969. *Euripides Helena*. Heidelberg.
Kaster, R. A., ed. 2011. Macrobius: Saturnalia. Loeb classical library, 3 vols. Cambridge, MA.
Katz, J. T. 2008. "Vergil Translates Aratus: *Phaenomena* 1–2 and *Georgics* 1.1–2." *MD* 60:105–23.
Katz, J. T. 2008a. "An Acrostic Ant Road in *Aeneid* 4." *MD* 59:77–86.
Katz, J. T. 2009. "Wordplay." In *Proceedings of the 20th Annual UCLA Indo-European Conference, Los Angeles, October 31–November 1, 2008*, ed. S. W. Jamison, H. C. Melchert, and B. Vine, 79–114. Bremen.
Katz, J. T. 2013. "The Muse at Play: An Introduction." In Kwapisz, Petrain, and M. Szymański 2013, 3–30.
Keith, A. M. 1992. "*Amores* 1.1: Propertius and the Ovidian Programme." In *SLLRH* 6, 327–44. Brussels.
Keith, A. M. 2008. "Etymological Wordplay in Flavian Epic." In *Papers of the Langford Latin Seminar* 13, ed. F. Cairns, 231–53. Cambridge.
Knox, P. E. 1995. *Ovid's* Heroides*: Select Epistles*. Cambridge.
Konstan, D. 2000. "A Pun in Virgil's *Aeneid* (4.492–93)?" *CP* 95.1: 74–76.

Korenjak, M. 1999. "*Vates: a vi mentis*. Eine Etymologie Varros und ihr Schicksal in der lateinischen Literatur der frühen Kaiserzeit." *GFA* 2:1–4.
Kraus, C. S. 1998. "Dangerous Supplements: Etymology and Genealogy in Euripides' *Heracles*." *PCPS* 44:137–57.
Krostenko, B. A. 2013. "Etymologizing the Convivium: Varro's *Nescis Quid Vesper Serus Vehat*." *Palamedes* 8.1: 113–39.
Kubiak, D. P. 2009. "*Scitus arator*: Germanicus, *Aratea* 13." *SIFC* 7.2: 248–55.
Kwapisz, J., D. Petrain, and M. Szymański, eds. 2013. *The Muse at Play: Riddles and Wordplay in Greek and Latin Poetry*. Berlin.
Kyriakidou, H. 2003. "Homer's Etymologising in the *Aeneid*: Simile and the Point of Concentration." In Nifadopoulos 2003, 131–41.
Levaniouk, O., ed. Forthcoming. *A Concise Inventory of Greek Etymologies*. Online journal *Classics@*, vol. 18. Center for Hellenic Studies, chs.harvard.edu.
Lipka, M. 2001. *Language in Vergil's Eclogues*. Berlin.
Lipka, M. 2002. "Notes on *Fagus* in Vergil's *Eclogues*." *Philologus* 146.1: 133–38.
Lowe, D. 2008. Review of Del Bello 2007. *BMCR* 2008.11.11. http://bmcr.brynmawr.edu/2008/2008-11-11.html
Maltby, R. 1991. *A Lexicon of Ancient Latin Etymologies*. ARCA Classical and Medieval Texts, Papers and Monographs 25. Leeds.
Maltby, R. 1993. "The Limits of Etymologising." Aevum *Antiquum* 6: 257–75.
Maltby, R. 1999. "Tibullus and the Language of Latin Elegy." In *Aspects of the Language of Latin Poetry*, ed. J. N. Adams and R. G. Mayer, 377–98. Oxford.
Maltby, R. ed. 2002. *Tibullus: Elegies*. Cambridge: Francis Cairns.
Maltby, R. 2003. "The Role of Etymology in Servius and Donatus." In Nifadopoulos 2003, 103–18.
Maltby, R. 2005. "Etymologising and the Structure of Argument in Lucretius 1." *Papers of the Langford Latin Seminar* 12:95–112.
Maltby, R. 2006. "Proper Names as a Linking Device in Martial." In Booth and Maltby 2006, 159–68.
Maltby, R. 2009. "Priscian's Etymologies: Sources, Function and Theoretical Basis." In *Priscien: Transmission et reformation de la grammaire de l'antiquite aux modernes*, ed. M. Baratin, B. Colombat, and L. Holtz, 239–46. Turnhout.
Maltby, R. 2014. "Etymologies and Onomastics in Lucretius." In *Telling Origins: On the Lookout for Aetiology*, ed. C. Reitz, and A. Walter, Spudasmata 162, 349–72. Hildesheim.
Marangoni, C. 2007. *Supplementum Etymologicum Latinum* 1. Trieste.
McGowan, M. M. 2002. "On the Etymology and Inflection of *Dares* in Vergil's Boxing Match, *Aeneid* 5.362–484." *CP* 97.1: 80–88.
Michalopoulos, A. 1996. "Some Etymologies of Proper Names in Catullus." *PLLS* 9:75–81.
Michalopoulos, A. 1997. "Etymologising on Proper Names in Latin Epigraphic Verse." *Sandalion* 20:125–34.
Michalopoulos, A. 1998. "Some Cases of Propertian Etymologizing." *PLLS* 10:235–50.
Michalopoulos, A. 2001. *Ancient Etymologies in Ovid's Metamorphoses: A Commented Lexicon*. Leeds.
Michalopoulos, A. 2003. "Working on an Established Etymological Background: Ovid and His Hellenistic Predecessors." In Nifadopoulos 2003, 165–75.

Michalopoulos, A. 2006. *Ovid* Heroides *16 and 17: Introduction, Text and Commentary*. Cambridge: Francis Cairns.

Mori, A. 2008. *The Politics of Apollonius Rhodius'* Argonautica. Cambridge.

Mulligan, B. 2011. "Ἱερὸς *Argus*: Bilingual Wordplay in Statius *Silvae* 5.4.11–13." *Mnemosyne* 64:471–80.

Muse, K. 2005. "'Don't Dally in This Valley': Wordplay in *Odyssey* 15.10 and *Aeneid* 4.271." *CQ* 55.2: 646–49.

Myers, M. Y. 2013. "Vergil's Underworld and the Afterlife of Love Poets." Paper delivered at the Symposium Cumanum, "*Aeneid* Six and Its Cultural Reception," held at the Villa Vergiliana, Cuma, and the University of Naples Federico II, Italy, June 25.

Nagle, B. R. 1980. *The Poetics of Exile: Program and Polemic in the* Tristia *and* Epistulae ex Ponto *of Ovid*. Collection Latomus 170. Brussels.

Nappa, C. 2002. "Cold-Blooded Virgil: Bilingual Wordplay at *Georgics* 2.483–9." *CQ* 52.2: 617–20.

Nappa, C. 2004. "Callimachus' *Aetia* and Aeneas' Sicily." *CQ* 54.2: 640–46.

Nelis, D. 2001. *Vergil's* Aeneid *and the* Argonautica *of Apollonius Rhodius*. Leeds.

Nelis, D. 2006. "Wordplay in Vergil and Claudian." *Dictynna* 3:255–63.

Nelis, D. 2010. "Vergil, *Georgics* 1.489–92: More Blood?" *Papers of the Langford Latin Seminar* 14:133–35. Cambridge: Francis Cairns.

Nelsestuen, G. 2015. *Varro the Agronomist: Political Philosophy, Satire, and Agriculture in the Late Republic*. Columbus, Ohio.

Nicolini, L. 2007. "*Ad (l)usum lectoris*: Giochi di parole nelle Metamorfosi di Apuleio." *MD* 58:115–79.

Nifadopoulos, C., ed. 2003. *Etymologia: Studies in Ancient Etymology*. Münster.

Nifadopoulos, C. 2003a. "Introduction." In Nifadopoulos 2003, 11–20.

Nisbet, R. G. M., and M. Hubbard. 1970. *A Commentary on Horace* Odes *I*. Oxford.

O'Hara, J. 1996. *True Names*. Ann Arbor. Reviewed by H. Stubbs, *Vergilius* 42 (1996): 136–40; R. Schork, *NECJ* 25 (1997): 20–21; R. Cormier, *Choice* 34.5 (1997); J. Wills, *BMCR* 97.12.17; J. Van Sickle, *CJ* 93 (1998): 211–16; P. Bleisch, *AJP* 119.2 (1998): 300–303; L. Morgan, *CR* 48 (1998): 27–29; S. J. Harrison, *EMC* 16 (1997): 521–23; A. Sharrock, *G&R* 42 (1997): 223–27; P. Hardie, *IJCT* 6 (1999): 284–86; W. Kissel, *Gnomon* 72 (2000): 455–57; R. Cormier, *Latomus* 60 (2001): 195–96.

O'Hara, J. 1996a. "Vergil's Best Reader? Ovidian Commentary on Vergilian Etymological Wordplay." *CJ* 91: 255–76. Reprinted in *Oxford Readings in Ovid*, ed. P. Knox, 100–122 (Oxford, 2007).

O'Hara, J. 1998. "Venus or the Muse as 'Ally' (Lucr. 1.24, Simon. Frag. Eleg. 11.20–22 W)." *CP* 93:69–74.

O'Hara, J. 2001. "Callimachean Influence on Vergilian Etymological Wordplay." *CJ* 96:369–400.

O'Hara, J. 2004. Review of Michalopoulos 2001. *CW* 97.2: 210–12.

O'Hara, J. 2007. *Inconsistency in Roman Epic: Studies in Catullus, Lucretius, Vergil, Ovid and Lucan*. Cambridge.

O'Hara, J. 2008. Review of Booth and Maltby. 2006. *BMCR* 2008.03.03; http://bmcr.brynmawr.edu/2008/2008-03-03.html

O'Hara, J. 2011. *Vergil:* Aeneid *Book 4*. Newburyport, MA: Focus Press.

O'Hara, J. Forthcoming. *Vergil:* Aeneid *Book 8*. Indianapolis: Hackett Press.
O'Hara, J. Forthcoming. "Genre, Gender, and the Etymology behind the Phrase *Lugentes campi* at *Aeneid* 6.441."
Pandey, N. 2013. "Caesar's Comet, the Julian Star, and the Invention of Augustus." *TAPA* 143:405–49.
Papaioannou, S. 2008–09. "What's in a Name? The Real Identity of Palinurus in Plautus' *Curculio*." *CJ* 104.2: 111–22.
Paschalis, M. 1995. "Names and Death in Horace's *Odes*." *CW* 88.3: 181–90.
Paschalis, M. 1997. *Virgil's Aeneid: Semantic Relations and Proper Names*. Oxford. Reviewed by E. Batinski, *CO* 76.4 (1998–99): 150–51; W. Briggs, *CW* 92.6 (1998–99): 578–79; J. Dangel, *REL* 76 (1998): 335–36; R. Maltby, *JRS* 89 (1999): 239–40; M. C. J. Putnam, *CJ* 94.2 (1998–99): 203–6; J. Thomas, *Latomus* 58.3 (1999): 682–84; J. Dingel, *Gnomon* 73.4 (2001): 354–57.
Paschalis, M. 2001. "*Semina Ignis*: The Interplay of Science and Myth in the Song of Silenus." *AJP* 122.2: 201–22.
Paschalis, M. 2003. "Etymology and *enargeia*: Re-reading Moschus' *Europa* vis-à-vis Hor. *C*. 3.2." In Nifadopoulos 2003, 153–63.
Paschalis, M. 2008. "Tityrus and Galatea (Virgil, *Eclogue* 1): An Expected Relationship." *Dictynna* 5. http://dictynna.revues.org/401
Pavlock, B. 2003. "Ulysses' Exploitation of Etymological Puns in *Metamorphoses* 13." In Nifadopoulos 2003, 143–51.
Peirano, I. 2009. "*Mutati artus*: Scylla, Philomela and the End of Silenus' Song in Virgil *Eclogue* 6." *CQ* 59.1: 187–95.
Pendergraft, M. L. B. 1995. "Euphony and Etymology: Aratus' Phaenomena." *SyllClass* 6:43–67.
Peraki-Kyriakidou, H. 2002. "Aspects of Ancient Etymologizing." *CQ* 52.2: 478–93.
Peraki-Kyriakidou, H. 2006. "Antonomasia and Metonymy in the Proem to Virgil's *Georgics*." In Booth and Maltby 2006, 83–99.
Petrain, D. 2000. "Hylas and *silva*: Etymological Wordplay in Propertius 1.20." *HSCP* 100:409–21.
Petrovitz, W. 2003. "Towards a Grammar of Allusion: A Cross-Linguistic Study of Vergil's Seventh *Bucolic*." *CW* 96.3: 259–70.
Possanza, D. M. 2001. "A Note on Lucretius *De Rerum Natura* 5.613." *Phoenix* 55:137–41.
Prioux, É. 2005. "Deux jeux de mots sur le nom d'Aratos: Note sur Virgile, *B*. III 42 et Aratos, *Phaen*. 2." *RPh* 79:309–17.
Putnam, M. 2005. "Virgil and Tibullus 1.1." *CP* 100.2: 123–41.
Reed, J. 2007. *Virgil's Gaze: Nation and Poetry in the* Aeneid. Ann Arbor.
Reed, J. 2008. "Another Greek Pun in the *Aeneid*." *Mnemosyne* 61.2: 300–302.
Reed, J. 2016. "*Mora* in the *Aeneid*." In *Wordplay and Powerplay in Latin Poetry*, ed. P. Mitsis and I. Ziogas, Festschrift for Frederick M. Ahl. Berlin.
Rivero García, L., and M. Librán Moreno. 2011. "New Light on Virgil's Mezentius: A New Homeric Model and Etymological Wordplay." *Paideia* 66:457–89.
Roche, P. 2013. "A Fawn in the Wood: *Inuleus* in Horace *Carmen* 1.23." *CP* 108.4: 346–51.
Rudd, N. 1989. *Horace* Epistles *Book II and Epistle to the Pisones* 'Ars Poetica'. Cambridge.

Savage, J.J.H. 1958. "The Art of the Third *Eclogue* of Vergil (55–111)." TAPA 89:142–58.

Sansone, D. 1996. "Virgil, *Aeneid* 5.835–6." *CQ* 46.2: 429–33.

Schawaller, D. 1987. "Semantische Wortspiele in Ovids Metamorphosen und Heroiden." *GB* 14:199–214.

Schironi, F. 2003. "Aristarchus and His Use of Etymology." In Nifadopoulos 2003, 71–78.

Schork, R. J. 1998. "Egyptian Etymology in Vergil." *Latomus* 57.4: 828–31.

Sharrock, A. 1997. Review of O'Hara 1996. *G&R* 42:223–27.

Shelton, C. 2013. "Religious Etymology and Poetic Syncretism at Rome." In *Poetic Language and Religion in Greece and Rome*, ed. J. V. García and A. Ruiz, 147–55. Newcastle.

Shelton, C. 2014. "Logical Complexity and Etymological Wordplay." *Latomus* 73:385–98.

Skempis, M. 2008. "Ery-Chthonios: Etymological Wordplay in Callimachus *Hec.* Fr. 70.9 H." *Hermes* 136.2: 143–52.

Skempis, M., and I. Ziogas. 2009. "Arete's Words: Etymology, Ehoie-Poetry and Gendered Narrative in the *Odyssey*." In *Narratology and Interpretation: The Content of Narrative Form in Ancient Literature*, ed. J. Grethlein and A. Rengakos, 213–40. Berlin.

Skutsch, O. 1987. "Helen, Her Name and Nature." *JHS* 107:188–93.

Somerville, T. 2010. "Note on a Reversed Acrostic in Vergil *Georgics* 1.429–33." *CP* 105.2: 202–8.

Stephens, S. A. 2002. *Seeing Double: Intercultural Poetics in Ptolemaic Alexandria.* Berkeley.

Sullivan, M. B. 2016. "Mind Your Tongues: Horace (Word)Plays Apollo (*Carm.* 3.1.1–4)." CQ 66.1: 402–6.

Tarrant, R. 2012. *Virgil:* Aeneid *Book XII.* Cambridge.

Thomas, R. F. 2003–04. "Torn between Jupiter and Saturn: Ideology, Rhetoric and Culture Wars in the *Aeneid*." *CJ* 100.2: 121–47.

Throop, P. 2006. *Isidore of Seville's Etymologies: Complete English Translation.* 2 vols. Charlotte, VT.

Tissol, G. 1997. *The Face of Nature: Wit, Narrative, and Cosmic Origins in Ovid's* Metamorphoses. Princeton.

Tsitsibakou-Vasalos, E. 2003. "Aphrodite in Homer and the Homeric Hymns: Poetic Etymology." In Nifadopoulos 2003, 119–29.

Tsitsibakou-Vasalos, E. 2007. *Ancient Poetic Etymology. The Pelopids: Fathers and Sons.* Stuttgart.

Tsitsiou-Chelidoni, C. 2003. "*Nomen Omen*: Scylla's Eloquent Name and Ovid's Reply (*Met.* 8,6–151)." *MD* 50:195–203.

Uría, J. 2006. "Personal Names and Invective in Cicero." In Booth and Maltby 2006, 13–31.

Vallat, D. 2006. "Bi-lingual Word-play on Personal Names in Martial." In Booth and Maltby 2006, 121–43.

Van Sickle, J. B. 2004. "Virgil *Bucolics* 1.1–2 and Interpretive Tradition: A Latin Roman Program for a Greek Genre." *CP* 99.4: 336–53.

Victor, B., D. Chassé, C. Dorey, F. Pezon and M. Vigneau. 2014. "Quelques étymologies et autres jeux de mots chez Lucrèce." *Phoenix* 68.1–2: 112–25.

Watson, L. 2003. *A Commentary on Horace's* Epodes. Oxford.

Wheeler, S. M. 1997. "Changing Names: The Miracle of Iphis in Ovid *Metamorphoses* 9." *Phoenix* 51.2: 190–202.

Wills, J. 1997. Review of O'Hara 1996. *BMCR* 97.12.17. http://bmcr.brynmawr.edu/1997/97.12.16.html

Yardley, J. C. 2001. "Word-Play in Propertius." In *Mélanges Pierre Rodrigue Brind'Amour*, ed. Pierre Senay, vol. 2 = *CEA* 38:129–34.

Ziogas, I. 2013. *Ovid and Hesiod: The Metamorphosis of the* Catalogue of Women. Cambridge.

# Introduction

In the *Homeric Hymn to Aphrodite,* Aphrodite explains that her son's name will be Aeneas because of the "awful grief" *(ainon achos)* that she feels for having slept with the mortal Anchises. In the *Iliad,* Hector's son is called Astyanax by the Trojans because his father is a protecting lord *(anax)* of the city *(astu).* In Aeschylus' *Agamemnon,* a chorus says that Helen has been rightly named because the root *hel-* means "destroy, destroyer." Less explicitly, Euripides' *Hippolytus* seems to play on Hippolytus as a "breaker of horses" *(hippoi + luo)* who is fatally "broken" by his own horses and chariot; the tragedy also often uses the verb *luo* of the breaking of nooses, knots, and oaths, and of the resolution of problems. The philosopher Heraclitus comments on how the name of the bow *(bios)* is associated with life *(bios,* with a different accent), although its work is the opposite, to bring death; Sophocles plays upon the near homonymy with the suggestion that to take away Philoctetes' bow is to take his life. A speaker in Plato's *Cratylus* argues, as do later Stoic philosophers, that the name Zeus, which is *Di-* in the oblique cases, is fitting for one who permeates, who goes through *(dia)* everything that exists; there are probably earlier allusions to this connection in Hesiod and Aeschylus. Among the Alexandrian poets of the third century B.C. and later, etymological wordplay becomes more frequent, more learned, and more focused on aetiology or the study of origins. Callimachus tells how the island of Delos received that name when its roots were fixed and it became no longer "inconspicuous" *(adelos).* Apollonius of Rhodes tells how an altar came to be dedicated to Apollo "of the Shore" *(Actios);* later he invokes the Muse Erato at the start of the story of Jason and Medea, because her "erotic" name makes her appropriate for such a context. Sometimes Alexandrian poets present competing etymologies, in the manner of scholars arguing for rival theories: Callimachus, Apollonius, and Euphorion seem to have offered different derivations for the name Achilles. At Rome, in Plautus' *Pseudolus* a character named Harpax says he is known for capturing *(rapio, = harpazo)* the enemy alive. Cicero, in both prose and poetry, discusses the derivation of the name of the constellation Hyades from the Greek word for rain; elsewhere he argues that "prudence" *(prudentia)* consists in seeing in advance *(providere).*[1]

These passages from archaic, classical, and Hellenistic Greek literature and philosophy, and from Republican Latin authors, are some of the almost countless examples of etymologizing or etymological wordplay to be found in ancient authors. This monograph aims to provide a reasonably comprehensive treatment of poetic etymological wordplay in Vergil's *Aeneid, Eclogues,* and *Georgics* and will present and discuss all plausible examples that I, or any other scholar of whose work I am aware, have found in Vergil's works.[2] Poetic etymological wordplay—to define it here briefly at the outset—consists of explicit reference or implicit allusion to the etymology of

---

1. For the name Aeneas, see on A. (= *Aeneid*) 12.945–47; for Astyanax, below in the discussion of Homer; for Helen, see my catalogue entry for A. 3.295; for Hippolytus, A. 7.761–77; for *bios,* below in the discussion of Sophocles; for Zeus, *Di-, dia,* G. 4.219–22; for Delos, A. 6.11–12; for *Actios,* A. 3.280; for Erato, A. 7.37–41; for Achilles, not in Vergil, below in section 1.1 for Homer, and 1.4 for the Alexandrians; for Harpax, A. 3.226–27; for Hyades, G. 1.137–38; for *prudentia,* A. 3.433.

2. This claim needs comment, for it is clear to me that I must have missed some suggestions in the vast secondary literature and some examples present in the text but not discernible to me. I have also omitted some suggestions from all periods that seemed to be so completely implausible as to be not worth printing; I have found little worth citing in Fulgentius, for example, whose etymologies seem to me like Mark Twain's derivation of Middletown from Moses (you take off the -oses, and add -iddletown–I owe my knowledge of this derivation to Carol Dougherty). A truly comprehensive collection of all possible examples would take a lifetime, but perhaps not be much more useful than this study, product of only a decade's work. I have used and greatly benefited from Maltby (1991), but much of my collection was developed from other sources and my own reading before its publication (Servius, Isidore, and Bartelink, who had already noted over half my examples, were especially important for me). One unavoidable limitation of Maltby's lexicon is its paucity of Greek material like that found in *Etym. Mag., Etym. Gen.,* and the Homeric and other scholia; my own search of Greek nonpoetic etymologizing that might be relevant to Vergil has been extensive (Mühmelt [1965] and the indices to Erbse [1969–88] have been helpful), but not exhaustive, and something more might be done with this when more Greek sources have been properly edited (cf. Dyck [1993] esp. 1–9 and Haslam [1994] esp. 1–3) and catalogued. A project under the direction of Professors Francis Cairns and Robert Maltby has been announced, with the goal of producing several lexica of Greek etymologies, modeled on Maltby (1991) but arranged by author or source; these will be a welcome tool. The completion of the Harvard edition of Servius may also offer an opportunity for improving upon what I have done here for the *Eclogues, Georgics,* and *Aeneid* 6–12 (cf. on A. 3.274, where Murgia has already restored a Servian comment on etymology). In addition, when our knowledge of Alexandrian poetic etymologizing is more complete, we will understand more of what is in Vergil; in section 1.4 I offer an extensive but still inadequate survey of Alexandrian etymologizing.

I invite all scholars who notice examples of etymologizing in Vergil that I have missed to send them to me.

one of the words a poet is using. A poet may simply explain or allude to the derivation of a word or may suggest further that the derivation of the name is appropriate because it corresponds to some essential feature of the thing named, or gives the true explanation *(etymos logos)* of the thing. But poetic etymologizing is more easily understood from examples than from definitions. Much of the Vergilian etymological wordplay to be discussed in this study will resemble the examples given above (in fact Vergil will allude to most of those etymologies), but the study will include a slightly broader range of wordplay, both to be more useful and because strenuous efforts to distinguish or separate etymological wordplay from "related phenomena," to use a phrase from the title of Rank's study of Homeric wordplay, are not worthwhile, and probably not true to the practice of the poets. There are abundant examples in Vergil, running the range from simple paronomasia or puns based on similar-sounding words, to explicit statements about the derivations of names, to more subtle, implicit etymologizing discernible only to the learned reader familiar with the scholarly and poetic tradition of etymologizing. I hope not to make the mistake of saying or implying that etymologizing was Vergil's main interest as he composed his careful hexameters, but etymological wordplay was a part of his technique and style, along with metaphor, simile, alliteration and assonance, metrical rhythm, allusion, imitation, and imagery. This technique he used sometimes casually and easily, sometimes with great care and erudition; at times for the reader to notice etymologizing provides only a slightly increased sense of pleasure in reading, but at other times to miss etymological wordplay is to miss important thematic suggestions, or at least significant markers of stylistic affinity to a tradition of etymologizing and etymological aetiology. With aetiology in particular the stylistic and thematic impulses behind etymologizing often come together: as both the *Georgics* and especially the *Aeneid* seek to explain how the world came to be as it is today, the two poems treat the origins of customs, traits, peoples, and also words. And so this study will argue against, and I hope provide material with which others will argue against, the notion that etymological wordplay is merely a game, for although such wordplay does have ludic aspects and may sometimes serve mainly to increase the reader's pleasure, it is also used to forward the poet's most serious themes. Thus this study should also play a role in the debate about the larger question of how to view or respond to the learned aspects of Alexandrian and Augustan poets.

This introduction has four sections. The first will trace, at some length but in a necessarily incomplete survey, the history of poetic etymologizing among the Greeks and Romans before Vergil, with special attention to both the Alexandrian or Hellenistic poets,[3] and the proto-Alexandrian features found already in archaic and classical Greek authors. The second will describe in some detail the typical features of Vergilian etymological wordplay. The third will discuss the functions of etymological wordplay in Vergil. The fourth will briefly describe the format of the annotated catalogue of examples from Vergil that follows. Brief justification will be given here now for the first two sections, which attempt to provide background for an evaluation of the heritage, extent, and nature of Vergilian etymologizing—an evaluation that may be useful for the study of etymological wordplay in any Roman poet.

Several factors combined to make etymological wordplay popular among Augustan poets: the long tradition of etymologizing in archaic and classical Greek literature, and in the ancient tradition of scholarly commentary on that literature; the popularity at Rome of Stoicism, which stressed the correspondence between words and the things for which they stood; the native Roman fondness both for etymological study, evident in the earliest Roman poetry and even in such nonpoetic types as the Roman jurists, and for wordplay of all kinds; the influence on the Augustans of the Alexandrian scholar-poets of the third and second centuries B.C., who made extensive demands upon the knowledge of the reader about matters mythological, aetiological, and etymological; and finally, the work of scholars such as Marcus Terentius Varro and Verrius Flaccus, just before and during the Augustan period. These factors or influences deserve consideration here, and so the next section will outline the history of etymological thinking and wordplay in antiquity up to Vergil's time. Exhaustive discussion is both impractical and unnecessary, and a monograph is expected from Robert Maltby as a followup to his enormously useful *Lexicon of Ancient Latin Etymologies*,[4] but a survey of the practices of earlier authors is needed to situate Vergilian etymologizing in its literary context and should prove useful to the readers of those authors as well.

The introduction's discussion of the typical features of Vergilian etymological wordplay should also prove useful. Scholarly interest in ety-

3. On these terms, of which Alexandrian is somewhat narrower than Hellenistic, see below at the start of section 1.4.

4. For now see Hecht (1882), Woodhead (1928), Stanford (1939), Reitzenstein (1909), Rank (1951), Collart (1954) 251–68, Curtius (1953) 495–500, Bartelink (1965) 5–27, Shechter (1975) esp. 358–59, Cairns (1979) 87–93, Snyder (1980) esp. 52–73, Amsler (1989) 15–55, Maltby (1993a).

mological wordplay in the Augustan poets has grown quickly in the last few years, with monographs, chapters in books, articles, and a growing attention to etymologizing even among those whose main concerns lie elsewhere. For Vergil the standard work is Bartelink's *Etymologisering bij Vergilius* (1965). Since the publication of that fine monograph a great number of scholars have added to our knowledge of Vergilian etymologizing, most of them ignorant of one another's work. More significantly, Bartelink also undervalues the importance of Alexandrian poetry for Vergil and has no analysis of the formal conventions of poetic etymologizing, and little analysis of the poetic function of etymologizing, which is seldom the gratuitous display of knowledge that it first appears but is generally serving some artistic purpose.[5] The purpose of my study—which would have been much more difficult without the existence of Bartelink's well-researched monograph—is not simply to update and expand Bartelink. Rather I hope to ask, and provide information that will help answer, a question not asked often enough in the first waves of study of etymological wordplay in Latin poets: How can I distinguish between an etymological wordplay made by the poet, which I have discovered, and one that I myself have invented, or forced upon the poet?[6] There is no easy or complete answer to this question, but I think we can at least point ourselves in the correct direction. One step must be to acknowledge the role of chance in producing some phrases that might merely look like etymological wordplay. Every scholar claiming to have discovered an example of poetic etymological wordplay must ask whether features of the text actually en-

5. In fact, most of this introduction focuses on aspects of Vergilian etymological wordplay given little attention in Bartelink. It may also be noted that Bartelink's Dutch monograph presents examples grouped in chapters by type of word and has no index locorum or verborum, which has made it somewhat difficult to consult. My catalogue provides full references to examples discussed by Bartelink and is now the best guide to finding information there.

6. Among those who have given this question some attention are Hanssen (1948), Due (1973), and more recently Maltby (1993a) and the skeptical Knox (1991).

The analysis by Starobinski (1979) 123, of Ferdinand de Saussure's numerous notebooks full of what he thought were anagrams in Latin poetry, provides a useful perspective on scholarly study of features like etymologizing:

> The error of Ferdinand de Saussure (if it be an error) will also provide an exemplary lesson. He will have taught us how difficult it is for the critic to avoid taking his own lucky find as the rule followed by the poet. The critic, thinking he has made a discovery, resigns himself with bad grace to accepting the possibility that the poet has neither consciously nor unconsciously *willed* what the analyst has only *assumed.* He resigns himself badly to remaining alone with his discovery. He wishes to share it with the poet. But the poet, having said all he has to say, remains strangely silent. One can produce any hypothesis about him: he neither accepts nor rejects it.

courage the reader to consider the derivations of the words involved.[7] This question, I realize, sounds a little like older, discredited appeals to simplistic notions of intentionality, but there are some difficult problems with dismissing intentionality completely in regard to poetic allusion. I do not endorse appeals to intentionality for most questions of meaning or interpretation, especially when such appeals involve ignoring the details of the text under study. But my observation has been that when etymological wordplay is significant in an Augustan poet, it is almost always a self-conscious poetic device.[8] I prefer, however, to focus not on the poet's thought processes, but on the reader's approach to the text itself. So my question might be restated like this: How can we determine whether an etymological wordplay is really in the text, or has been invented by an overly imaginative interpreter without the encouragement of the text? This is a difficult question, but I think a necessary first step is to recognize the conventions of etymological wordplay and its typical features: these are the focus of the second section of the introduction and can provide the circumstantial evidence, or clues, that I can use to help reassure myself that I am not simply foisting etymologies on the helpless poet. They will also help me to recognize some etymologizing that I might otherwise have overlooked, in other words to improve the "literary competence" with which I approach the text.[9] The second section of the introduction, then, has the twin goals of explaining some of these features and illustrating them with examples. Some examples will be quite simple, some rather involved. Some will be well known; several will be the result of my own observation. Discussion of most examples will be brief, with more details to be found in the catalogue. The second section will also provide, in

---

7. In lectures I have given on this problem, I have dramatized the problem of coincidence by showing audiences two photographs: one of the Augustus of Prima Porta, with the right arm raised in the air, the left arm holding a (modern) black staff against his body, the noticeable ponderation of the hips and legs, and the Cupid figure visible beyond the right leg; the other of Boston Red Sox Hall of Fame left fielder Carl Yastrzemski saluting the crowd in his final game, with his right arm raised in the air, the left arm holding a black bat against his body, the noticeable ponderation of the hips and legs, and the on-deck batter, made smaller by the photograph's perspective, visible just beyond the right leg.

8. Alternately, one might say that intentional wordplay is the only kind that I have any facility for discovering or discussing. I differentiate learned etymological wordplay from other kinds of punning, which of course need not be intentional: see Culler (1988a) esp. 10–16, Redfern (1984) passim, esp. 1–21, Ahl (1988) esp. 24–26.

On intention more generally see Patterson (1990) on the flaws of extreme views on both sides. For intentionality as it relates to allusion or Alexandrianism, cf. Farrell (1991) 21–23 and the reply of Conte (1992) 51 and n. 5.

9. On "literary competence" see e.g., the chapter of that name in Culler (1975); cf. too the discussion of Petronius in Slater (1990) 1–23.

footnotes appended to many of the categories, "features lists" that gather together examples to be found in Vergil of the feature in question. It must be noted, however, that not all examples of etymological wordplay treated in the catalogue are mentioned in the introduction. The introduction is meant to be illustrative, the catalogue, closer to being comprehensive.

## 1. Etymological Thinking and Wordplay before Vergil

This is not the place for a full discussion of Greek and early Roman etymologizing, but a survey with examples and some comments should prove useful. This section will touch upon archaic and classical Greek literature; philosophers from the fifth to third centuries; Alexandrian poets; grammarians and others who taught or discussed etymology at Rome and elsewhere; and Roman poets before Vergil. As noted earlier, my treatment of Alexandrian poetry will be extensive, both because of these poets' influence on Vergil and because they have been slighted or even scorned in some surveys of etymologizing; this section will also observe what may be called proto-Alexandrian features of earlier Greek poetry.

### 1.1. Homer, Hesiod, and the Hymns

Homer and Hesiod offer many examples of wordplay of several kinds not always easily distinguished, ranging from assonance or the simple collocation of similar sounds, to paronomasia or wordplay based on similar sounds, to glosses or explanations of what may be older or simply more difficult words, to glosses on proper names, either implicit or explicit, and finally to more developed etymological wordplay, which may include a stress on the name and the extent to which it seems to represent the essence of a thing or character.[10] Assonance, alliteration, or other considerations of euphony produce many collocations that might suggest etymological connections, and at times words originally connected only for euphony eventually are thought to

10. On Homer see esp. Rank (1951), but also Hecht (1882) 32–36, Woodhead (1928) passim, Stanford (1939) 99–114 and (1965) xxi, Curtius (1953) 495, Lendle (1957) 117–18, Dimock (1962), Bartelink (1965) 5–6, and more recently Cairns (1979) 92–93, Snyder (1980) 53–55, Macleod (1982) 50–53, Edwards (1987) 120–23, Haywood (1983), Dimock (1989), Peradotto (1990), Feeney (1991) 20–22, Baxter (1992) 113–17. On Greek material in general see Hecht (1882), McCartney (1918–19), Woodhead (1928), Fordyce (1932), (1932a), Rank (1951) 9–27, Lendle (1957) 117–21 ("Tabelle der Etymologien und Wortspiele in der archaischen Dichtung [und bei Aischylos]"), Quincey (1963), Bartelink (1965) 5–13, Cairns (1979) 87–93, Baxter (1992) esp. 107–63, Pollmann (1993), Dougherty (1993) 46–47 and index s.v. etymology.

be related etymologically.[11] In *Iliad* 13.481–82, Idomeneus says that he "terribly fears Aeneas" (δείδια δ' αἰνῶς / Αἰνείαν); as noted at the start of this introduction, the *Homeric Hymn to Aphrodite* explicitly derives the name Aeneas from the word αἰνός, "terrible." Homer also speaks of Πρόθοος θοός at *Iliad* 2.758 and uses the phrase τοῖον γὰρ ἄχος βεβίηκεν 'Αχαιούς at both *Iliad* 10.145 and 16.22. In the latter case the association of ἄχος, "grief," with the Achaeans may have greater thematic significance, if we are to believe Nagy's argument that original mythological connotations of names control how a myth develops in the epic, so that Achilles is the one "whose λαός ('people') has ἄχος."[12] This is certainly the theory of some of the *characters* who discuss the meanings of names in Greek tragedy, as several examples will show below. Four lines in *Iliad* 16 present elaborate wordplay or soundplay on πάλλειν (brandish), πῆλαι (aorist of preceding), Πηλιάς (adj., Pelian), Πηλίον (the mountain), and Πηλεύς (Achilles' father, not named but suggested by πατρὶ in 143).[13] Sometimes etymologizing provides practical assistance for the Homeric audience.

Since the language of Greek epic seems to have developed over several centuries, it preserves words that may have been obscure to later generations, and often Homer seems to offer glosses or explanations of rare words, especially those that occur only once either in Homer or in one or the other poem *(hapax legomena)*. When Thersites is described by the *hapax* ἀμετροεπής, "unmeasured in his words," there is added, as a gloss in a relative clause, "who knew many disorderly (ἄκοσμα) words."[14] Later poets will preserve

11. For a good and concise discussion of assonance and wordplay in Homer see Macleod (1982) 50–53.

12. Nagy (1979) 70 argues that this meaning of the name "is intrinsic to the function of Achilles in myth and epic." For the suggestions of Apollonius, Euphorion, and (perhaps) Callimachus see section 1.4.

13. *Il.* 16.141–44 (= 19.388–91):

βριθὺ μέγα στιβαρόν· τὸ μὲν οὐ δύνατ' ἄλλος 'Αχαιῶν
πάλλειν, ἀλλά μιν οἶος ἐπίστατο πῆλαι 'Αχιλλεὺς
Πηλιάδα μελίην, τὴν πατρὶ φίλῳ πόρε Χείρων
Πηλίου ἐκ κορυφῆς, φόνον ἔμμεναι ἡρώεσσιν.

With this Homeric passage may be compared the extensive plays, both euphonious and etymological, on the root *pal-* in both Vergil and Tibullus: see on G. 3.1–3.

14. *Il.* 2.212–13 ἀμετροεπὴς . . . / ὃς ἔπεα φρεσὶ ᾗσιν ἄκοσμά τε πολλά τε ᾔδη (it must be noted that ἄκοσμά is also an Homeric *hapax*). Cf. too *Od.* 5.67 εἰνάλιαι, τῇσίν τε θαλάσσια ἔργα μέμηλεν, *Il.* 1.238–39 δικασπόλοι, οἵ τε θέμιστας / πρὸς Διὸς εἰρύαται, *Il.* 5.63 ἀρχεκάκους, αἳ πᾶσι κακὸν Τρώεσσι γένοντο, *Il.* 5.403 σχέτλιος, ὀβριμοεργός, ὃς οὐκ ὄθετ' αἴσυλα ῥέζων, *Il.* 10.293 = *Od.* 3.383 ἀδμήτην, ἣν οὔ πω ὑπὸ ζυγὸν ἤγαγεν ἀνήρ. Fine discussion in Rank (1951) 76.

this practice by glossing a rare, often Homeric, word, and for Latin poets it will often be a word from Greek or other languages.

Much etymologizing in Homer, as throughout Greek and Roman literature, deals with names, which are often thought to be a key to the essence of a character. A well-known example occurs in *Odyssey* 19, where Autolycus says that because he himself is "hateful" or a "source of pain" (ὀδυσσάμενος) to many, his grandson should be named Odysseus.[15] The poem associates Odysseus with the word ὀδύσασθαι in a number of passages, and some recent studies stress the importance of the name, interpreted to mean something like "man of pain," for the poem as a whole.[16] Many other names are explicitly or implicitly etymologized, although for many examples the argument could be made that euphony, and not a suggested etymological link, motivates the collocation. The names of both Scylla and Charybdis seem to be glossed in *Odyssey* 12, where Scylla is linked with the word σκύλαξ, "puppy,"[17] and Charybdis with the verb ἀναρρυβδεῖ, "to swallow down."[18] The *Odyssey* suggests a connection between the name Telemachus and the word τῆλε, "far"; the other element in the name is linked with the root μαχ- (battle), in the *Iliad,* although both passages may reflect a desire for euphony rather than etymologizing.[19] *Odyssey* 18 explicitly explains the nickname Iros, given to

---

15. *Od.* 19.405–12:

τὴν δ' αὖτ' Αὐτόλυκος ἀπαμείβετο φώνησέν τε·  
"γαμβρὸς ἐμὸς θύγατέρ τε, τίθεσθ' ὄνομ' ὅττι κεν εἴπω·  
πολλοῖσιν γὰρ ἐγώ γε ὀδυσσάμενος τόδ' ἱκάνω,  
ἀνδράσιν ἠδὲ γυναιξὶν ἀνὰ χθόνα πουλυβότειραν·  
τῷ δ' Ὀδυσεὺς ὄνομ' ἔστω ἐπώνυμον. αὐτὰρ ἐγώ γε,  
ὁππότ' ἂν ἡβήσας μητρώιον ἐς μέγα δῶμα  
ἔλθῃ Παρνησόνδ', ὅθι πού μοι κτήματ' ἔασι,  
τῶν οἱ ἐγὼ δώσω καί μιν χαίροντ' ἀποπέμψω."

Dotted underlinings, as of τίθεσθ' ὄνομ' in 406, mark the naming constructions that often call attention to etymologizing or significant names (see sect. 2.6).

16. Cf. Dimock (1989) index s.v. Odysseus, name of, who suggests that the verb means "will pain to," Peradotto (1990) 120–42 and index s.v. names, Baxter (1992) 113, and the full discussion in Rank (1951) 50–63. See *Od.* 1.62 τί νύ οἱ τόσον ὠδύσαο, Ζεῦ; 5.339–40 κάμμορε, τίπτε τοι ὧδε Ποσειδάων ἐνοσίχθων / ὠδύσατ' ἐκπάγλως, ὅτι τοι κακὰ πολλὰ φυτεύει; 5.423 οἶδα γὰρ ὥς μοι ὀδώδυσται κλυτὸς ἐννοσίγαιος; 19.270–76 ὡς ἤδη Ὀδυσῆος ἐγὼ περὶ νόστου ἄκουσα / . . . ὀδύσαντο γὰρ αὐτῷ / Ζεύς τε καὶ Ἠέλιος.

17. 12.85–86 ἔνθα δ' ἐνὶ Σκύλλη ναίει δεινὸν λελακυῖα· / τῆς ἦ τοι φωνὴ μὲν ὅση σκύλακος νεογιλῆς. See on A. 3.432.

18. 12.104 τῷ δ' ὑπὸ δῖα Χάρυβδις ἀναρρυβδεῖ μέλαν ὕδωρ; 235–36 ἔνθεν γὰρ Σκύλλη, ἑτέρωθι δὲ δῖα Χάρυβδις / δεινὸν ἀνερροίβδησε θαλάσσης ἁλμυρὸν ὕδωρ.

19. *Od.* 15.10 Τηλέμαχ', οὐκέτι καλὰ δόμων ἄπο τῆλ' ἀλάλησαι; *Il.* 4.354 Τηλεμάχοιο φίλον πατέρα προμάχοισι μιγέντα.

a man who carries messages, like the goddess Iris.[20] *Iliad* 9 explicitly glosses Kleopatra's alternate name Alcyone: her mother wept like the seabird halcyon when Apollo took her daughter away.[21] Several passages connect the names of Hector and his son Astyanax with words that suggest Hector's importance to the city, and the hope that Astyanax will one day rule it. Hector's name is implicitly connected with the verb ἔχω, "to hold," which has a rough breathing in some tenses, since he "holds" or protects the city as its greatest warrior, although one might attribute this to assonance rather than etymological thinking. His son's name is connected with the words ἄστυ, "city," and ἄναξ, "lord, protecting chief."[22] The Catalogue of Ships seems to connect the name Protesilaos with the fact that he was the first (πρῶτος) to leap (cf. ἅλλομαι, Latin *salio)* from his ship when the Greeks landed at Troy.[23] *Odyssey* 19 seems to gloss the word nightingale (ἀηδών) by mentioning that it sings (ἀείδῃσιν).[24] In *Iliad* 7, Areithoos is called "clubfighter" (κορυνήτης), unsurprisingly, because he fights with a club (κορύνη).[25] This passage from *Iliad* 7 and several of the others call attention to an appellation by a naming formula such as "whom they call X"; this practice was adapted by many later poets and serves to call attention to wordplay in

---

20. *Od.* 18.6–7 Ἶρον δὲ νέοι κίκλησκον ἅπαντες, / οὕνεκ' ἀπαγγέλλεσκε κιών, ὅτε πού τις ἀνώγοι.

21. *Il.* 9.561–64:

τὴν δὲ τότ' ἐν μεγάροισι πατὴρ καὶ πότνια μήτηρ
Ἀλκυόνην καλέεσκον ἐπώνυμον, οὕνεκ' ἄρ' αὐτῆς
μήτηρ ἀλκυόνος πολυπενθέος οἶτον ἔχουσα
κλαῖεν ὅ μιν ἑκάεργος ἀνήρπασε Φοῖβος Ἀπόλλων.

22. *Il.* 5.472–73 Ἕκτορ, πῇ δή τοι μένος οἴχεται ὃ πρὶν ἔχεσκες; / φῆς που ἄτερ λαῶν πόλιν ἑξέμεν ἠδ' ἐπικούρων; 6.476–78 Ζεῦ ἄλλοι τε θεοί δότε δὴ καὶ τόνδε γενέσθαι / παῖδ' ἐμὸν, ὡς καὶ ἐγώ περ ἀριπρεπέα Τρώεσσιν, / ὧδε βίην τ' ἀγαθόν, καὶ Ἰλίου ἶφι ἀνάσσειν; 6.402–3 τόν ῥ' Ἕκτωρ καλέεσκε Σκαμάνδριον, αὐτὰρ οἱ ἄλλοι / Ἀστυάνακτ'· οἶος γὰρ ἐρύετο Ἴλιον Ἕκτωρ (suggesting also a connection between Ἕκτωρ and ἔχω); 22.506–7 Ἀστυάναξ, ὃν Τρῶες ἐπίκλησιν καλέουσιν· / οἶος γάρ σφιν ἔρυσο πύλας καὶ τείχεα μακρά. Plato's Socrates discusses Homer's glossing of both names at *Crat.* 392–93; cf. Rosenstock (1992).

23. *Il.* 2.698–702 τῶν αὖ Πρωτεσίλαος ἀρήιος ἡγεμόνευε / . . . / νηὸς ἀποθρῴσκοντα πολὺ πρώτιστον Ἀχαιῶν.

24. *Od.* 19.518–19 ὡς δ' ὅτε Πανδαρέου κούρη, χλωρηὶς ἀηδών, / καλὸν ἀείδῃσιν ἔαρος νέον ἱσταμένοιο. Cf. Cairns (1979) 93, Rank (1951) 35.

25. *Il.* 7.138–41:

τὸν ἐπίκλησιν κορυνήτην
ἄνδρες κίκλησκον καλλίζωνοί τε γυναῖκες
οὕνεκ' ἄρ' οὐ τόξοισι μαχέσκετο δουρί τε μακρῷ,
ἀλλὰ σιδηρείῃ κορύνῃ ῥήγνυσκε φάλαγγας.

Vergil as well.[26] Both in this introduction and in the catalogue, I highlight such naming constructions with dotted underlining; see below in section 2.6 for further discussion.

A final example from Homer will demonstrate the assumption of etymological thinking, which later Greeks will make more explicit, that a thing's name is a clue to its true essence. In Penelope's description of the gates of horn and ivory in *Odyssey* 19, etymological thinking underlies her explanation that dreams that pass through the gate of ivory (ἐλέφας) deceive (ἐλεφαίρονται), while those from the gate of horn (κέρας) "accomplish the truth" (ἔτυμα κραίνουσι; cf. κερ- and κρα-).[27] Vergil will imitate this passage closely at A. 6.893–98, but without directly alluding to etymology, unless the Homeric etymology should be thought of as implicitly reinforcing the points Vergil is making there.

Hesiod offers explicit or implied derivations for the names of several figures: Pandora, so called because all (πάντες) the Olympian gods gave a gift (δῶρον) to her;[28] the Cyclopes, named for their circular (κυκλοτερής) eyes;[29] Aphrodite, born from the foam (ἀφρός) of the sea;[30] the gray-haired

26. Rank (1951) 136–43 discusses this feature in Homer and other Greek authors.

27. *Od.* 19. 562–67:

δοιαὶ γάρ τε πύλαι ἀμενηνῶν εἰσὶν ὀνείρων·
αἱ μὲν γὰρ κεράεσσι τετεύχαται, αἱ δ' ἐλέφαντι.
τῶν οἳ μέν κ' ἔλθωσι διὰ πριστοῦ ἐλέφαντος,
οἵ ῥ' ἐλεφαίρονται, ἔπε' ἀκράαντα φέροντες·
οἳ δὲ διὰ ξεστῶν κεράων ἔλθωσι θύραζε,
οἵ ῥ' ἔτυμα κραίνουσι, βροτῶν ὅτε κέν τις ἴδηται.

Cf. Rank (1951) 104–8, and for further references Pollmann (1993); see also my entry on A. 6.893–98.

28. *Op.* 80–82 ὀνόμηνε δὲ τήνδε γυναῖκα / Πανδώρην, ὅτι πάντες Ὀλύμπια δώματ' ἔχοντες / δῶρον ἐδώρησαν.

On Hesiod I owe much to Hecht (1882) 46–52; cf. also West (1966) 77, Rank (1951) 137ff. and notes, Lendle (1957) 119–20, and Cairns (1979) 93.

29. *Th.* 144–45 Κύκλωπες δ' ὄνομ' ἦσαν ἐπώνυμον, οὕνεκ' ἄρα σφέων / κυκλοτερὴς ὀφθαλμὸς ἕεις ἐνέκειτο μετώπῳ. Cf. Rank (1951) 131, Cairns (1979) 93.

30. *Th.* 195–200:

ποσσὶν ὕπο ῥαδινοῖσιν ἀέξετο· τὴν δ' Ἀφροδίτην
[ἀφρογενέα τε θεὰν καὶ ἐυστέφανον Κυθέρειαν]
κικλήσκουσι θεοί τε καὶ ἀνέρες, οὕνεκ' ἐν ἀφρῷ
θρέφθη· ἀτὰρ Κυθέρειαν, ὅτι προσέκυρσε Κυθήροις·
Κυπρογενέα δ', ὅτι γέντο περικλύστῳ ἐνὶ Κύπρῳ·
[ἠδὲ φιλομμηδέα, ὅτι μηδέων ἐξεφαάνθη.]

Graiae;[31] Cymodocea, who calms the waves (κύματα);[32] Pegasus, born by the streams (πηγαί) of Ocean;[33] possibly the underworld dog Cerberus, said by Servius a millennium later to be named for being a meat eater (κρεοβόρος);[34] and the Titans who "strained" (τιταίνοντες) to commit a great crime, for which they receive punishment (τίσις).[35] The last example is a difficult one, because τιταίνω is hard to interpret, but also an important one, because Hesiod seems to be endorsing, in consecutive lines, two different derivations for the name Titan; we will see again that ancient authors were more prone to suggest that two etymologies are both true than our modern way of approaching etymology is willing to accept.[36]

The *Homeric Hymns* also often gloss the names or epithets of gods and mortals. I have mentioned the *Hymn to Aphrodite*'s derivation of the name Aeneas.[37] The *Hymn to Apollo* explains that the god is called Pythian because he killed the great serpent, whose body the heat of the sun then "made to rot" (πῦσε), Telephusian because of his victory over the stream Telephusa, and Delphinian because he appeared in the shape of a dolphin (δελφίς).[38] The *Hymn to Pan* connects Pan's name with πᾶς, "all," because as a boy he delighted all the gods.[39] Less overtly, the *Hymn to Dionysus* seems to derive

31. *Th.* 271 ἐκ γενετῆς πολιάς, τὰς δὴ Γραίας καλέουσιν.

32. *Th.* 252 Κυμοδόκη θ', ἣ κύματ' ἐν ἠεροειδέι πόντῳ. . . .

33. *Th.* 281–83 καὶ Πήγασος ἵππος· / τῷ μὲν ἐπώνυμον ἦν, ὅτ' ἄρ' Ὠκεανοῦ παρὰ πηγὰς / γένθ', ὃ δ' ἄορ χρύσειον ἔχων μετὰ χερσὶ φίλῃσιν.

34. *Th.* 311 Κέρβερον ὠμηστήν, Ἀίδεω κύνα γείνατο χαλκεόφωνον. Here ὠμηστήν may be a single-epithet gloss of the name Cerberus, glossed by Servius as κρεοβόρος, *id est, carnem vorans*. See on A. 8.296–87.

35. *Th.* 207–10:

τοὺς δὲ πατὴρ Τιτῆνας ἐπίκλησιν καλέεσκε
παῖδας νεικείων μέγας Οὐρανός, οὓς τέκεν αὐτός·
φάσκε δὲ τιταίνοντας ἀτασθαλίῃ μέγα ῥέξαι
ἔργον, τοῖο δ' ἔπειτα τίσιν μετόπισθεν ἔσεσθαι.

36. Rank (1951) 15 and West (1966) ad loc.; cf. Rank 51–63 and West on the name Odysseus.

37. *Hom. Hymn Aphr.* 198–99 τῷ δὲ καὶ Αἰνείας ὄνομ' ἔσσεται οὕνεκά μ' αἰνὸν / ἔσχεν ἄχος ἕνεκα βροτοῦ ἀνέρος ἔμπεσον εὐνῇ. On the *Hymns* I draw especially from Hecht (1882) 52–53, Woodhead (1928) 15, 29, and Lendle (1957) 120.

38. *Hom. Hymn Ap.* 372–74 ἐξ οὗ νῦν Πυθὼ κικλήσκεται, οἱ δὲ ἄνακτα / Πύθειον καλέουσιν ἐπώνυμον οὕνεκα κεῖθι / αὐτοῦ πῦσε πέλωρ μένος ὀξέος Ἠελίοιο; 385–87 ἔνθα δ' ἄνακτι / πάντες ἐπίκλησινΤελφουσίῳεὐχετόωνται/οὕνεκαΤελφούσηςἱερῆςᾔσχυνεῥέεθρα;493–96ὡςμὲνἐγὼ τὸπρῶτονἐνἠεροειδέιπόντῳ/εἰδόμενοςδελφῖνιθοῆςἐπὶνηὸςὄρουσα,/ὣςἐμοὶεὔχεσθαιδελφινίῳ· αὐτὰρὁβωμὸς/αὐτὸςδέλφειοςκαὶἐπόψιοςἔσσεταιαἰεί.OnDelphiniuscf.Callimachusinsection 1.4.

39. *Hom. Hymn* 19.47 Πᾶνα δέ μιν καλέεσκον ὅτι φρένα πᾶσιν ἔτερψε.

the god's name from that of his father Zeus (*Dios-* in the oblique cases) and the place where he grew up, Nysa; Vergil may allude to this etymology as well.[40]

## 1.2. Tragedy, Pre-Socratics and Sophists, and the *Cratylus*

Tragic poets show great interest in the derivation or meanings of names, and in other etymological wordplay.[41] I have mentioned Aeschylus' connection of the name Helen with the root ἑλ-, "destroy."[42] Aeschylean scholars have discussed such passages as examples of kledonomancy, "a system of divination which operates on the conviction that language possesses an enigmatic oracular capacity to bear an unexpected meaning not intended or even understood by the speaker," so that one's parents may bestow an ill-omened name unwittingly.[43] In the same play Cassandra says Apollo is the one destroying or killing (ἀπόλλων) her.[44] In the *Suppliants* and in *Prometheus,*

40. *Hom. Hymn* 26.2–5 Ζηνὸς καὶ Σεμέλης ἐρικυδέος ἀγλαὸν υἱόν, / ὃν τρέφον ἠύκομοι νύμφαι παρὰ πατρὸς ἄνακτος / δεξάμεναι κόλποισι καὶ ἐνδυκέως ἀτίταλλον / Νύσης ἐν γυάλοις. See Apollonius in section 1.4, and cf. on A. 6.805.

41. On etymologizing in tragedy (concentration on one tragedian indicated by A, S, or E) see Hecht (1882) 58–69, Woodhead (1928) 11–40, Kranz (1933) 287–89 (A), Schmid (1934) 297–98 (A), Stanford (1939) 137–79, Collart (1954) 254–55 n. 7, Lendle (1957) 121 (A), Zeitlin (1982) 38–40, 98–103, 133–34, 140–43 (A), Goldhill (1984) index s.v. etymology (A), Griffith (1983) index s.v. etymology (A), Cameron (1970) (A), Quincey (1963) (A), Dougherty (1991) (A) and (1993) 88–89 (A), Robinson (1969) 43–44 (S), Vernant (1981) 96–97 (S), Daly (1982) (S), Ahl (1991) (S), Platnauer (1938) 62–63 (E), Dodds (1960) 367 (E), Wilson (1968) (E), Zeitlin (1985) 58–64 and 191 (E), Segal (1982) 294–98 (E), Baxter (1992) 144–47. I have not seen H. Van Looy, "Figura etymologica et Étymologie dans l'oeuvre de Sophocle," *Mus. Phil. Lond.* 1 (1975) 109ff. (S) or id., "Παρετυμολογεῖ ὁ Εὐριπίδης," in *Zetemata,* Festschrift for Emile de Strijcker (Antwerp and Utrecht 1973) 345–66 (E).

42. *Ag.* 681–90:
τίς ποτ' ὠνόμαζεν ὧδ'
ἐς τὸ πᾶν ἐτητύμως
μή τις ὅντιν' οὐχ ὁρῶμεν προνοί-
αισι τοῦ πεπρωμένου
γλῶσσαν ἐν τύχᾳ νέμων; τὰν
δορίγαμβρον ἀμφινει-
κῆ θ' Ἑλέναν; ἐπεὶ πρεπόντως
ἑλένας ἕλανδρος ἑλέ-
πτολις.

43. Zeitlin (1982) 46; on Aeschylus, see Zeitlin passim, Cameron (1970) and Peradotto (1969); more generally, Woodhead (1928) 22–23, Pease (1963) 283–85 on Cic. *Div.* 1.102, and for more on the Romans see section 1.5.

44. *Ag.* 1080–82 ὤπολλον· ὤπολλον· / ἀγυιᾶτ', ἀπόλλων ἐμός· / ἀπώλεσας γὰρ οὐ μόλις τὸ δεύτερον.

Epaphus' name is derived from the "caress" (ἐπαφή) of his mother Io by Zeus.[45] The *Prometheus* also glosses the names Prometheus, said to be wrongly named since he is not "forethinking" (προμηθής); Bosporus (ox crossing); and Ionia, from the wandering or "going" of Io.[46] The *Septem* alludes to the etymology of the names Polyneices (much strife, πολὺ νεῖκος) and Parthenopaeus (cf. παρθένος, virgin).[47]

Sophocles refers explicitly to the derivations of the names Eurysakes (broad shield) and Parthenopaeus[48] and has Ajax lament the tragic appropriateness of his name, which he connects with the cry of woe αἰαῖ.[49] More subtly, the *Philoctetes* plays upon a possible derivation of the name Philoctetes from φίλος (friend) and κτάομαι or κτῆμα (possess, possession); in this passage the wordplay occurs with words at the ends of consecutive lines, a feature that will become more prominent in literature meant to be read.[50] I have mentioned the *Philoctetes*' wordplay with βιός (bow) and βίος (life).[51]

---

45. *Supp.* 17 βοὸς ἐξ ἐπαφῆς κἀξ ἐπιπνοίας; 46–48 ἔφαψιν ἐπωνυμίαν / δ' ἐπεκραίνετο μόρσιμος αἰὼν / εὐλόχως, Ἔπαφόν δ' ἐγέννασεν; 314–15 {ΒΑ.} τίς οὖν ὁ Δῖος πόρτις εὔχεται βοός; / {ΧΟ.} Ἔπαφος, ἀληθῶς ῥυσίων ἐπώνυμος; *PV* 848–51 ἐνταῦθα δή σε Ζεὺς τίθησ' ἐγκύμονα / ἐπαφῶν ἀταρβεῖ χειρὶ καὶ θιγὼν μόνον. / ἐπώνυμον δὲ τῶν Διὸς γεννημάτων / τέξεις κελαινὸν Ἔπαφον.

46. *PV* 85–87 ψευδωνύμως σε δαίμονες Προμηθέα / καλοῦσιν· αὐτὸν γάρ σε δεῖ προμηθέως, / ὅτῳ τρόπῳ τῆσδ' ἐκκυλισθήσῃ τέχνης; 732–34 ἔσται δὲ θνητοῖς εἰσαεὶ λόγος μέγας / τῆς σῆς πορείας, Βόσπορος δ' ἐπώνυμος / κεκλήσεται; 839–41 χρόνον δὲ τὸν μέλλοντα πόντιος μυχός, / σαφῶς ἐπίστασ', Ἰόνιος κεκλήσεται, / τῆς σῆς πορείας μνῆμα τοῖς πᾶσιν βροτοῖς. Euripides will derive Ionia from the same root, through a different myth; see below. I take no position here on whether *PV* is by Aeschylus or not.

47. *Sept.* 829–31 οἵ δῆτ' ὀρθῶς κατ' ἐπωνυμίαν / ⟨ ⟩ καὶ πολυνεικεῖς / ὤλοντ' ἀσεβεῖ διανοίαι; 536–37 ὁ δ' ὠμόν, οὔ τι παρθένων ἐπώνυμον / φρόνημα, γοργὸν δ' ὄμμ' ἔχων, προσίσταται. In the lacuna at 830, Wecklein's ἐτεόκλειτοι would also gloss the name Eteocles, suggesting perhaps "true fame," "truly called," or "truly bewept"; see Zeitlin (1982) 39, and for further play on the name Polyneices see *Sept.* 658, and the corrupt 576ff., with Cameron (1970) 106–7 and Zeitlin (1982) 133–34.

48. *Aj.* 574–76 ἀλλ' αὐτό μοι σύ, παῖ, λαβὼν τοὐπώνυμον, / Εὐρύσακες, ἴσχε διὰ πολυρράφου στρέφων / πόρπακος ἑπτάβοιον ἄρρηκτον σάκος; *OC* 1320–22 ἕκτος δὲ Παρθενοπαῖος Ἀρκὰς ὄρνυται, / ἐπώνυμος τῆς πρόσθεν ἀδμήτης χρόνῳ / μητρὸς λοχευθείς, πιστὸς Ἀταλάντης γόνος. For Parthenopaeus see also Aesch. *Sept.* 536–37, quoted above.

49. *Aj.* 430–33 αἰαῖ· τίς ἄν ποτ' ᾤεθ' ὧδ' ἐπώνυμον / τοὐμὸν ξυνοίσειν ὄνομα τοῖς ἐμοῖς κακοῖς; / νῦν γὰρ πάρεστι καὶ δὶς αἰάζειν ἐμοὶ. Cf. the play on the name in Pind. *I.* 5.53, quoted in the notes below in this section.

50. *Phil.* 670–73 {ΦΙ.} εὐεργετῶν γὰρ καὐτὸς αὔτ' ἐκτησάμην. / {ΝΕ.} οὐκ ἄχθομαί σ' ἰδών τε καὶ λαβὼν φίλον· / ὅστις γὰρ εὖ δρᾶν εὖ παθὼν ἐπίσταται, / παντὸς γένοιτ' ἂν κτήματος κρείσσων φίλος. See Daly (1982), who gives further references. For wordplay at the ends of consecutive lines see section 2.9.

51. *Phil.* 931 ἀπεστέρηκας τὸν βίον τὰ τόξ' ἑλών; 1281–83 οὐ γάρ ποτ' εὔνουν τὴν ἐμὴν

The *Oedipus Tyrannus* provides an explicit derivation of the king's name from the swelling (οἶδμα) of his foot (πούς), bound when he was exposed as an infant, but also exploits the suggestion of "knowing" (οἶδα) in his name and alludes to the πούς root in a number of passages, so that Vernant could say that the "whole of the tragedy of Oedipus seems to be contained in the play to which the riddle of his name lends itself."[52] A fragment of Sophocles also repeats the etymology of the name Odysseus found in Homer.[53]

Euripides has characters comment on the origins or connotations of a number of names: Polyneices again;[54] Aphrodite, said to be named for ἀφροσύνη, "thoughtlessness," instead of Hesiod's "foam" (ἀφρός);[55] Ion, whom Xuthus names because he met him as he was "exiting" (ἐξιόντι) the temple;[56] Thoas, whose speed makes him θοός, "swift";[57] Theonoe, so named because she "knows" (νοεῖ) "divine things" (τὰ θεῖα);[58] Meleager, whose name is glossed in a fragment as "hunter of the wretched hunt"

---

κτήσῃ φρένα. / ὅστις γ' ἐμοῦ δόλοισι τὸν βίον λαβὼν / ἀπεστέρηκας. Cf. Heraclitus fr. 48 D-K τῷ οὖν τόξῳ ὄνομα βίος, ἔργον δὲ θάνατος on which see e.g. Kahn (1979) 201–2. The claim of Jebb, repeated by Webster (1970) 126, that because the accent is different "no pun is intended or heard" in Sophocles was already fully refuted by Robinson (1969) 43–44. On quantity see also below in section 2.1.

52. *OT* 1034–36 {ΑΓ.} λύω σ' ἔχοντα διατόρους ποδοῖν ἀκμάς. / {ΟΙ.} δεινόν γ' ὄνειδος σπαργάνων ἀνειλόμην. / {ΑΓ.} ὥστ' ὠνομάσθης ἐκ τύχης ταύτης ὃς εἶ. Cf. Vernant (1981) 96: "The double meaning of Oedipus is to be found in the name itself in the opposition between the first two syllables and the third. Οἶδα: I know: this is one of the key words on the lips of Oedipus triumphant, of Oedipus the tyrant. Πούς: foot: the mark stamped at birth on one whose destiny is to end as he began, as one excluded like the wild beast whose *foot* makes it flee, whose *foot* isolates him from other men, who hopes in vain to escape the oracles, pursued by the curse of the terrible *foot* for having infringed the sacred laws with a *foot* raised high and unable henceforth to free his *foot* from the misfortunes into which he has cast himself by raising himself to the highest position of power. The whole of the tragedy . . ." (conclusion quoted above in text).

53. Fr. 880 Nauck = 965 Radt ὀρθῶς δ' Ὀδυσσεύς εἰμ' ἐπώνυμος κακῶν· / πολλοὶ γὰρ ὠδύσαντο δυσμενεῖς ἐμοί.

54. *Phoen.* 636–37 ἔξιθ' ἐκ χώρας· ἀληθῶς δ' ὄνομα Πολυνείκη πατὴρ / ἔθετό σοι θείᾳ προνοίᾳ νεικέων ἐπώνυμον. Cf. above on Aesch. *Sept.*

55. *Tro.* 989–90 τὰ μῶρα γὰρ πάντ' ἐστὶν Ἀφροδίτη βροτοῖς, / καὶ τοὔνομ' ὀρθῶς ἀφροσύνης ἄρχει θεᾶς. Hesiod's etymologizing is quoted in section 1.1.

56. *Ion* 661–63 Ἴωνα δ' ὀνομάζω σε τῇ τύχῃ πρέπον, / ὁθούνεκ' ἀδύτων ἐξιόντι μοι θεοῦ / ἴχνος συνῆψας πρῶτος. In a sense this whole play is an etymological *aition* of the name Ionia, Ionians; for Aeschylus' derivation from the same root but a different myth see above in this section.

57. *IT* 32–33 Θόας, ὃς ὠκὺν πόδα τιθεὶς ἴσον πτεροῖς / ἐς τοὔνομ' ἦλθε τόδε ποδωκείας χάριν.

58. *Hel.* 13–15 καλοῦσιν αὐτὴν Θεονόην· τὰ θεῖα γὰρ / τά τ' ὄντα καὶ μέλλοντα πάντ' ἠπίστατο, / προγόνου λαβοῦσα Νηρέως τιμὰς πάρα. Cf the etymology of Athena in *Crat.* 407, cited below in this section.

(μέλεος + ἄγρα);[59] and Oedipus.[60] More extensively, characters in the *Bacchae,* in keeping with Greek belief in kledonomancy, call attention to the connection of the name Pentheus with πένθος, "grief, sorrow," as though that name meant that he was fated to come to a bad end.[61]

These passages and others in fifth-century tragedy and more that could be cited from lyric, comedy, and even historiography, which I pass over here principally for reasons of economy,[62] show the age's ample interest in etymologizing, due in part to pre-Socratic and sophistic speculation about the nature and origin of language. Another passage from the *Bacchae,* in which Tiresias explains the mistaken myth of the birth of Dionysus from Zeus' thigh by linking the words μηρός (thigh), ὅμηρος (pledge, hostage), and μέρος (share, part), has been called "the most remarkable example of etymological argument in Greek poetry from Homer to Euripides," in which "we may detect the exaggerated methods of the sophists' eristic fallacies."[63]

---

59. Eur. fr. 517 Nauck Μελέαγρε, μελέαν γάρ ποτ' ἀγρεύεις ἄγραν.

60. *Phoen.* 26–27 σφυρῶν σιδηρᾶ κέντρα διαπείρας μέσον· / ὅθεν νιν Ἑλλὰς ὠνόμαζεν Οἰδίπουν.

61. *Bacch.* 367 Πενθεὺς δ' ὅπως μὴ πένθος εἰσοίσει δόμοις; 507–8 [ΠΕ.] Πενθεύς, Ἀγαύης παῖς, πατρὸς δ' Ἐχίονος. / {ΔΙ.} ἐνδυστυχῆσαι τοὔνομ' ἐπιτήδειος εἶ. Cf. Chaeremon fr. 4 Nauck Πενθεὺς ἐσομένης συμφορᾶς ἐπώνυμος (quoted in the brief discussion at Arist. *Rhet.* 1400 of arguments drawn ἀπὸ τοῦ ὀνόματος, quoted in section 1.3) and Theoc. 26.26 ἐξ ὄρεος πένθημα καὶ οὐ Πενθῆα φέροισαι.

62. For lyric, esp. Pindar, see Hecht (1882) 55–57, Bury (1888) (mainly implausible), Woodhead (1928) 11, 15, 21, 25, 30, Stanford (1939) 129–36, Lendle (1957) 120–21, Quincey (1963), Segal (1986) 19, Dougherty (1991) and (1993) index s.v. etymology. Stanford 129–30 lists the salient examples in Pindar: Hieron as ἱερῶν ἐπώνυμος in fr. 105 S-M, Ἐπιμαθεὺς ὀψίνοος in *P.* 5.27–28, Αἴας/αἰετός in *I.* 6.43–54 (cf. Sophocles, above in this sect.), Ἴαμος/ἴον/ἴος in *O.* 6.38–53, Λάχεσις/λάχος in *O.* 7.58–64, λᾶς/λαοί in *O.* 9.45–46 (see on G. 1.62–63), μήδεα/μῆτις/Μήδεια in *P.* 4.9–58 (cf. Apollonius, in sect. 1.4).

For historiography, esp. Herodotus and Hecataeus, cf. Woodhead (1928) 21–22, 28, 31, Pfeiffer (1968) 61, Dougherty (1992) and (1993) 106 (etymological puns in foundation oracles), Baxter (1992) 160 (who also mentions the *Dissoi Logoi*). For comedy, cf. Hecht (1882) 69–81, Woodhead (1928) 16–17, 28 and n. 3, MacDowell (1971) index s.v. puns; on the many significant names in comedy (which are somewhat different from etymological wordplay) see e.g. Olson (1992), with further references.

63. Stanford (1939) 175, commenting on *Bacch.* 286–97 (cf. also Feeney [1991] 21 n. 66: "I often wonder whether the speech of Tiresias . . . is not an extensive parody of the professors' talk on such topics"):

καὶ διαγελᾷς νιν, ὡς ἐνερράφη Διὸς
μηρῷ; διδάξω σ' ὡς καλῶς ἔχει τόδε.
ἐπεί νιν ἥρπασ' ἐκ πυρὸς κεραυνίου
Ζεύς, ἐς δ' Ὄλυμπον βρέφος ἀνήγαγεν νεόν,
Ἥρα νιν ἤθελ' ἐκβαλεῖν ἀπ' οὐρανοῦ,

We have a few fragments of such philosophers as Heraclitus and Democritus, and indications that the "correctness of names" (ὀνομάτων ὀρθότης) was discussed by Sophists like Prodicus and perhaps Protagoras,[64] but much of fifth-century etymological thought we know only through parodies or unflattering portraits, the most important of which is Plato's *Cratylus.*[65] In this dialogue Hermogenes argues that names are assigned to things only by convention *(nomos),* and Cratylus that by nature *(physis)* there is a connection between things and their names, so that the study of names leads to knowledge of the true nature of things. For much of the dialogue Socrates espouses and explores Cratylus' view, modified to allow for corruption of letters or whole words for the sake of euphony, and he provides numerous etymologies of gods' names, the names of virtues, and other words.[66] But then in the latter part of this aporetic dialogue, Socrates exposes the flaws behind the assumptions that words reflect the true nature of things. As in most parodies, there is much that is silly in the *Cratylus,* but also much that must have been taken seriously by some during Socrates' and Plato's day. It is difficult, however, and perhaps even impossible, to determine whether Plato is lampooning Heraclitus, whose views on "flux" are prominent in the discussion of ety-

---

Ζεὺς δ' ἀντεμηχανήσαθ' οἷα δὴ θεός·
ῥήξας μέρος τι τοῦ χθόν' ἐγκυκλουμένου
αἰθέρος, ἔδωκε τόνδ' ὅμηρον ἐκτιθεὶς
Διόνυσον Ἥρας νεικέων· χρόνῳ δέ νιν
βροτοὶ ῥαφῆναί φασιν ἐν μηρῷ Διός,
ὄνομα μεταστήσαντες, ὅτι θεᾷ θεὸς
Ἥρᾳ ποθ' ὡμήρευσε, συνθέντες λόγον.

64. On pre-Socratics and Sophists see Woodhead (1928) 47–48, Stanford (1939) 117, Collart (1954) 258–62 (who calls Heraclitus "la père de l'étymologie populaire"), Bartelink (1965) 7, Pfeiffer (1968) 12, 132, Kahn (1979) 201–2, Snyder (1980) 54–55, Kerferd (1981) 68–77, Feeney (1991) 20–21, Baxter (1992) 107–63.

65. For a sensible one-page discussion of the *Cratylus* see Kennedy (1991) 86–87; see also Woodhead (1928) 44–73 (includes a summary of the dialogue), Bartelink (1965) 10, Pfeiffer (1968) 59–64, Snyder (1980) 56–61, Kerferd (1981) 73–77, Amsler (1989) 20–21, 32–38, Rosenstock (1992), and now Baxter (1992), who argues that Plato is prescriptive, showing what names should be like, not what they are like, and offers an extensive survey of possible targets of Plato's parody. The humor of the dialogue should not be overlooked, and no scholar arguing for the importance of etymologizing to the Greeks should fail to mention that everything Socrates says about etymology is eventually undercut.

66. To list only some of the names or words treated: Astyanax, Hector, Orestes, Agamemnon, Atreus, Pelops, Tantalus, Zeus, Kronos, Ouranos, Hestia, Tethys, Poseidon, Pluto, Hades, Demeter, Hera, Persephone, Apollo, Muse, Leto, Artemis, Dionysus, Aphrodite, Pallas and Athena, Theonoe, Hephaestos, Ares, Hermes, Pan, θεός, δαίμων, ἥρως, ἄνθρωπος, ψυχή, σῶμα, οἶνος, ἥλιος, σελήνη, μείς, ἄστρα, ἀήρ, αἰθήρ, γῆ, ὧραι.

mologies, latter-day Heracliteans, or whatever Sophists were teaching about etymologies in the late fifth century.

Interest in using etymology to explain the poets, especially Homer, was widespread, and at one point in the *Cratylus,* "Socrates implies the existence of a veritable industry when he speaks of how the *majority* of the interpreters of Homer says that the poet represents Athena as mind and intellect."[67] As Woodhead explains, "side by side with the effort to interpret the Homeric and Hesiodic poems as allegories, and so to meet the hostile criticisms of Xenophanes, Heraclitus, and others, there developed an interest in etymological investigation of language." He cites the explanation in Xenophon of the name Ganymede (delighting [γάνυται] in wise counsels [μήδεα]).[68] Feeney has pointed to Theagenes of Rhegium as perhaps the first, back in the sixth century, to discuss "the *names* of the gods, attempting to show that these names referred to something other than their first apparent reference."[69] For readers of Vergil, one of the most important allegorical etymologies may be the connection of Hera (Ἥρα) and ἀήρ, which interprets the queen of the gods as a representation of "the lower air, the sphere for storms of wind and cloud."[70] The Derveni Orphic papyrus, which preserves a commentary, possibly from the late fifth century, on a *Theogony* attributed to Orpheus, includes etymologizing among its interpretive techniques.[71] Etymology as a part of allegorical or other commentary on the poets will be an important aspect of the centuries between classical Greek literature and Vergil, especially when the commentary is influenced by the thinking on etymology of the Stoics, to whom we turn our attention now.

---

67. Feeney (1991) 21, referring to *Crat.* 407 a–b ἐοίκασι δὴ καὶ οἱ παλαιοὶ τὴν Ἀθηνᾶν νομίζειν ὥσπερ οἱ νῦν περὶ Ὅμηρον δεινοί. καὶ γὰρ τούτων οἱ πολλοὶ ἐξηγούμενοι τὸν ποιητήν φασι τὴν Ἀθηνᾶν αὐτὸν νοῦν τε καὶ διάνοιαν πεποιηκέναι, καὶ ὁ τὰ ὀνόματα ποιῶν ἔοικε τοιοῦτόν τι περὶ αὐτῆς διανοεῖσθαι, ἔτι δὲ μειζόνως λέγων θεοῦ νόησιν ὡσπερεὶ λέγει ὅτι "ἁ θεονόα" ἐστὶν αὕτη, τῷ ἄλφα ξενικῶς ἀντὶ τοῦ ἦτα χρησάμενος καὶ τὸ ἰῶτα καὶ τὸ σῖγμα ἀφελών. See also Baxter (1992) 124–26.

68. *Symp.* 30, Woodhead (1928) 50. On both allegory and etymology cf. Richardson (1975), Long (1992), Baxter (1992) 107–63.

69. Feeney (1991) 8–11, discussing allegorizing responses to Xenophanes' criticisms of Homer. For allegorizing in Pherecydes of Syros cf. Baxter (1992) 114, 119–22 and the cautious words of Schibli (1990) 99–100 n. 54.

70. Feeney (1991) 132; cf. his index s.vv. Hera and Juno; he cites *Il.* 21.6–7 ἠέρα δ' Ἥρη / πίτνα πρόσθε βαθεῖαν ἐρυκέμεν, and Plato *Crat.* 404 c ἴσως δὲ μετεωρολογῶν ὁ νομοθέτης τὸν ἀέρα "Ἥραν" ὠνόμασεν ἐπικρυπτόμενος, θεὶς τὴν ἀρχὴν ἐπὶ τελευτήν· γνοίης δ' ἄν, εἰ πολλάκις λέγοις τὸ τῆς Ἥρας ὄνομα. See on A. 12.791–92.

71. Cronos from κρούω, "strike" (Col. X.7 in *ZPE* 47 [1982] after p. 300), Demeter = ἡ Γῆ Μήτηρ (XVIII.10); see Feeney (1991) 22–23, Rosenstock (1992) 405–11 on "Orphic/philosophical allegoresis" and "Orphic etymologizing fervor" as targets of parody in Plato *Crat.*, and Baxter (1992) 98, 130–39.

## 1.3. The Stoics (and Epicurus)

Stoic teaching on etymology resembles what is attributed to Cratylus in Plato's dialogue, and some have thought that views of the third-century Stoics go back to Heraclitus, or whoever Plato's target was, some that the Stoics were influenced directly by the *Cratylus.* We have more testimonia than fragments of the earliest Stoics on etymologizing, but it seems clear that they theorized that the first human words were closely imitative of the things they described, and that all later words derived from them.[72] Since the whole process was guided by the rational *logos* that the Stoics viewed as governing the physical universe, the connection between names and things remained

---

72. Origen *Contra Cels.* 1. 24 describes the views of Aristotle, the Stoics, and Epicurus when he mentions the

λόγος βαθὺς καὶ ἀπόρρητος, ὁ περὶ φύσεως ὀνομάτων· πότερον, ὡς οἴεται
Ἀριστοτέλης, θέσει εἰσὶ τὰ ὀνόματα ἤ, ὡς νομίζουσιν οἱ ἀπὸ τῆς Στοᾶς,
φύσει, μιμουμένων τῶν πρώτων φωνῶν τὰ πράγματα, καθ' ὧν τὰ ὀνόματα,
καθὸ καὶ στοιχεῖά τινα τῆς ἐτυμολογίας εἰσάγουσιν, ἤ, ὡς διδάσκει
Ἐπίκουρος, ἑτέρως ἢ ὡς οἴονται οἱ ἀπὸ τῆς Στοᾶς, φύσει ἐστὶ τὰ ὀνόματα,
ἀπορρηξάντων τῶν πρώτων ἀνθρώπων τινὰς φωνὰς κατὰ τῶν πραγμάτων.

On Stoic etymologizing cf. Woodhead (1928) 74–89, De Lacy (1948) 257–58, von Arnim (1921–24) 2.1060–1100 (pp. 312–20), Collart (1954) 262–63, Pease (1979) 705–33 and 1135–39 (on Cic. *ND* 2.63–69 and 3.62–63), Dahlmann (1964) 6–11, Jackson (1975) 127–29, Frede (1978) 68–74, Snyder (1980) 60–61, Colish (1985) 56–60, Rawson (1985) 117–20, Amsler (1989) 21–23, *OCD* s.v. etymology (Forbes), Long (1992).

For reasons of economy I largely pass over Aristotle, on whom see Woodhead (1928) 73–74, Collart (1954) 264–65, Snyder (1980) 61–63, and Quandt (1981); a more thorough treatment than this introduction can offer might well stress his influence. Cf. e.g. the appeal to arguments based on names at *Rhet.* 1400 b 17–25:

ἄλλος ἀπὸ τοῦ ὀνόματος, οἷον ὡς ὁ Σοφοκλῆς "σαφῶς σιδήρῳ καὶ
φοροῦσα τοὔνομα" (fr. 658 Radt, who prints Cobet's Σιδηρώ καὶ φρονοῦσα),
καὶ ὡς ἐν τοῖς τῶν θεῶν ἐπαίνοις εἰώθασι λέγειν, καὶ ὡς Κόνων Θρασύβουλον θρασύβουλον
ἐκάλει, καὶ Ἡρόδικος Θρασύμαχον "ἀεὶ
θρασύμαχος εἶ," καὶ Πῶλον "ἀεὶ σὺ πῶλος εἶ," καὶ Δράκοντα τὸν
νομοθέτην, ὅτι οὐκ [ἂν] ἀνθρώπου οἱ νόμοι ἀλλὰ δράκοντος (χαλεποὶ
γάρ)· καὶ ὡς ἡ Εὐριπίδου Ἑκάβη εἰς τὴν Ἀφροδίτην "καὶ τοὔνομ' ὀρθῶς
ἀφροσύνης ἄρχει θεᾶς" (*Tro.* 990), καὶ ὡς Χαιρήμων "Πενθεὺς ἐσομένης
συμφορᾶς ἐπώνυμος" (for the last two cf. above in this sect.).

At *Top.* 112a 32–38 he recommends arguments based on etymology for common words:

Ἔτι τὸ ἐπιχειρεῖν, μεταφέροντα τοὔνομα κατὰ τὸν λόγον, ὡς μᾶλλον
προσῆκον ἐκλαμβάνειν ἢ ὡς κεῖται τοὔνομα, οἷον εὔψυχον μὴ τὸν
ἀνδρεῖον, καθάπερ νῦν κεῖται, ἀλλὰ τὸν εὖ τὴν ψυχὴν ἔχοντα, καθάπερ
καὶ εὔελπιν τὸν ἀγαθὰ ἐλπίζοντα· ὁμοίως δὲ καὶ εὐδαίμονα οὗ ἂν ὁ δαίμων
ᾖ σπουδαῖος, καθάπερ Ξενοκράτης φησὶν εὐδαίμονα εἶναι τὸν τὴν ψυχὴν
ἔχοντα σπουδαίαν· ταύτην γὰρ ἑκάστου εἶναι δαίμονα.

Cf. the remarks of Cicero, below in section 1.5.

natural and dependable, as Cratylus had argued in Plato's dialogue. A treatise attributed to Augustine, but apparently preserving material from centuries earlier, explains the four principles by which nature formed from these basic words a full vocabulary, and by which derivations could be explained:[73]

1. κατὰ μίμησιν *(similitudo; res cum sono verbi aliqua similitudine concinat):* by imitating sounds, or by using sounds whose smoothness, harshness, and so on, mimicked that of the thing named;
2. καθ' ὁμοιότητα *(ipsarum inter se rerum similitudo):* from the similarity of one thing to another;
3. κατ' ἀναλογίαν *(per vicinitatem,* or *nomen non rei similis sed quasi vicinae):* by association, including by influence *(per efficientiam),* effects *(per effecta),* that which contains or is contained *(per id quo continetur . . . aut per id quod continet),* transference *(per abusionem),* whole from part or part from whole *(a parte totum . . . a toto pars);*
4. κατ' ἀντίφρασιν *(per contrarium):* a name indicates the opposite of a thing or of some property it has.

The last principle may be viewed from different perspectives as either extremely useful, or, to put it perhaps a little harshly, as cheating,[74] but it develops naturally from the recognition of euphemism in Greek naming, as in the name Eumenides, "kindly ones," for the Furies. Zeno, the founder of the Stoic school, and his successor Cleanthes seem to have used etymologizing in their allegorical explanations of the poets and their gods, but "all previous efforts pale before those of Chrysippus, the second founder of Stoicism,"[75] who is said to have written two treatises on etymologizing and proposed or argued for etymologies for the names Zeus, Cronos, Cypris,[76] Cytherea, Apollo, and for words like ἐγώ, διδάσκω, and ἀγκών. Despite frequent ridicule for its excesses, Stoic etymological thought exercised pro-

---

73. Aug. *de Dialectica* 6 (sometimes called *Principia Dialecticae;* see Jackson [1975], who supports Augustinian authorship, which many have doubted). Convenient summary, with the examples I omit here cited, in *OCD*² s.v. etymology (Forbes). Many have thought the long passage at the start of this treatise to be indebted to or even borrowed from Varro, and so Funaioli prints it as Varro fr. 265, *GRF* pp. 278–86; see Jackson (1975) 122.

74. Cf. the hostility of Collart (1954) 267–68, 290.

75. Woodhead (1928) 76–78:76, Dahlmann (1964) 8–10, Pease (1979) 1138, Pfeiffer (1968) 201, 241, 243, 260, Long (1992) 62–67 (on Zeno).

76. Zeus: ἀπὸ τοῦ πᾶσι δεδώκεναι τὸ ζῆν . . . Δία δὲ αὐτὸν λέγουσιν ὅτι πάντων ἐστιν αἴτιος καὶ δι' αὐτὸν πάντα (*SVF* ii, 1062; see Pease on Cic. *ND* 2.64, and below on G. 4.219–22); Cronos: ὅτι πρῶτος θεῶν εἰς κρίσιν ἐπέβαλε (*SVF* ii, 1090); Cypris: παρὰ τὸ κύειν παρέχειν (*SVF* ii, 1098).

found influence, both directly, through Stoic teachers and etymologists, and indirectly, through the impact of Stoic thought on the commentaries on the poets.[77]

The relationship between Epicurus' theory of language and poetic etymologizing has been explored in depth by Friedländer and by Snyder's monograph on Lucretian wordplay. Lucretius will be treated below in the section on poets at Rome; here we need only note that information on Epicurus' views is scanty, and subject to contested interpretation.[78] Epicurus seems to have posited a natural connection between the earliest, simplest sounds and the feelings (πάθη) or sense impressions (φαντάσματα) that occasioned them, but even in this earliest stage names differed from tribe to tribe, and later stages of the growth of language and naming are governed not by the Stoic *logos* but by arbitrary choice (see *Letter to Herodotus* 75–76).[79] Extensive wordplay in Lucretius and the recurring analogy he draws between letters rearranged to form different words and atoms rearranged to form different material objects have suggested to many that Epicureans also believed in a natural connection between words and things. Dalzell has questioned this view; I would comment that literal belief in etymological explanation is not required for a poet to make use of etymological wordplay. It seems worth noting, however, that the Roman Varro's eclectic but largely Stoic approach, to be discussed below, posits a largely arbitrary naming process; Varro also draws an analogy between the Epicurean notion of atoms *(principia)* and his own notion of the basic roots *(principia)* of words (*LL* 6.39).

## 1.4. The Alexandrian Poets

The age of the first Stoics also produced the Alexandrian[80] scholar-poets, whose influence upon Vergilian etymologizing was especially strong but is

77. Cf. Woodhead (1928) 79.

78. Friedländer (1941), De Lacy (1939), Konstan (1973) 44–51, Snyder (1980) esp. 11–30, Brown (1984) xxxvi–xxxix, Dalzell (1987). See also Origen *Contra Cels.* 1.24, quoted above in this section.

79. = Diog. Laert. 10.75–76 Ὅθεν καὶ τὰ ὀνόματα ἐξ ἀρχῆς μὴ θέσει γενέσθαι, ἀλλ' αὐτὰς τὰς φύσεις τῶν ἀνθρώπων καθ' ἕκαστα ἔθνη ἴδια πάσχουσας πάθη καὶ ἴδια λαμβανούσας φαντάσματα ἰδίως τὸν ἀέρα ἐκπέμπειν στελλόμενον ὑφ' ἑκάστων τῶν παθῶν καὶ τῶν φαντασμάτων, ὡς ἄν ποτε καὶ ἡ παρὰ τοὺς τόπους τῶν ἐθνῶν διαφορὰ ᾖ· ὕστερον δὲ κοινῶς καθ' ἕκαστα ἔθνη τὰ ἴδια τεθῆναι πρὸς τὸ τὰς δηλώσεις ἧττον ἀμφιβόλους γενέσθαι ἀλλήλοις καὶ συντομωτέρως δηλουμένας· τινὰ δὲ καὶ οὐ συνορώμενα πράγματα εἰσφέροντας τοὺς συνειδότας παρεγγυῆσαί τινας φθόγγους ἀναγκασθέντας ἀναφωνῆσαι, τοὺς δὲ τῷ λογισμῷ ἑλομένους κατὰ τὴν πλείστην αἰτίαν οὕτως ἑρμηνεῦσαι.

For a review of the many controversies about this passage see Konstan (1973) 46–49.

80. Here and in my title I use the term "Alexandrian" rather than "Hellenistic," but arguments could be made for the latter, especially as it is used in the titles of e.g. Cairns (1979),

overlooked or undervalued in some studies of Vergilian or other Roman etymologizing. The etymologizing that I have found in Vergil does resemble that found in classical and archaic Greek authors, but it is the Alexandrians like Callimachus, Apollonius of Rhodes, Aratus, and others whose learned etymological wordplay is most like Vergil's. Alexandrian etymologizing, though widely acknowledged or in more romantic times even lamented,[81] has not been studied as thoroughly as that of classical Greek authors, although numerous studies have discussed a few examples each.[82] Other basic characteristics of Alexandrian or Hellenistic poetry, and the nature of these poets' extensive influence on Roman poetry, have been well described in recent years and need only the barest rehearsal here.[83] These were scholar-

Clausen (1987), and Hollis (1992). I have stuck with "Alexandrian" to emphasize the central role of the poets of Alexandria, especially Callimachus and those influenced by him (so too Zanker [1987]). For recent discussion of the term see Zanker (1987) 1–3, Gelzer (1993) 130–34 (e.g., on Wilamowitz' wish to combat the negative connotations, in his day, of the term "Alexandrian"), and Henrichs (1993), who provides further references. Of the poets cited in this section, probably Rhianus must be called Hellenistic rather than Alexandrian (cf. Pfeiffer [1968] 148–49).

81. Cf. Lloyd-Jones (1990), who in his defense of Hellenistic poetry deals largely with "the Romantic prejudice against imitation," but his remarks are applicable to hostility toward learned poetry more generally.

82. The Alexandrians are only briefly treated in some of the surveys of Greek etymologizing: cf. Hecht (1882) 81–87, Woodhead (1928) 31–32, Bartelink (1965) 13–14. Nineteenth-century studies of Alexandrian poetry or of individual poets made important contributions: Meineke (1964) 50–51, 64, 88–89, 98–111, Dilthey (1863) 37–42, Von Jan (1893) 66–82. More recently, individual examples are regularly noted by editions and commentaries such as Pfeiffer (1949–53) 229, Bornmann (1968) 72, 94, 135, Livrea (1973), McLennan (1977) 50, Williams (1978) index s.v. jeu étymologique, Mineur (1982) index s.v. etymological word-play, Hopkinson (1984) index s.v. etymologising, Bulloch (1985) 202 (on these two see also Renehan [1987]), Hopkinson (1988) index s.v. etymology, Hunter (1989) index s.v. etymology. Etymological wordplay or aetiology is also discussed by such recent studies as Lapp (1965) 65–66, 99, 140–42, Levin (1971) index s.v. aetiological & etymological lore, Levitan (1978), Giangrande (1981) 401, Hopkinson (1984a), (1984b), Hunter (1986) 50–60, Koenen (1983) 177 n. 95, White (1987) index s.v. etymological word-games, Paskiewicz (1988), Bing (1988) 96–102 and (1990), Renkagos (1992) (who discusses many passages I do not), Calame (1993) 45–46, Depew (1993), Albis (1995). Studies of Latin poets also discuss Alexandrian etymologizing: Ross (1973), (1987) index s.v. etymology, Shechter (1975), Cairns (1979) index s.v. etymology, Thomas (1982a), (1982b), Rosen and Farrell (1986), O'Hara (1990) index s.v. etymology, (1990a), (1992), Hunter (1991), Weber (1991). Most of the studies in this note, however, treat only a few examples.

83. On the character of Alexandrian poetry see e.g. Fraser (1972) 553–674 and 717–93, Cairns (1979) esp. 6–32, Clausen (1987) esp. 1–14, Zanker (1987), Bing (1988) esp. 72–90, Hopkinson (1988) 6–11, Lloyd-Jones (1990). On Alexandrian scholarship cf. Pfeiffer (1968) 87–233, esp. 123–51, Fraser (1972) 447–79 and his comments scattered through 553–674 and 717–93.

poets, whose poetry demonstrates and makes effective use of their broad learning. For Callimachus, we know the titles of a number of prose treatises that indicate the range of scholarly information he controlled, and how great was his interest in names: *On Games, Non-Greek Customs, Marvels in All the Earth according to Locality, Local Nomenclature, On Winds, On Birds, Changes of Names of Fish, Local Month-Names, Foundations of Cities and Islands and Their Changes of Names, On the Rivers in the World, On the Rivers of Europe, Marvels of the Peloponnese and Italy,* and *On Nymphs.*[84] Writing in an age that studied and began to write commentaries on earlier poets, these poets produced works to be read and studied as well as heard; this self-conscious poetry also made some explicit and many implicit comments about its own place in the Greek literary tradition stretching back to Homer. This was poetry of wit, making demands upon the intelligence and learning of the reader in matters mythological, aetiological, and etymological, and poetry of irony, in which a simple, at times almost childlike, surface can overlay complex and learned subtexts. The poetry is characterized by attention to geography, ethnography, language, and aetiology, which includes the origins of customs, myths, and, most central to our concerns, words and names. Alexandrian aetiology in general is a particularly important part of the background to Vergilian etymological wordplay. These poets' concern with origins has some precedent in earlier Greek poetry, especially hymns, encomia, and the ends of many tragedies, but interest in *aitia* had never been so strong before.[85] Callimachus' central work, the *Aetia,* is a "compendium of tales attempting to explain the peculiarities of the present by reference to their 'causes' in the distant past, the very need for which bespeaks at once an awareness of the enormous gulf separating past and

84. Some titles are in Suid. s.v. Καλλίμαχος (cf. Pfeiffer [1949–53] xcv); others are given by the sources that quote fragments (cf. Pfeiffer [1949–53] 328–53), and some could be subheadings or alternate versions of the others: Περὶ ἀγώνων, Βαρβαρικὰ νόμιμα, Θαυμάτων τῶν εἰς ἅπασαν τὴν γῆν κατά τόπους ὄντων συναγωγή, Ἐθνικαὶ ὀνομασίαι, Περὶ ἀνέμων, Περὶ ὀρνέων, Περὶ μετονομασίας ἰχθύων, Μηνῶν προσηγορίαι κατὰ ἔθνος καὶ πόλεις, Κτίσεις νήσων καὶ πόλεων καὶ μετονομασίαι, Περὶ τῶν ἐν τῇ οἰκουμένῃ ποταμῶν, Περὶ τῶν ἐν Εὐρώπῃ ποταμῶν, Περὶ τῶν ἐν Πελοποννήσῳ καὶ Ἰταλίᾳ θαυμασίων καὶ παραδόξων, Περὶ νυμφῶν.

85. Cf. Fraser (1972) 626–33, 775–76, Shechter (1975), Zanker (1987) index s.v. aitia, Paskiewicz (1988), Depew (1993), Myers (1994a) index s.v. aetiology, *EV* s.v. aition (Fedeli), and Bing (1988) 71 n. 34: "One could establish a scale of aetiologial interest between Homer, at the one extreme, and Callimachus at the other. . . . While *aetia* are certainly present in pre-Hellenistic verse . . . they are not nearly as all-pervasive as they are in Hellenistic verse. There, the interest in forging a link between present and past seems to reach its height." I also expect a forthcoming study of Ovid by Garth Tissol to provide useful discussion of Alexandrian aetiology.

present."[86] Zanker well observes that "Apollonius' *Argonautica* is hardly less concerned with aetiology than . . . [the] *Aetia*" and calls attention to the way in which, in Alexandrian poetry, "the mythical past will have been 'verified' by the evidence of the still observable cults and institutions, which can be traced back into it."[87] He suggests that such aetiologies "will have helped alleviate the problem of cultural identity experienced by the early Alexandrian Greeks."[88] The relevance to Vergil of such an approach to the past should be clear; see below in section 2.5 and section 3 for more on Vergil and aetiology.

Since I know of no satisfactory collection and no extensive study of Alexandrian etymologizing, the next few pages will present, as concisely as possible, a good number of examples from the Alexandrian poets. I cite both explicit and implicit wordplay, the explicit not because readers have any difficulty in spotting them, but because the style and technique of explicit etymological aetiologies have much in common with that of more subtle wordplay, and so study of obvious and uncontroversial examples can help us develop the competence necessary to notice or recognize less explicit examples.[89] This is now the most extensive collection of such material of which I am aware, but it is far from comprehensive. A full study of etymologizing in the Alexandrians or in Hellenistic poetry might begin with the examples I cite here, then move to a more thorough survey of the authors than I have been able to do: this would not be a small task.

As in Homer and so many other Greek authors, a great many of the words etymologized by the Alexandrians are proper names, for which the poet usually offers an explanatory mythical *aition*. Apollonius of Rhodes, to begin with him, presents explicit derivations of many names, anticipating Vergilian technique in making the deeds of the heroic age responsible for many features of the modern world of his readers. The beach where the Argonauts "loosed" the Argo is "still" called Aphetae (cf. ἀφίημι).[90] An altar is offered to Apollo "of the shore" (Ἄκτιος) and "Embarker" (Ἐμβασίος) at the start of the expedition; Vergil will acknowledge this Actian Apollo when the

86. Bing (1988) 71; see too Depew (1993) on how Callimachus both presents and then ironizes the aetiological poet's authoritative stance toward the past.

87. Zanker (1987) 122–23; cf. too Paskiewicz (1988). (There is no longer any need even to discuss the now completely discredited theory of a quarrel between Callimachus and Apollonius.)

88. Zanker (1987) 121.

89. On "literary competence" see above n. 9.

90. 1.591 τὴν δ' ἀκτὴν <u>Ἀφέτας</u> Ἀργοῦς ἔτι κικλήσκουσιν.

epithet gains new meaning in the Augustan period.[91] Apollonius mentions the road named for Jason,[92] the place "still" called Sacred Rock because the Argonauts secured their ship to it,[93] the Spring of Jason made by Rhea for the Argonauts,[94] the island of Apollo of the Dawn, where Apollo appeared at daybreak,[95] the ravine or river mouth called Shipsaver because the Argonauts were saved by it from a storm,[96] and the islands whose name is changed to Strophades because there the Boreads "turned back" (ὑπέστρεφον) after pursuing the Harpies; this last name Vergil will also gloss.[97] The Argonauts' expedition also provides explanations for the names of the spot called Lyra, where Orpheus dedicated his lyre;[98] the place called Ram's Couch;[99] Colchian settlers named for Medea's brother Apsyrtus;[100] the har-

---

91. 1.402–4:

Ἔνθεν δ᾽ αὖ λάιγγας ἁλὸς σχεδὸν ὀχλίζοντες<br>
νήεον αὐτόθι βωμὸν ἐπάκτιον, Ἀπόλλωνος<br>
Ἀκτίου Ἐμβασίοιό τ᾽ ἐπώνυμον.

Cf. Callim. fr. 18.12 (quoted below), and A. 3.280, *Actia*que Iliacis celebramus *litora* ludis, where Vergil seems to allude to this original meaning of the epithet *Actius.*

92. 1.988 ἥδε δ᾽ Ἰησονίη πέφαται Ὁδός, ἥνπερ ἔβησαν.

93. 1.1019–20 αὐτονυχί (Ἱερὴ δὲ φατίζεται ἥδ᾽ ἔτι Πέτρη / ᾗ πέρι πείσματα νηὸς ἐπεσσύμενοι ἐβάλοντο).

94. 1.1148–49 Ἰησονίην δ᾽ ἐνέπουσιν / κεῖνο ποτὸν Κρήνην περιναιέται ἄνδρες ὀπίσσω.

95. 2.686–88:

Εἰ δ᾽ ἄγε δὴ νῆσον μὲν Ἑωίου Ἀπόλλωνος<br>
τήνδ᾽ ἱερὴν κλείωμεν, ἐπεὶ πάντεσσι φαάνθη<br>
ἠῷος μετιών· τὰ δὲ ῥέξομεν οἷα πάρεστιν.

96. 2.746–49:

τὸν μὲν ἐν ὀψιγόνοισι Σοωναύτην ὀνόμηναν<br>
Νισαῖοι Μεγαρῆες, ὅτε νάσσεσθαι ἔμελλον<br>
γῆν Μαριανδυνῶν· δὴ γάρ σφεας ἐξεσάωσεν<br>
αὐτῇσιν νήεσσι, κακῇ χρίμψαντας ἀέλλῃ.

97. 2.295–97:

οἱ δ᾽ ὅρκῳ εἴξαντες ὑπέστρεφον ἂψ ἐπὶ νῆα<br>
σώεσθαι Στροφάδας δὲ μετακλείουσ᾽ ἄνθρωποι<br>
νήσους τοῖο ἕκητι, πάρος Πλωτὰς καλέοντες.

Cf. on A. 3.210.

98. 2.928–29 βωμὸν δειμάμενοι μῆρ᾽ ἔφλεγον· ἂν δὲ καὶ Ὀρφεύς / θῆκε λύρην ἐκ τοῦ δὲ Λύρη πέλει οὔνομα χώρῳ. Cf. Paskiewicz (1988) 59 on Apollonius' departure from earlier tradition here.

99. 4.114–17:

τῆμος ἄρ᾽ Αἰσονίδης κούρη τ᾽ ἀπὸ νηὸς ἔβησαν<br>
ποιήεντ᾽ ἀνὰ χῶρον ἵνα Κριοῦ καλέονται<br>
Εὐναί, ὅθι πρῶτον κεκμηότα γούνατ᾽ ἔκαμψεν,<br>
νώτοισιν φορέων Μινυήιον υἷ᾽ Ἀθάμαντος.

100. 4.514–15 οἱ μὲν ἐπ᾽ αὐτάων νήσων ἔβαν ᾗσιν ἐπέσχον / ἥρωες, ναίουσι δ᾽ ἐπώνυμοι Ἀψύρτοιο.

bor on Aethalia named for the Argonauts;[101] the Cave of Medea;[102] and the island called Anaphe, where Apollo revealed (ἀνέφηνεν) himself, and where Apollo is called Αἰγλήτης, "radiant," because of his conspicuous "gleam" (αἴγλη).[103]

Apollonius also explicitly explains many names of persons and places involved in or passed by the Argonauts' expedition: the Argonauts' own alternate name Minyads,[104] the Mossynoeci, who live in μόσσυναι, "wooden towers";[105] the Muse Erato, whose name Apollonius calls "erotic," which may color Vergil's citation of this Muse near the start of A. 7;[106] Phaethon, who "outshone" the other young men;[107] the places called Callichorus (place of beautiful dances) and Aulion (bedchamber) because of Dionysus' ac-

101. 4.658 ἔνθα λιμὴν Ἀργῷος ἐπωνυμίην πεφάτισται.

102. 4.1153–55:

κεῖνο καὶ εἰσέτι νῦν ἱερὸν κλήιζεται Ἄντρον
Μηδείης, ὅθι τούσγε σὺν ἀλλήλοισιν ἔμειξαν,
τεινάμεναι ἑανοὺς εὐώδεας.

103. 4.1714–18:

φέγγεν ἀνερχομένη, τοὶ δ' ἀγλαὸν Ἀπόλλωνι
ἄλσει ἐνὶ σκιερῷ τέμενος σκιόεντά τε βωμόν
ποίεον, Αἰγλήτην μὲν ἐυσκόπου εἵνεκεν αἴγλης
Φοῖβον κεκλόμενοι, Ἀνάφην δέ τε λισσάδα νῆσον
ἴσκον, ὃ δὴ Φοῖβός μιν ἀτυζομένοις ἀνέφηνεν.

Callimachus may gloss the name Anaphe when he tells the same story, but there is no trace of this in fr. 18.

104. 1.229–32:

τοὺς μὲν ἀριστῆας Μινύας περιναιετάοντες
κίκλησκον μάλα πάντας, ἐπεὶ Μινύαο θυγατρῶν
οἱ πλεῖστοι καὶ ἄριστοι ἀφ' αἵματος εὐχετόωντο
ἔμμεναι.

105. 2.379–81:

τοῖς δ' ἐπὶ Μοσσύνοικοι ὁμούριοι ὑλήεσσαν
ἑξείης ἤπειρον ὑπωρείας τε νέμονται,
δουρατέοις †πύργοισιν ἐν οἰκία τεκτήναντες
κάλινα καὶ πύργους εὐπηγέας, οὓς καλέουσιν 381A
μόσσυνας, καὶ δ' αὐτοὶ ἐπώνυμοι ἔνθεν ἔασιν. 381B.

106. 3.1–5:

Εἰ δ' ἄγε νῦν Ἐρατώ, παρ' ἔμ' ἵστασο καί μοι ἔνισπε
ἔνθεν ὅπως ἐς Ἰωλκὸν ἀνήγαγε κῶας Ἰήσων
Μηδείης ὑπ' ἔρωτι. σὺ γὰρ καὶ Κύπριδος αἶσαν
ἔμμορες, ἀδμῆτας δὲ τεοῖς μελεδήμασι θέλγεις
παρθενικάς· τῷ καί τοι ἐπήρατον οὔνομ' ἀνῆπται.

Cf. Hunter (1989) on 4–5, and on A. 7.37–41.

107. 3.245–46 καί μιν Κόλχων υἷες ἐπωνυμίην Φαέθοντα / ἔκλεον, οὕνεκα πᾶσι μετέπρεπεν ἠιθέοισιν.

tivities there;[108] the place named for the nymph Sinope, carried off by Zeus but clever enough to remain a virgin;[109] the island of Philyra, which Apollonius innovatively links with the mother of Cheiron the centaur;[110] the drug named because it grew from the ichor of Prometheus, which Apollonius describes to an extent matched by some descriptions in the *Georgics;*[111] Black Corcyra,[112] perhaps the variously etymologized Achilles from α-χεῖλος as "the one who did not bring his lips to his mother's breast";[113] the bay named after the Ambracians;[114] and the island whose name is changed

108. 2.907–10:

στῆσαί τε χοροὺς ἄντροιο πάροιθεν
ᾧ ἐν ἀμειδήτους ἁγίας ηὐλίζετο νύκτας·
ἐξ οὗ Καλλίχορον ποταμὸν περιναιετάοντες
ἠδὲ καὶ Αὔλιον ἄντρον ἐπωνυμίην καλέουσιν.

109. 2.946–54; cf. Paskiewicz (1988) 60: she exacts a blind promise from Zeus, and then Apollo, and the river Halys.

110. 2.1232–41; cf. Paskiewicz (1988) 60.

111. 3.844–57:

ἡ δὲ τέως γλαφυρῆς ἐξείλετο φωριαμοῖο
φάρμακον ὅρρά τέ φασι Προμήθειον καλέεσθαι.
τῷ εἴ κεν, νυχίοισιν ἀρεσσάμενος θυέεσσιν
Δαῖραν μουνογένειαν, ἑὸν δέμας ἰκμαίνοιτο,
ἦ τ' ἂν ὅγ' οὔτε ῥηκτὸς ἔοι χαλκοῖο τυπῇσιν
οὔτε κεν αἰθομένῳ πυρὶ εἰκάθοι, ἀλλὰ καὶ ἀλκῇ
λωίτερος κεῖν' ἦμαρ ὁμῶς κάρτει τε πέλοιτο.
πρωτοφυὲς τόγ' ἀνέσχε καταστάξαντος ἔραζε
αἰετοῦ ὠμηστέω κνημοῖς ἔνι Καυκασίοισιν
αἱματόεντ' ἰχῶρα Προμηθῆος μογεροῖο.
τοῦ δ' ἤτοι ἄνθος μὲν ὅσον πήχυιον ὕπερθεν
χροιῇ Κωρυκίῳ ἴκελον κρόκῳ ἐξεφαάνθη,
καυλοῖσιν διδύμοισιν ἐπήορον· ἡ δ' ἐνὶ γαίῃ
σαρκὶ νεοτμήτῳ ἐναλιγκίη ἔπλετο ῥίζα.

Cf. on G. 2.126–41; I quote the passage in full here because its wealth of botanical detail resembles that of the key etymological aetiologies in the *Georgics* listed there.

112. 4.569–71:

μελαινομένην δέ μιν ἄνδρες
ναυτίλοι ἐκ πόντοιο κελαινῇ πάντοθεν ὕλῃ
δερκόμενοι, Κέρκυραν ἐπικλείουσι Μέλαιναν.

113. 4.812–13 ὃν . . . Νηιάδες κομέουσι τεοῦ λίπτοντα γάλακτος (Hera speaking to Thetis). See Hunter (1991) 255, whom I quote; he cites Richardson (1974) 237, who provides further information, but see also above in section 1.1 for the name Achilles in Homer, and below in this section for Callimachus and Euphorion.

114. 4.1228 ἤδη μὲν ὅποτὶ κόλπον ἐπώνυμον Ἀμβρακιήων.

from Oenoe, the name of a nymph, to Sicinus, the name of her son.[115] A spring is said to be named for the nymph Cleite, whose name is perhaps glossed by the word περικλεές, in a kind of double etymology, with derivations provided both for the place, and the person for whom the place is named, such as we will see several times in Vergil.[116] Apollonius also explains the name of the mountains called Ceraunian, because of Zeus' thunderbolts (κεραυνοί), and Vergil will allude to this etymology in the *Georgics*.[117]

For names contemporary with his story, especially personal as opposed to geographical names, Apollonius also presents a number of more subtle or implicit glosses. The Argo is apparently named after its builder (others, including later Catullus, offer other explanations).[118] The name Heracles, in Apollonius, Callimachus, Vergil, and Ovid, frames a line along with that of Hera, which may allude to a derivation of his name from hers attested in scholia and elsewhere.[119] The simple use of the verb near the name suggests a derivation of Harpies from ἁρπάζω (as in Vergil).[120] An epithet describing the Tibareni as "rich in sheep" may offer an etymology of their name, as single-word epithets often will in Vergil.[121] Apollonius seems to allude to

---

115. 1.623–26:

καὶ τὸν μὲν ἐς Οἰνοίην ἐρύσαντο  
(πρόσθεν, ἀτὰρ Σίκινόν γε μεθύστερον αὐδηθεῖσαν)  
νῆσον ἐπακτῆρες (Σικίνου ἄπο, τόν ῥα Θόαντι  
νηιὰς Οἰνοίη νύμφη τέκεν εὐνηθεῖσα).

116. 1.1067–69:

καί οἱ ἀπὸ βλεφάρων ὅσα δάκρυα χεύατ' ἔραζε,  
πάντα τάγε κρήνην τεῦξαν θεαί, ἣν καλέουσιν  
Κλείτην, δυστήνοιο περικλεὲς οὔνομα νύμφης.

Cf. in section 2.4b, "Names of Places."

117. 4.518–21:

οἱ δ' ἐν ὄρεσσιν  
ἐνναίουσιν ἅπερ τε Κεραύνια κικλήσκονται  
ἐκ τόθεν ἐξότε τούσγε Διὸς Κρονίδαο κεραυνοί  
νῆσον ἐς ἀντιπέραιαν ἀπέτραπον ὁρμηθῆναι.

Cf. O'Hara (1990b), and on G. 1.332.

118. 1.18–19 Νῆα μὲν οὖν οἱ πρόσθεν ἐπικλείουσιν ἀοιδοί / Ἄργον Ἀθηναίης καμέειν ὑποθημοσύνῃσι (18 ἔτι κλείουσιν codd.; ἐπικλείουσιν Brunck); 1.111–12 αὐτὴ γὰρ καὶ νῆα θοὴν κάμε, σὺν δέ οἱ Ἄργος/τεῦξεν Ἀρεστορίδης κείνης ὑποθημοσύνῃσι. Cf. Thomas (1982a).

119. 1.997 Ἥρη, Ζηνὸς ἄκοιτις, ἀέθλιον Ἡρακλῆι. Cf. Callim. *Hymn* 3.107–9, and see on A. 8.287–88.

120. 2.187–89 ἀλλὰ διὰ νεφέων ἄφνω πέλας ἀίσσουσαι / Ἅρπυιαι στόματος χειρῶν τ' ἀπὸ γαμφηλῇσι / συνεχέως ἥρπαζον, ἐλείπετο δ' ἄλλοτε φορβῆς; 2.223 Ἅρπυιαι στόματός μοι ἀφαρπάζουσιν ἐδωδήν. See on A. 3.226–27.

121. 2.377 πολύρρηνες Τιβαρηνοί; cf. Hecht (1882) 82.

etymologies of the names Dionysus, the Nysaean son of Zeus (Διός), as in a Homeric hymn mentioned above, and possibly also in Vergil;[122] Hera allegorized as ἀήρ, as we have seen in earlier authors, and will see several times in Vergil;[123] Medea (cf. μήδεα, counsels, schemes);[124] possibly Ariadne (bright, gleaming?); [125] Eurymedon (Perseus);[126] and possibly Tritogeneia (Athena), perhaps also glossed by Callimachus.[127] Among place-names, Haemonia may be considered "the land of blood,"[128] Avernus the place

---

122. 2.905 Διὸς Νυσήιον υἷα, 4.1134 κείνη δὴ πάμπρωτα Διὸς Νυσήιον υἷα. See Levin (1971) 194 n. 4, above in section 1.1 for *Homeric Hymns*, and cf. on A. 6.805.

123. 3.210–14:

τοῖσι δὲ νισσομένοις Ἥρη φίλα μητιόωσα  
ἠέρα πουλὺν ἐφῆκε δι' ἄστεος, ὄφρα λάθοιεν  
Κόλχων μυρίον ἔθνος ἐς Αἰήταο κιόντες·  
ὦκα δ' ὅτ' ἐκ πεδίοιο πόλιν καὶ δώμαθ' ἵκοντο  
Αἰήτεω, τότε δ' αὖτις ἀπεσκέδασεν νέφος Ἥρη.

See Hunter (1989) on 3.210–14, and above in section 1.2 for pre-Socratic allegorization.

124. 3.779–81 μοῖρα πέλει· πῶς γάρ κεν ἐμοὺς λελάθοιμι τοκῆας / φάρμακα μησαμένη, ποῖον δ' ἐπὶ μῦθον ἐνίψω; / τίς δὲ δόλος, τίς μῆτις ἐπίκλοπος ἔσσετ' ἀρωγῆς; 3.825–26 Ἔνθα κασιγνήτους μὲν ἔτ' αὐτόθι μεῖναι ἀνώγει / Ἄργος, ἵνα φράζοιντο νόον καὶ μήδεα κούρης; 3.1134–36 Ἑλλάδα ναιετάειν· ὧς γὰρ τόγε μήδετο Ἥρη, / ὄφρα κακὸν Πελίῃ ἱερὴν ἐς Ἰωλκὸν ἵκηται / Αἰαίη Μήδεια λιποῦσ' ἄπο πατρίδα γαῖαν. See Hunter (1989) on 3.825–27, citing the precedent at Pind. *P.* 4.27 (above in sect. 1.2).

125. 3.1074–76, 1096–1100 (see Hunter [1989] on 3.1075):

εἰπὲ δὲ κούρην  
ἥντινα τήνδ' ὀνόμηνας ἀριγνώτην γεγαυῖαν  
Πασιφάης, ἣ πατρὸς ὁμόγνιός ἐστιν ἐμεῖο.  
. . . . . . . . . . . . . . . . . . . . . . . . . . . . . . .  
ἀλλὰ τίη τάδε τοι μεταμώνια πάντ' ἀγορεύω,  
ἡμετέρους τε δόμους τηλεκλείτην τ' Ἀριάδνην,  
κούρην Μίνωος, τόπερ ἀγλαὸν οὔνομα κείνην  
παρθενικὴν καλέεσκον ἐπήρατον ἥν μ' ἐρεείνεις;  
αἴθε γάρ, ὡς Θησῆι τότε ξυναρέσσατο Μίνως.

126. 4.1513–15:

εὖτε γὰρ ἰσόθεος Λιβύην ὑπερέπτατο Περσεύς  
Εὐρυμέδων (καὶ γὰρ τὸ κάλεσκέ μιν οὔνομα μήτηρ)  
Γοργόνος ἀρτίτομον κεφαλὴν βασιλῆι κομίζων.

See Shechter (1975) 378–79.

127. 4.1309–11:

ἡρῶσσαι Λιβύης τιμήοροι, αἵ ποτ' Ἀθήνην  
ἦμος ὅτ' ἐκ πατρὸς κεφαλῆς θόρε παμφαίνουσα  
ἀντόμεναι Τρίτωνος ἐφ' ὕδασι χυτλώσαντο.

Cf. Callim. *Aet.* fr. 37, Lycophr. 528.

128. 3.1090 Αἱμονίην δὴ τήνγε περικτίονες καλέουσιν (see Hunter [1989] on 1086, and cf. on G. 1.491–92).

where no bird (ὄρνις) may fly, and the Rhipaen mountains named for the ῥιφή/ῥιπή (rush, gust) of its winds; Vergil will allude to the last two names and make a play on Haemus similar to (and more certain than) Apollonius' with Haemonia.[129] For Corcyra's alternate name Drepane (sickle) Apollonius offers two explanations, one apparently discussed by Callimachus and perhaps alluded to by Vergil.[130] A recent argument also proposes that Apollonius makes a punning reference to the name of Callimachus' *Aetia*.[131]

With Callimachus some etymologizing is uncertain for us, because of the loss of context for fragments, but many passages gloss names by reference to aetiological myths, explaining the present via the past, as in Apollonius. Among clear or possible explicit etymologies of proper names are those of an altar to Apollo the Embarker, linked to the Argonauts as in Apollonius, and perhaps in the same passage an altar to the Apollo "of the shore" (Ἄκτιος),[132] whom Augustus and Vergil will make famous. Callimachus also explains the names of the month Arneus (Linus was raised among lambs,

---

129. Avernus: 4.601–3 οὐδέ τις ὕδωρ κεῖνο διὰ πτερὰ κοῦφα τανύσσας / οἰωνὸς δύναται βαλέειν ὕπερ· ἀλλὰ μεσηγὺς / φλογμῷ ἐπιθρῴσκει πεποτημένος. See Livrea (1973) and cf. on A. 6.237–42. 4.286–87 πηγαὶ γὰρ ὑπὲρ πνοιῆς βορέαο / Ῥιπαίοις ἐν ὄρεσσιν ἀπόπροθι μορμύρουσιν. See Livrea (1973) and cf. on G. 3.382.

130. 4.982–92:

Ἔστι δέ τις πορθμοῖο παροιτέρη Ἰονίοιο
ἀμφιλαφὴς πίειρα Κεραυνίῃ εἰν ἁλὶ νῆσος,
ᾗ ὕπο δὴ κεῖσθαι δρέπανον φάτις (ἵλατε Μοῦσαι,
οὐκ ἐθέλων ἐνέπω προτέρων ἔπος) ᾧ ἀπὸ πατρός
μήδεα νηλειῶς ἔταμε Κρόνος (οἱ δέ ἑ Δηοῦς
κλείουσι χθονίης καλαμητόμον ἔμμεναι ἅρπην·
Δηὼ γὰρ κείνῃ ἐνὶ δή ποτε νάσσατο γαίῃ,
Τιτῆνας δ' ἔδαε στάχυν ὄμπνιον ἀμήσασθαι,
Μάκριδα φιλαμένη)· Δρεπάνη τόθεν ἐκλήισται
οὔνομα Φαιήκων ἱερὴ τροφός· ὧς δὲ καὶ αὐτοί
αἵματος Οὐρανίοιο γένος Φαίηκες ἔασιν.

Cf. Thomas (1988) on G. 2.406, Pfeiffer (1949–53) on Callim. *Aet.* fr. 14 and 43.68–71, Nic. fr. 21: καί τις καὶ Ζάγκλης ἐδάη δρεπανηίδος ἄστυ, Lycophr. 761–62 and 869, Ovid *F.* 4.474 *quique locus curvae nomina falcis habet.*

131. 1.414 (in a passage discussing matters also treated in Callim.): αὐτὸς γὰρ ἐπαίτιος ἔπλευ ἀέθλων (sc. Apollo); see Albis (1995), and cf. below in this section for Aratus' allusion to his own name.

132. *Aet.* fr. 18.12 ἐπώνυμον Ἐμβασίοιο. There is no reference in the extant traces of this passage to Apollo Aktios, but cf. Apoll. Rhod. 1.402–4, quoted above. Callimachus did discuss the ancient games dedicated to Apollo Aktios in his prose work *On Games* (fr. 403); for Apollo Actius in Vergil cf. on A. 3.280.

ἄρνες);[133] Drepane and another "sickle" name, Zancle (also glossed by Nicander);[134] the fountain named after Automate;[135] a tree named for Perseus;[136] possibly Kallichoros as place of beautiful dancing, as in Apollonius;[137] the town of Aenus, for which Vergil will provide a different *aition;*[138] a hill called "childbed of Rhea";[139] a stream named by Rhea for a nymph;[140] the Omphalian plain, where Zeus' navel fell off;[141] and the Palatid rocks, named for Pallas Athena.[142] Several more names explicitly etymologized by Callimachus will be implicitly glossed by Vergil. Apollo's bucolic epithet Nomios, also treated by Apollonius and Vergil, is linked by Callimachus to the god's service as herdsman to Admetus;[143] "starlike" Asterie[144] becomes "conspicuous" (οὐκέτ' ἄδηλος) Delos,[145] whence the epi-

---

133. *Aet.* fr. 26.1–2, 27.1–2:

Ἀρνεῖος μ[<br>
Ἀρνῆδας[<br>
. . . . . . . .<br>
ἄρνες τοι, φίλε κοῦρε, συνήλικες, ἄρνες ἑταῖροι<br>
ἔσκον, ἐνιαυθμοὶ δ' αὐλία καὶ βοτάναι.

134. *Aet.* 1, fr. 14 (Pliny *NH* 4.52): Corcyra . . . Homero dicta Scheria et Phaeacia, Callimacho etiam Drepane; *Aet.* fr. 43.69–71 οἱ κτίσται δρέπανον θέντο πε[ρὶ Κρόνιο]ν, / —κεῖθι γὰρ ᾧ τὰ γονῆος ἀπέθρισε [μήδε' ἐκ]ε[ῖν]ος / κέκρυπται γύπῃ ζάγκλον ὑπ[όχθονίῃ. Cf. Apoll. Rhod. 4.982–92, Nic. fr. 21, and see Thomas on G. 2.406.

135. *Aet.* fr. 65.1–2 Αὐτομά[της.] εὐναὲς ἐπών[υμον, ἀλ]λ' ἀπὸ σ[εῖ]ο / λούονται λοχίην οἰκέτιν [. . . . . . ]ης.

136. Fr. 655.1–2 καὶ τριτάτη Περσῆος ἐπώνυμος, ἧς ὀρόδαμνον / Αἰγύπτῳ κατέπηξεν.

137. Fr. 600 (test.).

138. Fr. 697 (test.) = Euphor. fr. 62; see on A. 3.17–18.

139. *Hymn* 1.13–14 ἑρπετὸν οὐδὲ γυνὴ ἐπιμίσγεται, ἀλλά ἑ Ῥείης / ὠγύγιον καλέουσι λεχώιον Ἀπιδανῆες. Contrast Euphor. fr. 13, below in this section.

140. *Hymn* 1.37–38 οὐδ' ἀλίην ἀπέτεισε θεὴ χάριν, ἀλλὰ τὸ χεῦμα / κεῖνο Νέδην ὀνόμηνε.

141. *Hymn* 1.44–45 τουτάκι τοι πέσε, δαῖμον, ἄπ' ὀμφαλός ἔνθεν ἐκεῖνο / Ὀμφάλιον μετέπειτα πέδον καλέουσι Κύδωνες.

142. *Hymn* 5.41–42 σὲ δέ, δαῖμον, ἀπορρώγεσσιν ἔθηκεν / ἐν πέτραις, αἷς νῦν οὔνομα Παλλατίδες. Cf. Shechter (1975) 369.

143. *Hymn* 2.47–48 Φοῖβον καὶ Νόμιον κικλήσκομεν ἐξέτι κείνου, / ἐξότ' ἐπ' Ἀμφρυσσῷ ζευγίτιδας ἔτρεφεν ἵππους. See Depew (1993) 74–75, and cf. on G. 3.1–3.

144. *Hymn* 4.36–38 οὔνομα δ' ἦν τοι / Ἀστερίη τὸ παλαιόν, ἐπεὶ βαθὺν ἥλαο τάφρον / οὐρανόθεν φεύγουσα Διὸς γάμον ἀστέρι ἴση. See Bing (1988) 96–102, who discusses the model in Pindar's *Hymn to Zeus.*

145. *Hymn* 4.51–54:

ἡνίκα δ' Ἀπόλλωνι γενέθλιον οὖδας ὑπέσχες,<br>
τοῦτό τοι ἀντημοιβὸν ἁλίπλοοι οὔνομ' ἔθεντο,

thet Delios, which Vergil seems to gloss;[146] Dictynna and Dicte are linked to δίκτυα, "nets," as Vergil seems to hint in the *Eclogues;* Vergil will also link Dicte and the herb *dictamnum.*[147]

Not explicitly but implicitly (unless a lost line made the derivation explicit) Callimachus offers derivation of the names of the fountain Hippocrene (horse fountain) created by the hoof of Pegasus;[148] the city alternately called Exile City or Polae;[149] the "not harmful" Ἀσινεῖς (σίνομαι = harm);[150] Athena's epithet Tritogeneia, from the waters of Libyan Triton as in Apollonius;[151] possibly "three-peaked" Sicily's alternate name Trinacria[152] and the Sicilian town of Selinus (the latter perhaps noticed by Vergil, in a passage that may owe several debts to Callimachus' discussion of Sicilian cities);[153] the name of Cydippe's lover Acontius, from ἀκοντίζω, glossed by Ovid and perhaps Vergil;[154] Etesian, from αἰτέω;[155] Epopsios the Watcher;[156] possibly Apollo Deipnias from δειπνέω;[157] Apollo Delphinius, possibly in two different ways, either from association with a dolphin as in the *Homeric Hymn* discussed above, or from the name of the serpent he

---

οὕνεκεν οὐκέτ' ἄδηλος ἐπέπλεες, ἀλλ' ἐνὶ πόντου
κύμασιν Αἰγαίοιο ποδῶν ἐνεθήκαο ῥίζας.

146. *Hymn* 4.268–69 δυσήροτος, ἀλλ' ἀπ' ἐμεῖο / Δήλιος Ἀπόλλων κεκλήσεται.

147. *Hymn* 3.193–200:

ὁ δ' ἐννέα μῆνας ἐφοίτα
παίπαλά τε κρημνούς τε καὶ οὐκ ἀνέπαυσε διωκτύν,
μέσφ' ὅτε μαρπτομένη καὶ δὴ σχεδὸν ἥλατο πόντον
πρηόνος ἐξ ὑπάτοιο καὶ ἔνθορεν εἰς ἁλιήων
δίκτυα, τά σφ' ἐσάωσαν· ὅθεν μετέπειτα Κύδωνες
νύμφην μὲν Δίκτυναν, ὄρος δ' ὅθεν ἥλατο νύμφη
Δικταῖον καλέουσιν, ἀνεστήσαντο δὲ βωμούς
ἱερά τε ῥέζουσι.

See Bornmann (1968) 94–95 and my notes on E. 6.55–60. On Dicte and *dictamnum,* see on A. 12.411–19.

148. *Aet.* fr. 2.1–2 ποιμ]ένι μῆλα νέμοντι παρ' ἴχνιον ὀξέος ἵππου / Ἡσιόδῳ Μουσέων ἑσμὸ[ς ὅτ' ἠντίασεν. Cf. Pfeiffer (1949–53) ad loc., and below in this section on Aratus.

149. *Aet.* fr. 11.5–6 ἄστυρον ἐκτίσσαντο, τό κεν "Φυγάδων" τις ἐνίσποι / Γραικός, ἀτὰρ κείνων γλῶσσ' ὀνόμηνε "Πόλας." Cf. Shechter (1975) 359.

150. *Aet.* fr. 25.1 δειλαιοῖς Ἀσινεῦσιν ἐπὶ τριπτῆρος †ἀπάσας† (see Pfeiffer's notes).

151. *Aet.* fr. 37 οἵη τε Τρίτωνος ἐφ' ὕδασιν Ἀσβύσταο.

152. *Aet.* fr. 40 (test.).

153. *Aet.* fr. 43.33; cf. on A. 3.705.

154. *Aet.* fr. 70.1–2 ἀλλ' ἀπὸ τόξου / αὐτὸς ὁ τοξευτὴς ἄρδιν ἔχων ἑτέρου. Cf. on E. 10.60.

155. *Aet.* fr. 75.36 αἰτεῖσθαι τὸ δ' ἄημα παραὶ Διὸς ᾧ τε θαμεινοί. Cf. Hopkinson (1988) ad loc.

156. *Aet.* fr. 85.14–15 ὅν]τινα κικλήσκουσιν Ἐπόψ[ιον,] ὅστις ἀλιτρούς / αὐγάζειν ἱθαραῖς οὐ δύναται λογάσιν.

157. *Aet.* fr. 87.1 Δειπνιὰς ἔνθεν μιν δειδέχαται.

killed at Delphi;[158] possibly Ciris from κείρω, glossed by Vergil;[159] possibly Hippolytus or Virbius (the former as implicitly in Euripides; both glossed by Vergil),[160] the much-discussed Athenian Glaukopion;[161] Scylla as "bitch" (glossed also by Homer and Vergil);[162] perhaps Hecale from καλέω,[163] perhaps Dardania/Samothrace[164] and the rocks called *Arae* (both possibly as precedent for Vergil);[165] possibly the river Imbrasos, whose name is discussed also in Euphorion;[166] possibly Achilles as one who brings ἄχος (sorrow) to those who live in "Ilium" (the name is glossed differently in Apollonius and Euphorion);[167] the Apidanians (who lacked water to drink, πίνω) and Azania (= Arcadia, which before Zeus's birth was both dry [cf. ἄζα] and ἀ-Ζην-, Zeus-less),[168] the Couretes, who helped Zeus when he was

---

158. *Aet.* fr. 88 (test.), *Lyr.* fr. 229.12–17:

χαῖρε δὲ Δελφ]ίνι' ἄ[ν]αξ, οὔν[ο]μα γά[ρ] τοι τόδ' ἐγὼ κατάρχω,
εἵνεκεν Οἰκούσ]ιον εἰς ἄ[σ]τυ σε δελφὶς ἀπ' ἔβησε Δήλου,
].[..].[..].[.......]α τιμᾷ, μετὰ δ' ἄψ [ἐ]ς ἄλλον
]υμω[ ]ον 'Ολύμπ[ο]υ θυόεν[τα] νηόν
]ουσο,[ φ]ιλήτωρ.[.]..εξεφο[.]β.[
]ατ' ἀνάκτων ἱερὴν γενέθλην.

159. *Aet.* fr. 113.4 Κ]εῖριν . . . ; see on G. 1.404–9 and E. 6.74–77.

160. *Aet.* fr. 190 (test.); see on A. 7.761–77.

161. *Hec.* fr. 238.11 Pf. = 17.11 Hollis †ἥ τ' ἄκρησθ† ἵνα Γλαυκώπιον ἵζει. See Pfeiffer and Hollis ad loc. and Von Jan (1893) 67–68.

162. *Hec.* fr. 288.1–2 Pf. = fr. 90 Hollis Σκύλλα γυνὴ κατακᾶσα καὶ οὐ ψύθος οὔνομ' ἔχουσα / πορφυρέην ἤμησε κρέκα. Cf. on E. 6.74–77.

163. *Hec.* fr. 342.1–2 Pf. = 81 Hollis τοῦτο γὰρ αὐτήν / κωμῆται κάλεον περιηγέες; *Hec.* fr. 231.1–2 = 2 Hollis τίον δέ ἑ πάντες ὁδῖται / ἦρα φιλοξενίης· ἔχε γὰρ τέγος ἀκλήιστον. See Pfeiffer and Hollis ad loc. and Dilthey (1863); Hollis is skeptical. And of course one point of the entire *Hecale* is to explain the name of the Athenian deme; see Hollis (1990) index s.v. Hecale, Attic deme.

164. Fr. 583 (test.). For Samothrace see on A. 7.206–8.

165. Fr. 584 (test.). For the Arae see on A. 1.108–10.

166. Fr. 599 ἀντὶ γὰρ ἐκλήθης Ἴμβρασε Παρθενίου (cf. Euphor., *SH* 431, below in this sect.).

167. Fr. 624 (test.); cf. Apoll. Rhod. 4.812–13, above in this section; Euphor. fr. 57, below in this section; and Nagy, above in section 1.1, on the *Iliad*.

168. *Hymn* 1.13–21:

ἑρπετὸν οὐδὲ γυνὴ ἐπιμίσγεται, ἀλλά ἑ Ῥείης
ὠγύγιον καλέουσι λεχώιον 'Απιδανῆες.
ἔνθα σ' ἐπεὶ μήτηρ μεγάλων ἀπεθήκατο κόλπων,
αὐτίκα δίζητο ῥόον ὕδατος, ᾧ κε τόκοιο
λύματα χυτλώσαιτο, τεὸν δ' ἐνὶ χρῶτα λοέσσαι.
Λάδων ἀλλ' οὔπω μέγας ἔρρεεν οὐδ' Ἐρύμανθος,
λευκότατος ποταμῶν, ἔτι δ' ἄβροχος ἦεν ἅπασα
'Αζηνίς· μέλλεν δὲ μάλ' εὔυδρος καλέεσθαι
αὖτις· ἐπεὶ τημόσδε, Ῥέη ὅτε λύσατο μίτρην.

a κοῦρος, and whose name is glossed also by Aratus, Lucretius, and Vergil;[169] Admetus, whose name is glossed by a single epithet suggesting he is an "unbroken" (α + δμα) virgin;[170] Cyrene (two suggestions at once: named for either the nymph or a spring);[171] possibly Heracles from Hera as possibly in Apollonius and Vergil;[172] Hermes Acacesios, apparently from the name of a mountain;[173] Cyclades (περιηγέας serves as a one-word gloss);[174] Dodona and Pelasgian, which are perhaps glossed κατ' ἀντίφρασιν as if from δίδωμι and πέλας, the former in a way apparently imitated by Vergil;[175] Pallas Athena for her killing of the giant Pallas;[176] and Erysichthon's nickname Aithon, glossed as "hungry."[177]

It will be clear that several names are treated by more than one poet; a characteristic feature of Alexandrian, and later of Augustan, etymologizing is that poets offer suggestions about disputed etymologies. Other features found in both Alexandrian and Vergilian etymologizing include attention to *metonomasia* or changes of names, framing a line with the words connected etymologically, juxtaposing such words vertically at the start or end of consecutive lines, suppression or omission of one of the words involved in etymological wordplay, and the use of naming constructions to draw attention to etymologies, a feature prominent also in earlier Greek poetry. These

---

See McLennan (1977), Wilamowitz (1924) 6 n. 4, Von Jan (1893) 80 n. 1, Hopkinson (1984), (1984b), and (1988), and Depew (1993) 75–76. The manuscripts offer the word Arcadia as the first word of 20: this is clearly a gloss that has replaced the original 'Αζηνίς.

169. *Hymn* 1.52–54 οὖλα δὲ Κούρητές σε περὶ πρύλιν ὠρχήσαντο / τεύχεα πεπλήγοντες, ἵνα Κρόνος οὔασιν ἠχήν / ἀσίδος εἰσαίοι καὶ μή σεο κουρίζοντος. Cf. Von Jan (1893) 80 n. 1, Shechter (1975) 370, Arat. *Phaen.* 32–35, and see on G. 4.149–52.

170. *Hymn* 2.49 ἠιθέου ὑπ' ἔρωτι κεκαυμένος 'Αδμήτοιο. See Williams (1978) ad loc., and esp. Depew (1993) 74–75.

171. *Hymn* 2.88–90 οἱ δ' οὔπω πηγῇσι Κύρης ἐδύναντο πελάσσαι / Δωριέες, πυκινὴν δὲ νάπῃσ' "Αζιλιν ἔναιον. / τοὺς μὲν ἄναξ ἴδεν αὐτός, ἑῇ δ' ἐπεδείξατο νύμφῃ. Williams (1978) 77: "Callim. in these lines . . . is playfully juxtaposing the two etymologies of 'Cyrene': cf. Steph. Byz.: Κυρήνη· πόλις Λιβύης, ἀπὸ Κυρήνης τοῦ 'Υψέως, ἢ Κύρης πηγῆς ἐγχωρίου." Cf. Dougherty (1993) 147 on both Pindar and Callimachus.

172. *Hymn* 3.108 "Ηρης ἐννεσίῃσιν, ἀέθλιον Ἡρακλῆι. Cf. on A. 8.287–88.

173. *Hymn* 3.142–43 ἔνθα τοι ἀντιόωντες ἐνὶ προμολῇσι δέχονται / ὅπλα μὲν Ἑρμείης 'Ακακήσιος. See Von Jan (1893) 66–67.

174. *Hymn* 4.198 Κυκλάδας ὀψομένη περιηγέας, οὔτι παλαιόν. Cf. on A. 3.126–27.

175. *Hymn* 4.284–85 ἃ Δωδώνηθε Πελασγοί / τηλόθεν ἐκβαίνοντα πολὺ πρώτιστα δέχονται. See Weber (1991), and my notes on G. 1.149.

176. *Hymn* 5.7–8; see Renehan (1987) 244.

177. *Hymn* 6.66–67 αὐτίκα οἱ χαλεπόν τε καὶ ἄγριον ἔμβαλε λιμόν / αἴθωνα κρατερόν, μεγάλα δ' ἐστρεύγετο νούσῳ. See Von Jan (1893) 80 n. 1, Hopkinson (1984) 136.

features should be easily observable by readers of this section and will be discussed in more detail in my treatment of the typical features of Vergilian etymological wordplay.

It is easy to focus on Apollonius of Rhodes and Callimachus, whose work was so influential in general and also deals with aetiological themes in a way directly relevant for Vergil's *Georgics* and especially *Aeneid.* Poems by other Alexandrian or Hellenistic figures, however, offer important general or even specific precedent for Roman poetic etymologizing, including the glosses of names.[178] In works no longer extant, Nicander discusses the origins of the names of Ortygia (Delos),[179] the "moonless mountains,"[180] and Zancle.[181] Nicander's lost *Metamorphoses* probably included etymological aetiologies, as in Ovid's poem of the same name, but we cannot tell for certain which details in the summaries of Antoninus Liberalis were found in the original.[182] Aratus' poem on the constellations, the *Phaenomena,* offers explicit glosses of many star names, some of which Vergil will borrow: Wagons,[183] the "kneeling" Ἐνγόνασιν,[184] Astraeus,[185] Dike,[186] the Knot of Tails or Ὑπουράιος (if that is the correct reading),[187] Aetos,[188] and Seirios (the last

178. For an important later Hellenistic poet see the discussion of Parthenius below in section 1.6.

179. Nic. fr. 5 (Schol. Apoll. Rhod. 1.419); cf. also Lycophr. 401.

180. Nic. fr. 6 (test.): see Gow and Scholfield ad loc.

181. Nic. fr. 21 καί τις καὶ Ζάγκλης ἐδάη δρεπανηίδος ἄστυ. Cf. Callim. fr. 43.69–71, Apoll. Rhod. 4.982–92, and Thomas (1988) on G. 2.405–7.

182. Cf. Hecht (1892) 85–86.

183. *Phaen.* 27 Ἄρκτοι ἅμα τροχόωσι· τὸ δὴ καλέονται Ἅμαξαι. See on G. 1.137–38.

184. *Phaen.* 65–67 ἀλλά μιν αὔτως / Ἐνγόνασιν καλέουσι. τὸ δ' αὖτ' ἐν γούνασι κάμνον / ὀκλάζοντι ἔοικεν.

185. *Phaen.* 98–99 εἴτ' οὖν Ἀστραίου κείνη γένος, ὅν ῥά τέ φασιν / ἄστρων ἀρχαῖοι πατέρ' ἔμμεναι, εἴτε τευ ἄλλου. See Shechter (1975) 366.

186. *Phaen.* 113 μυρία πάντα παρεῖχε Δίκη, δώτειρα δικαίων. See Hecht (1882) 86, Shechter (1975) 366.

187. *Phaen.* 242–45:

ἀμφοτέρων δέ σφεων ἀποτείνεται ἠΰτε δεσμὰ  
οὐραίων, ἑκάτερθεν ἐπισχερὼ εἰς ἓν ἰόντα.  
καὶ τὰ μὲν εἷς ἀστὴρ ἐπέχει καλός τε μέγας τε,  
ὅν ῥά τε καὶ σύνδεσμον ὑπουράιον καλέουσιν.

188. *Phaen.* 313–15:

σχεδόθεν δέ οἱ ἄλλος ἄηται  
οὐ τόσσος μεγέθει, χαλεπός γε μὲν ἐξ ἁλὸς ἐλθών  
νυκτὸς ἀπερχομένης· καί μιν καλέουσιν Ἀητόν.

picked up by Vergil).[189] Less explicitly, Aratus begins the *Phaenomena* with a play on his own name (Vergil may make a similar pun on Aratus' name and may also play with his own name),[190] and like Callimachus, he both connects Κούρητες and κουρίζω[191] and alludes to the etymology of Hippocrene.[192] Rhianus of Crete (best described as a Hellenistic rather than Alexandrian poet) suggests that Apia and the Apidanians were named for an eponymous king, instead of Callimachus' suggested derivation from α + πίνω. Hellenistic scholars seem to have argued often over whether mythological or topographical explanations for names were more likely to be correct.[193] In one passage, which has been likened to Evander's speech about the names of Italy at A. 8.328–32, Rhianus offers eponyms for Pyrrhaea, Haemonia, and Thessaly,[194] and a newer fragment seems to discuss names for the island of Samos.[195] Euphorion says Achilles was named because

---

189. *Phaen.* 328–32:

ἀλλὰ κατ' αὐτὴν
γαστέρα κυάνεος περιτέλλεται, ἡ δέ οἱ ἄκρη
ἀστέρι βέβληται δεινῷ γένυς, ὅς ῥα μάλιστα
ὀξέα σειριάει καί μιν καλέουσ' ἄνθρωποι
Σείριον.

Cf. on G. 4.425–28.

190. *Phaen.* 1–2 ἐκ Διὸς ἀρχώμεσθα, τὸν οὐδέποτ' ἄνδρες ἐῶμεν / ἄρρητον· μεσταὶ δὲ Διὸς πᾶσαι μὲν ἀγυιαί. Hopkinson (1988) ad loc., Bing (1990); for Vergil and the name Aratus see on E. 3.40–42, and for Vergil and his own name see on G. 1.427–35.

191. *Phaen.* 32–35 κουρίζοντα (sc. Δία) / δίκτῳ ἐν εὐώδει, ὄρεος σχεδὸν Ἰδαίοιο / . . . / Δικταῖοι Κούρητες ὅτε Κρόνον ἐψεύδοντο. See Shechter (1975) 370, and on G. 4.149–52 and A. 12.411–19 (where I explain the reading δίκτῳ, which might best be printed ΔΙΚΤΩΙ).

192. *Phaen.* 216–21:

Κεῖνον δὴ καί φασι καθ' ὑψηλοῦ Ἑλικῶνος
καλὸν ὕδωρ ἀγαγεῖν εὐαλδέος Ἱππουκρήνης.
Οὐ γάρ πω Ἑλικὼν ἄκρος κατελείβετο πηγαῖς·
ἀλλ' Ἵππος μιν ἔτυψε· τὸ δ' ἀθρόον αὐτόθεν ὕδωρ
ἐξέχυτο πληγῇ προτέρου ποδός· οἱ δὲ νομῆες
πρῶτοι κεῖνο ποτὸν διεφήμισαν Ἱππουκρήνην.

Cf. above in this section on Callim. *Aet.* fr. 2.1–2.

193. Rhian. fr. 13.2–3 τοῦ δὲ κλυτὸς ἐκγένετ' Ἆπις, / ὅς ῥ' Ἀπίην ἐφάτιξε καὶ ἀνέρας Ἀπιδανῆας. On mythological vs. topographical explanations see Von Jan (1893) 67–76.

194. Rhian. fr. 25.1–5:

Πυρραίην ποτὲ τήν γε παλαιότεροι καλέεσκον
Πύρρης Δευκαλίωνος ἀπ' ἀρχαίης ἀλόχοιο,
Αἱμονίην δ' ἐξαῦτις ἀφ' Αἵμονος, ὅν ῥα Πελασγὸς
γείνατο φέρτατον υἱόν· ὁ δ' αὖ τέκε Θεσσαλὸν Αἵμων,
τοῦ δ' ἄπο Θεσσαλίην λαοὶ μετεφημίξαντο.

Cf. Hollis (1992) 278.

195. *SH* 431; cf. Callim. fr. 599 (above in this sect.).

he had never tasted "fodder" (α + χιλός)[196] and also glosses the names Orchomenos (from dancing, ὄρχησις),[197] Iphigeneia (born from rape; old dative of ἴς = ἶφι),[198] the island of Naxos,[199] the herdsman Boiotos,[200] Perseus who sacked (πέρσεν) cities,[201] and the Saronic Gulf, where he says the hunter Saron drowned.[202] Possibly Euphorion connected the name Δαναοί with δάνος, "gift," in a way possibly imitated by Vergil.[203] Lycophron's relentlessly obscure *Alexandra* often plays with etymologies, many for mythological figures whose names he suppresses and only alludes to by means of etymology.[204] Both Theocritus and Vergil play on the association of the name Galatea with γάλα, "milk."[205] Theocritus offers glosses or at least puns connecting the name Pentheus with πένθημα, "suffering," and

---

196. Euphor. fr. 57 Ἐς Φθίην χιλοῖο κατήιε πάμπαν ἄπαστος· / τούνεκα Μυρμιδόνες μιν Ἀχιλέα φημίξαντο. Cf. above in section 1.1 on Homer, and above in this section on Apoll. Rhod. 4.812–13 and Callim. fr. 624; see Meineke (1964) 98–100.

197. Euphor. fr. 87 Ὀρχομενὸν Χαρίτεσσιν ἀφαρέσιν ὀρχηθέντα. See Meineke (1964) 106–7.

198. Euphor. fr. 90 Οὕνεκα δή μιν / ἶφι βιησαμένῳ Ἑλένη ὑπεγείνατο Θησεῖ. See Meineke (1964) 103–4.

199. Euphor. fr. 169 (test.) = Steph. Byz. s.v. Νάξος. Εὐφορίων δὲ παρὰ τὸ νάξαι, ὃ φασι θῦσαί τινες.

200. Euphor. fr. 96.3–4 Βοιωτὸν δ' ὀνόμηνε· τὸ γὰρ καλέσαντο νομῆες, / ὅττι ῥα πατρῴησι βοῶν ἀπεθήκατο κόπροις. See Powell ad loc. and Meineke (1964) 88–89.

201. Euphor. fr. 176 Τῷ μιν καὶ Περσῆα μετεκλήισσαν Ἀχαιοὶ / οὕνεκεν ἄστεα πέρσεν ἀπειρεσίων ἀνθρώπων. See Meineke (1964) 50–51, Hollis (1992) 279; Dilthey (1863) 40 suggests Callimachus as author.

202. Euphor. fr. 172 (test.); cf. Hollis (1993), who discusses Parthenius' different suggestion (see below in sect. 1.5).

203. See on A. 2.42–49.

204. I have probably only scratched the surface of Lycophron's etymologizing: he alludes to the origins of the names Hill of Doom (29), Scylla (45, 669; see my catalogue on A. 3.432), Cape Onugnathus (94), Myrtoan Sea (161), Neoptolemus (183; see on A. 2.469–75), Achilleius Dromus (193), Mnemon (240–41), Priam (338–39), Ortygia (401; cf. Nicander fr. 5, cited above, and on A. 3.693–94), Athena Tritogeneia (528; cf. above on Apoll. Rhod. 4.1309–11 and Callim. *Aet.* fr. 37), Protesilaus (528; cf. sect. 1.1 on *Il.* 2.698–702), Insulae Diomedeae (601), Ionian Sea (631), Balearic Isles (636; cf. G. 1.308–9), Pithecusae (691), Baiae (694), Phlegethon (699; cf. on A. 6.550–51), Melpomene (713), Parthenope (717–18), Leucosia (723–24), Corcyra/Drepane and Drepanum in Sicily (761–62, 869; see my note above on Apoll. Rhod. 4.982–92 for several poets), Hermes' Heel (835), Athena Agelaia (853), Trinacria (966), Ionians (987), Caulonia (1004), the Odyssean Hill (1030–31), Rome (ῥώμη, 1233; cf. on A. 1.273–77), Hellespont (1285), Euxine (1286), Aeolians (1377).

205. Theoc. 11.20 λευκοτέρα πακτᾶς ποτιδεῖν, ἁπαλωτέρα ἀρνός. Cf. Du Quesnay (1979) 44. See on A. 8.657–61.

Amycus with μυκάομαι, "roar, bellow."[206] Moschus offers two glosses found in fifth-century tragedy, for the Bosporos as bovine crossing, and for Io's son Epaphus, conceived from the "touch" (cf. ἐπαφάω) of Zeus.[207] In general, though, bucolic poets like Theocritus and Moschus seem to offer less etymological wordplay than other poets of the age. Vergil's bucolic *Eclogues* also contain comparatively fewer examples of etymological wordplay than his other works; this may be due to a sense that bucolic is less suitable for aetiology, or to the fact that Varro's *de Lingua Latina* had only recently been published when Vergil was writing.

Alexandrian poets offer implicit or, more rarely, explicit etymological suggestions about a number of common words as well. Many of these are rare or disputed Homeric words discussed in the Homeric scholia; glossing these words was part of both the poet's dual role as scholar and poet, and his way of claiming his own place in the epic tradition dominated by Homer.[208] Apollonius connects the disputed Homeric hapax ἀμφιλύκη, "morning twilight," with Lycia[209] and derives κερτομέω from κέαρ,[210] προαλὲς from ἅλις,[211]

---

206. Theoc. 26.26 ἐξ ὄρεος πένθημα καὶ οὐ Πενθῆα φέρουσαι (cf. Arist. *Rhet.* 1400, quoted above in sect. 1.3, Gow [1950] ad loc., Hecht [1882] 82); 22.75 ἦ ῥ' Ἄμυκος καὶ κόχλον ἑλὼν μυκήσατο κοῖλον (cf. Hecht [1882] 82, and my note on A. 5.372–73).

207. Mosch. *Eur.* 48–50 δοιοῦ δ' ἕστασαν ὑψοῦ ἐπ' ὀφρύσιν αἰγιαλοῖο / φῶτες ἀολλήδην θηεῦντο δὲ ποντοπόρον βοῦν. / ἐν δ' ἦν Ζεὺς Κρονίδης ἐπαφώμενος ἠρέμα χερσί. Cf. Aesch. *Supp.* 17, 46–48, 314–15, *PV* 732–35, 839–41, 848–51 (quoted above in sect. 1.2).

208. On this see (most give earlier references, e.g., to Erbse and Herter) Bing (1988) esp. 72–75, Pfeiffer (1968) 138–40, Fraser (1972) 633–34, Renkagos (1992), who discusses many words I do not, Hopkinson (1988) index s.v. Homer, echoes of Homeric diction and allusion to controversial readings.

209. Hunter (1986) 54–55, on Apoll. Rhod. 2.669–75:

Ἦμος δ' οὔτ' ἄρ πω φάος ἄμβροτον οὔτ' ἔτι λίην
ὀρφναίη πέλεται, λεπτὸν δ' ἐπιδέδρομε νυκτί
φέγγος, ὅτ' ἀμφιλύκην μιν ἀνεγρόμενοι καλέουσιν,
τῆμος ἐρημαίης νήσου λιμέν' εἰσελάσαντες
Θυνιάδος καμάτῳ πολυπήμονι βαῖνον ἔραζε.
τοῖσι δὲ Λητοῦς υἱός, ἀνερχόμενος Λυκίηθεν
τῆλ' ἐπ' ἀπείρονα δῆμον Ὑπερβορέων ἀνθρώπων.

Cf. too McKeown (1987) 52–53, who cites imitation of Apollonius in several passages in Ovid.

210. 3.56 Κερτομέεις, νῶιν δὲ κέαρ συνορίνεται ἄτη. See Hunter (1989) ad loc.

211. 3.66–68, 73:

καὶ δ' ἄλλως ἔτι καὶ πρὶν ἐμοὶ μέγα φίλατ' Ἰήσων,
ἐξότ' ἐπὶ προχοῇσιν ἅλις πλήθοντος Ἀναύρου
ἀνδρῶν εὐνομίης πειρωμένῃ ἀντεβόλησεν. . . .
. . . . . . . . . . . . . . . . . . . . . . . . . . . . . . . .
αὐτὸς ἑοῖς ὤμοισι διὲκ προαλὲς φέρεν ὕδωρ.

See Hunter (1989) ad loc.

ἠλίβατος from ἥλιος,[212] and ἐπίουρον from ἐπι-οράω.[213] Callimachus twice uses ὑποδράξ in a way reminiscent of Homeric τὸν δ' ἄρ' ὑπόδρα ἰδών (*Il.* 1.148, etc.), which may suggest derivation from δέρκομαι.[214] Elsewhere Callimachus "is perhaps hinting at the etymology which connected βλοσυρός with βλέπειν."[215] In a fragment he describes but does not name (i.e., he suppresses the name of) a fish in such a way as to point to and gloss the omitted name; Vergil will also gloss omitted names in this way.[216]

Both Apollonius and Callimachus, the former implicitly and the latter explicitly, explain the origin of the cry ἵη used in worship of Apollo, in telling of Apollo's shooting (ἵημι) of the serpent.[217] Apollonius glosses μύωψ by mentioning the μύκημα the gadfly produces in cattle, and Callimachus may have etymologized one or more of the words for gadfly, as Vergil will.[218] Apollonius glosses the adjective κατουλάς with the adjective ὀλοός,

---

212. 3.161–62 οὐρανίη· δοιὼ δὲ πόλοι ἀνέχουσι κάρηνα / οὐρέων ἠλιβάτων, κορυφαὶ χθονός, ἧχί τ' ἀερθείς. See Hunter (1989) ad loc.

213. 3.1179–82:

Κάδμος, ὅτ' Εὐρώπην διζήμενος εἰσαφίκανεν,
πέφνεν, Ἀρητιάδι κρήνῃ ἐπίουρον ἐόντα·
ἔνθα καὶ ἐννάσθη πομπῇ βοὸς ἥν οἱ Ἀπόλλων
ὤπασε μαντοσύνῃσι προηγήτειραν ὁδοῖο·

See Hunter (1989) ad loc.

214. Callim. *Iam.* fr. 194.101–2 τὴν δ' ἆρ' ὑποδρὰξ οἷα ταῦρος ἡ δάφνη / ἔβλεψε καὶ τάδ' εἶπεν, *Hec.* fr. 374 Pf. = 72 Hollis ἡ δὲ πελιδνωθεῖσα καὶ ὄμμασι λοξὸν ὑποδράξ. By using ὑποβλέψας in a third passage, he may be calling further attention to his own etymology: *Hymn* 6.50 τὰν δ' ἄρ' ὑποβλέψας χαλεπώτερον ἠὲ κυναγόν. See Hopkinson (1984) on *Hymn* 6.50.

215. Hopkinson (1984) on *Hymn* 6.52 ὠμοτόκος, τᾶς φαντὶ πέλειν βλοσυρώτατον ὄμμα; cf. too Renehan (1987) 252.

216. Fr. 378.1 ἢ μᾶλλον χρύσειον ἐν ὀφρύσιν ἱερὸν ἰχθύν; the fish is the χρύσοφρυς, the "gilthead" or "golden brow," as Athenaeus notes in quoting the fragment. For Vergil see e.g. on *G.* 3.425–34, where he is following Nicander's gloss of the name of a snake.

217. Cf. Apoll. Rhod. 2.701–13, Callim. *Hymn* 2.97–104, and see Williams (1978) on *Hymn* 2.103, Hunter (1986) 57–60, Shechter (1975) 360, Paskiewicz (1988) 58, and Calame (1993) 45–46. Cf. too the imitation of Apollonius by Varro of Atax, discussed below in section 1.6.

218. 1.1265–69:

ὡς δ' ὅτε τίς τε μύωπι τετυμμένος ἔσσυτο ταῦρος
πίσεά τε προλιπὼν καὶ ἑλεσπίδας, οὐδὲ νομήων
οὐδ' ἀγέλης ὄθεται, πρήσσει δ' ὁδὸν ἄλλοτ' ἄπαυστος,
ἄλλοτε δ' ἱστάμενος καὶ ἀνὰ πλατὺν αὐχέν' ἀείρων
ἵησιν μύκημα, κακῷ βεβολημένος οἴστρῳ.

3.275–77:

Τόφρα δ' Ἔρως πολιοῖο δι' ἠέρος ἷξεν ἄφαντος,
τετρηχὼς οἷόν τε νέαις ἐπὶ φορβάσιν οἶστρος
τέλλεται, ὅν τε μύωπα βοῶν κλείουσι νομῆες.

"deadly."[219] A fragment of Callimachus seems to allude to the connection made, both in archaic Greek poets and in Vergil, between λαός, "people," and λᾶας, "stone."[220] Callimachus seems also to gloss the words πανάκεια,[221] ἄκμων,[222] Homeric ἔνδιος[223] and θυμάρμενον,[224] νύξ,[225] and δόρκας.[226]

Nicander's poems on drugs and animals offer explicit or implicit etymologies for a number of plants and animals,[227] including aconite, also

---

Callim. *Hec.* fr. 301 Pf. (cf. 117 Hollis):

⟨οἶστρον⟩

βουσόον ὅν τε μύωπα βοῶν καλέουσιν ἀμορβοί.

Cf. Ross (1987) 158, and see on G. 3.146–56.

219. 4.1694–98:

αὐτίκα δὲ Κρηταῖον ὑπὲρ μέγα λαῖτμα θέοντας
νὺξ ἐφόβει τήνπερ τε κατουλάδα κικλήσκουσιν
νύκτ' ὀλοήν· οὐκ ἄστρα διίσχανεν, οὐκ ἀμαρυγαί
μήνης, οὐρανόθεν δὲ μέλαν χάος, ἠδέ τις ἄλλη
ὠρώρει σκοτίη μυχάτων ἀνιοῦσα βερέθρων.

Livrea cites the schol.: ἡ σκοτεινὴ νὺξ κατουλὰς καλεῖται παρὰ τὸ ὀλοόν.

220. *SH* 295 (= 496 + 533 Pf.) λαοὶ Δευκαλίωνος ὅσοι γενόμεσθα γενέθλης, / πουλὺ θαλασσαίων μυνδότεροι νεπόδων. See on G. 1.62–63.

221. *Hymn* 2.39–41 οὐ λίπος Ἀπόλλωνος ἀποστάζουσιν ἔθειραι, / ἀλλ' αὐτὴν πανάκειαν· ἐν ἄστει δ' ᾧ κεν ἐκεῖναι / πρῶκες ἔραζε πέσωσιν, ἀκήρια πάντ' ἐγένοντο; *Epig.* 46.4 ἦ πανακὲς πάντων φάρμακον ἁ σοφία. Cf. too Nic. *Ther.* 508.

222. From ἀκάματος. See *Hymn* 3.145–48:

νῦν δ' οὐκέτι Φοῖβος ἄεθλον
τοῦτον ἔχει, τοῖος γὰρ ἀεὶ Τιρύνθιος ἄκμων
ἕστηκε πρὸ πυλέων ποτιδέγμενος, εἴ τι φέρουσα
νεῖαι πῖον ἔδεσμα.

See Bornmann (1968) 72.

223. *Hec.* fr. 304.1–3 Pf. = 46.1–3 Hollis ἀμφὶ δέ οἱ κεφαλῇ νέον Αἱμονίηθεν / μεμβλωκὸς πίλημα περίτροχον ἄλκαρ ἔκειτο / εἴδεος ἐνδίοιο. See Von Jan (1893) 77–78.

224. *Hymn* 3.166–67 ἐν καὶ χρυσείας ὑποληνίδας ἐπλήσαντο / ὕδατος, ὄφρ' ἐλάφοισι ποτὸν θυμάρμενον εἴη. Von Jan (1893) 76.

225. *Hymn* 5.82 παιδὸς δ' ὄμματα νὺξ ἔλαβεν. See Renehan (1987) 248–49.

226. *Hymn* 5.90–92:

ὦ ὄρος, ὦ Ἑλικὼν οὐκέτι μοι παριτέ,
ἦ μεγάλ' ἀντ' ὀλίγων ἐπράξαο· δόρκας ὀλέσσας
καὶ πρόκας οὐ πολλὰς φάεα παιδὸς ἔχεις.

See Bulloch (1985), Hopkinson (1988), and Renehan (1987).

227. *Alex.* 36–40 τὴν μέν τε κλείουσι μυοκτόνον; *Alex.* 41–42 (with White [1987] 74–76) πολλάκι θηλυφόνον καὶ κάμμαρον· ἐν δ' Ἀκοναίοις / θηλήειν ἀκόνιτον ἐνεβλάστησεν ὀρόγκοις; *Alex.* 344–46 ἤ καί που δαμάλεις ἐριγάστορας ἄλλοτε μόσχους / πίμπραται ὁππότε θῆρα νομαζόμενοι δατέονται, / τοὔνεκα τὴν βούπρηστιν ἐπικλείουσι νομῆες; *Ther.* 411–12 Κῆρα δέ τοι δρυΐναο πιφαύσκεο, τόν τε χέλυδρον / ἐξέτεροι καλέουσιν· ὁ δ' ἐν δρυσὶν οἰκία τεύξας; *Ther.* 500–

apparently discussed by Euphorion,[228] panacea, as in Callimachus,[229] and the snake χέρσυδρος, whose name will be glossed in the *Georgics*.[230] A fragment of Nicander says that wine (οἶνος) was named by and after Oeneus.[231] Eratosthenes says that the word φωριαμός (chest, trunk) is so called because "secret" (φώριος) things are hidden in it.[232] Theocritus implicitly glosses the herb ἱππομανές, as if from ὅππος, "horse," and μανία, "madness," as Vergil will in an important passage in the *Georgics*.[233]

In sum, the etymological wordplay of the Alexandrian or Hellenistic poets was not so much a radical departure from that of classical Greek poetry as it was an intensification and change of emphasis.[234] Their wordplay was more frequent, more learned or often even obscure, and more closely tied to the aetiological poetry's appropriation of both the literary past (the work of earlier poets like Homer) and the mythological past (the heroic mythological subject matter of earlier poetry). It was more competitive, in that poets offered rival etymologies not merely to meet their own needs but even to revel in the competition. And it was above all more demanding on readers, who will appreciate and enjoy the poetry more to the extent that they are familiar with the extensive research and scholarship that underlies it. It also

---

501 πρώτην μὲν Χείρωνος ἐπαλθέα ῥίζαν ἑλέσθαι, / Κενταύρου Κρονίδαο φερώνυμον, ἥν ποτε Χείρων; *Ther.* 554–56 τὴν ἤτοι μελίφυλλον ἐπικλείουσι βοτῆρες, / οἱ δὲ μελίκταιναν· τῆς γὰρ περὶ φύλλα μέλισσαι / ὀδμῇ θελγόμεναι μέλιτος ῥοιζηδὸν ἵενται; *Ther.* 625–28 (cf. White [1987] 40–41), *Ther.* 666ff. Ἄλλην δ' Ἀλκιβίοιο φερώνυμον ἄγρεο ποίην; *Ther.* 685–88 (with Shechter [1975] 359).

228. *Alex.* 41–42 (with White [1987] 74–76) πολλάκι θηλυφόνον καὶ κάμμαρον· ἐν δ' Ἀκοναίοις / θηλήειν ἀκόνιτον ἐνεβλάστησεν ὀρόγκοις; cf. Euphor. fr. 37 (test.), as discussed by Hecht (1882) 84.

229. *Ther.* 508 παντὶ γὰρ ἄρκιός ἐστι· τό μιν πανάκειον ἔπουσιν. Cf. also *Ther.* 685–88, with Shechter (1975) 359, *Ther.* 801–4 (with White [1987] 55–56), Nic. fr. 74.27–29 ἃ κρίνα λείρια δ' ἄλλοι ἐπιφθέγγονται ἀοιδῶν, / οἱ δὲ καὶ ἀμβροσίην, πολέες δέ τε χάρμ' Ἀφροδίτης· / ἤρισε γὰρ χροιῇ.

230. *Ther.* 359–71 Νῦν δ' ἄγε χερσύδροιο καὶ ἀσπίδος εἴρεο μορφάς. / ἰσαίας. See on G. 3.425–34.

231. Nic. fr. 86 = Athen. 2.35A τὸν οἶνον ὁ Κολοφώνιος Νίκανδρος ὠνομάσθαι φησὶν ἀπὸ Οἰνέως· "Οἰνεὺς δ' ἐν κοίλοισιν ἀποθλίψας δεπάεσσιν / οἶνον ἔκλησε."

232. Eratosth. fr. 4 φωριαμὸν δ' ὀνόμηνεν, ὅ μιν κύθε φώρια ἄγρην· / ἐκ τοῦ φωριαμός κικλήσκεται ἀνθρώποισι.

233. Theoc. 2.48–49 ἱππομανὲς . . . τῷ δ' ἔπι πᾶσαι / καὶ πῶλοι μαινόνται ἀν' ὤρεα καὶ θοαὶ ἵπποι. See on G. 3.266–83.

234. So rightly Hopkinson (1988) 7–8, Parsons (1993) 155, who in a discussion of Hellenistic poetry speaks of the "dangers" of "all attempts to write literary history" and notes that "it is normally not a question of absolute novelties but of novel emphases."

involved a number of examples of etymological wordplay or etymologizing aetiology to which Vergil and other Roman poets will directly allude.

## 1.5. Etymological Thought and Rome

Although this study argues that the Alexandrian poets were of paramount importance for Vergilian etymologizing, a whole range of Roman influences and factors made Vergil and the other Augustan poets, and their readers or audience, inclined to be receptive to Alexandrian etymological wordplay. Romans seem naturally to have had a great interest in wordplay and puns, as the surveys of wordplay by McCartney and Wölfflin clearly show.[235] The influence on Rome of the culture and scholarship of *Graecia capta* included both theoretical and practical work on language, and soon Romans were producing their own studies of etymology. Rawson notes one practical incentive for etymological study at Rome: "traditionally-minded Romans needed assistance in understanding ancient documents of all kinds, and often found it in etymology and derivation."[236] This section will note briefly the work of several grammarians and others who taught or discussed etymology at Rome, or in a way that influenced Rome, with a somewhat more extensive treatment of the most important figure, Varro.[237] I begin in the second century; early poets such as Livius and Naevius, who have some claim to being the first philologists at Rome,[238] will be included in the next section's treatment of poets at Rome. Neither section claims to be a full treatment of the topic, which would be beyond the scope of this introduction; both seek to give some indication of the range and character of interest in etymologizing at Rome.

Early historians often glossed place-names and explained their origins.[239] Cato the elder (234–149 B.C.) seems to have discussed the etymologies of two city names alluded to by Vergil, that of *altum Praeneste* (A. 7.681–85), from the verb *praesto,* "stand out," because of its hilltop location, and that of *intempestae . . . Graviscae* (A. 10.184), from its "unwholesome air"

235. McCartney (1918–19), Wölfflin (1887).

236. Rawson (1985) 119.

237. This section owes much to Rawson (1985) 117–31, Woodhead (1928) 81–89, Bartelink (1965) 14–27, Porte (1985) 197–202, and of course Funaioli (1907) (= *GRF*), whose edition of the fragments of Roman grammarians includes many helpful comments.

238. Cf. Suet. *Gramm.* 1 = *GRF* p. ix: initium quoque eius [*sc.* grammaticae] mediocre extitit, siquidem antiquissimi doctorum, qui idem et poetae et semigraeci erant (Livium et Ennium dico . . .), nihil amplius quam Graecos interpretebantur, aut si quid ipsi Latine composuissent praelegebant.

239. Cf. Collart (1954) 255.

*(gravis aer).*[240] We know also of glosses by the historians Q. Fabius Pictor *(Vulsci* as a corruption of *Siculi),* L. Cincius Alimentus *(fana* from *Faunus),* A. Postumius Albinus (*Baiae* named for a Trojan nurse), L. Cassius Hemina (Crustumerium named after a *Clytemestra),* L. Calpurnius Piso Censorius Frugi (cens. 120, *Italia a vitulis),* Q. Lutatius Catulus (cos. 102, the name of Parthenope changed to Neapolis, "new city," *ob recentem institutionem),* and Valerias Antias (Ancus named for his bad elbow, ἀγκών).[241]

M. Fulvius Nobilior (cens. 179), the patron of Ennius who built the temple of *Hercules Musarum,* wrote on the derivations of the names of the months.[242] Servius tells us that the *libri pontificales* contained explanations of the names of the gods.[243] L. Aelius Stilo, who lived perhaps from 150 into the eighties and was called by his pupil Varro the most learned man of his age, had extensive interest in etymologies, and his derivations are mentioned often enough by Varro and others for us to know that he followed the Stoic view that etymology could explain natural relationships between words and the things for which they stood. He derived *caelum* either from *caelatum,* or κατ' ἀντίφρασιν from *celatum (quod apertum est); latro* from *latere, lepos* from *levipes* because of the rabbit's swiftness, and *miles* κατ' ἀντίφρασιν from *mollitia.* Stilo seems to have had a predilection (some might say weakness) for etymologies κατ' ἀντίφρασιν, and may be the source of the well-known gloss *lucus quia . . . parum luceat.*[244]

The work of several Greek scholars possibly influential on second- and first-century Rome may be mentioned. Apollodorus of Athens (180?–109?) wrote a Περὶ Ἐτυμολογιῶν, whose fragments preserve no proper names, only common nouns, and a Περὶ Θεῶν that focused "on Homeric nomenclature in particular"; this focus arguably "will have made the Περὶ Θεῶν required reading for a poet who knew the Homeric scholia as well as Vergil demonstrably did."[245] The *Art of Grammar* or Τεχνὴ Γραμματική attributed to Dionysius Thrax, a pupil of Aristarchus, discusses etymology, and may have been influential at Rome—or it may have been written as late as A.D.

240. Cf. *GRF* pp. 9–14.

241. Fabius Pictor and Cincius: *GRF* p. 7, Postumius and Hemina: p. 17, Piso: pp. 118–19, Catulus: pp. 122–23, Valerias Antias: p. 127.

242. *GRF* pp. 15–16.

243. Servius on G. 1.21: nomina haec numinum in indigitamentis inveniuntur, id est in libris pontificalibus, qui et nomina deorum et rationes ipsorum nominum continent.

244. Cf. *GRF* pp. 51–76, Collart (1954) 267–68, below in section 2.3, and my note on A. 1.441.

245. Weber (1991) 325–26; see also Pfeiffer (1968) 261–63, Rusten (1982) 30–33, Feeney (1991) 21.

200.[246] Crates of Mallos, whose unplanned stay at Rome after he fell into the opening of a sewer and broke his leg in 168 B.C. is said to have awakened Roman interest in scholarship, showed interest in etymology; he is quoted as deriving the name Zeus from διαίνω = πιαίνω, "fatten, enrich."[247] In the first century, the popularity and influence at Rome of the Stoic Posidonius will have lent weight to his citation of etymologies of gods' names (e.g., linking Zeus with διοικέω, govern, control) and especially the names of peoples discussed in his historical and ethnographic writings (e.g., linking the Cimbri and Cimmerians).[248] Hypsicrates, a *grammaticus* of the Sullan age, wrote of Latin words borrowed from Greek.[249] Later Philoxenus of Alexandria wrote a Περὶ τῆς τῶν Ῥωμαίων Διαλέκτου, of which several fragments remain; scholars disagree over whether he must have written after Varro, since he is not mentioned in the extant portion of *de Lingua Latina,* or whether a full text of Varro would show us that Philoxenus was an important source for him.[250] Of special interest as both poet and scholar is Parthenius of Nicea, whose enormous personal influence on Roman poets from Cinna to Vergil is now well understood.[251] The evidence is meager, but Parthenius is likely to have glossed a number of the learned names and rare words he clearly used; extant fragments show that he offered an etymology (in the verse or prose *Metamorphoses)* for the Saronic Gulf different from Euphorion's, and that he may have offered a unique gloss on the name Telephus, as if from τηλεφανής.[252] The prose *Erotica Pathemata* that Parthenius offered to Cornelius Gallus also offer a number of etymological aetiologies.[253]

246. Rawson (1985) 118–19; cf. too Amsler (1989) 17, with further references.

247. Lyd. *Mens.* 4.71.48 Κράτης (8 Wachsmuth) δὲ ἀπὸ τοῦ διαίνειν τουτέστι πιαίνειν τὴν γῆν βούλεται ὀνομασθῆναι τὸν Δία, τὸν εἰς πάντα διήκοντα. Cf. Kidd (1988) 413. For Crates' broken leg cf. Suet. *Gramm.* 2 = *GRF* pp. x–xi. On Crates cf. Porter (1992) and Hardie (1986) 27–29, who provide further references; Porter warns against facile assimilation of Crates to the Stoics.

248. See Kidd (1988) general index C s.v. etymology, and esp. pp. 77–78.

249. *GRF* pp. 107–8.

250. *GRF* pp. xx–xxi, 443–46; Theodoridis (1976) esp. 3–7, 12, with fragments at pp. 234–42; Rawson (1985) 125; see their references to Schmidt, Reitzenstein, and Wendel; Reitzenstein argued that Varro used Philoxenus. Horsfall (1991) 40 puts Philoxenus in a list of those whom the "young Vergil" could possibly have known.

251. Cf. Clausen (1987) 1–10; the skepticism of Courtney (1993) 212–14 is excessive: see O'Hara (1994).

252. Saronic Gulf: from the dragging (σύρω, or with Hollis [1993] σαρόω) of Scylla through the sea as punishment for treachery (for Scylla cf. on A. 3.432). Telephus: *SH* 650, where he is called ἀργειφόντης. Cf. also *SH* 664, on Nemausus in Gaul as named for one of the Heraclidae.

253. Cf. the ends of 11 (Biblys), 13 (Calchis), 15 (Daphne), 26 (the *heroon* of Trambelus), 30 (Celts), 32 (Epirus).

In the first century, work on etymologizing by Romans becomes more common. Writing probably in the eighties, the author of the treatise on oratory known as the *Rhetorica ad Herennium* discusses some examples of simple wordplay that show up in Vergil and Ovid; see below in the discussion of paronomasia in section 2.1. In the early first century the freedman Aurelius Opillus "explained and gave etymologies for poetic words . . . , mainly perhaps in his nine books called *The Muses*."[254] Nigidius Figulus, best known for his interest in Pythagoreanism, augury, and astrology, also wrote *Commentarii Grammatici* of uncertain date (he died in 45), in which he often appealed to etymology, for example, *frater est dictus quasi fere alter.*[255] Twice he may be part of the background to Vergilian etymologizing: once by discussing the gadfly, whose name Vergil will gloss, and possibly by being the first to derive *rudens,* "rope," from *rudeo,* "roar."[256] L. Ateius Praetextatus, also called Philologus, wrote a *Liber Glossematorum;* he died in old age sometime after 29.[257] Cicero's friend Q. Cornificius may have been both a learned poet, and the author of a Stoicizing treatise *de Etymis Deorum.* This work must have been written after 44, since a fragment refers to Cicero's *de Natura Deorum,* and before Verrius Flaccus, since it is often quoted in Festus. Cornificius offers often creative etymologies of Ianus *(ab eundo),* Apollo (ἀπὸ τοῦ ἀναπολεῖν), Phoebus (ἀπὸ τοῦ φοιτᾶν βίᾳ), and Minerva *(minitans armis).*[258] Other minor figures: the knight Servius Clodius; the *duodecim tabularum interpretes* mentioned by Varro; M. Iunius Gracchanus, whose *Libri de Potestatibus ad Pompeium* explained the origin of, for example, the name *quaestor (a genere quaerendi);* and Saufeius, an equestrian friend of Atticus, who derived Latium from *latere,* as Vergil's Evander will do (see on A. 8.319–27).[259]

The view of Cicero himself toward etymologizing may be described as ambivalent.[260] He discusses etymologies of gods' names in the de *Natura Deorum,* cites etymologies of key terms in his philosophical discussions, and plays with possible derivations of personal names in speeches, partly in jest,

254. Rawson (1985) 124; cf. *GRF* pp. 86–95.

255. *GRF* pp. 158–79 (*frater* = fr. 28, p. 171).

256. Gadfly: fr. 40, *GRF* p. 176, and see on G. 3.146–53; *rudens:* fr. dub. 47, *GRF* p. 178, and see on A. 1.87.

257. *GRF* pp. 136–41, Rawson (1985) 124.

258. Rawson (1985) 124, (1979), Courtney (1993) 225–27; cf. *GRF* pp. 473–80.

259. Servius Clodius: *GRF* pp. 95–98, XII tables: pp. 113–15, Iunius: pp. 120–21, Saufeius: pp. 438–39.

260. Cf. Pease (1979) 709–10 (with further references), Woodhead (1928) 83–89, Rawson (1985) 120, Snyder (1980) 66.

but perhaps in accord with his audience's tendency to believe in kledonomancy, or the power of names or chance utterances.[261] But in the *de Natura Deorum,* somewhat as in Plato's *Cratylus,* the etymologies are presented by speakers of whom the author does not fully approve. In book 2 Lucilius Balbus presents Stoic views and in 2.25.64–27.69 a long series of allegorical etymologies of gods' names,[262] but in book 3 Cotta attacks the Stoics on behalf of the Academy, at one point criticizing the Stoic (and Varronian; see below) flexibility in altering letters to explain derivations.[263] Recently Long

261. That Romans were seriously interested in the good and bad omens associated with some names is clear from the extensive survey at Pease (1963) 283–85 (for drawing my attention to which I thank Garth Tissol); on kledonomancy see also Ogilvie (1970) 752, and above in the discussion of Greek tragedy.

262. Cic. *ND* 2.25.64.–27.69: Saturnum autem eum esse voluerunt qui cursum et conversionem spatiorum ac temporum contineret. qui deus Graece id ipsum nomen habet: Κρόνος enim dicitur, qui est idem χρόνος id est spatium temporis. *Saturnus* autem est appellatus quod *saturaretur annis*. . . . sed ipse *Iuppiter,* id est *iuvans pater,* quem conversis casibus appellamus a *iuvando Iovem*. . . . *Aer* autem, ut Stoici disputant, interiectus inter mare et caelum *Iunonis nomine consecratur*. . . . sed *Iunonem a iuvando* credo nominatam. . . . nomenque productum *ut Portunus a porta sic Neptunus a nando,* paulum primis litteris immutatis. terrena autem vis omnis atque natura *Diti patri* dedicata est, qui *dives* ut apud Graecos Πλούτων, quia et recidunt omnia in terras et oriuntur e terris. . . . mater autem est *a gerendis frugibus Ceres* tamquam *geres,* casuque prima littera itidem immutata ut a Graecis; nam ab illis quoque Δημήτηρ quasi γῆ μήτηρ nominata est. iam qui *magna verteret Mavors, Minerva* autem quae vel *minueret vel minaretur*. . . . principem in sacrificando *Ianum* esse voluerunt, quod *ab eundo* nomen est ductum, ex quo transitiones perviae iani foresque in liminibus profanarum aedium ianuae nominantur. nam *Vestae* nomen *a Graecis* (ea est enim quae ab illis Ἑστία dicitur); *vis* autem eius ad aras et focos pertinet. . . . nec longe absunt ab hac vi di *Penates,* sive *a penu* ducto nomine (est enim omne quo vescuntur homines penus) sive ab eo quod *penitus* insident; ex quo etiam penetrales a poetis vocantur. iam Apollinis nomen est Graecum. quem solem esse volunt, Dianam autem et lunam eandem esse putant, cum *sol* dictus sit vel quia *solus* ex omnibus sideribus est tantus vel quia cum est exortus obscuratis omnibus *solus* apparet, *luna a lucendo* nominata sit; eadem est enim *Lucina,* itaque ut apud Graecos Dianam eamque Luciferam sic apud nostros Iunonem Lucinam in pariendo invocant. quae eadem Diana *Omnivaga* dicitur non a venando sed quod in septem numeratur tamquam *vagantibus; Diana* dicta quia noctu quasi *diem* efficeret. adhibetur autem ad partus, quod ii maturescunt aut septem non numquam aut ut plerumque novem lunae cursibus, qui quia mensa spatia conficiunt menses nominantur. . . . quae autem dea ad res omnes *veniret Venerem* nostri nominaverunt, atque ex ea potius venustas quam Venus ex venustate.

263. *ND* 3.24.62–24.63: Iam vero quid vos illa delectat explicatio fabularum et *enodatio nominum?* exsectum a filio Caelum, vinctum itidem a filio Saturnum, haec et alia generis eiusdem ita defenditis, ut ii qui ista finxerunt non modo non insani sed etiam fuisse sapientes videantur. *in enodandis autem nominibus quod miserandum sit laboratis:* "Saturnus quia se saturat annis, Mavors quia magna vertit, Minerva quia minuit aut quia minatur, Venus quia venit ad omnia, Ceres a gerendo." quam periculosa consuetudo. in multis enim nominibus

has warned that Cicero's perhaps unfair portrait of the Stoic position has produced unwarranted assumptions about Stoic views of poetry, but the treatise does at least provide evidence for perceptions about Stoic etymologizing.[264] Cicero himself will not hesitate to make any possible pun with the name of a forensic target (cf. *de Orat.* 2.63.256–57).[265] In *Topica* 35 he speaks of forensic occasions *cum ex vi nominis* (= a word) *argumentum elicitur* and cites an argument of Scaevola's about the etymology and therefore proper meaning of the word *postliminium* (return to former privileges).[266] The numerous but unadventurous derivations in the philosophical works probably conform to a fairly standard Roman practice of citing etymologies while explaining concepts.[267] Cicero's poetry also included ety-

---

haerebitis: quid Veiovi facies quid Volcano? quamquam, quoniam Neptunum a nando appellatum putas, *nullum erit nomen quod non possis una littera explicare unde ductum sit;* in quo quidem magis tu mihi natare visus es quam ipse Neptunus. Magnam molestiam suscepit et minime necessariam primus Zeno post Cleanthes deinde Chrysippus, commenticiarum fabularum reddere rationem, vocabulorum cur quidque ita appellatum sit causas explicare. quod cum facitis illud profecto confitemini, longe aliter se rem habere atque hominum opinio sit; eos enim qui di appellantur rerum naturas esse non figuras deorum.

On "cheating" cf. also Rawson (1985) 120 n. 15. At *Tusc.* 3.18 Cicero disparages the etymologies he suggests for *nequitia,* but he does not pass up the opportunity of using them to make his point.

264. Long (1992). But cf. too the end of the dialogue (3.40.95), where Cicero says: Haec cum essent dicta, ita discessimus, ut Velleio Cottae disputatio verior, mihi Balbi ad veritatis similitudinem videretur esse propensior.

265. On Cicero's wordplay cf. Wölfflin (1887) 189–93, 203, McCartney (1918–19), Curtius (1953) 495.

266. For Q. Mucius Scaevola (cos. 95 B.C.) see *GRF* pp. 124–26. For etymologizing by Roman jurists cf., e.g., M. Antisteus Labeo (d. A.D. 22) at *GRF* pp. 557–63, esp. frags. 6 (Pomerium quasi promoerium), 7 (soror appellata est quasi seorsum nascitur), 10 (viduam dictam esse sine duitate), 13, 14, (furtum a furvo [cf. on G. 3.406–8]), 17, 19, 23, 24.

In *Acad.* 1.8.32 Cicero has Varro, in his exposition of the views of the Old Academy, say: verborum etiam explicatio probabatur, id est, qua de causa quaeque essent ita nominata, quam ἐτυμολογίαν appellabant; post argumentis quibusdam et quasi rerum notis ducibus utebantur ad probandum et ad concludendum id quod explanari volebant; in quo tradebatur omnis dialecticae disciplina, id est, orationis ratione conclusae. Cf. too Arist. *Rhet.* 1400 b 17–25, quoted above in section 1.3.

267. Cf. *Amic.* 26: *amor* enim, ex quo *amicitia* nominata est, 100: sive amor sive *amicitia;* utrumque enim dictum est ab *amando; Fin.* 2.78: quid autem est *amare, e quo nomen ductum amicitiae est,* nisi velle bonis aliquem affici quam maximis, etiamsi ad se ex iis nihil redundet?; *Tusc.* 2.43: fortitudo, cuius munera duo sunt maxima: mortis dolorisque contemptio. utendum est igitur his, si virtutis compotes vel potius si viri volumus esse, quoniam *a viris virtus nomen est mutuata; Div.* 1.1.1: divinationem, quam Graeci μαντικὴν appellant id est praesensionem et scientiam rerum futurarum. . . . itaque ut alia nos melius multa quam Graeci, sic huic praestantissimae *rei nomen nostri a divis, Graeci* ut Plato interpretatur, *a furore duxerunt; Leg.* 1.19:

mologizing; his translations of Aratus' *Phaenomena* feature glosses both explicit (*Engonasin vocitant, genibus quia nixa feratur,* frag. XII S., *ND* 2.42.108) and implicit, as when two verses explain the name Ophiuchus, "snake holder": *quem claro perhibent* ***Ophiuchum*** nomine Grai. followed by *hic pressu duplici palmarum* ***continet Anguem*** (frags. XIV, XV S, *ND* 2.42.109). Elsewhere he comments on the Greek and Roman star names Hyades/Suculae (frag. XXVIII S, *ND* 2.43.111), and in this case we have evidence of discussion of the names by Cicero's freedman Tiro; later Vergil will gloss the name Hyades in both the *Georgics* and the *Aeneid.*[268]

Without doubt the Roman who influenced Vergilian etymologizing most was Marcus Terentius Varro, whose many writings, especially the *de Lingua Latina,* published in 45 or 44 B.C., provided Augustan poets with a wealth of etymological information and speculation in convenient and accessible form.[269] Of *de Lingua Latina*'s original twenty-five books, only six, books 5–10, survive; of these books 5–7 preserve a little of Varro's theoretical approach to etymologizing (there was more in books 2–3), and a great number of examples of derivations. Varro generally follows the Stoic line, like his teacher Aelius Stilo, but he seems pragmatic and eclectic,[270] citing also Aristophanes of Byzantium, Cleanthes, Chrysippus, Antipater of Tarsus,

---

eamque rem (sc. νόμον) illi Graeco putant nomine ⟨*a*⟩ *suum cuique tribuendo* appellatam, ego nostro a *legendo,* 2.11: *in ipso nomine legis* interpretando inesse vim et sententiam iusti et iuris *legendi; Rep.* 6.1: *prudentiam* . . . quae ipsum nomen hoc nacta est ex *providendo; Div.* 1.49.111: quos *prudentes* possumus dicere, id est, *providentes, Hort.* fr. 5.33 Müller (ap. Non. p. 41 M): *prudentiam* a *providendo* dictam dilucide ostendit M. Tullius in Hortensio (see on A. 3.433).

Note that Sallust *Iug.* 78 gives the etymology of *Syrtes: ab tractu nominatae* (cf. σύρειν, to sweep); see below on A. 1.108–10.

268. See on G. 1.137–38. For Engonasin cf. Arat. *Phaen.* 65–67 ἀλλά μιν αὔτως / Ἐνγόνασιν καλέουσι. τὸ δ' αὖτ' ἐν γούνασι κάμνον / ὀκλάζοντι ἔοικεν. Ophiuchus is perhaps glossed less precisely at *Phaen.* 82 Ὄφιος πεπονείαται.

For etymologizing in Cicero's poetry cf. also *levipes lepus* at *Arat.* 121, which echoes an etymology Varro *RR* 3.12.6 attributes to Stilo fr. 12, *GRF* p. 61, and *gelidos rores aurora remittit* at *Progn.* 4.7, which may suggest an etymological connection between the words for "dew" and "dawn" (see Soubiran [1972] ad loc., and also Weber [n.d.] on Catulus' Roscius epigram).

269. Collart (1954) esp. chap. 4, "L'étymologie," Dahlmann (1964) 1–51, Pfaffel (1981) (detailed analysis of Varro's etymological method, divided into types of derivation), Bartelink (1965) 19–25, Taylor (1974), Cairns (1979) 90–99, Ahl (1985) 22–31, 54–60 et passim, Rawson (1985) 125–29, Porte (1985) 199–202, Amsler (1989) 24–31, Horsfall (1991) index s.v. Varrone, and *EV* s.v. Varrone, L'Opera Varroniana e l'Eneide (Horsfall), Maltby (1993).

270. Dahlmann (1964) 11: "Er etymologisiert nicht als Philosoph, nicht als Stoiker, sondern als Grammatiker." On Varro's eclecticism cf. Collart (1954) 269–72, 278, 300–302, Taylor (1974) 68–70.

Democritus and Epicurus, Apollodorus of Athens, and the Roman Q. Cosconius. Varro distinguishes four levels of etymologizing: one accessible to the ordinary person, one to the grammarian, one to the philosopher, and the fourth, where the text is corrupt and the thought almost mystical, that of the *adytum et initia . . . regis,* which he hoped to reach.[271] Varro believes that a number of "primary words" were originally imposed on things by some number of name givers, and that these words produced all others through a process of change he called *declinatio*.[272] I mentioned earlier that at *LL* 6.39 Varro draws an analogy between the Epicurean notion that all things are made up of atoms *(principia),* and his own notion that a great number of words are derived from comparatively few *(mille)* roots *(principia verborum).* Difficulties in recognizing original roots are caused by changes in the appearance of words over the course of time; words are changed "by the subtraction or addition of letters, by the transposition or change of letters, or by lengthening syllables ⟨shortening them, or removing or adding syllables⟩ (most editors supplement the text to include the words in brackets).[273]

271. *LL* 5.7–9 nunc singulorum verborum origines expediam, quorum quattuor explanandi gradus. infimus [in] quo populus etiam venit. . . . secundus quo grammatica descendit antiqua. . . . tertius gradus, quo philosophia ascendens pervenit. . . . quartus, ubi est adytum et initia | regis: quo si non perveniam " " " scientiam, at opinionem aucupabor, quod etiam in salute nostra nonnunquam facit cum ⟨a⟩egrotamus medicus. quodsi summum gradum non attigero, tamen secundum praeteribo, quod non solum ad Aristophanis lucernam, sed etiam ad Cleant⟨h⟩is lucubravi. volui praeterire eos, qui poetarum modo verba ut sint ficta expediunt. See Collart (1954) 272–75, Rawson (1985) 126, Pfaffel (1981).

272. Cf. 5.13 genera prima . . . verborum, 6.36 verborum . . . primigenia, 6.39 principia, 8.7 illi qui primi nomina imposuerunt rebus, 8.27 cum utilitatis causa verba ideo sint imposita rebus ut ea⟨s⟩ significent. See Dahlmann (1964) 12–13, Pfaffel (1981) 7–10, Taylor (1974). Varro's term *declinatio* includes both inflection and etymological derivation.

273. Three passages are most informative; the words translated in the text are at the end of the second:

5.3 neque omnis impositio verborum exstat, quod vetustas quasdam delevit, nec quae extat sine mendo omnis imposita, nec quae recte est imposita, cuncta manet (multa enim verba li⟨t⟩teris commutatis sunt interpolata).

5.5–6 vetustas pauca non depravat, multa tollit. quem puerum vidisti formosum, hunc vides deformem in senecta. . . . non mediocris enim tenebrae in silva ubi haec captanda neque eo quo pervenire volumus semitae tritae, neque non in tramitibus quaedam obiecta quae euntem retinere possent: quorum verborum novorum ac veterum discordia omnis. in consuetudine com⟨m⟩uni quot modis litterarum commutatio sit facta qui animadverterit, facilius scrutari origines patietur verborum: reperiet enim esse commutata, ut in superioribus libris ostendi, maxime propter bis quaternas causas. litterarum enim fit demptione aut additione et propter earum tra⟨ie⟩c[ta]tionem aut commutationem, item syllabarum productione ⟨aut correptione, denique adiectione aut detrectione⟩.

6.1 huius rei auctor satis mihi Chrysippus et Antipater et illi in quibus, si non tantum

Varro's discussion of the mechanics by which the appearance of words changes appeared in the lost early books; in extant books he notes that archaic *C* may become *G* (5.64), that *S* may become *R* (7.26), that *L* and *S* often change places (5.138), and that *I* and *E,* as well as C and *G,* "have much in common" (6.95). And of course his myriad examples allow his practice to be observed; in particular we may note the fluidity with which he suggests that words with different vowel sounds are related etymologically.[274] Amsler aptly summarizes Varro's idea of the etymologist's task:

> From the etymological point of view, the ultimate external referent of a word is immanent, located within the word, behind/beneath its material surface. The etymologist must reverse the dynamic of *declinatio* and perform an archaeology in order to recover the immanent meaning.[275]

Varro will be cited often in the catalogue below; it should be noted that the text of Varro is often very uncertain.

One more scholar at Rome must be mentioned: the learned freedman Verrius Flaccus, some of whose *De Significatu Verborum* has been preserved in Paulus' eighth-century epitome of Festus' second-century epitome of Verrius. Although Verrius' work may slightly postdate Vergil, Paulus-Festus is an important source of Augustan notions about etymology.[276]

---

acuminis, at plus litterarum, in quo est Aristophanes et Apollodorus, qui omnes verba ex verbis ita declinari scribunt, ut verba litteras alia assumant, alia mittant, alia commutent, ut fit in turdo [in] turdario et turdelice. sic declinantes Graeci nostra nomina dicunt L[e]uci[en]um Λεύκι[εν]ον et Quin[c]tium Κοίντιον, et ⟨nostri illorum⟩ 'Αρίσταρχον Aristarchum et Δίωνα Dionem; sic, inquam, consuetudo nostra multa declinavit [ut] a vetere ut ab † solu solum, ab loebeso liberum, ab lasibus lares: quae obruta vetustate ut potero eruere conabor.

274. Cf. Collart (1954) 290–93, Rawson (1985) 128–29, Ahl (1985) 54–60; Rawson 120 n. 15 cites Cicero's complaints at *ND* 3.62 and *Tusc.* 3.18; see above in this section, and on quantity also section 2.1.

275. Amsler (1989) 29.

276. For actual fragments of Verrius see *GRF* pp. 509–23. Since "Paulus-Festus" can be confusing, I explain here my method of citing them: Lindsay's edition prints Paulus' epitome where only that is available, but where the large fragments of Festus, such as those in the lacunose Codex Farnesianus, are extant, he prints Festus on the left-hand page and Paulus on the right. My references to Festus or Paulus-Festus are to page number and line number in Lindsay's edition. References in Maltby are to the Mueller page, which Lindsay also prints; my use of the Lindsay pagination allows me to give line numbers as well.

## 1.6. Poets at Rome

Roman poetic precedent was also important for Vergilian etymologizing, and that I aim for concise treatment here is not to be taken as devaluation of Roman as opposed to Alexandrian influence.[277] In the interest of brevity this section will discuss only poets writing before Vergil began to write, providing bibliographical references only for Horace, Tibullus, Propertius, and Ovid.

Poetic etymologizing is evident in the earliest Roman poets. When Livius Andronicus in his translation of the *Odyssey* translates Musa as *Moneta,* Feeney sees etymological motivation and an allusion to the derivation of *Moneta* from *moneo* in the line *nam diva Monetas filia* ***docuit*** (fr. 21 B; for discussion see on A. 1.8).[278] Varro cites the explanations in Naevius' *Bellum Punicum* of the names Aventinus (*ab avibus;* see on A. 8.231–35) and Palatine (Balatinus, from the bleating *[balo]* of sheep; see on A. 8.53–54); Servius cites Naevius' connection of the name Prochyta to a kinswoman of Aeneas (see on A. 9.715–16). Vergil will gloss Aventinus in this way, and the Palatine (or Pallanteum) differently.

Ennius, who described himself as the first poet of Rome to be *dicti studiosus* (*Ann.* 208–9 Sk.), seems to have made extensive use of etymologizing; a few examples relevant to the study of Vergil will give some idea of his wordplay.[279] Ennius seems to have glossed the name Ceres: *quod gerit fruges* (*Var.* 49–50 V), as Vergil will in the *Georgics* (see on G. 1.7–8). At *Ann.* 48 Sk., *caeli caerula templa* may allude to a derivation of *caeruleus* from *caelum* (see on A. 3.192–94). Servius derives *sermo* from *sero* and sees allusion to the etymology in Vergil; Norden thinks the connection is of Ennian origin (see on A. 6.160). Three examples of etymological wordplay in A. 6.842–46 probably come from Ennius: wordplay between the name Scipio and the word *fulmen,* and between the name Serranus and the verb *sero,* and the obvious gloss of Quintus Fabius' cognomen Cunctator. At A. 7.517 *sulpurea Nar albus aqua,* Vergil has borrowed the gloss on *Nar* (= Sabine for sulfur) from Ennius *Ann.* 222 Sk.: *sulpureas posuit spiramina Naris ad undas.* Enn. *Var.* 57–58 V *(Epicharmus)* derives the name Jupiter from *iuvo,* as Vergil may (cf. on A. 9.128–29 and Feeney [1991] 120). Varro *LL* 5.55 cites Ennius (= *Ann.* fr. lix Sk.) for the sources of the names of the three Roman tribes:

277. Cf. Snyder (1980) esp. chap. 3, "Verbal Play in Theory and Practice before Lucretius," and chap. 4, "Lucretian Puns: Types and Functions," and also Woodhead (1928) 81–89, Bartelink (1965) 14–19, Ahl (1985), and the notes in this section.

278. Feeney (1991) 121. On Naevius cf. *GRF* pp. 6–7, Collart (1954) 255 n. 1.

279. Collart (1954) 255 n. 2, Snyder (1980) 69–72, Feeney (1991) 120–21, Thomas (1982a) 149ff., Skutsch (1985) 841 s.v. puns.

*Tribus . . . nominatae, ut ait Ennius, Titienses ab Tatio, Ramnenses ab Romulo, Luceres, ut Iunius* (*GRF* p. 121), *ab Lucumone* (see on A. 9.324–30, where Vergil links a Rhamnes with a Remus in a way that alludes to Romulus). Varro *LL* 7.82 criticizes etymologizing by Ennius that he finds too subtle, and less easily understandable than, in one case, Euripides:

> apud Ennium (*SRP* fr. 65 R = fr. 99 J) "Andromachae nomen qui indidit, recte indidit." item (fr. 38 R, 64 J) "quapropter Parim pastores nunc Alexandrum vocant." Imitari dum voluit Euripiden et ponere ἔτυμον, est lapsus; nam Euripides quod Graeca posuit, ἔτυμα sunt aperta. ille ait ideo nomen additum Andromachae, quod ἀνδρὶ μάχεται: hoc Ennii quis potest intellegere in versu[m] significare "Andromachae nomen qui indidit recte indidit," aut Alexandrum ab eo appellatum in Graecia qui Paris fuisset, a quo Herculem quoque cognominatum Alexicacon, ab eo quod defensor esset hominum? (See on A. 3.297)

In another tragedy, *Medea,* Ennius' introductory verses include a gloss on the name of the ship Argo: *Argo, quia Argivi in ea delecti viri;* Thomas has explained the history of the dispute over whether the ship was named for its builder Argos, as in the implicit etymology in Apollonius of Rhodes, for its swiftness (cf. Homeric ἀργός, swift), as in Diodorus Siculus and implicitly in Catullus 64, or for the Argives, as here; this etymology seems to be Ennius' own contribution.[280]

When Servius in the preface to his commentary on the *Eclogues* stops to observe that many characters in those poems have significant names, he cites the example of names in Terence's *Andria* and *Hecyra: sicut etiam in comoediis invenimus; nam Pamphilus est totum amans, Glycerium quasi dulcius mulier, Philumena amabilis.*[281] Roman comedy indeed provides ample evidence for interest in wordplay, soundplay, and to some extent etymologizing.[282] Plautus especially provides numerous examples of simple *figura etymologica: machinabor machinam* (*Bacch.* 232), *opsonabo opsonium* (*Stich.* 440), *familiaris . . . familiariter* (*Amph.* 355), *suavi suavitate* (*Pseud.* 882), *Venerem venerabor* (*Poen.* 278), *an Salutem te salutem?* (*Pseud.* 709).

280. Enn. *SRP* fr. 208–10 R, = 211–13 J = Enn. fr. 4, *GRF* p. 8; cf. Apoll. Rhod. 1.19–20, Diod. Sic. 4.41.3 (ὡς ἂν τῶν ἀρχαίων ἀργὸν τὸ ταχὺ προσαγορευόντων), Catullus 64.1–7 (below), Thomas (1982a) 149, Gaisser (1993) 363 n. 69.

281. Serv. *Praef.* E. (quoted in catalogue at start of *Eclogues*).

282. Duckworth (1952) 340–56, from whom the following examples are drawn, and who cites earlier scholarship. Cf. also Wright (1974) index s.vv. figura etymologica, paronomasia, and Maltby (1993a).

As Servius notes, Plautus has many "significant names" or names coined for humorous effect; he also makes a number of puns on names, both with an etymological basis—*Harpax* as plunderer (*Pseud.* 653ff., 1010), Lucris-*lucrum* (*Pers.* 626f., 668, 712f.), *opus est chryso Chrysalo* (*Bacch.* 240)—and without—Sosia-*socius* (*Amph.* 384). In some cases we see the same potentially deceptive pattern as in the earliest Greek poetry, where Homeric assonance becomes later etymologizing; so too wordplay in Roman comedy for the sake of alliteration, assonance, or other euphonic effects looks like later etymologizing, but may not be. In a number of passages Plautus or Terence associate the words *cor, cura,* and *uro:* Plaut. *Truc.* 454–55: quanta est *cura* in animo, quantum *corde* capio / dolorem, *Truc.* 773: una *cura cor* meum mouit; *Men.* 761: haec res mihi in pectore et *corde curaest; Pers.* 801: DO. *uritur cor* mi / TO. da illi cantharum, exstingue ignem, si / *cor uritur;* Ter. *Hec.* 347 *cura* ex *corde* excessit. These may look like allusions to an etymology such as Varro's *cura quod cor urit,* but Plautus and Terence may have been unaware of any such connection, and motivated simply by euphony.[283]

There has been no full study of etymologizing in Catullus, but several examples of learned etymological wordplay have been noted, most in recent years. A century ago Ellis suggested that *altas Alpes* in Catullus 11.9 and *reguli gaza* in 64.46 are glosses explaining non-Latin words, since *Alpes* is a Gallic word for high mountain, and *gaza* a Persian word for "royal treasure"; Vergil seems to gloss the word *Alpes* in the same way.[284] In the phrase *Uriosque apertos* at Catullus 36.12, the epithet *apertos* is a learned gloss on the place-name Urios, possibly coined for the sake of the pun, which transliterates into Greek as οὔριος, "windy, open to the wind."[285] In Catullus 7, "the combination of the word *harena* (line 3) and the reference to the oracle of Jupiter Ammon (line 5) hints at the learned etymology Ἄμμων - ἄμμος" (sand).[286] In another poem, "it seems very likely that Catullus is hinting through the use of *menstruo/metiens* (34.17–18) at a set of etymological links between *mensis* and *messis, metior* and *meto.*"[287] In 64.1–18, Catullus plays on the connection of the name of the ship Argo with the word ἀργός,

283. See on A. 1.208–9; cf. Maltby (1993a).

284. *Alpes:* G. 3.474, Ellis (1878) 42, 292; gaza: Serv. on A. 1.119 GAZA Persicus sermo est et significat divitias, Curt. 3.13.5 pecumiam regiam gazam Persae vocant (more in Maltby s.v.).

285. Ross (1973).

286. Cairns (1973) 18, who cites Servius on A. 4.196 and Shackleton Bailey (1956) 223 on Prop. 4.1.103; cf. Cerda (1612) 416, and also now Maltby s.v. Hammon, who cites Pliny *NH* 12.107 and Paul.-Fest. p. 91, 3 L.

287. Zetzel (1988) 81.

"swift," in a way that demonstrates his awareness of earlier etymologies, such as that by Ennius noted above.[288] In 64.72, when Catullus refers to Venus as *spinosas Erycina serens in pectore curas,* he glosses the name Erycina, as if to associate it with the word *ericius* (spiked instrument of war or [spiked] hedgehog); Venus is emphatically described as a producer of "thorny cares."[289] In 64.353–54, *aristas / sole sub ardenti,* and in 48.5–6 *aridis aristis,* Catullus plays upon the etymology *arista ab ariditate,* in a way probably noticed and imitated by both Vergil and Ovid.[290]

Lucretius' etymologizing has been amply discussed by Friedländer and then in more detail in Snyder's monograph.[291] I have mentioned Varro's analogy between the Epicurean notion of atoms *(principia),* and his own idea of roots of words *(principia verborum);* Lucretius several times cites the way that letters are rearranged to form different words in an attempt to explain how atoms form different combinations (1.196–98, 814–29, 907–14, 2.688–99, 1013–21). In 1.907–14 he notes the shared letters in the words *ignis* and *lignum* but, as Dalzell has argued, is probably not suggesting an etymological link between them. But he does engage in extensive etymological wordplay, which for a poet need not involve literal belief that one word derived from another. In 1.167–71 Lucretius explains that the Earth is a kind of mother not in any personified mythological way, but because it contains the matter *(materies)* from which all living things are fed; he reinforces his argument with wordplay between the words *mater terra* and *materies.*[292] Several instances of Lucretian etymological wordplay reappear in Vergil (it may be freely admitted that this introduction has a bias toward both finding and citing such wordplay). In 5.1230, *ventorum . . . paces animasque se-*

---

288. Thomas (1982a); see also now Maltby s.v.

289. O'Hara (1990a); see below, and on A. 1.719–22, for acknowledgment of Catullus' gloss by Vergil. On Catullus cf. also Keith (1992) 88 n. 55 and Barchiesi (1993) 364.

290. Ross (1987) 35; see on A. 7.720.

291. Friedländer (1941), Snyder (1980); cf. too Brown (1984) xxxv–xxxix, Farrell (1988), and the protests of Dalzell (1987), who argues that Lucretian wordplay does not imply etymological connection—but at some level this may be true of much poetic etymological wordplay.

292. 1.167–71:

quippe ubi non essent genitalia corpora cuique,
qui posset *mater* rebus consistere certa?
at nunc seminibus quia certis quaeque creantur,
inde enascitur atque oras in luminis exit,
*materies* ubi inest cuiusque et corpora prima.

Cf. Friedländer (1941), Snyder (1980) 93, and Brown (1984) ad loc.; they also cite Lucr. 2.991–1003, 5.795–96 and 821–22.

*cundas*, Lucretius probably plays on *animas* and ἄνεμος (wind), as Vergil will (see on A. 1.56–57). In 4.1059–60, Lucretius ends consecutive lines with *cor* and *cura*, probably alluding to the etymological connection *cura quod cor urit* (see on A. 1.208–9).[293] The passage at 6.740–44 presents at least one and probably two examples of etymologizing found also in Vergil. Lucretius explicitly glosses the name Avernus (see on A. 6.237–42) and also uses the words *volantes* and *vela* in a way that may indicate awareness of the derivation of the latter from the former for which our earliest explicit evidence is Isidore—although it may be that Isidore's etymology is simply derived from Lucretius and Vergil (see on A. 3.520).[294] In 1.277–97, the comparison of the movement and force of the winds with that of rivers is supported by the use of the terms *fluunt* (280), *flumine* (282), *fluctibus* (289), *flamina* (290), and *flumen* (291) (see on A. 4.438–43). Lucretius also plays on the meanings of the names Priscus and Superbus (the last Tarquins),[295] Scipio,[296] Curetes,[297] and Phoebus, and in ways similar to what Vergil will do later.[298]

Of late Republican poets no longer extant, three may be mentioned whose etymologizing may have been a precedent for Vergil.[299] Gallus may have glossed the name Atalanta or Atlas, since in a poem highly indebted to Gallus, Propertius uses the antonomasia *durae . . . Iasidos* to refer to Atalanta (1.1.10); *durae* glosses her name, as though from τλῆναι, "endure," and a similar gloss occurs at A. 4.247, *Atlantis duri*. Ross suggests a common source in Gallus (see on A. 4.247). Varro of Atax, author of a version of the *Argonautica*, is known to have derived the name Media from that of Medea, although it is not clear whether he did so in this poem or in a prose work (see

---

293. 4.1059–60 hinc illaec primum Veneris dulcedinis in *cor* / stillavit gutta et successit frigida *cura*.

294. 6.740–44.

Principio, quod *Averna* vocantur nomine, id ab re
impositumst, quia sunt *avibus* contraria cunctis,
e regione ea quod loca cum venere *volantes*,
remigii oblitae pennarum *vela* remittunt.

295. 5.1136–37 ergo regibus occisis subversa iacebat / *pristina* maiestas soliorum et sceptra *superba* (cf. on A. 6.817–18).

296. 3.1034 Scipiadas, belli fulmen, Carthaginis horror (see on A. 6.842–46).

297. 2.629–39 (see on G. 4.149–52).

298. 6.1197 candenti lumine solis (= *Phoebi*, glossed by *candenti*) (see on A. 8.720). On Lucretius cf. too on G. 1.326–27 *(fretum* and *fervere)* and on G. 2.328 *(avius* and *aves)*.

299. For etymologizing in the verse of Parthenius and Cicero see above in section 1.5. On Gallus see also Cairns (1984) on *miles* < *mollis* in elegy, Vergil, and Horace; this study came to my attention too late for me to make full use of it, especially on Vergil.

on G. 2.126–41).[300] In *Arg.* frag. 7 Courtney, *te nunc Coryciae tendentem spicula nymphae / hortantes "o Phoebe" et "ieie" conclamarunt,* Varro reproduces an etymological gloss in his Apollonian model (and in Callimachus): *tendentem spicula* explains *ieie,* as if from ἵημι, "shoot."[301] Varro may also have revived the learned Alexandrian debate about whether islands called Sickle (Drepane and Zancle) were named for Demeter's reaping hook or the tool used by Zeus to castrate Cronos.[302] Valerius Cato, author of a *Dictynna,* may well have provided a precedent for the glossing of *dictamnum* in the *Aeneid* and the pseudo-Vergilian *Ciris* (see on A. 12.411–19) and the connection of Dicte with the "nets" (δίκτυα) of fishermen found in Callimachus and probably in Vergil (see on E. 6.55–60, especially the references to Connors). These traces of evidence are clues that lost verse of the late Republican and early Augustan period may have involved a good deal of etymological wordplay.

Considerations of length do not permit discussion of Vergil's contemporaries, but recent work has shown extensive interest in etymologizing on the part of Horace,[303] Propertius (whose fourth book proclaims its Alexandrian aetiological goals at 4.1.69, *sacra diesque canam et cognomina prisca locorum),*[304] Tibullus,[305] Sulpicia,[306] and then later Ovid,[307] whose poetic "commentary" on Vergil will be featured below in section 2.14.

300. Some say the etymology may have been in a work *Chorographia;* cf. *GRF* p. 439, Courtney (1993) 253.

301. O'Hara (1994) 390; see in section 1.4 for 2.701–713, Callim. *Hymn* 2.97–104, and references to secondary literature on them.

302. See in section 1.4 for Callim. *Aet.* 1, fr. 14, *Aet.* fr. 43.69–71, Apoll. Rhod. 4.982–92, and Nic. fr. 21, and for Varro Thomas (1988) on G. 2.405–7.

303. On Horace cf. Horsfall (1973) on *Epode* 15.12, André (1975) 194 n. 6 on *Serm.* 2.3.142, Reckford (1966) on C. 1.34, Nisbet and Hubbard (1970) 257, 268, 371, Macleod (1979) on *Epode* 16.2 (on which see also Maltby [1993a] 269), Putnam (1986) 44–46, 90–91, 121, 165–66, 191, 240, 265 on C. IV, (1993) on C. 1.24 and (1994) on C. 1.17, Gini (1989) on the *Epistles;* Ahern (1991) on C. 1.6.13, Davis (1991) index s.v. names, symbolic, Hendry (1992) on C. 1.37, and Paschalis (1995) on several poems.

304. On Prop. cf. Courtney (1969) 80–81 on Acanthis and *spinae* in 4.5, Ross (1975) 61–65 on 1.1.10 *durae . . . Iasidos,* King (1980) 212–14 on 1.13, Koster (1983) 47–54 on several poems, Zetzel (1983) 92 on 2.1.8, Boyd (1984) on *Tarpeia-turpis* in 4.4, Bramble (1974) on 1.20, Shackleton Bailey (1956) 223, 260 on 4.1.103 and 9.38, and Cairns (1984) on *miles* < *mollis* in several poems.

305. On Tibullus cf. Cairns (1979) 87–110 and (1984), Maltby (1993a).

306. On Sulpicia see Roessel (1990).

307. On the extensive etymologizing in Ovid cf. Skutsch (1968), the neglected Lascu (1961), André (1975), Porte (1985) 197–264, Ahl (1985), McKeown (1987) 32–37, 45–62, Hinds (1985) and (1987), Kenney (1986) and (1989), Keith (1991) and (1992) index s.v. etymological wordplay, Barchiesi (1991), Myers (1992), (1994) and (1994a), and Maltby (1993a). A forthcoming study by G. Tissol should also be useful.

## 2. Typical Features of Vergilian Etymological Wordplay

Near the beginning of this introduction I argued for the importance of being able to distinguish actual examples of etymological wordplay from specious examples found by the overly diligent searches of investigators like me. A key factor in developing the competence as readers to make such distinctions must be familiarity with the characteristic features of ancient or Vergilian etymologizing.[308] One goal of the previous section's survey of earlier etymologizing has been to improve a reader's ability to recognize Alexandrian or simply ancient wordplay. This section will address Vergilian practice more directly, with a survey of the typical features of his wordplay.

Ahl and Cairns have provided useful surveys of the rules in Varro and other authors, some of which we have seen above, which describe what types of words can be connected etymologically, and both of these scholars recommend creative extrapolation from and extension of these rules. This study will employ a somewhat more cautious approach, exploring no less widely I hope, but with perhaps more self-criticism; it should be no surprise that I have more leisure for self-criticism than those groundbreaking works that saw themselves as introducing and arguing for the importance of a neglected feature of ancient literature. I now take the importance of etymological wordplay to be self-evident to most scholars of Latin literature. Rather than taking the rules and employing them in as creative a way as possible, my study will endorse mainly plays on etymological connections mentioned in antiquity or late antiquity, or at least those to which other poets seem to allude (although I do catalogue a great number of examples of which I am skeptical, for which I usually offer my grounds for doubt). Our theoretical discussions of etymologizing from antiquity are far less extensive than our examples, and it seemed best to extrapolate from the examples rather than the brief discussions in Varro and others, although I have taken them into account. Just as a rudimentary knowledge of the rules of any language, combined with earnest creativity, can produce nonidiomatic speech, it is easy for modern students of ancient etymologizing to use the poorly attested rules to claim to find etymological wordplay that would never have struck even the subconscious mind of any ancient reader. This study thus adopts an open-minded but cautious approach, which should prove most useful both for those who would wish to share my approach and for those who think a more creative approach is necessary.

Both the introduction and especially the catalogue, which is a kind of running commentary on all of Vergil's works, are a continuing discussion of

308. On "literary competence" see n. 9.

what is and is not characteristic of Vergilian (and perhaps Latin) etymologizing, a discussion of when etymologizing is or is not taking place. As noted above, I have been most confident about suggesting that Vergil is etymologizing when the words thus linked have been connected by another source. Here we face a slight difficulty. Many of the sources for explicit ancient etymologies postdate Vergil, so we face two types of problem. The first is that the derivation may simply have occurred only to persons living later than Vergil; in this sense evidence from the fourth century (such as Servius' commentary on Vergil) or even the seventh (such as Isidore of Seville's *Etymologiae,* also called *Origines*) is not much better than speculation from the twentieth. But the situation is in fact not so dire: much later etymologizing does seem conservatively to preserve information and principles from such early sources as Varro and Verrius Flaccus, or even from earlier Greek scholia.[309] The second problem involves a phenomenon similar to that observed above, where what may be no more than assonance in Homer ("I terribly fear Aeneas," δείδια δ' αἰνῶς Αἰνείαν) becomes etymology in a later text ("Aeneas, because *terrible* grief held me"). So too words juxtaposed by Vergil simply for assonance or other reasons may have seemed to later authors—in particular Servius, Isidore, or their sources—to have been connected etymologically simply because they are juxtaposed by Vergil, who was thought by some in late antiquity to have mastered all human knowledge. Thus their evidence is not independent of Vergil, and their conjectures are superior to our own only in that Latin was still a living language for them. This is not a major problem, although I have tried to take note of it in the catalogue (see on A. 1.164–65) and provide dates for ancient sources in my list of abbreviations.

It must be stressed that in judging the ancient evidence, the question of whether or not an etymology is true according to modern linguistics is completely irrelevant. At times whether the derivation is even literally true according to what the ancients knew will also be irrelevant. Often Vergil or a similar poet will indeed be suggesting that a word is derived from another, but their goals are not those of the scholar of language.[310] An etymology is a story, the story of the origin and development of a word, and poets play with details of the story in a way that may be compared with the way they play with myths. What scholars have learned about the distinction between an-

309. For Greek sources cf. Mühmelt (1965) passim, esp. 48–72, and also Fraenkel (1948); cf. also n. 2 on the Cairns/Maltby project.

310. On this see esp. Porte (1985) 202, 236–43 on Ovid.

cient and modern attitudes toward history, historiography, and myth[311] must be kept in mind by the student of poetic etymologizing. Failure to appreciate this distinction mars many studies from the last century or from the early part of this century[312] and still occurs as a kind of instinctive error even today. In Vergil, I see a willingness to use any etymology that suits his purposes; the question of whether the word *cura* is "really" derived from *cor urit* is only as important as the question of whether it was Dido or Anna that Aeneas "really" loved.

A list of the features of Vergilian etymologizing to be discussed in this section follows below. My categories are not all observably ancient, for I have found ancient categorizations insufficiently helpful. The categories are also of different types, some focusing on stylistic features, some on type of name etymologized, but the nature and variety of Vergilian etymologizing demands flexible organizational principles; the goal is to present a picture of the range of Vergilian etymological wordplay, not to separate examples into rigid categories. I have developed these categories largely from my reading of Vergil and Vergilian scholarship, but they should be useful for the study of wordplay in other poets as well (e.g., Apollonius, Lucretius, Ovid, Silver Latin epic). My categories are these:

1. Paronomasia: the poet links words of similar sounds.
   1a. Translation with paronomasia: the poet plays upon or creatively reproduces the sound of words in a Greek model.
2. The single-adjective gloss: the poet uses "modifiers that reflect the etymology of the word modified."
   2a. The reverse gloss: a noun expresses the etymology of an adjective modifying it.
3. Etymologizing κατ' ἀντίφρασιν: the poet glosses a word by reference to its opposite.
4. Etymologizing of proper names:
   4a. Names of gods;
   4b. Names of places;
   4c. Names of mortals.
5. The explicit gloss or derivation: the poet openly explains the origin of a word or name.

311. See conveniently Feeney (1991) 250–62, who discusses and provides references to important recent work by Veyne, Wiseman, and Woodman.

312. The survey of etymologies in Mustard (1892), for example, is greatly concerned to distinguish correct from incorrect etymologies in Vergil. So soon after the birth of modern linguistics, this is understandable, but still regrettable.

6. Naming constructions as etymological signposts: the poet uses an unnecessary naming construction to draw attention to a name, and so to its etymology.
7. Suppression: the poet omits but alludes to one of the words involved in the etymological wordplay.
8. Framing: the poet frames a line with the words to be connected etymologically.
   8a. Passage frame.
9. Vertical juxtaposition in consecutive lines: the words to be connected etymologically are at the start or end of successive lines.
10. Changes of names/alternate names.
    10a. Changes marked by the word *nunc.*
11. Etymologizing with languages other than Latin and Greek.
12. Clustering: the poet gives or alludes to the etymologies of several words, usually proper names, within a short passage.
13. Playing with the tradition, or allusion to earlier etymologizing.
14. Later comment: poets after Vergil (especially Ovid) allude to his etymologizing.

## 2.1 Paronomasia

Paronomasia, or to the Romans *adnominatio,* is wordplay by means of the collocation of words of similar sounds. Paronomasia has been amply discussed by many ancient and modern sources;[313] the treatments by the author of the *Rhetorica ad Herennium*[314] and by Quintilian[315] are full and

313. Harrison (1991) on A. 10.192 and 418, Austin (1977) on 6.43, Fordyce (1977) on 7.491, Cerda (1612) esp. 305–6, Norden (1981) on 6.204ff., Gransden (1976) on 8.441, and Maltby (1993a); more generally see Macleod (1982) 50–53, Woodhead (1928) 36–43, Wölfflin (1887), Snyder (1980) 67–73, 90–108 and passim, McCartney (1918–19).

314. *Rhet. Her.* 4.21.29–30 Adnominatio est cum ad idem verbum et nomen acceditur commutatione vocum aut litterarum, ut ad res dissimiles similia verba adcommodentur. ea multis et variis rationibus conficitur. adtenuatione aut conplexione eiusdem litterae, sic "hic qui se magnifice iactat atque ostentat, *venit* ante quam Romam *venit.*" et ex contrario: "hic quos homines alea *vincit,* eos ferro statim *vincit.*" productione eiusdem litterae, hoc modo: "hinc *avium* dulcedo ducit ad *avium.*" brevitate eiusdem litterae: "hic, tametsi videtur esse honoris cupidus, tantum tamen *curiam* diligit, quantum *Curiam?*" addendis litteris, hoc pacto: "hic sibi posset *temperare,* nisi amore⟨i⟩ mallet *obtemperare.*" demendis nunc litteris, sic: "si *lenones* vitasset tamquam *leones,* vitae tradidisset se." transferendis litteris, sic: "videte, iudices, utrum homini *navo* an *vano* credere malitis." commutandis hoc modo: "*deligere* oportet, quem velis *diligere.*" hae sunt adnominationes quae in litterarum brevi commutatione aut productione aut transiectione aut aliquo huiusmodi genere versantur. sunt autem aliae quae non habent tam propinquam in verbis similitudinem et tamen dissimiles non sunt.

315. *Inst.* 9.3.66–72 Tertium est genus figurarum quod aut similitudine aliqua vocum aut

useful, although it must be kept in mind that Quintilian's hostility to wordplay is more appropriate for the kinds of orators he hopes to produce than for poets. At A. 2.606–7, Vergil juxtaposes the noun *parens* and the verb *pareo* in a way that may suggest an etymology showing that it is natural to obey one's parent, but this example is more likely to be simple *paronomasia.* Other examples in Vergil involve the words *avius* and *avis; pareo* and *paro; cano* and *caneo; libro* and *liber, libri;* and *gemitus* and *geminant.*[316]

Since several of these examples of wordplay involve words with different vowel quantities, it will be useful here to discuss how vowel length affects wordplay and etymologizing. In my view, both the traditional assumption that differences in vowel quantity prevent wordplay and etymologizing the more recent claim that they are completely irrelevant to etymologizing are wrong. The Greeks and Romans clearly played on words with similar if not identical sounds and clearly thought that words with different vowel quan-

---

paribus aut contrariis convertit in se aures et animos excitat. hinc est παρονομασία, quae dicitur adnominatio. ea non uno modo fieri solet: ex vicinia quadam praedicti nominis ducta, casibus declinatis, ut Domitius Afer pro Cloatilla: "mulier omnium rerum imperita, in omnibus rebus infelix," et cum verbo idem verbum plus significans subiungitur: "quando homo hostis, homo." . . . aliter quoque voces aut eaedem [aut] diversa in significatione ponuntur aut productione tantum vel correptione mutatae: quod etiam in iocis frigidum equidem tradi inter praecepta miror, eorumque exempla vitandi potius quam imitandi gratia pono: "amari iucundum est, si curetur ne quid insit amari," "avium dulcedo ⟨ad⟩ avium ducit," et apud Ovidium ludentem: "cur ego non dicam, Furia, te furiam?" Cornificius hanc traductionem vocat, videlicet alterius intellectus ad alterum. sed elegantius quod est positum in distinguenda rei proprietate: "hanc rei publicae pestem paulisper reprimi, non in perpetuum comprimi posse"; et quae praepositionibus in contrarium mutantur: "non emissus ex urbe, sed inmissus in urbem esse videatur." melius atque acrius quod cum figura iucundum est, tum etiam sensu valet: "emit morte inmortalitatem." illa leviora: "non Pisonum sed pistorum" et "ex oratore arator." pessimum vero: "ne patres conscripti videantur circumscripti."

316. **Features list no. 1: Paronomasia**

(This is necessarily an incomplete list, and some of these may involve etymologizing as well. Some syllables have long vowels marked to show wordplay despite quantity.)

A. 1.331 orbis in oris; A. 1.399 puppesque tuae pubesque tuorum (with Quint. 9.3.75); A. 1.646 cari stat cura parentis; A. 2.606–7 parentis . . . praeceptis pārere; A. 4.271 teris otia terris; A. 2.313 clamorque . . . clangorque; A. 2.494 fit via vi; A. 4.238 pārere parabat; A. 4.359 auribus hausi; A. 6.42–43 latus ingens . . . quo lāti; A. 6.204 auri . . . aura; A. 7.164 aut acris tendunt arcus; A. 10.99 murmura venturos nautis prodentia ventos; A. 10.191–92 canit . . . cānentem; A. 10.735 furto . . . fortibus; A. 11.554–56 libro . . . librans; A. 11.644 tantus in arma patet. latos huic hasta per armos; A. 11.729 caedes cedentiaque agmina; A. 12.389 lato . . . latebram; A. 12.617–18 aura . . . auris; A. 12.713–14 gemitum . . . congeminant; A. 12.788 armis animisque; E. 3.109–10 amores . . . amaros; E. 7.5 pares . . . parati; G. 1.157 umbras . . . imbrem; G. 2.207 iratus . . . arator; G. 2.328 āvia . . . avibus (with *Rhet. Her.* quoted two notes earlier); G. 3.502 tactum tractanti.

tities could be related etymologically.[317] At the same time it would be wrong to ignore vowel quantities, or to assume that they were as unimportant to the Romans as they are in some modern classrooms. Vowel quantity was one of the things that made words different. If words seemed too different, etymologies might seem implausible, but changes in vowel quantities alone do not prevent etymologizing. To object to an alleged instance of etymological wordplay because of quantity alone is to show anachronistic concern for modern notions of linguistically correct etymology.

Paronomasia will not be a major concern of this monograph; for some entries in the catalogue, it will not be clear whether the poet is etymologizing or simply engaging in the kind of wordplay or soundplay that always delighted Romans.[318]

---

317. Varro *LL* 5.6 litterarum enim fit demptione aut additione et propter earum tra⟨ie⟩c[ta]tionem aut commutationem, item syllabarum productione. Cf. 5.22 for the derivation of sŏlum, "soil," from sōlus, "lone"; 7.54 cārĕre ("to card [wool]") a cărēndo (carere, "to lack"); 6.60 nōmen from nŏvus; and fr. 30a prŏceres qui prōcesserunt.

Cf. Ross (1987) 43, Ahl (1985) 56, Thomas (1992) 142 ("although restraint is needed in such matters, it is time we stopped seeing etymological play in Latin poetry as a branch of verse composition classes"), Gransden (1976) on A. 8.54 *Pallantis proavi de nomine Pallanteum* ("a characteristic wordplay which defies quantity, since the first syllable of Palatium is short") and 441, Keith (1992) 65 n. 2, and Clausen (1994) 223. See also the refutation by Robinson (1969) 43–44 of the claim by Webster and Jebb that Sophocles cannot play at *Phil.* 931 on βίος, "life," and βιός, "bow," because of the accent and pitch (he cites *Crat.* 399 a 6–9: πρῶτον μὲν γὰρ τὸ τοιόνδε δεῖ ἐννοῆσαι περὶ ὀνομάτων, ὅτι πολλάκις ἐπεμβάλλομεν γράμματα, τὰ δ' ἐξαιροῦμεν, παρ' ὃ βουλόμεθα ὀνομάζοντες, καὶ τὰς ὀξύτητας μεταβάλλομεν, Emped. fr. 68 apud Arist. *Gen. An.* 777 a 7, and Plato *Gorg.* 493 b 4 with Dodds' note). The suggestion of Rawson (1985) 129, that Varro's "tendency to neglect differences in vowel quantity" is "perhaps a sign of the interest in the written rather than the spoken word," is interesting but perhaps anachronistic.

See also the ancient and modern references in the last few notes on paronomasia, often with differing vowel quantities.

318. The question of anagrams arises. Plato's *Cratylus,* Lucretius, and Varro mention rearranging of letters, and *Rhet. Her.* 4.29 describes paronomasia between *navo* and *vano* as *transferendis litteris,* but I have seen little indication that ancient writers thought that words with the same letters, rearranged in any order whatsoever, were etymologically related (cf. too Dalzell [1987] on *ignis* and *lignis* in Lucretius). The rearrangement of letters in some of the etymologies in the *Cratylus* (many of which involve *l* and *r,* whose position in words does often change) is not the tip of the iceberg, indicating widespread ancient interest in anagrams, but reflects comic exaggeration. There is not much indication that Vergil engaged in etymologizing that involved the kind of complex rearranging of letters lampooned in the *Cratylus.* One plausible anagram has been detected in Vergil, in the phrase *Latiumque vocari maluit* at A. 8.322–23, but here there is no indication that the words *Latium* and *maluit* are related. Other examples of Vergilian wordplay may involve etymologies featuring letters that have been rearranged (cf. on A. 4.347 for *Roma/amor*), but I think only in modest ways that at least some ancients could find plausible. Varro's metaphor of a person whose appearance changes over time

*2.1a. Translation with Paronomasia*

Several passages in Vergil involve what we might call "mistranslation," "translation by homonym," "translation with paronomasia," or "sound imitation." The items in this category do not all involve the same kind of wordplay, and few involve etymological wordplay, but it should be useful to consider them together. The individual entries should be consulted for more details, including bibliographical information (here I do note in parentheses the scholar from whom I learned about some examples).[319]

At E. 1.1 and elsewhere in the *Eclogues, fagus,* which in Latin should mean "beech," is used to correspond to φάγος, "oak," as though *fagus* and φάγος were related etymologically. Similarly, G. 3.172 uses *faginus axis* to translate Homer's φήγινος ἄξων (*Il.* 5.838), although Latin *faginus* should be "beech," Homeric φήγινος "oak." At E. 2.18, *vaccinium,* which in Latin should describe a bilberry that has pink flowers (Du Quesnay) is instead used here to correspond to ὑάκινθος at Theoc. 10.28.

At E. 8.58, *omnia vel medium fiat mare,* Vergil adapts Theoc. 1.134, πάντα δ' ἔναλλα γένοιτο but translates ἔναλλα, "changed," as though it were ἐνάλια, "in the sea." At E. 10.22, *tua cura Lycoris,* the word *cura* is used to mean *amica* for the first time in extant Latin; Vergil is translating Theocritus 1.81–83, and *tua cura Lycoris* represents Theocritus' ἁ δέ τυ κώρα.

G. 1.277 has *pallidus Orcus* where the model in Hes. *Op.* 802 has Ὅρκος; Vergil suggests a connection between (or blurs the distinction between) Orcus the god of the dead and Horcus the god of oath. At G. 1.373, *aeriae* is used where one model at *Il.* 3.7 has ἠέριαι (Farrell). G. 2.528, *socii cratera coronant,* is "thought by some to be a mistranslation of the Homeric line κοῦροι μὲν κρατῆρας ἐπεστέψαντο ποτοῖο, 'the young men filled the bowls with wine,' *Il.* 1.470, *Od.* 1.148" but more likely reflects scholiastic debate on the word (Thomas). At G. 4.260–63, *ut . . . ut . . . ut* is used to correspond to οὔτε . . . οὔτε . . . οὔτε in the model at *Il.* 14.392–401 (Farrell).

In Juno's words at A. 1.37, *mene incepto desistere victam,* the sound of *mene in-* recalls that of *Il.* 1.1, Μῆνιν ἄειδε, θέα (Levitan). At A. 6.273–81, two of the figures at the entrance to the underworld, *Curae* and *Letum,* may echo the sounds of the names of figures in Hes. *Th.* 211ff., Κῆρες and Λήθη (Sider). At A. 9.716, Vergil's *Inarime* is a misreading or reinterpretation of εἰν Ἀρίμοις at *Il.* 2.783.

---

perhaps indicates the extent of change he would find plausible: *LL* 5.5–6 *vetustas pauca non depravat, multa tollit. quem puerum vidisti formosum, hunc vides deformem in senecta.*

For the report that Lycophron used anagrams (e.g., ἀπὸ μέλιτος = Πτολεμαῖος with no indication that etymologizing is involved), see *SH* 531. Cf. also above n. 6.

319. On "sound imitation," I have also benefited from McKeown (1994).

## 2.2. The Single-Adjective Gloss

The single-adjective gloss may be the oldest kind of poetic etymologizing,[320] as noted above in my remarks on Homer, and perhaps served the legitimate function in archaic epic of explaining old words that had fallen into disuse. In Augustan poetry the gloss sometimes fulfills this old function, but more often Vergil is challenging the reader to notice a learned gloss.[321] Often Servius will comment on these, to say that the epithet has been chosen well *(bene)*, because of the etymology, or to note that Vergil has glossed the name *(verbum de verbo expressit)*. The latter phrase is used of *Plemyrium undosum* at A. 3.693, where *undosum* is a gloss on *Plemyrium,* suggesting a derivation from πλημμυρίς, "tide, flood." This example becomes paradigmatic for Servius, who cites it when he notes that at A. 1.744, which is repeated at 3.516, *pluvias* is a gloss on the name *Hyades,* suggesting a derivation from ὕω, "rain," and when he suggests that at A. 4.268, the adjective *clarus* functions as a gloss on the name *Olympus,* suggesting a connection with ὁλολαμπής, "bright shining."

In the last section I mentioned single-epithet glosses possibly borrowed from earlier Latin authors. At A. 4.247 *Atlas* is glossed by the adjective

---

320. **Features list no. 2: The single-adjective gloss or, "modifiers that reflect the etymology of the word modified" (= title of McCartney [1927])**
A. 1.298 novae . . . Karthaginis; A. 1.366 novae Karthaginis; A. 1.522 novam . . . urbem; A. 1.742 errantem lunam; A. 1.744 = 3.516 pluviasque Hyadas; A. 2.469–70 Pyrrhus . . . coruscus; A. 2.529 ardens . . . Pyrrhus; A. 3.126–27? sparsas . . . Cycladas; A. 3.271 Neritos ardua; A. 3.402 parva . . . Petelia; A. 3.689? Thapsumque iacentem; A. 3.693 Plemyrium undosum; A. 3.698 stagnantis Helori; A. 3.702? immanisque Gela fluvii; A. 3.703 arduus . . . Acragas; A. 3.705 palmosa Selinus; A. 4.211 femina (Dido) . . . errans; A. 4.247 Atlantis duri; A. 4.268 claro . . . Olympo; A. 6.552? solidoque adamante; A. 6.570–71 ultrix . . . Tisiphone; A. 6.841? magne Cato; A. 7.81–82 Fauni, / fatidici genitoris; A. 7.457? curvo . . . cornu; A. 7.513? cornuque recurvo; A. 7.682 altum Praeneste; A. 7.713 Tetricae horrentis; A. 7.740 maliferae . . . Abellae; A. 8.340 vatis fatidicae (Carmentis); A. 8.663 exsultantis Salios; A. 8.720 candentis . . . Phoebi; A. 8.726? indignatus Araxes; A. 10.184 intempestaeque Graviscae; A. 10.199 fatidicae Mantus; A. 10.315 Lichan . . . exsectum; A. 10.560? piscesque impasti; A. 11.200–201 semustaque . . . busta; E. 7.29–30 parvus . . . Micon; E. 10.5? Doris amara; G. 1.7 alma Ceres; G. 1.8 pingui . . . arista; G. 1.17–18 Pan . . . favens; G. 1.58–59 virosaque . . . castorea; G. 1.75 tristisque lupini; G. 1.460 claro . . . Aquilone; G. 1.462? umidus Auster; G. 2.88 gravibusque volemis; G. 2.139? tota . . . Panchaia; G. 3.407? nocturnum . . . furem; G. 3.461? acerque Gelonus; G. 3.474 aerias Alpis; G. 4.126? niger . . . Galaesus; G. 4.426 torrens . . . Sirius; G. 4.521? nocturni . . . Bacchi.

321. On single-epithet glosses see McCartney (1927), Rehm (1932) Sachregister s.v. Etymologien, Knight (1944) 197–200; Hanssen (1948), Marouzeau (1940) 259–65 and (1949) 71–79; Fordyce (1977) on A. 7.684; Williams (1960) on A. 5.2 and (1961) on A. 3.693, Ross (1973), (1987) 35, O'Hara (1990b) and (1992).

*durus,* which points to a (possibly Gallan) derivation from τλάς or τλῆναι, "endure." At A. 10.184 *intempestae* is a gloss on *Graviscae,* following Cato's idea that the name reflects the city's "unwholesome air" *(gravis aer).* At G. 3.474, *aerias Alpis,* Vergil follows Catullus 11.9 in glossing the name *Alps,* said to be Gallic for "high mountain."

The frequency with which epithets suggest etymological glosses may lead us to suspect etymologizing in some cases where we cannot be certain that that is what Vergil intended. Rehm has suggested that at A. 3.702, *immanisque Gela* offers a gloss on the name *Gela* as though connected to Latin *gelu,* but this involves reading an allusion to cold or ice in the epithet in a way that may not be legitimate. At A. 3.689 *Thapsumque iacentem* may contain a gloss on *Thapsum,* which would thus be connected to the Greek θάπτω, "bury," but *iacentem* does not seem to be a close match for θάπτω. Both cases seem doubtful to me, even though both look at first glance like single-epithet glosses, and even though they occur in a section of A. 3 containing many glosses of geographical names.

I draw particular attention to single-epithet glosses in part for convenience, in part because they do seem to be a special class, but this introduction and especially the catalogue will cite many examples where other types of phrasing perform the same function as single-epithet glosses.

### 2.2a. *The Reverse Gloss*

In A. 7.683–84, we see a kind of reverse gloss, where the noun glosses the adjective: on the phrase *Hernica saxa* Servius tells us that *hernae* is the Sabine word for rocks, *saxa,* so Vergil's use of the noun *saxa* with *Hernica* alludes to that etymology. At A. 3.280, the phrase *Actia . . . litora* alludes to the old etymology of the newly significant epithet for Apollo, *Actius,* which as a Greek word referred to any ἀκτή, or shore; Apollonius provides an explicit etymology at *Argonautica* 1.402–5. Other examples of this phenomenon are perhaps less certain. At A. 11.143, Vergil uses the phrase *funereas faces.* Varro, Donatus, and Servius derive the word *funus* from the rope torches *(funalia)* that burn in funeral rites. Although the phrase "funereal torch" needs no etymological motivation, Vergil's *funereas faces* may allude to this etymology.[322]

---

322. **Features list no. 2a: glosses of adjective by noun**

A. 3.280 Actia . . . litora; A. 7.683–84 Hernica saxa; A. 11.143–44? funereas . . . faces; A. 12.225? genus . . . ingens; G. 1. 309? Balearis . . . fundae.

## 2.3. Etymologizing κατ' ἀντίφρασιν

My list of the Stoics' principles of etymologizing included the idea that names for things could be given κατ' ἀντίφρασιν and so indicate the opposite of a thing, or of some property it has.[323] Aelius Stilo and then somewhat more cautiously Varro popularized this idea among the Romans, and Quintilian's concise but unsympathetic summary is well known, especially the example *"lucus" quia umbra opacus parum luceat.*[324] In Vergil we see I think comparatively few examples. At G. 1.8 *pinguis arista, pinguis* = "rich, moist," and *arista* suggests aridity, as Servius explains, commenting also on Vergil's etymologizing: *adfectate ait pinguem aristam, cum proprie arista ab ariditate sit dicta.* At G. 1.462, *umidus Auster* may refer to an etymology κατ' ἀντίφρασιν for Auster that associates it too with "dryness," but ancient evidence for this is dubious.

## 2.4. Etymologizing of Proper Names

The etymologies of names are as prominent in Vergil as in the Greek and Roman sources discussed earlier. This section will present examples of Vergilian etymologizing of the names of gods, geographical places, and mortals—both characters in the poem, and men of Vergil's day linked by etymology to heroic times. It will be noted that this category is based on content, or type of name etymologized, rather than stylistic features.

---

323. **Features list no. 3: glosses** κατ' ἀντίφρασιν

A. 1.12–13? *urbs antiqua* fuit . . . *Karthago*
A. 1.441? *lucus* in urbe fuit media, laetissimus *umbrae*
A. 4.670 *Karthago* aut *antiqua* Tyros
A. 5.606–8 *Saturnia* . . . necdum . . . *saturata*
A. 6.139? *lucus* et obscuris claudunt convallibus *umbrae*
A. 6.392–93 *nec* vero Alciden *me sum laetatus* euntem / accepisse
E. 2.6? o crudelis *Alexi,* nihil mea carmina *curas?*
G. 1.8 Chaoniam *pingui* glandem mutavit *arista*
G. 1.149 victum Dodona negaret
G. 1.192 nequiquam *pinguis* palea teret *area* culmos
G. 1.364 atque *altam* supra volat *ardea* nubem
G. 1.460 et *claro* silvas cernas *Aquilone* moveri
G. 1.462? quod cogitet *umidus Auster*
G. 2.127 *felicis mali,* quo non praesentius ullum
G. 4.126? qua *niger* umectat flaventia culta *Galaesus*

324. Quint. 1.6.34 etiamne a contrariis aliqua sinemus trahi, ut "lucus" quia umbra opacus parum luceat, et "ludus" quia sit longissime a lusu, et "Ditis" quia minime dives? For a possible (but perhaps unlikely) allusion to this etymology see on A. 1.441.

For harsh disapproval of etymology κατ' ἀντίφρασιν see Collart (1954) 267–71.

### *2.4a. Names of Gods*

The derivation and meaning of gods' names[325] always received special attention both in classical and Alexandrian Greek sources, and closer to Vergil's time, in the work of Apollodorus, "Cornificius," Cicero in especially *de Natura Deorum,* and Varro's *de Lingua Latina.* I have also mentioned the explanations in the *libri pontificales* of the *nomina deorum et rationes ipsorum nominum,* attested by Servius on G.1.21. Vergil too glosses the names of numerous gods.

Four examples from *Aeneid* 4 involve divine names; two are uncertain, in ways that illustrate problems in identifying etymologizing. At 356, Mercury is called *interpres divum,* and Servius notes that Vergil is glossing the name Hermes, from ἑρμηνεύς = *interpres.* At 242–43, with the words *animas . . . mittit,* Vergil may provide Hermes/Mercury with a gloss that hints at the epithet Psychopompos, but this example must remain less certain, because the idea of Mercury as guide to souls need not imply etymology. In 609, *nocturnisque Hecate triviis ululata per urbes,* the word *triviis* alludes to the cult name Trivia, as if to say, "Hecate is called Trivia because she is howled for at the crossroads." At 510–11, when Vergil describes a priestess calling on "three hundred gods" and on "Hecate" *(ter centum tonat ore deos . . . tergeminamque Hecaten),* Servius reads *centum* as an allusion to the etymology of the name Hecate (cf. Greek ἑκατόν). Here Servius' claim is less plausible, but it is interesting to think of Servius or some ancient reader thinking it to be valid.

I have already mentioned Vergil's gloss of Apollo's epithet *Actius* at A. 3.280. Vergil also glosses the epithet *Delius* as if from δηλόω, "make clear," at A. 6.11–12, saying *Delius inspirat vates aperitque futura.* We saw above Callimachus' explanation of the name of the island of Delos, which once

---

325. **Features list no. 4a: names of gods/semidivine beings**
Agmentis A. 4.469?; Apollo Actius A. 3.280; Delius A. 6.11–12; Phoebus A. 8.720; Nomius G. 3.1–3; Atlas A. 4.246–49; Brontes; Steropes; Pyragmon A. 8.425; Ceres G. 1.7; Charon A. 6.299–300; 392–93; Dionysus A. 6.805?; Bacchus 4.300–303?; Thyias 4.300–303?; Nyctelius 4.300–303?, G. 4.521?; Lenaeus G. 2.4–6; Dirae A. 12.845–52?; Erato A. 7.37–41?; Faunus A. 7.81–82, G. 1.17–18; Hamadryades G. 1.11; Harpyiae A. 3.226–27; Hecate A. 4.509–11?; Trivia 4.609; Hercules A. 8.287–88?; Hercules Victor 8.203, 362–63; Hermes/Mercury Psychopompos A. 4.242–43?; Hermes 4.356, 378; Juno A. 1.50–156, 71–73?, 252, 12.791–92, 796, 810, 842; Juppiter A. 9.128–29?; Juppiter Lucetius 9.570?; Juturna A. 10.439–40, 12.813–14, 872, 878–84; Mercury Psychopompos A. 4.242–43; Musa A. 1.8?, 7.41, 7.645?; E. 7.19; Opis A. 11.836–37?; Pales G. 3.1–3; Portunus A. 5.241; Romulus Quirinus A. 6.859? G. 3.27?; Saturnus, Saturnius A. 5.606–8, 781–82, 785–86, 7.297–98, 310–12, G. 2.173? G. 2.538?; Scylla A. 3.432?; E. 6.74–77; Silvanus A. 8.600–601?; Tisiphone A. 6.570–72; Trivia A. 4.609; Venus Acidalia A. 1.719–22; Vulcan Mulciber A. 8.724–26; Zeus G. 4.126?

fixed instead of wandering became no longer "inconspicuous" (ἄδηλος). Vergil may also offer a Callimachean gloss on the epithet Nomius at G. 3.1–3, where Servius so reads the phrase *pastor ab Amphryso,* and gloss the name Phoebus as "bright, radiant" at A. 8.720, *candentis limine Phoebi.* Following Apollonius, Vergil invokes the Muse Erato at the beginning of the second half of his epic (7.37–41). Unlike Apollonius, Vergil does not call attention to the connection of the name with the word ἔρως, but that association may lie behind his invocation of Erato at the start of the half of the poem that deals much with the role of desire, broadly conceived to include all those things for which one may have *amor.*

Etymological glosses help define the roles of the goddesses Juturna, Juno, and Venus in the *Aeneid.* Varro and Servius derive the name of Juturna, the nymph who in Vergil is Turnus' sister, from the verb *iuvare,* "help." Vergil plays on this etymology several times, adding the notion that the name means "the one who helps *Turnus*":

A. 10.439–40: interea *soror* alma monet *succedere* Lauso / *Turnum*
A. 12.813–14: *Iuturnam* misero (fateor) *succurrere* fratri / suasi
A. 12.872: quid nunc te *tua,* Turne, potest *germana iuvare?*

The name is thus a complete expression of her principal function in the epic. Somewhat differently, at A. 12.878–84 the association Juturna/Diuturna may add to Juturna's lament about immortality. For Juno/Hera, the allegorizing connection with *aer,* "the upper air," found in Plato, Apollonius, Cicero, and other sources, seems to be alluded to in several passages in A. 12:

791–92: *Iunonem* interea rex omnipotentis Olympi
   adloquitur fulva pugnas *de nube* tuentem
796: aut qua spe *gelidis in nubibus* haeres?
810: nec tu me *aeria* solam nunc sede videres
842: interea excedit caelo *nubemque relinquit.*

On the first passage Servius makes the comment on *fulva . . . de nube,* that Juno speaks from the *aer,* her own element *(de aere, de elemento suo).* Feeney has suggested further that readers' awareness of the association of Hera and *aer* also would color Juno's first action in the poem, the sending of the storm in book 1; when the goddess of the *aer* sends a storm the poet thereby suggests an allegorical way of reading. Elsewhere "Saturnian" Juno is described three times as "insatiable," suggesting an etymology κατ' ἀντίφρασιν from *saturo* mentioned by Cicero:

A. 5.606–8: *Saturnia* Iuno . . . necdum antiquum *saturata* dolorem
A. 5.781: Iunonis gravis ira neque *exsaturabile* pectus
A. 7.297–98: at, credo, mea numina tandem
fessa iacent, odiis aut *exsaturata* quievi.

In the *Georgics,* Vergil may show awareness of the different derivation *ab satu Saturnus;* see on G. 2.173–74. At A. 1.715–22 Venus is called *mater Acidalia,* as Cupid, mindful of his Acidalian mother, begins to tempt Dido with love for Aeneas. Servius connects the rare Acidalia with Greek ἀκίς = "dart, care, arrows of Eros." Vergil's epithet thus suggests both *curae* and the arrows of Cupid, and both are appropriate to the context, where Venus' instructions to Cupid and later conspiracy with Juno will produce figurative *curae* (cares, worry) for Dido and for Aeneas.

### 2.4b. Names of Places

Alexandrian poetry displayed the results of geographical and mythological research on names of places.[326] Callimachus' treatises on islands and rivers

326. **Features list no. 4b: names of places**
(To facilitate consideration of possible influence of e.g., Callimachus' treatises on the names of rivers or islands (described above in sect. 1.4), I have marked names of rivers [fl.] and islands [is.]) Abella A. 7.740; Acesta/Segesta A. 5.718; Acragas A. 3.703; Aenus A. 3.17–18; Alba Longa A. 3.389–93, 8.43–48; loci Albani A. 9.386–88? mons A. 12.134–36?; Alpes G. 3.474; Amsanctus A. 7.563–66; Angitia A. 7.752–60; Arae (is.) A. 1.108–10; Araxes (fl.) A. 8.726?; Arcadia A. 8.367–68?; Ardea A. 7.411–12, A. 7.623–31; Argiletum A. 8.345–46; Argyripam A. 11.246–47; Aventinus collis A. 7.655–63, 8.200, 231–35; Avernus A. 6.237–42; Bebrycia A. 5.373?; Bursa A. 1.367–68; Caieta A. 7.1–4; Capua A. 10.145; Ceraunia G. 1.328–33; Chaonia A. 3.333–36; Circei A. 7.10–14; Cycladas (is.) A. 3.126–27; Dicte E. 6.55–60; Elysium A. 6.640–41?; Galaesus G. 4.126?; Gargara G. 1.103; Gela A. 3.701–2? (fl.); Gelonus G. 3.461?; Graviscae A. 10.184; Haemus G. 1.491–92; Helorus (fl.) A. 3.698; Hesperia/Italia A. 1.530–33 = 3.163–66; Ianiculum A. 8.357–58; Inarime A. 9.715–16; Karthago A. 1.12–13, 297–300, 366, 522, 4.260, 670; Latium A. 8.319–27; Lavinium A. 12.194; Lethe (fl.) A. 6.713–15; Leucata A. 3.274?; Lugentes campi A. 6.441?; Lupercal A. 8.342–44, 630–32?; Maenala E. 8.21?, E. 10.55–61?, G. 1.17–18?; Mantua A. 10.198–200; Media G. 2.126–41; Misenum A. 6.232–35; Nar (fl.) A. 7.517; Narycia G. 2.438?; Neritos (is.) A. 3.270–71; Nomentum A. 6.773–76; Olenos E. 3.104–5?; Olympus A. 4.268–69; Palinurus A. 6.378–83; Pallanteum/Palatium A. 8.53–54; Panchaia G. 2.139?; Parthenii saltus E. 10.55–61?; Pergamea A. 3.132–34; Petelia A. 3.401–2; Phlegethon (fl.) A. 6.550–51; Plemyrium/Ortygia A. 3.693–94; Porta Carmentalis A. 8.337–41; Praeneste A. 7.681–85; Riphaei montes G. 3.382; Roma A. 1.273–77, 4.347?; Rosea rura A. 7.712?, G. 2.201–2?; Samothracia A. 7.206–8; Saturnia A. 8.357–58; Selinus A. 3.705; Sila A. 12.715–17; Strophades (is.) A. 3.210; Styx (fl.) A. 6.438–39, G. 4.479–80; Taburnus A. 12.715–17; Tetrica mons A. 7.713; Thapsum A. 3.689?; Tiber (fl.) A. 8.62–64, A. 8.328–32, A. 9.815–17; Tiberinus/Xanthos (fl.) A. 7.30–32; Tibur A. 7.670–71.

come to mind, and Vergil probably benefited from the writings of Varro and other contemporaries as well.[327] I have already noted Vergil's single-epithet glosses of *Plemyrium undosum, intempestaeque Graviscae, claro . . . Olympo,* and *aerias Alpis.* At A. 7.412, ***magnum** manet **Ardea** nomen,* the word *magnum,* as Servius notes, glosses the name *Ardea,* which is thus to be associated with the word *arduus.* At 7.623–31, Vergil may connect the name *Ardea,* the first word in 631, with the verb *ardet,* the first word in 623, to suggest a natural association between Turnus' hometown and fire, but this is less certain. At G. 1.328–33, the lightning Jupiter hurls at Ceraunia makes clear the name's derivation from κεραυνός, which is given by Servius here and treated explicitly by Apollonius. At A. 3.210, ***Strophades** Graio stant nomine dictae,* Vergil calls attention to the name *Strophades,* derived, as Servius notes, and as Apollonius had made explicit, from the Greek στροφή, "turning," because there the winged Argonauts Zetes and Calais "turned back" after chasing the Harpies away from Phineus.

At A. 8.337–41, Vergil provides a kind of double etymology, explaining both the place-name and the etymology of the person for whom it is named:

> vix ea dicta, dehinc progressus monstrat et aram
> et *Carmentalem* Romani nomine portam
> quam memorant, nymphae priscum *Carmentis* honorem,
> vatis *fatidicae, cecinit* quae prima futuros
> Aeneadas magnos et nobile Pallanteum.

Vergil is explicit with one name (the Carmental gate is named for Carmenta), but more subtle with the other, as *cecinit* points to the association of Carmenta's name with *carmen.* My note on this passage lists examples of this type of double etymologizing.

Several explanations of place-names are found in the trip to the underworld in book 6 of the *Aeneid.* At 6.237–42, Vergil alludes, as had Lucretius and Apollonius, to the etymology of the name Avernus or Aornus from α + ὄρνις; an interpolator adds line 242 to make the etymology explicit. At 438–39, ***tristis** . . . palus **inamabilis** undae /. . . **Styx,*** Vergil makes the familiar association of the name Styx with στυγερός, "hateful," as he had earlier at G. 4.479–80. At A. 6.550–51, *flammis . . . torrentibus . . . Phlegethon,* Vergil points to the obvious root φλέγω. At 641 it may be that ***solemque suum, sua** sidera norunt* alludes to a derivation of the name Elysium from [H]elios = *sol,* but this is less clear.

327. On Vergil's place-names cf. Bartelink (1965) 35–60, Rehm (1932), Holland (1935), Harrison (1991) on A. 10.145, *EV* s.v. toponimi (Garuti). For Callimachus and Varro see above.

### 2.4c. Names of Mortals

A representative sampling of Vergil's glosses of personal names is found clustered together in the parade of heroes that Anchises identifies for Aeneas in the underworld.[328] In A. 6.763–65, Anchises refers to Silvius, Aeneas' son by Lavinia:

> *Silvius,* Albanum nomen, tua *postuma* proles
> quem tibi longaevo serum Lavinia coniunx
> educet *silvis.*

Other sources refer to this man as Silvius Postumus. Vergil etymologizes both of these names, one more explicitly *(educet silvis)* and the other, which he never mentions, by an implied or suppressed etymology (see below on suppression): ***tua postuma proles.*** The phrase *Albanum nomen* here is the etymological signpost (see below).

At 808–12, Anchises sees Rome's second king, Numa Pompilius:

> quis procul ille autem ramis insignis olivae
> sacra ferens? nosco crinis incanaque menta

---

328. **Features list no. 4c: names of mortals**
Aborigines A. 7.180–81; Achaemenides A. 3.613–18?; Achates A. 1.174?, 1.312?; Aconteus A. 11.615–17; Aeneas A. 12.496–99?, 945–47?; Alexis E. 2.6?; Amata A. 7.56–57?; Amycus A. 9.771–72?; Ancus Poplicius A. 6.815–16?; Andromache A. 3.297?; Anxur A. 10.545–49?; Aquiculus A. 9.684–87; Aratus E. 3.40–42; Aristaeus G. 1.14–15; Ascanius/Iulus A. 1.267–68, 9.640–50?, Ascanius Leontodamas A. 4.159?; Atius A. 5.568; Aventinus A. 7.655–63; Augustus? A. 8.364–67?; Baleares G. 1.308–9?; Butes A. 5.372?, 9.646–48?; Cacus A. 8.194; Caeculus A. 7.678–81; Caeneus A. 6.448–49; Caesar? A. 6.460?; Camilla A. 7.803–4?, 11.552–66?, 11.573–75?, 11.648–54?, 11.778–82?; Cato Maior A. 6.841?; Ciris G. 1.401–9, Claudius A. 7.709; Cluentius A. 5.123; Cunare A. 10.185–92; Cupencus A. 12.539–40; Danai A 2.42–49?; Dido A. 4.211, 6.450–54; Drances A. 11.122–23?; Epytides A. 5.547?; Evander A. 8.194, 10.369–70?; Fabius Maximus Cunctator A. 6.845–46; Galli A. 8.657–61; Haemon A. 9.684–87; Hernici A. 7.681–85; Hippolytus/Virbius A. 7.761–77; Iapyx Iasides A. 12.391–97; Iulius A. 1.267–68, 286–88, 6.789–90; Labici A. 7.796–98; Laurentes A. 7.59–63; Lausus A. 10.825?; Lichas A. 10.315; Ligures A. 10.185–92; Lucetius A. 9.570?; Lycus A. 9.556–59, 563–66; Manto A. 10.198–200; Memmius A. 5.117; Micon E. 7.29–30; Neoptolemus A. 2.263?, 469–75; Numa A. 6.808–12; Palinurus A. 6.339?, 350?, 362; Parthus E. 1.61–62?; Pompeius Magnus A. 2.558?; Pyrrhus A. 2.469–75, 529–30; Quercens A. 9.684–87; Quirites A. 7.709–10; Rhamnes A. 9.324–30; Rhea Silvia A. 7.655–63; Romani A. 1.273–77; Salii A. 8.663; Sarrastes A. 7.738; Scipiones Africani A. 6.842–43; Sergius A. 5.121; Serranus A. 6.844; Silvius Aeneas A. 6.768–69; Silvius Postumus A. 6.763–65; Sinon A. 2.79, 195, 259, 329; Tarquinius Superbus A. 6.817–18; Tityrus E. 1.9–10?; Tmarus A. 9.684–87; Turnus A. 7.56?; Ucalegon A. 2.310–12?; Veneti A. 1.247–52; Vergilius G. 1.427–35, 4.563–64; Virbius A. 7.761–77.

regis Romani primam qui *legibus* urbem
fundabit, Curibus parvis et paupere terra
missus in imperium magnum.

Numa is not named, but the reader easily supplies the name from the description. The suppression of the name (see below) involves an implied etymology, in the words *primam qui* ***legibus*** *urbem fundabit.* Servius explains, *Numa dictus est* ἀπὸ τῶν νόμων.

In lines 815–16, a scholarly problem is created by what may be another reference to a cognomen:

quem iuxta sequitur iactantior *Ancus*
nunc quoque iam nimium gaudens *popularibus* auris

The popularist tendencies of this Ancus, who must be the king Ancus Marcius, have puzzled scholars, because there is no trace of this theme in other references to Ancus. Skutsch has suggested that the king Ancus Marcius, who replaced Tullus Hostilius, is to be identified with an Ancus Poplicius, a Latin leader said to have fought against Tullus. The tradition of Ancus as *popularis* thus would have come from the name *Poplicius,* to which Vergil might here be alluding.

Another transference or confusion of cognomina comes in 817–18, where Vergil uses the adjective *superbus* to describe Brutus, right after mentioning the Tarquins. Although the word *superbus* is important for what Vergil is saying about Brutus here, it also reminds us of the name *Tarquinius Superbus,* the last Roman king. Lucretius uses the adjective in a more straightforward way to allude to the Tarquins.

At 6.842–46, we see a cluster of etymologies:

quis Gracchi genus aut geminos, duo *fulmina belli,*
*Scipiadas,* **cladem Libyae,** parvoque potentem
Fabricius vel te sulco, Serrane, serentem?
quo fessum rapitis, Fabii? tu *Maximus* ille es,
unus qui nobis *cunctando* restituis rem.

In 844, Vergil alludes to the simple etymology of the name Serranus from *sero,* "to sow." In 846, drawing from Ennius as often in the underworld, he does not give but allusively explains the name Cunctator, "delayer," given to Fabius Maximus. The etymology of the name Serranus, with both the name and the key word *serentem* given, is like the etymology of Silvius Postumus' nomen *Silvius* in 763–65. The gloss of the suppressed name Cunctator is like that of Silvius' cognomen Postumus. A similar technique is used in 842–43, *geminos, duo fulmina belli, / Scipiadas, cladem Libyae. Fulmina* refers to the association, found in a number of authors, of the name Scipio with σκηπτός, "thunderbolt." The words *cladem Libyae,* "destruction of Libya," refer to the agnomen *Africanus,* which both the elder and younger Scipio received for their victories in Africa. One name is given and glossed, one name glossed without being given.

My survey of Greek etymologizing noted instances where etymologies of names of central characters like Achilles, Odysseus, Oedipus, and Pentheus may be important for interpretation of an entire work. No single etymology of a proper name in Vergil is as important to interpretation of the poem as that of those names arguably is. The name Aeneas is probably not glossed at all, although one scholar has detected an allusion to the etymology from αἰνὸν ἄχος found in the *Homeric Hymn to Aphrodite* (see on A. 12.945–47). For the name Turnus an etymology may be offered, but not prominently (see on A. 7.56). The name Dido is glossed in an interesting way, which I shall discuss in section 3, on the function of etymologizing.

In Evander's story of Hercules and Cacus in *Aeneid* 8, the sense of Evander as "good man" (Εὔανδρος) and Cacus as "bad man" (κακός) seems present, although no particular line of Vergil's seems to allude to this (see on A. 8.194).

Some etymologizing of proper names has the function of linking families or persons of Vergil's day to Trojan or Italian families of heroic times; this is also true of the etymologies of many of the place names discussed just above. For this important aspect of the *Aeneid*'s etymologizing, see both section 3, on the function of etymologizing, and on A. 5.116–23.

## 2.5. The Explicit Gloss or Derivation

We saw earlier that explicit etymologies or etymological aetiologies appear at times in Homer and other archaic and classical Greek poets and are featured prominently in the Alexandrians. For the *Aeneid,* written in the learned style and tradition of Apollonius and Callimachus, and having as its subject the origins or *aitia* of the Roman people, explicit etymologies are a natural component.[329] Vergil (or one of his characters) discusses the name or naming

329. **Features list no. 5: explicit etymological aetiologies**

A. 1.267–68 at puer Ascanius, cui nunc cognomen *Iulo*
additur (*Ilus* erat, dum res stetit *Ilia* regno)

of the Romans, the Julian *gens,* Latium, the Italian promontories named after Misenus and Palinurus, Pallanteum, and other figures or features of Roman myth or topography; in all over thirty names are explained explicitly. I find no examples in Vergil outside of the *Aeneid.*

Explicit etymologies need little comment here. It may be noted again,

---

| | |
|---|---|
| A. 1.276–77 | *Romulus* excipiet gentem et Mavortia condet<br>moenia *Romanos*que suo de nomine dicet |
| A. 1.288 | *Iulius,* a magno demissum nomen *Iulo* |
| A. 1.532–33 =<br>3.165–66 | nunc fama minores<br>*Italiam* dixisse ducis de nomine *gentem* |
| A. 3.17–18 | moenia prima loco fatis ingressus iniquis<br>*Aeneadas*que meo nomen de nomine fingo |
| A. 3.132–34 | ergo avidus muros optatae molior urbis<br>Pergameamque voco, et laetam cognomine gentem<br>hortor amare focos arcemque attollere tectis |
| A. 3.334–35 | Heleno, qui *Chaonios* cognomine campos<br>*Chaoniam*que omnem Troiano a *Chaone* dixit |
| A. 3.702 | *immanis*que *Gela fluvii* cognomine dicta |
| A. 5.117, 121–23 | mox Italus *Mnestheus,* genus a quo nomine *Memmi*<br>. . . . . . . . . . . . . . . . . . . . . . . . . . . . .<br>*Sergestus*que, domus tenet a quo *Sergia* nomen,<br>Centauro invehitur magna, Scyllaque *Cloanthus*<br>caerulea, genus unde tibi, Romane *Cluenti* |
| A. 5.568–69 | alter *Atys,* genus unde *Atii* duxere Latini,<br>parvus *Atys* pueroque puer dilectus Iulo |
| A. 5.602 | Troiaque nunc pueri, Troianum dicitur agmen |
| A. 5.718 | urbem appellabunt permisso nomine *Acestam* |
| A. 6.234–35 | monte sub aerio, qui nunc Misenus ab illo<br>dicitur aeternumque tenet per saecula nomen |
| [A. 6.237–42 | unde locum Grai dixerunt nomine *Aornum*—only the interpolation is explicit] |
| A. 6.381 | aeternumque locus Palinuri nomen habebit |
| A. 6.768–69 | et qui te nomine reddet / Silvius Aeneas |
| A. 7.3–4 | et nunc servat honos sedem tuus, ossaque nomen<br>Hesperia in magna, si qua est ea gloria, signat |
| A. 7.208 | *Threiciam*que *Samum,* quae nunc *Samothracia* fertur |
| A. 7.671 | fratris *Tiburti* dictam cognomine gentem |
| A. 8.54 | *Pallantis* proavi de nomine *Pallanteum* |
| A. 8.322–23 | *Latium*que vocari / maluit, his quoniam *latuisset* tutus in oris |
| A. 8.330–32 | tum reges *asper*que immani corpore *Thybris,*<br>a quo post Itali fluvium cognomine *Thybrim*<br>diximus |
| A. 8.338–39 | et *Carmentalem* Romani nomine portam<br>quam memorant, nymphae priscum *Carmentis* honorem |
| A. 8.343–44 | *Lupercal* / Parrhasio dictum Panos de more *Lycaei* |

however, that the study of explicit etymologies is useful for the study of implicit or subtle ones: while some of the latter may appear to some to be simply products of the critic's imagination, the explicit etymologies are unmistakable, and thus good sources for many stylistic features common to both explicit and implicit etymologies. This should calm some fears about whether recent scholarship has exaggerated the importance of etymological wordplay in Vergil and other Latin poets.

The role of aetiology in the *Aeneid* will be discussed at greater length in section 3, on the function of Vergilian etymologizing.

## 2.6. Naming Constructions as Etymological Signposts

When Vergil calls attention to the fact that a name is a name,[330] by using words such as *nomen, cognomen, verum nomen, voco, dico, appello,* or

---

A. 8.345–46 nec non et sacri monstrat nemus *Argileti*
testaturque locum et *letum* docet hospitis *Argi*
A. 8.422 *Volcani* domus et *Volcania* nomine *tellus*
A. 10.145 et *Capys:* hinc nomen *Campanae* ducitur *urbi*
A. 10.199–200 *fatidicae Mantus* et Tusci filius amnis,
qui muros matrisque dedit tibi, *Mantua,* nomen
A. 11.246–47 ille urbem *Argyripam* patriae cognomine gentis
victor Gargani condebat *Iapygis* agris.
A. 11.542–43 matrisque vocavit / nomine Casmillae mutata parte Camillam
A. 12.194 *urbi*que dabit *Lavinia* nomen
A. 12.826–28, 835 "sit Latium, sint Albani per saecula reges,
sit Romana potens Itala virtute propago;
occidit, occideritque sinas cum nomine Troia."
. . . . . . . . . . . . . . . . . . . . . . . . .
"utque est nomen erit."

330. **Features list no. 6: naming constructions as signposts**
A. 1.109 saxa vocant Itali mediis quae in fluctibus Aras
A. 1.267–68 at puer Ascanius, cui nunc cognomen *Iulo* / additur
A. 1.277 *Romanos*que suo de nomine dicet
A. 1.288 *Iulius,* a magno demissum nomen *Iulo*
A. 1.367 facti de nomine Byrsam
A. 1.530? est locus, *Hesperiam* Grai cognomine dicunt
A. 1.533 *Italiam* dixisse ducis de nomine *gentem.*
A. 3.18 *Aeneadas*que meo nomen de nomine fingo
A. 3.133 Pergameamque voco, et laetam cognomine gentem
A. 3.210 Strophades Graio stant nomine dictae
A. 3.334–35 pars Heleno, qui Chaonios cognomine campos
Chaoniamque omnem Troiano a Chaone dixit
A. 3.693–94 Plemyrium undosum; nomen dixere priores / Ortygiam
A. 5.602 Troiaque nunc pueri, Troianum dicitur agmen

*perhibeo,* he may be calling attention to etymological wordplay, especially if the naming construction seems otherwise unnecessary.[331] I have found this feature to be an important and useful marker for wordplay, so besides the list of examples from Vergil provided here in the notes, the reader is urged to notice the signposts marked by dotted underlining above in the examples given from earlier poets. In Vergil naming constructions as signposts mark

---

| | |
|---|---|
| A. 5.718 | urbem appellabunt permisso nomine *Acestam* |
| A. 6.234–35 | monte sub aerio, qui nunc Misenus ab illo |
| | dicitur aeternumque tenet per saecula nomen |
| A. 6.441? | Lugentes campi; sic illos nomine dicunt |
| A. 6.763 | *Silvius,* Albanum nomen, tua *postuma* proles |
| A. 7.3–4 | et nunc servat honos sedem tuus, ossaque nomen |
| | Hesperia in magna, si qua est ea gloria, signat |
| A. 7.412 | magnum manet Ardea nomen |
| A. 7.607? | sunt *geminae* Belli portae (sic nomine dicunt) |
| A. 7.671 | fratris *Tiburti* dictam cognomine gentem |
| A. 7.777 | versoque ubi nomine Virbius esset |
| A. 8.48 | Ascanius *clari* condet cognominis *Albam* |
| A. 8.54 | *Pallantis* proavi de nomine *Pallanteum* |
| A. 8.322–23 | Latiumque vocari / maluit, his quoniam latuisset tutus in oris |
| A. 8.338–39 | Carmentalem Romani nomine portam / quam memorant |
| A. 8.344 | Parrhasio dictum Panos de more *Lycaei* |
| A. 8.422 | *Volcani* domus et *Volcania* nomine *tellus* |
| A. 9.387–88? | atque locos qui post Albae de nomine dicti /*Albani* |
| A. 10.200 | qui muros matrisque dedit tibi, *Mantua,* nomen |
| A. 10.369–70? | Per vos et *fortia facta,* / per *ducis Evandri* nomen devictaque bella |
| A. 11.246 | ille urbem Argyripam patriae cognomine gentis |
| A. 11.542–43 | matrisque vocavit / nomine Casmillae mutata parte Camillam |
| A. 12.845? | dicuntur geminae pestes cognomine *Dirae* |
| G. 1.137–38 | *navita* tum stellis numeros et nomina fecit |
| | *Pleiadas, Hyadas,* claramque Lycaonis Arcton |
| G. 2.238? | *salsa* autem tellus et quae perhibetur *amara* |
| G. 3.147–48 | volitans, cui *nomen;* asilo |
| | Romanum est, oestrum Grai vertere vocantes |
| G. 3.280–81 | hippomanes vero quod nomine dicunt / pastores |
| G. 4.271–72 | flos in pratis cui nomen amello / fecere agricolae. |

331. Maltby (1993a) calls attention to etymologies signaled by the use of the words *verus* or *nomen.* My list has some of those, but leans toward the use of verbs of naming or calling. Shechter (1975) 359 uses the term "signpost"; Hunter (1989) 217 stresses naming constructions in Apollonius; cf. Rank (1951) 136–43 (an appendix on "de Terminologie der etymologieën en benaming"), Woodhead (1928) 35, 38, 99 (discusses naming constructions, but also criticizes the excessive claims about signposts in Euripides by Verrall; cf. too Quincey [1963]); Williams (1961) on 133 ("Virgil often uses this word *[cognomen]* in a context which implies the meaning ἐπωνυμία, the calling of a new thing after an old"), McKeown (1989) 201–2, Keith (1992) 65–66. Cf. also below in this section on the "Alexandrian" or "illusory" footnote.

some examples of wordplay that is quite obvious to us (as in the example from A. 6, *Silvius, Albanum nomen,* mentioned above), some that is less explicit but now equally certain, and some examples that look like etymologizing, but which I have not been able to explain fully yet.

I have mentioned the gloss in A. 3.693 on *Plemyrium* as rainy; here we may quote more of the lines *(Plemyrium undosum; nomen dixere priores / Ortygiam)* to note that *nomen dixere* is a signpost calling attention to the names. In A. 3.210, *Strophades Graio stant nomine dictae,* the word *nomine* is a signpost calling attention to the name *Strophades* (Apollonius' explicit etymology also is marked with a signpost). In A. 8.48, *Ascanius clari condet cognominis Albam,* the word *cognominis* calls attention to the name Alba, whose derivation from *albus,* "white," is glossed here by the word *clarus.* In this instance, the literal meaning of *clarum cognomen* is "famous name," but the phrase also has connotations of "named for brightness (whiteness)." As Fordyce notes, "Virgil uses the word *[cognomine]* especially of the significant name, the ἔτυμον or αἴτιον."[332]

G. 3.280–81 presents a well-known example, with an interesting twist:

> hic demum, *hippomanes* vero quod nomine dicunt
> pastores, lentum destillat ab inguine *virus*

The words *vero quod nomine dicunt* call attention to the name and its etymology; indeed *vero . . . nomine* virtually translates *etymologia.* One etymology for *hippomanes* is that it comes from Greek μανία, "madness," and ἵππος, "horse," and scholars have noted that the phrase *furor equarum,* "madness of mares," occurs fifteen lines earlier in the text, at 266. Jacobson has also noticed that the word *destillat,* "ooze, drip down," in line 281, suggests the Latin verb *manat* from *mano, manare:* "flow, run, exude." So Vergil alludes to two etymologies, the second perhaps a playful "correction" of the first. "Correction" of a predecessor, or of the tradition generally, will be discussed below.

In G. 1.137–38, a significant naming construction does the work done elsewhere by the modifier as gloss. Vergil tells how sailors first gave names to stars such the Pleiades, the Hyades, and Arctos:

> *navita* tum stellis numeros et nomina fecit
> *Pleiadas, Hyadas,* claramque Lycaonis Arcton.

The words *nomina fecit* alert us the possibility of etymological play. Servius derives the name Pleiades from πλέω, "to sail," because their rising in the

332. Fordyce (1977) on 7.670.

spring marked the beginning of the sailing season, and Hyades from ὕω, "to rain," since their rising in the fall marked the beginning of the rainy season. As noted above, twice in the *Aeneid* Vergil uses the phrase *pluviasque Hyadas,* with the epithet *pluvias* as a gloss on the name. The etymologies of both the Pleiades and Hyades were contested in antiquity; by saying it was sailors who named the Pleiades and Hyades, Vergil takes a stand, as it were, and suggests the etymology from sailing for both words. The naming construction here functions in the same way as the more obvious gloss in the *Aeneid.* (This example drew the attention of Ovid; see section 2.14 below.)

Another example of the unnecessary naming construction is at A. 1.108–10:

> tris Notus abreptas in saxa latentia torquet
> (saxa vocant Itali mediis quae in fluctibus Aras,
> dorsum immane mari summo)

This is not quite etymologizing, but Vergil uses the naming signpost to call attention to the name of these rocks: *Arae,* Altars. He further calls attention to the name by means of the word *dorsum* in line 110. A number of the examples of naming constructions involve alternate names (see below). Servius' note on this passage tells us that some called these rocks ἵππου νῶτα, Horse's Back. In Vergil's line 110, *dorsum* is an allusion to this other name, Back; Vergil says in effect, "I am deliberately calling these rocks not 'Back,' as some do, but 'Altars.'" I have argued elsewhere that these rocks are called Altars because Vergil uses them to introduce the theme of sacrifice in the *Aeneid,* and because the men on the boat that goes down near them, the boat of Orontes, are to be seen as a sort of sacrifice.[333]

Two last examples of a naming construction are tantalizingly puzzling, for I cannot figure out exactly what is going on with them. At A. 6.441, Vergil refers to the location in the underworld of those who have died for love: *Lugentes campi; sic illos nomine dicunt.* Here we seem to have a clear etymological signpost, but we lack sufficient information to understand Vergil's point. Norden long ago suggested that *nomine dicunt* implies debt to a poetic predecessor, and in particular a source in lost Hellenistic poetry, perhaps a catalogue of women in the underworld. A Hellenistic source would also explain the "pathetic fallacy" of the phrase *Lugentes campi,* for normally "fields" cannot "mourn." He cites phrases parallel to *nomine dicunt* in Cicero, Lucretius, and elsewhere in Vergil (see catalogue): my additional observation is that each of the four passages he cites involves etymologizing.

333. O'Hara (1990) 19–24.

Servius suggests that the *Lugentes campi* are so called because they are *lucis egentis* (i.e., *lugentes* < *lu(cis e)gentes);* de la Cerda suggests instead a connection with the underworld Cocytus River, named from κωκύω, "mourn." Some such wordplay as this must have been made clear by Vergil's source.

A second, still more elusive case in that of A. 9.386–88:

> Nisus abit; iamque imprudens evaserat hostis
> atque locos qui post *Albae* de nomine dicti
> *Albani* (tum rex stabula alta Latinus habebat)

Nisus, fleeing the men that will capture Euryalus and eventually kill both of them, has reached the "places later called Alban, after the name of Alba, which now are serving as the stables of King Latinus." Why this detail? And what are these *loci Albani,* Alban places? I have no complete answer, although I offer a tentative suggestion. My sense is that because of the use of the etymological signpost, the full answer must somehow involve the significance of the name Alba, and possibly a Gallic or pre-Indo-European word meaning "high, lofty," which we have seen earlier in possible glosses by Catullus and Vergil on the name Alps.

The naming construction as etymological signpost may be looked on as similar to, or perhaps even part of, another phenomenon: what has been called the "Alexandrian footnote," or "illusory footnote," the practice of authors like Vergil of referring to what "they say," with expressions like *ferunt, dictum est, ut fama est,* as at times a means of indicating debt to a model, or at least adherence to a learned tradition.[334] The existence of the Alexandrian footnote means that some caution should be exercised when we claim to see etymological signposts.

## 2.7. Suppression

Vergil and other Augustan poets often suppress or omit a name or word that must be supplied by the reader,[335] so that the etymological wordplay only

334. See Norden (1981) on A. 6.14, Ross (1975) 78, Thomas (1988) on G. 1.247 (such expressions "often refer to traditional views, specifically poetic ones, and are sometimes to be seen as allusive references to precise sources; alternately they may even express *diffidentia,* a means of separating the poet from the reported information"), and now Horsfall (1989), (1990), (1991) 117–33, and (1991c) 33–34.

335. **Features list no. 7: suppression/antonomasia**

A. 1.317? *volucremque* fuga praevertitur *Hebrum*
A. 2.469–75 (Neoptolemus)
A. 2.682–98 (cometes)

really "takes place" when the missing word is supplied; the term "suppress" we take from Servius' *supprimens nomen.*[336] Alexandrian and Augustan scholar-poets use suppression (or *antonomasia* or "kenning") not only for etymological wordplay, but for a broad range of allusions to things not made

| | |
|---|---|
| A. 2.558? | iacet *ingens* litore truncus (Pompeius *Magnus*) |
| A. 2.679–98 | (cometes) |
| A. 3.390–93 | litoreis ingens inventa sub ilicibus sus<br>triginta capitum fetus enixa iacebit,<br>*alba* solo recubans, *albi* circum ubera nati,<br>is locus *urbis* erit, requies ea certa laborum (Alba Longa) |
| A. 4.211 | *femina,* quae nostris *errans* in finibus urbem (Dido) |
| A. 4.260 | Aenean fundantem arces ac tecta *novantem* (Carthago) |
| A. 4.356, 378 | *interpres divum* (Mercury/Hermes) |
| A. 4.469? | *Eumenidum* veluti demens videt *agmina* Pentheus (Agmentis) |
| A. 4.609 | nocturnisque Hecate *triviis* ululata per urbes (Trivia) |
| A. 6.27 | hic *labor* ille *domus* et inextricabilis error (labyrinthus) |
| A. 6.237–39, 242 | spelunca alta fuit vastoque immanis hiatu,<br>scrupea, tuta lacu nigro nemorumque tenebris,<br>quam super *haud ullae* poterant impune *volantes*<br>[unde locum Grai dixerunt nomine *Aornum.*] (Avernus, made explicit by interpolator) |
| A. 6.601–3? | quid memorem *Lapithas,* Ixiona Pirithoumque?<br>quos super atra *silex* iam iam *lapsura* cadentique (lapis) |
| A. 6.640–41? | largior hic campos aether et lumine vestit<br>purpureo, *solemque suum,* sua sidera norunt (Elysium) |
| A. 6.763 | Silvius, Albanum nomen, tua *postuma* proles (Postumus) |
| A. 6.810–11 | regis Romani primam qui *legibus* urbem / fundabit (Numa) |
| A. 6.843 | *Scipiadas, cladem Libyae* (Africani) |
| A. 6.846 | unus qui nobis *cunctando* restituis rem (Cunctator) |
| A. 7.10–11 | proxima *Circaeae* raduntur litora terrae,<br>dives inaccessos ubi *Solis filia* lucos (Circe) |
| A. 7.41 | tu vatem, tu, *diva, mone* (Musa) |
| A. 7.56–57? | Turnus, avis atavisque potens, quem *regia coniunx*<br>adiungi generum miro properabat *amore* (Amata) |
| A. 7.181 | aliique *ab origine* reges (Aborigines) |
| A. 8.281–82? | iamque sacerdotes primusque Potitius ibant<br>pellibus in morem cincti, *flammas*que ferebant (flamen) |
| A. 8.296–97? | te Stygii tremuere lacus, te *ianitor Orci*<br>*ossa* super recubans antro *semesa* cruento (Cerberus) |
| A. 8.653 | stabat pro templo et *Capitolia* celsa tenebat (Capitolinus) |
| A. 10.145 | et *Capys:* hinc nomen *Campanae* ducitur *urbi* (Capua) |
| A. 10.439–40 | interea *soror* alma monet *succedere* Lauso / Turnum (Juturna) |
| A. 10.825? | quid tibi nunc, miserande *puer,* pro *laudibus* istis? (Lausus) |
| A. 11.630? | bis reiecti armis respectant terga *tegentes* (clipeus) |
| A. 12.194 | *urbi*que dabit *Lavinia* nomen (Lavinium) |

explicit, but sufficiently clear to the learned readers for whom they wrote.[337] I have mentioned a number of these above, beginning in the section on earlier Roman poets with the gloss of the suppressed name Atalanta in *durae . . . Iasidos* at Propertius 1.1.10. In Vergil I have noted the allusions to the name Hermes at A. 4.356, *interpres diuum,* and Trivia at 4.609, *nocturnisque*

---

| | |
|---|---|
| A. 12.498? | *terribilis* saevam nullo discrimine caedem (Aeneas) |
| A. 12.862–64 | *alitis* in parvae subitam collecta figuram,<br>quae quondam in bustis aut culminibus desertis<br>*nocte* sedens *serum* canit importuna per umbras (noctua) |
| A. 12.872 | quid nunc te *tua,* Turne, potest *germana iuvare?* (Juturna) |
| A. 12.946–47? | furiis accensus et *ira* / *terribilis* (Aeneas) |
| E. 3.40–42 | in medio duo signa, Conon et—*quis fuit alter,*<br>descripsit radio totum qui gentibus orbem,<br>tempora quae messor, quae curvus *arator* haberet? (Aratus) |
| E. 10.5 | *Doris amara* suam non intermisceat undam (mare) |
| G. 1.14 | et *cultor* nemorum, cui *pinguia* Ceae (Aristaeus) |
| G. 1.17–18 | *Pan* ovium custos, tua si tibi Maenala curae,<br>adsis, o Tegeaee, *favens* (Faunus) |
| G. 1.217–18 | candidus auratis *aperit* cum cornibus annum / Taurus (Aprilis) |
| G. 1.406, 409 | quacumque illa levem fugiens *secat* aethera pennis . . .<br>illa levem fugiens raptim *secat* aethera pennis (ciris) |
| G. 1.462? | quod cogitet *umidus Auster* (Notus) |
| G. 2.126–41 | *Media* fert tristis sucos tardumque saporem<br>*felicis mali,* quo non praesentius ullum . . . (medica) |
| G. 2.380–83 | non aliam ob culpam Baccho *caper* omnibus aris<br>caeditur et veteres ineunt proscaenia ludi,<br>praemiaque ingeniis *pagos et compita* circum<br>Thesidae posuere (tragoedia, comoedia) |
| G. 3.1–3 | Te quoque, magna *Pales,* et te memorande canemus<br>*pastor* ab Amphryso, vos, silvae amnesque Lycaei.<br>cetera, quae vacuas tenuissent carmine mentes. . . (Nomius, Pan) |
| G. 3.34 | *stabunt* et Parii lapides, *spirantia signa* (statuae) |
| G. 4.42–44 | *fovere* larem (favus) |
| G. 4.521? | *nocturni*que orgia *Bacchi* (Nyctelius) |

336. For the term suppression cf. Servius ad G. 2.126 (Vergil's treatment of the *felix malum*): apud Medos nascitur quaedam arbor, ferens mala, quae medica vocantur: quam per perpiphrasin ostendit, eius *supprimens* nomen. Cf. Ross (1987) 36–37, 114, etc., and next note.

337. Cf. Thomas (1988b) 216: At G. 2.319–20, "the name of the white bird is suppressed and is to be recovered from its attributes. . . . In this poem such suppresssion . . . regularly points to a literary source" (his examples include the etymologizing at G. 3.1–2 and 425–34). Haslam (1992) 202, discussing suppression in a passage not involving etymology, offers healthy skepticism about how "absence can be converted into presence by what might be called the 'deafening silence' ploy," but the phenomenon is widespread enough to overcome justifiable initial hesitation. See also Horsfall (1991) 117–33, (1991a) 216, and (1991c) 35, with further references.

*Hecate triviis,* and the allusions to the names Numa, Postumus, Cunctator, and Africanus in A. 6.810–46.

Other examples: at A. 3.389–93 the stress on the whiteness of the sow and her young *(alba solo recubans, albi circum ubera nati),* and the word *urbis,* point to the name Alba Longa, which is not given. At G. 1.406–9 Vergil "glosses the (omitted) name of the bird: the *ciris,* which once cut (κείρω) her father's lock, now 'cuts' the air with her wings" (Thomas). At A. 2.469–75, the simile in which Achilles' son is compared to a snake shedding its skin and the word *novus* point to the common etymology of the first element of the name Neoptolemus, but that name only appears in other passages, and Achilles' son is called Pyrrhus in these lines. At A. 4.211 *femina, quae nostris errans in finibus urbem,* the word *errans* provides a gloss, to be discussed below, on the name Dido; here the word *femina* stands in for the suppressed name. An interesting case occurs at A. 6.237–41, where *haud ullae . . . volantes* glosses the suppressed name Avernus (α + ὄρνις), but then an interpolator adds 242 to make the etymology explicit: *unde locum Grai dixerunt nomine Aornum.* When Servius uses the phrase *supprimens nomen,* he is commenting on G. 2.126–41, where Vergil puns on *Media,* the fruit called *medica,* whose name he suppresses, and probably also the name Medea, also suppressed. At G. 4.42–44 Vergil says that some bees are said to warm their hive *(fovere larem)* by digging it into the ground. The word *larem* is part of the gentle personification of the bees, but the phrase really means *fovere favum.* Festus tells us that *favus* comes from the verb *faveo,* "to warm" *(favi a favendo).* So the bees "warm their place of warmth."

## 2.8. Framing

An explicit example of framing a line with words connected etymologically[338] is at A. 8.54: *Pallantis* proavi de nomine *Pallanteum,* where the

338. **Features list no. 8: framing**

A. 1.288 *Iulius,* a magno demissum nomen *Iulo.*

A. 1.441? *lucus* in urbe fuit media, laetissimus *umbrae*

A. 6.12 *Delius* inspirat vates *aperitque futura*

A. 8.54 *Pallantis* proavi de nomine *Pallanteum*

A. 7.539 *armenta* et terram centum vertebat *aratris*

A. 7.738 *Sarrastis* populos et quae rigat aequora *Sarnus*

A. 8.288? *Herculeas* et facta ferunt; ut prima *novercae*

A. 9.570 *Lucetium* portae subeuntem *ignisque ferentem*

A. 12.412 *dictamnum* genetrix *Cretaea* carpit *ab Ida*

A. 12.942 *balteus* et notis fulserunt cingula *bullis*

E. 2.30? *haedorum*que gregem viridi compellere *hibisco!*

E. 8.83 *Daphnis* me malus urit, ego hanc in *Daphnide laurum*

(Bartelink [1965] 53 cites the framing wordplay at 7.791 argumentum—Argus)

words connected etymologically start and finish the line.[339] An example from A. 7.738 is a little less explicit, but quite clear: *Sarrastis populos et quae rigat aequora Sarnus.* Clearly here either the Sarrastes were named after the river Sarnus, or vice versa, or perhaps both were named after the same thing—Servius suggests a river back in their Peloponnesian homeland.

A. 7.538–39 presents framing etymologizing that is less explicit, but no less certain:

Quinque greges illi balantum, quina redibant
*armenta* et terram centum vertebat *aratris*

Varro tells us that *armenta,* "cattle," are so called because the ancient ones raised them for plowing, *ad arandum.*

While noting that etymologizing sometimes frames a line we should remember that etymologizing mainly involves nouns and adjectives, which have a tendency to occur at the start and end of lines.

### *2.8a. Passage Frame*

Somewhat more tentatively, I would suggest that Vergil also uses words connected etymologically to "frame" a sentence, passage, or "paragraph," with such words at the beginning or end of the lines that begin or end the passage.[340] In the five-line sentence at A. 7.59–63, the name of the Lauren-

339. This is a little like framing a line with a noun-adjective pair. On etymological framing in Lucretius see Snyder (1980) 86; she also comments on the tendency to put words involved in etymological wordplay at the beginning or ends of lines (see in sect. 2.9).

340. **Features list no. 8a: passage frame**

A. 7.59–63 *laurus* erat tecti medio in penetralibus altis
sacra comam multosque metu servata per annos,
quam pater inventam, primas cum conderet arces,
ipse ferebatur Phoebo sacrasse Latinus,
*Laurentis*que ab ea nomen posuisse colonis.

A. 7.623–31 *ardet* inexcita Ausonia atque immobilis ante;
pars pedes ire parat campis, pars arduus altis
pulverulentus equis furit; omnes arma requirunt.
. . . . . . . . . . . . . . . . . . . . . . . . . . . . . . . . . . . . .
adeo magnae positis incudibus urbes
tela novant, Atina potens Tiburque superbum,
*Ardea* Crustumerique et turrigerae Antemnae.

A. 7.761–77 ibat et Hippolyti proles pulcherrima bello,
*Virbius,* insignem quem mater Aricia misit,
. . . . . . . . . . . . . . . . . . . . . . . . . . . . . .
at Trivia Hippolytum secretis alma recondit
sedibus et nymphae Egeriae nemorique relegat,

tians is explicitly connected with the laurel; *laurus* is the first word of 59, *Laurentis* the first word of 63. The effect is partly visual, although the highlighting/italics by which I call attention to the words in question might be considered a type of cheating. Less explicitly, Vergil seems to suggest at A. 7.623–31 a connection between the verb *ardet* at the start of 623 and the name of Turnus' city *Ardea* at the start of 731. At G. 1.160–62, a connection seems to be suggested between *arma* at the end of 160 and *aratri* at the end of 162; this is not much different from the framing of A. 7.539 by *armenta* and *aratris* mentioned just above.

More certainly, framing of a paragraph occurs in the glossing of the flower *amellus* at G. 4.271–78; the flower's name ends the first line, and the name of the river Mella comes at the end of the last:

> est etiam flos in pratis cui nomen *amello*
> fecere agricolae, facilis quaerentibus herba;
> namque uno ingentem tollit de caespite silvam
> aureus ipse, sed in foliis, quae plurima circum
> funduntur, violae sublucet purpura nigrae;
> saepe deum nexis ornatae torquibus arae;
> asper in ore sapor; tonsis in vallibus illum
> pastores et curua legunt *prope flumina Mellae.*

At A. 7.761–77, the repetition of the name Virbius at the start (second line) and finish of the story makes the name almost frame the lines; Vergil is alluding to the derivation of the name from *bis vir.*

*Aeneid* 12 presents a complicated example, where we see suppression, two types of slightly imperfect framing, and playful correction of the etymological tradition. This example is also a case where some odd use of language by Vergil is an important clue.

---

| | |
|---|---|
| | solus ubi in silvis Italis ignobilis aevum<br>exigeret versoque ubi nomine *Virbius* esset. |
| A. 12.411–19 | (quoted in text) |
| G. 1.160–62 | dicendum et quae sint duris agrestibus *arma,*<br>quis sine nec potuere seri nec surgere messes:<br>vomis et inflexi primum grave robur *aratri.* |
| G. 2.238–47? | *salsa* autem tellus et quae perhibetur *amara*<br>(frugibus infelix ea, nec mansuescit arando<br>nec Baccho genus aut pomis sua nomina servat)<br>tale dabit specimen. . . .<br>at sapor indicium faciet manifestus et ora<br>tristia temptantum sensu torquebit *amaro.* |
| G. 4.271–78 | (quoted in text). |

Hic Venus indigno nati concussa dolore
*dictamnum* genetrix *Cretaea* carpit *ab Ida,*
puberibus caulem foliis et flore comantem
purpureo; non illa feris incognita capris
gramina, cum tergo volucres haesere sagittae.
hic Venus obscuro faciem circumdata nimbo
detulit, hoc fusum labris splendentibus *amnem*
inficit occulte medicans, spargitque salubris
*ambrosiae* sucos et odoriferam *panaceam*

(12.411–19)

Venus uses the plant *dictamnum* to heal Aeneas' thigh wound. Commentators offer only weak suggestions to explain why Vergil uses the word *amnis,* "stream," in 417 of the water used to cleanse Aeneas' wound; I see etymologizing. In 412, *dictamnum* genetrix *Cretaea* carpit *ab Ida,* Vergil gives the name of the herb, then in explaining where it comes from alludes to the etymology, for *Cretaea carpit ab Ida* suggests the other famous Cretan mountain, Dicte, which the etymological tradition says gave the name to the herb. Thus the line is framed by the word *dictamnum* and the words that allude to its etymology. This frame is, as it were, borrowed from Aratus' *Phaenomena,* where Aratus plays, or at least was thought to have played, with the names of the herb and of the mountain, in a passage that also mentions Ida. At *Phaenomena* 32–33, Aratus speaks of the child Zeus, κουρίζοντα / ΔΙΚΤΩΙ ἐν εὐώδει, ὄρεος σχεδὸν Ἰδαίοιο (playing in fragrant "dicton," near the Idaean mountain). Most editors correct δίκτῳ to Δίκτῃ. But the mountain Dicte, as Strabo points out, is not at all near Mount Ida, and a scholiast reports that some understood the word δίκτον to be a shortened form for δίκταμνον, the plant. Aratus, who had no need to distinguish a proper from a common noun, may well be playfully obscuring the matter, so that only the learned who know the location of Dicte and Ida will understand his use of δίκτον. Or, with no need to choose an upper- or lowercase delta, Aratus may be using a word that could refer either to the mountain or to the herb. That Vergil is alluding to Aratus' wordplay seems likely in view of the position of the key words in Aratus' and Vergil's lines:

**ΔΙΚΤΩΙ** ἐν εὐώδει, ὄρεος σχεδὸν Ἰδαίοιο
**dictamnum** genetrix Cretaea carpit ab **Ida**

Vergil, however, goes further, in a way that only a Latin poet could. By his unusual use of *amnis* in 12.417, Vergil derives *dictamnum* from *Dicte* +

*amnis*. In 417, *hoc* refers to the *dictamnum;* without the pronoun the phrase would be ***dictamno*** *fusum labris splendentibus* ***amnem.*** There is thus in 417 a kind of suppressed pun. Looking at the passage as whole, the words *dictamnum* and *Cretaea carpit ab Ida* in 412, together with *amnem* in 417, in a loose sense can be said to frame the passage.

The examples in this section, besides illustrating this framing technique, also push the boundaries of how far apart words involved in etymological wordplay may be. I believe each example is legitimate, but it is clear that the greater the distance between words, the harder it is for the reader to see potential etymological connections.

## 2.9. Vertical Juxtaposition in Consecutive Lines

Vertical juxtaposition has been mentioned in the discussion of Greek etymologizing and is used several times by Vergil,[341] in both explicit and

341. **Features list no. 9: juxtaposition of words connected etymologically at the beginning or end of consecutive lines**

| | |
|---|---|
| A. 1.336–38? | virginibus Tyriis mos est gestare pharetram |
| | *purpureo*que alte suras vincire coturno |
| | *Punica* regna vides, Tyrios et Agenoris urbem |
| A. 1.367–68 | mercatique solum, facti de nomine *Byrsam,* |
| | *taurino* quantum possent circumdare *tergo* |
| A. 3.226–27 | *Harpyiae* et magnis quatiunt clangoribus alas |
| | *diripiunt*que dapes |
| A. 4.1–2 | at regina gravi iamdudum saucia *cura* |
| | vulnus alit venis et caeco carpitur *igni* |
| A. 5.122–23 | Scyllaque *Cloanthus* |
| | caerulea, genus unde tibi, Romane *Cluenti* |
| A. 7.56–57? | Turnus, avis atavisque potens, quem *regia coniunx* |
| | adiungi generum miro properabat *amore* |
| A. 8.330–31 | tum reges asperque immani corpore *Thybris,* |
| | a quo post Itali fluvium cognomine *Thybrim* |
| A. 8.343–44 | gelida monstrat sub rupe *Lupercal* |
| | Parrhasio dictum Panos de more *Lycaei* |
| A. 8.345–46 | nec non et sacri monstrat nemus *Argileti* |
| | testaturque locum et *letum* docet hospitis *Argi* |
| A. 10.324–27 | tu quoque, flaventem *prima lanugine malas* |
| | dum sequeris Clytium infelix, nova gaudia, *Cydon,* |
| A. 12.617–19? | attulit hunc illi caecis terroribus *aura* |
| | commixtum clamorem, arrectasque impulit *auris* |
| | confusae sonus urbis et inlaetabile murmur |
| A. 12.800–802 | desine iam tandem precibusque inflectere nostris, |
| | ne te tantus edit tacitam dolor et mihi *curae* |

implicit etymologies.[342] It appears three times in the explicit derivations of the place name Tiber, Lupercal, and Argiletum presented by Evander in his speech to Aeneas in *Aeneid* 8:

> tum reges asperque immani corpore *Thybris,*
> a quo post Itali fluvium cognomine *Thybrim* . . .
> . . . . . . . . . . . . . . . . . . . . . . . . . . . . . .
> . . . gelida monstrat sub rupe **Lupercal**
> Parrhasio dictum Panos de more **Lycaei.**
> nec non et sacri monstrat nemus Argileti
> testaturque locum et letum docet hospitis Argi.
>
> (8.330–31, 343–46)

This is largely a visual rather than an aural technique, but meter also makes it possible to function aurally as well. *Aeneid* 4 begins with lines that end with the words *cura* and *igni:*

> at regina gravi iamdudum saucia *cura*
> vulnus alit venis et caeco carpitur *igni.*

The fiery nature of Dido's *cura* is reinforced by allusion to an etymology found in both Varro and Servius: *cura . . . quod cor urit.* A similar wordplay,

---

saepe tuo dulci tristes ex ore *recursent*

E. 3.109–10 et vitula tu dignus et hic, et quisquis *amores*
aut metuet dulcis aut experietur *amaros*

G. 1.109–12 illa cadens raucum per levia murmur
saxa ciet, scatebrisque *ar*entia temperat *ar*va.
quid qui, ne gravidis procumbat culmus *ar*istis,
luxuriem segetum tenera depascit in herba . . .

G. 2.391–93 complentur vallesque cavae saltusque profundi
et quocumque deus circum caput egit *honestum.*
ergo rite suum Baccho dicemus *honorem*

G. 3.343–45 omnia secum
*armentarius* Afer agit, tectumque laremque
*arma*que Amyclaeumque canem Cressamque pharetram.

Compare also Lucr. 1.140–42
sed tua me virtus tamen et sperata voluptas
*suavis* amicitiae quemvis efferre laborem
*suadet* et inducit noctes vigilare serenas

and 2.942–43 contulit inter se motus, quibus *omnituentes*
accensi sensus animantem quamque *tuentur.*

342. Cf. Weber (1990) 209–14, who notes Vergil's tendency "to juxtapose related words vertically," Snyder (1980) 86, O'Hara (1990b) 371–72 and (1992) 53–54.

focusing not on the *urit* element of the element but on the root *cor,* appears in Lucretius, at the start of his discussion of the harmful effects of erotic passion, perhaps not coincidentally at the end of consecutive lines:

> hinc illaec primum Veneris dulcedinis in *cor*
> stillavit gutta et successit frigida *cura.*
>
> (4.1059–60)

In A 3.226–27, Vergil starts one line with the name Harpies, and the next with the verb *diripiunt,* clearly glossing their name by reference to ἁρπάζω, "snatch."

> *Harpyiae* et magnis quatiunt clangoribus alas
> *diripiunt*que dapes

## 2.10. Changes of Names or Alternate Names

Etymological wordplay often involves names that have been changed, or persons, places, or things called different names by different peoples.[343] For

343. **Features list no. 10: metonomasia or changed or alternate names**

| | |
|---|---|
| A. 1.108–110 | tris Notus abreptas in saxa latentia torquet<br>(saxa vocant Itali mediis quae in fluctibus *Aras,*<br>*dorsum* immane mari summo) |
| A. 1.267–68 | at puer Ascanius, cui nunc cognomen *Iulo*<br>additur (*Ilus* erat, dum res stetit *Ilia* regno) |
| A. 1.317? | *volucremque* fuga praevertitur *Hebrum* (Rhombus) |
| A. 1.530–33 = 3.163–66 | est locus, *Hesperiam* Grai cognomine dicunt,<br>terra antiqua, potens armis atque ubere glaebae;<br>Oenotri coluere viri; nunc fama minores<br>*Italiam* dixisse ducis de nomine *gentem.* |
| A. 2.469–75 | (Pyrrhus, Neoptolemus) |
| A. 3.210? | *Strophades* Graio stant nomine dictae |
| A. 3.693–94 | Plemyrium undosum; *nomen dixere* priores / Ortygiam |
| A. 4.159? | optat aprum, aut fulvum descendere monte *leonem* (Leontodamas, Ascanius) |
| A. 7.206–8? | Auruncos ita ferre senes, his ortus ut agris<br>*Dardanus* Idaeas Phrygiae penetrarit ad urbes<br>*Threiciam*que *Samum,* quae nunc *Samothracia* fertur |
| A. 7.774–77 | at Trivia Hippolytum secretis alma recondit<br>sedibus et nymphae Egeriae nemorique relegat,<br>solus ubi in silvis Italis ignobilis aevum<br>exigeret versoque ubi nomine *Virbius* esset |
| A. 8.322–23 | *Latium*que vocari / *maluit,* his quoniam latuisset tutus in oris |

such *metonomasia* the extensive Alexandrian precedent is most clear.[344] Callimachus, who wrote the treatises *Local Nomenclature* and *Foundations of Cities and Islands and Their Changes of Names,* explains how the name of the island is changed from its "old" name Asteria to Delos (*Hymn* 4.36–54), and how a city is called Exile City by some, Polae by others (*Aet.* fr. 11). Apollonius tells how after the Boreads "turned back" from their pursuit of the Harpies, the name of the islands where they did so is changed from Plotae to Strophades (*Arg.* 2.295–97). Rhianus explains how Thessaly was called first Pyrrhaia, then Haemonia, then Thessaly (fr. 25.1–5).[345] In Vergil's poem on the origins of the Roman people, *metonomasia* is a frequent con-

---

A. 8.328–32 tum manus Ausonia et gentes venere Sicanae,
saepius et nomen posuit Saturnia tellus;
tum reges *asper*que immani corpore *Thybris,*
a quo post Itali fluvium cognomine *Thybrim*
diximus; amisit verum vetus Albula nomen
A. 11.542–43 matrisque vocavit / nomine Casmillae mutata parte Camillam
G. 3.147–48 volitans, cui nomen asilo
Romanum est, oestrum Grai vertere vocantes

344. Cf. Hollis (1992) 278–79, Shechter (1975) 378, and Horsfall (1991) 113 and (1991c) 32, with further references.

345. Callim. *Hymn*
4.36–38 οὔνομα δ' ἦν τοι
Ἀστερίη τὸ παλαιόν, ἐπεὶ βαθὺν ἥλαο τάφρον
οὐρανόθεν φεύγουσα Διὸς γάμον ἀστέρι ἴση
4.51–54 ἡνίκα δ' Ἀπόλλωνι γενέθλιον οὖδας ὑπέσχες,
τοῦτό τοι ἀντημοιβὸν ἁλίπλοοι οὔνομ' ἔθεντο,
οὕνεκεν οὐκέτ' ἄδηλος ἐπέπλεες, ἀλλ' ἐνὶ πόντου
κύμασιν Αἰγαίοιο ποδῶν ἐνεθήκαο ῥίζας
4.268–69 δυσήροτος, ἀλλ' ἀπ' ἐμεῖο
Δήλιος Ἀπόλλων κεκλήσεται
5.41–42 σὲ δέ, δαῖμον, ἀπορρώγεσσιν ἔθηκεν
ἐν πέτραις, αἷς νῦν οὔνομα Παλλατίδες
Apoll. Rhod. 2.295–97 οἱ δ' ὅρκῳ εἴξαντες ὑπέστρεφον ἂψ ἐπὶ νῆα
σώεσθαι Στροφάδας δὲ μετακλείουσ' ἄνθρωποι
νήσους τοῖο ἕκητι, πάρος Πλωτὰς καλέοντες
Rhian. fr. 25.1–5 Πυρραίην ποτὲ τήν γε παλαιότεροι καλέεσκον
Πύρρης Δευκαλίωνος ἀπ' ἀρχαίης ἀλόχοιο,
Αἱμονίην δ' ἐξαῦτις ἀφ' Αἵμονος, ὅν ῥα Πελασγὸς
γείνατο φέρτατον υἱόν· ὁ δ' αὖ τέκε Θεσσαλὸν Αἵμων,
τοῦ δ' ἄπο Θεσσαλίην λαοὶ μετεφημίξαντο
Euphor. fr. 34.1–3 Ἀκτῆς δὲ παροίτερα φωνηθείσης
οἳ μὲν δὴ ἐνέπουσι καὶ Ἀσίδα κικλήσκεσθαι,
οἳ δὲ Ποσειδάωνος ἐπώνυμον αὐδηθῆναι.

Cf. too Enn. *Alex.* fr. 64 J (= 38 R = 53 V): quapropter Parim pastores nunc Alexandrum vocant.

cern, as are alternate names. Before Jupiter's prophecy explains that the Julian *gens* is named for Iulus, it tells at A. 1.267–68 how the cognomen Iulus is given to him, instead of the Ilus that recalls Ilium:

> at puer Ascanius, cui nunc cognomen *Iulo*
> additur (*Ilus* erat, dum res stetit *Ilia* regno)

Several passages discussing different names for Italy broadly resemble Rhianus' verses on Thessaly. The prophecy of Helenus at A. 3.163–66, and the words of Ilioneus at 1.530–33, tell of the names of the land the Trojans seek: *est locus, Hesperiam Grai cognomine dicunt, / . . . nunc fama minores / Italiam dixisse ducis de nomine gentem.* In Evander's words to Aeneas at A. 8.322–23, the statement that Saturn "preferred" to call Italy Latium *(Latiumque vocari / maluit)* implies that the name was changed from an earlier one. A few lines later Evander mentions a series of name changes, including those of both the land, and its major river:

> tum manus Ausonia et gentes venere Sicanae,
> saepius et nomen posuit Saturnia tellus;
> tum reges *asper*que immani corpore *Thybris,*
> a quo post Itali fluvium cognomine *Thybrim*
> diximus; amisit verum vetus Albula nomen.
>
> (A. 8.328–32)

I have mentioned how Vergil calls attention to the name *Arae* at A. 1.108–110 by alluding to another name for these rocks, Back. In glossing the name Plemyrium at 3.693, Vergil also mentions an older name: *Plemyrium undosum; nomen dixere priores / Ortygiam.* The glossing of the name Virbius at A. 7.761–77 calls attention to the fact that his name has been changed from Hippolytus: *versoque ubi nomine Virbius esset.* At G. 3.147–48, the learned discussion of the name for gadfly distinguishes Greek and Roman names and probably alludes to another Greek name.

### *2.10a. Changes Marked by the Word* Nunc

The word *nunc*[346] marks changes of names, the giving of a new name where

346. **Features list no. 10a:** *nunc* in etymologizing and naming

A. 1.267–68 at puer Ascanius, cui *nunc* cognomen Iulo / additur

A. 1.530–33 est locus, Hesperiam Grai cognomine dicunt,
terra antiqua, potens armis atque ubere glaebae;
Oenotri coluere viri; *nunc* fama minores

the old name is not mentioned, and, in *aitia,* names that survive to the present time.[347]

## 2.11. Etymologizing with Languages Other Than Latin and Greek

We have seen examples of wordplay in languages other than Latin and Greek already, such as in the reverse gloss of the Sabine adjective *Hernicus* in A. 7.684 *Hernica saxa colunt.*[348] The material has also been discussed in

---

| | |
|---|---|
| | Italiam dixisse ducis de nomine gentem |
| A. 5.602 | Troiaque nunc pueri, Troianum dicitur agmen |
| A. 6.234–35 | monte sub aerio, qui *nunc* Misenus ab illo<br>dicitur aeternumque tenet per saecula nomen |
| A. 6.776 | haec tum nomina erunt, *nunc* sunt sine nomine terrae |
| A. 7.3 | et *nunc* servat honos sedem tuus |
| A. 7.208 | Threiciamque Samum, quae *nunc* Samothracia fertur |
| A. 7.412 | *nunc* magnum manet Ardea nomen |
| A. 7.707–8 | Clausus . . . / Claudia *nunc* a quo diffunditur et tribus et gens |
| A. 12.134 | At Iuno ex summo (qui *nunc* Albanus habetur . . .) |

Cf. Enn. *Alex*. fr. 64 J (= 38 R = 53 V) quapropter Parim pastores *nunc* Alexandrum vocant; Callim. *Hymn* 5.42 (cited by Norden [1957] 197–98) ἐν πέτραις, αἷς νῦν οὔνομα Παλλατίδες; Apoll. Rhod. 4.1153–54 κεῖνο καὶ εἰσέτι νῦν ἱερὸν κληΐζεται Ἄντρον / Μηδείης.

347. For such expressions in Greek aetiological poetry cf. Zanker (1987) 16, Bing (1988) 71 n. 34, and above in section 1.4.

348. **Features list no. 11: etymologizing with languages other than Latin and Greek**

A. 1.12–13? urbs *antiqua* fuit (Tyrii tenuere coloni) / *Karthago* (Punic)
A. 1.298 novae . . . Karthaginis (Punic)
A. 1.366 moenia surgentemque *novae Karthaginis* arcem (Punic)
A. 1.367–68 mercatique solum, facti de nomine *Byrsam,*
*taurino* quantum possent circumdare *tergo* (Punic)
A. 1.522 o regina, *novam* cui condere Iuppiter *urbem* (Punic)
A. 4.211 *femina,* quae nostris *errans* in finibus urbem (Punic)
A. 4.247 *Atlantis duri* (N. Africa?)
A. 4.260? Aenean fundantem arces ac tecta *novantem* (Punic)
A. 4.670 *Karthago* aut *antiqua* Tyros (Punic)
A. 6.450–51 inter quas Phoenissa recens a vulnere *Dido* / *errabat* (Punic)
A. 7.56, etc.? Turnus (Etruscan)
A. 7.517 *sulpurea Nar* albus *aqua* (Sabine)
A. 7.684 Hernica saxa colunt (Sabine)
A. 7.740 et quos *maliferae* despectant moenia *Abellae* (Italic?)
A. 7.803–4 etc.? *Camilla* (Cretan?)
A. 9.570? *Lucetium* portae subeuntem *ignisque ferentem* (Oscan)
A. 12.134? At Iuno ex *summo* (qui nunc *Albanus* habetur . . .) ("pre-Indo-European"?)
A. 12.539–40 nec di texere *Cupencum* / Aenea veniente sui (Sabine)
E. 1.10 ludere quae vellem *calamo* permisit agresti (Italic-Doric)

Bartelink's fine chapter "Etymologizing of (Allusion to, Explanatory Translation of) Greek or Other Foreign Words."[349] Not all the examples cited by Servius must be correct, but there are at least possible examples of wordplay involving Punic, Etruscan, Sabine, Oscan, Scythian, an unspecified North African language, and other words of uncertain Indo-European or even pre-Indo-European tongues. Several times Vergil seems clearly to play on the Punic meaning of the name Carthage, New Town, mentioned explicitly by Livy. The *Etymologicum Magnum* and Timaeus tell us that Dido's name meant "wanderer" in Punic, and Vergil seem to show awareness of this etymology (see below). The learned Catalogue of Forces in *Aeneid* 7 glosses two Sabine names, *Nar,* which means "sulfur," at A. 7.517 *sulpurea Nar albus aqua* (borrowed from Ennius), and *Hernicus,* discussed above, and offers at 7.740 the well-known gloss *maliferae . . . Abellae,* which seems to suggest knowledge of an Indo-European word that is the ancestor or cousin of the word "apple." I have mentioned the possible gloss in the name Alps by Catullus and Vergil; in some passages dealing with the name Alba Vergil may suggest a connection not with the Latin word for "white" but with this same Gallic or pre-Indo-European root meaning "high, lofty" (see on G. 3.474 and A. 8.328–32).

## 2.12. Clustering

This needs little discussion, and most of the passages involved have been mentioned already. They include the sailing past Sicily at A. 3.692–708, where Vergil may be indebted to lost writings of Varro, and to the discussion of Sicilian cities in Callimachus' *Aetia* (see on A. 3.693–94); the parade of heroes in the underworld at A. 6.756–846; the Catalogue of Forces at A. 7.641–817, and Evander's tales of local history at A. 8.314–58.

## 2.13. Playing with the Tradition, or Allusion to Earlier Etymologizing

Vergil follows, alludes to, comments on, or "corrects" poetic etymological precedent, often in the case of words for which the tradition presents more than one possible etymology.[350] This may involve suggesting an etymology different from those given before, choosing between those offered before, or

E. 1.61–62? *exsul* / aut Ararim *Parthus* bibet aut Germania Tigrim (Scythians)

G. 3.474 aerias Alpis ("Gallic")

349. Bartelink (1965) 85–91 (I translate his chapter title); cf. also Ahl (1985) 60–63, Horsfall (1991) 20.

350. Much recent work on Augustan poets has described their fondness for what has been called "correction," "commentary," or "oppositio in imitando"; on Vergil see esp. Thomas

suggesting two different etymologies for the same word. The survey of etymologizing before Vergil showed that in classical Greek some etymologies were treated by several authors, at times with alternate derivations offered. Among the Alexandrians, this practice became almost professionalized, as poets offered either serious or playful suggestions and arguments about which etymology was correct. In a brief discussion of Catullus, we saw that he offers a learned gloss on the name of the ship Argo, which must be seen in the context of earlier glosses, one explicit in Ennius, another implicit in Apollonius of Rhodes. For Vergil, since my belief is that most of the examples of etymologizing endorsed in the catalogue deal with etymologies known in Vergil's time, it would be pointless to compile a list here of instances in which he plays with the tradition in one way or another. The next few paragraphs, then, will present a few examples where his use of the tradition seems to me interesting or informative and will give only an indication of the extent of Vergil's borrowings from a few authors. My survey of earlier etymologizing frequently commented on examples of wordplay that Vergil would imitate; this is especially true for Alexandrian poets. Scanning that section of the introduction looking for the word "Vergil" in the text will provide the information that might have been included in an overly cumbersome list here.

My discussion of the etymological signpost noted that at G. 1.137–38, Vergil offers subtle glosses of the star names Pleiades (from πλέω) and Hyades (from ὕω), and a single-epithet gloss in *pluviasque Hyadas* at A. 1.744 and 3.516. We have evidence of a wide variety of suggested derivations for both words; not all of these must predate Vergil, but I believe most do, and we have evidence of both Cicero and his freedman Tiro dismissing one derivation in favor of that from ὕω. Vergil's lines argue for the etymology from sailing weather for both words and also allude to passages in both Homer and Aratus. Later Ovid will comment on Vergil's gloss; see below, and on G. 1.137–38.

At A. 3.210, Vergil's *Strophades Graio stant nomine dictae* alludes to but does not explain the derivation from στροφή, "turning," of the name of these islands; Vergil's lines look to Apollonius of Rhodes, who explains the *aition* (from the story of the Boreads' "turning back" after pursuit of the Harpies) at *Arg.* 2.295–97. Several times in this section of A. 3 Vergilian etymologizing borrows from or points to Apollonius.[351] I have mentioned Vergil's gloss

(1982a) and (1986), Clausen (1987), Conte (1986), Cairns (1989), and Farrell (1991), who begins with a survey of earlier work. For Alexandrian poets see esp. the long note at Bing (1988) 73 n. 39.

351. I first observed this in O'Hara (1990b).

at 3.226–27 of the name Harpy, which comes directly from Apollonius. At 3.271 *Neritos ardua* glosses the name of the island (= immense) in a way that looks to Apollonius' use of the rare archaic word νήριτος. In 3.280 *Actia . . . litora* has been mentioned as a gloss in which the noun explains the adjective; here Vergil alludes to the original meaning of Apollo's epithet *Actius* (of the shore) as it appeared in an *aition* in the *Argonautica.* Other possible allusions to or borrowings from etymologizing by Apollonius include Vergil's treatments of Apollo Actius (A. 3.280), Erato (A.7.37–41), the Ceraunian mountains (G. 1.332), Herakles (A. 8.287–88), Dionysus (A. 6.805), Hera allegorized as ἀήρ (cf. A. 12.791–92), Avernus (A. 6.237–42), and the Rhipaen mountains (G. 3.382). Vergilian etymologizing that recalls an Apollonian model that itself has no etymological wordplay will be noted below.

At E. 6.74–77, Vergil may offer both a common and a rare etymologial connection for the name Scylla:

> Quid loquar aut ***Scyllam*** Nisi, quam fama secuta est
> candida succinctam *latrantibus* inguina monstris
> Dulichias **vexasse** rates et gurgite in alto
> a! timidos nautes *canibus* lacerasse marinis

The word *latrantibus* suggests an etymology connecting Scylla with σκύλαξ, "puppy, yelping," here as in Homer and Callimachus. But *vexasse* in line 75, a word criticized by some ancient readers as inappropriately mild for what Scylla does to ships, may connect the name with σκύλλω, "molest, trouble, annoy," although only one late source offers this derivation.

At G. 3.280–81, we have seen that Vergil's lines on *hippomanes* both allude to the traditional etymology, from "madness of mares," and also suggest a new etymology involving the word *mano,* "flow, run, exude."[352] At A. 12.411–19, discussed in the section above on framing, the extensive gloss of the word *dictamnum* includes a reworking of part of Aratus' lines on *dictamnum* at *Phaenomena* 32–33.

At G. 4.149–52, with the phrase *canoros / Curetum sonitus crepitantiaque aera* Vergil seems to allude to the derivation, found in both Callimachus and Aratus, of Curetes from κουρίζω, "to make infant sounds"; Lucretius also seems to gloss the name by mentioning *pueri* (= κοῦροι).

Vergil's borrowings from Callimachus are probably more extensive than our fragments of that poet indicate: they may include Vergil's treatment of

352. Thomas (1988) ad loc.: "This is Vergil at his most Alexandrian, subsuming and reshaping the tradition."

Apollo's epithets *Actius* (A. 3.280), *Nomius* (G. 3.1–3), and *Delius* (A. 6.11–12), the town of Aenus (A. 3.17–18), Dictynna and Dicte (E. 6.55–60 and A. 12.411–19), the Sicilian towns Aeneas passes at the end of A. 3 (see on A. 3.693–94), the names Acontius (E. 10.60), Ciris (G. 1.404–9), Hippolytus or Virbius (A. 7.761–77), Herakles (A. 8.287–88), the Couretes (above), Scylla (E. 6.74–77), Samothrace (A. 7.206–8), Dodona and Pelasgian (G. 1.149), and the rocks called Arae (A. 1.108–10).

Other examples of etymologizing possibly indebted to Lucretius include wordplay with *animos* (spirits, animosity) and ἄνεμος (wind) at A. 1.56–57, *cura* and *cor* at A. 1.208–9, *fretum* and *ferveo* at G. 1.326–27, and *avius* and *avis* at G. 2.328, and the glosses of *Avernus* at A. 6.237–42, and Scipio at A. 6.842–43, where Ennian precedent may be more significant for both Lucretius and Vergil.

I have noted, in the section on names of gods, that when Venus is called *mater Acidalia* at A. 1.715–22, the epithet suggests both *curae* and the arrows of Cupid (both ἀκίδες). This epithet recalls two models, in different ways, and is the subject of later learned commentary by Ovid, which will be discussed below.[353] One model is the scene in Apoll. Rhod. 3.111–66, where Aphrodite sends Eros after Medea, but Apollonius' Eros uses his traditional bow and arrow, while Vergil's Cupid puts away his weapons to use the more insidious trick of assuming the identity of Ascanius. The etymological significance of the epithet Acidalia brings the notion of arrows back, or at least alludes to what has been omitted from the model. The other model is in Catullus 64, where the lament for the sorrows that Venus has brought to Ariadne refers to Venus as "Erycina, sowing thorny cares in her heart" (*spinosas Erycina serens in pectore curas* [64.72]). The *spinosae curae* that Venus sows in Ariadne's heart are much like the ἀκίδες implied by Vergil's *mater Acidalia* and provide the epithet Erycina with a learned gloss, playing on the resemblance (despite the difference in vowel quantity) between Erycina and the word *ericius*, "(spiked) hedgehog," or "spiked instrument of war." Like Vergil's *mater Acidalia,* Venus Erycina is emphatically described as a producer of "thorny cares."

## 2.14. Later Comment

At times Vergil is the target, rather than the author, of poetic allusion calling attention to the tradition of etymology wordplay, as later authors allude to Vergilian wordplay in a way that functions almost as scholarly commentary.

353. For more detailed discussion of this example see O'Hara (1990a) and (1996).

These examples are valuable as evidence both for near-contemporary reaction to Vergil's etymologizing, and as further instances of poets showing awareness of and playing with the tradition. This topic deserves more space than I can give it here; this section will provide a few illustrative examples from Ovid,[354] and even for Ovid my discussion must be less than fully

354. **Features list no. 14: Ovidian comment on Vergilian etymologizing**
(This list offers both certain and uncertain examples; of the latter, there are some it is not certain that both poets are etymologizing, and perhaps some where both are clearly etymologizing, but it is not certain that Ovid is commenting on Vergil. In this list each unindented citation from Vergil begins a new example.)

A. 1.87? clamorque virum *stridor*que *rudentum*
  A. 3.561–62 primusque *rudentem* / contorsit laevas proram Palinurus ad undas
  *Met.* 11.495 quippe sonant clamore viri, stridore rudentes
A. 1.288 *Iulius,* a magno demissum nomen *Iulo*
  *F.* 4.39–40 nomen *Iuli,* / unde domus Teucros *Iulia* tangit avos
A. 1.493 bellatrix, audetque *viris* concurrere *virgo.*
  *Met.* 4.681–82 primo silet illa nec audet / adpellare *virum virgo*
A. 1.720 matris *Acidaliae*
  *Met.* 5.363–68 (Erycina)
A. 2.682–84, 692–94? *(comas . . . stella facem ducens)*
  A. 8.681 laeta vomunt *patrium*que aperitur vertice *sidus*
  A. 10.270–72 ardet apex capiti . . . non secus ac liquida si quando nocte *cometae*
  *Met.* 15.746–50 in sidus vertere novum stellamque comantem (sc. Caesarem)
A. 3.271 Dulichiumque Sameque et *Neritos ardua* saxis
  *Tr.* 1.5.57–58 pro duce *Neritio* docti mala nostra poetae
    scribite *Neritio* nam mala *plura* tuli
A. 3.660–61 lanigerae comitantur oves; ea *sola* voluptas / *solamen*que mali
  *Met.* 1.359–60 quo *sola* timorem / ferre modo posses? quo *consolante* dolores?
A. 3.701–2? campique *Geloi, / immanis*que *Gela fluvii* cognomine dicta
  *F.* 4.470 et te, verticibus non adeunde Gela.
A. 4.302–3? audito . . . *Baccho* / orgia *nocturnus*que vocat clamore Cithaeron
  G. 4.521 *nocturni*que orgia *Bacchi*
  *Ars* 1.565 *Nycteliumque* patrem *nocturnaque* sacra precare
A. 4.402–5? *formicae* farris acervum . . . praedamque per herbas / *convectant*
  *Ars* 1.93–94 *formica . . . granifero* solitum cum *vehit ore* cibum
  *Met.* 7.625 grande onus exiguo *formicas ore gerentes*
A. 5.241–43 *Portunus* . . . / impulit illa . . . / ad terram fugit et *portu* se condidit alto
  *F.* 6.546–47 in *portus* nato ius erit omne tuo,
    quem nos *Portunum,* sua lingua Palaemona dicet
A. 5.606–8 *Saturnia* Iuno / . . . / multa movens necdum antiquum *saturata* dolorem
  A. 5.781–86, 7.298–311 (Saturnia Iuno/saturata/satis)
  *Met.* 9.9.176–78 *Saturnia* . . . / corque ferum *satia* (cf. also 3.249–72?)
A. 6.570–71 continuo sontis *ultrix* accincta flagello / *Tisiphone* quatit insultans
  *Am.* 2.1.13 ulta est (Titan)
A. 6.714–15 *Lethaei* ad fluminis undam / *securos latices et longa oblivia potant*
  *Pont.* 2.4.23 securae pocula Lethes

satisfying.[355] One problem with Ovid is that when he makes wordplay found also in Vergil, he may be borrowing not from Vergil but from the *de Lingua Latina* or other works of Varro, or from the *de Significatu Verborum* of Verrius Flaccus, who probably wrote after Vergil and before Ovid (cf. above, end of sect. 1.5). Or Ovid may even be drawing on knowledge about

---

A. 6.763–65 *Silvius,* Albanum nomen, tua *postuma* proles, /
quem . . . Lavinia . . . / educet *silvis*
F. 4.41–42 Postumus hinc, qui, quod *silvis* fuit ortus in altis,
*Silvius* in Latia gente vocatus erat
A. 6.810–11 regis Romani primam qui *legibus* urbem / fundabit
*Am.* 2.17.18 *iusto . . . Numae*
A. 6.842–43 geminos, duo *fulmina belli, / Scipiadas, cladem Libyae*
*Am.* 2.1.17–20 clausit amica fores: ego cum Iove *fulmen* omisi;
excidit ingenio Iuppiter ipse meo.
Iuppiter, ignoscas: nil me tua *tela* iuvabant;
clausa tuo maius ianua *fulmen* habet
A. 6.859? tertiaque *arma* patri suspendet capta *Quirino*
G. 3.27 victorisque *arma Quirini*
F. 2.475–80 proxima lux vacua est, at tertia dicta *Quirino*
qui tenet hoc nomen (Romulus ante fuit),
sive quod hasta *'curis'* priscis est dicta Sabinis
(bellicus a telo venit in astra deus),
sive suum regi nomen posuere *Quirites,*
seu quia Romanis iunxerat ille *Cures.*
A. 7.1–4 (Caieta)
*Met.* 14.443–44 Hic me *Caietam* notae pietatis alumnus
ereptam Argolico quo debuit igne *cremavit*
A. 7.10–11 proxima *Circaeae* raduntur litora terrae,
dives inaccessos ubi *Solis filia* lucos . . .
*Met.* 14.348 nomine dicta suo *Circaea* reliquerat arva
A. 7.30–31 *Tiberinus* . . . / verticibus rapidis et multa *flavus* harena
*Met.* 2.245 *Xanthus flavusque Lycormas*
A. 7.37–41? (Erato; cf. Apoll. Rhod. 3.1–5)
F. 4.195–96 sic *Erato* . . . quod teneri nomen *Amoris* habet
*Ars* 2.16 nunc *Erato,* nam tu nomen *Amoris* habes
A. 7.411–12 locus Ardea quondam
dictus avis, et nunc *magnum* manet *Ardea* nomen
A. 7.623–31 *ardet* inexcita Ausonia atque immobilis ante; /. . . /
*Ardea* Crustumerique et turrigerae Antemnae
*Met.* 14.573–80 (city burned, then *ardea* emerges)
A. 7.709–10 . . . postquam in partem data Roma *Sabinis.*
*una ingens Amiterna cohors priscique Quirites*
F. 2.475–80 (quoted above on A. 6.859)
A. 7.720 vel cum sole novo densae *torrentur aristae*
*Her.* 5.111–12 et minus est in te quam summa pondus *arista,*
quae levis adsiduis *solibus usta* riget.

etymologizing common to every Roman schoolboy. But my research shows that Ovid alludes directly and unmistakably to Vergilian etymological wordplay more often than has been thought. Still, some examples, both in my text and especially in my longer list, may fall under the category of coincidental rather than planned resemblance.

---

A. 7.765–67 *Hippolytum* . . . turbatis *distractus equis*
F. 3.265 *Hippolytus* loris *direptus equorum*
5.309–10 *Hippolyte, . . . diripereris equis*
*Met.* 15.542–44 nomenque simul, quod possit *equorum* admonuisse, . . . / *Hippolytus*
A. 8.48 Ascanius *clari* condet cognominis *Albam*
*Met.* 14.612 *clarus* subit *Alba* Latinum
A. 8.105 una omnes *iuvenum* primi pauperque *senatus*
F. 5.63–64 nec nisi post annos patuit tunc curia *seros,*
nomen et *aetatis* mite *senatus* habet
A. 8.194 etc. semihominis Caci
F. 1.551–52 *Cacus,* Aventinae timor atque infamia silvae
non leve finitimis hospitibusque *malum*
A. 8.231–35 *Aventini* montem. . . . / *dirarum nidis domus opportuna volucrum*
F. 4.51–52 venit *Aventinus* post hos, locus unde vocatur, / mons quoque
*Met.* 14.620–21 Aventino, qui . . . eodem
monte iacet positus tribuitque vocabula monti
A. 8.287–88? qui carmine laudes / *Herculeas* et facta ferunt; ut prima *novercae* . . .
*Met.* 9.135 *Herculis* inplerant terras odiumque *novercae*
A. 8.322–23 *Latium*que vocari / maluit, his quoniam *latuisset* tutus in oris
F. 1.237–38 mansit Saturnia nomen; / dicta quoque est *Latium* terra, *latente* deo
A. 8.330–32 tum reges *asper*que immani corpore *Thybris,*
a quo post Itali fluvium cognomine *Thybrim*
diximus; amisit verum vetus Albula nomen
F. 2.389–90 Albula, quem *Tiberim* mersus *Tiberinus* in undis / reddidit
*Met.* 14.614–16 regnum *Tiberinus* ab illis
cepit et in *Tusci* demersus *fluminis* undis
nomina fecit aquae
A. 8.338–39 et *Carmentalem* Romani nomine portam
quam memorant, nymphae priscum *Carmentis* honorem,
F. 1.467 quae nomen habes a *carmine* ductum
A. 8.343–44 et gelida monstrat sub rupe *Lupercal*
Parrhasio dictum Panos de more *Lycaei*
A. 8.630–31 fecerat et viridi fetam Mavortis in *antro* / procubuisse *lupam,*
F. 2.421–24 illa (sc. *lupa*) loco nomen fecit, locus ipse *Lupercis;*
magna dati nutrix praemia lactis habet.
quid vetat Arcadio dictos de monte *Lupercos?*
Faunus in Arcadia templa *Lycaeus* habet

At times both poets allude to an etymology. Both gloss the name *Portunus,* from *portus,* though this may be coincidental (A. 5.241–43, *F.* 6.546–47). When both seem to allude to the original meaning of the rare epic word or name *Neritos* (= large), coincidence is less likely (A. 3.271, *Tr.* 1.5.57–58). Ovid seems to gloss the word for ant, *formica,* as though from *ferre micas,*

---

A. 8.357–58 hanc *Ianus* pater, hanc *Saturnus* condidit arcem;
*Ianiculum* huic, illi fuerat *Saturnia* nomen
Cf. *F.* 1.235–48
A. 8.425 Brontesque Steropesque et nudus membra Pyracmon
*F.* 4.288 Brontes et Steropes Acmonidesque solent
A. 8.663 *exsultantis Salios*
*F.* 3.387 iam dederat *Saliis* a *saltu* nomina ducta
A. 9.128–29? his *Iuppiter* ipse / *auxilium* solitum eripuit
*Am.* 2.1.19 *Iupiter,* ignoscas: nil me tua tela *iuvabunt*
A. 10.145 et *Capys* hinc nomen *Campanae* ducitur *urbi*
*F.* 4.45 ille dedit *Capyi* repetita vocabula Troiae
A. 12.521–28 ac velut . . . *ignes* /. . . / . . . non *segnius*
*Am.* 3.7.13–14 tacta tamen veluti *gelida* mea membra cicuta
*segnia* propositum destituere meum
E. 8.107 *Hylax* in limine *latrat*
Cf. *Met.* 3.224 acutae vocis *Hylactor*
E. 10.55–61? (Acontius)
*Her.* 21.211–12 mirabar quare tibi nomen *Acontius* esset;
quod faciat longe vulnus, *acumen* habes
G. 1.62–63 Deucalion vacuum *lapides* iactavit in orbem,
unde *homines* nati, *durum genus*
*Am.* 2.14.11–12 quique iterum iaceret generis primordia nostri
in vacuo *lapides* orbe, parandus erat
*Met.* 1.414 inde *genus durum* sumus experiensque laborum
G. 1.217–18 candidus auratis *aperit* cum cornibus annum / Taurus
*F.* 4.61–62, 85–87, 89 (cf. too 125ff.)
sed Veneris mensem Graio sermone notatum
auguror a *spumis* est dea dicta maris . . .
Quo non livor abit? sunt qui tibi menis honorem
eripuisse velint invideantque, Venus.
nam quia ver *aperit* tunc omnia . . . ,
*Aprilem* memorant ab *aperto* tempore dictum
G. 1.308–9? tum figere dammas / stuppea torquentem *Balearis* verbera *fundae*
*Met.* 2.727–28 Balearica plumbum / funda iacit
4.709–10 Balearica . . . / funda
G. 1.329–33 *fulmina* molitur dextra . . . ; / . . . ille flagranti /
aut Atho aut Rhodopen aut *alta Ceraunia telo* / deicit
*Am.* 2.11.19 *violenta Ceraunia*
G. 1.406, 409 illa (sc. Scylla = ciris) levem fugiens *secat* aethera pennis, /. . . /
illa levem fugiens raptim *secat* aethera pennis

even more clearly than Vergil (A. 4.402–7?, *Ars* 1.93–94, *Met.* 7.625). Both poets allude to the etymologies of the names Tisiphone (< τίσις: A. 6.571–72, *Am.* 2.1.13), Numa (< νόμοι: A. 6.808–12, *Am.* 2.17.18), and Hippolytus (*distractus equis,* A. 7.761–77; *loris direptus equorum; F.* 3.265; cf. too *F.* 5.309–10, *Met.* 15.542–44).

At times Vergil implies wordplay, and Ovid is more explicit. Vergil links *Silvius* and the woods (A. 6.763–65); Ovid is explicit: *quod silvis fuit ortus in altis, / Silvius . . . vocatus erat* (*F.* 4.41–42). Vergil juxtaposes *Carmenta* and *cecinit* (A. 8.338–39); Ovid explains: *nomen habes a carmine ductum* (*F.* 1.467). Vergil glosses with an explanatory epithet (*exsultantis Salios,* A. 8.663); Ovid is overt: *dederat Saliis a saltu nomina dicta* (*F.* 3.387). The name of the muse Erato is explicitly glossed in Apoll. Rhod. 3.1–5 and twice in Ovid (*F.* 4.196, teneri nomen *Amoris* habet, and *Ars* 2.16, nunc Erato, nam tu nomen *Amoris* habes); Ovid's explicit glosses may make us more inclined to think of the erotic connotations of the name in Vergil's invocation of Erato at A. 7.37 *(nunc age, qui reges, Erato).* At *Met.* 1.414, *inde* ***genus durum*** *sumus experiensque laborum,* Ovid borrows from G. 1.62–63, *Deucalion vacuum lapides iactavit in orbem, / unde homines nati,* ***durum genus,*** and both poets allude to the connection made between λαός, "people," and λᾶας, "stone."

Among more complicated examples, one involves the glosses of Venus' epithets Erycina in Catullus and Acidalia in Vergil, both linked to "thorny cares" as discussed just above. This seems a clear instance of Ovidian commentary. At *Met.* 5.363–68, Ovid uses the epithet *Erycina* to refer to Venus as she asks Cupid to shoot Pluto with an arrow so that he will love Persephone. Ovid's scene is directly modeled on the Venus-Cupid scene in A. 1, so Ovid uses Catullus' epithet *Erycina* as he imitates the scene in which Vergil calls Venus *Acidalia.* Ovid shows that he sees both what Vergil is doing, and that Catullus had done it before.[356]

---

*Met.* 8.150–51 vocatur / *Ciris* et a tonso est hoc nomen adepta capillo

G. 1.500? hunc saltem everso *iuvenem succurrere* saeclo

Ovid *Am.* 3.6.23 flumina debebant *iuvenes* in amore *iuvare*

G. 3.474 aerias Alpis

*Met.* 2.226 aeriaeque Alpes

G. 4.45–48 cubilia limo / unge *fovens* . . . /. . . neve rubentis / ure *foco* cancros

*F.* 6.301 *focus* a *flammis* et quod *fovet* omnia dictus

355. I discuss this topic in more depth in O'Hara (1996); I have treated some examples, including some of those given below in the text, in O'Hara (1990a) and (1992).

356. On such "double allusions" or "multiple references" see esp. Thomas (1986) 193–98, McKeown (1987) 37–45, Clausen (1987) 20 and passim; on this one O'Hara (1990a).

After Vergil glosses the star names Pleiades (from πλέω) and Hyades (from ὕω) at G. 1.137–38 *(**navita** tum stellis numeros et nomina fecit / **Pleiadas, Hyadas**),* Ovid offers commentary, at *F.* 5.163–82, of which I quote here the first four lines, and the last:

> at simul inducent obscura crepuscula noctem,
> pars Hyadum toto de *grege* nulla latet.
> ora micant Tauri septem radiantia flammis,
> *navita quas Hyadas Graius ab imbre vocat;*
> . . . *nomina fecit Hyas.*

At 166 Ovid mentions the etymology of Hyades implicit in Vergil (cf. *navita* at the start of a line in both), but in 182 he says instead that they were named for their brother Hyas. The words *nomina fecit* in 182 occur before Ovid only in the subtle Vergilian gloss to which Ovid, in the explicit style he uses more often than Vergil, is offering an alternative. But Ovid's lines also contain a third, implicit suggested derivation: in 164 *grex* is an unusual term for a group of stars, not seen before in extant Latin, and so Ovid is probably alluding to the derivation of Hyades from ὗς, "pig," found in many sources. In addition, Ovid's reference in line 167 to Bacchus as having been nursed by the Hyades *(pars Bacchum nutrisse putat)* alludes to another etymology. Euphorion fr. 14.1 and the scholia to Aratus that preserve the line tell us that Hyas was a name for Dionysus, and so the Hyades were named for having nursed him. Thus Ovid's lines allude to Vergil's etymologizing and mention or allude to three rival derivations.

At *F.* 4.87–89, *nam, quia ver aperit tunc omnia . . . Aprilem memorant ab aperto tempore dictum,* Ovid explicitly mentions the derivation of *Aprilis* from *aperio* implied by Vergil at G. 1.217–18, but Ovid is rejecting the derivation from *aperio,* favoring instead an etymology involving the name Aphrodite, to whom *F.* 4.85–132 is addressed. Porte has shown, however, that by stressing the way things open up and bloom in the spring, Ovid is at the same time arguing for the validity of both the derivation from *aperio,* and that from Aphrodite.

My last example is one of my favorites. In A. 8, Vergil offers two etymologies, one explicit and one only implicit, for the cave known as the Lupercal. Both connect it with the word *lupa,* "wolf," but Evander, as noted above in section 2.9, links the Lupercal with the Arcadian Pan Lycaeus: *et gelida monstrat sub rupe **Lupercal** / Parrhasio dictum Panos de more **Lycaei*** (A. 8.343–44). On the shield of Aeneas, however, Vergil seems to connect the Lupercal, the *antrum* in 630, with the wolf that nourished Romulus and Remus:

fecerat et viridi fetam Mavortis in *antro*
procubuisse *lupam*, geminos huic ubera circum
ludere pendentis pueros et lambere matrem
impavidos, illam tereti cervice reflexa
mulcere alternos et corpora fingere lingua.

(A. 8.630–34)

In *F.* 2.381–424, Ovid gives tentative endorsement to both theories, although he concentrates on the Romulus and Remus connection to which Vergil only alludes, with language echoing that of the Vergilian shield: *F.* 2.418, *et **fingit lingua corpora** bina sua*, recalls A. 8.634, *mulcere alternos et **corpora fingere lingua.*** Then Ovid also endorses the rival theory, which derives the name from the Arcadian Lupercal:

illa (sc. *lupa*) loco nomen fecit, locus ipse *Lupercis;*
   magna dati nutrix praemia lactis habet.
quid vetat Arcadio dictos de monte *Lupercos?*
   Faunus in Arcadia templa *Lycaeus* habet

(*F.* 2.421–24)

While at 418 Ovid echoed the Vergilian shield, here in 423–24 he echoes the Evander passage: cf. Ovid's *quid vetat Arcadio dictos de monte Lupercos? / . . . Lycaeus* with Vergil's *Lupercal / Parrhasio dictum Panos de more Lycaei* (A. 8.343–44). Just like a commentator, then, Ovid cites both Vergilian passages offering etymologies for the Lupercal; for the shield passage, he brings to the surface something only implicit, or easy to miss, in Vergil.

This section of the introduction, then, has surveyed what I have found to be the salient typical features of Vergilian etymologizing. The organizational principles that I have chosen are not the only ones possible, but I believe my survey has given a sense of what Vergil's wordplay is and is not like.

### 3. The Poetic Function of Vergilian Etymologizing

This section will treat the function of etymological wordplay in Vergil, although some attention has been given to this topic during the course of earlier parts of this introduction. It must be stressed at the start that this monograph is unlikely to provide the final word on the subject. Besides the suggestions about poetic function that I make here, I hope that this study provides both information that will enable others to reassess the function of Vergilian or other etymological wordplay, and incentive for others to conduct inquiries into how Vergil's nearly ubiquitous etymologizing interacts with the poem's complex layers of thematic suggestion. My own earlier work on the interpretation of the *Aeneid,* especially parts of my monograph on prophecy in the poem, was stimulated by the observations about Vergilian etymologizing by Bartelink and others. My strong belief is that Vergil etymologized not in order to be pedantic or to contribute to his reader's knowledge of etymologies, but because he saw etymological wordplay as one effective way of achieving some of the goals of his poems. This must be, though it has not always been, an important part of the study of etymological wordplay. But it is also a dangerous area for me if I want to avoid foisting my own fantasies about etymological wordplay onto Vergil. That an etymological wordplay would fit nicely into a larger argument about the poem is not a guarantee of authenticity. In discussing the thematic integration of poetic etymologizing, we face the danger not only of being fooled by coincidence, but of building complex interpretations on a foundation made of sand. Appropriate caution should minimize the danger, however, and discussion of the poetic function of etymological wordplay must be an integral part of the modern reassessment of Alexandrianism in Latin poetry. In this section I begin with three important general observations, before moving to a series of specific examples.

One of the most important functions of etymologizing may be the most subtle, and hardest to illustrate. For Vergil learned etymological wordplay helps create a sense of tone, style, and allegiance to a tradition. Conte has suggested that one function of learned poetic allusion is to call attention to one's own literariness, to announce, "I too am a poet."[357] Poetic etymological wordplay, especially the implicit rather than explicit wordplay, also marks the text as other than ordinary nonfictional discourse. Vergilian etymologizing makes the announcement more specific: "I too am a poet in the learned Alexandrian tradition." To engage in learned wordplay is to announce that one is writing in the tradition of Callimachus and Apollonius of Rhodes, which for my purposes includes also those learned aspects of the poetry written before them, and under their influence after them. This announcement is both a claim to a position in literary history and also an indication to the reader that scholarship must be a tool of the reader as it was a resource of the poet.

A second function of etymologizing that must be stressed, but also does not lend itself to lengthy discussion, involves what must have been one of the prime functions of any display of Alexandrian learning in an Augustan poem: pleasure for the reader. This is related to the profession of the poet's

357. Conte (1986) 42.

Alexandrianism just mentioned. Whether or not a modern critic considers Alexandrian poetry or poetics important for reading Augustan poets often depends on whether that critic thinks of reading and mastering the Alexandrian poets as a boring chore or as an exciting source of intellectual pleasure. For Vergil the latter must certainly have been the case: he must have read the Alexandrians not as would a modern graduate student nervously preparing for an exam, but as some modern musicians and filmmakers eagerly devour all specimens of good earlier work they can get their hands on. For centuries poets had been also scholars, philologists, editors, commentators, masters of the poetry that had gone before them, and interested in every aspect of mythology, geography, astronomy, ethnology, religion, and language. Neither our romantic heritage, nor our comparative lack of facility with Latin and especially Greek, nor our loss of much of the literature known to Vergil, some of which is available to us only in frustrating fragments, must blind us to this. With learned etymological wordplay, the reader who was able to read clues and recognize allusions to etymological controversy, adaptations of earlier poetic wordplay, or simply new suggestions about derivations for words must have felt a pleasure akin to that of a reader recognizing a well-constructed narrative, or spotting an allusion to an earlier poet. Joseph Farrell, in discussing some approaches to Vergilian allusion, speaks with some unease of "an aesthetic response, difficult to define, that is closely tied to the excitement of philological discovery and thus accessible only to those who revel in such abstract joys."[358] His study, like the rest of this section of my introduction, usefully turns from this "aesthetic response" to discuss what he discovers to be the thematic import of Vergilian allusion in the *Georgics*, but we should not dismiss the role of excitement, pleasure, and the joy of discovery in the reader's experience of learned poetry.

A third crucial function of much Vergilian etymological wordplay is no less Alexandrian, but thematic rather than aesthetic. This involves aetiology, or the poetry of origins, which we saw above was one of the elements of etymologizing stressed by the Alexandrians. Both the *Aeneid* and to some extent the *Georgics* are poems of origins, works that wrestle with the question of what the (Roman) world is like, and how it got to be that way. Aetiology and etymological aetiology help to explain the world of today by tracing its roots in the past; discussion of or allusion to the origins of words

358. Farrell (1991) 18. On the reader's role in recognizing etymological wordplay see Cairns (1979) 93–100; there is perhaps some exaggeration, but also much truth, in his claim that "the reader . . . was supposed . . . to be engaged while reading in constant speculation about and discovery of etymological and other verbal complexes present in the text." On the pleasures of Alexandrianism, cf. now Horsfall (1988) 49, (1991c), and especially (1991) passim.

and especially names is a part of the *Aeneid*'s larger concerns with the origins of customs, peoples, and the characteristic strengths and weaknesses of the Roman people. Examples of such aetiological etymologizing will be discussed below in this section.

The rest of this section will be devoted to explaining the thematic import of specific examples of etymological wordplay in Vergil. Conte's description of allusion as a kind of trope is useful here, for etymologizing is basically a kind of allusion. Conte speaks of the "gap produced between the immediate, surface meaning of the word or phrase in the text and the thought produced by the allusion," and of "the simultaneous coexistence of both a denotative and a connotative semiotic."[359] Poetic etymological wordplay may also function as a kind of trope offering more suggestions to the reader than is first apparent from the surface of the text. Allusion to etymology is one way to open up more levels of signification or suggestiveness, more ways to say more than one appears to be saying. Of this a number of examples follow, which illustrate different types of thematic suggestions made through etymologizing. Many involve etymologizing cited or discussed above, although some examples reappear with more detail here, and others appear first here. The catalogue also discusses thematic matters a number of times, although both here and there I have tried to limit the amount of subjective interpretive material, in order to make the monograph as broadly useful for as long a time as possible. In other words: I have not held back from making comments about thematic material but have tried not to link my work on etymologizing too intimately with the stands on controversial matters I have taken elsewhere. Judgments of my success at this may vary.

At the start of this introduction I suggested that etymological wordplay was for Vergil a part of his technique and style, along with such things as imagery. At times etymologizing functions both like and with imagery; two characteristic examples were discussed in the last section. Book 4 of the *Aeneid* begins with the image of Dido wounded and burning with love:

> at regina gravi iamdudum saucia *cura*
> vulnus alit venis et caeco carpitur *igni.*
>
> (A. 4.1–2)

The allusion, in the vertical juxtaposition of *cura* and *igni,* to the Varronian etymology *cura . . . quod cor urit,* extends and deepens the fire imagery. In

359. Conte (1986) 23–24; cf. also 40. Cf. too Zeitlin (1982) 47 on name wordplay in Aeschylus: "the operation of a kledonomatic system attests to the basic instability and ambiguity of language, where one discourse can lie concealed behind another."

A. 1, when Venus sends Cupid after Dido, the image of wounding, literally present when Cupid shoots an arrow at Medea in the model in Apollonius, but until her suicide only metaphorically present in the story of Dido, seems to be suggested by Venus' epithet *Acidalia* (720). Elsewhere in A. 1 Vergil speaks of Dido "drinking in" the love for Aeneas that Cupid inspires (1.749, *longumque bibebat amorem*); this follows from Venus' commands to Cupid that he attack her with both fire and "poison" (1.688, *occultum inspires ignem fallasque veneno*), and again the usage is metaphorical, although it does occur in a banqueting scene. Due has suggested that the metaphor is underscored by a presumed connection between the words Venus and *venenum,* but this suggestion must remain tentative, since ancient awareness of the perhaps genuine connection between Venus and *venenum* is not clearly attested, and wordplay in Vergil here is not certain (see on A. 1.688–89 and 4.1–5). We must be careful to distinguish between what Vergil does and what we might like him to have done; the "excitement of philological discovery" sometimes makes it difficult to separate insightful discovery from fabricated supplements to the text.

At least twice etymologizing seems to underscore fire imagery. In A. 2 Knox has described the function of the image of fire in the story of the fall of Troy; in one part of the book Neoptolemus or Pyrrhus is associated with the destructive power of fire both through imagery and through allusion to the etymology of the name Pyrrhus (flame-colored, red-headed; see on A. 2.469–75 and esp. 529 *ardens . . . Pyrrhus).* A. 7.623–31, describing how Italy "burns" for war, begins and ends with the words *ardet* and *Ardea* in first position in the hexameter and may suggest a natural association of the name Turnus' town with fire; Turnus, like Pyrrhus, is often associated with fire.

In earlier sections of this introduction I have mentioned other examples that can be discussed in terms of larger themes. The Altars (Arae) of A. 1.108–10, to which Vergil calls attention by using the language of poetic etymologizing to stress their "Italian" name *(saxa vocant Itali)* while alluding to a Greek name, are connected to the important theme of sacrifice, suggesting that the men on the first ship to sink in the storm die in some sense in place of Aeneas, as Palinurus later will; I have discussed this pattern of sacrifice in my earlier book.[360] Earlier I identified G. 4.43 *fovere larem* as a gloss on the suppressed word *favus,* derived by Festus from *faveo,* "to warm"; thematically, this etymologizing contributes to the stress on the balance of hot, cold, wet, and dry in the *Georgics,* the importance of which Ross has established. Ross has also explained the central importance to the

360. O'Hara (1990) 19–24, 104–111; on sacrifice cf. now also Hardie (1993) 19–56.

*Georgics* of four extensive etymological aetiologies, which are linked to one another by style, structure, cross-references, and thematic suggestiveness. These involve the citron, or *medica,* used as an antidote for the poisons of stepmothers (2.126–41), the *amellus* used to try to cure sick bees (4.271–78), the *hippomanes* used as a drug by evil stepmothers (3.280–83), and the gadfly, or *asilus,* that torments cattle (3.146–53); all are involved with the *Georgics'* picture of a natural world where forces of disease or destruction do battle with forces of healing or amelioration. Vergil's gloss in the *Aeneid* of the healing herb *dictamnum,* which Venus uses to heal her son Aeneas' thigh wound at a crucial point before the final battle with Turnus (12.411–17; see also above in section 2.8a), resembles these in many ways, and I suspect it is of similar thematic importance, although I myself have not yet been able to fashion a single convincing explanation of its thematic function.

Two simple examples of the thematic importance of etymology involve the word for a crucial Roman concept: *virtus,* "courage, excellence, acting like a man," whose etymology from the word *vir,* "man," was clear to the ancient reader. Passages in a number of authors associate the words *vir* and *virtus;* most interestingly, Vergil twice juxtaposes the word *virtus* to the word *puer,* "boy." At A. 9.641, after Ascanius has by shooting an arrow killed a man for the first time, Apollo says to him, *macte nova* ***virtute, puer,*** which we might paraphrase as, "congratulations on your first act as a *man, boy.*" At A. 12.435, Aeneas says to Ascanius, in the only words addressed by this father to his son in the poem, *disce,* ***puer, virtutem*** *ex me verumque laborem, / fortunam ex aliis,* "Learn, *boy, man*liness from me and true *labor,* but learn luck from others." The exploitation of the etymology of *virtus* in both these passages underscores the fact that both these scenes have something to tell us about what it means to be a *puer,* or a *vir,* and more interestingly what it means to go from being a *puer* to being a *vir.*[361]

The sections on the history of etymologizing and on features of Vergilian wordplay noted how often gods' names are etymologized, and that this tendency is prominent in archaic, classical, and Alexandrian Greek poetry, in the *Cratylus,* in fragments attributed to the Stoics, in the reports of the *libri annales* of the pontiffs, and in Varro and Cicero. Often in the *Aeneid* allusions to the etymology of gods' names gloss their function in the poem, in ways both simple and complex. One etymological connection mentioned several times in the survey of earlier etymologizing is that between Hera or Juno and ἀήρ or *aer.* This connection will be alluded to several times in the *Aeneid* (see on A. 12.791–92). Feeney has even suggested that when Juno

---

361. Cf. Hardie (1994) on A. 9.641, Petrini (n.d.) chap. 5.

has Aeolus send the storm against Aeneas in book 1, Vergil's allusion to this connection introduces to the reader the notion of an allegorical interpretation of the actions of the gods in the poem (see on A. 1.50–156). In the previous section I also noted Vergil's allusions to the etymology of the name of Turnus' sister Juturna as "the one who helps *(iuvat)* Turnus," so that the name and the glosses on its origin express her principal function in the poem.

Near the start of book 7, Vergil invokes the Muse Erato to inspire him to tell the story of the war in Italy. Apollonius had begun *Argonautica* 3 by invoking Erato, with explicit reference to her name's connection with ἔρως. In Vergil neither the "erotic" etymology, nor its possible relevance, is as clear as in Apollonius (who is about to tell of the love of Jason and Medea), but the borrowing from Apollonius probably alludes to the etymology as well and so makes a kind of comment or narrative prediction about the role to be played in the second half of the poem by passion, broadly conceived to include both amorous and other forms of desire. Since Vergil does not allude directly to the etymology, however, some may resist such an interpretation here (see on A. 7.37–41).

At the beginning of Jupiter's speech to Venus, at A. 1.261–62, wordplay between *fabor* (I shall speak) and *fata* (fate, what is spoken) suggests that whatever Jupiter says equals fate; in my reading this etymologizing sets up an expectation that will be frustrated, as events of the poem prove to be more complicated than Jupiter's deceptively reassuring words to Venus promise. Part of this development involves etymological aetiologies: the speech of Venus that precedes Jupiter's prophecy stresses the example of Antenor, who settled in Italy and gave a name to a people (248, *genti nomen dedit*); Jupiter's prophecy mentions Romulus' naming of the city after himself (276–77) and the living on of the name Iulus in the Julian *gens* (see on A. 1.273–77 and 286–88) but does not mention that the Trojan name will die out, and that the Italian name and language will predominate. That compromise between Jupiter and Juno in book 12 is also an etymological *aition,* which resonates, not without significant tension, with those of the conversation between Jupiter and Venus in book 1 (see on A. 12.826–35). The mention in Jupiter's speech of Romulus' naming of the city is also phrased in such a way as to call to the reader's mind the full story of how Romulus came to name the city, namely in the competition with Remus that eventually led to Remus' death.

As I have noted at the start of this section, and briefly in the discussion of etymologizing of names of mortals in the features section, this kind of naming of peoples and cities makes etymological aetiology a part of the *Aeneid*'s central concerns, for the poem itself is at heart an *aition* for the Roman state and people, and as such has a basic generic affinity with the aetiological works of Callimachus, Apollonius, and other Greek poets. There is a significant overlap of the *Aeneid's* general concern with the origins of the Roman people and its frequent concern for the origins of words or names: in its interest in aetiology the *Aeneid* is simultaneously most Roman and most Alexandrian. Besides the instances mentioned in the last paragraph, for example, in A. 5.116–23, Vergil explicitly links the Memmii, the Sergii, and the Cluentii to the boat captains Mnestheus, Sergestus, and Cloanthus; etymologizing is thus involved in some of the occasions when Vergil "turns repeatedly to the importance of the *gens* and the values (or dangers) it transmits."[362] In 5.718 Vergil links the Sicilian town Segesta with Acestes, prefiguring through etymology and aetiology alliances of later ages. At A. 8.357–58, Evander tells Aeneas that two citadels were named for their founders, Janus and Saturn: the name Ianiculum remains in Vergil's day, but the Saturnian hill is (apparently) now that of Jupiter Capitolinus, so the aetiology calls attention to the way in which the age of Saturn has yielded to that of Jupiter. In A. 7.706–9, Vergil links Livia's *gens Claudia* to the Sabine Clausus, and the *gens Atia* of Augustus' mother to the Trojan boy Atys. Most significantly, at A. 1.267–68, 1.288, and 6.789–90 Vergil prominently traces the Iulian *gens* back to Aeneas' son Ascanius/Iulus: *Iulius, a magno demissum nomen Iulo* (1.288). Williams puts it well: "Virgil's fondness for aetiological name associations was encouraged by the use made of them in Hellenistic poetry, and sometimes it is a reflection of simple antiquarian interest; but much more often it is directly related to the national theme of the *Aeneid,* to the pride in Roman tradition which links the names and places of the present with the events of the distant past."[363] Etymological aetiology seeks to explain the present in terms of the past: it strives for knowledge of the "causes of things" (cf. G. 2.490, *rerum cognoscere causas,* with, however, a different context).

362. Horsfall (1991b) 204; for problematic aspects of the continuity of the gens cf. Feeney (1986), Hardie (1993) 88–91.

363. Williams (1960) on 5.116; cf. Heinze (1915) 373, Horsfall (1991b) esp. 204, 208 ("Genealogy is the strongest symbol of continuity; Virgil's particularly Roman emphasis on familial and national descent through the noble *gentes* rests on recent pseudo-scholarly work, especially by M. Terentius Varro: fashionable semi-learned tinkerings in the service of gentile pretensions is transposed . . . into a serious and major instrument . . . of cohesion between mythical and historical worlds"), *EV* s.v. anacronismi (Horsfall) and *aition* (Fedeli). Horsfall (*EV* s.v. Varrone, L'Opera Varroniana e l'Eneide) also calls attention to possible influence on Vergil of Varro's *Aetia.* For Alexandrian aetiology see esp. the references above at the start of section 1.4 to important recent work by Bing, Zanker, and Depew, which has been helpful to me in thinking about Vergil, as have comments on aetiology by Garth Tissol *per litteras.* See also on A. 5.116–23.

As noted also in the section on names of mortals, for the main characters in the *Aeneid* I have found little of the type of extended and thematically significant etymologizing such as has been found, for example, for Odysseus in the *Odyssey*, Pentheus in the *Bacchae*, and Oedipus in Sophocles (see above in sects. 1.1 and 1.2). Countless minor characters in Vergil have significant names, and names in the *Eclogues* seem often to have been chosen for their etymological significance or suggestiveness, although in many cases nothing in the poem calls attention to the etymology in a way that I would call etymological wordplay (see introductory note to *Eclogues)*. The suggestion has been made that "in essence Turnus is a bad king" in part because etymologically "[h]is name in itself indicates this," being connected to an Etruscan word for "tyrant," but I am not convinced by this argument (see on A. 7.56).

Vergil does, however, involve Dido in a complicated series of interlinked examples of etymological wordplay that are thematically suggestive.[364] This example will end this section.

At G. 1.337, Vergil refers to the "wandering" of the planet Mercury: *quos ignis caelo Cyllenius erret in orbis*. Servius comments that "the word *'erret'* is well chosen, because planets are so called after the Greek word πλάνη, which means 'wandering.'" At A. 1.742, Vergil uses the phrase *errantem lunam* in his description of the song of Iopas at Dido's banquet; to the ancient mind, the moon is just as much a planet or "wanderer" as is Mercury. Vergil also alludes to the etymological connotations of wandering for the name Dido. At A. 4.211 Dido is referred to as *femina, quae nostris errans in finibus,* "a woman, wandering in our land." Pease noted the suppressed pun, based on an etymology found in the *Etymologicum Magnum* and in Timaeus connecting the name Dido and the Greek words πλάνη or πλανῆτις. Vergil connects Dido to wandering at least two more times. At A. 4.68, the lovesick Dido wanders around the city; here the word is not *errat* but *uagatur:*

> uritur infelix Dido totaque *vagatur*
> urbe furens, qualis coniecta cerva sagitta.

Dido also wanders in the underworld at A. 6.450–54:

> inter quas Phoenissa recens a vulnere *Dido*
> *errabat* silva in magna; quam Troius heros
> ut primum iuxta stetit agnovitque per umbras

364. For another set of examples linked from several parts of the poem see on A. 2.682–98 on etymological connections between the words for comet and hair that help link several passages involving star/comets (including the *Sidus Iulium*), flames, heads, and hair.

obscuram, qualem primo qui surgere mense
aut videt aut vidisse putat per nubila *lunam*.

In this passage Vergil uses the verb *errare* of Dido; he also, in the haunting simile of the next few lines, compares her to the moon. So the etymologizing of the word planet is linked to that of the name Dido. This extended word-play links Dido closely to the verb *errare,* to suggest that this verb is somehow central to her. The *Etymologicum Magnum* suggests that Dido is called wanderer because she wandered around after leaving her home. But wandering is also a characteristic feature of the lover in elegy and eclogue, so it may be that the connection between Dido and wandering suggests elegy, or more broadly speaking the nonepic love poetry of the few decades preceding the writing of the *Aeneid*—Propertius, the Gallus of the *Eclogues,* perhaps Gallus' own poetry, and that of Calvus.[365] Vergil's etymologizing with the name Dido helps him evoke this tradition, and in a sense to cross genre boundaries, to include elegiac material in an epic to broaden the scope and suggestive power of the poetry.

## 4. About the Catalogue

The catalogue presents and discusses all plausible examples that I or any other scholar whose work I know have found in Vergil's works.[366] My catalogue is more heavily annotated than, for example, Knauer's lists of Vergilian borrowings from Homer or Moskalew's list of repetitions within Vergil. Each of them offers full discussions supported by those extremely useful lists, which are presented almost as appendices. This volume's introduction, by contrast, is what its name implies: an introduction to what I consider to be the more valuable and more informative part of the book, the annotated catalogue.

Entries in the catalogue typically take the following format (although there will not be information for each of these categories for each entry):

1. I first quote the passage, with a question mark after the book and line reference for uncertain examples.[367] I highlight the words in-

365. Cf. Callim. *Hymn* 3.190–91 (Minos roaming Cretan hills mad for Britomartis); E. 6.52 a virgo infelix, tu nunc in montibus erras (on *erras* see Thomas [1979]); E. 6.64 errantem Permessi ad flumina Gallum; Prop. 1.1.11 (Milanion) nam modo Partheniis amens errabat in antris (where Ross [1975] 61–65 sees a precedent in Gallus); Ovid *Ars* 1.527 Cnosis in ignotis amens errabat harenis.

366. See my caveats above n. 2.

367. My method of dealing with doubtful examples differs sharply from Bartelink's. He

volved in the etymologizing with italics or, for the few passages with more than one example, with italics, bold, and underlining; if one word is in italics, one both bold and in italics, and one in bold, the word with both kinds of highlighting will be interacting independently with each of the other words. In some sense this may be looked upon as cheating, since in most cases I am claiming that Roman readers would have noticed etymologizing in a text without highlighting, but it is hoped that the reader can compensate in making judgments about whether my suggestions or those of others are plausible. As in the introduction, I have marked instances of naming constructions functioning as etymological signposts with dotted underlining.

2. Next I explain the wordplay or possible wordplay, often mentioning relevant passages from other authors or from elsewhere in Vergil, and discussing factors bearing on the legitimacy of uncertain examples. Often cross-references either to the introduction or to other entries in the catalogue are given; where cross-references within the catalogue are given, the one with the main discussion of each phenomenon is in bold.
3. After the discussion come passages from ancient grammarians or poets that explicitly mention the derivation, where these are available, so that we have some idea whether and at what date the ancients suspected a connection between the words. It must be stressed that these lists are not always comprehensive, just extensive enough to help readers decide whether wordplay is taking place; at times I will note that Maltby's *Lexicon of Ancient Latin Etymologies* offers more examples. I offer here another reminder that the Key to Abbreviations offers dates by century for my sources.
4. Next come passages from elsewhere in Vergil and from other poets, principally but not exclusively the Greek Alexandrians and the Augustan Roman poets, alluding to the same or similar etymologies. Often some passages will have been mentioned or even quoted in full in the discussion above; repetition is then avoided. As in the discussion, cross-references to a Vergilian passage with my main

mentions such examples only after the last footnote of the section in which they would have appeared had he found them credible (cf. e.g. Bartelink [1965] 89 n. 1, on the name Arae at A. 1.108–10, which I found more interesting than he had); I place them in the catalogue, with question marks and often with discussion of the problem, in part because what looks implausible to me may look more plausible to another.

discussion of a particular phenomenon are highlighted in bold.
5. Last come bibliographical references.

The catalogue deals with the *Aeneid, Eclogues,* and *Georgics* in that order. I could argue that this is the order of Servius and say that my order is a tribute to the role of his commentary in preserving knowledge about ancient etymologizing. But my actual motivation is more practical: I thought that the first book of the *Aeneid* had more interesting examples than did the *Eclogues* and so could better serve as a practical introduction to my method.

I have given much thought to the question of whether to present the material in the current catalogue form, preceded by this introduction, or instead to organize the material into groupings as Bartelink did, adding one feature that Bartelink lacks, an index.[368] In the end it seemed to me that though the latter alternative might provide more pleasure for the first-time reader, it had serious disadvantages. For one, this monograph is not meant to be read through only once, but both to be read and to be consulted by the student, teacher, or scholar reading or working on particular passages; since Vergil is read in pieces, the running commentary format of the catalogue seemed best. More importantly, it seemed both too difficult and even unhelpful to group all my examples into rigid categories, since most belong to several categories. The introduction presents some groupings, but it must be remembered that not all catalogue entries are even mentioned in the introduction.

368. Bartelink has chapters on the etymologizing of (to translate his titles) "geographical names," "names of peoples, family names, and proper names of persons," "other proper names," "Greek and other foreign words," "etymological cognates, or words considered to be cognates, used near one another."

# Catalogue of Etymological Wordplay

## The *Aeneid*

**A. 1.8?:** *Musa,* mihi causas *memora*

This line and others in Vergil could allude to the etymological connection of the name Musa or Mousa with words for memory such as *moneo, memini.*

The earliest Roman epic verse, Livius Andronicus' translation of the *Odyssey,* may provide a kind of model for muse-memory wordplay here. In fr. 21, *nam diva Monetas filia docuit,* Livius uses Moneta as his Latin name for Mnemosyne, the mother of the Muses, and that Moneta is derived from *moneo* seems to be suggested by his reference to her "teaching" *(docuit)* (so Feeney).

E. 7.19: alternos *Musae meminisse* volebant; A. 7.645: et *meministis* enim, *divae,* et *memorare* potestis; A. 7.41: tu vatem, tu, *diva, mone;* A. 6.511–14: *monimenta . . . meminisse;* E. 1.16–17?: *mens . . . memini.*

Coleman (1977) on E. 7.19, Bartelink (1965) 93, Feeney (1991) 121; on the etymology, which I have not seen in an explicit ancient source, cf. Rank (1951) 50–51, Nagy (1979) 17.

**A. 1.12–13?:** *urbs antiqua* fuit (Tyrii tenuere coloni) / *Karthago*

Elsewhere Vergil clearly alludes to the Punic etymology of the name Carthage as *nova civitas* (see on **A. 1.297–300** [throughout this catalogue, cross-references to my main discussion of a recurring etymology will appear in bold]). Here *urbs antiqua* may allude to that derivation by the use of an adjective opposite to *novus* (on such glosses κατ' ἀντίφρασιν see intro. 2.3).

**A. 1.37:** *mene in*-cepto desistere victam

Not strictly involving etymological play, but still worthy of note, is Levitan's observation that in Juno's words here, which are "the first words spoken in the *Aeneid,*" Vergil recalls with *mene in-* the sound of *Il.* 1.1 Μῆνιν ἄειδε, θεά. He compares the echo of *Od.* 1.1 Ἄνδρα μοι ἔννεπε, Μοῦσα by Ezra Pound, *Cantos* 1.1 "*And* then went down to the ship." Skeptics should note that Vergil's context in 1.1–50 is full of *ira* = μῆνις; cf. esp. 4 *saevae memorem Iunonis ob iram,* 11 *tantaene animis caelestibus irae?,* 25 *causae irarum saevique dolores,* and Feeney's discussion of Vergil's question at 1.11 in the context of "centuries of philosophical debate concerned with denying the gods such motivations of anger."

Several times Vergil will reproduce the sound of a model with different words; for such "mistranslation," "translation by homonym," "translation with paronomasia," or "sound imitation," see intro. 2.1a.

Levitan (1993); cf. Feeney (1991) 130, McKeown (1994); the detailed imitation of the *Iliad* at the start of the *Aeneid* described by Weber (1987) also supports Levitan's suggestion.

**A. 1.50–56:** (the storm)

Feeney suggests that when Juno has Aeolus send the storm against Aeneas, the tradition of allegorical etymologizing that linked Juno or Hera with the *aer* adds significant resonance to her action:

> We are introduced to another way of apprehending the goddess, now according to the systems which allegorized the gods as forces in the natural world. By this tradition of interpretation, Vergil's audience will have known Juno as *aer,* the lower air, the sphere for storms of wind and cloud.

On Juno/Hera = *aer,* see on **A. 12.791–92**; for a different etymological connection for Juno see below on A. 1.71–73.

Feeney (1991) 132.

**A. 1.56–57:** celsa sedet Aeolus arce / sceptra tenens mollitque *animos* et temperat iras.

Aeolus controls the *animos* of the winds. Servius notes the play here between *animos* (anger, spirits, animosity) and Greek ἄνεμος (wind).

SERV. 57: MOLLITQVE ANIMOS id est, ventos, ἀπὸ τῶν ἀνέμων, ut ipse alibi (8.403) "quantum ignes animaeque valent" et Horatius (C. 4.12.2) "inpellunt animae lintea Thraciae" (cf. too Serv. A. 8.403, and two passages in Cassiod. cited by Maltby); LACT. *Opif.* 17.2: alii (dixerunt animam esse) ventum, unde anima, vel animus, quod graece ventus ἄνεμος dicitur.

A. 10.356–57: magno discordes aethere *venti* / proelia ceu tollunt *animis* et viribus aequis; A. 8.403: quantum ignes *animae*que valent; G. 2.441: animosi Furi LUCR. 5.1230: ventorum . . . paces *animas*que secundas.

Austin (1971) on 57; on Serv. here cf. Mühmelt (1965) 70.

**A. 1.71–73?:** sunt mihi bis septem praestanti corpore Nymphae, / quarum quae forma pulcherrima Deiopea, / conubio *iungam* stabili propriamque dicabo

Feeney sees in *conubio iungam stabili,* which will be repeated in 4.126 when Juno and Venus discuss Aeneas and Dido, allusion to and glossing of Juno's epithet *Iuga* or *Iugalis* (cf. Ἥρα Ζυγίη), or even a suggested "connection between . . . *iungo* and *Iuno,* the 'dear *coniunx* of Jupiter.'" He suggests that Valerius Flaccus "appears to pick up Vergil's etymology."

Feeney suggests that "there may be another play on this etymology at 1.252, where Venus complains that she and the Trojans are being 'disjoined' from Italy by Juno": *prodimur atque Italis longe disiungimur oris.*

More broadly, he sees the "etymological force" of Juno's name suggested in the way that Juno's storms provide "structural cohesion" between books 1–6 and 7–12, and in her role in the final "synthesis" in the compromise with Jupiter in book 12.

For the different notion of Juno/Hera = *aer* see above on A. 1.50–156 and esp. **A. 12.791–92.**

PAUL.-Fest. p. 92, 29 L: Iunonis Iugae, quam putabant matrimoniam iungere.

VAL. Fla. 6.540: Iuno duci sociam coniungere quaerit.

Feeney (1991) 133.

**A. 1.87?:** clamorque virum *stridor*que *rudentum*

Depending on context, *rudens* can mean either "rope" or "bellowing, braying"; Nonius and Isidore derive the former meaning from the latter. Both in Vergil's phrase *stridorque rudentum,* and in the phrase *rudentum sibilus* that Servius Auctus quotes from Pacuvius here, the noun *(stridor, sibilus)* may call to mind the homonyms (Ahl says "releases the double entendre latent in *rudens*"), although *rudentum* as "bellowing" ultimately makes no sense in the syntax of 87. Similar wordplay seems to take place in A. 3.

NON. p. 51, 13 M (= Nigid. Fig. fr. dub. 47, *GRF* p. 178): rudentes ea causa sapientissimi dictos volunt, quod funes, cum vento verberentur, rudere existimeretur; ISID. 19.4.1: rudentes sunt funes navium ex nimio stridore ita dicti.

A. 3.561–62: primusque *rudentem* / contorsit laevas proram Palinurus ad undas; VARRO *LL* 5.7 quotes Pacuvius *Teucer, SRP* 336 R as: rudentum sibilus; SERV. Auct. 87: Pacuvius in Teucro "armamentum stridor et rudentum sibilus"; CAELIUS (*ad Fam.* 8.2.1): strepitus fremitus clamor tonitruum et rudentum sibilus; OVID *Met.* 11.495 (for Ovid cf. intro. 2.14): quippe sonant clamore viri, stridore rudentes.

Cerda (1612) 21, Ahl (1985) 29.

**A. 1.108–10:** tris Notus abreptas in saxa latentia torquet / (saxa vocant Itali mediis quae in fluctibus *Aras,* / dorsum immane mari summo)

The signpost *saxa vocant Itali* calls attention to the name Arae (for signposts see intro. 2.6). Less obviously, *dorsum immane mari summo* alludes to an alternate name for the rocks, found in Sinnius Capito, ἵππου νῶτα. Vergil gives one name, Aras, but alludes to another (*dorsum* in 110 = νῶτα, back), to stress that he is making a choice. Etymologizing often involves alternate names, or changes of names such as would have been discussed in Callimachus' prose treatise *Foundations of Cities and Islands and Their Changes of Names;* see intro. 2.10. I have argued that Vergil calls the rocks Altars, in a line useless but for this purpose, in order to suggest that near them the first of many sacrifices in the *Aeneid* takes place, with the death of Orontes and the men of his ship.

Sallust *Iug.* 78 gives the etymology of *Syrtes*: *ab tractu nominatae* (cf. σύρω, to sweep), right before telling the story of the altars of the Philaeni. Vergil mentions the nearby Syrtes in 1.111, and Servius ad loc. quotes the description of them in *Iug.* 78. Pliny *NH* 5.28 mentions the altars of the Philaeni, then in the next sentence cites Callimachus for the name of the swamp Pallantias, and for its location in respect to the Syrtes. Could a lost Callimachean discussion of the Arae be Vergil's model?

SERV. Auct. on 110: "dorsum" autem hoc loco non absurde ait, quia Graece arae ipsae ἵππου νῶτα dicuntur, ut Sinnius Capito tradidit (fr. 5, *GRF* p. 460); cf. Serv. on 246, where Vergil uses *mare* to refer to the Timavus River: amat poeta rem historiae carmini suo coniungere; Varro enim dicit hunc fluvium ab incolis mare nominari. PLINY *NH* 5.28: in intimo sinu fuit ora Lotophagon, quos quidam Machroas dixere, ad Philaenorum aras; ex harena sunt hae. ab iis non procul a continente palus vasta amnem Tritonem nomenque ab eo accepit, Pallantias appellata Callimacho (fr. 584 Pf.) et citra Minorem Syrtim esse dicta, multis vero inter duas Syrtis. GLOSS. (Goetz) 4.439.21: dorsum immane saxa sunt inter Africam et Siciliam, quae est Sardinia.

O'Hara (1990) 19–22, Clay (1988) 203 n. 23; cf. Bandera (1981) 215–16; Bartelink (1965) 89 n. 1 cites Serv. with skepticism; Funaioli (1907) 460 notes that Sinn. Cap. may or may not be commenting on Vergil.

**A. 1.117:** *rapidus vorat* aequore *vertex*

*Rapidus* juxtaposed with *vorat* may suggest *rapere,* as at E. 1.65 *rapidum cretae veniemus Oaxen,* where Servius thinks of the verb: *RAPIDUM CRETAE. . . . quod rapit cretam.* There may also be a connection suggested between *vortex* and *vorare.*

Bartelink (1965) 29, 101 (skeptical), Marouzeau (1940) 261–62.

**A. 1.164–65?:** tum silvis *scaena* coruscis / desuper, horrentique atrum nemus imminet *umbra*

Vergil here innovatively uses *scaena* to refer not to the building that serves as the background for a drama, but to what we would call "scenery," a natural backdrop, "an original idea which has no parallel in classical Latin" (Austin). Servius derives *scaena* ἀπὸ τῆς σκιᾶς, "from shade" or "shadows," on the theory that the oldest dramatic backdrop was not a painted wall but natural foliage. Vergil's *umbra* at the end of 165 may allude to this etymology, which in part legitimizes his new usage (Servius glosses *scaena* with *inumbratio*). Servius' etymology, however, could simply be deduced from Vergil's line (for other possible examples of etymologies deduced by grammarians from Vergil's text cf. on A. 3.520, 4.359, 6.160, 6.204, 7.64–67, 8.641, G. 4.257 and 4.310; see also intro. 2.Praef.).

SERV. 164: "Scaena" inumbratio. et dicta scaena ἀπὸ τῆς σκιᾶς. apud antiquos enim theatralis scaena parietem non habuit, sed de frondibus umbracula quaerebant. postea tabulata conponere coeperunt in modum parietis.

Bartelink (1965) 89 n. 1 ("dubious case"); Austin (1971) on 164: "Virgil . . . has transferred *scaena* from its normal use to describe natural 'scenery'"; cf. too Williams (1968) 642ff., and on the caution needed for using grammarians see Maltby (1993a).

**A. 1.174?:** ac primum *silici scintillam* excudit *Achates*

Servius says that Vergil plays on the name Achates, also the name of a kind of rock, and so appropriate for producing the spark of fire. Perhaps.

See on **A. 1.312** for the etymology from Greek ἄχος proposed by Servius.

SERV. 174: ACHATES adlusit ad nomen, nam achates lapidis species est. bene ergo ipsum dicit ignem excusisse. unde etiam Achaten eius comitem dixit.

Bartelink (1965) 62 n. 3 ("very improbable") Hanssen (1948) 121 ("perhaps we ought to accept Servius' explanation"), Due (1973) 270–73, Harrison (1991) on 10.331–32, *EV* s.v. Acate (Speranza).

**A. 1.178–79:** *frugesque* receptas / et *torrere* parant flammis et frangere saxo

De la Cerda suggests that *torrere* glosses *fruges,* alluding to an etymology from φρύγω = *torreo,* "roast."

PRISC. *Gramm. Lat.* 2.278.12 K: frux . . . frugis facit genitivum, quia ἀπὸ τοῦ φρύγω Graeco verbo nascitur.

Cerda (1612) 39.

**A. 1.180–81?:** Aeneas *scopulum* interea conscendit et omnem / *prospectum* late pelago petit

Vergil may be playing with the words *scopulum,* from the Greek σκοπεῖν, "to look, watch," and *prospectum,* from the Latin *spectare.* Servius glosses *scopulum* with the more natural Latin *speculam.*

SERV. 180: SCOPVLVM id est, speculam; SERV. 45: "scopulus" autem aut a speculando dictus est, aut a tegimento navium, ἀπὸ τοῦ σκεπάζειν (sim. at Isid. 16.3.2); *speculam* is used at A. 3.239.

Cf. A. 10.45: utque leo, *specula* cum *vidit* ab alta; see on E. 8.59, where Vergil's *specula* reflects Theocritus' σκοπιάζεται; APOLL. Rhod. 3.1276: τοὺς μὲν Καυκασίοισιν ἐφεσταότας σκοπέλοισιν, with Hunter's note, citing Schol. *Il.* 2.396.

Cerda (1612) 40 (citing J.C. Scaliger, and Hesychius on σκόπελος), Bartelink (1965) 89, Hunter (1988) on 3.1275–77.

**A. 1.208:** talia voce refert *curis*que ingentibus aeger / spem vultu simulat, premit altum *corde* dolorem

Vergil plays with *cura* in a number of ways. Here and elsewhere he alludes to the etymology found in Varro and Servius, *cura, quod cor urat.*

For other wordplay with *cura* see on E. 10.22 tua *cura* Lycoris (= κούρη, κόρη), A. 1.720 *matris Acidaliae,* and A. 1.662, 4.1–3, 12.801–2 *cura* and *recursat.*

SERV. 208: cura dicta ab eo quod cor urat. denique paulo post ait (209) "premit altum corde dolorem"; VARRO *LL* 6.46: cura, quod cur urat; PAUL.-Fest. p. 43, 14 L: cura dicta est, quasi coreda, vel quia cor urat; *RHET. Her.* 4.14.21 cites the wordplay in *cur eam rem tam studiose curas, quae tibi multas dabit curas?* For Quintilian's comment, see on G. 2.328 and intro. 2.1.

A. 1.662: *urit* atrox Iuno et sub noctem *cura* recursat; A. 4.1–2: at regina gravi iamdudum saucia *cura* / vulnus alit venis et caeco carpitur *igni;* A. 9.225: laxabant *curas* et *corda* oblita laborum.

In other poets (the earlier examples are assonance or paronomasia rather than etymologizing; see intro. 2.1): PLAUT. *Truc.* 454–55: quanta est *cura* in animo, quantum *corde* capio / dolorem; *Truc.* 773: una *cura cor* meum movit; *Men.* 761: haec res mihi in pectore et *corde curaest; Pers.* 801: DO. *uritur cor* mi / TO. da illi cantharum, exstingue ignem, si / *cor uritur . . . ;* TER. *Hec.* 347: *cura* ex *corde* excessit; VALERIUS Aedituus 1.1 (Buechner, *FPL* p. 55 = Courtney p. 70): dicere cum conor *curam* tibi, Pamphila, *cordis;* LUCR. 3.116: *curas cordis* inanis; [VERG.] *Culex* 91: haec *cura* est subdita *cordi;* HOR. *AP* 98: si *curat cor* spectantis tetigisse querella; OVID *Tr.* 3.2.16 (for Ovid cf. intro. 2.14): fallebat *curas* aegraque *corda* labor; LUCR. 4.1059–60: hinc illaec primum Veneris dulcedinis in *cor* / stillavit gutta et successit frigida *cura;* SIL. 7.285–87: at non Sidonium *curis* flagrantia *corda* / ductorem vigilesque metus haurire sinebant / dona soporiferae noctis.

Cf. also Cat. 66.23 and Ovid *Am.* 2.19.43 for allusion to the etymology *cura dicta est, quasi coreda* (see McKeown, and for Ovid cf. intro. 2.14).

Bartelink (1965) 105, Due (1973) 276–79, Ross (1975) 69 n. 1, McKeown (1987) 53.

## A. 1.247–52:

hic (sc. Antenor) tamen ille urbem Patavi sedesque locavit
Teucrorum et *genti nomen dedit* armaque fixit
Troia, nunc placida compostus pace quiescit:
nos, tua progenies, caeli quibus adnuis arcem,
navibus (infandum!) amissis unius ob iram
prodimur atque Italis longe disiungimur oris.

Venus descibes Antenor as "giving a name to a people"; Vergil probably alludes to the tradition by which the Veneti "were identified with the Eneti led by Antenor" (Austin). Venus contrasts the Trojans' inability, so far, to found and name; Vergil will make the distinction permanent with the agreement by Jupiter and Juno in A. 12 that the Trojan name will fade (see on A. 12.826–35; the connection is made by Servius).

LIVY 1.1: Antenorum cum multitudine Enetum . . . venisse in intimum maris Hadriatici sinum. . . . Et in quem primum egressi sunt locum Troia vocatur pagoque inde Troiano nome est: gens universa Veneti appellati; SERV. Auct. 248: ET GENTI NOMEN DEDIT hoc est quod ne victori quidem concedetur Aeneae; quod scimus a

Iunone esse perfectum, sicut in XII (824) ait "nunc Troias fieri iubeas Teucrosque vocari," et Iuppiter ait (835) "commixti corpore tantum."

Austin (1971) on 248, Ogilvie (1970) 35–36, O'Hara (1990) 143–44.

**A. 1.252?:** prodimur atque Italis longe *disiungimur* oris

When "Venus complains that she and the Trojans are being 'disjoined' from Italy by Juno," Feeney sees possible allusion to a connection between Juno and *iungo;* see on **A. 1.71–73.** Perhaps unlikely here, because insufficiently marked.

Feeney (1991) 133 n. 15.

**A. 1.261–62:** *fabor* enim, quando haec te cura remordet, / longius et volvens *fatorum* arcana movebo

The Romans were well aware of the connection between *fatum* and the verb *for, fari.* I have argued that here the etymological subtext suggests that what Jupiter says *(fabor)* should correspond exactly to what is fated to happen *(fatum),* but does not.

Cf. on A. 10.225, *fandi doctissima Cymodocea,* and *fama/fata* at A. 7.79, 8.731.

VARRO *LL* 6.52: ab hoc (sc. fando) tempora quod tum pueris constituant Parcae fando, dictum fatum et res fatales; ISID. 8.11.90: Fatum autem dicunt esse, quidquid dii fantur, quidquid Iuppiter fatur. A fando igitur fatum dicunt, id est a loquendo (more in Maltby).

Bartelink (1965) 95–96, 105–6, Commager (1981) 101–14, Austin (1971) on 262, O'Hara (1990) 137–38, Keith (1992) 87–92 (on Ovid).

**A. 1.267–68:** at puer Ascanius, cui nunc cognomen *Iulo* / additur (*Ilus* erat, dum res stetit *Ilia* regno)

An explicit etymological aetiology, with further implicit connotations. In lines marked by the etymological signpost *cui nunc cognomen,* Jupiter says that Ascanius' *cognomen* is being changed from Ilus to Iulus, and that the name Ilus was connected with Ilium, Troy. Julius Caesar, in his *laudatio* for his aunt Julia in 69 B.C., claimed descent from Venus for his family (*a Venere Iulii, cuius gentis familia est nostra,* Suet. *Iul.* 6). The report that Ascanius' cognomen was changed from Ilus to Iulus stresses the connection of the *gens Iulia* with Iulus, and that of Iulus/Ascanius with Troy/Ilium (instead of letting him be a son of the Italian Lavinia, as in some versions of the myth). The picture is completed by 1.288 *Iulius, a magno demissum nomen Iulo,* and 6.789–90 *Caesar et omnis Iuli / progenies.*

Servius mentions two derivations of the name Iulus, both stemming from his killing of Mezentius by archery (in the non-Vergilian myth): either from ἰοβόλος, "the archer," or from ἴουλος, the young man's first beard that he wore at the tender age at which he killed Mezentius. Vergil may (but probably does not) allude to the derivation from ἰοβόλος in 9.640–50 (see there).

On connections between Romans of Vergil's time and Trojan families see on **5.116–23.**

For naming signposts like *cognomen* see intro. 2.6; for changes of names or alternate names, and for *nunc* in etymological aetiologies, see intro. 2.10 and 10a, and above on 110.

SERV. Auct. 267: CVI NVNC COGNOMEN IVLO ADDITVR . . . secundum Catonem historiae hoc habet fides: . . . et occiso Mezentio Ascanium sicut L. Caesar scribit Iulum coeptum vocari, vel quasi ἰοβόλον, id est sagittandi peritum, vel a prima barbae lanugine, quam ἴουλον Graeci dicunt, quae ei tempore victoriae nascebatur. sciendum est autem hunc primo Ascanium dictum, a Phrygiae flumine Ascanio, ut est "transque sonantem Ascanium" (G. 3.269); deinde Ilum dictum a rege Ilo, unde et Ilium, postea Iulum occiso Mezentio: de quibus nominibus hoc loco dicit; nam ideo ait "at puer Ascanius cui nunc cognomen Iulo additur, Ilus erat." ab hac autem historia ita discedit Vergilius, ut aliquibus locis ostendat non se per ignorantiam, sed per artem poeticam hoc fecisse. . . ; LIVY 1.3.2: Iulum . . . Iulia gens auctorem nominis sui nuncupat (more in Ogilvie ad loc. and Maltby s.vv. Iulus, Iulia gens).

Bartelink (1965) 64; for inconsistencies in the handling of Ascanius see Norden (1966) 391–93, O'Hara (1990) 145–47 with references in 147 n. 52, Horsfall (1991) 97 with references to his earlier work, Ogilvie (1970) 42–43; for Servius' derivation from ἴουλος cf. Mühmelt (1965) 70.

### A. 1.273–77:

regina sacerdos
Marte gravis geminam partu dabit Ilia prolem.
inde lupae fulvo nutricis tegmine laetus
*Romulus* excipiet gentem et Mavortia condet
moenia *Romanos*que suo de nomine dicet.

Vergil explicitly explains that Romulus named the Romans after himself, with the etymological signpost *suo de nomine dicet*. The subtext tells more of the story of Rome's naming. Feeney:

> Jupiter describes the birth of the *twins* . . . (274). The first five feet of the next line allude to the wolf who nursed the twins. . . , and it is with considerable shock that we reach the final word and discover that it is *singular (laetus)*. We carry on to find Romulus as the subject . . . (276). *Remo scilicet interempto,* comments Servius. Just so. We continue: *Mavortia condet / moenia Romanosque suo de nomine dicet* (276–77). It was when Remus jumped over Romulus' *moenia* that he was killed, while the naming of the people after Romulus rather than after Remus was a result of Romulus' victory in the contest of auspices: *certabant urbem Romam Remoramne vocarent* (Enn. *Ann.* 77 Sk.).

For more explanations of Rome's name see the long entry at Maltby s.v. Roma.

Bartelink (1965) 67, Feeney (1986) 9, O'Hara (1990) 151–55.

**A. 1.286–88:** nascetur pulchra Troianus origine Caesar, / imperium Oceano, famam qui terminet astris, / *Iulius*, a magno demissum nomen *Iulo*

Vergil continues to stress the connection of the Julian *gens* with Iulus and Troy (see above on 1.267–68). In the explicit etymologizing here, *nomen* is the etymological signpost (see intro. 2.6), and the words connected etymologically, *Iulius* and *Iulo*, frame the line (see intro. 2.8). These lines also present a notorious problem: do they refer to Julius Caesar the dictator or to his grandnephew Augustus, who by adoption became a C. Julius Caesar? I have argued that the lines are unavoidably ambiguous and do not refer clearly either to Julius or to Augustus, as Jupiter deceives Venus by presenting a composite picture of an unreservedly positive Trojan Caesar, and Vergil forces the reader to think about the similarities between Julius and Augustus.

Cf. on 1.267–68 and 6.789–90.

OVID *F.* 4.39–40 (for Ovid cf. intro. 2.14): venimus ad felix aliquando nomen Iuli, / unde domus Teucros Iulia tangit avos.

O'Hara (1990) 153–63 (contra Kraggerud [1992] and the response O'Hara [1994b], Bartelink (1965) 65, Austin (1971) 108–111 (arguing for ambiguity, but then in Austin [1977] 243 "less inclined to take [286] as an allusion to Julius"); for more on "Julius Caesar in Augustan Rome" cf. White (1988).

**A. 1.297–300:**

haec ait et Maia genitum demittit ab alto,
ut terrae utque **novae** pateant **Karthaginis** *arces*
hospitio Teucris, ne fati nescia Dido
finibus *arceret.*

Two examples in these lines. Servius, citing Livy, and Solinus, citing Cato, tell us that *Carthago* means *nova civitas* in Punic. Vergil plays on this etymology here with the gloss *novae,* and several other times.

With *arceret* in 300 after *arces* in 298 Vergil may also allude to Varro's derivation of *arx* from *arceo.*

Nova Karthago: SERV. 1.366: NOVAE CARTHAGINIS "Carthago" est lingua Poenorum "nova civitas," ut docet Livius (= Livy fr. 6 W-M; probably in book 16, of which the Periochae tell us "origo Carthaginiensium et primordia urbis eorum referuntur"); CATO *Orig.* fr. 37.4 (= Solinus 27.10): urbem istam, ut Cato in oratione senatoria autumat . . . Elissa . . . Carthadam dixit, quod Phoenicum ore exprimit civitatem novam. mox sermone verso in verbum Punicum . . . Carthago dicta est (cf. Isid. 15.1.30); SERV. 1.522: NOVAM VRBEM iuxta Poenorum opinionem dixit, qui novam civitatem Carthaginem dicunt (more in Maltby s.v. Carthago).

A. 1.12–13? urbs *antiqua* fuit (Tyrii tenuere coloni) / *Karthago;* 1.366: moenia surgentemque *novae Karthaginis* arcem; 1.522: o regina, *novam* cui condere Iuppiter *urbem. . . ;* 4.260: Aenean fundantem arces ac tecta *novantem. . . ;* 4.670: *Karthago* aut *antiqua* Tyros.

Arx: VARRO *LL* 5.151: arx ab arcendo, quod is locus munitissimus urbis, a quo facillime possit hostis prohiberi; SERV. Auct. A. 1.20: arces autem ab eo quod est "arceo" dictae, quia inde hostes arcentur, id est prohibentur (a bit more in Maltby s.v. arx).

Carthago: Bartelink (1965) 45, McCartney (1927) 188, Austin (1971) on 298. Arx: Bartelink (1965) 95 n. 2.

**A. 1.312?:** ipse uno graditur comitatus Achate

Servius connects Achates' name with the Greek word ἄχος, "grief, worry," and says that Achates is Aeneas' companion, because worry is the companion of kings. I see little or no allusion to this etymology in the *Aeneid.*

Cf. on 1.174 *primum silici scintillam excudit Achates.*

SERV. 312: COMITATVS ACHATE . . . dictum est quaeri, cur Achates Aeneae sit comes. varia quidem dicuntur, melius tamen hoc fingitur, ut tractum nomen sit a Graeca etymologia; ἄχος enim dicitur sollicitudo, quae regum semper est comes; SCHOL. *Il.* 1.1.h connects the name Achilles with ἄχος, and Callimachus seems to have given this derivation as well (see fr. 624, intro. 1.4). A *Homeric Hymn* derives the name Aeneas from αἰνὸν ἄχος (see on A. 12.945–47), but there αἰνὸν is the important element.

Cf. Due (1973) 270–73, Bartelink (1965) 62 n. 3 ("very improbable"), Hanssen (1948) 121; on Achilles cf. Nagy (1979) 69–71.

**A. 1.317?:** *volucremque* fuga praevertitur *Hebrum*

De la Cerda notes the story in the *de Fluviis* falsely attributed to Plutarch that this river was named because of the whirling stream of its waters and suggests that *volucrem* glosses the name (see intro. 2.2). Some editors of *de Fluviis,* however, suspect that a reference to the river's previous name, Rhombus, should be restored to the text, since it can be more plausibly linked to whirling waters. The story, in which the name is changed after a king's son named Hebrus falls into it, may have been discussed e.g. in Callimachus' work on the names of rivers (on *metonomasia* see intro. 2.10); [Plutarch] cites Timotheos' *de Fluviis.* Vergil may thus offer a single-epithet gloss for old name, which is suppressed (see intro. 2.7).

[PLUT.] *de Fluv.* 3.1: Ἕβρος ποταμός ἐστι τῆς Θρᾴκης . . . [ἐκαλεῖτο δὲ πρότερον Ῥόμβος, τὴν] προσηγορίαν εἰληφὼς ἀπὸ τῆς καταφορᾶς τοῦ ὕδατος.

Cerda (1612) 317; this example was suggested to me by G. Tissol.

**A. 1.336–38:** virginibus Tyriis mos est **gestare pharetram** / *purpureo*que alte suras vincire coturno. / *Punica* regna vides, Tyrios et Agenoris urbem

Austin suggests a play on *purpureo* and *Punica,* alluding to the latter word's connection with *puniceus.* Weber notes this as an example of Vergil's tendency to "juxtapose related words vertically"; for wordplay at the start of consecutive lines see intro. 2.9.

In 336, could *gestare pharetram* allude to a derivation of pharetram from φέφω or *fero,* such as is found in Isidore?

ISID. 18.9.1: faretra sagittarum theca, a ferendo iacula dicta.

Cf. LUCAN 1.214: puniceus (= ruber) Rubicon.

Austin (1971) on 337, Weber (1990) 212; on Lucan, McCartney (1927) 187.

**A. 1.366:** moenia surgentemque *novae Karthaginis* arcem

For Vergil's several allusions to "new city" as an etymology of Carthage see on **A. 1.297–300.**

SERV. 366: NOVAE CARTHAGINIS "Carthago" enim est lingua Poenorum "nova civitas," ut docet Livius.

**A. 1.367–68:** mercatique solum, facti de nomine *Byrsam, / taurino* quantum possent circumdare *tergo*

Austin: "the Greek βύρσα means a bull's hide; the Greeks identified it with the Phoenician name for the citadel of Carthage, *Bosra.*" Vergil glosses *Byrsa* in 367 with *taurino . . . tergo* in 368. The words *facti de nomine* serve as an etymological signpost (see intro. 2.6). The words most closely connected etymologically, *Byrsa* and *tergo,* are juxtaposed at the end of consecutive lines (see intro. 2.9). For etymologizing with languages other than Latin and Greek, see intro. 2.11.

SERV. Auct. 367: MERCATIQVE SOLVM, FACTI DE NOMINE BYRSAM Dido adpulsa ad Libyam, cum ad Hiarba pelleretur, petit callide ut emeret tantum terrae, quantum posset corium bovis tenere. tum corium in fila propemodum sectum tetendit occupavitque stadia viginti duo; quam rem leviter tangit Vergilius dicendo "facti de nomine" et non "tegere," sed (368) "circumdare." "facti de nomine" vero de causae qualitate, quia "byrsa" Graece corium dicitur. dicendo ergo "circumdare," ostendit corrigiam de corio factam (cf. too Claud. Don. on A. 1.365).

Cerda (1612) 73 (citing Joseph Scaliger), Austin (1971) ad loc., Bartelink (1965) 44.

**A. 1.441?:** *lucus* in urbe fuit media, laetissimus *umbrae*

The framing of the line with *lucus* and *umbrae,* here and at 6.138–39 (hunc tegit omnis / *lucus* et obscuris claudunt convallibus *umbrae*) may allude to the famous κατ' ἀντίφρασιν etymology, *lucus a non lucendo.* Caution is called for; groves are shady even without the help of etymology.

For framing see intro. 2.8, for κατ' ἀντίφρασιν cf. intro. 1.6 (on Aelius Stilo) and 2.3.

SERV. 441: "lucus" autem dicitur quod non luceat, non quod sint ibi lumina causa religionis, ut quidam volunt; SERV. A. 1.22: et dictae sunt Parcae κατὰ ἀντίφρασιν, quod nulli parcant, sicut lucus a non lucendo, bellum a nulla re bella; QUINT. 1.6.34: etiamne a contrariis aliqua sinemus trahi, ut "lucus" quia umbra opacus parum luceat? (=? Aelius Stilo fr. 59, *GRF* p. 72).

**A. 1.493:** bellatrix, audetque *viris* concurrere *virgo*

Both paronomasia and etymological thought conect *virgo* and *vir,* Paratore says the "alliterazione antifrastica" throws into relief the usual actions of a girl among men. As many have noted, the Homeric model at *Il.* 3.188 calls the Amazons ἀντιάνειραι, "a match for men"; de la Cerda suggests that Vergil's wordplay constitutes an allusion to the Homeric epithet.

FEST. p. 314, 14 L: feminas antiqui . . . viras appellebant; unde adhuc permanent virgines et viragines; *VULG. Gen.* 2.23: vocabitur virgo, quoniam de viro sumpta est.

CIC. *Off.* 1.18.61 (citing an unidentified poet): "Vos enim, iuvenes, animum geritis muliebrem, illa (sc. Cloelia) *virgo viri*"; OVID *Met.* 4.681–82 (for Ovid cf. intro. 2.14): primo silet illa nec audet / adpellare *virum virgo* (sc. Andromeda).

Cerda (1612) 95; cf. Conington (1963), Page (1894), and Paratore (1978–83) on 493; this example was called to my attention by G. Tissol.

*

**A. 1.522:** o regina, *novam* cui condere Iuppiter *urbem*

For Vergil's several allusions to "new city" as an etymology of Carthage see on 1.297–300.

SERV. 522: NOVAM VRBEM iuxta Poenorum opinionem dixit, qui novam civitatem Carthaginem dicunt.

**A. 1.530–33:**

est locus, *Hesperiam* Grai cognomine dicunt,
terra antiqua, potens armis atque ubere glaebae;
*Oenotri* coluere viri; nunc fama minores
**Italiam** dixisse **ducis** de nomine **gentem.**

The reference to the name *Hesperia* looks like an etymological signpost (*Grai cognomine dicunt;* see intro. 2.6), although no wordplay or reference to Land of the Evening seems intended. Vergil seems instead to allude to the earlier poetic history of the word—this is the second major function of naming constructions like *dicunt.* Line 530 adapts Enn. *Ann.* 20 Sk.: *est locus Hesperiam quam mortales perhibebant. Hesperia,* "the Western Land," is a "Greek poetic name of Italy" (Skutsch ad Enn. loc. cit.) found in Apoll. Rhod. 3.311 (of Circe's home), Agathyllus ap. D.H. 1.49.2, D.H. 1.35.3. Skutsch argues that in Ennius as in Vergil, a reference to the name *Italia* must have followed, to provide a contrast between the former name (imperfect *per-*

*hibebant*) and the present one. Skutsch thus rejects the view of some "that it was the neoterics who first in imitation of Callimachus (e.g., *Hymn. Dian.* 58) lengthened the first syllable" of *Italia.*

Line 533 presents an explicit etymology of the name *Italia,* which is derived from the name of a king Italus (mentioned in Thucydides, Aristotle, and A. 7). Servius Auctus mentions another (historically probable?) derivation, which connected the name with Greek ἰταλός, "calf" (cf. Latin *vitulus*).

The reference to *Oenotri viri* in 532 alludes to another name of Italy, *Oenotria,* named either after a Sabine or Arcadian king, or for its good wine (οἶνος).

These lines are repeated at A. 3.163–66. Vergil also treats different names of Italy at 8.319–32.

For *metonomasia* and for *nunc* in aetiologies see intro. 2.10 and 2.10a.

Italia from ἰταλός is in Serv. and in Timaeus and Varro ap. Aul. Gell. 11.1.1; Italus is an ancestor of Latinus at A. 7.178, a Sicilian king in Thuc. 6.2.4 and Serv. on A. 1.533, and king of Oenotria in Arist. *Pol.* 7.9.2 (more in Maltby); SERV. 532: OENOTRI COLVERE VIRI . . . "Oenotria" autem dicta est vel a vino optimo, quod in Italia nascitur, vel, ut Varro dicit, ab Oenotro, rege Sabinorum; SERV. Auct. 533: ITALIAM DIXISSE Italus, rex Siciliae, ad eam partem venit in qua regnavit Turnus, quam a suo nomine appellavit Italiam; unde est (11.317) "fines super usque Sicanos" non "usque ad Siciliam"–nec enim poterat fieri–sed "usque ad ea loca quae tenuerunt Sicani," id est Siculi a Sicano, Itali fratre. alii "Italiam" a bubus quibus est Italia fertilis, quia Graeci boves ἰταλούς, nos "vitulos" dicimus; alii a rege Ligurum Italo; alii ab advena Molossio; alii a Corcyreo; alii a Veneris filio, rege Lucanorum; alii a quodam augure, qui cum Sicilis in haec loca venerit . . . ; SERV. A. 1.2: Italus enim rex Siculorum profectus de Sicilia venit ad loca quae sunt iuxta Tiberim, et ex nomine suo appellavit Italiam; for Hesperia see the sources in Maltby s.v.

Cf. Cerda (1612) 101–2.

*

**A. 1.565–66:** quis genus Aeneadum, quis Troiae nesciat urbem, / *virtutes*que *viros*que aut tanti incendia belli?

Here and elsewhere Vergil plays on the connection, natural and familiar to the Romans but weakened at times by our English translations, between the words *vir* and *virtus,* in passages in which *virtus* is not just "courage" or "virtue" but "manliness, the essence of being a *vir* (as opposed to a *puer*)."

VARRO *LL* 5.73.4: virtus ut viritus a virilitate; CIC. *Tusc.* 2.43: appellata est . . . ex viro virtus; LACT. *Opif.* 12.16: vir itaque nuncupatus est, quod maior in eo vis est quam in femina, et hinc virtus nomen accepit; cf. ISID. 18.22: virtus est immensitas virium in labore et pondere corporis vocata (more in Maltby).

A. 3.342: antiquam *virtutem* animosque *virilis;* 4.3: multa *viri virtus* animo multusque recursat; 8.500: flos veterum *virtus*que *virum;* 9.641: macte nova *vir*tute, *puer*; 12.435: disce, *puer, vir*tutem ex me; cf. the different wordplay at 1.493: audetque *viris* concurrere *virgo*; CAT. 68.90: Troia *virum* et *virtutum* omnium acerba cinis;

HOR. *Epist.* 1.17.41–42: aut *virtus* nomen inane est, / aut decus et pretium recte petit experiens *vir;* cf. PLAUT. *Amph.* 212: magnanimi *viri* freti *virtute* et *viribus.*

See Bartelink (1965) 110–11, Ahl (1986) 28–29, Petrini (n.d.) chap. 5.

**A. 1.662:** *urit* atrox Iuno et sub noctem ***cura*** **recursat**

There are two kinds of wordplay here. For *urit* and *cura,* see on **1.208** for the etymology *cura quod cor urat.* Also, Austin notes that the verb *recurso* occurs three times in Vergil, each time with or near *cura;* Petrini calls it a *schema etymologicum.*

A. 4.1–3: at regina gravi iamdudum saucia *cura* / vulnus alit venis et caeco carpitur igni. / multa viri virtus animo multusque *recursat;* A. 12.801–2: ne . . . mihi *curae* / saepe tuo dulci tristes ex ore *recursent.*

Austin (1955) on 4.3, Kristol (1990) 92, Petrini (n.d.) chap. 5.

**A. 1.688–89?:** occultum inspires ignem fallasque *veneno.* / paret Amor dictis carae *genetricis* (sc. *Veneris*), et alas

This is an example for which there is no explicit ancient support. *Venenum* is related etymologically to *Venus* (cf. Ernout-Meillet and Walde-Hofmann s.v. venenum), and has the basic meaning "love potion." We have no explicit testimony for ancient awareness of this connection, only Lucretius' "loose association . . . of *Venus* with *venenum*" (Snyder) at *DRN* 5.895–900 and 1009–17, and this passage of Vergil, where *veneno* in 688 is spoken by Venus, and in the next line *genetricis* = *Veneris.*

Servius Auctus says that *venenum* is so called because it goes through the veins *(quod per venas eat),* and connects this passage with 1.749 *longumque bibebat amorem.* Due sees these two passages connected by the association of *Venus* with *venenum* (cf. on **4.1–5**).

For plausible but unattested etymologies see on **A. 3.192–94.**

SERV. Auct. 688: venenum dictum ab eo, quod per venas eat. ideo post ait (749) "longumque bibebat amorem."

Due (1973) 278, Snyder (1980) 106 (notes the collocation in Vergil as well).

**A. 1.701–2:** dant *manibus* famuli lymphas Cereremque canistris / expediunt tonsisque ferunt *mantelia* villis.

The word *manibus* may gloss *mantelia,* both here and at G. 4.376–77, even though the Homeric model at *Od.* 1.146 also mentions hands: ὕδωρ ἐπὶ χεῖρας ἔχευαν.

VARRO *LL* 6.85: mantelium, ubi manus terguntur; SERV. 702: "mantelia" vero a tergendis manibus dicta; ISID. 19.26.6: mantelia . . . ut nomen ipsud indicat, olim tergendis manibus praebebantur.

G. 4.376–77: *manibus* liquidos dant ordine fontis / germanae, tonsisque ferunt *mantelia* villis.

**A. 1.703–4:** quinquaginta intus famulae, quibus ordine longam / cura *penum* struere et flammis adolere *penatis*

Cicero and Varro mention the possible derivation of *penates* from *penus* or from *penitus.*

CIC. *ND* 2.27.68: penates sive a penu ducto nomine . . . sive ab eo quod penitus insident; ex quo etiam penetrales a poetis vocatur; SERV. Auct. A. 3.12 (citing Varro): quos (sc. penates) Romani penitus in cultu habent . . . , qui ideo penates appellantur, quod in penetralibus aedium coli soleant; nam et ipsum penetral penus dicitur . . . ; cf. VARRO fr. 374, *GRF* p. 344; PAUL.-Fest. p. 231, 1 L; SERV. Auct. A. 2.296; MACROB. 3.4.8.

Bartelink (1965) 80, Kenney (1979) 116 and n. 58.

**A. 1.719–22:**

at memor ille (sc. Amor)
matris *Acidaliae* paulatim abolere Sychaeum
incipit et vivo temptat praevertere amore
iam pridem resides animos desuetaque corda

Servius connects the rare Acidalia with Greek ἀκίς, "arrow, dart, care, pang." Acidalia thus suggests both *curae* and the arrows of Cupid, both appropriate to the context, where Venus' instructions to Cupid and plotting with Juno will produce *curae* for Dido and for Aeneas. Vergil's *mater Acidalia* seems to be the "mother who produces sharp *curae.*"

I have argued that Catullus 64.72 provides a parallel and perhaps a model for Vergil, by referring to Venus as *spinosas Erycina serens in pectore curas. Spinosus,* "thorny," describing *cura* only here in Latin literature, glosses Erycina, as if to associate it with *ericius.* This word is used of a spiked military apparatus used to ward off the enemy; literally it refers to the hedgehog, which is covered with spikes, *spinae,* which are mentioned in most references to it. So in Catullus too Venus is emphatically described as a producer of "thorny cares."

At *Met.* 5.363–68, Ovid is imitating Vergil's Cupid-Venus scene from A. 1, but uses Catullus' epithet for Venus, Erycina, perhaps to show that he sees both what Vergil is doing, and that Catullus had done it before (cf. intro. 2.14).

As Hollis has noticed, the *Etymologicum Genuinum* explains the epithet Κιδαλία, in a fragment of verse without attribution but that may be Callimachean, as the poet's misreading (we might say, scholarly interpretation) of the words χεῖρ' Ἀκιδαλίας in a fragment of Pindar as χεῖρα Κιδαλίας (cf. Callim. fr. inc. 751). If Vergil were aware of the passages from Pindar and (?)Callimachus, he could be entering the scholarly debate to offer his support for the reading χεῖρ' Ἀκιδαλίας.

For wordplay involving thorns cf. on G. 3.338 *acalanthida dumi*. For more on this passage, including another model in Apollonius of Rhodes, cf. intro. 2.13, and my article cited below.

Acidalia: PIND. fr. 244 S-M: χεῖρ' Ἀκιδαλία; MENOPHIL. Damasc. (date uncertain): φαιδρὴν εἶδον ἅπασαν ἐειδομένη Χαρίτεσσιν/ἐρχομέναις πρὸς Ὄλυμπον Ἀκιδαλίης ἀπὸ πηγῆς (*SH* 558.14–15); MART. 9.13.3: nomen Acidalia meruit quod harundine pingi, / quod Cytherea sua scribere gaudet acu; *ETYM. GEN.* B s.v. Κιδαλία: ἡ γὰρ λίμνη Ἀκιδαλία ἐκαλεῖτο· οἷον 'Κιδαλίης κρηνῖδος'· ἐλπίζω δὲ ὅτι ἐπλανήθη ἐκ τοῦ Πινδαρικοῦ· ἄλλως γὰρ διέστειλε καὶ ἐπλανήθη ΧΕΙΡΑΚΙΔΑΛΙΑΣ (= Pind. fr. 244); *ETYM. MAG.* s.v. Ἀκιδαλίη: ἔστιν δὲ ὄνομα κρήνης· ἔστιν Ἄκις ἄκιδος, ὄνομα κύριον· καὶ ἐκ τούτου Ἀκίδαλος, καὶ Ἀκιδαλίη; SERV. 720: "Acidalia" Venus dicitur vel quia inicit curas, quas Graeci ἀκίδας dicunt, vel certe a fonte Acidalio, qui est in Orchomeno, Boeotiae civitate, in quo se abluunt Gratiae, quas Veneri constat esse sacratas; ipsius enim et Liberi filiae sunt: nec immerito; gratiae enim per horum fere numinum munera conciliantur.

Ericius: SALL. *Hist.* fr. 3.36; CAESAR *Civ.* 3.67.5 and 6; RABIRIUS fr. 5 Morel: portarumque fuit custos ericius [codd.; Erucius Baehrens, cf. A. 9.176 Nisus erat portae custos]; ISID. 12.3.7: ericium animal spinis coopertum; SCHOL. Juv. 6.276: the *eruca* is a *genus animalis . . . spinosi, ut ericius.*

More in O'Hara (1990a) and (1996), Hollis (1992).

**A. 1.742:** hic canit *errantem lunam* solisque labores

Serv. G. 1.337 *(quos ignis caelo Cyllenius erret in orbis)* notes that Vergil is playing there on the etymology of the word planet: "the word *'erret'* is well chosen, because planets are so called after the Greek word πλάνη, which means 'wandering.'" At A. 1.742, Vergil's phrase *errantem lunam* alludes to the same etymology, again with *planetes* not expressed (see intro. 2.7); to the ancient mind, the moon is just as much a planet or "wanderer" as is Mercury.

Iopas' song is at Dido's banquet; see on **A. 4.211** for Vergil's wordplay on Dido, *planetes,* and the verb *erro.*

SERV. G. 1.337: bene "erret"; nam planetae vocantur ἀπὸ τῆς πλάνης, id est ab errore.

**A. 1.742–44:** hic canit . . . / unde hominum genus et pecudes, unde *imber* et ignes, / Arcturum *pluviasque Hyadas* geminosque Triones

Here *pluvias,* as Servius notes, is a gloss on the name *Hyadas,* as if from ὕω, "to rain." The Hyades' rising in late May marked the beginning of the spring rains. (Cf. single-adjective glosses in intro. 2.2.)

SERV. 744: PLVVIASQVE HYADAS hyades stellae sunt in fronte tauri, quae quotiens nascuntur pluvias creant; unde et Graece ὑάδες dictae sunt ἀπὸ τοῦ ὕειν, Latine "suculae" a suco. sic ergo ait "pluviasque hyades," ut (3.693) "Plemyrium undosum." alii dicunt hyadas dictas vel ab Υ littera vel ἀπὸ τοῦ ὑὸς, id est, sue, in cuius formatae sunt faciem.

A. 3.516 = 1.744; **G. 1.137–38:** *navita* tum stellis numeros et nomina fecit / *Pleiadas, Hyadas,* claramque Lycaonis Arcton.

Bartelink (1965) 76, O'Hara (1992); cf. Brown (1990).

**A. 2.1:** conticuere omnes *intenti*que ora *tenebant*
Juxtaposition of cognates.

Bartelink (1965) 93.

**A. 2.42–49?:**

et procul "o miseri, quae tanta insania, cives?
creditis avectos hostis? aut ulla putatis
*dona* carere dolis *Danaum?* sic notus Vlixes?
aut hoc inclusi ligno occultantur Achivi,
aut haec in nostros fabricata est machina muros,
inspectura domos venturaque desuper urbi,
aut aliquis latet error; equo ne credite, Teucri.
quidquid id est, timeo *Danaos* et *dona* ferentis."

Moskalew suggests wordplay between *Danai,* which is used as a name for the Greeks more often in A. 2 than elsewhere, and *dona,* possibly in imitation of a lost Hellenistic poet who "may well have connected Δαναοί with the rare poeticism δάνος, meaning gift." He names Euphorion, who uses δάνος in fr. 42 P, as one candidate for such wordplay.

Moskalew (1990).

**A. 2.199–200?:** hic aliud maius miseris multoque tremendum / *obicitur* magis atque improvida pectora turbat
Kleinknecht suggests that in this reference to the portent of the snakes that devour Laocoon, *obicitur* evokes the idea contained etymologically in *ostentum,* "portent" (from **obs-tentum*). He compares **A. 5.522–23,** hic oculis subitum *obicitur* magnoque futurum / augurio *monstrum.*

Kleinknecht (1963) 431.

**A. 2.79, 195, 259, 329?:** Sinon
Knox suggests that Sinon's name, "with its resemblance to *sinus, sinuo,* etc.," helps to bring out the suggestion that Sinon, like the other "principal instruments of the Trojan downfall," is "linked with the image of the serpent." It is difficult to see

exactly where the name works in this way. De la Cerda suggests a connection with σίνομαι, "harm, hurt."

Cerda (1612) 158, Knox (1950) 390.

**A. 2.227?:** sub pedibusque deae *clipei*que sub orbe *teguntur*.

De la Cerda sees possible allusion to a derivation of *clipeus* from κλέπτω, "conceal, keep secret," or καλύπτω, "cover, protect," here and at A. 11.630.

SERV. A. 2.389: "clipeos" maiora scuta, quibus latemus, ἀπὸ τοῦ κλέπτειν τὸ σῶμα; LYD. *Mag.* 1.10. p. 16.3 W: κλίπεον δὲ Ῥωμαῖοι τὸν θυρεὸν καλοῦσιν ἀπὸ τοῦ κλέπτειν καὶ καλύπτειν τὸν ἐπιφερόμενον αὐτόν (more in Maltby).

Cerda (1612) 182.

**A. 2.263?:** Pelidesque Neoptolemus primusque Machaon

Here "*primus* is a puzzle" (Austin). Mørland suggests a series of associations involving Neoptomelos = νέος πτόλεμος = νέος (primus) + μάχη (Machaon). Cf. on 2.469–75.

SERV. 263: NEOPTOLEMVS quia ad bellum ductus est puer, Pyrrhus vero a capillorum qualitate vocitatus est.

Austin (1964) on 263, Mørland (1960) 23; Mackail (1930) on 261–64 on the question "why *primus*?": "Why not?"

**A. 2.310–12?:** iam *Deiphobi* dedit ampla ruinam / Volcano superante domus, iam proximus ardet / *Ucalegon*

Ucalegon or Οὐκάλεγων appears first in *Il.* 3.148; his name means "not caring" (οὐκ ἀλέγων). Kraggerud and Gantat argue that Ucalegon, who does not care or is not worried, is to be contrasted with Deiphobus, whose name suggests φόβος, "fear." They note that in A. 6, Deiphobus describes himself as worried when going to bed (6.520–21: tum me confectum *curis* somnoque gravatum / infelix habuit thalamus), in contrast to most Trojans, who are carefree after the apparent departure of the Greeks. Gantat argues that the "indifferent" Ucalegon is in *Il.* 3 to be contrasted with the circumspect Antenor, and that the other appearance of the name, at Juv. 3.198, suggests a man "indifferent" to the dangers of the city.

Nothing in the texts of Homer, Vergil, or Juvenal actually draws attention to the etymology of the name.

Cerda (1612) 201, Kraggerud (1960) 36–38, Gantat (1971) 1–6.

## A. 2.469–75:

vestibulum ante ipsum primoque in limine *Pyrrhus*
exsultat telis et *luce coruscus aena:*
qualis ubi in lucem coluber mala gramina pastus,
frigida sub terra tumidum quem bruma tegebat,
nunc, positis **novus** exuviis nitidusque iuventa,
lubrica convolvit sublato pectore terga
arduus ad solem, et linguis micat ore trisulcis.

In several passages Vergil plays with the associations of the two names for Achilles' son, Pyrrhus and Neoptolemus. Pyrrhus, which first appears in 469, is associated with πυρρός, "flame colored, redheaded"; Servius says Pyrrhus is so called after the color of his hair. Knox has described the extensive thematic association of Pyrrhus with the fire (πῦρ) that destroys Troy. Vergil may allude to this in 470 by describing Pyrrhus as *luce coruscus aena,* "a flash of brazen-lustrous arms" (Austin's translation). More certainly, he alludes to the association in 529 *ardens . . . Pyrrhus.*

The name Neoptolemus, which first appears in 263, is from νέος, "new," and πτόλεμος, "war." Servius says he is so called because he is brought to war while a *puer;* Austin calls him the "young fighter." In the snake simile of 471-75, *novus,* as Knox notes, alludes to the νέος, "new," element in the name Neoptolemus, here suppressed (see intro. 2.7). Knox finds here an allusion not only to "the renewal of the old war, the rebirth of the old warrior," since "Pyrrhus is Achilles reborn in his son," but also the brighter future, and the rebirth of a "new" Troy in Italy. The snake simile seems grimmer to me: in Italy, the Trojans will find "new war" and another new Achilles (in some respects) in Turnus.

Bowie, in discussing allegorical associations of the death of Priam with that of Pompey, suggests that "Virgil wins a new pun from the name" Neoptolemus, associating him as the killer of Priam with Ptolemy the killer of Pompey: "Pyrrhus really is a new Ptolemy." Some may be uncomfortable with such detailed allegorical interpretation.

For alternate names cf. intro. 2.10.

SERV. 469: PYRRHVS a colore comae dictus, qui Latine "burrus" dicitur. ita et Sallustius "Crispus"; SERV. 263: NEOPTOLEMVS quia ad bellum ductus est puer, Pyrrhus vero a capillorum qualitate vocitatus est; LYCOPH. 183: οὐλαμώνυμος (οὐλαμός = armed throng); CIC. *de Orat.* 2.63.257: ut ego nuper Nummium divisorem, ut Neoptolemum ad Troiam, sic illum in Campo Martio nomen invenisse; SCHOL. *Il.* 19.326: Νεοπτόλεμος δὲ ἀπὸ τοῦ πατρὸς ὠνόμασται, ὅτι νέος ὢν ἐπολέμησεν; PAUS. 10.26.4: τὰ δὲ Κύπρια ἔπη (fr. XIV, pp. 122-23 Allen) φησὶν ὑπὸ Λυκομήδους μέν Πύρρον, Νεοπτόλεμον δὲ ὄνομα ὑπὸ Φοίνικος αὐτῷ τεθῆναι, ὅτι Ἀχιλλεὺς ἡλικίᾳ ἔτι νέος πολεμεῖν ἤρξατο.

Knox (1950) 394 (fnn. not in Commager reprint), with refs., Rank (1951) 92–93, Kenney (1979) 105–12, Austin (1964) on 263 and on 469, Mørland (1960) 24, Mühmelt (1965) 61, Bowie (1990) 478.

**A. 2.529–30:** illum *ardens* infesto vulnere *Pyrrhus* / insequitur

*Ardens* is a single-adjective gloss (see intro. 2.2) on the name Pyrrhus (cf. πῦρ), alluding to the thematic connections of Neoptolemus with the fire that burns Troy. See on 2.469–75.

On fire in *A.* 2 see Knox (1950), but Knox does not mention 2.529; see too Kenney (1979) 105. Austin (1964) on 529 notes that *ardens* is "chosen to suit Pyrrhus' name."

**A. 2.557?:** iacet *ingens* litore truncus

Servius Auctus suggests that Vergil alludes to the fate of Pompeius Magnus, whose cognomen is perhaps suggested by *ingens.*

SERV. Auct. 557: IACET INGENS LITORE TRVNCVS Pompei tangit historiam, cum "ingens" dicit, non "magnus."

Kenney (1979) 118 and n. 67, Williams (1973) ad loc., Moles (1983) (on the source in Asinius Pollio), Feeney (1986a) (Lucan's plays on the name *Magnus*), Bowie (1990).

**A. 2.606–7:** tu ne qua *parentis* / iussa time neu praeceptis *parere* recusa

Simple wordplay between *părens,* "parent," and *pāreo,* "obey." On such paronomasia see intro. 2.1, and cf. esp. A. 4.238 *pārere părabat,* and Vell. Pat. 2.39.3 *parendi . . . parens.*

Cf. Austin (1955) on 4.238, Ahl (1985) 107.

**A. 2.682–84, 692–98:**

ecce levis summo de vertice visus Iuli
fundere lumen apex, tactuque innoxia mollis
lambere flamma *comas* et circum tempora pasci.
. . . . . . . . . . . . . . . . . . . . . . . . . . . . . . .
. . . . . . . . . . . . . . . . . . . . . . subitoque fragore
intonuit laevum, et de caelo lapsa per umbras
*stella facem ducens* multa cum luce cucurrit.
illam summa super labentem culmina tecti
cernimus Idaea claram se condere silva
signantemque vias; tum longo limite sulcus
dat lucem et late circum loca sulphure fumant.

The omen of the fire that licks Ascanius' head without burning him is confirmed, in response to Anchises' request, by the omen of the falling star. The connection between the two omens is underscored by the etymological connection between *comas* in 681 and *cometes,* alluded to but not expressed (i.e., suppressed in the Alexandrian manner; cf. intro. 2.7) in 694 *stella facem ducens.* A *cometes* or *crinita* (Greek κομήτης) is so called because it seems to have hair (*coma*/*crines*/κώμη).

The etymological connection between the words for comet and hair is one of the features that link several passages involving stars/comets, flames, heads, and hair. Linked to Ascanius' flaming head and the falling star are Acestes' flaming arrow (5.527–28), the omen of Lavinia's flaming hair (7.71–80), the appearance of the Sidus Iulium behind Augustus' head at the battle of Actium (8.678–81), the flame that seems to leap from Aeneas helmet as he arrives at the battle, which is compared to a star (10.270), and perhaps Aeneas' use of a line Vergil has adapted from Catullus' *Coma Berenices* (6.46). Knox has suggested that Ovid's use of the wordplay recalls Callimachus' *Coma* (*Aet.* fr. 110); in some way this poem may lie behind Vergil's etymologizing as well.

Pliny *NH* 2.89: cometas Graeci vocant, nostri crinitas, horrentes crine sanguineo et comarum modo in vertice hispidas; SERV. A. 10.272: cometae autem latine crinitae appellantur (ISID. 3.71.17 adds: quia in modum crinium flammas spargunt); CIC. *ND* 2.14: stellis his, quas Graeci κομήτας, nostri cincinnatas vocant (more in Maltby).

OVID *Met.* 15.746–50 (for Ovid cf. intro. 2.14): quem (sc. Caesarem) . . . in sidus vertere novum stellamque comantem; LUCAN 1.528–29: crinemque timendi sideris; PETRON. *BC* 139 (*Sat.* 122): fax stellis comitata novis incendia duxit; A. 5.527–28: caelo ceu saepe refixa / transcurrunt *crinem*que volantia *sidera* ducunt; A. 8.678–81: hinc Augustus agens Italos in proelia *Caesar* / cum patribus populoque, penatibus et magnis dis, / stans celsa in puppi, geminas cui tempora flammas / laeta vomunt *patrium*que aperitur vertice *sidus;* A. 10.270–73: ardet apex capiti cristisque a vertice flamma / funditur et vastos umbo vomit aureus ignis: / non secus ac liquida si quando nocte *cometae* / sanguinei lugubre rubent.

Skulsky (1985) 447–55, esp. 452, Knox (1986) 76, Connors (1989) 104–5 (on Lucan and Petronius, who, she suggests, offers an alternate derivation from *comitata*), Nadeau (1982), Scott (1941) ("The Sidus Iulium and the Apotheosis of Caesar").

**A. 2.761–63:** et iam porticibus vacuis Iunonis *asylo* / custodes lecti Phoenix et dirus Vlixes / *praedam* adservabant.

At this first occurrence of *asylum* in extant Latin poetry (Austin), Vergil provides an ironic gloss. Servius Auctus explains that *asylum* is from the verb συλάω, "carry off as spoil," presumably with an α- privative, meaning "place from which persons or plunder cannot be removed." This is where the Greeks keep their *praeda.*

SERV. 761: IUNONIS ASYLO templo; unde nullus possit ad supplicum extrahi. dictum asylum quasi "asyrum" (see below on text); SERV. Auct. continues: alii asylum ideo dictum, quod nullus inde tolleretur, id est, quod συλᾶσθαι, hoc est, abripi nullus inde poterat; vel quod fugienti illuc spolia non detraherentur; σῦλα enim Graece aut furta aut spolia dicuntur (more in Maltby).

Bartelink (1965) 86, Hanssen (1948) 122; on Serv. see Fraenkel (1948) 142–43, who would "complete" Serv. by adding ⟨ad quod quisquis confugiebat nefas erat inde trahi⟩, and Mühmelt (1965) 61–62.

**A. 3.17–18:** moenia prima loco fatis ingressus iniquis / *Aeneadas*que meo nomen de nomine fingo.

Here *nomen de nomine* is an etymological signpost (see intro. 2.6). Williams: "Virgil is not specific about the name of the town, perhaps because of confusion between two different places," namely Aenus at the mouth of the Hebrus River, and Aeneia in Chalcidice. Servius notes that Callimachus and Euphorion say that Aenus was named after a companion of Odysseus buried there; Vergil perhaps offers a polemical countersuggestion.

Williams: "There was a town called Aenus at the mouth of the Hebrus where according to Pliny (*NH* 4.43) the tomb of Polydorus was shown; see also Pomp. Mela 2.28. It is referred to by Homer (*Il.* 4.520), so it evidently became part of the Aeneas legend because of its name rather than vice versa. The town Aeneia in Chalcidice was said to have been founded by Aeneas (D.H. 1.49.4, Livy 40.4.9) and that part of the world was strongly associated with the Aeneas legend, but it seems too far west to be in question here."

SERV. 17: Euphorion (fr. 62 P) et Callimachus (fr. 697) hoc dicunt etiam, quod Aenum dicatur a socio Ulixis illic sepulto eo tempore quo missus est ad frumenta portanda; cf. also EUPHOR. *SH* 416.3 and the scholia, which seem to discuss a name change from Poltymbria (named after Poltys) to Aenus.

Bartelink (1965) 38, Williams (1962) on 18.

## A. 3.22–26, 37–41, 45–46:

> forte fuit iuxta tumulus, quo cornea summo
> virgulta et densis *hastilibus* horrida myrtus.
> accessi viridemque ab humo convellere silvam
> conatus, ramis tegerem ut frondentibus aras,
> horrendum et dictu video mirabile monstrum.
> . . . . . . . . . . . . . . . . . . . . . . . . . . . .
> tertia sed postquam maiore *hastilia* nisu
> adgredior genibusque adversae obluctor harenae,
> (eloquar an sileam?) gemitus lacrimabilis imo
> auditur tumulo et vox reddita fertur ad auris:
> "quid miserum, Aenea, laceras?
> . . . . . . . . . . . . . . . . . . . . . .
> nam Polydorus ego. hic confixum *ferrea* texit
> *telorum seges* et *iaculis* increvit acutis."

The word *hastilia* can refer to a "spear-like stem or rod, cane" (*OLD*, cf. *TLL* s.v. 2557 41ff.), as at G. 2.358, and here seems first to denote "the spiky growth of the tree" (Williams), but as the scene plays out we see that these are the real spear shafts with which Polydorus was killed *(ferrea seges* and *iaculis* in 45–46 perhaps suggest *hasta).* The real or etymological meaning of the word "prepares us for the portent that follows" (Conington).

Bartelink (1965) 106, Conington (1963) on 23, Williams (1962) on 22–23; on the scene see also Thomas (1988a).

**A. 3.126–27:** *sparsas*que per aequor / *Cycladas,* et crebris legimus freta *concita* terris

The word *sparsas* modifies Cycladas but could serve as a gloss on or allusion to the name Sporades, the islands "scattered" off the West Coast of Asia Minor, as opposed to the Cyclades, thought to be further off the coast, around Delos. Servius Auctus reports that some thought Vergil was using the name Cyclades of the Sporades, since the Sporades are the ones that are *sparsae,* "scattered"; see *EV* for ancient confusion of the names.

For a transferred adjective, or one that alludes to a noun other than the one it modifies, cf. the use of *superbus* of Brutus at A. 6.817–18, next to a reference to the Tarquins, the last of whom was Tarquinius Superbus.

The name Sporades may have been discussed by Callimachus; see Pliny *NH* 4.65–71, which in discussing the Cyclades and Sporades cites Callimachus a number of times (probably from an intermediary). Callimachus *Hymn* 4.198, Κυκλάδας . . . περιηγέας, offers a gloss of the name Cyclades, "lying in a circle." Ovid repeats Vergil's epithet *sparsas,* and perhaps the wordplay (cf. intro. 2.14).

In 127 Hirtzel printed not *concita* but *consita,* with the comment "consita deteriores pauci, probat Bentley"; this participle (Williams:) "would refer etymologically to the Sporades, the group of islands south and East of the Cyclades (σπείρειν, *serere*). But I would prefer to retain the reading *concita* ('made rough by')."

SERV. 126: SPARSASQVE PER AEQVOR CYCLADAS et hae quas dixit Cyclades sunt; unde minus est "et alias." "sparsas" autem, quia nullo ordine continentur, ut stoechades, quae ἀπὸ τοῦ στοίχου dictae sunt; rectae enim sunt. Cyclades vero non ideo dicuntur, quia in rotunditate sunt, sed quod longo ordine eas circumire necesse est (more on Cyclades in Maltby s.v.); SERV. Auct. 126: alii Sporadas nomine Cycladum dictas tradunt, quod sparsae sunt; PARAPHR. Dionys. Perieg. 130: ἐκ τοῦ σποράδην ἐν τῷ πελάγει κεῖσθαι Σποράδες καλοῦνται; POMP. Mela 2.7.111: hae quia dispersae sunt Sporades.

OVID *Met.* 2.263–64: quod modo pontus erat, quoque altum texerat aequor, / exsistunt montes et *sparsas Cycladas* augent.

Cerda (1612) 300, Bartelink (1965) 56 (mentions possible play in the variant *consita*), Williams (1962) on 127, Hirtzel (1990), *EV* s.v. Cicladi (Bonamente); on Cycladas here more generally see Hardie (1986) 102 n. 47; on Callimachus, Mineur (1984) 183.

**A. 3.132–34:** ergo avidus muros optatae molior urbis / Pergameamque voco, et laetam cognomine gentem / hortor amare focos arcemque attollere tectis.

An explicit etymological *aition* for the naming of a town in Crete (mentioned by Velleius 1.1.2 and Pliny *NH* 4.59) after the Trojan citadel. Servius Auctus tells two stories about Pergamum, one that it was founded by Aeneas, another that it was founded by Trojans who left Troy as Agamemnon's captives, and then later named after another Aeneas.

Williams on *cognomine:* "Virgil often uses this word in a context which implies the meaning ἐπωνυμία, the calling of a new thing after an old." See also intro. 2.6.

Williams (1961) on 133.

## A. 3.163–66:

est locus, *Hesperiam* Grai cognomine dicunt,
terra antiqua, potens armis atque ubere glaebae;
Oenotri coluere viri; nunc fama minores
*Italiam* dixisse ducis de nomine *gentem*

Repeated from **A. 1.530–33.**

**A. 3.192–94:** Postquam altum tenuere rates nec iam amplius ullae / apparent terrae, *caelum* undique et undique pontus, / tum mihi *caeruleus* supra caput astitit imber

*Caeruleus* is probably derived from *caelum* (see Walde-Hofmann and Ernout-Meillet s.v.; Eden translates it "sky-like"). No ancient source explicitly comments on this (so Maltby), but it is tempting to think that the juxtaposition of these words in Ennius, Lucretius, and Vergil alludes to the etymological connection.

A. 5.8–10 (almost = 3.192–94); 8.64: caeruleus Thybris, caelo gratissimus amnis; ENN. *Ann.* 48 Sk.: caeli caerula templa; LUCR. 6.96: caerula caeli.

Other examples of possible etymologizing, where the etymology is plausible, but anattested in ancient sources: A. 1.688–89?: occultum inspires ignem fallasque *veneno.* / paret Amor dictis carae *genetricis* (sc. *Veneris*), et alas; A. 5.8–10: ut pelagus tenuere rates nec iam amplius ulla / occurrit tellus, maria undique et undique *caelum,* / olli *caeruleus* supra caput astitit imber.

Bartelink (1965) 104, Ellis (1985) 4, Eden (1975) on 8.64; on *caerula* cf. also Skutsch (1985) 281.

**A. 3.210:** *Strophades* Graio stant nomine dictae

With the etymological signpost *Graio . . . nomine dictae* (see intro. 2.6), Vergil calls attention to the name *Strophades,* which is derived, as Servius notes, from the Greek στροφή, "turning," because there the winged Argonauts Zetes and Calais "turned back" after chasing the Harpies away from Phineus. Apollonius of Rhodes made the etymology explicit in the passage cited below.

Williams notes (with disapproval) that some have seen in *stant* at A. 3.210 an allusion to the former name Plotae, Floating Islands. Such an allusion would be modeled on Callim. *Hymn* 4.36–54, where the name of the floating island Asterie is changed to Delos when after the birth of Apollo the island becomes rooted and no longer "obscure" (ἄδηλος). More generally one thinks of Callimachus' prose treatise *Foundations of Cities and Islands and Their Changes of Names*; see Callim. fr. 601

with Pfeiffer's notes for changes of island names in Callimachus' poetry, and cf. intro. 2.10, and also the names of islands marked in intro. 2.4b.

In A. 3.210–80 Vergil follows the etymologizing or verbal learning of Apollonius in several passages: see on 226 *(Harpyiae)*, 270 *(Neritos ardua)*, and 280 *(Actia litora)*.

SERV. 209: Argonautae Zethum et Calain, filios Boreae et Orithyiae, alatos iuvenes, ad pellendas harpyias miserunt; quas cum strictis gladiis persequerentur pulsas de Arcadia, pervenerunt ad insulas quae appellabantur Plotae. et cum ulterius vellent tendere, ab Iride admoniti ut desisterent a Iovis canibus, suos converterunt volatus; quorum conversio, id est στροφή, nomen insulis dedit. quod Apollonius plenissime exequitur.

APOLL. Rhod. 2.295–97: οἱ δ' ὅρκῳ εἴξαντες ὑπέστρεφον ἂψ ἐπὶ νῆα / σώεσθαι· Στροφάδας δὲ μετακλείουσ' ἄνθρωποι / νήσους τοῖο ἕκητι, πάρος Πλωτὰς καλέοντες; cf. too HES. *Cat.* fr. 156 M-W (from the scholia to Apollonius); VAL. Fla. 4.512–13, *iamque et ad Ionii metas atque intima tendunt / saxa; vocat magni Strophades nunc incola ponti;* and APOLLOD. 1.9.21.

Bartelink (1965) 56, O'Hara (1990b), Williams (1962) on 209–10.

**A. 3.226–27:** *Harpyiae* et magnis quatiunt clangoribus alas / *diripiunt*que dapes

With the verb *diripiunt* Vergil glosses the name Harpies, alluding to the derivation from ἁρπάζω, "snatch." Vergil is following Apollonius, who glosses the name twice, both times with the word also at the start of the hexameter. In Vergil the words connected etymologically are juxtaposed at the start of consecutive lines, as often (see intro. 2.9).

APOLL. Rhod. 2.187–89: ἀλλὰ διὰ νεφέων ἄφνω πέλας ἀίσσουσαι / Ἅρπυιαι στόματος χειρῶν τ' ἀπὸ γαμφηλῇσι / συνεχέως ἥρπαζον, ἐλείπετο δ' ἄλλοτε φορβῆς; 2.223: Ἅρπυιαι στόματός μοι ἀφαρπάζουσιν ἐδωδήν; VAL. Fla. repeats Vergil's *diripiunt* to describe the activity of the Harpies at his *Arg.* 4.454–55 *diripiunt verruntque dapes foedataque turbant / pocula;* cf. APUL. *Met.* 10.15: Harpyiae . . . quae diripiebant Phineias dapes; PLAUT. *Pseud.* 655: HARPAX: hostis vivos rapere soleo ex acie: eo hoc nomen mihi est.

Bartelink (1965) 81 n. 2 (calls it less probable), O'Hara (1990b); on possible etymologizing of the name in Homer see Rank (1951) 39–40; on Plautus, Duckworth (1952) 348.

**A. 3.250?:** *accipite ergo* animis atque haec mea figite dicta

Ahl: "Celaeno, the birdlike harpy, i.e. 'snatcher,' tells Aeneas to 'grab onto' her words: ACCIPITE ERgo. . . . ACCIPITER is Latin for 'hawk.'"

When Jupiter begins a speech with *accipite ergo* at A. 10.104, there seems to be no wordplay. Cf. the play on *accipiter . . . sacer ales* at A. 11.721.

ISID. *in Deut.* 10.1: accipere . . . aliquando dicimus auferre. unde et aves illae quae rapiendi sunt avidae accipitres vocantur; *Etym.* 12.7.55: accipiter . . . ab accipiendo, id est a capiendo, nomen sumpsit.

Ahl (1985) 63.

**A. 3.270–71:** iam medio apparet fluctu nemorosa Zacynthos / Dulichiumque Sameque et *Neritos ardua* saxis.

Vergil provides a learned gloss, *ardua saxis,* "steep with rocks, lofty," that alludes to the meaning of the name *Neritos,* "immense" (cf. intro. 2.2). This is one of Vergil's several plays on words like *arduus, altus* (see below); Vergil also shows awareness of the complex history of the word.

In Hesiod νήριτος is used only at *Op.* 511, to modify ὕλη, probably "forest of countless trees." Hesiod also has μεγήριτα at *Th.* 240 of "numerous Nereids." In the *Iliad,* the word appears only as a proper noun in the Catalogue of Ships (2.631–32). The *Odyssey* has two references to a mountain on Ithaca named Neritos (9.22 and 13.351), and one to a man named Neritos (17.207). Hoekstra speaks of an original word νήριτος equivalent to ἀνάριθμος, "countless," which "became the name of a mountain and afterwards that of its eponymous hero." So Hesiod uses the word in the original sense, Homeric epic only the proper noun, with no indication of awareness of the probable original meaning.

Apollonius uses the word twice (3.1288–89 and 4.156–59). In book 3 it describes the tracks of Aeetes' bulls, and the scholia gloss νήριτα with τὰ μεγάλα καὶ ἀναρίθμητα, "large," and "countless." In book 4 the word describes the scent of Medea's drugs; the gloss in the scholia is πολλή, "great, immense"; of a scent, we might say "powerful, penetrating." On the basis of 4.158, Campbell suggests that the notion of size may fit 3.1288 as well, in the sense that the bulls' tracks are "deeply imprinted."

Vergil's gloss *ardua saxis* shows his awareness of the meaning of the adjective νήριτος in either Hesiod or Apollonius, or, more probably, both. See on **3.210** for Vergil's allusions to Apollonius in this part of book 3.

For *arduus* as a gloss meaning "large," cf. Serv. 7.412: MAGNVM TENET ARDEA NOMEN bene adlusit: nam Ardea quasi ardua dicta est, id est magna et nobilis. Hinds argues that Ovid plays on the connotation of "countless" in the epithet *Neritius* (cf. intro. 2.14). For this island name, one thinks also of Callimachus' prose treatise *Foundations of Cities and Islands and Their Changes of Names.* For islands in Vergil cf. intro. 2.4b.

Cf. OVID *Tr.* 1.5.57–58: pro duce *Neritio* docti mala nostra poetae / scribite: *Neritio* nam mala *plura* tuli.

VERGIL's plays on arduus, etc.: A. 3.703: arduus inde Acragas; 7.412: *magnum* manet *Ardea* nomen; 7.682: altum Praeneste; A. 9.387–88?: locos qui post Albae de nomine dicti / *Albani;* A. 12.134–36?: At Iuno ex *summo* (qui nunc Albanus habetur; / tum neque nomen erat neque honos aut gloria monti) / prospiciens *tumulo* campum aspectabat; G. 1.332: alta *Ceraunia;* 1.364: *altam* supra volat *ardea* nubem; 3.474: aerias Alpis.

Hoekstra ap. Heubeck and Hoekstra (1989) 159, Campbell (1983) 82, Hinds (n.d.); this argument with more detail in O'Hara (1990c).

**A. 3.274?:** *Leucatae nimbosa* cacumina montis

The adjective *nimbosus* may suggest a gloss on the name *Leucata,* which Servius (on 8.677) derives from the shine or whiteness of the rocks on the mountain's peak (cf. Greek λευκ-). *Nimbosus* would suggest that the peak is white because enshrouded in clouds.

Cf. the aetiology of the name Alba at A. 8.43–48.

SERV. Auct. 8.677: LEVCATEN in promontorio Epiri est mons Leucata: quod quia saxa nuda in cacumine habuit, ex horum candore Leucates appellatus est; Murgia restores the etymology also to the text of SERV. Auct. 3.274: "For *hic locus vocatur allo* should be read *hic locus vocatur* ⟨*ab*⟩ *albo*. Leucate is the place in question, and it gets its name 'from white' (translation of ἀπὸ τοῦ λευκοῦ)"; SERV. 279 mentions an eponymous *puer* said to have jumped from the rocks.

Murgia (1987) 316 (without comment on *nimbosa*).

**A. 3.280:** *Actia*que Iliacis celebramus *litora* ludis

The adjective *Actius* in 280 (also in 8.675 and 704) is familiar, but is a poetic form, as Williams notes. The adjective formed from Actium should be *Actiacus,* which occurs a number of times. *Actius* is convenient for the hexameter, and Vergil often forms a proper adjective directly from a noun, without the adjectival suffix. But the Greek adjective ἄκτιος is used in Hellenistic poetry as an epithet of gods and refers not to Actium but to any shore, or ἀκτή. Thus at Theoc. 5.14 Πάν ἄκτιος is Pan of the Shore. At Apoll. Rhod. 1.402–5, the Argonauts build an altar on the shore to Apollo Actios, and Apollonius makes clear the significance of the epithet:

> Ἔνθεν δ' αὖ λάιγγας ἁλὸς σχεδὸν ὀχλίζοντες,
> νήεον αὐτόθι βωμὸν ἐπάκτιον Ἀπόλλωνος,
> Ἀκτίου Ἐμβασίοιό τ' ἐπώνυμον·

Here ἐπώνυμον serves as a signpost calling attention to the name (see intro. 2.6), and the adjective ἐπάκτιον provides the simple gloss for the epithet Ἄκτιος. At A. 3.280, *Actia* means "of Actium" but modifies a word that alludes to the original Greek meaning of Ἄκτιος: *Actia litora* suggests ἄκτιοι ἀκταί or *litorea litora* (at *Achill.* 1.285 Statius refers to *Palladi litoreae,* and *litoreus* = ἄκτιος). This is a reverse gloss, of *Hernica saxa* type (see intro. 2.2a); the noun alludes to the etymology of the adjective.

At 1.402–5 Apollonius seems to be following Callim. fr. 18, where in speaking of the Argonauts Callimachus apparently also referred to the temple of Apollo Actios (cf. Hyg. *Astr.* ii 37 p. 74 B, quoted by Pfeiffer ad loc.). We do not know whether he alludes to the etymology; of the crucial line 18.12 only the last two words, ἐπώνυμον Ἐμβασίοιο, are extant. We do know that in a scholarly work Callimachus mentioned the "old" Actian games (fr. 403).

Cf. Prop. 2.34.61–62, ***Actia** Vergilium custodis **litora** Phoebi, / Caesaris et fortis dicere posse ratis*. Propertius may anticipate Vergil; more probably, he is borrowing from a section of the *Aeneid* that he has seen or heard. His next two lines, 63–64, will "echo" A. 1.1ff.

See on **3.210** for Vergil's several allusions to Apollonius in this part of book 3.

Koster suggests that Prop. 4.6.67–68 *(Actius hinc traxit Phoebus monumenta, quod eius / una decem vicit missa sagitta ratis)* alludes to a derivation of this epithet for the sun-god (Phoebus) from ἀκτίς, ἀκτῖνος, "ray, sunbeam," but I see little allusion to this in the text of Propertius.

Other significant epithets of Apollo: A. 6.12 *Delius;* E. 6.3 *Cynthius* (see Clausen).

O'Hara (1990b), Pfeiffer (1949–53) on Callim. fr. 18, Koster (1983) 53–54, Clausen (1976) and (1977), Williams (1962) on 280.

**A. 3.295?:** Priamiden *Helenum Graias* regnare per urbis

Mørland suggests wordplay in the juxtaposition of *Helenum* (Ἕλενος) and *Graias* (cf. Ἕλληνες). Perhaps unlikely, but cf. the plays on the name Helen at Aesch. *Ag.* 681–98 (see intro. 1.2).

Mørland (1960) 23.

**A. 3.297?:** Et patrio *Andro*machen iterum cessisse *marito*

Mørland suggests wordplay between the name Andromache and *marito* (= Greek ἀνήρ, ἀνδρός). Perhaps unlikely.

Wordplay by Euripides imitated by Ennius is cited at Varro *LL* 7.82: apud Ennium (*SRP* fr. 65 R = 99 J) "Andromachae nomen qui indidit, recte indidit." . . . Euripides . . . ait ideo nomen additum Andromachae, quod ἀνδρὶ μάχεται (see intro. 1.5 for Varro's criticism of Ennius).

Mørland (1960) 23, Woodhead (1928) 21 (not mentioning Vergil).

**A. 3.333–36:**

morte Neoptolemi regnorum reddita cessit
pars Heleno, qui *Chaonios* cognomine campos
*Chaoniam*que omnem Troiano a *Chaone* dixit,
Pergamaque Iliacamque iugis hanc addidit arcem.

Explicit etymological aetiology, with *cognomine* and *dixit* as etymological signposts (see intro. 2.6). Williams: "this etymological association . . . seems to be Vergil's own. Chaon is not heard of elsewhere, and the general tradition about the Chaonians was that they existed before the Trojan War." Williams also neatly summarizes Servius Auctus, who "says a lot about Helenus' friend Chaon, and relates various stories about a King Campus who gave his name to this area." Possibly Vergil alludes to a change of name from Campania to Chaonia; for Alexandrian *metonomasia* see intro. 2.10.

SERV. Auct. 334: CHAONIOS COGNOMINE CAMPOS Epirum campos non habere omnibus notum est, sed constat ibi olim regem nomine Campum fuisse eiusque posteros Campylidas dictos et Epirum Campaniam vocatam, sicut Alexarchus, historicus Graecus, et Aristonicus referunt. Varro filiam Campi Campam dictam, unde provinciae nomen; post vero, sicut dictum est, Chaoniam ab Heleno appellatam, qui fratrem suum Chaonem, vel ut alii dicunt comitem, dum venaretur occiderat. alii filiam Campi Cestriam ab Heleno ductam uxorem, et de nomine soceri Campos, de nomine Chaone Chaonas dixisse; SERV. Auct. 335: TROIANO CHAONE . . . quidam dicunt hunc Chaonem pro omnium incolumitate, cum pestilentia laborarent socii Heleni, ex responso immolandum se obtulisse, unde in honorem eius Epirum, quae Campania dicebatur, Chaoniam nominatam. alii dicunt, [quod] cum Helenus cum Pyrrho ab Ilio navigaret et tempestate iactarentur, Chaonem, unum e Troianis, amicum Heleni, vovisse, ut si illi periculum evasissent, se pro eorum incolumitate interimeret; qui se, postquam illi evaserunt, sicut promisit, occidit; unde factum est, ut ex eius nomine Helenus, adeptus regnum, Epirum Chaoniam nominaret.

Williams (1962) on 334–35.

**A. 3.342–43:** ecquid in antiquam *virtutem* animosque *virilis* / et pater Aeneas at avunculus excitat Hector?

On the frequent association of *virtus* and *vir,* see on **A. 1.566.**

**A. 3.389–93:**

cum tibi sollicito secreti ad fluminis undam
litoreis ingens inventa sub ilicibus sus
triginta capitum fetus enixa iacebit,
*alba* solo recubans, *albi* circum ubera nati,
is locus *urbis* erit, requies ea certa laborum.

For the white *(alba)* sow as an etymological *aition* for Alba Longa, see on **8.43–48** (where 43–45 = 3.390–92). Here, *urbis* in 393 = *Albae Longae,* so we have a suppressed *figura etymologica* (line 393 is also interpolated with minor changes as 8.46).

Cf. Williams on the associations between the sow and the name of the city of Troy: "It is possible that there is a connection between this Trojan legend and the Latin word *troia* (French *truie*) meaning a sow (though *troia* is not found before the eighth century). This would give the word an etymological association comparable with that of the *lusus Troiae*" (see on **5.602** *Troia nunc pueri, Troianum dicitur agmen*).

For suppression see intro. 2.7.

Williams (1962) on 389ff.

**A. 3.401–2:** hic illa ducis Meliboei / *parva* Philoctetae subnixa *Petelia* muro.

Williams: "note the etymological epithet *parva;* Petelia is presumably connected with the old Latin word *petilus,* 'thin, small.'"

For the single-adjective gloss see intro. 2.2.

Differently SERV. 402: "Petilia" dicta vel ἀπὸ τοῦ πέτασθαι, id est "volare," quod captato augurio est condita, vel quod post relictum Ilium, quo ducebatur a Graecis, eam petivit civitatem.

Williams (1962) on 401–2.

## A. 3.420–24?:

dextrum Scylla latus, laevum implacata Charybdis
obsidet, atque imo *barathri* ter gurgite vastos
*sorbet in abruptum* fluctus rursusque sub auras
erigit alternos, et sidera verberat unda.

Servius perhaps reads *sorbet in abruptum* as a gloss on the Greek word *barathrum.* Catullus used *abruptum* to modify *barathrum.*

SERV. 421: barathrum est inmensae altitudinis nomen: unde sequitur "sorbet in abruptum": quod Graece βάραθρον dicitur.

CAT. 68.107–8: tanto te *absorbens* vertice amoris / aestus in *abruptum* detulerat *barathrum.*

Bartelink (1965) 89 n. 1 ("very dubious case"); cf. Fordyce (1961) on Cat. 68.108ff.: "*barathrum* is an old borrowing from Greek . . . , already a familiar word in Plautus."

**A. 3.432?:** *Scyllam* et caeruleis *canibus* resonantia saxo

Williams on 424f. notes that in the *Odyssey* Scylla "has a voice like a new-born hound (σκύλακος); this seems to be the origin of the later version, which Virgil follows, that she has wolves or dogs below the waist." Vergil also seems to play on or gloss the name (*Scylla-canibus*-σκύλαξ), as he had in E. 6, and as Callimachus had more explicitly in the *Hecale,* although Vergil's mention of dogs need not have etymological motivation.

E. 6.74–77: ***Scyllam*** . . . *latrantibus* inguina monstris . . . **vexasse** rates et . . . timidos nautes *canibus* lacerasse marinis; E. 8.107: Hylax . . . latrat; HOM. *Od.* 12.85–86: ἔνθα δ' ἐνὶ Σκύλλη ναίει δεινὸν λελακυῖα. / τῆς ἦ τοι φωνὴ μὲν ὅση σκύλακος νεογιλλῆς; CALLIM. *Hec.* fr. 288 Pf. = fr. 90 H (note the clear signpost): Σκύλλα γυνὴ κατακᾶσα καὶ οὐ ψύθος οὔνομ' ἔχουσα / πορφυρέην ἤμησε κρέκα (Pfeiffer ad loc.: Call. . . . dixisse videtur Scyllam vero nomine "canem" esse, i.e., impudentem [vix de σκύλλειν sc. capillum cogitavit]; see Pfeiffer's citation of the canine etymology in Greek sources; differently Schechter: "the abstruse κατακᾶσα, denoting 'wanton,' aids in explaining Σκύλλα in the sense 'shameless bitch' . . . , and it attracts attention to another literal meaning of Σκύλλα, which ἤμησε κρέκα ['cut the hair'] also etymologizes, as if 'Snipper' were meant [cf. Nic. *Alex.* 410 σκύλαιο κάρη, 'shave the head']"); LYCOPH. 45: ἀγρίαν κύνα, 669 ποία δ' Ἐρινὺς μιξοπάρθενος κύων; CAT. 60.2: Scylla latrans infima inguinum parte; LUCR. 5.892–93: rabidis canibus succinctas semimarinis / corporibus Scyllas; cf. G. 1.406–9, for *secat* as gloss on the name Ciris, given to the other Scylla (on the two Scyllas, see on E. 6.74–77); could Callim. also be glossing the name Ciris in the *Hecale* fragment?

Williams (1962); on Callim. see Pfeiffer (1949–53) ad loc., Hollis (1990) 278, Schechter (1975) 358–59.

**A. 3.433:** praeterea, si qua est Heleno *prudentia* vati

Cicero glosses *prudens* with *providens,* "seeing ahead of time." The use of *prudentia* by and of the prophet Helenus seems to play upon this sense of the word.

CIC. *Div.* 1.49.111: quos prudentes possumus dicere, id est, providentes; *Rep.* 6.1: Prudentiam . . . quae ipsum nomen hoc nacta est ex providendo; *Hort.* fr. 5.33 Müller (ap. Non. p. 41, 28 M): prudentiam a providendo dictam dilucide ostendit M. Tullius in Hortensio.

Bartelink (1965) 30, Pease (1963) on Cic. *Div.* 1.49.111.

**A. 3.444?:** fata canit foliisque *notas* et *nomina* mandat

Juxtaposition of apparent cognates, perhaps simply for the sake of euphony. Cf. G. 3.158 *continuoque notas et nomina gentis inurunt.*

PAUL.-Fest. p. 179, 13 L: nomen dictum quasi novimen, quod notitiam facit.

Bartelink (1965) 108–9.

**A. 3.516:** Arcturum *pluviasque Hyadas* geminosque Triones

*Pluvias* is a gloss on *Hyades,* as if from Greek ὕω, "to rain." Cf. **A. 1.744** (= A. 3.516), **G. 1.138.**

Bartelink (1965) 76.

**A. 3.520:** temptamusque viam et *velorum* pandimus *alas.*

Citing this passage, Isidore derives *velum,* "sail," from *volatus,* "flight." If Isidore is not simply deriving the etymology from this line of Vergil's, both Vergil and before him Lucretius may allude to this etymology. For Lucretius, see on A. 6.237–47; Lucretius is explaining the name Avernus.

For other possible examples of etymologies deduced by grammarians from Vergil's text cf. on **A. 1.164–65.**

ISID. 19.31.1: apud Latinos autem vela a volatu dicta. unde est illud (A. 3.520) velorum pandimus alas; differently CIC. *de Orat.* 153 (from *vexillum*).

LUCR. 6.742–43: e regione ea quod loca cum venere *volantes,* / remigi oblitae pennarum *vela* remittunt . . .

**A. 3.540:** bello *armantur* equi, bellum haec *armenta* minantur

Servius and Paulus-Festus (and so perhaps the Augustan Verrius Flaccus) connect *armenta,* "cattle," with *arma,* "arms"; Vergil plays with this connection both here and in the *Georgics.* He elsewhere connects *armenta* with *arare,* "to plow."

SERV. 540: armenta dicta sunt quasi apta armis: nam equi intersunt proeliis, boves armant ex coriis (cf. too Serv. Auct. A. 1.185); ISID. 12.1.8: armenta, vel quod sint apta armis, id est bello, vel quod his in armis utimur. Alii armenta tantum boves intellegunt, ab arando, quasi aramenta; PAUL.-Fest. p. 4, 5–6 L: Armentum id genus pecoris appellatur, quod est idoneum ad opus armorum.

G. 3.343–45: omnia secum / *armentarius* Afer agit, tectumque laremque / *arma*que Amyclaeumque canem Cressamque pharetram; cf. armenta < arare A. 7.538–39: Quinque greges illi balantum, quina redebant / *armenta* et terram centum vertebat *aratris;* cf. the association of *arma* and *aratrum* at G. 1.160–62.

Bartelink (1965) 94, Williams (1962) ad loc.

**A. 3.561–62:** primusque *rudentem* / contorsit laevas proram Palinurus ad undas

At **A. 1.87** *stridorque rudentum,* the word *rudens* = rope, but *stridor* alludes to *rudens* = "bellowing, braying." Here *rudens* = "roaring," but in this nautical context there is temporary ambiguity in *primusque rudentem / contorsit*: "until the middle of line 561, the Latin appears to mean 'first he twisted the rope' " (Ahl).

Williams reports (in order to reject the view) that "Heinsius and Bentley were so hostile to the unusual verb that they wished to read *tridentem,*" in part because *rudens* is not ordinarily used with an inanimate subject. This unusual use of the verb calls attention to Vergil's wordplay.

Ahl (1985) 29, Williams (1962) on 561–62.

**A. 3.608–9?:** qui sit *fari,* quo sanguine cretus, / hortamur, quae deinde agitet fortuna *fateri.*

Varro connects *fari* and *fateor;* still their proximity here could be accidental.

VARRO *LL* 6.55: ab eodem verbo fari . . . fassi ac confessi, qui fati id quod ab [h]is quaesitum.

Bartelink (1965) 92.

**A. 613–18?:**

sum patria ex Ithaca, comes infelicis Vlixi,
nomine *Achaemenides*
. . . . . . . . . . . . . . . . . . . . .
hic me . . . immemores socii . . . *deseruere.*

Heinze observed that Romans might connect the *Achae-* element of the name of this Greek, *Achaemenides,* with *Achaeus,* Achaean. Mørland goes further, connecting the *-men-* element with the Greek word μένω, "remain, stay behind," so that Achaemenides = "the left-behind Greek" (cf. *deseruere* in 618).

Heinze (1915) 112 n. 3, Mørland (1957) 87–88, Bartelink (1965) 62.

**A. 3.660–61:** lanigerae comitantur oves; ea *sola* voluptas / *solamen*que mali.
Isidore connects *consolator* and *solamen* with *solus,* and several authors seem to play on such a connection.

ISID. 10.38: et inde dictus consolator, quod soli se adplicat cui loquitur, et solitudinem levat adloquio suo. hinc et solacium.

PLAUT. *Trin.* 394: sed hoc *unum consolatur* me atque animum meum; OVID *Met.* 1.359–60 (for Ovid cf. intro. 2.14): quo *sola* timorem / ferre modo posses? quo *consolante* dolores?; SEN. *Med.* 945–46: *unicum* afflictae domus / *solamen;* CIC. *Cat.* 4.4.8: spem quae *sola* hominem in miseriis *consolari* solet; STAT. *Theb.* 10.590: *unum* rebus *solamen* in artis.

Bartelink (1965) 110, Ahl (1985) 119.

*

**A. 3.689?:** Pantagiae Megarosque sinus *Thapsum*que *iacentem*
Rehm suggests (following Isidore) that *iacentem* may be a single-epithet gloss of *Thapsum,* as if from θάπτω, "bury" (cf. intro. 2.2) but *iacentem* is perhaps not so helpful a gloss for θάπτω. Geymonat notes that "the artful setting of three geographical names in [this] verse has the look of a self-conscious poetic allusion"; cf. on 693–94 for possible Callimachean precedent for 687–714.

ISID. 14.6.35: Thapsus insula stadiis decem a Sicilia remota iacens et planior, unde et nuncupata. De qua Vergilius (A. 3.689) Thapsumque iacentem.

Rehm (1932) 37 ("Veilleicht steckt dahinter, wie bei so vielen der folgenden Verse, eine Etymologie [ἀπὸ τοῦ θάπτειν?]"), Hanssen (1948) 120–21 (skeptical), Bartelink (1965) 57, Geymonat (1993) 325.

**A. 3.693–94:** *Plemyrium undosum*; nomen dixere priores / Ortygiam.

Here *undosum,* as Servius notes, is a single-epithet gloss (see intro. 2.2) on *Plemyrium,* suggesting a derivation from πλημμυρίς, "tide, flood." The signpost *nomen dixere priores / Ortygiam* calls attention to a change of name, as many do (see intro. 2.6 and 10).

Williams suggests that for his brief descriptions of Sicilian cities in 692ff., "Virgil's source material was probably a book on the foundation of Sicilian cities with their local oracles." Rehm and Bartelink suggest a lost treatment by Varro of the cities of Sicily. But we must not overlook the discussion of Sicilian cities in Callim. *Aet.* 2 fr. 43 (about 130 lines, half with only a word or two preserved, first published in 1927). This section of the *Aetia* may lie behind much of A. 3.687–714 (as Geymonat has lately suggested).

Ortygia, the former name of Plemyrium, is also a former or alternate name of the island of Delos; see A. 3.154, Schol. Callim. *Hymn* 2.59, Nic. fr. 5, Serv. A. 3.73 (more in Maltby s.v. Ortygia).

SERV. 693: PLEMYRIVM VNDOSVM verbum de verbo expressit; hoc est enim "undosum," quod "Plemyrium." This example becomes paradigmatic for Serv.; cf. on A. 1.744: PLVVIASQVE HYADAS . . . ὑάδες dictae sunt ἀπὸ τοῦ ὕειν. . . . sic ergo ait "pluviasque hyades," ut "Plemyrium undosum"; and on A. 4.268: Olympos quasi ὁλολαμπής . . . unde addidit "claro," ut "Plemyrium undosum"; SCHOL. Veron. ad loc.: dictum autem ἀπὸ πλημμυρίας, id est, quod undique fluctibus undisque adluatur.

Bartelink (1965) 54, 59, Rehm (1932) 37, 106, Hanssen (1948) 116, Williams (1962) on 692ff., Geymonat (1993).

**A. 3.698:** praepingue solum *stagnantis Helori*

As Servius Auctus notes, *stagnantis* is a single-epithet gloss (see intro. 2.2) on *Helori,* from ἕλος, "marsh."

Propertius seems to use *stagnabant* to suggest a derivation from ἕλος for the name Velabra, for which Varro and perhaps Tibullus offer other suggestions.

SERV. Auct. 698: STAGNANTIS HELORI fluvii qui ad imitationem Nili superfunditur campis. et Graeci stagna ἕλη dicunt; unde ait "stagnantis Helori"; STRABO 9.2.17: Ἕλος τε καὶ Ἑλεὼν καὶ Εἰλέσιον ἐκλήθη διὰ τὸ ἐπὶ τοῖς ἕλεσιν ἱδρῦσθαι; cf. SERV. Auct. A. 6.359: Velia . . . dicta est a paludibus, quibus cingitur, quas Graeci ἕλη dicunt. fuit ergo Elia, sed accepit digamma et facta est Velia, ut Enetus Venetus (cf. D.H. 1.20.2–3); VARRO *LL* 5.156: quod ibi vehebantur lintribus, velabrum (cf. Tibullus 2.5.33–36, with Ross and Cairns).

PROP. 4.9.5: qua Velabra suo stagnabant flumine quoque / nauta per urbanas velificabat aquas.

Rehm (1932) 37, Bartelink (1965) 48, Hanssen (1948) 116, Williams (1962) ad loc., Ross (1975) 156, Cairns (1979) 81.

**A. 3.701–2?:** apparet Camerina procul campique *Geloi, / immanis*que *Gela fluvii* cognomine dicta

Here we see an explicit etymology found also in Thucydides, Callimachus (cf. above on 3.693–94) and others: the fields and the city are named after the river Gela. There may also be more etymological play involving the name Gela. Rehm points to the connection made in ancient sources between the name Gela and a local word for frost or ice, perhaps Latin *gelu*. In *immanis* he sees a suggestion of "dangerously packed with ice": "immanis scil. gelu sive frigore." Williams too refers it to "the winter torrent of the river"; cf. Ovid *F.* 4.470 *et te, verticibus non adeunde Gela* (for Ovid cf. intro. 2.14). Rehm's argument is perhaps not fully convincing, since the suggestion of ice in *immanis* is weak at best, but for similar double etymologies (one explicit, one implicit) cf. on **A. 8.337–41.**

Knight says they are "plains of laughter" in contrast with the *Lugentes campi* at 6.441. Williams notes that Aristophanes twice (*Ach.* 606, fr. 629 Kassel-Austin) plays on the name's similarity to γέλως, "laughter." But there is nothing in Vergil to trigger this association.

Henry suggests that "*immanis* is no so very extraordinary or out-of-the-way epithet to be applied to the insignificant Gela," but it is a little odd.

Cf. also on G. 3.461, *acerque Gelonus.*

THUC. 6.4.3: τῇ . . . πόλει ἀπὸ τοῦ Γελὰ ποταμοῦ τοὔνομα ἐγένετο; CALLIM. *Aet.* fr. 43.46: οἶδα Γελὰ ποταμοῦ κεφαλῇ ἔπι κείμενον ἄστυ (cf. Pfeiffer ad loc.); DIOD. Sic. 8.23.1 (quoting a Delphic oracle): πὰρ προχοὰς ποταμοῖο Γέλα συνομώνυμον ἁγνοῦ; SIL. 14.218: venit ab amne trahens nomen Gela; CLAUD. *de Rapt. Pros.* 2.58: nomenque Gelan qui praebuit urbi; STEPH. Byz. s.v. Γέλα: καλεῖται δὲ ἀπὸ ποταμοῦ Γέλα, ὁ δὲ ποταμὸς ὅτι πολλὴν πάχνην γεννᾷ —ταύτην γὰρ τῇ τῶν Ὀπικῶν φωνῇ καὶ Σικελῶν γέλαν λέγεσθαι; TZETZES in Schol. Thuc. 6.4: οὕτως Ἐπαφρόδιτος, ὡς λέγεις, γράφει. Γέλας δ' ἐκλήθη τῷ πάχνην πολλὴν φέρειν, κλῆσιν ἐκεῖ γὰρ πάχνη ταύτην φέρει (Epaphr. is Neronian, but see Pfeiffer on Callim. loc. cit. for the idea that a commentary on Callimachus is the source of this); for *immanis* Rehm cites AMMIAN. Marc. 25.4.10: patientia frigorum immanium.

Rehm (1932) 38, Hanssen (1948) 118–19 (skeptical), Bartelink (1965) 46, Henry (1873–93) 2.533, Geymonat (1993) 330, Knight (1944) 198, Williams (1962) on 702.

**A. 3.703–5: arduus** inde **Acragas** ostentat maxima longe / moenia, magnanimum quondam generator equorum; / teque datis linquo ventis, *palmosa Selinus*

Vergil glosses two names in these lines. In 703, as Williams notes, "*arduus* (= ἄκρος) is a clear etymological epithet of Acragas." In 705, Vergil calls Selinus *palmosa,* although "there were no palm trees at Selinus" (Williams). Williams: "the explanation is that Vergil is using another etymological epithet. . . . The plant σέλινον (*apium,* a kind of parsley), which figured on the coins of Selinus, was one of the plants used for the victor's crown at the great games of Greece. . . . Virgil has just been speaking of Acragas and the games, and nothing should be more natural than that his thoughts should turn to the connexion of Selinus with these games."

Selinus is discussed by Callimachus in the fragmentary *Aet.* fr. 43.33 (see above on 3.693–94), where the scholia indicate that the etymology may have been at issue.

Diogenes Laertius quotes an epigram, which he attributes to Empedocles or Simonides, playing on the name Acragas, the adjective ἄκρος, and a personal name Acron.

For the single-adjective gloss, see intro. 2.2, and for Vergil's several plays involving words like *arduus* and *altus,* see on **3.270–71.**

SERV. 3.506 notes the connection between height and the Acr- root: Ceraunia sunt montes Epiri, a crebris fulminibus propter altitudinem nominati; unde Horatius (C. 1.3.20) expressius dixit "Acroceraunia" propter altitudinem et fulminum iactus; EMPED. fr. dub. 157 D-K (= Diog. Laert. 8.63):

> ἄκρον ἰατρὸν Ἄκρων᾽ Ἀκραγαντῖνον πατρὸς Ἄκρου
> κρύπτει κρημνὸς ἄκρος πατρίδος ἀκροτάτης.
> τινὲς δὲ τὸν δεύτερον στίχον ὅυτω προσφέρονται ᾽ἀκροτάτης κορυφῆς τύμβος ἄκρος κατέχει᾽. τοῦτο τινες Σιμωνίδου φασὶν εἶναι.

On Acragas: Bartelink (1965) 38, Rehm (1932) 39, Williams (1962) on 703, Hecht (1882) 83. On Selinus: Rehm (1932) 39–40, Marouzeau (1949) 74, Hanssen (1948) 116–18 (skeptical), Bartelink (1965) 55, Williams (1962) on 705.

## A. 4.1–5:

> at regina gravi iamdudum saucia *cura*
> vulnus alit venis et caeco carpitur *igni.*
> multa viri virtus animo multusque **recursat**
> gentis honos; haerent infixi pectore vultus
> verbaque nec placidam membris dat *cura* quietem

There is ample wordplay in these lines, much of it discussed by Due. In 1–2, the words *cura* and *igni,* significantly placed at the ends of consecutive lines, play upon the etymology found in Varro and Servius: *cura . . . quod cor urit.* See on **A. 1.208–9,** for several allusions in Vergil and other poets to this etymology; in Lucretius, *cor* and *cura* also end consecutive lines (see too intro. 2.9).

In 2, *venis* may allude to the etymology of *venenum* given by Serv. A. 1.688: *venenum . . . quod per venas eat,* "*venenum,* because it goes through the veins." In 1.688, Venus tells Cupid to deceive Dido with his poison (or love-potion): *occultum inspires ignem fallasque veneno;* soon afterwards Vergil speaks of Dido "drinking" love: *longumque bibebat amorem* (1.749). Servius cites 1.749 and mentions *venenum* in his explanation of *venas.* In the language of 4.2, *caeco . . . igni* recalls the *occultum . . . ignem* of 1.688; this aids recollection of the use of *venenum* there (where it may be the subject of different wordplay with its cognate *Venus*).

In 3, Vergil juxtaposes *viri* and *virtus:* for the frequent etymological association of these words, see on **A. 1.566.**

The word *recursat* appears only three times in Vergil, each time near *cura.* Here the word is placed two lines after the *cura* at the end of line 1, and two lines before the *cura* near the end of line 5. See on **A. 1.662.**

SERV. 4.2: CVRA . . . ab eo quod cor urat. . . . VENIS quia per venas amor currit, sicut venenum. inde dictum (1.688) "fallasque veneno," item (1.749) "longumque bibebat amorem"; SERV. Auct.: nam venenum ideo dicitur, quia per venas currit; SERV. Auct. 1.688: venenum dictum ab eo, quod per venas eat. ideo post ait (749) "longumque bibebat amorem."

Cerda (1612) 379 (on *viri virtus*), Due (1973) 276–79.

**A. 4.9:** Anna soror, quae me suspensam *insomnia* terrent!

Knight explores the interesting etymological connotations of Vergil's word *insomnia:*

> In Latin a dream is *somnium,* but there is also a word *insomnia* for sleeplessness. Vergil uses . . . *insomnium* in the plural, *insomnia,* to mean dreams. Through the ivory gate of sleep the spirits send false dreams, *insomnia.* Dido says, *quae me suspensam insomnia terrent?* "What are these dreams that affright me, so anxious?" That ought to mean, if anything, "What sleeplessness . . . ?" But, primarily at least, the word means dreams. . . . Vergil has made an equation between the Latin word, in which *in-* should mean a negative, and the Greek word for a dream, ἐνύπνιον, . . . also neuter with the plural in -α, . . . also ending with the word ὕπνος, . . . sleep, and beginning too, with a corresponding prefix ἐν- . . . , *in-*; but it corresponds to *in-* in the sense of "in," not in the negative sense, and the Greek word legitimately means something that happens in sleep, and so a dream. . . . The impulse may have been instinctive. . . . But there is also a possible reasoned motive. Dido may be meant to have been frightened both by dreams, and, intermittently, by sleeplessness. *Suspensam* suggests it. Then *insomnia* means both [dreams and sleeplessness].

SERV. 9: INSOMNIA TERRENT et "terret" et "terrent" legitur. sed si "terret" legerimus, "insomnia" erit vigilia; hoc enim maiores inter vigilias et ea quae videmus in somnis interesse voluerunt, ut "insomnia" generis feminini numeri singularis vigiliam significaret, "insomnia" vero generis neutri numeri pluralis ea per somnium videmus, ut (6.896) "sed falsa ad caelum mittunt insomnia manes." sciendum igitur quia, si "terret" dixerimus, antiqua erit elocutio: "insomnia" enim, licet et Pacuvius et Ennius frequenter dixerit, Plinius tamen exclusit et de usu removit. sed ambiguitatem lectionis haec res fecit, quod non ex aperto vigilasse se dixit, sed habuisse quietem inplacidam, id est somniis interruptam, ut intellegamus eam et insomniis territam, et propter terrorem somniorum vigilias quoque perpessam.

Knight (1944) 201, Bartelink (1965) 33; more references on the word in Kaster (1980) 236 n. 61.

**A. 4.11:** quem sese ore ferens, quam forti pectore et *armis!*

Raven suggests a play on or ambiguity between *arma* = "weapons" and *armi* = "shoulders."

SERV. 4.495: proprie enim arma sunt quae armos tegunt.

Cf. A. 12.433: Ascanium fusis circum complectitur *armis;* A. 11.644–45: tantus in *arma* patet. latos huic hasta per *armos* / hasta tremit.

Raven (1975) 147–48; cf. Edwards quoted on A. 12.433; Austin (1955) on 3f. and Henry (1873–92) 2.560–65 argue for *armus;* Bartelink (1965) 103 n. 1; cf. also Egan (1983) 24.

**A. 4.80–81:** post ubi digressi, *lumen*que obscura vicissim / *luna* premit suadentque cadentia sidera somnos

Cicero and Varro derive *luna* from *luceo;* Vergil juxtaposes *luna* and *lumen* or *luceo* three times (although the moon would shine even without the help of the etymologist).

Cf. the connection between *lumine* and *inlustrem* at A. 7.76–80.

VARRO *LL* 5.68.2: luna, quod sola lucet noctu; CIC. *ND* 2.27.68: luna a lucendo nominata sit (cf. too Isid. 3.17.2).

A. 6.725: *lucentem* globum *lunae;* A. 7.8–9: aspirant aurae in noctem nec candida cursus / *luna* negat, splendet tremulo sub *lumine* pontus; A. 8.22–23: sicut aquae tremulum labris ubi *lumen* aenis / sole repercussum aut radiantis imagine *lunae;* CAT. 34.15–16: et notho es / dicta *lumine Luna.*

Norden (1981) 310, Bartelink (1965) 107.

**A. 4.99–100:** quin potius *pacem* aeternam *pactos*que hymenaeos / exercemus?

The derivation of *pax* from *pango* or *pactus* can be traced to the Augustan Sinnius Capito.

SINN. Cap. (fr. 10, *GRF* p. 461 = Fest. p. 260, 13 L): pacem a pactione condicionum putat dictam Sinnius Capito, quae utrique inter se populo sit observanda; ISID. 18.1.11: pacis vocabulum videtur a pacto sumptum.

A. 10.79–80: quid soceros legere et gremiis abducere *pactas, / pacem* orare manu, praefigere puppibus arma?; A. 11.133: bis senos *pepigere* dies, et *pace* sequestra.

Bartelink (1965) 98–99.

**A. 4.159?:** optat aprum, aut fulvum descendere monte *leonem*

Servius says that Leontodamas was another of Ascanius' names, and claims (implausibly) that Vergil alludes to that name here.

On the names of Ascanius see on A. 1.267–68 and 9.640–50, and on alternate names see intro. 2.10.

SERV. 159: MONTE LEONEM per transitum tangit historiam; nam Ascanius praeter Iulum et Ilium, quae habuit nomina, etiam Dardanus et Leontodamas dictus est, ad extinctorum fratrum solacium: ideo nunc eum dicit optare adventum leonis, paulo post (163) "Dardaniusque nepos Veneris."

**A. 4.211:** *femina,* quae nostris *errans* in finibus urbem

Dido, whose name is suppressed here (see intro. 2.7), is the *femina* said to have been wandering *(errans).* Pease calls attention to the etymology, found in both the *Etymologicum Magnum* and in Timaeus, which says that the Punic name Dido means πλάνη, "wandering," or πλανῆτις, "wanderer, planet." By suppressing Dido's name and then using *errans* of her here, Vergil probably alludes to this explanation of the name.

Vergil several times plays with words connected with πλάνη, in passages that seem linked and seem to suggest that wandering is an essential characteristic of Dido. At G. 1.337, Vergil refers to the "wandering" of the planet Mercury: *quos ignis caelo Cyllenius erret in orbis,* and Servius notes that "the word '*erret*' is well chosen, because planets are so called after πλάνη, which means 'wandering.'" At A. 1.742, Vergil uses the phrase *errantem lunam* in his description of the song of Iopas at Dido's banquet; to the ancient mind, the moon is just as much a planet or wanderer as is Mercury. Then at A. 4.211 Dido is referred to as *femina, quae nostris errans in finibus,* so both Dido and the moon are connected to the word πλάνη. Vergil connects Dido to wandering at least three more times. As she is dying, Dido is said to look up *oculis errantibus* (4.691). At A. 4.68–69, the lovesick Dido wanders around the city; here the word is not *errat* but *vagatur: uritur infelix Dido totaque **vagatur** / urbe furens, qualis coniecta cerva sagitta.* Dido also wanders in the underworld at A. 6.450–54:

> inter quas Phoenissa recens a vulnere *Dido*
> *errabat* silva in magna; quam Troius heros
> ut primum iuxta stetit agnovitque per umbras
> obscuram, qualem primo qui surgere mense
> aut videt aut vidisse putat per nubila *lunam.*

In this passage Vergil uses the verb *errare* of Dido, and then compares her to the moon.

*ETYM. MAG.* s.v. Διδώ: . . . φασὶ δὲ αὐτὴν . . . κληθῆναι ὕστερον τῇ Τυρίων φωνῇ Διδώ, διὰ τὸ πολλὰ πλανηθῆναι ἀπὸ Φοινίκης ἀπάρασαν ἐπὶ Καρχηδόνα. τῇ γὰρ Φοινίκων φωνῇ τὴν πλανῆτιν Διδὼ προσαγορεύουσι; TIMAEUS *FGrH* 566 F82: καὶ ὑπὸ τῶν Λιβύων διὰ τὴν πολλὴν αὐτῆς πλάνην Δειδὼ προσηγορεύθη ἐπιχωρίως; SERV. Auct. A. 1.340: post interitum a Poenis Dido appellata est, id est virago Punica lingua; SERV. G. 1.337: bene "erret"; nam planetae vocantur ἀπὸ της πλάνης, id est ab errore.

Cf. Bartelink (1965) 64, Thomas (1982a) 152, Hanssen (1948) 121, Pease (1935) 540, and now for Punic etymologies esp. Hexter (1992) 348 and nn.

**A. 4.238–39:** ille patris magni parere parabat / imperio

Austin describes *pārere părabat* as "a type of rhetorical assonance . . . involving something like a word-play, which seems to have pleased Roman ears." Cf. on A. 2.606, and intro. 2.1.

Austin (1955) on 238.

**A. 4.242–43?:** tum virgam capit: hac *animas* ille evocat Orco / pallentis, alias sub Tartara tristia *mittit*

Here the words *animas . . . mittit* may gloss the Greek epithet Psychopompos, occasionally applied to Hermes/Mercury in antiquity.

Psychopompos is used of Hermes by Diod. Sic. 1.1.96 and Cornutus *ND* 22.6, and of Charon by Eurip. *Alc.* 361. The word is not used by Homer, although the scene at *Od.* 24.1ff. in which Hermes leads the souls of the suitors to the underworld is one of Vergil's models here (*mittit* has no model in the Greek).

Norden says the Orphic *Hymn to Hermes* 57.6–9 is Vergil's immediate model here (cf. 6: αἰνυμόροις ψυχαῖς πομπὸς κατὰ γαῖαν ὑπάρχων).

Bartelink (1965) 89, Marouzeau (1949) 74, Norden (1981) 312.

## A. 4.246–49:

iamque volans apicem et latera ardua cernit
*Atlantis duri* caelum qui vertice fulcit,
*Atlantis,* cinctum adsidue cui nubibus atris
piniferum caput et vento pulsatur et imbri

Here the name *Atlas,* repeated so as to have "a curious prominence" (Austin) is glossed by the adjective *durus,* which points to an etymology of Atlas from an intensifying prefix α-, and τλάς or τλῆναι, "endure." For the single-epithet gloss cf. intro. 2.2.

Crutwell suggests that Vergil alludes "also to the Roman slang name of Durus for Mount Atlas," which may have been the way soldiers during the Jugurthine War pronounced a local name Duris or Diris (see Strabo and Pliny quoted below).

Ross notes that Vergil's gloss *Atlantis duri* resembles that of Prop. 1.1.10 *durae . . . Iasidos,* where *durae* glosses the suppressed name Atalanta; he suggests that Gallus is the ultimate source of the etymological gloss.

STRABO 17.3.2: ἔξω δὲ προελθόντι τοῦ κατὰ τὰς Στήλας πορθμοῦ, τὴν Λιβύην ἐν ἀριστερᾷ ἔχοντι ὄρος ἐστίν, ὅπερ οἱ μὲν Ἕλληνες Ἄτλαντα καλοῦσιν, οἱ βάρβαροι δὲ Δύριν; PLINY *NH* 5.13: ab eo ad Dirim—hoc enim Atlanti nomen esse eorum lingua convenit.

Knight (1944) 198–99, Cruttwell (1945), McGushin (1964), Bartelink (1965) 73, Doig (1968) 2, Ross (1975) 61–65, esp. 62, Morwood (1985), Hardie (1986) 280 n. 132.

**A. 4.260?:** Aenean fundantem arces ac tecta *novantem*

For Vergil's several allusions to "new city" as an etymology of Carthage see on **A. 1.297–300**. Here there may not be enough indication of wordplay.

Bartelink (1965) 45.

**A. 4.268–69:** ipse deum tibi me *claro* demittit *Olympo* / regnator

Servius connects the name Olympus with the Greek ὁλολαμπής, "shining all over," and sees this etymology as explaining the epithet *claro*. The phrase *claro . . . Olympo* represents Homeric αἰγλήεντος Ὀλύμπου; some may feel that the Homeric precedent alone accounts for Vergil's epithet.

See intro. 2.2 for the single-epithet gloss.

SERV. 268: CLARO DEMITTIT OLYMPO Olympus quasi ὁλολαμπής dictus est sive mons sit Macedoniae, qui dicitur esse diversorium deorum, sive caelum; unde addidit "claro," ut (3.693) Plemyrium undosum (sim. on A. 10.1 and in Prisc. *Gramm. Lat.* 3.507.11 and Isid. 14.8.9; see Maltby).

Cerda (1612) 429, Bartelink (1965) 70 n. 4 (unduly skeptical); for this etymology in ancient allegorizations of Homer see Porter (1992) 84–88.

**A. 4.271:** aut qua spe Libycis *teris* otia *terris?*

Varro cites Aelius Stilo for the derivation of *terra* from *tero,* "wear down, rub," because people tread upon it.

VARRO *LL* 5.21: terra dicta ab eo ut Aelius (fr. 39, *GRF* p. 67) scribit, quod teritur; ISID. 14.1.1: terra dicta a superiori parte, qua teritur.

Ahl (1985) 31.

**A. 4.300–303?:**

> saevit inops animi totamque incensa per urbem
> *bacchatur,* qualis commotis excita sacris
> *Thyias,* ubi audito stimulant trieterica ***Baccho***
> orgia **nocturnus**que vocat clamore Cithaeron.

Perhaps more than one example of wordplay. There is an obvious connection between *bacchatur* in 301 and *Baccho* in 302; the position of the two words at the opposite ends of successive lines is a variation on the etymological framing of lines.

Servius Auctus mentions a derivation of *Thyias,* Bacchant, from the Greek verb θύω, which he glosses as *insane currere,* "run madly"; a similar gloss is found in the scholia to Apollonius. This etymological connotation would fit all of 300–303, although nothing in the text really points to the etymology. Conceivably the word before Thyias, *sacris* at the end of 301, could point to a connection between Thyias and the other word θύω, "sacrifice." A scholiast on Horace seems to allude to this connection.

Servius connects *nocturnus* with an epithet of Bacchus or his rites, Nyctelius. There could be but need not be wordplay here; a more likely example is found in Ovid, as André notes (for Ovid cf. intro. 2.14).

For an etymology of the name Dionysus see on A. 6.805, ***Liber***, *agens celso* ***Nysae*** *de vertice tigris.*

Thyias: SERV. 302: THYIAS . . . a Thyoneo Thyiades dicuntur. (Serv. Auct. adds:) quidam ἀπὸ τοῦ θύειν, quod est "insane currere," dictas volunt; SCHOL. Apoll. Rhod. 1.636: θυιάσιν . . . παρὰ τὸ θύειν καὶ ὁρμᾶν μαινομένας (cf. too on 3.755); SCHOL. Hor. C. 2.19.19: Thiades Bacchas dixit a sacrificio velut Theadas; then enim Graece deum, ita et sacrificium vocaverunt; SCHOL. Stat. *Theb.* 5.9.2: Thias Baccha ἀπὸ θυίειν βακχᾶν id est bacchari.

Nyctelius: SERV. 303: NOCTVRNVSQVE nocte celebratus; unde ipsa sacra "nyctelia" dicebantur (sim. on G. 4.520).

G. 4.521: *nocturni*que orgia *Bacchi;* OVID *Ars* 1.565: *Nycteliumque* patrem *nocturnaque* sacra precare.

André (1975) 194 (on Ovid alone); on Thyias see too Fordyce (1961) on Cat. 64.392; on Serv. and the schol. to Apoll. Rhod., Mühmelt (1965) 64–65.

**A. 4.347?:** hic amor, haec patria est

Skulsky: "Juxtaposing *amor* and *patria,* Virgil provides what seems to be the first allusion in extant Latin literature to Amor as the ὄνομα τελεστικόν of Rome, the city's occult ritual name." The idea of a secret name for Rome was discussed as early as Varro (see Serv. A. 1.277); that the name was thought by some to be Amor is suggested by Lyd. *Mens.* 4.73, and a Pompeian graffito where Roma and Amor appear in palindromic quadrate form:

R O M A
O I I M
M I I O
A M O R

(*CIL* IV, Suppl., pt. 3.1, 8297)

That Vergil alludes to the secret name Amor here seems less than certain.

Skulsky (1985) 447–55, quotation from 450, Cairns (1989) 118; on the secret name see Skulsky and also Stanley (1963).

**A. 4.356:** nunc etiam *interpres divum* Iove missus ab ipso

As Servius notes, in 356 and again in 378 the phrase *interpres divum* alludes to and glosses the Greek name for Mercury, Hermes = Ἑρμῆς < ἑρμηνεύς, "interpreter, go-between." Cf. the allusion to the epithet Psychopompos in A. 4.242–43, and cf. intro. 2.7 for suppression, or glossing of words not expressed.

SERV. 356: INTERPRES DIVVM Hermes; expressit verbum de verbo; SERV. 242: Ἑρμῆς autem Graece dicitur ἀπὸ τῆς ἑρμηνείας, Latine "interpres"; HYG. *Fab.* 143.2: Mercurius sermones hominum interpretatus est, unde ἑρμηνευτὴς dicitur esse interpres (Mercurius enim Graece Ἑρμῆς vocatur); MACROB. 1.17.5 (cf. also 1.19.9): nam quia sermo interpretatur cogitationes latentes, Ἑρμῆς ἀπὸ τοῦ ἑρμηνεύειν . . . vocitatus est; PLATO *Crat.* 407 e: ἀλλὰ μὴν τοῦτό γε ἔοικε περὶ λόγον τι εἶναι ὁ "Ἑρμῆς," καὶ ὁ ἑρμηνέα εἶναι καὶ ὁ ἄγγελον.

On Serv. here cf. Mühmelt (1965) 76; on Plato, Baxter (1992) 125–26.

**A. 4.359?:** vocemque his *auribus hausi*

Lactantius and Isidore derive *aures* from *(h)aurio,* but this could be a deduction based simply on Vergil's assonance-based juxtaposition. On this problem see on **1.164–65**; see also intro. 2.1 on paronomasia.

LACT. *Opif.* 8.8 : aures—quibus est inditum nomen a vocibus hauriendis, unde Vergilius "vocemque his auribus ausit"; aut quia vocem ipsam Graeci vocant αὐδὴν ab auditu, per immutationem litterae aures velut audes sunt nominatae; ISID. 11.1.46: aurium inditum nomen a vocibus auriendis, unde et Vergilius "vocemque his auribus ausit" (more references in Maltby); differently: VARRO *LL* 6.83: auris ab aveo.

Cerda (1612) 440, Bartelink (1965) 95.

**A. 4.377–78:** nunc Lyciae sortes, nunc et Iove missus ab ipso / *interpres divum* fert horrida iussa per auras.

Here *interpres divum* = Mercury = Hermes = Ἑρμῆς < ἑρμηνεύς, "interpreter, go-between." See on **A. 4.356.**

**A. 4.402–7?:**

ac velut ingentem *formicae* farris acervum
cum populant hiemis memores tectoque reponunt,
it nigrum campis agmen praedamque per herbas
*convectant* calle angusto; pars grandia trudunt
obnixae frumenta umeris, pars agmina cogunt
castigantque moras, opere omnis semita fervet.

Due notes Servius' derivation of *formica* from the ant's "carrying of crumbs" *(micas ferat* or *ore micas ferat)*. He cites clear allusions to this etymology in Ovid (for Ovid cf. intro. 2.14), but is (rightly) uncertain about whether in Vergil this etymological association means that *formicae* in 402 provides a kind of preview of the content of the following lines.

SERV. 402: sane "formica" dicta est ab eo, quod micas ferat (Serv. Auct.: quod ore micas ferat). (Murgia argues that the reading *quod ferat micas,* found in some mss. and in Isid. 12.3.9, is correct, "since such is the order in *formica.*" But in Serv. Auct. *ore* would seem to account for the *-or-* of *formica.* Ovid's two allusions to the etymology both include *ore.*)

OVID *Ars* 1.93–94: *formica . . . granifero* solitum cum *vehit ore* cibum; *Met.* 7.625: grande onus exiguo *formicas ore gerentes.*

Due (1973) 273–74, Murgia (1967) 337–38.

**A. 4.438–43?:**

sed nullis ille movetur
*fletibus* aut voces ullas tractabilis audit;
fata obstant placidasque viri deus obstruit auris.
ac velut annoso validam cum robore quercum
Alpini Boreae nunc hinc nunc *flatibus* illinc
eruere inter se certant

There is at least a punning connection between the tears *(fletibus)* that fail to move Aeneas, and the winds *(flatibus)* that cannot topple the old tree in the simile.

In Lucretius 1.277–97, the comparison of the movement and force of the winds with that of rivers is supported by the use of the terms *fluunt* (280), *flumine* (282), *fluctibus* (289), *flamine* (290), and *flumen* (291). Isidore derives *fluctus* from *flatus,* but does not mention *fletus.*

Cf. ISID. 13.20.2: fluctus dicti quod flatibus fiant.

West (1969) 45.

**A. 4.469?:** *Eumenidum* veluti demens videt *agmina* Pentheus

Ancient and modern scholars have wondered why Vergil here and in A. 6 speaks of "columns" or "troops" of Furies, when before the Silver Age there were generally only thought to be three of them. Waszink surveys previous attempts to solve the problem and suggests that Vergil is alluding to the (suppressed; see intro. 2.7) name *Agmentis,* which appears with *Pecmentis* and *Furina* in a list of Furies' names in the scholia to a ninth-century manuscript (Cod. Par. lat. 7930), which may preserve information from Varro's *Antiquitates Divinae*. Courtney, however, rejects Waszink's suggestion, at least for this passage. He argues that since Pentheus never has any reason to see the Furies, we should accept S. Allen's emendation of *Eumenidum* to *Euiadum,* "Bacchants."

Cf. 6.571–72, Tisiphone . . . vocat *agmina* saeva *sororum.*

Courtney (1981) 22, Waszink (1963) 7–11, who cites Savage (1925), (1925a); Mackie (1992) argues for widespread belief that the three Furies were Allecto, Megaera, and Tisiphone.

**A. 4.509–11?:** stant arae circum et crinis effusa sacerdos / *ter centum* tonat ore deos, Erebumque Chaosque / *tergeminam*que *Hecaten,* tria virginis ora Dianae.

Servius, perhaps implausibly, sees in *centum* in 510 an allusion to the association of the name Hecate with the Greek ἑκατόν, "hundred," explaining that she is to be thought of as "having a hundred (or 'countless') powers." Servius Auctus gives other etymologies for the name. Cf. Austin: "*ter centum:* of any large number," and see on A. 4.609: *nocturnisque Hecate* ***triviis*** *ululata per urbes.*

SERV. 510: TER CENTVM TONAT ORE DEOS non "tercentum deos" sed "tonat ter centum numina Hecates"; unde Hecate dicta est, ἑκατὸν, id est, centum potestates habens; SERV. Auct. 511: TERGEMINAMQVE HECATEN quidam Hecaten dictam esse tradunt, quod eadem et Diana sit et Proserpina, ἀπὸ τῶν ἑκατέρων; vel quod Apollinis soror sit, qui est ἑκατηβόλος.

Cf. Tupet (1976) 248, Pease (1935) 418, Austin (1955) on 510.

**A. 4.609:** nocturnisque Hecate *triviis* ululata per urbes

The word *triviis,* next to the name Hecate, alludes to the cult name Trivia, used by Vergil eight times in the *Aeneid,* but here suppressed (see intro. 2.7). The phrase *triviis ululata per urbes* is a full gloss on the name, as if to say, "Hecate is called Trivia because she is howled for at the crossroads."

Cf. *ter centum* in 509.

VARRO *LL* 7.16: Trivia Diana est, ab eo dicta Trivia, quod in trivio ponitur fere in oppidis graecis vel quod luna dicitur esse, quae in caelo tribus viis movetur, in altitudinem et latitudinem et longitudinem.

On Hecate and crossroads see Johnston (1991).

**A. 4.670?:** *Karthago* aut *antiqua* Tyros

For Vergil's several allusions to "new city" as an etymology of Carthage see on **A. 1.297–300**. The word *antiqua* would make this a gloss κατ' ἀντίφρασιν, as perhaps in A. 1.12–13.

Bartelink (1965) 45.

**A. 5.2?:** fluctusque *atros Aquilone* secabat

The juxtaposition of the words *atros* and *Aquilone* may allude to a derivation of the name Aquilo from *aquilus,* "dark colored," or at least a punning association of the words.

PAUL.-Fest. p. 20, 7 L: Aquilus color est fuscus et subniger; but note that PAUL.-Fest. p. 20, 14 L connects Aquilo with *aquila,* "eagle": Aquilo ventus a vehementissimo volatu ad instar aquilae appellatur.

G. 1.460: et *claro* silvas cernes *Aquilone* moveri.

Knight (1934) 124–25, (1944) 199, Bartelink (1965) 101, Williams (1960) ad loc.

**A. 5.8–10:** ut pelagus tenuere rates nec iam amplius ulla / occurrit tellus, maria undique et undique *caelum,* / olli *caeruleus* supra caput astitit imber

On the derivation of *caeruleus* from *caelum* (not explicitly mentioned in antiquity) see on **3.192–94**.

**A. 5.53–54:** *annua* vota tamen *sollemnis*que ordine pompas / exsequerer

Ancient sources seem to derive *sollemnis* from *annus.*

SERV. Auct. A. 8.173: anniversaria sacrificia, id est sollemnia; SERV. Auct. 3.301: SOLLEMNES legitimas, anniversarias; FEST. p. 384, 36 L: sollemne quod omnibus annis praestari debet; FEST. p. 466, 26 L: sollemnia sacra dicuntur quae certis temporibus annisque fieri solent.

A. 8.102, 172–74, 185?:

> forte die *sollemnem* illo rex Arcas honorem
> . . . . . . . . . . . . . . . . . . . . . . . . . . . . . .
> interea sacra haec, quando huc venistis amici,
> *annua,* quae differre nefas, celebrate faventes
> nobiscum. . . .
> . . . . . . . . . . .
> rex Evandrus ait: "non haec *sollemnia* nobis."

Bartelink (1965) 101.

**A. 5.116–23:**

> velocem Mnestheus agit acri remige Pristim,

mox Italus *Mnestheus*, genus a quo nomine *Memmi*
ingentemque Gyas ingenti mole Chimaeram,
urbis opus, triplici pubes quam Dardana versu
impellunt, terno consurgunt ordine remi;
**Sergestus**que, domus tenet a quo **Sergia** nomen,
Centauro invehitur magna, Scyllaque Cloanthus
caerulea, genus unde tibi, Romane Cluenti.

Vergil connects the names of three contestants in the boat race with family names of his day. In 117, he links the Memmii, the best known of whom "was the propraetor of Bithynia whom Catullus accompanied, and to whom Lucretius dedicated his poem" (Williams), to Mnestheus. Williams notes that "the philological justification for connecting the Memmii with Mnestheus seems particularly slight" and speculates that "Virgil was thinking of [a connection like that between] μεμνῆσθαι and *meminisse*."

In 121–23, Vergil explicitly links the *gens Sergia* to Sergestus, and the Cluentii to Cloanthus (with the words connected etymologically ending consecutive lines; see intro. 2.9). Williams notes that "the most famous of the gens Sergia was Catiline; and we know relatively little of the Cluentii, one of whom was defended by Cicero."

Vergil does not link Gyas in 118 to any contemporary family, but as Williams notes, "Servius tells us that the gens Gegania (of whom a number appear in the pages of Livy) was descended from Gyas; it is suggested that Virgil omitted mention of them because the family had died out by his time."

Vergil's genealogies here and elsewhere combine his own Callimachean interest in origins with the interest of contemporary Roman families in identifying Trojan or other legendary ancestors. Cornelius Nepos (*Att.* 18.2) says that Atticus wrote a treatise *de Familiis Romanis;* Servius (on A. 5.389 and 704) says that both Varro and Hyginus wrote *de Familiis Troianis*. Dionysius of Halicarnassus (1.85.3) says that in his day there were fifty Trojan families at Rome.

SERV. 117: et bene laudat familias nobilium: nam a Sergesto Sergia familia fuit, a Cloantho Cluentia, a Gya Gegania, cuius nunc facit mentionem; SERV. 121: DOMVS SERGIA familia . . . et inde est Sergius Catilina.

A. 1.267–68: at puer Ascanius, cui nunc cognomen *Iulo* / additur (*Ilus* erat, dum res stetit *Ilia* regno); 1.288: Iulius, a magno demissum nomen Iulo; A. 5.568–69: alter *Atys*, genus unde *Atii* duxere Latini, / parvus *Atys* pueroque puer dilectus Iulo; A. 6.789–90: hic Caesar et omnis *Iuli* / progenies magnum caeli ventura sub axem; A. 7.707–8: agmen agens *Clausus* magnique ipse agminis instar, / *Claudia* nunc a quo diffunditur et tribus et gens; A. 9.324–25: sic memorat vocemque premit, simul ense superbum / *Rhamnetem* adgreditur, qui forte tapetibus altis.

Heinze (1915) 152, Williams (1960) on 117, Bartelink (1965) 63–64, 66, 69, Saunders (1940); on fondness for Trojan or Italian genealogies in Vergil's time see Wiseman (1974) and Toohey (1984), Zanker (1987) 14, 44, and also intro. 2.4c and 3.

**A. 5.241–43:** et pater ipse manu magna *Portunus* euntem / impulit: illa Noto citius volucrique sagitta / ad terram fugit et *portu* se condidit alto.

Cicero and others derive the name *Portunus* from *portus,* "harbor"; Vergil seems to allude to that etymology here. Some sources link the name instead with *porta,* "gate."

CIC. *ND* 2.26.66: Portunus a portu; SERV. 241: PORTVNVS deus marinus qui portubus praeest; VARRO *LL* 6.19: Portunalia dicta a Portuno cui eo die aedes in portu Tiberino facta et feriae institutae; for *porta* cf. VARRO fr. 376 (*GRF* p. 345 = Schol. Veron. A. 5.241), PAUL.-Fest. p. 48 L, more in Pease and Frazer; OVID *F.* 6.546–47 (for Ovid cf. intro. 2.14): in *portus* nato ius erit omne tuo, / quem nos *Portunum,* sua lingua Palaemona dicet.

Bartelink (1965) 81, Pease (1979) ad Cic. *ND* 2.66 (p. 719), Frazer (1931) 441–42.

### A. 5.350, 353–54:

me liceat *casus* miserari insontis amici . . .
. . . . . . . . . . . . . . . . . . . . . . . . . . . . . . .
hic Nisus "si tanta" inquit "sunt praemia victis,
et te *lapsorum* miseret. . . ."

Williams: *casus* has "enough latent ambiguity for Nisus to take Aeneas up . . . on the literal meaning ('fall')."

Note that *casus* in 350 is followed by *miserari, lapsorum* in 354 by *miseret.*

SERV. 350: CASVS adlusit, a cadendo; CIC. *Div.* 2.15: quid est . . . aliud fors . . . quid casus, quid eventus, nisi cum sic aliquid cecidit, sic evenit, ut vel aliter cadere atque evenire potuerit; PAUL.-Fest. p. 51, 5 L: casus dicimus non modo ea, quae fortuita hominibus accidunt, sed etiam vocabulorum formas, quia in aliam atque aliam cadunt effigiem.

A. 6.30–34:

tu quoque magnam
partem opere in tanto, sineret dolor, Icare, haberes.
bis conatus erat *casus* effingere in auro,
bis patriae *cecidere* manus.

Williams (1960) on 350.

**A. 5.372–73?:** victorem *Buten* immani corpore, qui se / *Bebrycia* veniens *Amyci* de gente ferebat

Kraggerud suggests bovine wordplay connecting the names Butes (cf. βοῦς, bull, ox); Bebrycia (cf. βρυχάομαι, roar, bellow), and Amycus (cf. μυκάομαι, low, bellow, linked with the name in a line of Theocritus). He notes that an ox is the prize for the winner of the fight; in the model in *Il.* 23 it was a mule.

THEOC. 22.75: ἦ ῥ' <u>Ἄμυκος</u> καὶ κόχλον ἑλὼν <u>μυκήσατο</u> κοῖλον; cf. APOLL. Rhod. 1.1265–69 (and see on G. 3.146–53):

ὡς δ' ὅτε τίς τε μύωπι τετυμμένος ἔσσυτο ταῦρος
πίσεά τε προλιπὼν καὶ ἑλεσπίδας, οὐδὲ νομήων
οὐδ' ἀγέλης ὄθεται, πρήσσει δ' ὁδὸν ἄλλοτ' ἄπαυστος,
ἄλλοτε δ' ἱστάμενος καὶ ἀνὰ πλατὺν αὐχέν' ἀείρων
ἵησιν μύκημα, κακῷ βεβολημένος οἴστρῳ.

Kraggerud (1960) 31–32, Hecht (1882) 82 (on Theoc.), Ross (1987) 157–63 (on Apoll.).

**A. 5.522–23?:** hic oculis subitum *obicitur* magnoque futurum / augurio *monstrum*

Kleinknecht suggests that in this reference to the portent of the burning arrow, *obicitur* evokes the idea contained etymologically in *ostentum,* "portent" (from **obstentum*), suggested here also by *monstrum.* He compares A. 2.199–200: *hic aliud maius miseris multoque tremendum / obicitur magis atque improvida pectora turbat.*

CIC. *ND* 2.3.7: praedictiones vero et praesensiones rerum futurarum quid aliud declarant nisi hominibus ea quae sint ostendi monstrari portendi praedici, ex quo illa ostenta monstra portenta prodigia dicuntur; VARRO fr. 440 (*GRF* p. 365, ap. Serv. Auct. A. 3.366): ostentum, quod aliquid hominibus ostendit (more references in *GRF* and in Maltby s.v. ostentum).

Kleinknecht (1963) 431.

**A. 5.525–28:**

namque volans liquidis in nubibus arsit harundo
signavitque viam flammis tenuisque recessit
consumpta in ventos, caelo ceu saepe refixa
transcurrunt *crinem*que volantia *sidera* ducunt.

The word *crinem* in 528 alludes to the derivation of the words for comet, *cometes* and *crinita* (here suppressed; see intro. 2.7), from *coma* and *crines,* "hair." Both the motif of the comet or shooting star, and the implied etymology, link this omen, the fire that burns in Ascanius' hair, the fire that burns in Lavina's hair, the *sidus Iulium,* and the star that appears over Aeneas' head.

Cf. on **2.679–98.**

**A. 5.547?:** Epytiden vocat

Kraggerud suggests that the juxtaposition of the words *Epytiden* and *vocat* alludes to a connection of the name with the verb ἠπύω, "call out loudly," mentioned by the Homeric scholia and Eustathius.

Cf. 579 *Epytides . . . insonuitque flagello.*

SCHOL. *Il.* 17.324 (κήρυκι Ἠπυτίδῃ): ἔστιν οὖν παράγωγον ἀπὸ τοῦ "ἠπύτα κήρυξ" (7.384); cf. Eustath. ad loc.

Kraggerud (1960) 33 n. 1, Stanford (1939) 100–101.

**A. 5.560–61:** *tres* equitum numero *turmae terni*que vagantur / ductores

Varro and others derive *turma*, "troop, squadron," from *ter* or *ter deni.*

VARRO *LL* 5.91.1: turma terima (E in U abiit), quod terdeni equites ex tribus tribubus Titiensium, Ramnium, Lucerum fiebant; PAUL.-Fest. p. 484, 9 L = Curiatius fr. 3, *GRF* p. 389: turmam equitum dictam esse ait Curiatius quase terimam: quod ter deni equites ex tribus Titiensium, Ramnium, Lucerum fiebant; ISID. 9.3.51: turma triginta equites sunt.

Cerda (1612) 572, Bartelink (1965) 110.

**A. 5.568–69:** alter *Atys*, genus unde *Atii* duxere Latini, / parvus *Atys* pueroque puer dilectus Iulo

As Servius notes, Vergil explicitly links the Atii, the *gens* of Augustus' mother, to Atys, whose friendship with Iulus looks forward to the ties between the Iulii and the Atii.

On Roman names traced back to Trojan families see on **A. 5.116–23.**

SERV. 568: GENVS VNDE ATII DVXERE LATINI propter Atiam dicit, matrem Augusti, de qua Antonius ait "Aricina mater"; vult enim eius etiam maternum esse genus antiquum.

Bartelink (1965) 62, Williams (1960) on 568.

**A. 5.602:** Troiaque nunc pueri, Troianum dicitur agmen

The reference to naming works as a signpost for an etymological aetiology. Vergil is explaining that the *lusus Troiae* is so called because it was brought to Rome /Italy by the Trojans.

Williams explains a different possible origin for the name: "Lejay (on 5.553) cites Festus' explanation of the archaic verbs *amptruare, redamptruare,* as describing the movements of dancing, which would suggest a noun *troia* meaning 'movement,' 'evolution,' and on a sixth-century oenochoe found at Tragliatella there are figures of horsemen and a labyrinth, and the Etruscan word *Truia*. . . . When the legend of Rome's Trojan origins became widespread, the *lusus Troiae* would easily be associated with Troy." See also Clark for "the widespread association of labyrinths in northern Europe with the name *Troia* or *Truia*."

Cf. on A. 3.389–93 for the sow, Troy, and the word *troia*. For *nunc* in etymologies and aetiologies see intro. 2.10a for signposts, intro. 2.6.

SERV. 602: TROIAQVE NVNC PVERI TROIANVM DICITVR AGMEN ut ait Suetonius Tranquillus, lusus ipse, quem vulgo pyrrhicham appellant, Troia vocatur, cuius originem expressit in libro de puerorum lusibus (Suet. *Lus. Puer*. 197, p. 345 Reiffersch).

Williams (1960) on 545f., Clark (1978) 135–36, *EV* s.v. Ludus Troiae (Polverini).

**A. 5.606–8:** Irim de caelo misit *Saturnia* Iuno / Iliacam ad classem ventosque aspirat eunti, / multa movens necdum antiquum *saturata* dolorem.

Cicero links the name *Saturnus* to the verb *saturo,* "to fill, satisfy." Vergil several times describes the *in*satiability of Saturnian Juno, with ironic allusion to this etymology.

For possible allusion to or awareness of the derivation *ab satu Saturnus,* see on **G. 2.173–74**. For etymology κατ' ἀντίφρασιν see intro. 2.3.

CIC. *ND* 2.64: Saturnus autem est appellatus quod saturaretur annis; 3.62: Saturnus quia se saturat annis; see Pease's citations from Aug., Fulg., Isid. 8.11.30, and the idea that Cicero's etymology is related to the association of Cronos with κόρον νοῦ (Plato *Crat.* 396 b, etc.).

A. 5.781–82, 785–86:

> Iunonis gravis ira neque *exsaturabile* pectus
> cogunt me, Neptune, preces descendere in omnis;
> . . . . . . . . . . . . . . . . . . . . . . . . . . . . . . .
> non media de gente Phrygum exedisse nefandis
> urbem odiis *satis* est

A. 7.297–98, 310–12:

> at, credo, mea numina tandem
> fessa iacent, odiis aut *exsaturata* quievi.
> . . . . . . . . . . . . . . . . . . . . . . . . . . . .
> vincor ab Aenea. quod si mea numina non sunt
> magna *satis,* dubitem haud equidem implorare quod usquam est:
> flectere si nequeo superos, Acheronta movebo.

OVID *Met.* 9.9.176–78: *Saturnia* . . . / corque ferum *satia* (cf. too 3.249–72?, and also intro. 2.14).

Anderson (1958) 519–32, esp. 522–25, Pease (1979) on *ND* 2.64, Lyne (1989) 173–77, Feeney (1991) 201 (on the parallel or imitative wordplay in Ovid).

**A. 5.638–39?:** iam tempus *agi* res, / nec tantis mora *prodigiis*

Kleinknecht sees wordplay between *agere* and *prodigium,* especially with the similar-sounding *agi res* and *prodigiis* at line end and sentence end, respectively. Nonius derives *prodigium* from *porro adigenda;* most ancient sources connect *prodigium* with *praedicere* (Cicero) or *porro dirigit* (Varro). Kleinknecht argues that a *prodigium* is to be seen as a divine "act" that does not simply reveal the future, but instead helps to propel human beings toward their fate. (The snakes that devour Laocoon and his sons in book 2 are his best example of this.)

Cf. A. 6.379, *prodigiis acti caelestibus.*

NON. p. 44, 17 M: prodigia dicta sunt porro adigenda; differently CIC. *Div.* 1.93, *ND* 2.7, VARRO ap. Serv. Auct. A. 3.366 (= fr. 440, *GRF* p. 365); more in Maltby.

Kleinknecht (1963) 446–47, 485–88.

**A. 5.718:** urbem appellabunt permisso nomine *Acestam*

Vergil derives the name of the town Segesta (called Egesta by the Greeks) from the name Acestes. Note the etymological signpost (intro. 2.6).

Bartelink suggests too a possible connection between the name Acesta and Greek ἀκεῖσθαι, "heal," since some of Aeneas' followers find an end to toils there. But there is nothing in the text to point to this.

Bartelink (1965) 38, Williams (1960) on 718.

**A. 5.781–88:**

Iunonis gravis ira neque *exsaturabile* pectus
cogunt me, Neptune, preces descendere in omnis;
quam nec longa dies pietas nec mitigat ulla,
nec Iovis imperio fatisque infracta quiescit.
non media de gente Phrygum *exedisse* nefandis
urbem odiis *satis* est nec poenam traxe per omnem
reliquias Troiae: cineres atque ossa peremptae
insequitur. causas tanti sciat illa furoris.

For Vergil's plays on *Saturnia Juno* and words like *saturata* and *satis* see on **A. 5.606–8**. Lyne notes that Vergil alludes in 5.785 to *Il.* 4.35, where Zeus says that Hera would be satisfied only by eating raw Priam and his sons.

Neptune too is called *Saturnius* at 5.799, as he begins his reply to this speech of Venus.

Lyne (1989) 175.

**A. 6.11–12:** antrum immane, petit, magnam cui mentem animumque / *Delius* inspirat vates *aperitque futura*

Servius suggests that the island of Apollo's birth is called *Delos* from δῆλος, "clear, apparent" and δηλόω, "make clear," because from that site Apollo gives not obscure but clear oracles. *Aperitque futura* may therefore gloss the epithet *Delius*. Callimachus also derives Delos from δῆλος, though on different grounds (also found amoung Servius' explanations): the floating island Asterie was allowed to become rooted as a gift for its role in Apollo's birth, and was given the name Delos because it was no longer "obscure" (ἄδηλος). Macrobius in discussing the name glosses δῆλα with *aperta*.

On this passage Servius offers the implausible suggestion that with the words *mentem animumque* in 11, Vergil offers a gloss on the name Sibylla, as if from σιοῦ (= Aeolic for "god") βουλή. That etymology is found in Varro but probably is not alluded to in A. 6.11–12.

SERV. A. 3.73: Delos . . . quia diu latuit et post apparuit—nam δῆλον Graeci "manifestum" dicunt—vel quod verius est, quia cum ubique Apollinis responsa obscura sint, manifesta illic dantur oracula; PLINY *NH* 4.66: (Delum) Aristoteles ita appellatam tradidit, quoniam repente apparuit enata; MACROB. 1.17.56: haec insula ideo Delos vocatur, quia ortus et quasi partus luminum omnia facit δῆλα id est aperta clarescere (more in Maltby); SERV. 12: bene autem Sibylla quid sit expressit "magnam cui mentem animumque Delius inspirat vates": nam, ut supra (3.445) diximus, Sibylla dicta est quasi σιοῦ βουλή, id est dei sententia. Aeolici enim σιοὺς deos dicunt; cf. Varro ap. Lact. *Inst.* 1.6.7 (fr. 179, *GRF* p. 247).

Callim. *Hymn* 4.51–54:

> ἡνίκα δ' Ἀπόλλωνι γενέθλιον οὖδας ὑπέσχες,
> τοῦτό τοι ἀντημοιβὸν ἁελίπλοοι οὔνομ' ἔθεντο,
> οὕνεκεν οὐκέτ' ἄδηλος ἐπέπλεες, ἀλλ' ἐνὶ πόντου
> κύμασιν Αἰγαίοιο ποδῶν ἐνεθήκαο ῥίζας.

Bartelink (1965) 75.

**A. 6.27:** hic *labor* ille *domus* et inextricabilis error

Vergil's alludes to but does not use (i.e., he suppresses; see intro. 2.7) the word *labyrinthus*. Norden suggests that Vergil's unusual expression *labor ille domus* alludes to an etymology of *labyrinthus* from *labor,* and perhaps even to the spelling *laborinthus,* common in the medieval period. Norden refers to this etymology as "much-discussed in antiquity," but I know only of references to it in medieval sources, some of them not fully published, which are described by Doob. Doob also explores the connection between labyrinthine imagery and *labor* throughout the poem.

Doob cites and discusses medieval etymologies such as *labor intus.*

Norden (1981) on 6.27 (p. 129), Hanssen (1948) 122, Bartelink (1965) 87, Fitzgerald (1984) 55, Kristol (1990) 46 n. 21, Doob (1990) 95–100, 227–53, Petrini (n.d.) chap. 5.

**A. 6.30–33:**

> tu quoque magnam
> partem opere in tanto, sineret dolor, Icare, haberes.
> bis conatus erat *casus* effingere in auro,
> bis patriae *cecidere* manus.

The word *casus* in 33 both means "misfortune" and suggests Icarus' "fall"; then *cecidere* in 34 reinforces the connotation of "fall."

Cf. **A.** 5.350–54 *casus . . . lapsorum.*

I owe this observation to my student Daniel Mackta.

**A. 6.130:** *ardens* evexit ad *aethera* virtus

As Servius Auctus notes on A. 1.394, *aether* is from Greek αἴθω, "to burn." Here *ardens* alludes to that etymology.

For Norden, the caesura and alliteration here suggest borrowing from earlier poetry.

Cf. A. 7.281 *semine ab* ***aetherio*** *spirantis naribus* ***ignem.***

SERV. Auct. A. 1.394: aether altior est aere, vicinus caelo, ἀπὸ τοῦ αἴθειν, id est ardere; ISID. 13.5.1: aether locus est in quo sidera sunt, et significat eum ignem qui a toto mundo in altum separatus est; APUL. *Mund.* 1: aether vocatur, non ut quidam putant, quod ignitus sit et incensus, sed quod cursibus rapidis semper rotetur (= [Aristot.] *Mund.* 392a5ff., διὰ τὸ ἀεὶ θεῖν); *ETYM. GUD.*: αἰθήρ· παρὰ το αἴθεσθαι. πυρώδης γάρ.

Bartelink (1965) 86, Norden (1981) on 130; on Greek sources, cf. Rank (1951) 10–11.

**A. 6.138–39?:** hunc tegit omnis / *lucus* et obscuris claudunt convallibus *umbrae.*
An allusion κατ' ἀντίφρασιν to the etymology, *lucus a non lucendo?* Perhaps unlikely. See on **A. 1.441.**

**A. 6.160:** multa inter sese vario *sermone serebant*
Servius derives *sermo* from *sero.* Norden thinks the connection is of Ennian origin. Possibly the grammarians' etymology has been simply derived from the assonantal collocation in Vergil and other poets (for this problem cf. on **A. 1.164–65**).

SERV. 160: SERMONE SEREBANT hic proprie dictus est sermo, qui inter utrumque seritur; ISID. 6.8.3: sermo autem dictus quia inter utrumque seritur. unde in Vergilio (A. 6.160): Multa inter se serebant; SERV. A. 4.277: sermo est conseratio orationis et confabulatio duorum vel plurium; differently VARRO *LL* 6.64: sermo . . . est a serie.

PLAUT. *Curc.* 193: sermonem . . . serat; LIVY 7.39.6: haec . . . occultis sermonibus serunt; cf. too on *Serrane, serentem* at A. 6.844.

Cerda (1612) 636, Norden (1981) 182 and 373, Bartelink (1965) 100.

**A. 6.204:** discolor unde *auri* per ramos *aura* refulsit
Servius derives the word for gold, *aurum,* from *aura,* but this could be derived from Vergil's own phrase (cf. on **A. 1.164–65**). Certainly we have at least an effectve use of soundplay (see Norden's extensive discussion, and for paronomasia cf. too intro. 2.1)
Fordyce compares Horace C. 1.5.9–12: *qui nunc te fruitur credulus* ***aurea,*** */ qui semper vacuam, semper amabilem / sperat, nescius* ***aurae*** */ fallacis.* He considers both examples to be "calculated to appeal to the ear."

SERV. 204: AVRI AVRA splendor auri . . . hinc et aurum dicitur a splendore, qui est in eo metallo: hinc et aurarii dicti, quorum favor splendidos reddit (sim. at Isid. 16.18.1; cf. Maltby); not in MACROB. 6.6.8 ("Servius" speaking): quid est enim aura auri, aut quem ad modum aura refulget? sed tamen pulchre usurpavit.

Fordyce (1977) on 7.491; cf. Brooks (1966) 273, Norden (1981) 192–93, Ahl (1985) 304, Finkelpearl (1990) 342.

**A. 6.232–35:**

at pius Aeneas ingenti mole sepulcrum
imponit suaque arma viro remumque tubamque
monte sub aerio, qui nunc Misenus ab illo

dicitur aeternumque tenet per saecula nomen.

An explicit etymological aetiology, linking the Promontorium Misenum to the Trojan trumpeter Misenus. Note the etymological signpost, for which see intro. 2.6, and see intro. 2.10a for the use of *nunc*. The aetiology of the headland named after Palinurus at 6.378–83 is similar.

D.H. 1.53.3: τελευτήσαντος . . . αὐτόθι Μισηνοῦ . . . ἀπ' ἐκείνου τὸν λιμένα ὠνόμασαν; PAUL.-Fest. p. 110, 10 L: Misenum promontorium a Miseno tubicine Aeneae ibi sepultum est appellatum; [AUR. Vict.] *Orig.* 9.6: ex cuius nomine urbem Misenon appellatam, ut scribit etiam Caesar Pontificalium libro primo (cf. also Sol. 2.13, cited by Maltby).

Austin (1977) on 162 (cites other sources linking Misenus and Misenum) and on 235 ("the manner is Alexandrian"), Norden (1981) 197–98.

## A. 6.237–42:

spelunca alta fuit vastoque immanis hiatu,
scrupea, tuta lacu nigro nemorumque tenebris,
quam super *haud ullae* poterant impune *volantes*
tendere iter pennis: talis sese halitus atris
faucibus effundens supera ad convexa ferebat.
[unde locum Grai dixerunt nomine *Aornum*.]

Vergil alludes to the etymology of the name Avernus or Aornus from α- privative + ὄρνις, "bird." The name Avernus or Aornus is suppressed in these lines (cf. intro. 2.7), although Avernus was mentioned by Vergil at 6.201, *fauces grave olentis Averni,* and the interpolator of 242 adds Aornus. Apollonius glosses the name without mentioning it, and Lucretius glosses the name more explictly but perhaps connects it not with ὄρνις but with *avis*. Perhaps without the interpolated line, Vergil would seem to connect it with *avis* too? Varro discussed the phenomenon of the birds' dying, and is likely to have commented on the etymology.

For wordplay with *avis* cf. on A. 8.231–35 *Aventini*.

VARRO ap. Pliny *NH* 31.21: Caelius (sc. tradit) apud nos in Averno etiam folia subsidere, Varro aves quae advolaverint emori (Varro fr. 381, *GRF* p. 347); SERV. A. 3.442: odor gravissimus supervolantes aves necaret; unde et Avernus dictus est, quasi ἄορνις; NON. p. 14, 4 M: Avernus lacus idcirco appellatus est, quia est odor eius avibus infestissimus; ISID. 13.19.8: Avernus autem lacus vocatus quod aves ibi supervolare non possent.

APOLL. Rhod. 4.601–3:

οὐδέ τις ὕδωρ κεῖνο διὰ πτερὰ κοῦφα τανύσσας
οἰωνὸς δύναται βαλέειν ὕπερ· ἀλλὰ μεσηγὺς
φλογμῷ ἐπιθρῴσκει πεποτημένος.

LUCR. 6.740–43:

Principio, quod *Averna* vocantur nomine, id ab re
impositumst, quia sunt *avibus* contraria cunctis,
e regione ea quod loca cum venere *volantes,*
remigii oblitae pennarum vela remittunt.

Norden (1981) 201–2, Bartelink (1965) 41, Brooks (1966) 277 ("The creatures of heaven cannot enter hell"). On Apollonius, see Livrea (1973) ad loc., on Lucretius, Snyder (1980) 105, who follows Merrill in thinking that Lucretius connects Avernus with *avis*. On 242 see Bartelink, and Norden and Austin ad loc.

## A. 6.273–81?:

vestibulum ante ipsum primisque in faucibus Orci
Luctus et ultrices posuere cubilia *Curae,*
pallentesque habitant Morbi tristisque Senectus,
et Metus et malesuada Fames ac turpis Egestas,
terribiles visu formae, *Letum*que Labosque;
tum consanguineus Leti Sopor et mala mentis
Gaudia, mortiferumque adverso in limine Bellum,
ferreique Eumenidum thalami et Discordia demens
vipereum crinem vittis innexa cruentis.

Wordplay or soundplay. Sider suggests that two of the figures at the entrance to the underworld, *Curae* and *Letum*, may echo the sounds of the names of figures in Hes. *Th.* 211ff., Κῆρες and Λήθη.

For other such "mistranslations" see intro. 2.1a. For a gloss of the name Lethe cf. A. 6.713–15.

Cf. VARRO *LL* 7.42: in funeribus indictivis, quo dicitur "ollus *leto* datus est," quod Graecus dicit λήθη, id est oblivioni (sim. Paul.-Fest. p. 102, 19 L).

Sider (1988) 18.

*

**A. 6.299–300:** terribili squalore *Charon,* cui plurima mento / canities inculta iacet, stant *lumina flamma*

De la Cerda suggests that Vergil alludes to an explanation of the name Charon that connected it with χαροπός, a Homeric word of disputed meaning (fierce? with a look full of the joy of battle?), later used of eyes in the sense "flashing, bright" (LSJ 2). The poetic form χάρων, -ωνος is used at Euphorion 84 and Lycophron 260, 455, and 660.

For a different etymology of Charon see on 6.392–93.

Cerda (1612) 664, Norden (1981) 221, Roscher (1884–1937) s.v. Charon.

## A. 6.309–12?:

quam multa in silvis autumni *frigore* primo
lapsa cadunt folia, aut ad terram gurgite ab alto
quam multae glomerantur aves, ubi *frigidus* annus

trans pontum fugat et terris immittit *apricis.*

Paulus-Festus and Servius derive *apricus* from the Greek ἄτερ φρίκης, which Servius glosses as *sine frigore,* "without cold." If this etymology was known in Vergil's day, Vergil may be alluding to it by using the words *frigore* and *frigidus* before *apricis* in 312.

SERV. 312: INMITTIT APRICIS quasi ἄτερ φρίκης, id est sine frigore, ut diximus supra (5.128): unde non nulli et Africam dictam volunt; PAUL.-Fest. p. 2, 16 L: apricum locum a sole apertum. a Graeco vocabulo φρίκη appellatur, quasi ἀφρικής, id est sine horrore, videlicet frigoris, unde etiam putatur et Africa appellari (more in Maltby s.vv. apricus, Africa).

Cf. *EV* s.v. apricus (Vinchesi).

**A. 6.339?:** exciderat puppi
See on **A. 6.362** for possible allusion to the name Palinurus.

**A. 6.350?:** cui datus haerebam custos
See on **A. 6.362** for possible allusion to the name Palinurus.

**A. 6.362:** nunc me fluctus habet *versant*que in litore *venti*
Ambrose argues that *versant . . . venti* represents an etymological play on Palinurus' name, as is from πάλιν, "back, backward, from behind," and οὖρος, "(fair) wind." Brenk finds that Palinurus suggests Paliouros, "the contrary wind." Merkelbach sees allusion also to a possible derivation from πάλιν and οὖρος, "watcher, guardian," in 339 *exciderat puppi* (Παλιν-) and 350 *(gubernaclum) cui datus haerebam custos* (-ουρος).

Cf. MARTIAL 3.78.2: *meiere* vis *iterum?* iam Palinurus eris (cf. πάλιν + οὐρέω).

Ambrose (1980) 449–57, Brenk (1984) 777 and n. 4, Merkelbach (1972) 83, O'Hara (1990) 110 n. 44.

**A. 6.378–83:**

"nam tua finitimi, longe lateque per urbes
prodigiis acti caelestibus, ossa piabunt
et statuent tumulum et tumulo sollemnia mittent,
aeternumque locus Palinuri nomen habebit."
his dictis curae emotae pulsusque parumper
corde dolor tristi; gaudet cognomine terra.

An explicit etymological aetiology, explaining why the headland in Lucania has the name Palinurus (Maltby offers more sources). The aetiology of the Promontorium Misenum at A. 6.232–35 is similar.

There is a textual problem in 383: the manuscripts have the genitive *terrae;* Servius has the ablative *terra,* which makes *cognomine* a rare adjective (Servius and Austin cite Plaut. *Bacch.* 39), and seems to be the better reading.

**A. 6.379:** prodigiis acti caelestibus

See on **A. 5.638–39** (iam tempus *agi* res, / nec tantis mora *prodigiis*) for a possible etymological connection between *agere* and *prodigium.*

Kleinknecht (1963) 446–47, 485–88.

**A. 6.392–93:** *nec* vero Alciden *me sum laetatus* euntem / accepisse

The name Charon is given at 299 and glossed by Servius with the antithetical etymology, *quasi* ἀχαίρων. Norden notes the wordplay in 392–93 between Charon / Χάρων and *nec . . . laetatus* (cf. χαίρω).

For a different etymology of Charon see on 6.299–300. For glosses κατ' ἀντίφρασιν see intro. 2.3.

SERV. 6.299: CHARON κατὰ ἀντίφρασιν quasi ἀχαίρων.

ARISTOPH. *Ranae* 184: χαῖρ' ὦ Χάρων, χαῖρ' ὦ Χάρων, χαῖρ' ὦ Χάρων; also in ACHAEUS fr. 11 (*TGF* p. 118 Sn.), cited by Schol. *Ranae* 184, and in Eustathius 16.33 (on *Il.* 1.3), cited by Mühmelt.

Norden (1981) 237: "Diese Worte bekommen ihre Pointe erst, wenn man sie sich griechische denkt: οὐδὲ μὲν Ἡρακλῆα χαρεὶς δεχόμην κατιόντα, denn das antithetische Wortspiel zwischen Χάρων und χαίρειν war sehr beliebt"; Mühmelt (1965) 65.

**A. 6.438–39:** fas obstat, tristisque palus *inamabilis* undae / alligat et novies *Styx* interfusa coercet.

Greek authors, and Servius, connect the name Styx with Greek στυγέω, "hate," and στυγερός, "hateful." Vergil's *inamabilis* is thus a gloss on the name.

Henrichs provides a wealth of information on the name Styx, with a list of passages that play on the connection between the name Styx and στυγέω and στυγερός. He claims that Vergil's *inamabilis undae* / . . . *Styx* borrows from the new Aesch. fr. 273A.11–13: ⟨ἀ⟩μέγαρτο⟨ν⟩ ὕδωρ / . . . / Στυγίοις (the supplement is plausible).

Cf. G. 4.479–80 *inamabilis . . . Styx.*

SERV. 6.134: Styx maerorem significat, unde ἀπὸ τοῦ στυγεροῦ, id est a tristitia Styx dicta est; SERV. 439: tristitia . . . , id est Styx; ISID. 14.9.6: Styx ἀπὸ τοῦ στυγερός, id est a tristitia, dicta, eo quod tristes faciat vel quod tristitiam gignat.

Bartelink (1965) 82, Henrichs (1989) 1–19, esp. 11 n. 30.

**A. 6.441?:** Lugentes campi; sic illos nomine dicunt

These lines present a puzzle I cannot quite solve, but I can outline the interesting problem. *Nomine dicunt* looks like an etymological signpost (cf. intro. 2.6), but it is not clear exactly what kind of etymologizing might be involved. Norden thinks the phrase *nomine dicunt* is a sign that Vergil is drawing upon a lost source; he compares four other uses of *nomine* in the fifth dactyl. Often such "footnotes" refer to sources, but I would add that all four seem to involve etymologizing (see my entries on the two Vergilian passages):

A. 7.607, where he sees an Ennian model and I see allusion to a name; G. 3.280, where he suspects a source in a Hellenistic model, perhaps Euphorion, and Vergil is clearly etymologizing; LUCR. 2.629–30, where Friedländer suggests allusion to the derivation of Κούρητες from κοῦροι (see on G. 4.149–52); and CIC. *Arat.* fr. xiii S, in quoting which Cic. *ND* 2.109 glosses Ophiouchum with Anguitenens.

In general on the whole passage at 6.440–76, with its catalogue of women doomed by *durus Amor,* Norden is probably right to think of a Hellenistic precedent, perhaps even a *Catalogue of Famous Women in Hades,* which itself would have been modeled upon *Od.* 11.225–332, but probably with the Hellenistic taste for pathos of both Parthenius' *Erotika Pathemata* and Vergil's lines. The pathetic fallacy evident in the phrase *Lugentes campi* is Hellenistic; Fletcher notes that "the Latin expression is a strange one," for "fields cannot mourn." Norden points to Nic. *Alex.* 301, where a pine mourns for Marsyas, and Ovid *Met.* 11.44–49, where trees mourn for Orpheus; see also Fordyce on A. 7.514ff. and 760.

Two suggestions may be noted about possible etymologizing here or in Vergil's source. Servius glosses the phrase *Lugentes campi* as *lucis egentes,* and Isidore repeats the gloss with a bit more information, namely that this is the origin of *luctus* as well. De la Cerda explains *Lugentes campi* by reference to the Cocytus River, whose name is commonly derived from κωκύω, "mourn" (see Servius on A. 6.312 and Maltby s.v.); de la Cerda explains that the fields next to the Cocytus could thus similarly be called Mourning Fields. By itself these observations do not provide a satisfactory motivation for Vergil's phrase, but I think we have improved upon Norden's suggesting of a Hellenistic source by tentatively specifying a Hellenistic or Roman-Alexandrian source that featured an etymology of the *Lugentes campi* or that connected them either with lack of light or with the Cocytus. The Hellenistic model is likely to have made clear what is being suggested about the name *Lugentes campi.*

Knight contrasts A. 3.701 *campique Geloi,* perhaps "plains of laughter," with these *Lugentes campi.*

Austin notes that the phrase *nomine dicunt* "impl[ies] a received tradition . . . but one would prefer not to accept the implication." Such romantic hostility to the use of a model is inappropriate for the criticism of Vergil.

SERV. 441: LVGENTES CAMPI quasi "lucis egentes": quod et amoribus congruit; ISID. *Diff.* 1.227: lugentes cero dicti, quasi luce egentes, unde et luctus dicitur (some manuscripts have *lucus*).

A. 7.607: sunt geminae Belli portae (sic nomine dicunt); G. 3.280: hippomanes vero quod nomine dicunt; LUCR. 2.629–30: Curetas nomine Grai / quos memorant; CIC. *Arat.* fr. xiii: quem claro perhibent Ophiuchum nomine Graii.

Cerda (1612) 684, Norden (1981) 249, Knight (1944) 198, Fletcher (1961) on 441, Austin (1977) on 441, Fordyce (1977) on A. 7.514ff. and 760; Friedländer (1941) 21 and Snyder (1980) 96 on Lucretius.

**A. 6.448–49:** it comes et iuvenis quondam, nunc femina, *Caeneus* / rursus et in *veterem* fato revoluta figuram.

Norden speaks of antithetical wordplay between the name Caeneus, which is here, he says, associated with Greek καινός, "new," and *veterem* "old, former."

Norden (1981) 251 ("Καινεύς, 'Neumann' von καινός, statt 'Mörder' von καίνω"), Mørland (1960) 21, Kraggerud (1965) 66–71, Austin (1977) ad loc. (notes that in Vergil alone Caeneus becomes a woman again in the underworld).

## A. 6.450–54:

inter quas Phoenissa recens a vulnere *Dido*
*errabat* silva in magna; quam Troius heros
ut primum iuxta stetit agnovitque per umbras
obscuram, qualem primo qui surgere mense
aut videt aut vidisse putat per nubila *lunam*

Earlier Vergil has linked first the moon (A. 1.742 *errantem lunam*) and then Dido (see on **A. 4.211** *femina, quae nostris errans in finibus*) with the word *erro* and by implication with πλάνη. The word πλανῆτις or *planeta* is said to derived from πλάνη, because the planets "wander," and Dido's name is said to mean πλανῆτις. In this passage Vergil again uses the verb *errare* of Dido, and then he compares her to the moon.

**A. 6.460?:** invitus, regina, tuo de litore cessi

Among the many discussions of this line, two connect it with etymological wordplay, although not at all convincingly. This line adapts Catullus 66.39, *invita, o regina, tuo de vertice cessi,* spoken, in Catullus' version of Callimachus' *Coma Berenices* (fr. 110), by the lock of hair made into a star. Nadeau and Skulsky point to the etymological connection between *caesaries,* "head of hair," which is used of the lock at Cat. 66.8, and the name Caesar, suggested in A. 6 (represented allegorically, Nadeau would say) by the ancestor of Julius and Augustus, Aeneas. In Catullus, the lock *(caesaries)* speaks to the queen of Egypt, Berenice; in Vergil Aeneas (= ?Caesar) speaks to a Carthaginian queen, Dido, who has literary associations with the Egyptian queens Berenice and Cleopatra. The claim that there are such precise allegorical correspondences seems unconvincing to me.

If the association *caesaries*/star/Caesar is felt, it would link this line to the system of omens and wordplay involving Ascanius' flaming head and the falling star, Acestes' flaming arrow, Lavinia's flaming hair, the appearance of the Sidus Iulium behind Augustus at Actium, and the flame from Aeneas helmet as he arrives at battle (see on **A. 2.679–98**).

PAUL.-Fest. p. 50, 7 L: Caesar, quod est cognomen Iuliorum, a caesarie dictus est, quia scilicet cum caesarie natus est; GLOSS. (Goetz) 5.177.30: cesariem comam unde et omnes imperatores antiqui caesares dicti sunt quod comti essent.

Nadeau (1982), Skulsky (1985). Cf. Knox (1982) 76, who suggests that Ovid's use of the wordplay recalls Callimachus. On Vergil and Catullus here, see Clausen (1970) 92 and Tatum (1984).

**A. 6.511–14:**

> sed me fata mea et scelus exitiale Lacaenae
> his mersere malis; illa haec *monimenta* reliquit.
> namque ut supremam falsa inter gaudia noctem
> egerimus, nosti: et nimium *meminisse* necesse est.

Vergil seems to suggest a link between *monimenta* and *meminisse;* Varro and others connect *monimentum* with *memoria* and/or *moneo.*

The two forms Vergil uses have the same metrical shape (even the same distribution of vowels and consonants) and appear in the same metrical position. For other wordplay involving *memoria* or *memini* see **A. 1.8** *Musa,* mihi causas *memora,* and passages cited there.

VARRO *LL* 6.49: Meminisse a memoria, cum id quod remansit in mente . . . rursus movetur; quae a manendo ut manimoria potest esse dicta. . . . Ab eodem monere, quod is qui monet, proinde sit ac memoria; sic monimenta quae in sepulcris, et ideo secundum viam, quo pratereuntis admoneant et se fuisse et illos esse mortalis. ab eo cetera quae scripta ac facta memoriae causa monimenta dicta; CIC. ap. Non. p. 32, 15 M: monumenti proprietatem a monendo M. Tullius exprimendam putavit ad Caesarem Epistula (2,7) "sed ego, quae monimenti ratio sit, nomine ipso admoneor. ad memoriam magis spectare debet posteritatis quam ad praesentis temporis gratiam"; PAUL.-Fest. p. 123, 7 L: monimentum est . . . quicquid ob memoriam alicuius factum est; cf. SERV. A. 6.512: MONVMENTA sermo est medius, dictus ab eo quod moneat mentem; SERV. A. 3.486: "monumenta" autem a mentis admonitione sunt dicta; SERV. A. 12.945: MONVMENTA DOLORIS proprie; nam et monumentum ab eo quod mentem moneat, dictum est (more sources in Maltby s.v. monumentum).

Bartelink (1965) 30.

**A. 6.550–51:** quae rapidus **flammis** *ambit* torrentibus *amnis,* / Tartareus **Phlegethon**

Varro derives *amnis,* "stream," from *ambitus,* "circuit, going around" (for other wordplay involving *amnis,* this time as a root, see on A. 12.412–17 *dictamnum*). Also, line 650 glosses the name *Phlegethon,* from Greek φλέγω, "burn" (cf. on A. 6.715, *Lethaei ad fluminis,* and on A. 6.438–39, *Styx*).

Amnis: VARRO *LL* 5.28.1: amnis id flumen quod circuit aliquod: nam ab ambitu amnis; PAUL.-Fest. p. 15, 24 L.: amnis proprie dicitur a circumnando, quoniam am ex Graeca praepositione sumptum, quae est ἀμφί, significat circum, et nare fluere; cf. HOR. *Ars* 17: et properantis *aquae* per amoenos *ambitus* agros.

Phlegethon: PLATO *Phaedo* 113.a5–b6: τρίτος δὲ ποταμὸς τούτων κατὰ μέσον ἐκβάλλει, καὶ ἐγγὺς τῆς ἐκβολῆς ἐκπίπτει εἰς τόπον μέγαν πυρὶ πολλῷ καόμενον, καὶ λίμνην ποιεῖ μείζω τῆς παρ' ἡμῖν θαλάττης, ζέουσαν ὕδατος καὶ πηλοῦ· ἐντεῦθεν δὲ χωρεῖ κύκλῳ θολερὸς καὶ πηλώδης, περιελιττόμενος δὲ τῇ γῇ ἄλλοσέ τε ἀφικνεῖται καὶ παρ' ἔσχατα τῆς 'Αχερουσιάδος λίμνης, οὐ συμμειγνύμενος τῷ ὕδατι· περιελιχθεὶς δὲ πολλάκις ὑπὸ γῆς ἐμβάλλει κατωτέρω τοῦ Ταρτάρου· οὗτος δ' ἐστὶν ὃν ἐπονομάζουσιν Πυριφλεγέθοντα, οὗ καὶ οἱ ῥύακες ἀποσπάσματα ἀναφυσῶσιν ὅπῃ ἂν τύχωσι τῆς γῆς;

SERV. A. 6.265: per Phlegethonta, inferorum fluvium, ignem significat: nam φλὸξ graece, latine ignis est.

Amnis: Norden (1981) 272 ("etymologische Verbindung"), Bartelink (1965) 94. Phlegethon: Bartelink (1965) 81, Doig (1968) 1 (quotes the several meaningful underworld river names at *Od.* 10.513–15, on which see Rank [1951] 131, Stanford ad loc., and Milton *PL* 2.51ff.).

**A. 6.552?:** *solido*que *adamante* columnae

Pliny says the name *adamas* means *indomita,* implying an etymology from α privative + δαμάζω, "overpower, conquer." *Solido* here could be an etymological gloss; cf. Servius' *tantae soliditatis.*

At Horace C. 1.6.13, *Martem tunica tectum adamantina,* Ahern sees a "sly" allusion to the etymology: the word "literally means 'unconquered' . . . , but Horace applies it to Mars at the moment of his confrontation with Diomedes, precisely when he will be wounded."

Cf. intro. 2.2 for single-adjective glosses.

SERV. 552: SOLIDOQUE ADAMANTE lapis est durissimus et tantae soliditatis, ut nec ferro possit infringi; the manuscript that Thilo-Hagen call D (Dresdensis) adds: unde etymologia est ab α sine et δαμάζω domo, id est lapis indomitus; PLINY *NH* 37.57: quippe duritia (sc. adamantis) est inenarrabilis, simulque ignium victrix natura et numquam incalescens, unde et nomen [interpretatione Graeca indomita vis] accepit (some have thought *interpretatione* . . . *vis* to be an interpolated gloss; sim. at Isid. 16.13.2); *NH* 24.162: adamantida . . . nominis causam esse quod conteri nequeat.

Bartelink (1965) 85 n. 2 (says "improbable"), Ahern (1991) 306–7.

**A. 6.570–72:** continuo sontis *ultrix* accincta flagello / *Tisiphone* quatit insultans, torvosque sinistra / intentans anguis vocat **agmina** saeva **sororum.**

Servius elsewhere notes that *ultrix,* "avenging," alludes to the first part of the name *Tisiphone,* from τίσις, "vengeance, punishment." In 572, the reference to *agmina . . . sororum,* "columns" or "troops" of Furies, might allude to the name Agmentis; see on **A. 4.469.**

SERV. A. 4.609: "ultrix" vero, hoc est Tisiphone: nam Graece τίσις ultio dicitur (cf. on G. 4.453: τίσις φόνου).

OVID *Am.* 2.1.13: ulta est (Titan) (see McKeown; cf. intro. 2.14); STAT. 8.757–58: ultrix / Tisiphone; HES. *Th.* 207–210:

τοὺς δὲ πατὴρ Τιτῆνας ἐπίκλησιν καλέεσκε
παῖδας νεικείων μέγας Οὐρανός, οὓς τέκεν αὐτός·
φάσκε δὲ τιταίνοντας ἀτασθαλίῃ μέγα ῥέξαι
ἔργον, τοῖο δ' ἔπειτα τίσιν μετόπισθεν ἔσεσθαι.

Tisiphone: Cerda (1612) 701, Norden (1981) 280, Bartelink (1965) 83, Rank (1951) 15 and West (1966) on *Th.* 207–10, McKeown (1987) 46, Mühmelt (1965) 62–63; *agmina*: Waszink (1963) 7–11.

**A. 6.601–3?:** quid memorem *Lapithas,* Ixiona Pirithoumque? / quos super atra *silex* iam iam *lapsura* cadentique / imminet adsimilis

Putnam suggests that both *lapsura* and *silex* are connected by *figura etymologica* with the name Lapiths, *lapsura* more obviously, and *silex* by what I would call a suppressed pun, since through it "we hear and understand the noun *lapis,* for which *silex* is a metonymy." See his discussion of the literary significance of the wordplay.

For suppression see intro. 2.7.

Putnam (1990).

**A. 6.640–41?:** largior hic campos aether et lumine vestit / purpureo, *solemque suum,* sua sidera norunt.

Thornton: "It is possible that the description of Elysium as knowing its own sun is an allusion to the etymology connecting the word 'Elysium' with the word *helios,* the sun." She cites a fragment of Porphyry that seems to allude to this etymology; the name Elysium would be suppressed here, but easily supplied from the context—and from its mention in 542. For suppression see intro. 2.7.

PORPHYRY apud Stob. *Eclog.* 41.61: Πάλιν αἰνιττόμενος ὅτι ταῖς τῶν εὐσεβῶς βεβιωκότων ψυχαῖς Μετὰ τὴν τελευτὴν οἰκεῖος ἐστι τόπος ὁ περὶ τὴν σελήνην, ὑπεδήλωσεν (sc. Πορφύριος) εἰπών

ἀλλά σ' ἐς ἠλύσιον πεδίον καὶ πείρατα γαίης
ἀθάνατοι πέμψουσι, ὅτι ζανθὸς Ῥαδάμανθυς,

ἠλύσιον μέν πεδίον εἰκότως προσειπὼν τὴν τῆς σελήνης ἐπιφάνειαν ὑφ' ἡλίου καταλαμπομένην "ὅτ' ἀέξεται ἀλίου αὐγαῖς" ὥς φησι Τιμόθεος.

Differently SERV. Auct. 5.735: Elysium ἀπὸ τῆς λύσεως, ab "solutione."

Thornton (1976) 66, citing Buffière (1956) 489–95.

**A. 6.713–15:** animae, quibus altera fato / corpora debentur, *Lethaei* ad fluminis undam / *securos latices et longa oblivia potant.*

Line 715 glosses the name of the river Lethe, from Greek λήθη, "forgetfulness," first by calling its waters *securos latices,* "waters that make one be without care *(sine cura)*"—Norden compares the Ἀμέλης ποταμός of Plato *Rep.* 10.621A—then more explicitly with the more abstract *longa oblivia potant.*

For a possible "translation by homonym" involving Lethe cf. A. 6.273–81. For names of underworld rivers see on 6.551 (Phlegethon) and A. 6.438–39 (Styx). For names of rivers in general see the annotations in intro. 2.4b.

OVID *Pont.* 2.4.23 (for Ovid cf. intro. 2.14): securae pocula Lethes.

Norden (1981) 307, Bartelink (1965) 79; cf. too Paschalis (1995) on Lethe and *oblivia* in Hor. *Epode* 14.1–4.

**A. 6.725:** *lucentem*que globum *lunae*

For the derivation of *luna* from *lux* or *luceo* see on **A. 4.80–81,** *lumen*que obscura vicissim / *luna* premit.

Norden (1981) 310.

**A. 6.763–65:** *Silvius,* Albanum nomen, tua *postuma* proles, / quem tibi longaevo serum Lavinia coniunx / educet *silvis* regem regumque parentem

Anchises refers to Silvius, Aeneas' son by Lavinia. Other sources refer to this man as Silvius Postumus. Vergil etymologizes both of these names, Silvius more explicitly: "Silvius, whom Lavina will raise in the woods, *silvis,*" and Postumus, which is never mentioned, by an implied or suppressed etymology: *Silvius, Albanum nomen, tua* ***postuma*** *proles,* "Silvius, your posthumous offspring." The phrase *Albanum nomen* is an etymological signpost (see intro. 2.6, and for suppression, intro. 2.7).

LIVY 1.3.6: deinde regnat Ascani filius, casu quodam in silvis natus; OVID *F.* 4.41–42 (for Ovid cf. intro. 2.14): Postumus hinc, qui, quod *silvis* fuit ortus in altis, / *Silvius* in Latia gente vocatus erat; D.H. 1.70: Σιλούιον ὀνομάσας ἀπὸ τῆς ὕλης, ὥσπερ ἂν εἴ τις Ἑλλάδι γλώσσῃ λέξειεν Ὑλαῖον; AUL. Gell. 2.16: Silvius, ita ut in omnium ferme annalium monumentis scriptum est, post ⟨patris⟩ mortem natus est ob eamque causam praenomen ei Postumo fuit; cf. FEST. p. 460, 7 L.

Cf. (?) A. 8.600–601: *Silvano* fama est veteres sacrasse Pelasgos, / arvorum pecorisque deo, *lucum*que diemque.

Bartelink (1965) 70, Ahl (1985) 304, Norden (1981) 317.

**A. 6.768–69:** et qui te nomine reddet / Silvius Aeneas

An explicit reference to Silvius Aeneas being named after Aeneas.

**A. 6.773–76:**

hi tibi *Nomentum* et Gabios urbemque Fidenam,
hi Collatinas imponent montibus arces,
Pometios Castrumque Inui Bolamque Coramque;
haec *tum nomina* erunt, nunc sunt *sine nomine* terrae.

Feeney (citing Ahl and an oral comment of S. Goldhill) observes that Vergil plays upon the name of Nomentum, a Latin town not yet founded in Aeneas' time, but in the Empire "a by-word for an out of the way backwater in Seneca and Martial," with the words *tum nomina* (cf. *nomen-tum*) and *sine nomine* in 676.

Nomentum is mentioned in 7.712 in the wordplay cluster of the Catalogue of Italian Forces.

Ahl (1985) 307–8, (1976) 211–22, Feeney (1986) 7–8; on Nomentum see e.g. Ogilvie (1965) 155–56 (on Livy 1.38.4).

**A. 6.789–90:** hic Caesar et omnis *Iuli* / progenies magnum caeli ventura sub axem.

For the connection of the *gens Iulia* to *Iulus* see on **A. 1.288** Iulius, a magno demissum nomen Iulo.

**A. 6.805?:** *Liber,* agens celso *Nysae* de vertice tigris.

Apollonius of Rhodes seems to gloss the name Dionysus as "Nysaean" son of Zeus (genitive Διὸς); this derivation also appears in the *Iliad* scholia, and perhaps in a Homeric hymn, and Euripides. Vergil may allude to such an etymology here for the suppressed name Dionysus (for suppression see intro. 2.7). Antiquity offers a number of other derivations for the name.

SERV. 805: NYSAE DE VERTICE mons est Indiae, de quo loquitur. ceterum est et Nysa civitas, in qua Liber colitur, unde Nysaeus dictus est (sim. in Isid. 8.11.44) HYG. *Fab.* 167.3: Liberum . . . Nyso dedit (sc. Iupiter) nutriendum, unde Dionysus est appellatus; SCHOL. *Il.* 14.325: Διόνυσος ἀπὸ Διὸς καὶ Νύσης τοῦ ὄρους; Erbse suggests that Epaphroditus (A.D. I) is the source, but he may have used earlier material. See Erbse too for other derivations.

APOLL. Rhod. 2.904–5: ὦκα δὲ Καλλιχόροιο παρὰ προχοὰς ποταμοῖο / ἤλυθον, ἔνθ' ἐνέπουσι Διὸς Νυσήιον υἷα (Levin suggests etymologizing here; Apollonius gives two explicit etymologies in 907–10); *Hom. Hymn* 26.1–5 gives the name Dionysus in 1, says that he is the son of Zeus in 2 and that he grew up Νύσης ἐν γυάλοις in 5; EUR. *Bacch.* 1–2: Ἥκω Διὸς παῖς . . . / Διόνυσος; Saunders notes that similarities between the names of Vergil's Trojans and figures in Nonnus' *Dionysiaca* suggests a common source in one or more poems on Dionysus by Alexandrians such as Euphorion; Rank notes the assonantal use of Διωνύσοιο and Νυσήιον at *Il.* 6.132–33.

Cerda (1612) 744, Erbse (1969–88) 3.643, Rank (1951) 45, Saunders (1940) 541–42; on Apollonius cf. Levin (1971) 194 n. 4; on the Homeric hymn, Woodhead (1928) 15; on Euripides, Dodds (1960) ad loc.

**A. 6.808–12:**

quis procul ille autem ramis insignis olivae
sacra ferens? nosco crinis incanaque menta
regis Romani primam qui *legibus* urbem
fundabit Curibus parvis et paupere terra
missus in imperium magnum.

Anchises' descriptions of future Romans include many etymological glosses (cf. intro. 2.4c. and my next several entries). Here Numa is not named, but the suppressed name is easily supplied from the description. The name is precisely glossed by the words *primam qui* ***legibus*** *urbem fundabit* in line 810. Serv. 808 explains, "Numa is so called after the Greek word for laws" (νόμοι). For suppression see intro. 2.7.

Ovid *Am.* 2.17.18 *iusto . . . Numae,* perhaps alludes to the same etymology (McKeown; cf. intro. 2.14).

SERV. 808: Numa dictus est ἀπὸ τῶν νόμων; SERV. Auct.: ab inventione et constitutione legis, nam proprium nomen Pompilius habuit; differently SCHOL. Pers. 2.59: Numa dictus est, eo quod numinibus deserviret.

Cerda (1612) 744, McKeown (1987) 53; on Serv. here cf. Mühmelt (1965) 72.

**A. 6.815–16?:** quem iuxta sequitur iactantior *Ancus* / nunc quoque iam nimium gaudens *popularibus* auris.

This "popularist" Ancus, who must be the king Ancus Marcius, is curious, because there is no trace of this theme in other references to him. Skutsch has suggested that the king Ancus Marcius, who replaced Tullus Hostilius, is to be identified with an Ancus Poplicius, a Latin leader said to have fought against Tullus (D.H. 3.34.3). The tradition of Ancus as *popularis* thus would have come from the name Poplicius, to which Vergil might here be alluding.

Zetzel, however, sees the description of Ancus as *popularis* as one of a number of inconsistencies or oddities in Vergil's underworld by means of which Vergil raises "questions of truth and causation essential to historical understanding."

Skutsch (1972) 13–16 and Badian apud Skutsch (1972) 34–35 (skeptical), Zetzel (1989); cf. Feeney (1986) 9–10.

**A. 6.817–18:** vis et *Tarquinios* reges animamque *superbam* / ultoris Bruti, fascisque videre receptos?

Vergil uses the adjective *superbus* to describe Brutus, right after mentioning the Tarquins. Although *superbus* is important for what Vergil is saying about Brutus here, it also reminds us of the name Tarquinius Superbus, the last Roman king. Lucretius uses the adjective in one passage to allude to the Tarquins without mentioning them.

For the adjective modifying the "wrong" figure and suggesting another name, cf. the allusion to the Sporades in *sparsas . . . Cyclades* in A. 3.126–27.

LUCR. 5.1136–37: ergo regibus occisis subversa iacebat / pristina maiestas soliorum et sceptra *superba.*

**A. 6.841?:** quis te, *magne Cato,* tacitum aut te, Cosse, relinquat

Another allusion to a (type of) cognomen. Feeney describes the reference to *magne Cato* as a "riddle": "The commentators tell us that Cato the Censor is meant here. In Vergil's time he would be called *Cato maior,* 'Cato the elder.' [Feeney acknowledges that the evidence for this is not extensive.] When Anchises addresses someone as '*great* Cato,' then the positive form of the adjective, if it prompts thoughts of the comparative, is perhaps disconcerting. . . . Which Cato *was* the greater?"

Feeney (1986) 12–13, citing Ahl (1976) 140.

**A. 6.842–46:**

quis Gracchi genus aut geminos, duo *fulmina belli,*
*Scipiadas,* **cladem Libyae,** parvoque potentem
Fabricium vel te sulco, Serrane, serentem?

quo fessum rapitis, Fabii? tu *Maximus* ille es,
unus qui nobis *cunctando* restituis rem.

At least three examples of etymological wordplay in these lines, each one probably coming from Ennius.

In 842–43, *geminos, duo fulmina belli, / Scipiadas, cladem Libyae,* Vergil refers to the elder and younger Scipio Africanus (at least; cf. Feeney below), and he etymologizes both an expressed and an implied name.

*Fulmina* refers to the supposed etymology of the name Scipio from σκηπτός, "thunderbolt." The wordplay was perhaps encouraged by the Scipios as they fought against the house of Hamilcar Barca—Norden notes that "Barkas" means lightning, Richardson compares Hebrew *baraq* (cf. *TLL* s.v. barac), and Hardie and others point to an allusion to the name in Silius. L&S say that Barca means "a gleaming, or a gleaming sword." The play on Scipio-*fulmina* probably occurred in Ennius, as well as in Cicero, and in Lucretius 3.1034, "in a context that has clear Ennian colour" (Austin).

Austin notes that in reality, "Scipio means 'support,' 'staff': according to Macrob. 1.6.26 it was first borne by a Cornelius who acted as a *baculum* for his blind father," and suggests that Cicero may allude to a connection between *fulmentum,* "support," and *fulmina;* Ovid may play on that sense once as well at *Am.* 2.1.17–20 (see Skutsch and McKeown, and cf. intro. 2.14).

The words *cladem Libyae,* "destroyers of Libya," refer to the agnomen *Africanus,* which each received for his victories in Africa, and which is suppressed here (see intro. 2.7).

Feeney suggests that Vergil refers ambiguously both to the Scipios who died in Spain in 211 and to the more successful Scipiones Africani.

In 844–46 we again see glossing of both an expressed name and a suppressed name, but this time for two different men. In 844, Vergil alludes to the etymology of Serranus from *sero,* "to sow." M. Atilius Regulus (cos. 257, 250 B.C.) was said to have been called Serranus because he was sowing a field when news came that he had been chosen consul.

In 846, Vergil suppresses but, following Ennius, alludes to and explains the name Cunctator, Delayer, given to Fabius Maximus, whose dilatory techniques were successful in containing Hannibal in the Second Punic War *(tu Maximus ille es, / unus qui nobis* ***cunctando*** *restituis rem).* Hardie suggests allusion to the cognomen, this time with additional pointed wordplay between *unus* and *cuncta,* in Sil. 7.1–10.

(Stanton argues that Cunctator is not considered a cognomen for Fabius until the second century A.D., but his attempt to distinguish between uses of the word as "epithet" and "name" is overly subtle. On early *cognomina* living "in a no-man's land between name and description" see Badian.)

Scipios: MACROB. 1.6.26: non aliter dicti Scipiones nisi quod Cornelius, qui cognominem patrem luminibus carentem pro baculo regebat, Scipio cognominatus nomen ex cognomine posteris dedit; ISID. 18.2.5: licet et Scipio baculum sit quo homines innituntur. unde et ille primus Cornelius Scipio appellatus est, quia in foro pater eius caecus innixus eo ambulabat; LUCR. 3.1034: Scipiadas, belli fulmen, Carthaginis horror; CIC. *Balb.* 34: cum Carthago nixa duabus Hispaniis huic imperio immineret et cum duo fulmina nostri imperi subito in Hispania, Cn. et P. Scipiones, exstincti occidissent; OVID *Am.* 2.1.17–20:

> clausit amica fores: ego cum Iove *fulmen* omisi;
> excidit ingenio Iuppiter ipse meo.
> Iuppiter, ignoscas: nil me tua *tela* iuvabant;
> clausa tuo maius ianua *fulmen* habet;

SIL. 15.664: fulmen subitum Carthaginis Hannibal; SIL. 7.106–7: ubi sunt nunc fulmina gentis / Scipiadae?

Serranus: SERV. 844: Atilius quidam senator fuit, qui cum agrum suum coleret, evocatus propter virtutem meruit dictaturam. Serranus autem a serendo dictus est; PLINY *NH* 18.20 (cf. *GRF* p. 342 adn.; Funaioli thinks Varro is Pliny's source): serentem invenerunt dati honores Serranum, unde cognomen; cf. too on *sermone serebant* at A. 6.160.

Fabius: ENN. *Ann.* 363 Sk.: unus homo nobis cunctando restituis rem; on which see Skutsch (1985).

On Scipios: Bartelink (1965) 67–68, Hanssen (1948) 99, Knight (1944) 199, Norden (1981) 333, Skutsch (1968) 145–50, McKeown (1989) 132 (on *Am.* 1.6.16), Feeney (1986) 13–14, Hardie (1993) 64 n. 9, *EV* s.v. Scipiadi (Càssola). On Serranus: Bartelink (1965) 69–70, Austin (1977) on 844; on "direct quotation from Ennius" see Richardson (1942) and Wigodsky (1972) 72 n. 362. On Fabius: Stanton (1971), Badian (1988), Hardie (1993) 9.

**A. 6.859?:** tertiaque *arma* patri suspendet capta *Quirino*

Austin notes that "the normal tradition made Marcellus dedicate his *spolia* to Iuppiter Feretrius . . . as Romulus and Cossus, the only earlier winners, had done. . . . So Virgil causes a problem." As with the reference to the popularist Ancus in 815–16 and the *anima superba* of Brutus in 817–18, the "problem" may involve wordplay. Ovid, Plutarch, and Paulus (and so perhaps the Augustan Verrius Flaccus) offer a derivation of the name Quirinus from *curis,* a Sabine word for spear, which Romulus was said to carry (each mentions other possibilities as well). Vergil mentions *arma* two of the three times he uses the name Quirinus; there may be a suggestion of the etymology *Quirinus* from *curis*. Or, this could just be coincidental. Austin discusses other attempts to explain why *spolia* are offered to Quirinus.

PAUL.-Fest. p. 43, 1 L: curis est Sabine hasta. Unde Romulus Quirinus, quia eam ferebat, est dictus; et Romani a Quirino Quirites dicuntur. Quidam eum dictum putant a Curibus, quae fuit urbs opulentissima Sabinorum; ISID. 9.2.84: hi (sc. Romani) et Quirites dicti, quia Quirinus dictus est Romulus, quod semper hasta utebatur, quae Sabinorum lingua curis dicitur; SERV. A. 1.292: Romulus autem ideo "Quirinus" dictus est, vel quod hasta utebatur, quae Sabinorum lingua "curis" dicitur . . . vel a κοίρανος, qui Graece rex dicitur; cf. too Plut. *Rom.* 29, Macrob. 1.9.16; more in Maltby s.v. Quirinus.

OVID *F.* 2.475–80 (for Ovid cf. intro. 2.14):

proxima lux vacua est, at tertia dicta Quirino:
    qui tenet hoc nomen (Romulus ante fuit),
sive quod hasta "curis" priscis est dicta Sabinis
    (bellicus a telo venit in astra deus),
sive suum regi nomen posuere Quirites,
    seu quia Romanis iunxerat ille Cures.

Cf. G. 3.27 victorisque arma Quirini; no wordplay at A. 1.292–93: Remo cum fratre Quirinus / iura dabunt.

Austin (1977) on 859; on Ovid see Porte (1985) 258–59.

*

## A. 6.893–98?:

sunt geminae Somni portae, quarum altera fertur
cornea, qua veris facilis datur exitus umbris,
altera candenti perfecta nitens elephanto,
sed falsa ad caelum mittunt insomnia Manes.
his ibi tum natum Anchises unaque Sibyllam
prosequitur dictis portaque emittit eburna

Vergil's model at *Od.* 19. 562–67 features etymological interpretation of the names of the gates of ivory (ἐλέφας), through which come dreams that deceive (ἐλεφαίρονται), and of horn (κέρας), through which come those that "accomplish the truth" (ἔτυμα κραίνουσι; cf. κερ- and κρα-). Nothing in Vergil points to etymology, unless his words *elephanto, / sed falsa* point to Homer's ἐλέφαντος, / οἵ ῥ' ἐλεφαίρονται, roughly in the same position in the verse but in a different metrical shape. Servius reports rather strained allegorical connotations of horn and ivory with truth and falsehood.

Cockburn has made the unattractive suggestion that *veris* in 894 be changed to *falsis, falsa* in 896 be changed to *vera,* and *sed* in 896 be changed to *hac* or *qua,* thus allowing our hero Aeneas to leave the underworld "by the shining-white gate of true dreams." His claim is that etymology supports the change, with *cornu* linked in the ancient mind to "falsehood." Varro does derive *cornu* from *curvatus,* but only in the literal sense in which most horns are, indeed, "crooked," and with no connotations of "falsehood"; etymology offers nothing to support Cockburn.

SERV. 893: physiologia vero hoc habet: per portam corneam oculi significantur, qui et cornei sunt coloris et duriores ceteris membris: nam frigus non sentiunt, sicut et Cicero dicit in libris de natura deorum (cf. 2.57). per eburneam vero portam os significatur a dentibus. et scimus quia quae loquimur falsa esse possunt, ea vero quae videmus sine dubio vera sunt. ideo Aeneas per eburneam emittitur portam; VARRO *LL* 7.25: cornua a curvore dicta, quod pleraque curva.

*Od.* 19. 562–67:

δοιαὶ γάρ τε πύλαι ἀμενηνῶν εἰσὶν ὀνείρων·
αἱ μὲν γὰρ κεράεσσι τετεύχαται, αἱ δ' ἐλέφαντι.

τῶν οἳ μέν κ' ἔλθωσι διὰ πριστοῦ ἐλέφαντος,
οἵ ῥ' ἐλεφαίρονται, ἔπε' ἀκράαντα φέροντες·
οἳ δὲ διὰ ξεστῶν κεράων ἔλθωσι θύραζε,
οἵ ῥ' ἔτυμα κραίνουσι, βροτῶν ὅτε κέν τις ἴδηται.

Pollmann (1993) (better on Homer than on Vergil; on Homer see also intro. 1.1), Cockburn (1992), O'Hara (n.d.).

## A. 7.1–4:

Tu quoque litoribus nostris, Aeneia nutrix,
aeternam moriens famam, Caieta, dedisti;
et nunc servat honos sedem tuus, ossaque nomen
Hesperia in magna, si qua est ea gloria, signat.

Explicit etymological aetiology linking the port of Caieta with Aeneas' nurse. Servius preserves a different explanation: Caieta is where the Trojan ships were burned, and so named from the Greek for "burn," καίω. Ovid's epitaph for the woman Caieta (in a passage in which Vergil's geographical aetiology is probably implicit) makes prominent mention of the burning of her pyre, probably playing on that association of the name—and alluding to the derivation that Vergil omitted.

For *nunc* in etymological aetiologies see intro. 2.10a; for Ovid cf. intro. 2.14.

SERV. 7.1: lectum tamen est in philologis in hoc loco classem Troianorum casu concrematam, unde Caieta dicta est, ἀπὸ τοῦ καίειν (several more sources in Maltby).

OVID *Met.* 14.443–44: Hic me *Caietam* notae pietatis alumnus / ereptam Argolico quo debuit *igne cremavit.*

Cerda (1617) 2, Fordyce (1977) ad loc.; on the legends of the burning of the ships see Williams (1960) on 5.604f.; cf. *EV* s.v. Caieta (Barchiesi) and also Myers (1994a) 104.

**A. 7.8–9:** aspirant aurae in noctem nec candida cursus / *luna* negat, splendet tremulo sub *lumine* pontus.

For the derivation of *luna* from *lux* or *luceo* see on **A. 4.80–81:** *lumen*que obscura vicissim / *luna* premit.

A. 6.725: *lucentem*que globum *lunae*; A. 8.22–23: *lumen* . . . *lunae.*

Bartelink (1965) 107.

## A. 7.10–14:

proxima *Circaeae* raduntur litora terrae,
dives inaccessos ubi *Solis filia* lucos
adsiduo resonat cantu, tectisque superbis
urit odoratam nocturna in lumina cedrum
arguto tenuis percurrens pectine telas.

Vergil follows tradition by linking Circei to Circe, whose name is suppressed here (11: *Solis filia*). Fordyce notes that the name was probably originally Cercei and so unconnected to Circe, but the association precedes Vergil.

For suppression see intro. 2.7.

Cf. e.g. CIC. *ND* 3.48: Circen quoque coloni nostri Cercienses religiose colunt (some mss. have Circ-; see Pease); OVID *Met.* 14.348 (for Ovid cf. intro. 2.14): nomine dicta suo *Circaea* reliquerat arva.

Fordyce (1977) ad loc.; cf. *RE* 3.2565–67 (Hülsen), Pease (1979) 1077–78, Hunter (1989) 133.

**A. 7.30–32:** hunc inter fluvio *Tiberinus* amoeno / verticibus rapidis et multa *flavus* harena / in mare prorumpit.

At A. 6.88–89, Servius saw an allusion to the Italian rivers Tiber and Numicus, in the Sibyl's prediction that the Simois and Xanthus will not be absent from the wars in Italy: *NON SIMOIS TIBI NEC XANTHVS Tiberis et Numicus, in quem cecidit.* The Xanthus is further linked to the Tiber by the wordplay *Tiberinus . . . flavus* (7.30–31), where ξανθός = Xanthus. The connection seems to occur again at 9.816, *cum gurgite flavo*. The pun on Xanthus-ξανθός-*flavus* was popular with the Augustans; cf. Ovid *Met.* 2.245: *Xanthus flavusque Lycormas* (for Ovid cf. intro. 2.14), and Prop. 2.9.12: *flavis in Simoente vadis*. The Homeric scholia say the Xanthus was so called because it made hair blonde.

But for the Tiber keep in mind Fordyce on 31f.: "*flavus* is a regular description of the Tiber (Hor. C. 1.2.13, 1.8.8, 2.3.18; Ovid *Tr.* 5.1.31). . . . The lower Tiber is still a yellow river, carrying down large quantities of eroded rock."

SCHOL. *Il.* 6.4c: Ξάνθος δὲ ὠνόμασται διὰ τὸ ξανθίζειν τὰς τρίχας (cf. too Erbse 5.18 on Schol. *Il.* 20.73–74).

Norden (1981) on 6.88, Christmann (1976) 272, O'Hara (1990) 107 n. 37, Fordyce (1977); on Propertius Enk (1962); on the Xanthus also Rank (1951) 117–19.

**A. 7.37–40?:**

> nunc age, qui reges, *Erato,* quae tempora rerum,
> quis Latio antiquo fuerit status, advena classem
> cum primum Ausoniis exercitus appulit oris,
> expediam, et primae revocabo exordia pugnae.

Apollonius invokes the muse Erato at *Arg.* 3.1–5 and refers to her "erotic name" (ἐπήρατον οὔνομ', 5; cf. also ὑπ' ἔρωτι in 3), which makes her appropriate for the story of Medea's love. Vergil certainly borrows from Apollonius here (cf. *nunc age, qui reges, Erato,* with Εἰ δ' ἄγε νῦν Ἐρατώ); does he evoke the thematic and etymological associations of the name Erato as well?

Williams is probably right to say that "The Muse of love is invoked probably because the whole conflict about to be described arises from Turnus' refusal to give up his bride Lavinia to the Trojan stranger." More broadly speaking, the role of "desire," erotic or otherwise, will be prominent in the stories of Turnus, Amata, Ascanius,

Nisus and Euryalus, and Pallas (see passages quoted below). Nothing in Vergil's lines calls attention to the etymology, but the allusion to Apollonius may be enough.

APOLL. Rhod. 3.1–5:

> Εἰ δ' ἄγε νῦν Ἐρατώ, παρ' ἔμ' ἵστασο καί μοι ἔνισπε
> ἔνθεν ὅπως ἐς Ἰωλκὸν ἀνήγαγε κῶας Ἰήσων
> Μηδείης ὑπ' ἔρωτι· σὺ γὰρ καὶ Κύπριδος αἶσαν
> ἔμμορες, ἀδμῆτας δὲ τεοῖς μελεδήμασι θέλγεις
> παρθενικάς· τῶ καί τοι ἐπήρατον οὔνομ' ἀνῆπται.

OVID *F.* 4.195–96 (for Ovid cf. intro. 2.14): sic Erato (mensis Cythereius illi / cessit, quod teneri nomen *Amoris* habet); *Ars* 2.16: nunc Erato, nam tu nomen *Amoris* habes.

A selection of references to *amor* in A. 7–12: 7.56–57 Turnus . . . quem regia coniunx / adiungi generum miro properabat amore, 461 saevit amor ferri et scelerata insania belli, 496–97 ipse etiam eximiae laudis succensus amore / Ascanius, 550 accendamque animos insani Martis amore, 8.327 et belli rabies et amor successit habendi, 9.182 his amor unus erat pariterque in bella ruebant, 10.789–90 ingemuit cari graviter genitoris amore . . . Lausus, 12.70 illum (sc. Turnum) turbat amor figitque in virgine vultus, 282 sic omnis amor unus habet decernere ferro, 688 et furiis agitatus amor et conscia virtus.

Williams (1973) on 37; cf. Putnam (1985), Toll (1989).

**A. 7.41:** tu vatem, tu, *diva, mone.*

See on **A. 1.8** for the etymological connection between *Musa,* suppressed here but suggested here by *diva,* and words connected to memory like *moneo* and *memini.* For suppression see intro. 2.7.

Cerda (1617) 10.

**A. 7.56, etc.?:** Turnus

Cairns: "In essence Turnus is a bad king. His name in itself indicates this, for whatever other etymologies antiquity may have offered for it, the true derivation, from the Etruscan version of Greek τύρρανος ('tyrant'), will surely have been known in the circle of Virgil's patron, the Etruscan Maecenas, so that 'Turnus' would have suggested the interplay between 'king' and 'tyrant.' "

I see no specific allusion to this in book 7 (see on 9.327 and 10.446–48 for possible allusion), or any evidence that the name Turnus would suggest "*bad* king." Modern notions of a true derivation are irrelevant to poetic etymologizing. Brandenstein, whom Cairns cites, says that Turnus must be derived from Etruscan *turan,* "ruler," but may more precisely be derived from *turns,* perhaps "son of the ruler," which Brandenstein says fits Vergil's Turnus, whose father is still living.

Cairns and Brandenstein also mention "the historically false (but in antiquity perfectly credible) etymology from Τυρρηνός (Etruscan)" (Cairns).

A. 9.327: rex idem et *regi Turno* gratissimus augur; 10.446–48: miratus stupet in *Turno* corpusque per ingens / lumina volvit obitque truci procul omnia visu, / talibus et dictis it contra dicta *tyranni.*

Cairns (1989) 67, Brandenstein, *RE* s.v. Turnus, col. 1409. McKeown (1987) 55 cites Horace's use of an Etruscan derivation "as a compliment to Maecenas' descent."

**A. 7.56–57?:** Turnus, avis atavisque potens, quem *regia coniunx* / adiungi generum miro properabat *amore*

*Regia coniunx* in 56 stands for the name Amata, which is not given until 343. If the suppressed name is mentally supplied here, the ends of consecutive lines (a frequent locus of etymologizing; see intro. 2.9) may feature wordplay on *Amata* and *amore*. For the actual origins of the name Amata (not from *amo*), see Fordyce, but that would not hinder wordplay.

The first appearance of Juturna in the poem provides an interesting parallel. Juturna's name is not give until book 12, but at 10.439–40 she is called simply Turnus' *soror,* possibly with allusion to the etymology *Iuturna quod iuvaret,* "because she helps." See on **10.439–40**.

For wordplay with *amor* and *amarus* see on E. 3.109–10; between *amor* and *Roma,* on A. 4.347. For suppression see intro. 2.7.

On suggestions of the erotic in Vergil's treatment of Amata see Lyne (1987) 13–27, esp. 13–15 on Amata's name; cf. also Fordyce (1977) on 7.343, Horsfall (1988) 39.

**A. 7.59–63:**

> *laurus* erat tecti medio in penetralibus altis
> sacra comam multosque metu servata per annos,
> quam pater inventam, primas cum conderet arces,
> ipse ferebatur Phoebo sacrasse Latinus,

*Laurentis*que ab ea nomen posuisse colonis.

Vergil explicitly derives the name of the Laurentians from Latinus' sacred laurel. The words *laurus* and *Laurentis,* each at the start of its line, frame the sentence (see intro. 2.8a).

Cerda (1617) 15, Bartelink (1965) 78.

**A. 7.64–67?:**

> huius *apes* summum densae (mirabile dictu)
> stridore ingenti liquidum trans aethera vectae
> obsedere apicem, et *pedibus per mutua nexis*
> examen subitum ramo frondente pependit.

For a possible (but unlikely?) etymological connection between *apes* and the phrase *pedibus per mutua nexis* see on G. **4.257**, *aut illae pedibus conexae ad limina pendent.*

## A. 7.67–70:

> *examen* subitum ramo frondente pependit.
> continuo vates "externum cernimus" inquit
> "adventare virum et partis petere *agmen* easdem
> partibus ex isdem et summa dominarier arce."

The connection between the swarm of bees in the omen and the Trojans in the interpretation of the omen is underscored by the etymological connection between *agmen* and *exa(g)men*. Compare the connection between omen and interpretation suggested by *lumine* and *inlustrem* at A. 7.76–80, and the connection between two omens suggested by *comas* and the (suppressed) *cometes* at A. 2.679–98.

Bartelink (1965) 105, Willams (1973) on 69–70; cf. Ernout-Meillet (1967) and Walde-Hofmann (1930–56) for the etymological connection.

## A. 7.76–80:

> tum fumida *lumine* fulvo
> involvi ac totis Volcanum spargere tectis.
> id vero horrendum ac visu mirabile ferri:
> namque fore *inlustrem* fama fatisque canebant
> ipsam, sed populo magnum portendere bellum.

The connection between the omen and its interpretation is underscored by the etymological connection between *lumine,* "light (of the flame)," and *inlustrem,* "she will be illustrious." Compare the connection between omen and interpretation in **A. 7.67–70.**

For the etymological connection involving *lux, lumen* etc., see on **A. 4.80–81.**

Bartelink (1965) 107.

**A. 7.79:** namque fore inlustrem *fama fatisque* canebant

Juxtaposition of cognates. Cf. 8.731 *famamque et fata nepotum,* and see also **A. 1.261–62** on *fari-fatum.*

VARRO *LL* 6.55: hinc (sc. a fando) fama et famosi (more sources in Maltby).

Bartelink (1965) 105.

**A. 7.81–82:** at rex sollicitus monstris oracula *Fauni, / fatidici* genitoris, adit

*Fatidici* provides a gloss on the name *Faunus,* said by Servius and Varro to come from the verb *fari,* in the sense of "prophesy," or from Greek φωνή, "voice," because he showed the future by means of a voice (cf. *-dici*), not signs.

Vergil glosses the name Faunus differently at **G. 1.17–18,** *Pan* . . . adsis, o Tegeaee, *favens.*

The names Carmenta, at 8.341, and Manto, at 10.199, are also glossed by *fatidicus.*

VARRO *LL* 7.36: in silvestribus locis traditum est solitos fari ⟨a⟩ quo fando faunos dictos (cf. Serv. Auct. G. 1.11); SERV. Auct. A. 7.47: dicti autem sunt Faunus et Fauna a vaticinando, id est fando, unde et fatuos dicimus inconsiderate loquentes; SERV. Auct. A. 7.81: Faunus ἀπὸ τῆς φωνῆς dictus, quod voce, non signis ostendit futura.

Bartelink (1965) 75.

**A. 7.116:** heus, etiam mensas consumimus?

Ascanius' joke, in which the cakes onto which fruit had been piled are described as "tables," marks the fulfillment of the prophecy of the Harpy Celaeno, who said that the Trojans would eat their tables before they would wall their city. Underlying the harmless fulfillment of the prophecy is a pun, or an allusion to the origin of *mensa,* which "originally designated precisely a round sacrificial cake on which offerings were heaped" (Vine). Fordyce suggests that "the story of the 'eating of the tables' looks like an aetiological legend invented to account for the special sacrificial meaning of *mensa.*"

SERV. Auct. A. 3.257: maiores enim nostri has mensas habebant in honore deorum, panicias scilicet; SERV. 1.736: (Romani) panicias sacratasque mensas habebant, in quas libabant, ut est (7.116) "heus, etiam mensas consumimus, inquit Iulus."

Vine (1986) 111–12; cf. too Ernout-Meillett (1967) p. 397, Williams (1973) on 116, and Fordyce (1977) on 116 with further references.

**A. 7.177–81:**

quin etiam veterum effigies ex ordine avorum
antiqua e cedro, Italusque paterque Sabinus
*vitisator* curvam servans sub imagine falcem,
Saturnusque senex Ianique bifrontis imago
vestibulo astabant, aliique *ab origine* reges

Servius sees in 181 a reference to the *Aborigines,* the name given to original inhabitants of Italy in Cato, Varro, Livy, and other—mostly Republican—authors. If so, their name, which, as Servius notes, would not fit a hexameter, is thereby glossed.

In 179 *vitisator* Horsfall suggests that Vergil "alludes obliquely to the Sabinus-*serere* etymology" found in Lydus, by depicting Sabinus with a "pruning-knife" *(falx vinitoria).*

SERV. 181: AB ORIGINE pro "Aboriginum reges," sed est metro prohibitus; LYD. *Mens.* 1.5: Σαβῖνος ἐκ τῆς περὶ τὸν οἶνον γεωργίας φερωνύμος ὠνομάσθη. τὸ γὰρ Σαβῖνος ὄνομα σπορέα καὶ φυτευτὴν οἴνου διασημαίνει; SERV. A. 1.532: "Oenotria" autem dicta est vel a vino optimo, quod in Italia nascitur, vel, ut Varro dicit, ab Oenotro, rege Sabinorum; the Aborigines are mentioned by Cato *Orig.* fr. 5–7, Tuditanus (fr. 1 Peter), Sall. *Cat.* 6.1, Cic. *Rep.* 2.5, Livy 1.1–2, and Varro *LL* 5.53; for other derivations (from *error,* wandering, or ὄρη, mountains) see Maltby.

Bartelink (1965) 61 (not improbable but . . . ); on etymologizing with names that do not fit verse see Woodhead (1928) 42; Horsfall (1981) 148 (Aborigines) and (1978) (Sabinus); on Aborigines see Ogilvie (1970) 38 on Livy 1.1.5 and Linderski (1992).

*

**A. 7.206–8:** Auruncos ita ferre senes, his ortus ut agris / *Dardanus* Idaeas Phrygiae penetrarit ad urbes / *Threiciam*que *Samum,* quae nunc *Samothracia* fertur.

An obvious explanation of the name *Samothracia,* perhaps following Callimachus, whom Pliny cites as using the old name Dardania for Samothrace, and certainly an example of Callimachean interest in *metonomasia.* Vergil might be explicitly glossing the name Samothrace, and by the mention of Dardanus alluding to the name Dardania and its origin (cf. intro. 2.10 on *metonomasia*).

PLINY *NH* 4.73: insula Samothrace. . . . Callimachus eam antiquo nomine Dardaniam vocat (= Callim. fr. 583—see further references in Pfeiffer).

**A. 7.281:** semine ab *aetherio* spirantis naribus *ignem*

For the connection between *aether* and αἴθω, "burn," see on **A. 6.130** *ardens evexit ad aethera virtus.*

**A. 7.297–98, 310–12:**

> at, credo, mea numina tandem
> fessa iacent, odiis aut *exsaturata* quievi.
> . . . . . . . . . . . . . . . . . . . . . . . . . . .
> vincor ab Aenea. quod si mea numina non sunt
> magna *satis,* dubitem haud equidem implorare quod usquam est:
> flectere si nequeo superos, Acheronta movebo.

For Vergil's plays on *Saturnia* Juno and *saturata* see on **A. 5.606–8.**

**A. 7.328–29:** tot sese vertit in ora, / tam saevae facies, tot *pullulat atra colubris.*

*Pullulat* here means "sprouts"; the verb is related to the noun *pullus,* "young animal," or *pullulus,* "young sprout." Weber suggests that Vergil's phrase *pullulat atra colubris* implies an alternate etymology and meaning, as if connected with *pullus,* "dark colored," or the rare (attested only in some manuscripts of Colum. 2.2.19) word *pullulus,* "blackish."

Weber (1990) 210–12.

**A. 7.376?:** tum vero infelix *ingentibus* excita *monstris* (sc. Amata)

Feeney suggests that etymological wordplay here contributes to the ambiguity about whether Allecto acts on humans as an external force, or brings out qualities already present in her victims:

> *Monstra* are portents which signal a supernatural involvement of some sort, but the epithet *ingens,* "huge," points to Amata's own nature, by way of an etymological play on *ingenium* ("natural character"). Amata is presented in these three words as stirred up by something at once supernatural and innate.

For the association of *ingens* with what is "innate" or "natural" see on **G. 2.131.** As in other passages with wordplay with *ingens,* the meaning "huge" would add little to the passage.

Feeney (1991) 167.

**A. 7.411–12:** locus Ardea quondam / dictus avis, et nunc *magnum* manet *Ardea* nomen

The word *magnum,* as Servius notes, glosses the name *Ardea,* which is thus to be associated with *ardua.*

For other plays on *arduus* see on 3.270–71, *Neritos ardua.* For *nunc* in etymologies see intro. 2.10a.

At 7.623–31, Vergil may connect the name Ardea with the verb *ardens.*

Ahl calls attention to the similarity of *avīs* to *avĭs:* "Hence we have: 'a place, once called Ardea by our ancestors,' with undertones of 'a place, Ardea, once called a bird.'" Ovid *Met.* 14.573–80 connects the bird *ardea* with the city Ardea (for Ovid cf. intro. 2.14). Vergil certainly plays on the name of the bird *ardea* at **G. 1.364:** ***altam*** *supra volat* ***ardea*** *nubem.*

SERV. 412: MAGNVM TENET ARDEA NOMEN bene adlusit: nam Ardea quasi ardua dicta est, id est magna et nobilis, licet Hyginus in Italicis urbibus ab augurio avis ardeae dictam velit. illud namque Ovidii in Metamorphoseos (14.547) fabulosum est, incensam ab Hannibale Ardeam in hanc avem esse conversam.

Cerda (1617) 72, Bartelink (1965) 42, Fordyce (1977) ad loc., Ahl (1985) 265 n. 29, Hardie (1992) 77 n. 16 and 81 n. 81.

**A. 7.457?:** Ascanius *curvo* derexit spicula *cornu*

Varro derives *cornu* from *curvus,* since most horns are curved. Vergil may be alluding to that here and in 513 *pastorale canit signum* ***cornuque recurvo,*** with a single-epithet gloss (see intro. 2.2), but if most horns are curved the collocation need not necessarily imply etymology.

VARRO *LL* 7.25: dicere apparet cornutum a cornibus; cornua a curvore dicta, quod pleraque curva.

**A. 7.513?:** pastorale canit signum *cornu*que *recurvo*

See on 457 for the idea that *recurvo* may be a single-epithet gloss (see intro. 2.2) of *cornu.*

**A. 7.517:** *sulpurea Nar* albus *aqua*

Servius says that *nar* is the Sabine word for sulfur, so the reference to *sulpurea . . . aqua* is a gloss on the name of the river. Vergil has borrowed the etymology from Enn *Ann.* 222 Sk. *sulpureas posuit spiramina Naris ad undas,* where there may be double wordplay. Skutsch discusses the idea that *Naris* in Ennius also suggests "nose," and so "Ennius may have meant to suggest that the holes *[spiramina]* in or near the river's banks were in fact the nostrils of hell, thus giving an etymology of Nar." He continues, "it is possible that Lucan's *spiramina naris* [2.183] . . . echoes the secondary sense (or nonsense) of the line." Vergil's borrowing from Ennius here becomes more interesting when we recall that the whole Ennian passage probably described "the breaking open of the Gates of War by a Fury."

For etymologizing with a Sabine word cf. *Hernica saxa* in 7.683; cf. also intro. 2.11.

SERV. Auct. 517: Sabini lingua sua nar dicunt sulphur. ergo hunc fluvium ideo dicunt esse Nar appellatum, quod odore sulphureo nares contingat, sive quod in modum narium geminos habeat exitus.

Bartelink (1965) 51, McCartney (1927) 187 (compares Lucan 1.214 *puniceus* [= *ruber*] *Rubicon*), Marouzeau (1940) 260–61, Skutsch (1985) 392, citing Norden (1915).

**A. 7.538–39:** Quinque greges illi balantum, quina redibant / *armenta* et terram centum vertebat *aratris*

Varro tells us that *armenta,* "cattle," are so called because the ancient ones raised them for plowing: *ad arandum.* The words connected etymologically frame the line (see intro. 2.8). For the alternative derivation of *armenta* from *armare* see on **A. 3.540.**

VARRO *LL* 5.96: *armenta,* quod boves ideo maxime parabant, ut inde eligerent ad *arandum;* ISID. 12.1.8: alii armenta tantum boves intellegunt, ab arando, quasi aramenta; COLUM. 6.praef.3: iumenta et armenta nomina a re traxere, quod nostrum laborem vel onera subvectando vel arando iuvarent.

Bartelink (1965) 103.

**A. 7.563–66:**

est locus Italiae medio sub montibus altis,
nobilis et fama multis memoratus in oris,
*Amsancti* valles; densis hunc frondibus atrum
urget *utrim*que latus nemoris

Norden noted that Vergil's *utrimque* in 566 shows awareness of the etymological explanation of Amsanctus (quoted by Servius) as "sacred on all sides." Varro discusses other words formed from the root *ambo,* "around," and may (as Norden suggests) have given the etymology of Amsanctus.

SERV. 565: AMSANCTI VALLES loci amsancti, id est omni parte sancti: quem dicit et silvis cinctum et fragoso fluvio torrente; SERV. 7.125: hoc est apud nos "ac," quod apud Graecos ἀμ. hinc est (565) "amsancti valles," is est undique sancti; VARRO *LL* 7.30: ambages . . . profectum a verbo ambe, quod inest in ambitu et ambitioso; *LL* 7.43: ancilia dicta ab ambecisu, quod ea arma ab utraque parte ut Thracum incisa (followed by Ovid *F.* 3.377; see Porte).

Norden (1915) 23, Rehm (1932) 75–76, Bartelink (1965) 40, Porte (1985) 227.

**A. 7.607?:** sunt *geminae* Belli portae (sic nomine dicunt)

Here *sic nomine dicunt* looks like an etymological signpost (see intro. 2.6), or at least an acknowledgment of poetic precedent. Serv. 7.622 quotes Enn. *Ann.* 225–26 Sk.: *postquam Discordia taetra / Belli ferratos postes portasque refregit.* Skutsch thinks that Ennius must be referring to the opening of the doors of the *Ianus Geminus,* "a small rectangular structure with double doors at each end, [which] lay in the Forum near the Curia where the Argiletum entered" (Ogilvie), in 241 or 235 B.C. Vergil's word *geminae,* not in the Ennian model, probably alludes to the name Ianus Geminus (mentioned by Varro *LL* 5.156).

MACROB. 1.9.15: in sacris quoque invocamus Ianum Geminum, Ianum Patrem, Ianum Iunonium, Ianum Consivium, Ianum Quirinum, Ianum Patulcium et Clusivium.

For the phrasing cf. A. 1.294: claudentur Belli portae; A. 6.893: sunt geminae Somni portae; **A. 6.441:** Lugentes Campi: sic illos nomine dicunt; G. 3.280: hippomanes vero quod nomine dicunt.

Skutsch (1985) 401–5, Norden (1981) 249, Ogilvie (1970) 93, Fordyce (1977) on 607ff. (calling the structure Ianus Quirinus as in Suet. *Aug.* 22).

## A. 7.623–31:

*ardet* inexcita Ausonia atque immobilis ante;
pars pedes ire parat campis, pars arduus altis
pulverulentus equis furit; omnes arma requirunt.
pars levis clipeos et spicula lucida tergent
arvina pingui subiguntque in cote securis;
signaque ferre iuvat sonitusque audire tubarum.
quinque adeo magnae positis incudibus urbes
tela novant, Atina potens Tiburque superbum,
*Ardea* Crustumerique et turrigerae Antemnae.

This passage describing how Italy "burns" in preparation for war may suggest a connection between *ardet* at the start of 623 and the name *Ardea* at the start of 731. Turnus is often associated with fire; this wordplay would link his city to fire as well.

This would be wordplay that as it were frames a passage rather than a line, as at A. 7.59–63 *laurus . . . Laurentes* (both at the start of the line—for more on framing of passages see intro. 2.8a).

At *Met.* 14.573–80, Ovid tells the story of how the city of Ardea is destroyed and burned, and then the bird *ardea* rose from the city's ashes, possibly also suggesting a connection between *Ardea* and *ardeo* (for Ovid cf. intro. 2.14).

For other wordplay on Ardea see on A. 7.411–12 *locus Ardea quondam / dictus avis, et nunc* ***magnum*** manet ***Ardea*** nomen.

For a survey of numerous passages connecting Turnus with fire see von Duhn (1957) 64–79 (she begins with Allecto's torch at 7.456–57).

**A. 7.645?:** et *meministis* enim, divae, et *memorare* potestis

Conington noted that Vergil "has chosen two verbs which suggest the connection of memory with the Muses." Nagy and others have suggested that *Mousa* is from the same root as the Greek words for "remember" and "memory." Here *divae* = *Musae;* the wordplay would be with a suppressed name (for suppression see intro. 2.7).

This line is repeated by the manuscript R at 9.529, but is omitted by most editors.

E. 7.19: alternos *Musae meminisse* volebant (where Nagy is cited); **A. 1.8:** *Musa* mihi causas *memora.*

Bartelink (1965) 93, Conington (1963) on 645.

## A. 7.655–63:

post hos insignem palma per gramina currum
victoresque ostentat equos satus Hercule pulchro
pulcher *Aventinus,* clipeoque insigne paternum
centum anguis cinctamque gerit serpentibus Hydram;
*collis Aventini* **silva** quem **Rhea** sacerdos
furtivum partu sub luminis edidit oras,
mixta deo mulier, postquam Laurentia victor
Geryone exstincto Tirynthius attigit arva,
Tyrrhenoque boves in flumine lavit Hiberas.

Aventinus seems to be named after the hill where he was born. Servius' note (quoted on A. 8.231–35) lists etymologies for the hill. Cf. *Aventini* montem . . . dirarum nidis domus opportuna *volucrum* in **A. 8.231–35.**

The story of the furtive birth of Aventinus to Rhea resembles that of Romulus and Remus to Rhea Silvia, and *silva* in 659 here alludes to her name. Cf. the description of Silvius Postumus in 6.763.

OVID *F.* 4.51–52 (on an Alban king; for Ovid cf. intro. 2.14): venit *Aventinus* post hos, locus unde vocatur, / mons quoque.

Cf. Williams (1973) on 659ff.

**A. 7.670–71:** tum gemini fratres *Tiburtia* moenia linquunt, / fratris *Tiburti* dictam cognomine gentem

Explicit derivation of the name of Tibur from the founder (in some versions; see Fordyce ad loc. and Maltby s.v. Tibur) Tiburtus. Here *dictam cognomine* is an etymological signpost (see intro. 2.6), as noted by Fordyce: "*cognomine:* Virgil uses the word especially of the significant name, the ἔτυμον or αἴτιον."

Fordyce (1977) on 670.

## A. 7.678–81:

nec Praenestinae fundator defuit urbis,
Volcano genitum pecora inter agrestia regem
*inventumque focis* omnis quem credidit aetas,
*Caeculus.*

Servius and the Scholia Veronensia (quoting Cato) suggest that Caeculus was so named because he was found in the hearth, and had little eyes because of his exposure to the smoke; the connection being made is between the name Caeculus and the adjective *caecus,* "blind." Vergil's *inventumque focis* seems to allude to this etymology, which may have been in Varro's *Res Humanae* (so Horsfall).

SCHOL. Veron. on 681: [Ca]to in Origines ait Caeculum virgines aquam petentes in foco invenisse ideoque Vulcani [filium eum ex]istimasse et, quod oculos exiguos haberet, Caeculum appellatum; SERV. 678: Caeculus autem ideo, quia oculis minoribus fuit: quam rem frequenter efficit fumus.

Fordyce (1977) on 678ff., Horsfall ap. Horsfall and Bremmer (1987).

## A. 7.681–85:

hunc legio late comitatur agrestis:
quique *altum Praeneste* viri quique arva Gabinae
Iunonis gelidumque Anienem et roscida rivis
**Hernica saxa** colunt, quos dives Anagnia pascis,
quos Amasene pater.

In 682 *altum* is an etymological gloss (see intro. 2.2) on the name Praeneste. Servius Auctus cites Cato for the derivation of the name from the verb *praesto,* "stand out," because of its hilltop location. See on **A. 3.270–71** for other plays on *altum, arduus.*

In 683–84, the noun *saxa* glosses the etymology of the adjective *Hernica.* Servius tells us that *hernae* was a Sabine word for *saxa,* "rocks." This example of an etymological gloss is unusual: most often, an adjective glosses a noun, but here, a noun glosses an adjective. For other examples of this kind of gloss of adjective by noun see intro. 2.2a. For the Sabine etymology cf. on A. 7.517 *sulpurea Nar albus aqua,* and cf. intro. 2.11.

Praeneste: SERV. Auct. 682: ALTVM PRAENESTE Cato (*Orig.* fr. 60 P, *GRF* p. 11, fr. 7) dicit quia is locus montibus praestet, Praeneste oppido nomen dedit. ergo "altum," quia in montibus locatum; FEST. p. 250, 22 L: Praeneste dicta est, quia is locus, quo condita est, montibus praestet (sim. in Schol. Veron. on A. 7.684); differently SERV. 678: Praeneste locus est haud longe ab urbe, dictus ἀπὸ τῶν πρίνων, id est ab ilicibus, quae illic abundant (other suggestions in Maltby).

Hernica saxa: SERV. 684: HERNICA SAXA COLVNT Sabinorum lingua saxa hernae vocantur. quidam dux magnus Sabinos de suis locis elicuit et habitare secum fecit in saxosis montibus: unde dicta sunt Hernica loca et populi Hernici; PAUL.-Fest. p. 89, 24 L: Hernici dicti a saxis, quae Marsi herna dicunt.

Praeneste: Hanssen (1948) 121, Bartelink (1965) 54, Horsfall (1987) 60 (suggesting that the scholiasts found Cato's etymology in Varro's *Res Humanae*). Hernica saxa: Bartelink (1965) 48, Ahl (1985) 63, Marouzeau (1940) 261, Fordyce (1977) ad loc., Horsfall (1991) 20.

**A. 7.706–14:**

ecce Sabinorum prisco de sanguine magnum
agmen agens *Clausus* magnique ipse agminis instar,
*Claudia* nunc a quo diffunditur et tribus et gens
per Latium, postquam in partem data Roma **Sabinis.**
una ingens Amiterna cohors priscique **Quirites,**
Ereti manus omnis oliviferaeque Mutuscae;
qui Nomentum urbem, qui *Rosea rura* Velini,
qui Tetricae horrentis rupes montemque Severum
Casperiamque colunt Forulosque et flumen Himellae

In 707–8, we see explicit etymologizing linking a Roman family of Vergil's day to the Sabines of Aeneas' time. Fordyce: "Clausus, the Sabine leader, is an ancestor of that Clausus or Claudius from whom the patrician *gens Claudia* claimed descent (as the Emperor [Claudius] proudly declared, Tac. *Ann.* 11.24)." For links between families of Vergil's day and those of Aeneas' see on **A. 5.116–23.**

In 709–10 we see, as Fordyce explains, "an allusion to the fanciful theory . . . which made *Quirites* equivalent to *Curenses* and derived the use of the name for the people of Rome from the incorporation of Tatius' Sabines in the time of Romulus." Note that the words that suggest the etymology are at the end of consecutive lines (see intro. 2.9). Cf. also on A. 6.859 Quirinus-curis.

Ross sees simple wordplay in 712 *Rosea rura Velini* (cf. *ros, rus*). In addition, Servius cites a comment of Varro on the *Rosulanus ager,* and Paulus-Festus preserves a fragment of Varro connecting the name with *ros,* "dew." Vergil seems to have played with this connection in the *Georgics* and may here suggest "the dewy farms of Velinus."

Nomentum, mentioned in 712, was the subject of a pun at **A. 6.773–76:** *hi tibi* ***Nomentum*** *et Gabios urbemque Fidenam / . . . , haec* ***tum nomina*** *erunt, nunc sunt* ***sine nomine*** *terrae.*

In 713 *Tetricae horrentis rupes, horrentis* is a gloss (cf. intro. 2.2) on the mountain name Tetrica (cf. the adjectives *taeter,* "foul, horrible" and *tetricus,* "frowning, severe"). Servius notes the connection, but implausibly suggests that the adjective is derived from the name of the mountain, rather than the other way around. As 713 continues, *montemque Severum* (or *severum*) is either another mountain with a Latin adjective for a name, or a further gloss on *Tetrica.* Both *tetricus* and *severus* are fitting adjectives or names for a Sabine mountain (cf. 8.638 *Curibusque severis*). The ethnographer's notion that harsh lands make harsh peoples is also in evidence.

In 707, *agmen agens* juxtaposes cognates; cf. on **A. 11.433.**

Claudius: LIVY 2.16.4–5: Attius Clausus cui postea Appio Claudio fuit Romae nomen (more references in Maltby).

Quirites (more sources in Maltby): VARRO *LL* 6.68: Quirites a Curensibus; ab his cum Tatio rege in societatem venerunt civitatis (cf. 5.51); SERV. 710: unde et Romani Quirites dicti sunt, quod nomen Sabinorum fuerat a civitate Curibus; FEST. p. 304, 16 L: Quirina tribus a Curensibus Sabinis appellationem videtur traxisse; OVID *F.* 2.475–80 (for Ovid cf. intro. 2.14):

proxima lux vacua est; at tertia dicta *Quirino;*
  qui tenet hoc nomen (Romulus ante fuit),
sive quod hasta "*curis*" priscis est dicta Sabinis
  (bellicus a telo venit in astra deus);
sive suum regi nomen posuere *Quirites,*
  seu quia Romanis iunxerat ille *Cures.*

Rosea rura: G. **2.201–2:** et quantum longis carpent armenta diebus / exigua tantum gelidus *ros* nocte reponet.

SERV. G. 2.201: ut in Aeneide (7.712) diximus, hoc dicit Varro fuisse in Rosulano agro, postquam Velinus siccatus est lacus: ubi longam perticam magnitudo superabat herbarum; VARRO *RR* 1.7.10: Caesar Vopiscus, aedilicius causam cum ageret apud censores, campos Roseae Italiae dixit esse sumen, in quo relicta pertica postridie non appareret propter herbam; VARRO fr. 403 (= Paul.-Fest. p. 355, 5–6 L = *GRF* p. 352): Rosea in agro Reatino campus appellatur, quod in eo arva rore umida semper seruntur; VARRO *RR* 3.2.9: villa tua . . . in Rosia; CIC. *ad Att.* 4.15.5: Rosia; PLINY *NH* 3.108: Velinos accolunt lacus, roscidis collibus.

Tetrica: SERV. 713: TETRICAE HORRENTIS RVPES Tetricus mons in Sabinis asperrimus, unde tristes homines tetricos dicimus. MONTEMQUE SEVERVM proprium nomem montis est, sicunt agri Roseus.

Clausus: Bartelink (1965) 63, Fordyce (1977) on 707; on the Claudii see *RE* 3 col. 2663 s.v. Claudius and e.g. Wiseman (1979) 57–139 ("The Legends of the Patrician Claudii"). Quirites: Bartelink (1965) 66, Rehm (1932) 17, 96, Fordyce (1977) on 710. Rosea rura: Bartelink (1965) 54, Ross (1973) 62, Marouzeau (1940) 260, Horsfall (1991) 113 and *EV* s.v. Rosea rura (Horsfall, skeptical). Tetrica: Rehm (1932), Bartelink (1965) 57, Ross (1973) 62, Fordyce (1977) ad loc., and *EV* s.v. Tetrica (Horsfall).

**A. 7.720:** vel cum sole novo densae *torrentur aristae*

Servius derives *arista* from *ariditas,* "dryness." With *torrentur,* "are scorched," Vergil plays on that etymology here as in the *Georgics* (see on **G. 1.7–8**).

SERV. 720: aristae, quas ab ariditate dictas esse constat.

CAT. 48.5–6: non si densior *aridis aristis* / sit nostrae seges osculationis; CAT. 64.353–54: namque velut densas praeceprens messor *aristas* / sole sub *ardenti* flaventia demetit arva; OVID *Her.* 5.111–12 (for Ovid cf. intro. 2.14): et minus est in te quam summa pondus *arista,* / quae levis adsiduis *solibus usta* riget.

Ross (1987) 35. He cites Cat. 48, where *aridis* is a gloss on *aristis,* and 64 as models for A. 7.720: "Virgil quite obviously has both Catullan lines in mind." He also suggests that Ovid "looks to both Virgil and Catullus" in *Her.* 5.

**A. 7.738:** *Sarrastis* populos et quae rigat aequora *Sarnus*

Here either the Sarrastes ("otherwise unknown," according to Fordyce) were named after the river Sarnus, or vice versa, or perhaps both were named after the same thing—Servius Auctus suggests a river back in their Peloponnesian homeland. The words connected etymologically frame the line (see intro. 2.8).

SERV. Auct. 738: Conon in eo libro, quem de Italia scripsit, quosdam Pelasgos aliosque ex Peloponneso convenas ad eum locum Italiae venisse dicit, cui nullum antea nomen fuerit, et flumini quem incolerent, Sarro nomen inposuisse ex appellatione patrii fluminis, et se Sarrastras appellasse.

Fordyce (1977) on 738.

### A. 7.740: et quos *maliferae* despectant moenia *Abellae*

A famous example in which Vergil seems to show awareness of a word otherwise unattested this early. Fordyce: "There is ground for thinking that the name *Abella* preserves an Italic word for 'apple,' a cognate of those existing in the Northern groups of I.G. languages (Teutonic, Celtic, and Baltic), which was supplanted in Latin by *malum,* borrowed from Greek. If *Abella* was 'apple-town,' *maliferae . . . Abellae* is another Virgilian etymological play." For single-epithet glosses cf. intro. 2.2.

Most manuscripts and Servius read Bellae, which Rehm defends.

Differently SERV. Auct. 740: ab nucibus Abellanis Abella nomen accepit. alii quod inbelle vulgus et otiosum ibi fuerit, ideo Abellam appellatam.

Vergil's other plays on *mala:* A. 10.324–25: tu quoque, flaventem *prima lanugine malas* / dum sequeris Clytium *infelix,* nova gaudia, *Cydon;* E. 2.51: ipse ego cana legam *tenera lanugine mala;* G. 2.126–27: *Media* fert tristis sucos tardumque saporem / *felicis mali,* quo non praesentius ullum.

Bartelink (1965) 36, Rehm (1932) 34–35, Hanssen (1948) 119–20, Marouzeau (1940) 261, Ross (1973) 61, Fordyce (1977) on 740, Ahl (1985) 63 and (1982) 402–10, Horsfall (1991) 20; cf. too Wölfflin (1887) 206 for a pun on *mala* (troubles) and μῆλα at Cic. *ad Fam.* 9.20.1.

### A. 7.752–60:

fortissimus Vmbro,
*vipereo generi et graviter spirantibus hydris*
spargere qui somnos cantuque manuque solebat,
mulcebatque iras et morsus arte levabat.
sed non Dardaniae medicari cuspidis ictum
evaluit neque eum iuvere in vulnera cantus
somniferi et Marsis quaesitae montibus herbae.
te nemus *Angitiae,* vitrea te Fucinus unda,
te liquidi flevere lacus.

The name Angitia may be connected to Umbro's ability to charm snakes with song, in either of two ways (or perhaps both). Servius says that the Marrubians called Medea *Angitia* because her *carmina* could choke *(angere)* snakes. Or the name Angitia could be directly connected with *anguis,* "snake" (Wagner and Conington read Anguitia, found in some manuscripts).

SERV. 750: Medea . . . docuit remedia contra serpentes. . . . hi ergo populi Medeam Angitiam nominaverunt ab eo quod eius carminibus serpentes angerent.

Bartelink (1965) 40.

## A. 7.761–69, 774–77:

ibat et Hippolyti proles pulcherrima bello,
*Virbius,* insignem quem mater Aricia misit,
eductum Egeriae lucis umentia circum
litora, pinguis ubi et placabilis ara Dianae.
namque ferunt fama Hippolytum, postquam arte novercae
occiderit patriasque explerit sanguine poenas
turbatis distractus equis, ad sidera rursus
aetheria et superas caeli venisse sub auras,
Paeoniis revocatum herbis et amore Dianae.
. . . . . . . . . . . . . . . . . . . . . . . . . . . . .
at Trivia Hippolytum secretis alma recondit
sedibus et nymphae Egeriae nemorique relegat,
solus ubi in silvis Italis ignobilis aevum
exigeret versoque ubi nomine *Virbius* esset.

The repetition of the name Virbius at the start and finish of the story makes the name almost frame the lines, and *verso . . . nomine* in 777 both calls attention to the name as an etymological signpost (cf. intro. 2.6) and links the passage to Alexandrian concern for *metonomasia* (see intro. 2.6 and 10). Servius gives the etymology of the name, from *bis vir,* "twice a man" (i.e., "twice alive"), and reports that Callimachus told the story in the *Aetia;* Horsfall suggests that "detailed and extended borrowing" from Callimachus by Vergil "is likely." (The scholia to Ovid's *Ibis* attribute four verses, quoted in Latin, to Callimachus; Pfeiffer is properly skeptical about them [so too *EV*]).

Ahl notes that in 767, "*distractus equis,* 'torn apart by his horses,' . . . translates the popular . . . Greek etymology of the name," as if from Greek ἵππος, "horse," + λύω, "to loose, break up."

Virbius: SERV. 761: sed Diana Hippolytum, revocatum ab inferis, in Aricia nymphae commendavit Egeriae et eum Virbium, quasi bis virum, iussit vocari; SERV. 778: VNDE ETIAM TRIVIAE TEMPLO exponit τὸ αἴτιον: nam Callimachus scripsit αἴτια, in quibus etiam hoc commemorat (= Callim. fr. 190); SCHOL. Pers. 6.56: Virbius . . . id est Hippolytus, quod bis in vita prolatus sit . . . ; Diana . . . Virbium vocavit merito, quod bis in vita prolatus esset; SCHOL. G to Ovid, *Ibis* 279: Tangit fabulam de Hippolyto. Unde Callimachus:

Noluit Hippolytus Phaedrae violare pudorem,
Et quia noluerat, habuit pro munere mortem.
Sed qui recta facit quod in aeternum moriatur,
Denegat Hippolytus, qui vitae *bis* reparatur.

Hippolytus: OVID *F.* 3.265 (for Ovid cf. intro. 2.14): Hippolytus loris *direptus equorum; F.* 5.309–10: Hippolyte infelix, velles coluisse Dianam, / cum consternatis *diripereris equis; Met.* 15.542–44: nomenque simul, quod possit *equorum* / admonuisse, iubet deponere, "qui" que "fuisti / *Hippolytus*" dixit, "nunc idem Virbius esto"; PRUD. *Peristeph.* 11.85–88:

> "quis," inquit (sc. iudex),
>   "dicitur?" adfirmant dicier Hippolytum.
> "ergo sit Hippolytus, quatiat turbetque iugales,
>   intereatque feris *dilaceratus equis.*"

Pfeiffer (1949–53) on Callim. fr. 190, Fordyce (1977) ad loc., Horsfall (1981) 149 and (1991) 109–10, Mørland (1960) 24–25 (suggests a derivation from *vir* + βίος), Ahl (1985) 63, *EV* s.v. Virbio (Caviglia), Paschalis (1995) on Hor. *C.* 4.7. Mørland (1960) 24–25 connects -olytus with ὄλλυμι. On Ovid, see Knox (1986) 74; on the etymology in Euripides' play see Zeitlin (1985) 58–64 and 191 n. 16. On Prudentius, Malamud (1989) 81–83, 96. Hollis (1992) compares the Vergilian passage with Callim. fr. 664, on why there are no dogs on Delos.

**A. 7.796–98?:** et Sacranae acies et picti *scuta Labici;* / qui saltus, Tiberine, tuos sacrumque Numici / litus arant

Servius says that the Labici were so called after the name Labicus given to Glaucus, who showed himself worthy to rule them by inventing a kind of shield (cf. λαβή, shield handle). The juxtaposition of the words *scuta* and *Labici* may signal an allusion to this story.

SERV. 796: PICTI SCVTA LABICI Glaucus, Minois filius, venit ad Italiam. et cum sibi imperium posceret nec acciperet, ideo quod nihil praestabat, sicut eius pater praestiterat zonam eis transmittendo, cum antehac discincti essent, ostendit scutum: a quo et ipse Labicus dictus est, et ex eo populi ἀπὸ τῆς λαβῆς quam latine amplam vocamus.

Rehm (1932) 29, Hanssen (1948) 121, Bartelink (1965) 65 n. 3, Williams (1973) on 796, Horsfall (1991) 113.

**A. 7.803–4?:** Hos super advenit Volsca de gente *Camilla* / **agmen agens** equitum et florentis *aere* catervas

Egan suggests a chain of derivations linking the name Camilla with words for weapons. Vergil connects the name Camilla with that of her mother, Casmilla (A. 11.542–43 *matrisque vocavit / nomine Casmillae mutata parte Camillam*). Egan:

> Varro (*LL* 7.34) explains the Latin nouns *camillus* and *camilla* as being related to the name of the Samothracian deity Kasmilos, and the latter name is also attested in the variant form Kadmilos. . . . Kadmilos had a connection, real or imagined, with Kadmos. . . . [A] gloss in Hesychius explains the word κάδμος as a Cretan noun which means δόρυ, λόφος, ἀσπίς—that is, "armor," or "arms". . . . [In] the Greek mythographer Konon, there is a punning connection between Κάδμος and the remarkable armor of the Spartoi. . . . It appears the casm-, the initial part of Casmilla, can be identified with a Greek element

> which . . . meant or connoted "arms" or "armor." "Casmilla," accordingly, should mean something like "armor woman."

Egan argues that several passages seem to look to this special connection of Camilla with arms.

De la Cerda notes that the phrase *agmen agens* juxtaposes cognates (cf. on **A. 11.433**).

A. 11.552–55, 561–66:

> *telum* immane manu valida quod forte gerebat
> bellator, solidum nodis et robore cocto,
> huic natam libro et silvestri subere clausam
> implicat atque habilem mediae circumligat *hastae;*
> . . . . . . . . . . . . . . . . . . . . . . . . . . . . . . . .
> dixit, et adducto contortum *hastile* lacerto
> immittit: sonuere undae, rapidum super amnem
> infelix fugit in *iaculo* stridente Camilla.
> at Metabus magna propius iam urgente caterva
> dat sese fluvio, atque *hastam* cum virgine victor
> gramineo, donum Triviae, de caespite vellit.

A. 11.573–75:

> utque pedum primis infans vestigia plantis
> institerat, *iaculo* palmas *armavit* acuto
> *spicula*que ex umero parvae suspendit et *arcum.*

A. 11.648–54:

> at medias inter caedes exsultat Amazon
> unum exserta latus pugnae, *pharetrata* Camilla,
> et nunc lenta manu spargens *hastilia* denset,
> nunc validam dextra rapit indefessa *bipennem;*
> aureus ex umero sonat *arcus* et *arma* Dianae.
> illa etiam, si quando in tergum pulsa recessit,
> *spicula* converso fugientia derigit *arcu.*

A. 11.778–82:

> hunc virgo, sive ut templis praefigeret *arma*
> Troia, captivo sive ut se ferret in auro
> venatrix, unum ex omni certamine pugnae
> caeca sequebatur totumque incauta per agmen
> femineo praedae et spoliorum ardebat amore.

Egan (1983), Cerda (1617) 143; on the name Camilla see also Köves-Zulauf (1978) 420–36, Fordyce (1977) on 803ff., Horsfall (1988) 38–39.

**A. 8.22–23:** sicut aquae tremulum labris ubi *lumen* aenis / sole repercussum aut radiantis imagine *lunae*

For the derivation of *luna* from *lux* or *luceo* see on **A. 4.80–81** ***lumenque*** *obscura vicissim* / ***luna*** *premit.*

**A. 8.43–48:**

litoreis ingens inventa sub ilicibus sus
triginta capitum fetus enixa iacebit,
*alba* solo recubans, *albi* circum ubera nati.
[hic locus urbis erit, requies ea certa laborum,]
ex quo ter denis urbem redeuntibus annis
Ascanius *clari* condet cognominis *Albam.*

*Cognominis* in 48 is an etymological signpost (cf. intro. 2.6); *alba* and *albi* in 45 suggest that the name Alba is associated with the omen of the white sow. Conington comments further: " 'Clari' seems rightly taken by Heyne to refer to 'Alba' by a play on the word. The town was really named from the white rocks on which it stood." Ovid offers a similar gloss for a king described as *clarus . . . Alba* at *Met.* 14.612, perhaps as an allusion to Vergil's gloss here (for Ovid cf. intro. 2.14).

Lycophron 1253–60 has a black (κελαινή) sow, the early annalist Fabius Pictor (Diod. Sic. 7.5 = fr. 4 *HRR* Peter) a white sow. Eden: "it looks as if an important detail has been changed . . . to form an aetiological myth to explain the name Alba."

Cf. A. 3.389–93 (where 390–93 = 8.43–46). For more on the name Alba see on **A. 9.387–88.** For other wordplay involving words for "white" see on A. 3.274, ***Leucatae nimbosa*** *cacumina montis,* and A. 8.657–61, *Galli . . . lactea colla.*

VARRO *LL* 5.144: propter colorem suis et loci naturam Alba Longa dicta; SERV. A. 1.270: Albam Longam . . . dictam ab omine albae porcae repertae vel situ civitatis.

PROP. 4.1.35: et stetit *Alba* potens, *albae suis* omine nata; TIB. 1.7.58: *candida*que antiquo detinet *Alba* Lare; LYCOPH. 1253–60:

κτίσει δὲ χώραν ἐν τόποις Βορειγόνων
ὑπὲρ Λατίνους Δαυνίους τ' ᾠκισμένην,
πύργους τριάκοντ', ἐξαριθμήσας γονὰς
συὸς κελαινῆς, ἣν ἀπ' Ἰδαίων λόφων
καὶ Δαρδανείων ἐκ τόπων ναυσθλώσεται,
ἰσηρίθμων θρέπτειραν ἐν τόκοις κάπρων·
ἧς καὶ πόλει δείκηλον ἀνθήσει μιᾷ
χαλκῷ τυπώσας καὶ τέκνων γλαγοτρόφων.

A. 9.387–88: locos qui post Albae de nomine dicti / *Albani;* **A. 12.134–36:** At Iuno ex summo (qui nunc Albanus habetur; / tum neque nomen erat).

Conington (1963) on 48, Bartelink (1965) 39, Marouzeau (1940) 260, Ahl (1985) 303, Eden (1975) on 43–48.

**A. 8.53–54:** delegere locum et posuere in montibus urbem / *Pallantis* proavi de nomine *Pallanteum.*

Vergil implicitly derives the name of the *mons Palatinus* (for which antiquity offered several explanations) from the Arcadian name Pallanteum (cf. Παλλαντεῖον at Paus. 8.43.1–2), and explicitly derives that name from the personal name of Pallas, the grandfather (apparently) of Evander and great-grandfather of Pallas. The words connected etymologically frame line 54 (see intro. 2.8); *nomine* is an etymological signpost (see intro. 2.6).

Gransden: "a characteristic wordplay which defies quantity, since the first syllable of Palatium is short" (on quantity see intro. 2.1). On the Palatine see also the systematic etymologizing at Tib. 2.5.25–30 (quoted below on G. 3.1–3), linking *pasco, Palatia, Pan, Pales,* and *pastor.*

For this kind of two-stage etymologizing, cf. on **A. 8.337–41** on the Carmental Gate.

SERV. 51: Evander Arcas fuit, nepos Pallantis, regis Arcadiae. hic patrem suum occidit, suadente matre Nicostrata, quae etiam Carmentis dicta est, quia carminibus vaticinabatur. . . . hic autem mons Palatinus secundum Vergilium a Pallante, avo Evandri, est dictus, secundum Varronem et alios a filia Evandri Pallantia, ab Hercule vitiata et postea illic sepulta, vel certe a Pallante eius filio illic sepulto *(Serv. Auct. adds:)* inmaturae aetatis: alii a filio Evandri, qui post mortem patris seditione occisus est: *(Serv. continues:)* alii a balatu ovium Balanteum volunt dictum, et exinde per antistichon Pallanteum dictum; VARRO *LL* 5.53: Palatium, quod Pallantes cum Evandro venerunt, qui et Palatini; ⟨alii quod Palatini⟩, aborigines ex agro Reatino, qui appellatur Palatium, ibi conse⟨de⟩runt; sed hoc alii a Palanto uxore Latini putarunt. eundem hunc locum a pecore dictum putant quidam; itaque Naevius (fr. 2, *GRF* p. 6) Balatium appellat; LIVY 1.5.1–2: et a Pallanteo, urbe Arcadica Pallantium, dein Palatium montem appellatum; PLINY *NH* 4.20: Pallantium (sc. Arcadiae) unde Palatium Romae; PAUL.-Fest. p. 245, 3 L: Palatium . . . appellatus est, quod ibi pecus pascens balare consueverit, vel quod palare, id est errare, ibi pecudes solerent; alii quod ibi Hyperborei filia Palanto habitaverit, quae ex Hercule Latinum peperit; alii eundem, quod Pallas ibi sepultus sit, aestimant appellari; ISID. 15.3.5: Palatium a Pallante principe Arcadum dictum (more sources in Maltby).

Bartelink (1965) 52, Fordyce (1977) ad 8.51ff., Edwards (1960) 163, O'Hara (1990) 48–49, Horsfall (1981) 142, Ross (1975) 155–57 (on Tibullus), Gransden (1976) on 51–54.

**A. 8.62–64:** ego sum pleno quem flumine cernis / *stringentem* ripas et *pinguia culta secantem,* / **caeruleus** *Thybris* **caelo** gratissimus amnis

In the phrase *stringentem ripas,* Servius (perhaps implausibly) sees an allusion to an old name for the Tiber, Rumon, *quasi ripas ruminans et exedens.* (More implausibly, he sees another allusion to the name Rumon in 8.90, *rumore secundo ["rumore" pro "Rumone" posuit; nam, ut supra diximus, Rumon dictus est].*) In 63, *pinguia culta secantem,* Servius sees an allusion to an old name Serra (cf. *serra,* saw). Cf. on 8.330 asper Thybris.

In 64 the words *caeruleus . . . caelo* may allude to the derivation of *caeruleus* from *caelum* (not explicitly mentioned in antiquity; see on **3.192–94**). Eden suggests that Vergil "was attracted by the sound-echo between *caelo* and its derivative *caerul(e)us* (originally *caelulus*); wordplay is the obvious point of Ennius' *caeli caerula templa* (*Ann.* 49 V [= 48 Sk.]), imitated by Lucretius 1.1090 *per caeli caerula.*" Cf. also A. 5.8–10.

SERV. 63: STRINGENTEM RIPAS radentem, inminuentem: nam hoc est Tiberini fluminis proprium, adeo ut ab antiquis Rumon dictus sit, quasi ripas ruminans et exedens. in sacris etiam Serra dicebatur, unde ait nunc "et pinguia culta secantem." in aliqua etiam urbis parte Tarentum dicitur eo quod ripas terat. (*Auct.*:) alii "stringentem" iuxta veterem morem dictum intellegunt: "stringere" enim significare dicunt tactu modico praeterire, ut ipse ait (10.478) "magno strinxit de corpore Turni"; SERV. 90: RVMORE SECVNDO hoc est bona fama, cum neminem laederent: aut certe dicit eos ante venisse, quam fama nuntiaret venturos. aut "rumore" pro "Rumone" posuit; nam, ut supra (63) diximus, Rumon dictus est: unde et ficus ruminalis, ad quam eiecti sunt Remus et Romulus. quae fuit ubi nunc est lupercal in circo: hac enim labebatur Tiberis, antequam Vertumno factis sacrificiis averteretur. quamvis ficum ruminalem alii a Romulo velint dictum, quasi Romularem, alii a lacte infantibus dato: nam pars gutturis ruma dicitur. ergo si fuerit "Rumone secundo," favente fluvio intellegimus.

Servius' names for the Tiber are noted by Gransden (1976) 63; on *caeruleus*: Eden (1975) on 64, Fordyce (1977) on 64.

## A. 8.102, 172–74, 185?:

> forte die *sollemnem* illo rex Arcas honorem
> . . . . . . . . . . . . . . . . . . . . . . . . . . . .
> interea sacra haec, quando huc venistis amici,
> *annua,* quae differre nefas, celebrate faventes
> nobiscum. . . .
> . . . . . . . . . . .
> rex Evandrus ait: "non haec *sollemnia* nobis . . ."

For the connection between *sollemnis* and *annus* see on **A. 5.53** *annua* vota tamen *sollemnis*que ordine pompas. This example is less certain, because of the distance between the words.

Bartelink (1965) 101.

**A. 8.105:** una omnes *iuvenum* primi pauperque *senatus*

The pairing of *iuvenum primi* and *senatus* here may allude to the etymological connection between *senatus* and *senex* or *senectas:* both young and old have come to the rites.

CIC. *Sen.* 6.19: quae (consilium ratio sententia) nisi essent in seniores, non summum consilium maiores nostri appellassent senatum; FEST. p. 454, 11 L: Senatores a senectute dici satis constat; VARRO *LL* 5.156: senaculum vocatum, ubi senatus aut ubi seniores consisterent, dictum ut γερουσία apud Graecos; OVID *F.* 5.63–64 (for Ovid cf. intro. 2.14): nec nisi post annos patuit tunc curia *seros*, / nomen et *aetatis* mite *senatus* habet.

Cerda (1617) 165, Ellis (1985) 33.

**A. 8.194 (etc.):** semihominis Caci

When Vergil has Evander tell the story of Hercules and Cacus, the sense of Evander as "good man" (Εὔανδρος) and Cacus as "bad man" (Κακός) seems present, although no particular line of Vergil's seems to allude to this.

Servius notes that Cacus = κακός, but in the context of a rationalized version of the story in which Cacus is a slave who stole from Evander.

Cf. the possible (unlikely?) play on *ducis Evandri nomen* and εὐανδρία, "courage," at **A. 10.369–70.**

SERV. 190: Cacus secundum fabulam Vulcani filius fuit, ore ignem ac fumum vomens, qui vicina omnia populabatur. veritas tamen secundum philologos et historicos hoc habet, hunc fuisse Evandri nequissimum servum ac furem. novimus autem malum a Graecis κακόν dici: quem ita illo tempore Arcades appellabant. postea translato accentu Cacus dictus est; AUG. *Civ.* 19.12: tam . . . malitia singularis, ut ex hac ei nomen inventum sit—Graece namque malus κακός dicitur, quod ille (sc. Cacus) vocabatur; Ovid *F.* 1.551–52 (for Ovid cf. intro. 2.14): *Cacus*, Aventinae timor atque infamiae silvae, / non leve finitimis hospitibusque *malum*.

Cerda (1617) 178, Hardie (1986) 111, Gransden (1976) on 190–305, Ogilvie (1970) 56, Clausen (1994) 223 (citing Ovid).

**A. 8.200–201:** attulit et nobis aliquando optantibus aetas / auxilium *adventum*que dei.

Ellis sees a connection between *adventus* used of the arrival of Hercules here and the name of the Aventine hill. See on **A. 8.231–35.**

VARRO *LL* 5.43: alii Aventinum ab adventu hominum, quod com⟨m⟩mune Latinorum ibi Dianae templum sit constitutum.

Ellis (1985) 41.

**A. 8.203:** *Alcides* aderat taurosque hac *victor* agebat

Serv. 8.363 sees an allusion both here and there to the worship of Hercules Victor at Rome. See on **A. 8.363** ***"haec" inquit "limina victor / Alcides subiit."***

Cerda (1617) 180.

**A. 8.231–35:**

lustrat *Aventini* montem, ter saxea temptat
limina nequiquam, ter fessus valle resedit.
stabat acuta silex praecisis undique saxis

speluncae dorso insurgens, altissima visu,
*dirarum nidis domus opportuna volucrum.*

Varro and Servius present (among alternatives) the derivation of the name of the Aventine hill from *avis,* "bird"; Varro says that this is Naevius' derivation. Line 235, *dirarum nidis domus opportuna volucrum,* may allude to this etymology.

VARRO *LL* 5.43: Aventinum aliquot de causis dicunt. Naevius (fr. 4, *GRF* p. 115) ab avibus, quod eo se ab Tiberi ferrent aves, alii ab rege Aventino Albano, quod ⟨ibi⟩ sit sepultus, alii Aventinum ab adventu hominum, quod com⟨m⟩mune Latinorum ibi Dianae templum sit constitutum. ego maxime puto, quod ab advectu: nam olim paludibus mons erat ab reliquis disclusus. itaque eo ex urbe advehebantur ratibus; SERV. A. 7.657: PVLCHER AVENTINVS Aventinus mons urbis Romae est, quem constat ab avibus esse nominatum, quae de Tiberi ascendentes illic sedebant, ut in octavo (235) legimus "dirarum nidis domus opportuna volucrum." quidam etiam rex Aboriginum, Aventinus nomine, illic et occisus et sepultus est, sicut etiam Albanorum rex Aventinus, cui successit Procas. Varro tamen dicit in gente populi Romani, Sabinos a Romulo susceptos istum accepisse montem, quem ab Avente, fluvio provinciae suae, Aventinum appellaverunt. constat ergo varias has opiniones postea secutas, nam a principio Aventinus est dictus ab avibus vel a rege Aboriginum: unde hunc Herculis filium constat nomen a monte accepisse, non ei praestitisse (many more sources in Maltby).

Cf. Aornon at A. 6.239–42; Aventinus heros < Aventinus collis at A. 7.657–60; the possible etymologizing at 8.201 adventus; etymologies for the other hills: Palatine (see on A. 8.53–54), Ianiculum (A. 8.357–58); OVID *F.* 4.51–52 (on the Alban king; for Ovid cf. intro. 2.14): venit Aventinus post hos, locus unde vocatur, / mons quoque; *Met.* 14.620–21: Aventino, qui, quo regnaret, eodem / monte iacet positus tribuitque vocabula monti.

Bartelink (1965) 43, Marouzeau (1949) 73.

**A. 8.281–82?:** iamque sacerdotes primusque Potitius ibant / pellibus in morem cincti, *flammas*que ferebant.

Ellis sees in this description of priests *(sacerdotes)* carrying flames *(flammas)* a suggestion of an etymological connection between *flamen,* the name for a priest assigned to the worship of a particular deity, and *flamma.* This would be wordplay with one term suppressed (*flamen;* see intro. 2.7). Varro and Paulus-Festus point to a derivation from *filum,* the woolen band worn around the hair, but some modern scholars have pointed to a connection with *flamma* (cf. Lewis and Short, Ogilvie).

VARRO *LL* 5.84: flamines, quod in Latio capite velato erant semper ac caput cinctum habebant filo, f⟨i⟩lamines dicti; PAUL.-Fest. p. 77, 28 L: Flamen Dialis dictus, quod filo assidue veletur; indeque appellatur flamen, quasi filamen; SERV. A. 8.664: a filo quo utebantur, flamines dicti, quasi filamines (more sources in Maltby).

Ellis (1985) 54–55, Ogilvie (1970) 97.

**A. 8.287–88?:** qui carmine laudes / *Herculeas* et facta ferunt; ut prima *novercae*

The words that frame 288, *Herculeas* and *novercae,* may suggest an etymology of the name Hercules. A number of ancient sources derive the Greek name Herakles from the name Hera (= Juno) and a word like κλέος, "fame, glory." In 288 the *noverca* is Juno-Hera; the name is suppressed in the Hellenistic manner (see intro. 2.7). Both Callimachus and Apollonius have lines framed by the names Hera and Herakles, suggesting at least soundplay, and probably an allusion to the etymology. Vergil probably alludes to both the etymology, and these Alexandrian precedents.

On framing see intro. 2.8.

Ovid also has a line framed by the name Hercules and *noverca* (for Ovid cf. intro. 2.14).

Cf. on A. 8.203 and 363 for references to the name Hercules Victor; for wordplay on the name Hera see also on A. 12.792.

[PROB.] E. 7.61: Pindarus initio Alciden nominatum, postea Herculem dicit ab Ἥρα, quam Iunonem dicimus, quod eius imperiis opinionem famamque virtutis sit consecutus; SCHOL. T on *Il.* 14.324: ὁ δὲ Πύθιος (fr. 443 P.-W.) "Ἡρακλέην δέ σε Φοῖβος ἐπώνυμον ἐξονομάζει· / ἦρα γὰρ ἀνθρώποισι φέρων κλέος ἄφθιτον ἕξεις." οἱ δὲ ὅτι Πορφυρίωνος ἐρασθέντος Ἥρας, προσκαλεσαμένης αὐτῆς, ἐλθὼν ἐβοήθησε· διὸ παρὰ τὸ ὑπὸ τῆς Ἥρας κληθῆναι Ἡρακλῆς λέγεται; DIOD. Sic. 4.10.1: ἡ μὲν Ἥρα δύο δράκοντας ἀπέστειλε τοὺς ἀναλώσοντας τὸ βρέφος, ὁ δὲ παῖς οὐ καταπλαγεὶς ἑκατέρᾳ τῶν χειρῶν τὸν αὐχένα σφίγξας ἀπέπνιξε τοὺς δράκοντας. διόπερ Ἀργεῖοι πυθόμενοι τὸ γεγονὸς Ἡρακλέα προσηγόρευσαν, ὅτι δι' Ἥραν ἔσχε κλέος, Ἀλκαῖον πρότερον καλούμενον; MACROB. 1.20.10: et re vera Herculem solem esse vel ex nomine claret. Ἡρακλῆς enim quid aliud est nisi Ἥρας id est aeris, κλέος? quae porro alia aeris gloria est nisi solis illuminatio . . . ? cf. too *Etym. Mag.* p. 435, 3ff. (that and more cited or quoted by Zwicker, *RE* v. 8, pt. 1 s.v. Herakles, col. 524).

CALLIM. *Hymn* 3.107–9: τὴν δὲ μίαν Κελάδοντος ὑπὲρ ποταμοῖο φυγοῦσαν / Ἥρης ἐννεσίῃσιν, ἀέθλιον Ἡρακλῆι / ὕστερον ὄφρα γένοιτο, πάγος Κερύνειος ἔδεκτο; APOLL. Rhod. 1.996–97: δὴ γάρ που καὶ κεῖνα θεὰ τρέφεν αἰνὰ πέλωρα / Ἥρη, Ζηνὸς ἄκοιτις, ἀέθλιον Ἡρακλῆι; OVID *Met.* 9.134–35: actaque magni / *Herculis* inplerant terras odiumque *novercae.*

**A. 8.296–97?**: te Stygii tremuere lacus, te *ianitor Orci* / *ossa* super recubans antro *semesa* cruento

Scholars have wondered where in the insubstantial underworld Cerberus found blood and bones; Eden rightly notes that "the germ of the idea" here "is probably Hesiod's ὠμηστής (*Theog.* 311, cf. 772f.)." But Servius suggests that the name Cerberus means "meat eater," as if from κρεοβόρος. Possibly we could read Hesiod's Κέρβερον ὠμηστήν as a single-epithet gloss (see intro. 1.1 and 2.2), and Vergil's allusion to meat eating as an allusion to the etymology of the suppressed name (for suppression see intro. 2.7). Allegorical interpretations of underworld mythology may underlie such wordplay: Servius explains that Cerberus is the earth, which consumes all bones, and Lucretius 3.1011 mentions Cerberus when he rationalizes underworld myths, although he offers no details.

SERV. A. 6.395: quod autem dicitur (sc. Hercules) traxisse ab inferis Cerberum, haec ratio est, quia omnes cupiditates et cuncta vitia terrena contempsit et domuit: nam

Cerberus terra est, id est consumptrix omnium corporum. unde et Cerberus dictus est, quasi κρεοβόρος, id est, carnem vorans: unde legitur (8.297) "ossa super recubans": nam non ossa citius terra consumit; SERV. A. 8.297: OSSA SVPER RECUBANS aut ad terrorem dictum est: aut certe illud est quod etiam supra (6.395) diximus, Cerberum esse terram, quae corpora sepulta consumit; nam inde Cerberus dictus est, quasi κρεοβόρος. alii pueriliter volunt a cerbero Amphiarai ossa consumi, qui hiatu terrae secundum Statium descendit ad inferos; ISID. 11.3.33: Cerberum inferorum name tria capita habentem, significantes per eum tres aetates per quas mors hominuem devorat, id est infantiam, iuventutem et senectutem. quem quidam ideo dictum Cerberum putant quasi κρεοβόρος id est carnem vocans; Maltby also cites Fulg. *Myth.* 1, 6 p. 20, 15 and Lyd. *Mens.* 3, 8 p. 42.4 W.

Conington (1963) on 297 (mentioning Servius) and Eden (1975) on 297; on Lucretius cf. Wallach (1976) 83–90.

## A. 8.319–27:

primus ab aetherio venit Saturnus Olympo
arma Iovis fugiens et regnis exsul ademptis.
is genus indocile ac dispersum montibus altis
composuit legesque dedit, *Latium*que vocari
maluit, his quoniam *latuisset* tutus in oris.
aurea quae perhibent illo sub rege fuere
saecula: sic placida populos in pace regebat,
deterior donec paulatim ac decolor aetas
et belli rabies et amor successit habendi.

Names are prominent in Evander's history of Italy. Vergil (or Evander) derives the name *Latium* from the fact that Saturnus hid there *(latuisset);* others derived the name, e.g., from that of Latinus, or from its geographical position hiding between the Alps and the Appenines. Here *vocari* is an etymological signpost (see intro. 2.6), and *maluit,* as Servius notes, calls attention to the fact that Latium had other names (see intro. 2.10 for *metonomasia*).

Ahl notes that *maluit* is "a perfect anagram of Latium, which neatly complements the idea of Saturnus' concealment in Latium" (cf. intro. n. 318).

SERV. 322: bene "maluit": nam et Saturnia dicta est, ut (329) "et nomen posuit Saturnia tellus." et Vergilus Latium vult dici, quod illic Saturnus latuit. Varro (fr. 394, *GRF* p. 350) autem Latium dici putat, quod latet Italia inter praecipitia Alpium et Appennini; SERV. Auct. 322: quidam ferunt a Latino dictum Latium, alii ipsum Latinum a Latio; VARRO *LL* 5.32.5: qua regnum fuit Latini, universus ager dictus Latius; SERV. Auct. 1.6 (*GRF* p. 438): Latium autem dictum est quod illic Saturnus latuerit. Saufeius Latium dictum ait quod ibi latuerunt incolae, qui quoniam in cavis montium . . . habitaverint, Casci vocati sunt, quos posteri Aborigines cognominarunt, quoniam ⟨nullis⟩ aliis ortos esse recognoscebant, ex quibus Latinos etiam dictos; OVID *F.* 1.237–38 (for Ovid cf. intro. 2.14): inde diu genti mansit Saturnia nomen; / dicta quoque est *Latium* terra, *latente* deo; ISID. 14.4.18: mox et

Latium dicta eo quod idem Saturnus a Iove sedibus suis pulsus ibi latuerit; 15.1.50: a Saturno Saturnia atque Latium conditum, eo quod ibi fugiens latuisset cognominatum (more sources in Maltby).

Bartelink (1965) 49, Eden (1975), Fordyce (1977), Gransden (1976), Thomas (1982) 101 and n. 45, Ahl (1985) 47–48, Linderski (1992).

## A. 8.328–32:

> tum manus Ausonia et gentes venere Sicanae,
> saepius et nomen posuit Saturnia tellus;
> tum reges *asper*que immani corpore *Thybris,*
> a quo post Itali fluvium cognomine *Thybrim*
> diximus; amisit verum vetus Albula nomen.

Evander's concern with names continues. In 329, he says that the Saturnian land often put off its old name. In the previous line, the adjective *Ausonia* suggests that "'learned' or romantic name for Italy" in the Hellenistic poets (Fordyce, citing Apoll. Rhod. 4.660 Αὐσονίης ἀκτὰς Τυρσηνίδας—see too Livrea ad loc.). In 330–32, Vergil gives an explicit aetiology deriving the river name Thybris from the name of the king Thybris. Servius' note connects that name with the Greek word ὕβρις; if Vergil's *asper* is a gloss referring to this idea, we would have the familiar pattern in which a place name is explicitly traced to the name of a person, then that person's name is subtly glossed (see on **A. 8.337–41,** Carmentalis porta/Carmenta/carmen).

Line 332 gives Albula as the former "true name" of the Tiber; Servius' note says it was so called after its color *(alba).* Cf. Ogilvie: "Alba as used as the name of the mountains, the town, and the river has no connection with the Latin *albus,* 'white' but is a pre-Indo-European word meaning 'mountain' (cf. Alps . . . ). Hence the substitution of Tiber for Albula represents the victory of the Etruscan language (Thebris) over the indigenous." (More on this at **A. 9.386–88.**)

Vergil continues to show Callimachean interest in changes of names (see intro. 2.10; Hollis notes the general similarity between Vergil's lines and a fragment of Rhianus). On Italy's changes of names see also on A. 1. 530–33; on the name of the Tiber see on A. 8.62–64; cf. also the *flavus*/Xanthous plays at A. 7.30–32, *Tiberinus . . . flavus,* and 9.816, *gurgite flavo.*

SERV. 330: INMANI CORPORE THYBRIS hic Tuscorum rex fuit, qui iuxta hunc fluvium pugnans cecidit et ei nomen inposuit: alii volunt istum ipsum regem latrocinatum esse circa huius fluminis ripas et transeuntibus crebras iniurias intulisse, unde Thybris quasi ὕβρις dictus est ἀπὸ τῆς ὕβρεως, id est ab iniuria: nam amabant maiores ubi aspiratio erat Θ ponere. alii, ut supra (3.500) diximus, volunt eos qui de Sicilia venerunt, Thybrin dixisse ad similitudinem fossae Syracusanae, quam fecerunt per iniuriam Afri et Athenienses iuxta civitatis murum: nam quod Livius (1.3.8) dicit, ab Albano rege Tiberino Thybrin dictum, non procedit ideo, quia etiam ante Albam Thybris dictus invenitur (more suggestions in Serv. Auct.; see too Maltby s.vv. Thybris, Tiberis); on 332: ALBVLA NOMEN antiquum hoc nomen a colore habuit.

OVID *F.* 2.389–90 (for Ovid cf. intro. 2.14): Albula, quem Tiberim mersus Tiberinus in undis / reddidit (cf. too *Met.* 14.614–16, *F.* 4.47–48); RHIANUS fr. 25.1–5 P:

Πυρραίην ποτὲ τήν γε παλαιότεροι καλέεσκον
Πύρρης Δευκαλίωνος ἀπ' ἀρχαίης ἀλόχοιο,
Αἱμονίην δ' ἐξαῦτις ἀφ' Αἵμονος, ὅν ῥα Πελασγὸς
γείνατο φέρτατον υἱόν· ὁ δ' αὖ τέκε Θεσσαλὸν Αἵμων,
τοῦ δ' ἄπο Θεσσαλίην λαοὶ μετεφημίξαντο.

Fordyce (1977) on 7.39, Eden (1975), Gransden 1976 ad loc., Hollis (1992); Ogilvie (1970) on Livy 1.3.3, O'Hara (1996).

## A. 8.337–41:

vix ea dicta, dehinc progressus monstrat et aram
et *Carmentalem* Romani nomine portam
quam memorant, nymphae priscum *Carmentis* honorem,
uatis *fatidicae, cecinit* quae prima futuros
Aeneadas magnos et nobile Pallanteum.

There are two etymologies here: using the signpost *Romani nomine . . . quam memorant,* Vergil explicitly tells us that the Porta Carmentalis is named for Carmentis, and then with *fatidicae* and *cecinit* glosses her name to tell us it means "one who sings prophecies." Varro probably connected *cano* and Carmentis, to judge from Augustine.

For the etymological signpost cf. intro. 2.6.

The names Faunus, at 7.81–83, and Manto, at 10.199, are also glossed by *fatidicus.*

The same pattern of person/place double etymologizing is followed at A. 10.198–200, where the name of the town of Mantua is explicitly derived from the name Manto, which is also etymologized by the gloss *fatidicae,* at A. 8.53–54, where the name of the Palatine Hill is (implicitly) derived from the Arcadian name Pallanteum, which is then explicitly said to be named for an ancestor of Evander's named Pallas, and perhaps in A. 8.328–32.

SERV. Auct. 8.336: sed ideo Carmentis appellata a suis, quod divinatione fata caneret: nam antiqui vates carmentes dicebantur; AUG. *Civ.* 4.11 (Varro fr. 149, *GRF* p. 240): quae fata nascentibus canunt et vocantur Carmentes; OVID *F.* 1.467 (suppressing the name, but otherwise, in keeping with the goals of the *Fasti,* typically explicit where Vergil is not; for Ovid cf. intro. 2.14): quae nomen habes a carmine ductum; cf. [VERG.] *Catalepton* 11.61–62, LIVY 1.7.8; more sources in Maltby s.vv. Carmenta, Carmentalis Porta.

Bartelink (1965) 73–74, Gransden (1976) on 340–41.

**A. 8.342–44:** hinc lucum ingentem, quem Romulus acer asylum / rettulit, et gelida monstrat sub rupe *Lupercal* / Parrhasio dictum Panos de more *Lycaei.*

The well-known connection of Latin *lupus* with Greek λύκος underlies this explicit connection (with signpost *dictum;* cf. intro. 2.6) of the name of the Roman Lupercal with Pan Lycaeus. Servius' note suggests that Lupercal is to be derived from *lupus* and *arceo,* because Pan keeps the wolves away from the flock, but Vergil seems not to allude to this.

The words connected etymologically come at the ends of consecutive lines (see intro. 2.9).

Servius and Ovid also mention the explanation that the Lupercal was so called because it was where the wolf *(lupa)* nursed Romulus and Remus; Ovid gives both that derivation, and the one Evander offers here (for Ovid cf. intro. 2.14). Vergil too alludes to this derivation at 8.630–31 (*fetam Mavortis in **antro** / procubuisse **lupam*** . . . ), but of course Evander speaks 8.342–44, and can speak only of pre-Romulan myths.

For λυκ-, lup- see also on A. 9.556–66.

SERV. 343: GELIDA MONSTRAT SVB RVPE LVPERCAL sub monte Palatino est quaedam spelunca, in qua de capro luebatur, id est sacrificabatur: unde et lupercal non nulli dictum putant. alii quod illic lupa Remum et Romulum nutrierit: alii, quod et Vergilius, locum esse hunc sacratum Pani, deo Arcadiae, cui etiam mons Lycaeus in Arcadia consecratus est. et dictus Lycaeus, quod lupos non sinat in oves saevire. ergo ideo et Evander deo gentis suae sacravit locum et nominavit lupercal, quod praesidio ipsius numinis lupi a pecudibus arcerentur; AUG. *Civ.* 18.17 (Varro *Gen. Pop. Rom.* fr. 189, *GRF* p. 250): nec idem propter aliud arbitratur historicus [Varro] in Arcadia tale nomen adfictum Pani Lycaeo et Iovi Lycaeo nisi propter hanc in lupos hominum mutationem. . . . lupus enim graece λύκος dicitur, unde Lycaei nomen apparet inflexum; OVID *F.* 2.421–24:

> illa (sc. lupa) loco nomen fecit, locus ipse Lupercis;
>   magna dati nutrix praemia lactis habet.
> quid vetat Arcadio dictos de monte Lupercos?
>   Faunus in Arcadia templa Lycaeus habet.

Bartelink (1965) 50–51, Gransden (1976), Eden (1975), Fordyce (1977), Porte (1985) 247–48, Ahl (1985) 69–74 (much on λυκ-, *lup-*) and 85 (on Lupercal here), Horsfall (1991) 112, Putnam (1994) 359, O'Hara (1996).

**A. 8.345–46:** nec non et sacri monstrat nemus *Argileti* / testaturque locum et *letum* docet hospitis *Argi*

Varro and Servius connect the name Argiletum either with an Argus (if the text of Varro is correct) said to be buried there or (probably correctly) with *argilla,* the white clay found there. Vergil follows the mythical etymology; in fact here Evander seems to explain to Aeneas the etymology of the name.

The words connected etymologically come at the ends of consecutive lines (see intro. 2.9).

SERV. 345: sane Argiletum, quasi argilletum, multi volunt a pingui terra; alii a fabula. nam Evander Argum quendam suscepit hospitio. qui cum de eius cogitaret interitu, ut ipse regnaret, Evandro hoc non sentiente socii intellexerunt et Argum necarunt: cui Evander et sepulchrum fecit et locum sacravit, non quod ille merebatur, sed hospitalitatis causa. bene autem in hac re Evander inmoratur et docet causas, ne apud hospitem veniat in suspitionem. ergo Argiletum ab Argo illic sacrato et sepulto. (Auct.:) alii Argum occisum dicunt ab ipso Evandro, auxiliante sibi Hercule, quod is ex hospite factus esset inimicus. alii . . . (several more theories); VARRO *LL* 5.157:

Argiletum sunt qui scripserunt ab Argo La⟨ri⟩saeo (Kent; MSS argolaseu), quod is huc venerit ibique sit sepultus, alii ab argilla, quod ibi id genus terrae sit.

Bartelink (1965) 42, Eden (1975).

**A. 8.357–58:** hanc *Ianus* pater, hanc *Saturnus* condidit arcem; / *Ianiculum* huic, illi fuerat *Saturnia* nomen

Explicit aetiologies of the ancient towns of Janus (Ianiculum) and Saturnus (Saturnia), with an implied aetiology of the name of the Ianiculum Hill (which Paulus-Festus connects instead with the verb "to go," *ire*). The difference between the fates of the names Ianiculum, which survives to Vergil's day, and Saturnia, which does not, calls attention to Saturnia. Varro *LL* 5.42 explains that Saturnia was on the Capitoline Hill. Vergil may be calling attention to the way in which Saturn was supplanted by Juppiter Capitolinus—thus another allusion to change of name, and to the end of the Saturnian and beginning of the Jovian age.

Cf. the aetiologies of the names Palatine (see on A. 8.53–54) and Aventine (see on A. 8.231–35).

AUG. *Civ.* 7.4 (following Varro): Saturnum fugientem benignus excepit (Ianus); cum hospite partitus est regnum, ut etiam civitates singulas conderent, iste Ianiculum, ille Saturniam; cf. also Ovid *F.* 1.235–48 (for Ovid cf. intro. 2.14), and many more sources in Maltby s.vv. Ianiculum, Saturnius; differently PAUL.-Fest. p. 93, 1 L: Ianiculum dictum, quod per eum Romanos populus primitus transierit in agrum Etruscum.

On the topography cf. Williams (1973), Eden (1975), and Fordyce (1977). On Saturn and Jupiter in general cf. Thomas (1982); in this passage, O'Hara (1994a) 222 n. 48.

**A. 8.362–63:** "haec" inquit "limina *victor* / *Alcides* subiit"

Servius Auctus sees an allusion both here and at 8.203 to the worship of Hercules Victor at Rome.

Ross notes that at Prop. 4.9.3, *invictos . . . montes* alludes to Hercules Invictus, "the aetiological subject of the poem."

SERV. Auct. 363: Vergilium non tantum ad victoriam praesentem victorem dixisse, sed occulte perpetuo eius epitheto usum debemus accipere, quippe quem Romae sub hoc nomine sacratum coli videbat: nam supra ait (203) "taurosque hac victor agebat," cum de pugna eius alia loqueretur; MACROB. 3.6.9: ut servavit (sc. Vergilius) Apollonis Genitoris proprietatem patrem vocando, idem curavit Herculem vocando victorem: "haec, inquit, limina victor Alcides subiit." Varro Divinarum libro quarto victorem Herculem putat dictum, quod omne genus animalium vicerit.

A. 8.203: Alcides aderat taurosque hac victor agebat; OVID also calls Hercules *victor,* after his version of the Cacus story, at *F.* 1.580 (for Ovid cf. intro. 2.14); cf. too on A. 8.288, Herculeas . . . novercae.

On Propertius, Ross (1975) 156.

**A. 8.364–67?:**

> "aude, hospes, contemnere opes et te quoque dignum
> finge deo, rebusque veni non asper egenis."
> dixit, et *angusti* subter fastigia tecti
> ingentem Aenean duxit stratisque locavit

Gransden: "*angusti:* can a poet of V.'s extraordinary sensitivity to words have failed to intend a word-play on *Augusti* (especially in view of the topography of this passage)?" Perhaps.

Gransden (1976) on 366.

**A. 8.367–68?:** ingentem Aenean duxit stratisque locavit / effultum foliis et pelle Libystidis *ursae*

Tracy suggests that *ursa* here, through its Greek equivalent ἄρκτος or ἄρκας, is suggestive of both the name Arcadia, and the "pioneer simplicity" that Evander is urging upon Aeneas. Caution is perhaps warranted; we will probably not understand this passage until we know why Vergil uses the adjective *Libystis*, which appears in A. 5.37, and previously only in Callim. fr. 676 and Apoll. Rhod. 4.1753.

Tracy (1963) 30; on *Libystis* see Fordyce (1977) ad loc., Clausen (1987) 153 n. 21, and Ahl (1985) 309.

**A. 8.383:** genetrix nato

Bartelink notes the juxtaposition of the apparent cognates *genetrix (g)nato* here and *genitor (g)nati* at 10.800.

Bartelink (1965) 106.

**A. 8.403:** quantum ignes *animae*que valent

There is wordplay here as elsewhere between *animae,* "breath (of the bellows)," and Greek ἄνεμος (wind). See on **A. 1.56–57** *celsa sedet Aeolus arce / sceptra tenens mollitque* ***animos*** *et temperat iras.*

SERV. 403: ANIMAE venti, ἀπὸ τῶν ἀνέμων.

**A. 8.416–17, 422:**

> insula Sicanium iuxta latus Aeoliamque
> erigitur Liparen fumantibus ardua saxis,
> . . . . . . . . . . . . . . . . . . . . . . . . . . .
> *Volcani* domus et *Volcania* nomine *tellus*

At first glance a simple explicit etymology, with a typical etymological signpost in *nomine* (cf. intro. 2.6): the island closest to Sicily is named for Vulcan. Possibly Vergil is alluding to a learned controversy over where Vulcan's workshop was located: see the information in Pfeiffer, Pease, and Fordyce. Aeolia is so called because Aeolus is said to keep the winds there (A. 1.52).

CIC. *ND* 3.22.55: Volcani item complures . . . , quartus Maemalio natus, qui tenuit insulas propter Siciliam quae Volcaniae nominabantur; ISID. 14.6.36: Aeoliae insulae . . . et Volcaniae vocantur, quod et ipsae sicut Aethna ardeant; SERV. 416: physiologia est, cur Vulcanus in his locis officinam habere fingatur inter Aetnam et Liparen: scilicet propter ignem et ventos, quae apta sunt fabris.

Pfeiffer (1949–53) on Callim. *Aet.* fr. 115.11, Pease (1979) on Cic. loc. cit. (pp. 1104–7), Fordyce (1977) 252.

**A. 8.425:** Brontesque Steropesque et nudus membra Pyracmon

As Servius notes, the three Cyclopes are named for their work: Brontes from βροντή, "thunder"; Steropes from στεροπή, "lightning," and Pyracmon from πῦρ, "fire," and, ἄκμων, "anvil."

The first two names are from Hes. *Th.* 140, Βρόντην τε Στερόπην τε καὶ Ἄργην ὀβριμόθυμον (Vergil lengthens his first *-que* in imitation of the Greek practice). Callimachus begins a line with Ἄργην ἢ Στερόπην, with Brontes mentioned at the start of a line seven lines later (*Hymn* 3.68, 75). Apoll. Rhod. 1.510 has the collocation βροντῇ τε στεροπῇ τε; they are common nouns, not names, but occur in a discussion of Cyclopes. Pyracmon occurs first here and is perhaps borrowed from a lost source (see Thomas on transliteration and conflation, although he does not discuss this line).

Mühmelt compares Servius' note with the scholia to Hesiod, which cite an allegorical interpretation of the Cyclopes' names by Zeno.

Ovid puts Brontes and Steropes in a line with Acmonides, a name found in Callim. fr. 498 (see Pfeiffer's notes; for Ovid cf. intro. 2.14).

SERV. 425: BRONTESQVE quid facturi sint ex nominibus docet: nam Brontes a tonitru dictus est, Steropes a fulgetra, ἀπὸ τῆς στεροπῆς. Pyragmon vero, qui numquam a calenti incude discedit, ἀπὸ τοῦ πυρὸς καὶ τοῦ ἄκμονος; nam πῦρ ignis est, ἄκμων incus; SCHOL. Hes. *Th.* 139: Ζήνων (*SVF* 1.118 Arn.) φυσικώτερον τὰς ἐγκυκλίους περιφορὰς εἰρῆσθαι· ἐν χρόνῳ γάρ τινι ἐγένοντο ἐγκύκλιοι περιφοραί τοῦ πυρὸς καὶ τοῦ ἀέρος. καὶ (one manuscript has διὸ καὶ) τὰ ὀνόματα αὐτῶν Βρόντην καὶ Στερόπην· Ἄργην δέ, ἐπειδή φασιν ἀργῆτα κεραυνόν.

Cf. Quercus etc. in A. 9.684–87; OVID *F.* 4.288: Brontes et Steropes Acmonidesque solent.

Thomas (1986) 193–95, Mühmelt (1965) 64 (preferring some different readings in the Hesiod scholia; I print the text of Di Gregorio), Hardie (1986) 103 n. 48.

**A. 8.500:** flos veterum *virtus*que *virum*

On the frequent association of *virtus* and *vir,* see on **A. 1.566.**

**A. 8.600–601?:** *Silvano* fama est veteres sacrasse Pelasgos, / arvorum pecorisque deo, *lucum*que diemque

Perhaps the reference to a *lucus* looks to the obvious meaning of the name *Silvanus*. Cf. on A. 6.763–65: Silvius . . . silvis.

Bartelink (1965) 70 n. 4 (mentions almost in passing).

**A. 8.630–32:** fecerat et viridi fetam Mavortis in *antro* / procubuisse *lupam*, geminos huic ubera circum / ludere pendentis pueros et lambere matrem

The grotto here seems to be the Lupercal, whose name was derived, in lines 343–44 above, from the connection between *lupus* and Pan Lykaeus. These lines suggest an alternate derivation, that the Lupercal is so called because the *lupa* nourished Romulus and Remus there. Both Ovid in the *Fasti* and Servius mention this explanation, and Ovid like Vergil offers both; see on **8.342–44**, and esp. intro. 2.14, for Ovid's commentary on these Vergilian lines.

O'Hara (1996).

**A. 8.641:** caesa iungebant foedera porca

Servius derives *foedera* from *porca foede occisa,* "a pig foully slaughtered"; Vergil may allude to that etymology here, unless Servius or a source has simply invented it on the basis of Vergil's line. On this problem see on **A. 1.164–65.**

SERV. 641: IVNGEBANT FOEDERA PORCA foedera, ut diximus supra (1.62), dicta sunt a porca foede et crudeliter occisa; *(Auct.:)* nam cum ante gladiis configeretur, a fetialibus inventum ut silice feriretur ea causa, quod antiqui Iovis signum lapidem silicem putaverunt esse. Cicero foedera a fide putat dicta; SERV. A. 1.62: "foedus" . . . dictum vel a fetialibus, . . . per quos fiunt foedera, vel a porca foede, hoc est lapidibus occisa; AUG. *Dialect.* 6.10ff.: foederis nomen quod res foeda non sit; quod si a foeditate porci dictum est . . . , redit origo ad illam vicinitatem, cum id quod fit ab eo per quod fit nominatur . . . , aut per efficientiam . . . , ut hoc ipsum a foeditate porci, per quem foedus efficiatur; alternate derivations (e.g. *a fide*) in Maltby.

Ahl (1985) 304–7.

**A. 8.652–53:** in summo custos Tarpeiae *Manlius* arcis / stabat pro templo et *Capitolia* celsa tenebat

Vergil alludes to and explains the cognomen *Capitolinus,* awarded to Manlius after he (and the geese) helped ward off the Gauls, and still worn by a branch of the Manlii in Vergil's day. For glosses of suppressed names see intro. 2.7.

Ogilvie says that "In reality the Manlii, like the Sestii and the Quinctii, assumed the cognomen to distinguish one branch of the family which lived on the Capitol."

Cf. the allusion to Manlius' son's cognomen Torquatus in 8.661.

LIVY 5.31: M. Manlius, cui postea Capitolino fuit cognomen (for the story cf. Livy 5.47).

Ogilvie (1970) 694, 734, Gransden (1976) on 652–72.

## A. 8.657, 659–61:

> *Galli* per dumos aderant. . . .
> . . . . . . . . . . . . . . . . .
> aurea caesaries ollis atque aurea vestis,
> virgatis lucent sagulis, tum *lactea* colla
> **auro** *innectuntur*

Isidore says that Vergil gives the Gauls "milky-white throats" *(lactea colla)* because the name *Gallus* is derived from Greek γάλα, "milk," because of the Gauls' light skin coloring. The etymology may have been derived from this passage, but Hardie notes that A. 8.660 and 10.137 (Ascanius) present the first uses of *lacteus* of flesh (he sees in the word an allusion to an ivory relief on the doors of the Palatine temple of Apollo dedicated in 28 B.C.).

Williams notes the allusive *aition* in 660–61: "*auro innectuntur* refers to the famous Gallic *torques,* the necklace from which Manlius' son got his cognomen Torquatus." Cf. the allusion to Manlius' cognomen Capitolinus in 8.652–53, and for glosses of names not expressed see intro. 2.7.

Gallus: ISID. 9.2.104 (sim. at 14.4.25 and Hier. *ad Galat.* 1.2 [citing Lactantius]): Galli a candore corporis nuncupati sunt: γάλα enim graece lac dicitur. unde Sibylla sic eos appellat, cum ait de his (Verg. A. 8.660) tunc lactea colla / auro innectuntur; cf. on G. 4.126, where Nisbet suggests a connection between the river Galesus and γάλα; cf. THEOC. 11.19–20: ὦ λευκὰ Γαλάτεια . . . λευκοτέρα πακτᾶς, where "the etymological wordplay . . . is intended to point to the connection of the name Galatea and γάλα (milk)" (Du Quesnay, who translates, "o white Galatea . . . whiter than cream cheese"—cf. on E. 2.6).

Torquatus: QUADRIG. ap. Aul. Gell. 9.13.18–19: (Titus Manlius) torquem (Gallo) detraxit eamque sanguinolentam sibi in collum imponit. quo ex facto ipse posterique eius Torquati sunt cognominati (cf. Cic. *Off.* 3.112 and *Fin.* 1.23, Livy 1.10.13).

Cerda (1617) 259, Bartelink (1965) 70 n. 1 (skeptical), Hardie (1986) 120–25 (on *lacteus* see also Harrison [1991] on 10.137–38), Du Quesnay (1979) 44, Williams (1973) on 660.

## A. 8.663: exsultantis Salios

Varro and others (full references in Maltby) derive the name of the dancing priests, the Salii, from the verb *salio*, "to leap," or *sal(i)to*, "to dance." Vergil's *exsultantis* is a gloss alluding to that etymology. Servius Auctus and others also mention a derivation from the name of Salius, a companion of Aeneas mentioned at A. 5.298, 321.

Ovid explicitly derives the name from *saltus* (for Ovid cf. intro. 2.14).

SERV. 663: dicti Salii ideo quod circa aras saliunt et triupdiant. *(Auct.:)* alii a Salio, Aeneae comite, dictos volunt; VARRO *LL* 5.85: Salii ab salitando; ISID. 18.50: Saltatores autem nominatos Varro dicit ab Arcade Salio, quem Aeneas in Italiam secum adduxit, quique primo docuit Romanos adolescentes nobiles saltare; FEST. p. 438, 27 L: Salios a saliendo et saltando dictos esse quamvis dubitari non debeat, tamen Polemon ait Arcada quendam fuisse, nomine Salium, quem Aeneas a Mantinea in Italiam deduxerit, qui iuvenes Italicos ἐνόπλιον saltationem docuerit; OVID *F.* 3.387: iam dederat (sc. Numa) Saliis a saltu nomina ducta.

Bartelink (1965) 82, Eden (1975) on 663f., Porte (1985) 245.

## A. 8.678–81?:

hinc Augustus agens Italos in proelia *Caesar*
cum patribus populoque, penatibus et magnis dis,
stans celsa in puppi, geminas cui tempora flammas
laeta vomunt *patrium*que aperitur vertice *sidus*

This picture may be part of the network of omens and etymological wordplay involving shooting stars/comets/*coma*/*caesaries*/Caesar; see on **A. 2.679–98.**

**A. 8.720:** ipse sedens niveo *candentis* limine *Phoebi*

*Candentis* glosses the name *Phoebus* = Φοῖβος, "bright, radiant" (see intro. 2.2). The idea of Apollo as sun god may be felt here, especially as Vergil's line echoes Lucretius 6.1197, *candenti lumine solis* (= *Phoebi,* also glossed by *candenti*).

Cf. **A. 4.268–69** *ipse deum tibi me* ***claro*** *demittit* ***Olympo,*** where Servius says, *Olympus quasi* ὁλολαμπής . . . *unde addidit "claro," ut (3.693) Plemyrium undosum.*

Cf. Hardie (1986) 356 n. 64, who provides references for the syncretism of Apollo and the sun, and Fordyce (1977) on 720, who notes however that Apollo is here "identified with his temple," which "was of white marble"; he suggests that "*candentis* reinforces *niveo.*"

**A. 8.724–26:** hic Nomadum genus et discinctos *Mulciber* Afros, / hic Lelagas Carasque sagittiferosque Gelonos / finxerat; Euphrates ibat iam *mollior* undis

Vulcan is called *Mulciber* as he shapes the shield; Servius and Macrobius note the connection with *mulceo,* "stroke, soften." Paulus-Festus (and so probably the Augustan Verrius Flaccus) connects the name with *mulceo* and *mollio;* could *mollior* in 726 allude to this?

SERV. 724: MULCIBER Vulcanus, ab eo quod totum ignis permulcet: *(Auct.:)* aut quod ipse mulcatus pedes sit, sicut quibusdam videtur: aut quod igni mulceatur; MACROB. 6.5.2: "et discinctos Mulciber Afros" Mulciber est Vulcanus quod ignis sit et omnia mulceat ac domet. Accius in Philoctete: "heu Mulciber arma ignavo invicta es fabricatus manu"; PAUL.-Fest. p. 129, 5 L: Mulciber Vulcanus a molliendo scilicet ferro dictus. mulcere enim mollire sive lenire est (more sources in Maltby).

Hardie (1986) 361 n. 79, Eden (1975) on 724, Clausen (1987) 121, Ahl (1985) 172–73.

**A. 8.728?:** indomitique Dahae, et pontem *indignatus Araxes*

Citing the scholia to Aeschylus, Hardie suggests a connection between the Araxes and the verb ἀράσσω, "strike hard, beat," and that "the name is perhaps chosen for . . . its violent connotations."

For names of rivers see the annotations to intro. 2.4b.

SCHOL. Aesch. *PV* 717: τόν Ἀράξην, παρὰ τὸ ἀράσσειν καὶ ἠχεῖν τὰ κύματα αὐτοῦ; ISID. 13.21.16: Araxis amnis Armeniae . . . dictus quod rapacitate cuncta prosternit.

Cerda (1617) 276, Hardie (1986) 208 n. 132.

**A. 8.730–31:** miratur rerumque ignarus imagine gaudet / attollens umero *famam*que et *fata* nepotum.

For the connection see on **A. 7.79** *illustrem fama fatisque.*

Bartelink (1965) 105.

**A. 9.33–36:**

hic subitam nigro *glomerari* pulvere nubem
prospiciunt Teucri ac tenebras insurgere campis.
primus ab adversa conclamat mole Caicus:
"quis *globus*, o cives, caligine volvitur atra?"

Conington: "'Globus' is explained by 'glomerari.'"

ISID. 16.1.3: gleba, quod sit globus; pulveris enim collectione conpingitur et in uno adunatur; GLOSS. (Goetz) 5.547.2: glomeravit insini vel globi rotundam efficit.

Conington (1963) on 36, Bartelink (1965) 98.

**A. 9.80–81?:** tempore quo primum Phrygia *formabat* in *Ida* / Aeneas classem

Hardie suggests that "V. may . . . pun on the similarity between Ida and ἰδέα (Platonic) 'form,'" but I am somewhat skeptical.

Hardie (1994) on 80.

**A. 9.128–29?:** his *Iuppiter* ipse / *auxilium* solitum eripuit

Servius sees an allusion to the derivation of the name *Iuppiter* from *iuvans pater,* "the father who helps." But this is perhaps to miss the point of *solitum,* which Turnus applies to the Trojans' "customary means of escape," flight. Servius Auctus offers the latter view. Cf. the play on *Iuturna-iuvare* at **A. 10.439–40**, 12.813–14, and 12.872.

SERV. 126: IVPPITER IPSE scilicet qui omnibus praestare consuevit: unde et Iuppiter dictus est, quasi iuvans pater. ergo "auxilium solitum" non circa Troianos accipimus, sed quod ipse praestare consuevit; SERV. Auct.: alii "auxilium solitum" auxilium fugae accipiunt; ENN. *Var.* 57–58 V *(Epicharmus):* Haec propter *Iupiter* sunt ista quae dico tibi, / qua mortalis atque urbes beluasque omnis *iuvat;* OVID *Am.* 2.1.19: *Iupiter,* ignoscas: nil me tua tela *iuvabunt* (note framing; for Ovid cf. intro. 2.14); cf. the paronomasia at PLAUT. *Pers.* 755: quam bene nos, *Iuppiter, iuvisti* (more sources in Maltby).

Hardie (1994) on 128; on Ovid, see McKeown (1987) 49, on Ennius, Feeney (1991) 120–21.

**A. 9.215:** absenti *ferat* in*fer*ias **decoretque sepulcro**

*Inferiae* was thought to be connected with the verb *infero.* Cf. also Hardie: "the collocation [of *sepulcro*] with *decoret* may suggest a pun on *pulc(h)er;* see Maltby s.v. *sepulcrum.*"

PAUL.-Fest. p. 99, 26 L (sim. 10, 23): inferiae sacrificia, quae dis Manibus inferebant.

Bartelink (1965) 98, Hardie (1994) ad loc.

**A. 9.225:** laxabant *curas* et *corda* oblita laborum

Citing Varro's *cura quod cor urat* (*LL* 6.46), Hardie calls *curas* et *corda* "an assonance probably based on an etymological pun." Cf. on **A. 1.208–9,** *curisque ingentibus aeger . . . premit altum corde dolorem.*

Hardie (1994) ad loc.

**A. 9.324–30:**

sic memorat vocemque premit, simul ense superbum
*Rhamnetem* adgreditur, qui forte tapetibus altis
exstructus toto proflabat pectore somnum,
rex idem et **regi Turno** gratissimus augur,
sed non augurio potuit depellere pestem.
tris iuxta famulos temere inter tela iacentis
armigerumque *Remi* premit

The connection of a man named Rhamnes with a man named Remus alludes to the derivation of one of the old Roman tribes, the R(h)amnenses, from the name Romulus (further suggested here by the name of his brother Remus).

In 327, could the collocation *regi Turno* allude to a connection between the name Turnus and an Etruscan word for "ruler?" See on **A. 7.56.**

VARRO *LL* 5.55 (= Enn. *Ann.* fr. lix Sk.): Tribus . . . nominatae, ut ait Ennius, Titienses ab Tatio, Ramnenses ab Romulo, Luceres, ut Iunius (*GRF* p. 121), ab Lucumone; sed omnia haec vocabula tusca, ut Volnius (*GRF* p. 126), qui tragoedias tuscas scripsit, dicebat; CIC. *Rep.* 2.8.14: populumque et suo et Tati nomine et Lucumonis; SERV. A. 5.560: alteram Ramnetum a Romulo; more in *RE* 1 s.v. Ramnes, col. 137–39 (Rosenberg).

Bréguet (1956) 54–62, *EV* s.v. Ramnete (Fo).

**A. 9.386–88?:** Nisus abit; iamque imprudens evaserat hostis / atque locos qui post *Albae* de nomine dicti / *Albani* (tum rex stabula alta Latinus habebat)

A problematic passage. Nisus has reached the "places later called Alban, after the name of Alba, which then were serving as the stables of King Latinus." Why this detail? The stress on the name resembles that of the name *Arae* at A. 1.108–10, which, like 9.387–88, some editors have wanted to delete. And what are these *loci Albani,* Alban places? Or are they Alban groves, *lucos,* as some manuscripts have, despite the quantity, or perhaps lakes, *lacus*? The etymological signpost (cf. intro. 2.6) suggests that the answer must somehow involve the significance of the name Alba. Elsewhere the connection of the name Alba with the "white" sow that appears to Aeneas is stressed (cf. on **A. 3.389–93**), but there is no clear allusion to that here.

Another possibility is that here and at 12.134–36 Vergil alludes to a derivation from a "pre-Indo-European word meaning 'mountain'" (Ogilvie). As Servius notes, Vergil probably glosses the name Alps as being from this root at G. 3.474 *aerias Alpis* (see there). There is no clear allusion to that etymology here (*alta* in 388 seems to mean something like "deep"; Norden thinks *stabula alta* at A. 6.179ff. is borrowed from an earlier poet). The words *summo* and *tumulo* are featured in 12.134–36, which also has an otherwise unnecessary signpost.

For Vergil's plays on *arduus, altus,* etc. see on 3.270–71 *Neritos ardua.*

SERV. 385: ALBAE DE NOMINE vel porcae, vel civitatis, vel regis Albani, cui successit Procas; LIVY 1.3.3: Ascanius . . . novam ipse aliam (sc. urbem) sub Albano monte condidit quae ab situ porrectae in dorso urbis Longa Alba appellata (Bertoldi may be wrong to quote this passage of Livy to support his claim that Alba = "mountain," because Livy's reference to *situ* seems to refer instead to the second part of the name, *Longa*).

A. 12.134–36: At Iuno ex *summo* (qui nunc Albanus habetur; / tum neque nomen erat neque honos aut gloria monti) / prospiciens tumulo campum aspectabat.

Ogilvie (1970) on Livy 1.3.3 (p. 43, quoted above on A. 8.328–32); on Alba = mountain, Bertoldi (1936) 179–88; Williams (1973) on 9.386f.: ("nothing is known of the *loci Albani,* and some editors read *lacus Albani,* but the lake was too far away from the Trojan camp to make sense here"); Hardie (1994) on 387–88; *EV* s.v. Albani loci (Castagnoli); Norden (1981) on 6.179ff. On excising the lines cf. the apparatus of Ribbeck (1966).

**A. 9.463–64?:** acratasque *acies* in proelia cogunt, / quisque suos, variisque *acuunt* rumoribus iras.

Hardie suggests "word-play on the literal sense of *acies* 'sharp edge,'" brought out by *acuunt* in 464.

Hardie (1994) ad loc.

**A. 9.495–96?:** aut tu, magne pater divum, miserere, tuoque / *invisum* hoc detrude caput sub *Tartara* telo

Hardie suggests that in addition to the primary meaning on *invisum,* "hated," these lines also offer "perhaps a hint of the other *invisiu* 'unseen,' taken proleptically: "thrust me down to Tartarus [ = Hades, 'Α-ίδης 'the unseen'] where I shall be unseen." Perhaps.

Hardie (1994) ad loc.

### A. 9.556–59, 563–66:

> at pedibus longe melior *Lycus* inter et hostis
> inter et arma fuga muros tenet, altaque certat
> prendere tecta manu sociumque attingere dextras.
> quem Turnus pariter cursu teloque secutus
> . . . . . . . . . . . . . . . . . . . . . . . . . . . . .
> qualis ubi aut leporem aut candenti corpore cycnum
> sustulit alta petens pedibus Iovis armiger uncis,
> quaesitum aut matri multis balatibus agnum
> Martius a stabulis rapuit *lupus*.

Lycus is compared to a wolf; his name = λύκος, "wolf." See on A. 8.342–44, *Lupercal* / Parrhasio dictum Panos de more *Lycaei*.

Ahl (1985) 320.

**A. 9.570?:** *Lucetium* portae subeuntem *ignisque ferentem*

Servius says that this is the only name in Vergil found in no other author, and that it is an Oscan name for Jupiter, derived from *lux*, "light," which Jupiter brings to mortals. Could the derivation from *lux* be suggested by *ignisque ferentem,* with the etymological wordplay thus framing the line? See intro. 2.8 for framing.

SERV. 567: LVCETIVM solum hoc nomen est, quod dictum a Vergilio in nullo alio reperitur auctore. sane lingua Osca Lucetius est Iuppiter, dictus a luce, quam praestare hominibus dicitur. ipse est nostra lingua Diespiter, id est diei pater: Horatius (C. 1.34.5–7) "namque Diespiter . . . plerumque per purum"; AUL. Gell. 5.12.6: (Iupiter) dictus est . . . Lucetius, quod nos die et luce quasi vita ipsa afficeret et iuvaret. "lucetium" autem Iovem Cn. Naevius in libris Belli Poenici appellat; PAUL.-Fest. p. 102, 4 L: Lucetium Iovem appellabant, quod eum lucis esse causam credebant; MACROB. 1.15.14: cum Iovem accipiamus lucis auctorem, unde et Lucetium Salii in carminibus canunt.

Saunders (1940) 554, Hardie (1994) ad loc.

**A. 9.618:** biforem dat tibia cantum

Hardie suggests that "*biforem* . . . may hint at an etymology of διθύραμβος, in antiquity often derived from δί-θυρος = *biforis* 'having two doors'" (cf. *Etym. Mag.* and Maltby s.v.). He points to the etymology of tragedy implied at G. 2.380–83.

Hardie (1994) ad loc.

**A. 9.640, 652?:** (Apollo) his victorem adfatur *Iulum* . . . atque his ardentem dictis adfatur *Iulum*

Servius Auctus elsewhere, citing an L. Caesar (whom some would associate with the *Origo Gentis Romanae,* while others like Thilo would emend to make him a I[ulius] Caesar), says that Ascanius was first called Iulus after he had (in the non-Vergilian version) killed Mezentius. The name is said to be derived either from ἰοβόλος, "skilled at archery," or ἴουλος, "first beard," because he was a young man when he made the kill. There *may* be some significance here in Apollo using this name after Ascanius has killed Numanus Remulus with bow and arrow. At 7.475–99, when Ascanius kills Silvia's deer with his bow, he is called Iulus twice (478, 493), but Ascanius once (497). All in all, however, Vergil uses *Ascanius* 42 times, *Iulus* 35; this makes it difficult to claim significance in any particular choice.

SERV. Auct. 1.267: et occiso Mezentio Ascanium, sicut L. Caesar scribit, Iulum coeptum vocari, vel quasi ἰοβόλον, id est, sagittandi peritum, vel a prima barbae lanugine, quam ἴουλον Graeci dicunt, quae ei tempore victoriae nascebatur.

Hardie (1994) on 590–91.

**A. 9.641:** macte nova *vir*tute, *puer*

On the frequent association of the words *virtus* and *vir,* see on **A. 1.566**. Here and at A. 12.435 *(disce, puer, virtutem ex me)* the words *vir* and *puer* (in both cases addressed to Ascanius) are virtually juxtaposed. The exploitation of the etymology of *virtus* in both passages suggests that both scenes have something to tell us about what it means to be a *puer,* or a *vir,* and more interestingly what it means to go from being a *puer* to being a *vir*.

Hardie (1994) ad loc., Petrini (n.d.) chap. 5.

**A. 9.646–48?:** Ascaniumque petit; forma tum vertitur oris / antiquum in *Buten*. hic Dardanio Anchisae / *armiger* ante fuit fidusque ad limina custos

Kraggerud connects Butes with the constellation Bootes and sees connections between *currus* (ἅρμα) and *arma, custos* and *Arcturus*.

Kraggerud (1960) 32–36.

**A. 9.684–87:**

continuo *Quercens* et pulcher *Aquiculus* armis
et praeceps animi *Tmarus* et Mavortius *Haemon*
agminibus totis aut versi terga dedere
aut ipso portae posuere in limine vitam.

In 679–82, Pandarus and Bitias are compared to oaks *(quercus)*. In 684–85 the four warriors seem to have etymologically obvious names suggestive of Latin words in 684 (Quercens—quercus, Aquiculus—aqua) and Greek words in 685 (Tmarus—τέμνω, τμῆσις, Haemon—αἵμα [as at G. 1.491–92 sanguine—Haemi]). I see no motivation here, but the suggestive names somewhat resemble the "speaking names" of the Cyclopes at 8.425.

Cf. Hardie (1994) ad loc.

**A. 9.715–16:** tum sonitu Prochyta alta tremit durumque cubile / *Inarime* Iovis imperiis imposta Typhoeo.

Conington: Vergil "has identified Pithecusa or Aenaria with the Homeric Ἄριμα (ὄρη), which he calls 'Inarime,' apparently mistaking *Il.* 2.783 εἰν Ἀρίμοις, ὅθι φασὶ Τυφωέος ἔμμεναι εὐνάς."

But such "mistakes" are often deliberate in Vergil (see intro. 2.1a). Servius' note and other ancient sources (see e.g. Kirk) show that the location and name of Arima were a subject of debate in antiquity. Vergil's "error" may also be described as a reinterpretation of a text with no word division (see on A. 1.719–22 on *Acidalia/ Kidalia*).

For a gloss on the name Pithecusae (to which Vergil does not seem to allude), see Lycophron 691.

SERV. Auct. 712: Hanc (Prochytam) Naevius in primo belli Punici de cognata Aeneae nomen accepisse dicit. sed Inarime nunc Aenaria dicitur. et saepe fulgoribus petitur ob hoc quod Typhoeum premat, et quia in † eamdi contumeliam simiae missae sunt, quas Etruscorum lingua arimos dicunt: ob quam causam Pithecusam etiam vocitant: licet diversi auctores varie dicant: nam alii hanc insulam Typhoeum, alii Enceladum tradunt premere. et putatur nove dictum "Inarime," quod et singulari numero, et addita syllaba dixerit, cum Homerus εἰν Ἀρίμοις posuerit, ut prior syllaba praepositionis locum obtineat. Livius in libro nonagesimo quarto Inarimen in Maeoniae partibus esse dicit, ubi per quinquaginta milia terrae igni exustae sunt. hoc etiam Homerum significasse vult.

Conington (1963) ad loc., Hardie (1994) ad loc., Kirk (1985) on *Il.* 2.781–84: "It is clear that ancient critics did not know which particular region that signified, and that local claims were made on behalf of several different apparently lightning-blasted or generally volcanic areas."

**A. 9.753–54?:** conlapsos *artus* atque *arma* cruenta cerebro / sternit humi moriens

Hardie suggests "etymological play in *artus* atque *arma*," but I am skeptical.

Hardie (1994) ad loc.

**A. 9.771–72?:** ferarum / vastatorem Amycum

Mørland suggests a connection between the name Amycus and the verb ἀμύσσω, "scratch, wound," and an allusion to this in the description of Amycus as *ferarum vastatorem*. Perhaps doubtful.

Mørland (1965) 72.

**A. 9.815–17:** tum demum praeceps saltu sese omnibus armis / in fluvium dedit. ille suo cum gurgite *flavo* / accepit venientem

The Tiber may be linked to the Homeric Xanthus River by the description of its waters as *flavus* = ξανθός = Xanthus. See on **A. 7.30–32**.

**A. 10.2?:** *concilium*que *vocat* diuum pater atque hominum rex

One derivation in Festus links *concilium* with *concalo* = *voco*, a verb perhaps coined for the sake of the etymology on the analogy of καλέω. If this were known in Vergil's day, this line could offer a gloss.

PAUL.-Fest. p. 33, 39 L: concilium dicitur a populi consensu; sive concilium dicitur a concalando, id est vocando.

This example was suggested to me by Stephen Wheeler.

**A. 10.79–80:** quid soceros legere et gremiis abducere *pactas, / pacem* orare manu, praefigere puppibus arma?

For the derivation of *pax* from *pango,* see on **A. 4.99,** ***pacem** aeternam **pactos**que hymenaeos.*

**A. 10.145:** et *Capys:* hinc nomen *Campanae* ducitur *urbi*

Williams: "Capys has already been mentioned several times; here Virgil pauses to link him etymologically with the famous Campanian town of Capua." The actual name Capua is suppressed here (see intro. 2.7).

SERV. 145: ET CAPYS HINC NOMEN CAMPANAE DVCITVR VRBI iste quidem dicit a Capy dictam Campaniam. sed Livius (4.37.1) vult a locis campestribus dictam, in quibus sita est. sed constat eam a Tuscis conditam viso falconis augurio, qui Tusca lingua capys dicitur, unde est Campania nominata. Tuscos autem omnem paene Italiam subiugasse manifestum est; SERV. Auct.: HINC NOMEN CAMPANAE DVCITVR VRBI iste quidem hoc dicit, sicut Ovidius (*F.* 4.45), qui Capyn de Troianis esse commemorat "ille dedit Capyi repetita vocabula Troiae," Coeliusque Troianum Capyn condidisse Capuam tradidit eumque Aeneae fuisse sobrinum; PAUL.-Fest. p. 38, 9 L: quidam a Capye appellatum ferunt . . . alii a planitie regionis; OVID *F.* 4.45 (quoted by Serv., for Ovid cf. intro. 2.14); LIVY 4.37: Capuamque ab duce eorum Capye vel, quod proprius vero est, a campestri agro appellatam.

Bartelink (1965) 45, Ogilvie (1970) 591, Williams (1973) on 145, Harrison (1991) on 145.

**A. 10.184:** et Pyrgi veteres *intempestae*que *Graviscae*

Here *intempestae* is a gloss on *Graviscae,* named (as Servius says, citing Cato) from its "unwholesome air" *(gravis aer).* For single-epithet glosses cf. intro. 2.2.

SERV. 184: ut ait Cato (= fr. 5, *GRF* p. 11), ideo Graviscae dictae sunt, quod gravem aerem sustinent.

Bartelink (1965) 48, Knight (1944) 198, Rehm (1932) 13, 72, Marouzeau (1940) 72, Harrison (1991) on 184.

**A. 10.185–92:**

Non ego te, *Ligurum* ductor fortissime bello,
transierim, *Cunare,* et paucis comitate Cupavo,
cuius olorinae surgunt de vertice pennae
(crimen, Amor, vestrum) formaeque insigne paternae.
namque ferunt *luctu Cycnum* Phaethontis amati,

populeas inter frondes umbramque sororum
dum ***canit*** et maestum Musa solatur amorem,
**canentem** molli pluma duxisse senectam

Ahl suggests that the identification of a singer named Cycnus (Swan) as a Ligurian "involves a wordplay with the Greek λιγύς, 'clear and melancholy.'"

Ahl also suggests a connection between the name *Cunare* (variously spelled in the manuscripts as Cinyr(a)e, Cynir(a)e, Cinire, as Mynors' ap. crit. notes) and the Greek verb κινύρομαι (cf. *luctu* in 189) or, more interestingly, the noun κινυρός, which occurs only once in Apoll. Rhod. (at 4.605) and once in Homer (*Il.* 17.5).

For the simple wordplay between *cănit* and *cānentem* cf. 10.417–18 *cănens-cānentia,* and on **A. 2.606–7** *pareo-parentis.*

PLATO *Phaedr.* 237 a 7: Ἄγετε δή, ὦ Μοῦσαι, εἴτε δι' ᾠδῆς εἶδος λίγειαι, εἴτε διὰ γένος μουσικὸν τὸ Λιγύων ταύτην ἔσχετ' ἐπωνυμίαν.

Ahl (1985) 33, Woodhead (1928) 68, Putnam (1986) 43–45 (on Vergil and on Ligurinus in Hor. *C.* 4.1.33), Keith (1992) 145.

**A. 10.198–200:** ille etiam patriis agmen ciet Ocnus ab oris, / *fatidicae Mantus* et Tusci filius amnis, / qui muros matrisque dedit tibi, *Mantua*, nomen

A double etymology, with *nomen* as a signpost (cf. intro. 2.6). The name of the town Mantua is explicitly derived from the name Manto, whom Servius identifies as the daughter of the prophet Tiresias. Her name is then implicitly etymologized by the gloss *fatidicae* (as if Manto < μαντεύεσθαι). For the explicit etymology of a place-name from a personal name, along with an implied etymology of the personal name, cf. **A. 8.337–41,** on Carmenta.

The names Faunus, at A. 7.81–82, and Carmenta, at 8.341, are also glossed by *fatidicus.*

SERV. 198: Ocnus . . . Mantuam dicitur condidisse, quam a matris nomine appellavit: nam fuit filius Tiberis et Mantus, Tiresiae Thebani vatis filiae, quae post patris interitum ad Italiam venit; SERV. Auct.: alii Manto, filiam Herculis, vatem fuisse dicunt. . . . alii a Tarchone Tyrrheni fratre conditam dicunt: Mantuam autem ideo nominatam, quod Etrusca lingua Mantum Ditem patrem appellant, cui cum ceteris urbibus et hanc consecrauit.

Bartelink (1965) 65, Harrison (1991) on 199.

**A. 10.225:** fandi doctissima Cymodocea

In *fandi doctissima* Vergil plays with the connection of the verb *fari* with the noun *fata,* "fate." Cymodocea is not just "best at speaking"; she is "best at speaking prophetically." Vergil virtually translates the phrase πολυφράδμων ὑποφήτης ("very wise [or very eloquent] spokesman"), used by Apollonius at *Arg.* 1.1310–11 to describe Glaucus, who swims up to the Argo, grabs the ship's keel (as Cymodocea grabs Aeneas' ship), and prophesies to the Argonauts.

On the connection between *for, fari,* and *fatum* see on **A. 1.261–62:** ***fabor*** *enim, quando haec te cura remordet, / longius et volvens* ***fatorum*** *arcana movebo.*

O'Hara (1990) 40–41.

## A. 10.270–73?:

ardet apex capiti cristisque a vertice flamma
funditur et vastos umbo vomit aureus ignis:
non secus ac liquida si quando nocte *cometae*
sanguinei lugubre rubent

The comparison of the flame from or behind Aeneas' head to comets puts this picture into the network of omens and possible etymological wordplay involving shooting stars/comets/*coma*/*caesaries*/Caesar; see on **A. 2.679–98.**

**A. 10.308–9:** nec Turnum segnis retinet mora, sed rapit *acer* / totam *aciem* in Teucros et contra in litore sistit.

For the use of these cognates (cf. Walde-Hofmann s.v. *acies*) near one another cf. also 12.661–62: *Messapus et acer Atinas / sustentant acies.*

ENN. *Trag.* fr. 333 J: acrem aciem; cf. SEN. *NQ* 7.11.

Bartelink (1965) 101.

**A. 10.315:** inde *Lichan* ferit *exsectum* iam matre perempta

Saunders notes that Hesychius glosses λιχάς with ἀπότομος and suggests that *exsectum* may gloss the name Lichas in Vergil. See intro. 2.2 for single-epithet glosses.

Saunders (1940) 540.

**

## A. 10.324–27:

tu quoque, flaventem *prima lanugine malas*
dum sequeris Clytium *infelix*, nova gaudia, *Cydon,*
Dardania stratus dextra, securus amorum
qui iuvenum tibi semper erant, miseranda iaceres

Subtle and erudite etymologizing involving self-imitation by Vergil. The phrase *prima lanugine malas,* "cheeks with the first fuzz of a beard," recalls the *tenera lanugine mala,* "apples with soft fuzz," of E. 2.51, especially when followed by the name Cydon. Servius, albeit with some degree of botanical imprecision (see Boyd, and below on **E. 2.51**), identified the *mala* of E. 2 as *Cydonia mala,* "quinces," and saw an allusion to the well-known Cretan (Cydonian = Cretan) love for boys in that passage as well.

Boyd:

> by describing Cydon's beloved in words reminiscent of *Ecl.* 2.51 . . . Virgil has effected a clever word-play. Through the collocation of the words *lanugine*

> *malas* and *Cydon* at successive line-ends, Virgil not only recalls the homosexual love for Alexis [in *Ecl.* 2] but also suggests that an etymological connection exists between *malum* and *mala*. . . .
>
> The epithet *infelix* used to describe Cydon makes the Virgilian pun even more elaborate: aside from the predominant sense of *felix/infelix* as happy/unhappy or lucky/unlucky, Virgil recalls the literal sense [of *infelix* as "infertile"] as described by Cato (Paul. ex Fest. p. 92): *felices arbores Cato dixit, quae fructum ferunt, infelices quae non ferunt.*

For wordplay at the end of consecutive lines see intro. 2.9. For other Vergilian wordplay involving *mala* see on **A. 7.740** *maliferae . . . Abellae.*

Boyd (1983), Harrison (1991) on 324 (unduly skeptical, because of vowel quantities of Cȳdon and Cy̆donius); on vowel quantities see intro. 2.1.

**A. 10.356–57:** magno discordes aethere *venti* / proelia ceu tollunt *animis* et viribus aequis

West notes the play here between *animos* (anger, spirits, animosity) and Greek ἄνεμος (wind). See on **A. 1.56–57,** *celsa sedet Aeolus arce / sceptra tenens mollitque* ***animos*** *et temperat iras.*

West (1969) 48 n. 6, Harrison (1991) on 356–57.

**A. 10.369–70?:** Per vos et *fortia facta* / per *ducis Evandri* nomen devictaque bella

Mørland suggests a play on *fortis* in the sense of "brave, courageous," and the name Evander, suggestive of εὐανδρία, "courage"; thus *per ducis Evandri nomen* (with *nomen* as signpost) = *per* εὐανδρίαν, *per virtutem* (= *fortia facta*).

Cf. on **A. 8.194,** where Cacus = κακός, Evander = good man.

Mørland (1960) 23.

**A. 10.389:** Anchemolum thalamos ausum incestare novercae

Harrison: "Anchemolus' name . . . characterizes his mythical role: it suggests ἀγχίμολος, 'coming near' (*Il.* 4.529), and given the common euphemism 'come near' for sexual congress (Pind. *Nem.* 10.81, Aesch. fr. 175.1 Radt, Stevens on Eur. *And.* 25), his name might mark the man who 'came near' his stepmother."

For a play on *Anchi-* in the name *Anchialus* in Ovid *Tr.* 1.10.36 see André.

Harrison (1991) on 388–89, André (1975) 194.

**A. 10.417–18:** fata *canens* silvis genitor celarat Halaesum; / ut senior leto *canentia* lumina solvit

For the simple wordplay between *cănens,* and *cānentia,* cf. 10.191–92 *canit-canentem,* and see intro. 2.1.

**A. 10.439–40:** interea *soror* alma monet *succedere* Lauso / Turnum

The name Juturna is suppressed here and not given until 12.146 (for suppression see intro. 2.7). The suppression accompanies a glossing of the name Iuturna by the verb *succedere,* "move into the position of, relieve militarily," and so, in a sense, "help." Varro and Servius derive the name Iuturna from the verb *iuvare,* "help," because she comes to the aid of the sick and others. Vergil clearly plays on this etymology in 12.814 *(succurrere)* and 12.872 *(iuvare).* The names of both Jupiter (cf. on A. 9.128–29) and Juno (Varro *LL* 5.67, Serv. A. 1.4) are also connected to the verb *iuvare.*

In commenting on 12.872, Barchiesi suggests that Vergil may be going beyond the traditional etymology *Iuturna quae iuvat* to suggest *Iuturna quae iuvat Turnum.* That may be going on in 10.439–40 as well, with *Turnum* at the start of 440, and in 12.813 *succurrere fratri* [= *Turno*]. The similarity between the names of brother and sister is unsurprising. For such Vergilian addition to a traditional etymology cf. on G. 3.280–83 *(hippomanes)* and A. 12.411–19 *(dictamnum).*

The name of Amata is also suppressed when she is first mentioned, in a passage that might involve wordplay (see on A. 7.56–57).

VARRO *LL* 5.71.2: lympha Iuturna quod iuvaret, itaque multi aegroti propter id nomen hanc aquam petere solent; SERV. A. 12.139: Iuturna . . . cui nomen a iuvando est inditum; SERV. Auct. A. 12.139: quae laborantibus iuvare consuevit.

A. 12.813–14: *Iuturnam* misero (fateor) *succurrere* fratri / suasi; 12.872: quid nunc te *tua,* Turne, potest *germana iuvare?;* cf. also on A. 12.878–84 for the possible connection *Juturna/Duiturna/vita aeterna.*

Bartelink (1965) 78, Barchiesi (1978) 103 n. 4, McKeown (1987) 1.49–50, Ahl (1985) 319–20, Harrison (1991) on 139.

**A. 10.446–48?:** miratus stupet in *Turno* corpusque per ingens / lumina volvit obitque truci procul omnia visu, / talibus et dictis it contra dicta *tyranni*

The reference to Turnus as *tyrannus* may allude to a connection between the name and an Etruscan word for king; see Cairns, quoted on **A. 7.56.**

**A. 10.454:** utque leo, *specula* cum *vidit* ab alta

For the connection between *specula* and *specto* = *video,* cf. on **A. 1.180–81** *scopulum . . . prospectum.*

Bartelink (1965) 89.

**A. 10.523?:** et genua *amplectens* effatur talia *supplex*

Here *amplectens* seems to gloss *supplex.*

**A. 10.545–49?:**

Dardanides contra furit: *Anxuris* ense sinistram
et totum clipei ferro deiecerat orbem
(dixerat ille aliquid magnum vimque adfore verbo
crediderat, caeloque animum fortasse ferebat
canitiemque sibi et longos promiserat annos)

Kraggerud quotes Servius' explanation on A. 7.799 that Jupiter Anxuris is so called because the young Jupiter has not shaved and so is ἄνευ ξυροῦ, "without razor," and suggests an ironic contradiction between Anxur's name and his expectations of a long life.

The etymological connection is like that of the connection by Servius Auctus elsewhere of the name Iulus and Greek ἴουλος, "first beard" (see on A. 9.640, 652).

SERV. A. 7.799: CIRCAEVMQVE IVGVM circa hunc tractum Campaniae colebatur puer Iuppiter, qui Anxyrus dicebatur, quasi ἄνευ ξυροῦ, id est sine novacula, quia barbam numquam rasisset; SERV. Auct. 1.267: et occiso Mezentio Ascanium sicut L. Caesar scribit, Iulum coeptum vocari, vel quasi ἰοβόλον, id est, sagittandi peritum, vel a prima barbae lanugine, quam ἴουλον Graeci dicunt, quae ei tempore victoriae nascebatur.

Kraggerud (1960) 39.

**A. 10.560?:** . . . *pisces*que *impasti* vulnera lambent.

De la Cerda suggests that Vergil alludes to a derivation of *piscis* from *pasco,* found in extant texts only in Isidore. Perhaps. For single-epithet glosses cf. intro. 2.2.

ISID. 12.6.1: pisces dicti unde et pecus, a pascendo scilicet.

Cerda (1617) 496.

*

**A. 10.730–31, 737?:**

*sternitur* infelix *Acron* et calcibus atram
tundit humum exspirans infractaque tela cruentat.
. . . . . . . . . . . . . . . . . . . . . . . . . . . . . . . . .
"pars belli haud temnenda, viri, *iacet altus Orodes.*"

Harrison: in 730, "the verb *[sternitur]* suggests an ironic play on the name: the lofty Acron (ἄκρος, 'highest') is laid low." In 737, "the antithesis between *iacet,* 'lies low' (i.e. in death) and *altus,* 'lofty' . . . is deliberate and ironic, and augmented by the punning juxtaposition *altus Orodes;* the proper name can mean 'mountainous' (ὀρώδης)."

For other examples of wordplay on words like *altus,* ἄκρο-, see on **A. 3.270–71** *Neritos ardua.*

Harrison (1991) on 730–31 and 737; on Orodes he cites Saunders (1940) 553 (although a misprint makes it 533; 553 is correct).

**A. 10.747?:** *Caedicus* Alcathoum *obtruncat, Sacrator* Hydaspen

Harrison: the name Caedicus "may . . . be chosen here as appropriate to a slayer . . . , especially with *Sacrator* in the same line"; note also *obtruncat.*

Harrison (1991) on 747.

**A. 10.752:** quem tamen haud expers *Valerus virtutis avitae*

Harrison: "*virtutis avitae* suggests the traditional derivation of *Valerius* from *valere.*"

Harrison (1991) on 752, citing the discussion of Valerius as a name of good omen at Pease (1963) 285.

**A. 10.825?:** quid tibi nunc, miserande *puer,* pro *laudibus* istis

Mørland suggests a connection between *laudibus* and the name Lausus, which one might say is suppressed here (for suppression see intro. 2.7), and replaced by *puer;* with *quid tibi, Lause, pro laudibus tuis* we would have a figura etymologica, or at least paronomasia. The wordplay may strike us as inappropriate for this moment of pathos, but that the Romans may have felt differently is suggested by McCartney's list of puns in sepulchral inscriptions *(Antho . . . male deflorentibus annis, Crescens . . . non adcrevi, Felicitas . . . parentes infelices).*

Mørland (1960) 23, McCartney (1918–19) 350–51.

**A. 11.78–79:** multaque praeterea Laurentis *praemia* pugnae / aggerat et longo *praedam* iubet ordine duci

Vergil may be alluding to the etymological connection (suggested by Varro) between *praemium* and *praeda.*

VARRO *LL* 5.178: praemium a praeda.

Bartelink (1965) 109.

**A. 11.122–23?:** tum senior *semperque odiis et crimine Drances / infensus* iuveni Turno

Mørland suggests that *semperque odiis et crimine . . . infensus* is a gloss on the name *Drances.* Hesychius glosses δραγκαλακτᾶν with βριμοῦσθαι (snort with anger, be indignant).

Mørland (1960) 25.

**A. 11.133:** bis senos *pepigere* dies, et *pace* sequestra

For the derivation of *pax* from *pango* see on **A. 4.99** *pacem* aeternam *pactos*que hymenaeos.

**A. 11.142–44:** Arcades ad portas ruere et de more vetusto / *funereas* rapuere *faces;* lucet via longo / ordine flammarum et late discriminat agros

Varro, Donatus, and Servius derive *funus* from the rope torches *(funalia)* that burn in funeral rites. Although the phrase "funereal torch" needs no etymological motivation, Vergil's *funereas faces* may allude to this etymology.

In a variation on the gloss in which a modifier explains the noun modified, here the adjective modifies a noun that explains the etymology of the adjective: cf. on **A. 7.784** *Hernica saxa,* and intro. 2.2a.

SERV. Auct. 143: RAPVERE FACES . . . apud Romanos moris fuit ut noctis tempore efferrentur ad funalia—unde etiam funus dictum est—quia in religiosa civitate cavebant, ne aut magistratibus occurrerent aut sacerdotibus, quorum oculos nolebant alieno funere violari. . . . funera autem alii a funalibus candelis, sebo vel cera circumdatis, dicta (tradunt), quod his praelucentibus noctu efferrentur mortui: alii a fungendo, quod eo supremo in eo qui decessit, officio fungimur, vel quod hi qui mortui sunt "vita functi" dicuntur; SERV. 6.224: FACEM de fune, ut Varro dicit (= fr. 428, *GRF* p. 361): unde et funus dictum est; DON. on Ter. *Andr.* I 1 81: "funus" est pompa exsequiarum, dictum a funalibus; 88: funus . . . a funalibus dictum est, id est uncis et aculeis candelabrorum, quibus delibuti funes et [ingenium] cerei fomites infiguntur; cf. SERV. A. 1.727, ISID. 11.2.34, 19.4.1, 20.10.5; differently PAUL.-Fest. p. 74, 11 L: Furvum nigrum, vel atrum. Hinc dicta furnus, Furiae, funus.

Cerda (1617) 564.

**A. 11.200–201:** ardentis spectant socios *semusta*que servant / *busta*

Ancient sources derive *bustum* from *uro,* "burn," *ustum,* "burnt." Thus *semusta* is a gloss on *busta* (see intro. 2.2).

PAUL.-Fest. p. 29, 8 L: bustum, quasi bene ustum; SERV. A. 11.185: "bustum" vero iam exustum vocatur (sim. Isid. 20.10.9); COMMENT. Lucan 8.778: bustum est ubi ustum est cadaver.

Bartelink (1965) 99.

**A. 11.246–47:** ille urbem *Argyripam* patriae cognomine gentis / victor Gargani condebat Iapygis agris.

Servius explains that the name of Argyripam (or Arpi) is a corruption of Argos Hippion (Ἄργος Ἵππιον), referring to Diomedes' hometown of Argos (in 246 *patriae* = Argos). In 246 *cognomine* is the obvious signpost; cf. intro. 2.6.

SERV. 246: ARGYRIPAM Diomedes fuit de civitate quae Argos Hippion dicitur, de qua Homerus Ἄργεος ἱπποβότοιο, Horatius "aptum" dicet "equis Argos" (C. 1.7.9). hic in Apulia condidit civitatem, quam patriae suae nomine appellavit et Argos Hippion dixit: quod nomen postea vetustate corruptum est, et factum ut civitas Argyrippa diceretur: quod rursus corruptum Arpos fecit; SCHOL. Lycophr. 592: ἔκτισε πόλιν, ἥντινα Ἵππιον Ἄργος ἐκάλεσεν; PLINY *NH* 3.104: Arpi, aliquando Argos Hippium Diomede condente, mox Argyripa dicta.

Bartelink (1965) 43, Rehm (1932) 35.

*

**A. 11.433:** *agmen agens* equitum et florentis aere catervas

De la Cerda notes that the phrase, in a line repeated from A. 7.433, juxtaposes cognates. The phrase occurs also in A. 7.707.

COMMENT. Lucan 1.478: in agmine esse proprie dicitur qui iter agit; ISID. 9.3.64: agmen dictur cum exercitus iter facit, ab agendo vocatum, id est, eundo.

Cerda (1617) 143.

**A. 11.542–43:** matrisque vocavit / nomine Casmillae mutata parte Camillam

On the name Camilla see on A. 7.803–4. Here *nomine* is an etymological signpost (see intro. 2.6), as Vergil says that Camilla was named for her mother Casmilla; cf. also intro. 2.10 for the Alexandrian *metonomasia.*

Cf. Tissol (1992) 268 n. 12 for possible Callimachean precedent (see fr. 723) here.

**A. 11.552–56, 561–66, 573–75?:**

*telum* immane manu valida quod forte gerebat
bellator, solidum nodis et robore cocto,
huic natam *libro* et silvestri subere clausam
implicat atque habilem mediae circumligat *hastae;*
quam dextra ingenti *librans* ita ad aethera fatur. . . .
. . . . . . . . . . . . . . . . . . . . . . . . . . . . . . *
**dixit, et adducto contortum** *hastile* lacerto
immittit: sonuere undae, rapidum super amnem
infelix fugit in *iaculo* stridente Camilla.
at Metabus magna propius iam urgente caterva
dat sese fluvio, atque *hastam* cum virgine victor
gramineo, donum Triviae, de caespite vellit.
. . . . . . . . . . . . . . . . . . . . . . . . . .
utque pedum primis infans vestigia plantis
institerat, *iaculo* palmas *armavit* acuto
*spicula*que ex umero parvae suspendit et *arcum.*

See on A. 7.803–4 for Egan's idea that the use of words for weapons used in contexts that feature Camilla constitutes allusion to an etymology of her name as "something like 'armor woman.' "

For such simple wordplay as here between *libro* (bark) in 554 and *librans* (balance, poise to throw) in 556 see on **A. 2.606–7** *parentis . . . parere.* **

**A. 11.615–17:** excussus *Aconteus / fulminis in morem aut tormento ponderis acti /* praecipitat longe et vitam dispergit in auras.

The simile in 616 plays on the name Aconteus and Greek ἄκων, "javelin," and the verb ἀκοντίζω, "hurl the javelin." Aconteus is thrown like a weapon.

See **E. 10.55–61** for a play on *spicula* and the name Acontius, and A. 1.720 on the epithet *Acidalia* and Greek ἀκίς.

Saunders (1940) 553–54, Bartelink (1965) 85 n. 2 ("possible"), Hardie (1986) 178 n. 61 (cites *TLL* 1.420.36ff. for puns on the root, gives references, including some on the use of of ἀκοντ- words for "flash," "meteors," and "shooting stars").

**A. 11.630?:** bis reiecti armis respectant terga *tegentes.*

De la Cerda sees allusion here to the derivation of *clipeus* (suppressed here; see intro. 2.7) from κλέπτω, "hide," or καλύπτω, here as at **A. 2.227.**

Cerda (1617) 627.

**A. 11.644–45?:** tantus in *arma* patet. latos huic hasta per *armos* / hasta tremit.
Bartelink mentions what he calls "unlikely" possible etymologizing between *armus* and *arma* here. Cf. on **A. 4.11** *quem sese ore ferens, quam forti pectore et* ***armis!***

Bartelink (1965) 103 n. 1.

*

## A. 11.648–54?:

at medias inter caedes exsultat Amazon
unum exserta latus pugnae, *pharetrata* Camilla,
et nunc lenta manu spargens *hastilia* denset,
nunc validam dextra rapit indefessa *bipennem;*
aureus ex umero sonat *arcus* et *arma* Dianae.
illa etiam, si quando in tergum pulsa recessit,
*spicula* converso fugientia derigit *arcu.*

See on **A. 7.803–4** for Egan's idea that the large number of words for weapons used in contexts that feature Camilla constitutes allusion to an etymology of her name that would have it mean "something like 'armor woman.'"

**A. 11.721–22:** quam facile *accipiter* saxo *sacer* ales ab alto / consequitur pennis sublimem in nube columbam

As Servius explains, *accipiter,* "hawk," corresponds to Greek ἱέραξ; *sacer ales* alludes to this name because of the resemblance between ἱέραξ and ἱερεύς, "priest," or ἱερός, "divine, sacred." We know that Callimachus discussed types of hawks in his Περὶ Ὀρνέων (fr. 420).

Cf. the possible play on *accipiter* at A. 3.250?

SERV. 721: ACCIPITER SAXO SACER ALES AB ALTO "sacer" ideo, quia Marti est consecratus: aut "sacer" avibus execrabilis, ut (3.57) "auri sacra fames": aut, quod verius est, Graecum nomen expressit: nam ἱέραξ dicitur, hoc est sacer: ἱερεύς enim sacerdos vocatur. cur autem graece ita dictus sit, ratione non caret, quae nota est sacrorum peritis.

Cerda (1617) 637, Bartelink (1965) 85.

## A. 11.778–82?:

hunc virgo, sive ut templis praefigeret *arma*
Troia, captivo sive ut se ferret in auro
venatrix, unum ex omni certamine pugnae
caeca sequebatur totumque incauta per agmen
femineo praedae et spoliorum ardebat amore

See on **A. 7.803–4** for Egan's idea that the large number of words for weapons used in contexts that feature Camilla constitutes allusion to an etymology of her name that would have it mean "something like 'armor woman.'"

**A. 11.790–91:** non exuvias *pulsaeve tropaeum* / virginis aut spolia ulla peto

Varro suggests that a *tropaeum* is awarded for "turning away" the enemy, as if from τροπή; *pulsae* in 790 would allude to this etymology and would mean not "wound" but "beat away"—although in 793 *(pulsa cadat) pulsa* seems to mean "struck, wounded."

SERV. 790: EXVVIAS PVLSAEVE TROPAEVM exuvias occisae, pulsae tropaeum. et proprie: nam ut supra (10.775) diximus, de occisis hostibus triumphabant, de pulsis figebant tropaea; SERV. 10.775: TROPAEVM tropaeum dictum est ἀπὸ τοῦ τρέπεσθαι, id est ab hostium conversione: unde qui hostem fugasset, merebatur tropaeum, qui autem occidisset, triumphum, ἀπὸ τοῦ θριαμβεύειν, id est ab exultatione; VARRO ap. Non. p. 55, 8 M (fr. 98, *GRF* p. 224): ideo fuga hostium graece vocatur τροπή. hinc spolia capta fixa in stipitibus appellantur tropaea.

Bartelink (1965) 90–91, Conington (1963) on 790, Mühmelt (1965) 63.

**A. 11.836–37?:** At Triviae custos iamdudum in montibus *Opis* / alta sedet summis *spectat*que interrita pugnas

Köves-Zulauf sees in *Opis . . . spectat* and in other passages allusions to the connection of the name Opis with sight. Cf. on 11.853 speculatur.

Cf. SERV. Auct. A. 11.532 and Thilo-Hagen's ap. crit.

Köves-Zulauf (1978) 187–91.

**A. 12.45–46, 67–69?:**

haudquaquam dictis *violentia* Turni
flectitur. . . .
. . . . . . . . .
Indum sanguineo veluti *violaverit* ostro
si quis ebur, aut mixta rubent ubi lilia multa
alba rosa, talis virgo dabat ore colores.

As Johnson and others have noted, Vergil connects the *violentia* of Turnus with the staining of the ivory in the simile used to describe Lavinia's blush. The wordplay or echo (admittedly twenty lines apart, but with the same five-syllable metrical position and shape) of *violentia* and *violaverit* (both suggest *vis*) establishes the link; Lyne observes that Vergil's *violaverit* has connotations of force and violence lacking in the μιαίνω of the model at *Il.* 4.141.

Johnson (1976) 54–59 (57: *violaverit* echoes the *violentia* of Turnus that dominates this scene), Lyne (1987) 120.

**A. 12.134–36?:** At Iuno ex *summo* (qui nunc *Albanus* habetur; / tum neque nomen erat neque honos aut gloria monti) / prospiciens *tumulo* campum aspectabat

The reference to the name of Juno's perch seems prolix and unnecessary, unless it is a signpost that etymologizing is intended (cf. intro. 2.6). With *summo* and *tumulo*, could Vergil be alluding to a derivation of the name Alba from a "pre-Indo-European word meaning 'mountain'" (Ogilvie)? Cf. on **A. 9.387–88.**

For the phrasing here cf. A. 6.776 *haec tum nomina erunt, nunc sunt sine nomine terrae*. See intro. 2.10a for *nunc.*

SERV. Auct. 134: NVNC ALBANVS HABETVR Catonem sequitur, qui Albanum montem ab Alba Longa putat dictum; 135: "nomen" quis ignorat a longa Alba † tractaturi?

A. 9.387–88: locos qui post *Albae de nomine dicti* / *Albani.*

Ogilvie (1970) 43.

**A. 12.194:** *urbi*que dabit *Lavinia* nomen

Explicit connection of the names of Lavinium (suppressed, = *urbi*) and Lavinia. For suppression see intro. 2.7.

VARRO *LL* 5.144: Lavinium . . . a Latini filia, quae coniuncta Aeneae, Lavinia, appellatum; many other sources in Maltby, including D.H. 1.59.3 (who cites both this derivation and one from Lavinia, the daughter of Anius, king of the Delians), and Serv. A.1.2, who says the city was first called Lavinum, after Latinus' brother.

**A. 12.224–26:** formam adsimulata Camerti, / cui *genus* a proavis *ingens* clarumque paternae / nomen erat virtutis, et ipse acerrimus armis

Mackail and Conway suggest a real or imagined connection of *ingens* with *gens* or *genus; genus . . . ingens* here is at least wordplay, and perhaps an etymological gloss, of the more rare *Hernica saxa* type, in which the noun alludes to the etymology of an adjective modifying it.

For *Hernica saxa* cf. intro. 2.2a; for *ingens* cf. on **G. 2.131.**

Mackail (1912), Conway (1912).

**A. 12.275–76?:** egregium forma iuvenem et *fulgentibus* armis, / transadigit costas *fulva*que effundit harena.

Some modern scholars have suggested an etymological connection between *fulvus* and *fulgeo.*

Bartelink (1965) 97–98, Ernout-Meillet (1967) s.v. fulvus (p. 462), Walde-Hofmann (1930–56) s.v. fulvus (p. 561).

*

**A. 12.391–97:**

iamque aderat Phoebo ante alios dilectus *Iapyx*
*Iasides,* acri quondam cui captus amore
ipse suas artis, sua munera, laetus Apollo
augurium citharamque dabat celerisque sagittas.

ille, ut depositi proferret fata parentis,
scire potestates herbarum usumque *medendi*
maluit et mutas agitare inglorius artis.

Both the name and patronymic of the doctor Iapyx Iasides suggest the Greek word for healing, ἰάομαι.

SERV. Auct. 391: IAPIX aptum nomen medico: nam ἰᾶσθαι Graeci dicunt "curare."

Cerda (1617) 716, Saunders (1940) 545, Ambrose (1980) 457, Eden (1975) on A. 8.425; on Jason (Iason) as healer in Pindar *P.* 4 see Segal (1986) 19, with references.

## A. 12.411–19:

hic Venus indigno nati concussa dolore
*dictamnum* genetrix *Cretaea* carpit ab *Ida,*
puberibus caulem foliis et flore comantem
purpureo; non illa feris incognita capris
gramina, cum tergo volucres haesere sagittae.
hic Venus obscuro faciem circumdata nimbo
detulit, hoc fusum labris splendentibus *amnem*
inficit occulte medicans, spargitque salubris
*ambrosiae* sucos et odoriferam *panaceam.*

In 412 Vergil names the herb *dictamnum* (or *dictamnus;* sources give both), then in explaining where it comes from alludes to the etymology, for *Cretaea carpit ab Ida* suggests the other famous Cretan mountain, Dicte, which Servius says gave the name to the herb. Thus the line is framed by *dictamnum,* and the words that allude to its etymology, just as in Arat. *Phaen.* 33 δίκτῳ ἐν εὐώδει, ὄρεος σχεδὸν Ἰδαίοιο (see below on the text of this line).

Vergil improves on the traditional etymology in a way open only to a Latin poet, as he did with *hippomanes* at G. 3.266–83, where he suggests a hybrid derivation from Greek *hippos,* "horse," but Latin *manare:* "flow, run, exude." Commentators offer only weak suggestions about why at 12.417–18, Vergil uses *amnis,* "stream," of the water used to cleanse Aeneas' wound. This unusual use of the word suggests that *dictamnum* comes from *Dicte* and *amnis.* (See below for derivations involving *amnis* in Propertius, Ovid, and Varro.) In A. 12.417, *hoc* = *dictamnum;* without the pronoun it would be ***dictamno*** *fusum labris splendentibus* ***amnem.*** There is thus in 417 a kind of suppressed pun (for suppression see intro. 2.7).

This extensive description and etymology of an herb resemble the four major etymological aetiologies in the *Georgics* that Ross has described: the *felix malum* at G. 2.126–41, the *asilus* at G. 3.146–53, *hippomanes* at G. 3.280–83, and the *amellus* at G. 4.271–78 (see on those passages).

Connors points to an allusion to *dictamnum* at *Ciris* 299–300, complete with *Dictaeas* "as a punning etymological gloss"; she suggests a model in Valerius Cato's *Dictynna,* which would also have influenced Vergil here, and points also to A. 4.72–73, *illa fuga silvas saltusque peragrat / Dictaeos,* and to Servius' notes, which suggest that the deer is to be imagined as searching for *dictamnum*. Cf. too on E. 6.55–60 *Dictaeae,* and the passage from Callimachus cited there.

Harrison suggests that Vergil models his lines on the description of μῶλυ at *Od.* 10.302–5—cf. 305, μῶλυ δέ μιν καλέουσι θεοί, but there seems to be no etymologizing there. Harrison suggests Theophrastus, *History of Plants* 9.16 as Vergil's source for information about μῶλυ. It may also be relevant that Euphorion 111 mentions *dictamnum,* but we have too little of the context to say more than that.

(On Arat. *Phaen.* 33 most editors print Δίκτη, the usual form of the name of the mountain, but some ancient readers understood the masculine form to be not a proper noun but a variant name for *dictamnum* [see intro. 2.8a, O'Hara (1993a) 15 n. 6, with references to the notes in the editions of Aratus by Martin and Mair]. Aratus may have written a deliberately ambiguous form: either a rare masc. form of the mountain's name, or a rare short form of the name of the herb.)

SERV. Auct. 412: DICTAMNVM haec herba licet ubique nascatur, melior in Creta est, quae Dicta dicitur, unde proprium herbae nomen; VARRO fr. 392 (*GRF* p. 350): Interamnae et Antemnae dictae sunt, quod inter amnes sint positae vel ante se habeant amnes.

[VERG.] *Ciris* 299–300: Cnosia nec Partho contendens spicula cornu / *Dictaeas* ageres ad *gramina nota* capellas; PROP. 4.2.10: *Vertumnus verso* dicor ab *amne* deus; OVID *F.* 3.654: *amne perenne* latens *Anna Perenna* vocor; *F.* 6.410: nomen ab averso ceperat *amne deus* (sc. *Vertumnus*); EUPHOR. 111: στεψαμένη θαλεροῖσι συνήντετο δικτάμνοισι, quoted by Schol. Arat. *Phaen.* 33, who says Euphor. is talking about Eileithuia.

Cerda (1617) 720, Harrison (1990), Connors (1991) and (1992), O'Hara (1993a) 15 n. 6, *EV* s.v. dittamo (Maggiulli).

**A. 12.433–34:** Ascanium fusis circum complectitur *armis* / summaque per galeam delibans oscula fatur

Edwards suggests that the ambiguous word *armis,* which can mean "arms (weapons)" or "shoulders," is carefully chosen: "Realization of the twofold meaning of *armis,* the vagueness of reference of *fusis* ('throwing his arms around him' or 'having donned his armour'?) and the ambiguity of the ablatives ('instrument' or ablative absolute?) makes it suddenly and strikingly clear that the embrace is one in which both of them are surrounded not only by the arms of the loved one but by the horrors of the war in present, past, and probably future."

The ambiguity is underscored by the ancient notion that *arma,* "weapons," is related etymologically to *armus,* "shoulder."

Cf. on **A. 4.11** *quem sese ore ferens, quam forti pectore et **armis**!* Contra e.g. Williams: "*Armis* is from *arma* (weapons), not from *armus* (shoulder)."

SERV. Auct. 4.495: proprie enim arma sunt quae armos tegunt.

Edwards (1960) 163, Williams (1973) on 433.

**A. 12.435–36:** disce, *puer, vir*tutem ex me verumque laborem, / fortunam ex aliis.

For the etymology of *virtus* from *vir,* see on **A. 1.566;** for the juxtaposition of *puer* and *vir*tus see on **A. 9.641** *(macte nova virtute, puer).* For the thematic importance of the difference between *puer* and *vir* see Petrini.

Vergil is adapting earlier poets here; cf. *Il.* 6.476–77, Soph. *Aj.* 550–51, and the quotation at Macrob. 6.1.58 of Accius' *Armorum Iudicum* (fr. 156 Ribbeck): *virtuti sis par, dispar Fortunis patris.*

Petrini (n.d.) chap. 5.

## A. 12.496–99?:

multa Iovem et laesi testatus foederis aras
iam tandem invadit medios et Marte secundo
*terribilis* saevam nullo discrimine caedem
suscitat, irarumque omnis effundit habenas.

See on **A. 12.945–47** for the possible suggestion in the adjective *terribilis,* used of Aeneas both here and there, of the presumed etymological connection between the name Aeneas and Greek αἰνός, "dread, dire, terrible."

## A. 12.521–28:

ac velut immissi diversis partibus *ignes*
. . . . . . . . . . . . . . . . . . . . . . . . . .
non *segnius* ambo
Aeneas Turnusque ruunt per proelia

Servius Auctus explains *segnis* as *sine igne* and sees a connection between the *ignes* of the simile and the words *non segnius* as applied to Aeneas and Turnus.

Cf. the possible play on *insincerus* and *cera* at G. 4.283–85.

SERV. Auct. 525: "non segnius" ad ignem retulit, quia segnis quasi sine igne sit; SERV. Auct. A. 2.374: "segnis" autem est proprie "frigidus," "sine igni," ut "securus" "sine cura," "sedulus" "sine dolo" (more references in Maltby).

OVID *Am.* 3.7.13–14 (for Ovid cf. intro. 2.14): tacta tamen veluti *gelida* mea membra cicuta / *segnia* propositum destituere meum.

McKeown (1987) 1.50–51 (cites both Vergil and Ovid); Williams (1973) on 525 notes that *non segnius* occurs after a simile also in 4.149, 7.383, 8.414, and 10.657.

**A. 12.539–40:** nec di texere *Cupencum* / Aenea veniente sui

Servius says that *cupencus* is a Sabine word for "priest," and that Vergil alludes to this by saying *nec di texere Cupencum.*

SERV. Auct. 538: sane sciendum cupencum Sabinorum lingua sacerdotem vocari, ut apud Romanos flaminem et pontificem, sacerdotem. sunt autem cupenci Herculis sacerdotes. ergo quia huic proprium nomen de sacerdote finxit, bene dixit "nec dii texere sui."

Cerda (1617) 734, Eden (1975) on 8.425.

**A. 12.617–19?:** attulit hunc illi caecis terroribus *aura* / commixtum clamorem, arrectasque impulit *auris* / confusae sonus urbis et inlaetabile murmur.

Wordplay or soundplay at the ends of consecutive lines (see intro. 2.1 and 2.9) between *aura,* "breeze," and *aures,* "ears." Maltby lists no ancient source, however, that connects the words etymologically.

Cf. the possible play at A. 6.204 between *auri* and *aura.*

**A. 12.646–47:** vos o mihi, *Manes* / este *boni*

Ancient sources say that the *manes,* "spirits of the dead," were so called as a euphemism, or κατ' ἀντίφρασιν (see intro. 2.3), because the old word *manus* meant "good." Vergil alludes to that etymology here.

VARRO *LL* 6.4: bonum antiqui dicebant manum; PAUL.-Fest. p. 109, 5 L: inferi di Manes (dicti), ut subpliciter appellati bono essent, et in carmine Saliari Ceres manus intellegitur creator bonus (cf. also pp. 112, 151); ISID. 10.139: manum enim bonum dicitur. unde et κατ' ἀντίφρασιν dii Manes, minime boni; cf. also MACROB. 1.3.13, and many sources in Maltby s.vv. manes, immanis.

Bartelink (1965) 108.

**A. 12.661–62:** soli pro portis Messapus et *acer* Atinas / sustentant *acies.*

For the connection between *acer* and *acies* cf. on 10.308–9, *rapit **acer** / totam **aciem** in Teucros.*

Bartelink (1965) 101.

**A. 12.713–14:** dat *gemitum* tellus; tum crebros ensibus ictus / con*geminant,* fors et virtus miscetur in unum.

Probably simple wordplay (cf. intro. 2.1), although Cassiodorus does derive *gemitus* from *geminat.* Cf. on A. 2.606–7 *tu ne qua **parentis** / iussa time neu praeceptis **parere** recusa.*

CASSIOD. *In Psalm.* 6.7: gemitus . . . dictus est geminatus luctus.

**A. 12.715–17:** ac velut ingenti *Sila* summove *Taburno* / cum duo conversis inimica in proelia tauri / frontibus incurrunt

As they begin their single combat, Aeneas and Turnus are compared to fighting bulls, whom Vergil oddly places in some seldom-mentioned Italian locations, Sila and Taburnus. Thomas suggests that these obscure place-names call to mind the two Latin words for gadfly, *asilus* and *tabanus.* At G. 3.146–56, Vergil suggested a connection between *asilus* and the place-name *Silarus;* see there for the Alexandrian tradition of playing with the etymology of words for gadfly. For the suggestion here of the gadfly that Juno sent to torment Io, see Ross and O'Hara.

Thomas (1982b) 84 n. 13, Ross (1987) 157–63, O'Hara (1990) 79–80.

**A. 12.717–19:** pavidi cessere magistri, / stat pecus omne metu *mutum, mussant*que iuvencae / quis nemori imperitet, quem tota armenta sequantur

Wheeler shows that by juxtaposing *mutum* and *mussant* in 718, Vergil is alluding to the connection between the words suggested by Varro.

VARRO *LL* 7.101: mussare dictum quod muti non amplius quam μῦ dicunt.

Wheeler (1993).

**A. 12.791–92:** *Iunonem* interea rex omnipotentis Olympi / adloquitur fulva pugnas *de nube* tuentem

Feeney calls attention to Servius' comment that Juno watches *de nube* because that is the *aer,* her own element: "the identification is based on the allegorists' equation of Ἥρα and ἀήρ." He notes that several other passages in this section of book 12 may allude to this connection, and also suggests a broader significance to the connection in A. 1.

SERV. 792: FVLVA DE NVBE de aere, de elemento suo; PLATO *Crat.* 404 c: ἴσως δὲ μετεωρολογῶν ὁ νομοθέτης τὸν ἀέρα "'Ἥραν" ὠνόμασεν ἐπικρυπτόμενος, θεὶς τὴν ἀρχὴν ἐπὶ τελευτήν· γνοίης δ' ἄν, εἰ πολλάκις λέγοις τὸ τῆς Ἥρας ὄνομα; CIC. *ND* 2.66: aer autem, ut Stoici disputant, interiectus inter mare et caelum Iunonis nomine consecratur; MENAND. Rhet. p. 337 Sp.: καὶ περὶ Ἥρας ὅτι ἀήρ, καὶ Ζεὺς τό θερμόν· οἱ γὰρ τοιοῦτοι ὕμνοι φυσιολογικοί (many more sources in Pease).

A. 12.796: aut qua spe gelidis in nubibus haeres; 810: aeria . . . sede; 842: interea excedit caelo nubemque reliquit; A. 1.50–156 (the storm); *Il.* 21.6–7: ἠέρα δ' Ἥρη / πίτνα πρόσθε βαθεῖαν ἐρυκέμεν; APOLL. Rhod. 3.210–14:

τοῖσι δὲ νισσομένοις Ἥρη φίλα μητιόωσα
ἠέρα πουλὺν ἐφῆκε δι' ἄστεος, ὄφρα λάθοιεν
Κόλχων μυρίον ἔθνος ἐς Αἰήταο κιόντες·
ὦκα δ' ὅτ' ἐκ πεδίοιο πόλιν καὶ δώμαθ' ἵκοντο
Αἰήτεω, τότε δ' αὖτις ἀπεσκέδασεν νέφος Ἥρη.

Heinze (1915) 299, Feeney (1984) 184 and (1991) 9, 21, 132 and index s.vv. "Hera" and "Juno," Buffière (1956) 106–10, Pease (1979) 716–17, Hunter (1989) on Apoll. Rhod. 3.210–14, Murrin (1980) 3–25. See also my Index of Words Glossed s.v. Iuno.

**A. 12.796:** aut qua spe gelidis in *nubibus* haeres

See on **A. 12.791–92** for possible allusions to the equation Juno/Hera = *aer* in these words spoken by Jupiter to Juno and elsewhere.

**A. 12.800–802:** desine iam tandem precibusque inflectere nostri, / ne te tantus edit tacitam dolor et mihi *curae* / saepe tuo dulci tristes ex ore *recursent*

The verb *recurso* occurs three times in Vergil, each time with or near *cura.* See on **A. 1.662.** The words here occur at the ends of consecutive lines (see intro. 2.9).

**A. 12.810:** nec tu me *aeria* solam nunc sede videres

See on **A. 12.791–92** for possible allusions to the equation Juno/Hera = *aer* in these words spoken by Juno and elsewhere.

**A. 12.813–14:** *Iuturnam* misero (fateor) *succurrere* fratri / suasi

Here *succurrere,* "come to the aid of," alludes to the derivation of the name Juturna from *iuvo,* "help, aid"; the phrase *succurrere fratri* (= *Turno*) may allude to Vergil's more innovative etymology *Iuturna quae Turnum iuvat.* The term *iuvat* is suppressed here; see intro. 2.7.

Cf. on **A. 10.439–40,** interea *soror* alma monet *succedere* Lauso / Turnum, and A. 12.872, quid nunc te *tua,* Turne, potest *germana iuvare?* At G. 1.500, *hunc saltem everso* ***iuvenem succurrere*** *saeclo,* Vergil seems also to use *succurrere* to suggest derivation of *iuvenis* from *iuvo.*

## A. 12.826–28, 835:

"sit Latium, sint Albani per saecula reges,
sit Romana potens Itala virtute propago; *
occidit, occideritque sinas cum nomine Troia."
. . . . . . . . . . . . . . . . . . . . . . . . . . . . .
"utque est nomen erit."

This conversation between Juno and Jupiter provides an aetiological explanation of why the Trojans, though nominally victorious in the battle with Turnus and the Latins, did not give their name to the mixture of Trojans and Italians.

O'Hara (1990) 137–51, Horsfall (1989) 22–23.

**A. 12.842:** interea excedit caelo *nubem*que relinquit

See on **A. 12.791–92** for possible allusions to the equation Juno/Hera = *aer* in these words (spoken of Juno) and elsewhere.

## A. 12.845–52?:

dicuntur geminae pestes cognomine *Dirae,*
quas et Tartaream Nox intempesta Megaeram
uno eodemque tulit partu, paribusque revinxit
serpentum spiris ventosasque addidit alas.
hae Iovis ad solium *saevi*que in limine *regis*
apparent acuuntque metum mortalibus aegris,
si quando letum horrificum morbosque deum rex
molitur, meritas aut bello territat urbes.

In 845 *dicuntur* and *cognomine* call attention (as signposts; cf. intro. 2.6) to the name *Dirae.* Ancient sources connect *dira* with *deorum ira;* this connotation of *dira* fits the reference to Jupiter as *saevus rex* in 849, although it may seem implausible to claim that *saevi* alludes to the etymology. Hardie puts it this way: "*Dei ira,* the just anger of Jupiter, turns out to be a *Dira,* a Fury."

PAUL.-Fest. p. 61, 1 L: dirus dei ira natus; SERV. 845: PESTES COGNOMINE DIRAE proprie "pestes" vocantur, "dirae" vero cognomine. et dictae "dirae," quod non nisi ante iratum Iovem videntur, ut (849) "saevique in limine regis apparent"; SERV. A. 2.519: "dira" . . . est deorum ira (so too Serv. A. 6.373, Serv. Auct. 4.453; several more references in Maltby).

Cf. Hardie (1993) 73, and on Vergil's Dirae in general Mackie (1992).

**A. 12.862–64:** *alitis* in parvae subitam collecta (sc. Dira) figuram, / quae quondam in bustis aut culminibus desertis / *nocte* sedens *serum* canit importuna per umbras

Vergil does not name the bird (for suppression see intro. 2.7), but by specifying that it sings *nocte,* he is probably alluding to and glossing the name of the *noctua,* the night-owl, which he names and perhaps glosses in an ill-omened context in G. 1.403 (several words from that passage reappear in these lines), and whose name Varro and others explain.

SERV. 863: noctuam dicit, non bubonem; nam ait "alitis in parvae": bubo autem maior est; VARRO *LL* 5.76: noctua, quod noctu canit ac vigilat; PAUL.-Fest. p. 179, 14 L (cf. Fest. p. 178, 29 L): noctua a tempore noctis dicta, quo canit vel volat; ISID. 12.7.40: noctua dicta pro eo quod nocte circumvolat.

G. 1.402–3: solis et occasum servans de culmine summo / nequiquam *seros* exercet *noctua cantus.*

Cf. Cerda (1617) 771.

**A. 12.872:** quid nunc te *tua,* Turne, potest *germana iuvare?*

Vergil alludes again to the derivation of the name *Iuturna* from *iuvo,* "help." In 872 *germana* = *Iuturna,* so we see here a suppressed figura etymologica. For suppression see intro. 2.7.

Barchiesi suggests that Vergil may be going beyond the traditional etymology *Iuturna quae iuvat* to suggest *Iuturna quae iuvat Turnum.* Cf. on **A. 10.439–40** *soror alma monet* **succedere** *Lauso / Turnum.*

Cerda (1617) 773, Bartelink (1965) 78, Barchiesi (1978) 103 n. 4.

**A. 12.878–84?:**

haec pro virginitate reponit?
*quo vitam dedit aeternam?* cur mortis adempta est
condicio? possem tantos finire dolores
nunc certe, et misero fratri comes ire per umbras!
*immortalis ego?* at quicquam mihi dulce meorum
te sine, frater, erit? o quae satis ima dehiscat
terra mihi, Manisque deam demittat ad imos?

Juturna complains about the disadvantages of immortality. Her name is Diuturna in *CIL* 6, 3700, in one manuscript of Florus 1.28, and some manuscripts of Cic. *Cluent.* 101. If this is the original spelling of the name, could the meaning of that name, "long lasting," underscore the connection of Juturna with the theme of immortality?

On Juturna and immortality see Barchiesi (1978), O'Hara (1990) 114–16 and (1993); in the latter I argue for printing *at* instead of *aut* in 882.

**A. 12.897–98?:** saxum antiquum ingens, campo quod forte iacebat, / *limes* agro positus *litem* ut discerneret arvis.

Isidore derives *lis* from *limen,* and Vergil may allude to such a connection here. But Isidore may have derived his etymology from Vergil's text, which he cites, and so is perhaps not independent evidence. (For this problem see on **A. 1.164–65.**)

ISID. 18.15.4: lis a contentione limitis prius nomen sumpsit. de qua Vergilius "limes erat positus litem ut discerneret arvis."

Cerda (1617) 777.

**A. 12.941–42:** infelix umero cum apparuit alto / *balteus* et notis fulserunt cingula *bullis*

Varro connects *balteus* and *bulla;* the words connected etymologically frame the line (see intro. 2.8).

VARRO *LL* 5.116: balteum, quod cingulum e corio habebant bullatum, balteum dictum; VARRO ap. Char. *Gramm.* p. 97, 20 B: Varro in Scauro (fr. II R) baltea dixit et Tuscum vocabulum ait esse.

Bartelink (1965) 104.

**A. 12.945–47?:** *ille,* oculis postquam saevi monimenta doloris / exuviasque hausit, furiis accensus et *ira / terribilis*

Du Quesnay suggests that with *ira terribilis* Vergil alludes to the derivation, in the *Homeric Hymn to Aphrodite,* of the name Aeneas from Greek αἰνός, "dread, dire, terrible."

In the same discussion, Jocelyn is "skeptical," noting that "αἰνός has not as definite a meaning as *terribilis* with its derivation from *terreo:* it is 'grim,' 'horrible,' but it is not so serious, and its exact meaning is unclear."

Cf. on 12.496–99, where Aeneas is also called *terribilis* (498).

*Hom. Hymn Aphr.* 198–99: τῷ δὲ καὶ Αἰνείας ὄνομ' ἔσσεται οὕνεκα μ' αἰνὸν / ἔσχεν ἄχος ἕνεκα βροτοῦ ἀνέρος ἔμπεσον εὐνῇ; Rank discusses the wordplay or assonance at *Il.* 13.481, δείδια δ' αἰνῶς Αἰνείαν; cf. also Woodhead.

Du Quesnay apud Du Quesnay et al. (1977) 139, Jocelyn apud Du Quesnay et al. (1977), Rank (1951) 37, Woodhead (1928) 36.

# The *Eclogues*

I have found comparatively few certain examples of etymological wordplay in the *Eclogues*. This may be because they were written not so very long after the publication of Varro's *de Lingua Latina* in 45 or 44, or because aetiology and origins are not a major thematic concern here as in the *Georgics* and *Aeneid*. I have also noted a similar tendency for the bucolic poetry of Theocritus and Moschus to have comparatively fewer examples of etymological wordplay than we find in the other Hellenistic poets (see the end of intro. 1.4). It is true, as Servius notes in his preface to the poems, that the names of most characters in the *Eclogues* seem to have been chosen for their significance in Greek or other languages, but I have not chosen to comment on these unless the text calls attention to the name. Commentators, and also Van Sickle, offer helpful comments on these names.

SERV. Praef. E.: etiam hoc sciendum, personas huius operis ex maiore parte nomina de rebus rusticis habere conficta, ut Meliboeus, ὅτι μέλει αὐτῷ τῶν βοῶν, id est quia curam gerit boum, et ut Tityrus; nam Laconum lingua tityrus dicitur aries maior, qui gregem anteire consuevit: sicut etiam in comoediis invenimus; nam Pamphilus est totum amans, Glycerium quasi dulcius mulier, Philumena amabilis.

Van Sickle (1978) index s.v. etymology.

**E. 1.1:** Tityre, tu patulae recubans sub tegmine *fagi*

This is not quite etymological wordplay, but a related phenomenon. Commentators have noted that Vergil's reference to the shade of the *fagus* ("beyond all others, perhaps, the tree of the *Eclogues*"-Ross) seems to recall the reference to the shade of the φηγός at Theoc. 12.8: σκιερὴν δ' ὑπὸ φηγόν, and that *fagus* seems to correspond to φηγός in several other passages (the most certain in the *Georgics*). But in Latin *fagus* should be "beech," while φηγός is "oak." For such "mistranslations" or "translation by homonym" see intro. 2.1a.

For this example, scholars have called attention to the comparative rarity of the word *fagus* in Latin poetry and suggested that Vergil may have had a precedent for the identification in either Catullus or a lost passage of Gallus. Varro also seems to have mentioned the identification.

VARRO *Gen. Pop. Rom.* fr. 185, *GRF* p. 249: fagus Varro de gente p. R.: "fagus quas Graece φηγούς vocant"; SERV. E. 1.1: antea . . . homines glandibus vescebantur, unde etiam fagus dicta est ἀπὸ τοῦ φαγεῖν (sim. Isid. 17.7.28).

Not all of the following passages necessarily offer *fagus* = φηγός, but all should be considered in weighing the question of poetic precedent for Vergil; this list contains all occurrences in the *Eclogues:* CAT. 64.288–89: namque ille tulit radicitus altas / *fagos* ac recto proceras stipite laurus (see Williams, who notes that in Tempe, the setting of this scene, "beeches surprise a little, while oaks would not"); NIC. *Geo.* fr. 69 G-S: φηγοὶ Πανὸς ἄγαλμα; PROP. 1.18.19–20: vos eritis testes, si quos habet arbor amores, / *fagus* et Arcadio pinus amica deo (Cairns cites Arist. *Ep.* 1.10.57 Mazal: μόνον δὲ φηγοῖς ὑποκαθήμενος ἢ πτελέαις, and suggests a model in Callimachus' *Acontius and Cydippe*); E. 2.3: tantum inter densas, umbrosa cacumina, fagos (see Ross on the suggestion of Gallus in the "neoteric appositional construction" here and in E. 9.9); E. 3.12–13: aut hic ad veteres fagos cum Daphnidis arcum / fregisti et calamos; E. 3.36–37: pocula ponam / fagina, caelatum diuini opus Alcimedontis; E. 5.13–14: immo haec, in viridi nuper quae cortice fagi / carmina descripsi et modulans alterna notavi; E. 9.9: usque ad aquam et veteres, iam fracta cacumina, fagos; G. 3.172: post valido nitens sub pondere *faginus axis;* HOM. *Il.* 5.838–39: μέγα δ' ἔβραχε φήγινος ἄξων βριθοσύνῃ (φήγινος appears once only in Homer, once in extant fragments of Callimachus [*Epig.* 34.1] and then once in the *Eclogues* and once in the *Georgics*).

Du Quesnay (1979) 40, (1981) 50, Williams (1968) 317–19, Cairns (1969), Ross (1975) 72, Kenney (1983) 49–50, Thomas (1988) on G. 3.172, Mynors (1990) on G. 3.172–3, Clausen (1994) on E. 2.3.

**E. 1.9–10?:** ille meas errare boves, ut cernis, et ipsum / ludere quae vellem *calamo* permisit agresti.

Coleman suggests wordplay on the name Tityrus: "*calamo* is for the normal Latin *harundine*. The loan-word from Greek *kalamos* occurs as early as Cato *Agr.* 105.2 and may not by now have seemed exotic. However, as Tityrus has been playing an oaten pipe, there may be reference to the fact that *titurinos* was the Italian Doric word for the single reed pipe *kalaminos aulos* (Athen. 4.182d)." Cf. above in the introductory note to the *Eclogues* for Servius' idea that Tityrus = "ram."

Tityrus speaks these lines.

For wordplay with languages other than Latin or Greek see intro. 2.11.

Coleman (1977) on 10; cf. several suggestions in Cerda (1608) 2.

**E. 1.16–17?:** saepe malum hoc nobis, si *mens* non laeva fuisset, / de caelo tactas *memini* praedicere quercus.

Du Quesnay points to what he calls "the *figura etymologica* of *mens-memini.*"

For other wordplay on words for memory cf. on **A. 1.8.**

VARRO *LL* 6.44: ab eadem mente meminisse dictum; ISID. 11.1.12: mens . . . vocata, quod emineat in anima, vel quod meminit.

Du Quesnay (1981) 70 and 148 n. 184.

**E. 1.61–62?:** ante pererratis amborum finibus *exsul* / aut Ararim *Parthus* bibet aut Germania Tigrim

Du Quesnay suggests that the association of the words *exsul* and *Parthus* alludes to the Scythians' reported use of *parthi* to mean *exsules*. For wordplay with languages other than Latin or Greek see intro. 2.11.

ISID. 9.2.44: Scythico sermone exules "parthi" dicuntur; IUST. 41.1.2: Parthi . . . Scythorum exules fuere . . .; Scythico sermone exules "parthi" dicuntur; differently COMMENT. Lucan 8.300: Parthi dicti eo, quod virtute praestent nec habeant pares.

Du Quesnay (1981) 137.

**E. 1.64–66:** at nos hinc alii sitientis ibimus Afros, / pars Scythiam et *rapidum* cretae veniemus Oaxen / et penitus toto divisos orbe Britannos.

As Servius notes, *rapidum* in 65 is used in a way that exploits its connection with *rapere,* "to seize."

Some have thought that RAPIDUM CRETAE in 65 is ambiguous, suggesting both "snatching up chalk" and "swift (river) of Crete." Many have argued that *Cretae* could not have this meaning.

SERV. 65: ET RAPIDUM CRETAE OAXEN hoc est lutulentum quod rapit cretam.

Knight (1944) 202–3 (argues for ambiguity), Coleman (1977) on 65 ("*Cretae* is impossible"), Wellesley (1968) 139–41 (cannot be Crete).

**E. 1.77–78:** carmina nulla canam; non me pascente, *capellae,* / florentem cytisum et salices *carpetis* amaras.

De la Cerda suggests an allusion to the derivation, found in Varro and elsewhere, of *caper* from *carpo*.

VARRO *RR* 2.3.7: a carpendo caprae nominatae; PAUL.-Fest. p. 42, 7 L: caprae dictae, quod omne virgultum carpant, sive a crepitu crurum; ISID. 12.1.15: capros et capras a carpendis virgultis quidam dixerunt. alii quod captent aspera. nonulli a crepitu crurum.

Cerda (1608) 19.

**E. 2.1?:** *formosum* pastor Corydon *ardebat* Alexin

Du Quesnay suggests that Vergil may be "hinting at" an assumed etymological connection, mentioned by Servius in a note on the *Aeneid,* between *formosus* and heat.

SERV. A. 8.453: forvum est calidum: unde et formosos dicimus quibus calor sanguinis ex rubore pulchritudinem creat; SCHOL. Veron. A. 4.149: formonsum non aliunde dicimus quam a calido; formum enim dicebant antiqui calidum (more sources in Maltby, including suggestions of a derivation from *forma*).

Du Quesnay (1979) 213 n. 121.

**E. 2.6?:** o crudelis *Alexi,* nihil mea carmina *curas?*

Du Quesnay suggests that among the many adaptations of Theocritus' *Idyll* 11 in E. 2 is an indirect imitation of "the etymological wordplay in (19f.) ὦ λευκὰ Γαλάτεια . . . λευκοτέρα πακτᾶς ('o white Galatea . . . whiter than cream cheese'), which is intended to point to the connection of the name Galatea and γάλα (milk)." He suggests that Vergil uses the principle of etymologizing from opposites "to suggest a derivation of the name Alexis from ἀλέξω (to protect, defend) or from ἀλέγω (to care). The effect is to produce a sort of oxymoron: 'o cruel savior . . . will you compel me to die?' 'o caring one . . . do you not care for my songs?' In Virgil the etymology is not used as part of a pretty compliment but plays a full part of the argument: Alexis is being urged to live up to his name and not to belie his character."

For etymologizing κατ' ἀντίφρασιν see intro. 2.3.

VARRO *LL* 7.82 on Enn. *Alex.* fr. 64 J (= 38 R = 53 V, quapropter Parim pastores nunc Alexandrum vocant), explains: Alexandrum ab eo appellatum in Graecia qui Paris fuisset, a quo Herculem quoque cognominatum Alexicacon, ab eo quod defensor esset hominum.

Cerda (1608) 23, Du Quesnay (1979) 44; cf. Van Sickle (1978) 120 on Galatea, 125 on Alexis; on Alexander, Rank (1951) 110–12.

**E. 2.18?:** alba ligustra cadunt, *vaccinia* nigra leguntur

Du Quesnay notes that *vaccinium,* which in Latin should describe a "bilberry which has pink flowers," is instead used here to correspond to ὑάκινθος at Theoc. 10.28 (καὶ τό ἴον μέλαν ἐστί, καὶ ἁ γραπτὰ ὑάκινθος), presumably because of the resemblance in sound. He points to the epithet *niger,* which recalls μέλας in Theocritus (even though there applied to a different flower).

For such "mistranslations" or "translation by homonym" see intro. 2.1a.

Du Quesnay (1979) 40 and 210 n. 49.

**E. 2.20?:** quam *dives pecoris,* nivei quam lactis abundans

Du Quesnay: "the phrase *dives pecoris* . . . reminds the reader of the standard etymology *pecunia a pecu: a pastoribus enim horum vocabulorum origo*" (Varro *LL* 5.92).

Du Quesnay (1979) 64.

**E. 2.30?:** *haedorum*que gregem viridi compellere *hibisco!*

Du Quesnay: "*haedorum* and *hibiscum* frame the line . . . perhaps hinting at an etymological explanation of *hibiscum* as derived from *haedus* and *esca.*" He points to Theoc. 5.128 αἴγιλον αἶγες ἔδοντι, but the hint, if there is one, does not seem strong.

For framing of a line with words connected etymologically see intro. 2.8.

Du Quesnay (1979) 39.

**E. 2.51:** ipse ego cana legam *tenera lanugine mala*

Boyd, drawing on Servius' suggestion that Vergil is alluding to the Cretans' reputation for love of boys, suggests a play here betweeen *mala,* "apples," and *malae,* "cheeks": "down-covered fruits *(tenera lanugine mala)* are a particularly suitable gift for a youth whose beard has just begun *(tenera lanugine malae).*" See Boyd for more details on this wordplay; more certain than the wordplay here is her suggestion that the *prima lanugine malas* of A. 10.324 alludes to E. 2.51, and plays with *malae* and *mala.*

See on A. 10. 324–25, *flaventem prima lanugine malas / dum sequeris Clytium infelix.*

For other Vergilian wordplay with *mala* see on A. 7.740, *maliferae . . . Abellae.*

SERV. 51: mala dicit Cydonia, quae lanuginis plena sunt: sed non praeter obliquitatem. nam ut in Aeneide (10.325) diximus, apud Cretenses infamiae genus iuvenibus fuerat non amatos fuisse.

Boyd (1983), citing also Du Quesnay (1979) 40 and 210 n. 50.

**E. 3.40–42:** in medio duo signa, Conon et—*quis fuit alter, /* descripsit radio totum qui gentibus orbem, / tempora quae messor, quae curvus *arator* haberet?

Springer suggests that wordplay is the key to the riddle of these lines, seeing in *arator* in 42 a punning reference to the suppressed name Aratus (for suppression see intro. 2.7).

For wordplay and riddles see on E. 3.104–5.

Without mentioning E. 2, Bing has suggested that Aratus puns on his own name, which is suppressed, at *Phaen.* 1–2: ἐκ Διὸς ἀρχώμεσθηα, τὸν οὐδέποτ' ἄνδρες ἐῶμεν / ἄρρητον. He finds allusions to Aratus' pun in Callim. *Epig.* 27, Leonidas *Anth. Pal.* 9.25, and G. 1.429–33.

Springer (1983–84) 131–34, Bing (1990) 281–85 and (1993) 105 (citing earlier comments by Levitan, Kidd, and Hopkinson); cf. too Albis (1995) on allusion by Apoll. Rhod. to the name of Callim. *Aetia.*

**E. 3.104–5?:** dic *quibus in terris* (et eris mihi magnus Apollo) / tris pateat caeli spatium non amplius *ulnas.*

Putnam suggests that wordplay figures in the solution to this riddle: Latin *ulna* suggests Greek ὠλένη, which suggests the city of Olenos, birthplace of (and source of the standard epithet for) the goat Amalthea, who nourished the infant Jupiter.

The goat later was elevated to the stars with her two kids (cf. Arat. *Phaen.* 162–66), which could account, Putnam suggests, for *caeli spatium* and (less precisely) *tris . . . ulnas.* The quotation of Aratus at E. 3.60 *(ab Iove principium)* helps to suggest both Aratus and Jupiter's birth (Putnam also cites Ovid *F.* 5.111–28).

For wordplay and riddles see on E. 3.40–42.

SERV. 105: dicta ulna ἀπὸ τῶν ὠλενῶν, id est a brachiis.

Putnam (1965) 150–54.

**E. 3.109–10:** et vitula tu dignus et hic, et quisquis *amores* / aut metuet dulcis aut experietur *amaros.*

*Rhet. Her.* 4.14.21 cites the play on *amo* and *amarus* in *nam amari iucundum sit, si curetur nequid insit amari.* Quint. 9.3.69–71 (see intro. 2.1) cites the same sentence, with disapproval, calling it *frigidum* and a type of pun to be avoided by the orator. Vergil's wordplay involves words at the ends of consecutive lines (see intro. 2.9).

Cf. E. 10.4–6, *Doris amara . . . amores.*

Cf. PLAUT. *Cist.* 67: eho an amare occipere amarum est opsecro?; *Trin.* 260: amor amara dat.

Snyder (1980) 65, 114.

## E. 6.55–60:

claudite, Nymphae,
*Dictaeae* Nymphae, nemorum iam claudite saltus,
si qua forte ferant oculis sese obvia nostris
errabunda bovis vestigia; forsitan illum
aut herba captum viridi aut armenta secutum
perducant aliquae stabula ad Gortynia vaccae.

Van Sickle suggests that in this "desperate invocation to enclose and catch" the bull for whom Pasiphae lusts, the use of *Dictaeae* alludes to Callimachus' etymological aetiology for the epithet, which derives it from the "nets" (δίκτυα) of fishermen.

Cf. on A. 12.412–17 *dictamnum.*

CALLIM. *Hymn* 3.193–200 (summ. in *Brev. Exp.* G. 2.536 and Comment. Lucan 6.214):

ὁ δ' ἐννέα μῆνας ἐφοίτα
παίπαλά τε κρημνούς τε καὶ οὐκ ἀνέπαυσε διωκτύν,
μέσφ' ὅτε μαρπτομένη καὶ δὴ σχεδὸν ἥλατο πόντον
πρηόνος ἐξ ὑπάτοιο καὶ ἔνθορεν εἰς ἁλιήων
δίκτυα, τά σφ' ἐσάωσαν· ὅθεν μετέπειτα Κύδωνες
νύμφην μὲν Δίκτυναν, ὄρος δ' ὅθεν ἥλατο νύμφη
Δικταῖον καλέουσιν, ἀνεστήσαντο δὲ βωμούς
ἱερά τε ῥέζουσι.

Van Sickle (1978) 156–57; on etymologies for Dictynna see also Connors (1991).

## E. 6.74–77:

Quid loquar aut ***Scyllam*** Nisi, quam fama secuta est
candida succinctam *latrantibus* inguina monstris
Dulichias vexasse rates et gurgite in alto
a! timidos nautes *canibus* lacerasse marinis

Coleman and others note the wordplay with the name Scylla and σκύλαξ, "puppy, yelping," here as in *Od.* 12.85–86, and a fragment of Callimachus (where the play is on Scylla as "bitch").

Another derivation of the name may be suggested by the use of *vexasse* in 76. A late Latin gloss connects the name with σκύλλω, "molest, trouble, annoy," and derives it specifically from her harassment of ships (a spoliando sive vexando nautas), which may mean the note derives from a commentary on this passage. This would solve a bit of a problem, because passages in Aul. Gell. 2.6, Macrob. 6.7.4–12, and Servius ad loc. indicate ancient dissatisfaction with *vexasse,* thought to be too gentle a word for Scylla's activity. Servius' note shows that Probus offered one explanation; Vergilian desire to suggest an alternate etymology for the name Scylla would be another.

Cf. the close adaptation of this passage at [Verg.] *Ciris* 58–61; cf. also **A. 3.432** ***Scyllam*** *et caeruleis* ***canibus*** *resonantia saxo,* and E. 8.107, ***Hylax*** *in limine* ***latrat.***

BEDA *Gramm. Lat.* 7.289.9 K: Scylla habet nomen a spoliando sive vexando nautas: spolio enim et vexo Latine, Graece dicitur scyllo.

Cerda (1608) 125, Coleman (1977) on 74ff., Van Sickle (1978) 148, Pfeiffer (1949–53) 268 (who mentions the late gloss and cites the *Ciris* passage), *EV* s.v. Scilla (Pinotti).

**E. 7.19:** alternos *Musae meminisse* volebant

Coleman: "The Muses were the daughters of Mnemosyne 'Memory' and their name *Mousai* is etymologically connected with *moneo, memini;* cf. A. 7.645 *et* **meministis** enim, divae, et **memorare** potestis."

Cf. too **A. 1.8** ***Musa,*** *mihi causas* ***memora,*** and other passages cited there.

Coleman (1977) on 19, Bartelink (1965) 93, on the etymology cf. Nagy (1979) 17.

**E. 7.29–30:** Saetosi caput hoc apri tibi, Delia, *parvus* / et ramosa *Micon* vivacis cornua cervi

Garson: "In *parvus* / . . . *Micon* . . . Corydon is Virgil's mouthpiece for an etymological pun involving the Doric form μικκός" (= μικρός, small, little). See intro. 2.2 for single-adjective glosses.

Garson (1971) 199, Coleman (1977) ad loc., Clausen (1994) ad loc.

**E. 8.21 etc.?:** incipe *Maenalios* mecum, mea tibia, versus

Doig on this repeated refrain: "if we take into consideration the circumstances, the frenzied despair of a jilted lover about to commit suicide, does this word not also call to mind the root in the Greek μαίνεσθαι ('to be mad' or 'in a state of frenzy')?"

I would prefer more of a signal in the text that Vergil was alluding to or calling upon this root.

Cf. the possible plays on Maenala at E. 10.55–61 and G. 1.17–18.

Doig (1968) 4.

**E. 8.58?:** omnia vel medium fiat mare

Vergil is adapting Theoc. 1.134, πάντα δ' ἔναλλα γένοιτο, "let all things become altered." He translates ἔναλλα, "changed," as though it were ἐνάλια, "in the sea"; Doig suggests that this is improvement upon a model, not an error, and praises the way Vergil's word choice "evokes the picture of the sea overwhelming or confusing all the old order." The resemblance between ἔναλλα and ἐνάλια in a sense justifies or points to the change.

For Theocritus, Gow prints ἄναλλα, "topsy-turvy" (LSJ), found in several manuscripts.

For other instances of "mistranslation," or "translation with paronomasia," see intro. 2.1a.

Knight (1944) 202, Bartelink (1965) 33, Doig (1968) 3; cf. also Rank (1951) 79 on a Homeric gloss of ἐνάλια.

**E. 8.59–60:** praeceps aerii *specula* de montis in undas / deferar;

Vergil uses *specula,* "lookout," where his Theocritean model has "I will . . . leap in the waves from the cliff where Olpis, the fisherman, watches (σκοπιάζεται) for the tunny" (Gow translation).

See on A. 1.180–81 *Aeneas* ***scopulum*** *interea conscendit et omnem /* ***prospectum*** *late pelago petit.*

THEOC. 3.25–27: τὰν βαίταν ἀποδὺς ἐς κύματα τηνῶ ἀλεῦμαι, / ὧπερ τὼς θύννως σκοπιάζεται Ὄλπις ὁ γριπεύς· / καὶ κα δὴ 'ποθάνω, τό γε μὲν τεὸν ἁδὺ τέτυκται.

Cf. Coleman (1977) on 59.

**E. 8.82–83:** sparge molam et fragilis incende bitumine *lauros: / Daphnis* me malus urit, ego hanc in *Daphnide laurum.*

As Servius notes, the laurel is appropriate for working magic on Daphnis because his name suggests δάφνη, "laurel." The words *Daphnis* and *laurum* frame line 83 (see intro. 2.8).

SERV. 83: IN DAPHNIDE LAURUM aut archaismos est pro "in Daphnidem": aut intellegamus supra Daphidis effigiem eam laurum incendere propter nominis similitudem; SERV. Auct. E. 5.20: hunc pastores invenerunt inter lauros et Daphnin vocaverunt.

THEOC. 2.23–24: Δέλφις ἔμ' ἀνίασεν· ἐγὼ δ' ἐπὶ Δέλφιδι δάφναν / αἴθω.

Bartelink (1965) 64, Doig (1968) 2–4, Coleman (1977) on 83, Van Sickle (1978) 139.

**E. 8.107:** *Hylax* in limine *latrat*

*Latrat* glosses the dog's name Hylax, from ὑλακτέω, "bark." Cf. on E. 6.74–77 *Scyllam . . . latrantibus,* and **A. 3.432** *Scyllam . . . canibus.*

Cf. OVID *Met.* 3.224 (for Ovid cf. intro. 2.14): acutae vocis Hylactor; PROP. 4.3.55: Craugidos et catulae vox est mihi grata querentis (with Fedeli's ap. crit.).

Bartelink (1965) 78, Doig (1968) 2.

**E. 9.32–34:** et me *fecere poetam* / Pierides, sunt et mihi carmina, me quoque dicunt / vatem pastores

The use of the verb *facio*, "make," next to the Greek loan word *poeta* alludes to the derivation of *poeta*/ποιητής from ποιέω, although it is not the poet who is the subject of the verb.

The etymologizing is not in the model at Theoc. 7.37–38 ἀοιδόν ἄριστον.

For passages in which poets remark that "shepherds" or "herdsmen" have named something see on **G. 3.280–81:** *hippomanes vero quod nomine dicunt / pastores.*

DON. on Ter. *Andr.* prol. 3: poetae a faciendo dicti sunt, ἀπὸ τοῦ ποιεῖν; SUET. ap. Isid. 8.7.2: poetae unde sint dicti, sic ait Tranquillus (*de Poet.* 2) ". . . quia forma quadam efficitut, quae ποιότης dicitur, poema vocitatum est, eiusque fictores poetae"; MAR. Victor. *Gramm. Lat.* 6.56.16 K: qui versus facit παρὰ τὸ ποιεῖν dictus est ποιητής.

PROP. 4.6.1: sacra facit vates (but *vates* here is not poet); POLLIANUS *Anth. Pal.* 11.127: αἵ σε ποίουσι ποιητήν; GALLUS fr. 2.6 Courtney: fecerunt c[ar]mina Musae (cf. Verducci).

Griffiths (1969–70) 19 n. 11, Verducci (1984) 129.

**E. 10.4–6:** sic tibi, cum fluctus subterlabere Sicanos, / *Doris* ***amara*** suam non intermisceat undam, / incipe: sollicitos Galli dicamus **amores**

Perhaps two kinds of wordplay with *amara* in 5. Servius notes that *Doris* in 5 is metonymy for *mare*, "sea." Vergil suppresses the wordplay or jingle *mare amarum* (for suppression see intro. 2.7). This may be an etymological gloss, because Isidore says that the *mare* is so called because its waters are bitter *(amarae)*. See G. 2.238–47 for what seems to be wordplay involving *amarus* and *mare.*

Then with *amores* in 6 Vergil seems to allude again to the wordplay *amor*/*amarus* as in **E. 3.109–10.**

SERV.: DORIS AMARA mater nympharum est, quam pro mari posuit; ISID. 13.14.1: proprie autem mare appellatum eo quod aquae eius amarae sint.

E. 3.109–10: quisquis *amores* / aut metuet dulcis aut experietur *amaros.*

**E. 10.21–23:** venit Apollo: / "Galle, quid insanis?" inquit. "tua *cura* Lycoris / perque nives alium perque horrida castra secuta est."

Ross explains that "*cura* . . . with the meaning '*amica*' first occurs" here. In 21–23, Vergil is translating Theoc. 1.81–83, and *tua cura Lycoris* represents Theocritus' ἁ δέ τυ κώρα, "your girl." "Virgil has put *Lycoris* in the same position in his line as Theocritus' κώρα, and glossed it with *tua cura* (κούρη, Ionic and always in Homer = κώρα)."

Ross suggests that "this play on *cura* = κούρη/κώρα = *Lycoris*" may have "originated with Gallus"; he notes that Propertius uses *cura* to mean *amica* at 1.1.36, "looking to the Tenth Eclogue, or to the poet Gallus behind it." (It is on E. 10.46 that Servius, perhaps with some degree of exaggeration, says, *hi autem omnes versus Gallis sunt, de ipsius translati carminibus.*)

For the several other plays on *cura* in Vergil see on **A. 1.208–9.**

For translation or mistranslation by homonym see intro. 2.1a.

Ross (1975) 68–69.

## E. 10.55–61:

interea mixtis lustrabo *Maenala* Nymphis,
aut acris venabor apros. non me ulla vetabunt
frigora **Parthenios** canibus circumdare saltus.
iam mihi per rupes videor lucosque sonantis
ire, libet Partho torquere Cydonia cornu
spicula—tamquam haec sit nostri medicina furoris,
aut deus ille malis hominum mitescere discat.

Rosen and Farrell argue that in 59–60, *Cydonia spicula* provides a gloss on the name Acontius (*spicula* = ἄκοντας), as Vergil alludes to one of his models for the Gallus figure here. Callimachus glossed Acontius' name by calling him a bowman (τοξευτής). Gallus himself, both Ross and then Rosen and Farrell have argued, treated the myth of Acontius and Cydippe in the lost *Amores,* probably associating himself as elegiac lover with Acontius. Gallus may have made some use of the wordplay.

Ovid *Her.* 21.211–12 makes the etymology explicit: *mirabar quare tibi nomen* ***Acontius*** *esset; / quod faciat longe vulnus,* ***acumen*** *habes* (for Ovid cf. intro. 2.14).

Rosen and Farrell also repeat the suggestion of Doig that in 55–57, the movement in the geographical epithets from *Maenala* to *Parthenios saltus* "stands for Gallus' passage from a life of amatory *furor* (μανία, μαίνομαι—Μαίναλα) to one of renunciation (παρθενία—*Parthenios*)." I see little in the text pointing to these etymological associations.

On Cydonia in 59, Rosen and Farrell, after Boyd, also see an allusion to the *(Cydonia) mala* alluded to in E. 2.51, *ipse ego cana legam tenera lanugine mala.*

On Maenala see on E. 8.21, *incipe Maenalios mecum, mea tibi, versus* (where Doig also sees a suggestion of *furor*), and G. 1.17, *Pan ovium custos, tua si tibi Maenala curae.* For a possible play on the name Aconteus, see A. 11.615–17 *excussus Aconteus / fulminis in morem aut tormento ponderis acti.* For the association between Venus' epithet Acidalia and Greek ἀκίς, "dart, care," see on A. 1.719–22.

CALLIM. fr. 70: ἀλλ' ἀπὸ τόξου / αὐτὸς ὁ τοξευτῆς ἄρδιν ἔχων ἑτέρου.

Rosen and Farrell (1986), Ross (1975) 89–91, Boyd (1983), Doig (1968) 4–5.

# The *Georgics*

**G. 1.7–8:** Liber et *alma Ceres,* vestro si munere tellus / Chaoniam **pingui** glandem mutavit **arista**

Ross notes that *alma,* with its root meaning "nourishing" (*ab alendo,* as Servius says), is a gloss on the name Ceres, which is said to be from *creare* (Servius) or from *fruges gerere* (Ennius(?), Varro, Cicero). For the single-epithet gloss see intro. 2.2.

*Pingui* seems to gloss *arista* in 2. Ross paraphrases and interprets Servius: "the word *arista* (the ear of grain) is derived from 'dryness' *(ab ariditate),* and Virgil studiously indicates this etymology by glossing the term with an adjective meaning the opposite, *pinguis* ('fat, oily, plump, succulent')." See Ross' explanation of the significance of this gloss for the poem.

See on **A. 7.720** for glosses on *arista* in Catullus and Ovid.

For glosses κατ' ἀντίφρασιν see intro. 2.3.

alma Ceres: SERV. 7: "alma" ab alendo, "Ceres" a creando dicta; VARRO *LL* 5.64: ut ait Ennius, quae "quod gerit fruges, Ceres"; (=*Var.* 49–50 V—but possibly only the preceding line of Varro belongs to Ennius) antiquis enim quod nunc G C; CIC. *ND* 2.67: Mater autem est a gerendis frugibus Ceres tamquam geres; PAUL.-Fest. p. 6, 28 L: alma sancta sive pulchra, vel alens, ab alendo scilicet; ISID. *Diff.* 1.498: alma . . . ab alendo dicta, unde . . . alma Ceres dicta est, alimentorum inventrix (more sources in Maltby).

pinguis arista: SERV. 8: adfectate ait pinguem aristam, cum proprie arista ab ariditate sit dicta (sim. Brev. Exp. 8); VARRO *RR* 1.48.2: arista dicta, quod arescit prima; SERV. A. 7.720: aristae, quas ab ariditate dictas esse constat.

G. 1.14: et *cultor* nemorum, cui *pinguia* Ceae; 1.192: nequiquam *pinguis* palea teret *area* culmos; 1.297–98: at rubicunda Ceres medio succiditur aestu / et medio tostas aestu terit *area* fruges; 1.462: quid cogitet *umidus Auster;* A. 7.720: vel cum sole novo densae *torrentur aristae.*

alma Ceres: Ross (1987) 33–34, Cerda (1608) 226 on G. 1.147; cf. McCartney (1927) 195 (cites *alma nutrix* at Lucr. 5.230), and see Feeney (1991) 121 and Pease (1979) on Cic. *ND* 2.67 (p. 722) for more on Ceres. pinguis arista: Ross (1987) 34–38; cf. Cerda (1608) 199.

**G. 1.11?:** ferte *simul* Faunique pedem *Dryadesque* puellae

By using *simul* in a line with *Dryadas,* Vergil may be alluding to the etymology of the term *Hamadryades,* from ἅμα = *simul* + Dryades ([Prob.] ad loc. mentions the derivation). The Hamadryads are the subject of discussion at Callim. *Hymn* 4.79–85 and may have been treated in his work *On Nymphs,* and Roman poets seem to have paid attention to Callimachus' lines. Full details cannot be given here, but for "the genealogy of the term hamadryad, . . . descended in a line from Hesiod, Callimachus, Catullus, and Gallus, to Vergil and Propertius," see Myers, who discusses the use of *hamadryadas* at Ovid *Met.* 14.624 (for Ovid cf. intro. 2.14).

[PROB.] G. 1.11: "Dryadas puellas" dicit, quas alii Hamadryadas vocant, et eas cum quercu nasci et simul interire, sed diuturnas esse, et inde Hamadryadas dictas. quercus enim Graece appellatur δρῦς, ἅμα significat simul (somewhat sim. Serv. E. 10.62; cf. Schol. Apoll. Rhod. 2.477).

Myers (1994) 230–32, Bing (1988) 41 (neither mentioning this line).

**G. 1.14–15:** et *cultor* nemorum, cui *pinguia* Ceae / ter centum nivei tondent dumeta iuvenci

In 14, the *cultor* is Aristaeus, whose name is suppressed (see intro. 2.7); he is associated with *pinguis* here, in a play that echoes that of *pinguis* and *arista* above in 8.

Ross (1987) 36–37 (notes that Schol. Bern. tell the story of Aristaeus, who is not mentioned until 14, in a note on 8 *arista,* perhaps echoing an earlier note about the wordplay).

**G. 1.17–18:** *Pan* **ovium** custos, tua si tibi **Maenala** curae, / adsis, o Tegeaee, *favens*

Thomas: "*favens:* a gloss in the learned manner . . . on the name Faunus (the Italian Pan), to which *faveo* is related." On the omission or suppression of the term glossed see intro. 2.7. Vergil glosses the name Faunus in line with a derivation from *for,* at **A. 7.81–82** oracula *Fauni, / fatidici* genitoris.

Servius derives the name *Maenala* from Greek μῆλα = *oves;* the presence of *ovium* and *Maenala* in 17 may allude to that etymology. Vergil may play on the name Maenala and Greek μανία in E. 8.21 and 10.52–61. For plays on μῆλα/mala = "apples" see on A. 7.740 *maliferae . . . Abellae.*

SERV. Auct. G. 1.10: Faunus, quid dictus est a fando. . . . quidam faunos putant dictos ab eo, quod frugibus faveant; MACROB. 1.12.22: Faunam quod omni usui animantium favet; SERV. 17: MAENALA mons Arcadia, dictus ἀπὸ τῶν μήλων, is est ab ovibus, quibus plenus est.

Thomas (1988) on 16–18; see Bartelink (1965) 76 for more on *Faunus* and *faveo.*

**G. 1.56–59:**

nonne vides, croceos ut Tmolus odores,
India mittit ebur, molles sua tura Sabaei,
at Chalybes nudi ferrum *virosa*que Pontus
*castorea,* Eliadum palmas Epiros equarum?

Ross:

> Beavers were trapped not for their fur but for the glandular secretion, used medicinally, which was popularly thought to be secreted by their testicles. . . . Virgil's point . . . is conveyed . . . by the gloss *virosa (castorea),* not simply "strong (smelling)," but "manly," which lends then further significance to the topic [in these lines] of the manly West. But Servius records as well the comment, " 'virosa' autem venenata . . . et 'virosa' dicta ab eo, quod est virus." . . . Poison . . . is a frequent motif in the poem, and thus is set forward in this characteristic, and poetically vivid, "learned" manner. *Vīrosa* . . . includes . . . the meanings of *vīrus* ("animal sperm," "poison") and *vĭr* ("man"—ancient etymologies are not concerned with vowel quantities, of course), with inevitably as well an echo of *vīres* ("strength").

SERV. 58: castores autem a castrando dicti sunt. . . . "virosa" dicta ab eo, quod est virus; alii fortia accipiunt a viribus.

Ross (1987) 42–43 (see for more details); on vowel quantities see intro. 2.1.

**G. 1.62–63:** Deucalion vacuum *lapides* iactavit in orbem, / unde *homines* nati, *durum genus.*

While telling the aetiological story of how humans were made from rocks, Vergil alludes to the connection made between λαός, "people," and λᾶας, "stone." This mythological wordplay appears certainly in Pindar, and probably in fragments of Hesiod and Callimachus. Ovid twice alludes to the wordplay, once echoing Vergil's *durum genus* (for Ovid cf. intro. 2.14).

SERV. 63: expressit τὸ αἴτιον, id est causativum; nam et graece populi λαοὶ dicuntur a lapidibus; APOLLOD. 1.48.7: καὶ Διὸς εἰπόντος ὑπὲρ κεφαλῆς ἔβαλλεν αἴρων λίθους, καὶ οὓς μὲν ἔβαλε Δευκαλίων, ἄνδρες ἐγένοντο, οὓς δὲ Πύρρα, γυναῖκες. ὅθεν καὶ λαοὶ μεταφορικῶς ὠνομάσθησαν ἀπὸ τοῦ λᾶας ὁ λίθος.

HES. fr. 234 M-W: ἤτοι γὰρ Λοκρὸς Λελέγων ἡγήσατο λαῶν, / τούς ῥά ποτε Κρονίδης Ζεὺς ἄφθιτα μήδεα εἰδὼς / λεκτοὺς ἐκ γαίης ΛΑΟΥΣ πόρε Δευκαλίωνι; PIND. *O.* 9.45: κτισσάσθαν λίθινον γόνον· / λαοὶ δ' ὀνύμασθεν; CALLIM. fr. 496: ΛΑΟΙ Δευκαλίωνος ὅσοι γενόμεσθα; OVID *Am.* 2.14.11–12: quique iterum iaceret generis primordia nostri / in vacuo lapides orbe, parandus erat; *Met.* 1.414 (Deucalion and Pyrrha, borrows from and alludes to Vergil): inde genus durum sumus experiensque laborum; cf. too HYG. *Fab.* 153, and in the myth of Niobe at *Il.* 24.611 λαοὺς δὲ λίθους ποίησε Κρονίων (see Rank).

Cerda (1608) 211, Ahl (1985) 104–5, McKeown (1987) 47, Rank (1951) 101–3.

**G. 1.75–76:** aut tenuis fetus viciae *tristis*que *lupini* / sustuleris fragilis calamos silvamque sonantem.

Thomas: "the epithet no doubt describes the bitterness of the seed . . . , but V[ergil] may also intend a (false) etymological gloss (λύπη, 'sadness,' 'grief')."

Cerda (1608) 211, Coleman (1984) 30, Thomas (1988) on 75.

**G. 1.103:** ipsa suas mirantur *Gargara* messis

Nisbet and others suggest an etymological pun here on Greek γάργαρα, "heaps." Mynors notes that "Macrobius . . . thinks V[ergil]'s choice was influenced by the Greek use of γάργαρα proverbially of a large number." Serv. A. 9.85 and Schol. Stat. *Theb.* 1.549 instead suggest a derivation from κάρα = "head, peak, top."

MACROB. 5.20.11–13: haec Gargara tanta frugum copia erant ut qui magnum cuiusque rei numerum vellet exprimere pro multitudine immensa Gargara nominaret. testis Alcaeus, qui in κωμῳδοτραγῳδίᾳ (fr. 19 Kock) sic ait:

ἐτύγχανον μὲν ἀγρόθεν πλείστους φέρων
εἰς τὴν ἑορτὴν ὅσσον οἷον εἴκοσι.
ὁρῶ δ' ἄνωθεν Γάργαρ' ἀνθρώπων κύκλῳ.

Aristophanes autem comicus composito nomine ex harena et Gargaris innumerabilem, ut eius lepos est, numerum conatur exprimere. in fabula enim Acharneusin (*Ach.* 3) ait,

ἄδ' ὠδυνήθην ψαμμακοσιογάργαρα.

ψαμμακόσια autem seorsum pro multis Varro saepe in Menippeis suis posuit, sed Aristophanes adiecit γάργαρα ad significationem numerositatis innumerae.

Nisbet (1990) 261, Mynors (1990) on 103, *EV* s.v. Gargaro (Bevilacqua).

**G. 1.109–12:**

illa cadens raucum per levia murmur
saxa ciet, scatebrisque *arentia* temperat *ar*va.
quid qui, ne gravidis procumbat culmus *ar*istis,
luxuriem segetum tenera depascit in herba

Ross notes that Vergil is playing again on the etymology *arista ab ariditate* (see on G. 1.7–8). In 110, *arentia . . . arva* alludes to the etymology of the last word in 111, *aristis* (see intro. 2.9 for wordplay at ends of consecutive lines).

Ross (1987) 48–49.

**G. 1.123:** *curis* acuens mortalia *corda*

For the etymology *cura dicta ab eo quod cor urat,* and other plays on *cura,* see on A. 1.208–9.

Due (1973) 276–77, Bartelink (1965) 105.

**G. 1.127–28?:** ipsaque tellus / omnia liberius nullo poscente ferebat

Petersmann suggests, perhaps unpersuasively, allusion to the etymology that connected Dodona with δίδωμι (see on **G. 1.149**).

Petersmann (1987) 8.

**G. 1.137–38:** *navita* tum stellis numeros et nomina fecit / *Pleiadas, Hyadas,* claramque Lycaonis Arcton.

Vergil tells how sailors first named the Pleiades, the Hyades, and Arctos: the signpost *nomina fecit* alerts us to etymological wordplay (see intro. 2.6). The etymologies of the names of the Pleiades and Hyades were contested in antiquity; here Vergil offers his opinion.

Servius derives Pleiades from πλέω, "to sail," because their spring rising marked the beginning of the sailing season, and Hyades from ὕω, "to rain," because their May rising marked the start of spring rains. Sources suggest that the Pleiades are named because they are daughters of Pleione; are useful to many (πλείοσι), or to sailors (τοῖς πλέουσι); were metamorphosed into doves (πέλειαι) as they fled Orion; go around (πολέω) in rotation. Evidence for discussion of the name Hyades includes **A. 1.744** and 3.516, where *pluvias* is a gloss on the name, and passages from Cicero, Tiro, and Ovid. Hyades is derived from ὗς, Latin *sus,* "pig," from their resemblance to the letter upsilon, or from their brother Hyas. Cicero and Tiro dismiss the derivation from ὗς, preferring that from ὕω.

By saying that sailors named the Pleiades and Hyades, Vergil argues for the etymology from sailing and weather for both words. That *navita* and *Pleiadas* begin consecutive lines helps the suggestion (see intro. 2.9).

In *Fasti* 5, Ovid mentions the derivation from ὕω in a line that seems to allude to Vergil (166: ***navita** quas Hyadas Graius ab imbre vocat*), but Ovid explicitly derives the name from the brother Hyas, and may also allude (in 164 *grege*) to the derivation from ὗς, "pig." Ovid seems to be acknowledging and commenting on what Vergil is doing in the *Georgics.* (For Ovidian comment on Vergilian etymologizing see also intro. 2.14; note esp. what I say there about Hyas-Dionysus.)

Line 138 is a conflation of *Iliad* 18.486, which starts Πληιάδας θ' Ὑάδας τε, and Callimachus *Hymn* 1.41, which ends Λυκαονίης ἄρκτοιο. See also Farrell for discussion of Hesiod *Op.* 615, which begins Πληιάδες θ' Ὑάδες τε.

Pleiades (more in O'Hara and in Maltby s.v.): SERV. G. 1.138: PLEIADES . . . ortu suo primae navigationis tempus ostendunt: unde graece pleiades dicuntur ἀπὸ τοῦ πλέειν, latine vergiliae a verni temporis significatione, quo oriuntur; ISID. 3.71.13: Has Latini Vergilias dicunt a temporis significatione, quod est ver, quando exoriuntur. Nam occasu suo hiemem, ortu aestatem, primaeque navigationis tempus ostendunt; SCHOL. Arat. *Phaen.* 254–55 (Martin, p. 202; Maass, p. 387): Ἄτλαντος δὲ καὶ Πληιόνης γενεαλογοῦνται Πλειάδες, παρ' ὃ καὶ λέγονται· ἢ ἐπεὶ πλείοσιν εἰσὶ χρειώδεις, τοῖς τε πλέουσι καὶ γεωργοῦσι· ἢ ὅτι εἰς πελείας μετεμορφώθησαν τὸν Ὠρίωνα φεύγουσαι· ἢ ἀπὸ τοῦ πολεῖν ἐκ περίοδου καὶ συμπληροῦν τὸν ἐνιαυτόν. Later manuscripts add (Martin p. 548; cf. Maass p. 386): καλοῦνται δὲ αἱ Πλειάδες τῷ ὀνόματι τούτῳ ἀπὸ Πλειόνης τῆς ἑαυτῶν μητρός, ἢ ἀπὸ τοῦ πελειάδας γενέσθαι φευγούσας τὸν Ὠρίωνα, ἢ ἀπὸ τοῦ εἰς πολλὰ χρησιμεύειν (σημαντικαὶ γὰρ καὶ θέρους καὶ σπόρου), ἢ ὅτι πλησίον ἀλλήλων κεῖνται παρὰ τὸ λαιὸν γόνυ τοῦ Περσέως, ἢ ὅτι χρήσιμοί εἰσι τοῖς πλέουσιν; SERV. Auct. G. 1.138: pleiades dicuntur . . . vel quod Pliones et Atlantis filiae sint; BREV. EXP. G. 1.138: ἀπὸ τοῦ πλείονες; ISID. 3.71.13: Pliades a pluralitate dictae, quia pluralitatem Graeci ἀπὸ τοῦ πλεῖστον appellant; they lie near (πλησίον) to one another: Hyg. *Fab.* 192.

Hyades (more in O'Hara and in Maltby s.v.): CIC. *ND* 2.111.1 (commenting on his translation of Aratus): eius (sc. Tauri) caput stellis conspersum est frequentibus; "has Graeci stellas Hyadas vocitare suerunt" ⟨*Arat.* fr. 29 S⟩ a pluendo (ὕειν enim est pluere), nostri imperite Suculas, quasi a subus essent non ab imbribus nominatae; AUL. GELL. 13.9 = Tullius Tiro fr. 13, *GRF* p. 402: sed ὑάδες οὐκ ἀπὸ τῶν ὑῶν, id est non a subus ita ut nostri Opici putaverunt, sed ab eo, quod est ὕειν, appellantur; nam et cum oriuntur et cum occidunt, tempestates pluvias largosque umbres cient. Pluere autem Graeca lingua ὕειν dicitur; SERV. Auct. G. 1.138: hae sunt in fronte tauri, in formam Υ litterae, unde etiam hyadas dici volunt. . . . alii hyadas a porcis, quas Graeci ὗας dicunt, a nobis sues appellantur, non a pluviis, quas ὑετοὺς vocant, dictas accipiunt: nam ideo et suculas dici a suibis; SERV. Auct. A. 1.744: quidam hyadas ab Hyante fratre, quem inventum extinctum usque ad mortem doluerunt, dictas putant.

OVID *F.* 5.163–72, 179–82:

at simul inducent obscura crepuscula noctem,
   pars Hyadum toto de grege nulla latet.
ora micant Tauri septem radiantia flammis,
   *navita quas Hyadas Graius ab imbre vocat;*
pars Bacchum nutrisse putat, pars credidit esse
   Tethyos has neptes Oceanique senis.
nondum stabat Atlas umeros oneratus Olympo,
   cum satus est forma conspiciendus Hyas;
hunc stirps Oceani maturis nixibus Aethra
   edidit et nymphas, sed prior ortus Hyas.
. . . . . . . . . . . . . . . . . . . . . . . . . . . . . . .
mater Hyan et Hyan maestae flevere sorores
   cervicemque polo subpositurus Atlas,
victus uterque parens tamen est pietate sororum:
   illa dedit caelum, *nomina fecit Hyas.*

See O'Hara (1992) and (1996) for more evidence, and a more extensive discussion of Ovid; on conflation, Thomas (1988) on 138 and (1986) 193–94; cf. too Farrell (1991) 214–16, Cerda (1608) 224.

**G. 1.149:** victum Dodona negaret

Weber cites the gloss of the name Dodona in Apollodorus' Περὶ Θεῶν (δίδωσιν . . . τὰ ἀγαθά) and notes that Vergil's phrase "*victum . . . negaret* is an exact inversion of Apollodorus' gloss," so Vergil suggests "that there was once a time when Dodona belied its name." He points to a gloss of the name Dodona κατ' ἀντίφρασιν with the verb δέχομαι in Callimachus and suggests that Vergil is recalling both Callimachus and the gloss in Apollodorus that "holds the key" to what Callimachus is doing. For glosses κατ' ἀντίφρασιν see intro. 2.3.

APOLLOD. Ath. Περὶ Θεῶν (*FGrH* 244, fr. 88): καθάπερ οἱ τὸν Δία Δωδωναῖον μὲν καλοῦντες ὅτι δίδωσιν ἡμῖν τὰ ἀγαθά; SCHOL. *Il.* 16.233: τινὲς δὲ "'αναδωδωναῖε" ὑφ' ἕν, παρὰ τὴν ἀνάδοσιν τῶν ἀγαθῶν. . . . τινὲς δὲ Δωδώνην τὴν γῆν, παρόσον πάντα δίδωσι.

SIMMIAS Rhod. fr. 10 P: ὑπεδέξετο Δωδώ (Weber calls this an antithetical pairing: give/receive); CALLIM. *Hymn* 4.284–85: ἅ Δωδώνηθε Πελασγοί / τηλόθεν ἐκβαίνοντα πολὺ πρώτιστα δέχονται; cf. also G. 1.127–28?: ipsaque tellus / omnia liberius nullo poscente ferebat.

Weber (1991).

**G. 1.160–62:** dicendum et quae sint duris agrestibus *arma,* / quis sine nec potuere seri nec surgere messes: / vomis et inflexi primum grave robur *aratri*

Marouzeau notes that these lines suggest a connection between *arma* and *arare,* like that between *arare* and *armentum* or *arma* and *armentum.* The wordplay would resemble that between words at the end of consecutive lines (see intro. 2.9).

For *arare* and *armentum* see on **A. 7.538–39,** *quina redibant / **armenta** et terram centum vertebat **aratris;*** for *arma* and *armentum,* see on **A. 3.540,** *bello **armantur** equi, bella haec **armenta** minantur.*

Bartelink (1965) 102–3, Marouzeau (1940) 262, Ross (1987) 52–53, 82–83.

**G. 1.192:** nequiquam *pinguis* palea teret *area* culmos.

Varro and Servius Auctus connect the words *area* and *aresco,* "to dry." Ross notes that "Virgil clearly glosses the word" *area* in G. 1.298; he suggests that in 192, Vergil brings wet *(pinguis)* and dry *(area)* together to echo "the fundamental opposition of fire and water" of G. 1.7 *pinguis . . . arista.*

SERV. Auct. G. 1.178: area est locus vacuus . . . quasi qui exaruerit (cf. Brev. Exp. G. 1.178, Paul.-Fest. p. 10, 10 L); VARRO *LL* 5.38: ubi frumenta secta, ut terantur, arescunt, area.

Cf. **G. 1.7–8:** pinguis . . . arista; G. 1.297–98: at rubicunda Ceres medio succiditur aestu / et medio tostas aestu terit *area* fruges.

Ross (1987) 75–76.

**G. 1.208?:** *Libra* die somnique *pares* ubi *fecerit* horas

In this reference to the autumnal equinox, Bartelink sees in *pares . . . fecerat* a gloss on the name *libra,* since *pares facere* = *librare.* He compares two passages in Lucan. But given Libra's function, such a reference need not be etymologizing.

ISID. 3.71.29: Libram . . . vocaverunt ab aequalitate mensis ipsius, quia VIII Kal. Octobres sol per illud signum aequinoctium facit.

Lucan 4.58–59: atque iterum aequatis ad iustae ponderis Librae / temporibus vicere dies; 8.467: tempus erat quo Libra pares examinat horas; COLUM. 10.42: cum paribus Titan orbem libraverit horis.

Bartelink (1965) 79.

**G. 1.217–18:** candidus auratis *aperit* cum cornibus annum / Taurus

Thomas describes this "elegant periphrasis for April, with *aperit* functioning as a gloss on the unstated month." For suppression of the term glossed see intro. 2.7.

Ovid in the *Fasti* explicitly mentions the same gloss, while arguing for the derivation from Aphrodite, but probably, as Porte suggests, accepting both derivations (for Ovid cf. intro. 2.14).

VARRO *LL* 6.33: secundus (sc. mensis), ut Fulvius scribit et Iunius, a venere, quod ea sit Aphrodite; cuius nomen ego antiquis litteris quod nusquam inveni, magis puto dictum, quod ver omnia aperit, Aprilem; ISID. 5.33.7: Aprilis pro Venere dicitur, quasi Aphrodis; Graece enim 'Αφροδίτη Venus dicitur; vel quia hoc mense omnia aperiuntur in florem, quasi Aperilis; cf. too VARRO fr. 409 (*GRF* p. 355): eaque omnia verno id est hoc mense aperiantur, arbores quoque nec minus cetera, quae continet terra, aperire se in germen incipiant, ab his omnibus mensem Aprilem dici merito credendum est quasi Aperilem; SERV. G. 1.43: Aprilis dictus est quasi terras tepore aperiens (more sources for both derivations in Maltby).

OVID *F.* 4.61–62, 85–87, 89:

> sed Veneris mensem Graio sermone notatum
>     auguror: a spumis est dea dicta maris
> . . . . . . . . . . . . . . . . . . . . . . . .
> Quo non livor abit? sunt qui tibi menis honorem
>     eripuisse velint invideantque, Venus.
> nam quia ver *aperit* tunc omnia . . . ,
> . . . . . . . . . . . . . . . . . . . . . . . .
> *Aprilem* memorant ab aperto tempore dictum.

Thomas (1988) on 217, Bartelink (1965) 72, Porte (1985) 229, McKeown (1987) 55, Mynors (1990) on 217–18, O'Hara (1996).

**G. 1.277:** pallidus Orcus

By saying *pallidus Orcus* where the model in Hes. *Op.* 802 has Ὅρκος, Vergil suggests a connection between (or blurs the distinction between) Orcus the god of the dead and Horcus the god of oath.

For such "mistranslations" or "translation by homonym" see intro. 2.1a.

Bartelink (1965) 33–34, Doig (1968) 3; on Orcus see Wagenvoort (1956) 102–31, esp. 104–5, and Mynors (1990) on 277.

**G. 1.297–98:** at rubicunda Ceres medio succiditur aestu / et medio tostas aestu terit *area* fruges.

Varro and Servius connect *area* with *aresco,* "to dry." Ross says Vergil "clearly glosses the word" in 298. See on **G. 1.7–8,** *pinguis . . . arista,* and on **G. 1.192,** where *pinguis* and *area* are opposed.

Ross (1987) 75–76.

**G. 1.308–9?:** tum figere dammas / stuppea torquentem *Balearis* verbera *fundae*

Servius Auctus derives the name *Balearis* from βάλλω, "hurl," because of the use (or invention) of the sling on the islands so named. Thus *Balearis . . . funda* may be a kind of reverse gloss, like *Hernica saxa* (see on **A. 7.683–84**), where Balearis modifies a noun, *funda,* that hints at its etymology. Some may feel that the association of the islanders with the sling makes an etymological explanation of Vergil's lines unnecessary.

SERV. Auct. 309: BALEARIS FVNDAE quia apud insulas Baleares fundarum usus inventus est. et insulae Baleares primo Gymnasiae dictae: post vero cum a Graecis occupatae sunt, quia cum lapidibus fundas rotantes adversarios submoverent, insulas, quas incolebant, παρὰ τοῦ βάλλειν Baleares appellarunt (sim. in Isid. 14.6.44); DIOD. Sic. 5.17.1: προσαγορεύονται βαλιαρίδες ἀπὸ τοῦ βάλλειν ταῖς σφενδόναις λίθους μεγάλους κάλλιστα τῶν ἁπάντων ἀνθρώπων; LIVY *Perioch*. 60: Baleares a teli missu appellati vel a Balio, Herculis comite ibi relicto; cf. LYCOPH. 633–47, where the name is suppressed.

OVID *Met.* 2.727–28 (for Ovid cf. intro. 2.14): Balearica plumbum / funda iacit; 4.709–10: Balearica . . . funda; cf. the play on the name Ballista in the verses attributed to the young Vergil by the Suetonian *Vita Verg.* 17 (discussed by Hanssen).

Cf. Cerda (1608) 251, Hanssen (1948) 124–25.

**G. 1.326–27:** implentur fossae et cava flumina crescunt / cum sonitu *fervet*que *fretis* spirantibus aequor.

Varro and Servius derive *fretum* from the verb *fervere.* Cf. Lucr. 6.427–28: *freta circum / fervescunt.*

VARRO *LL* 7.22: dictum fretum ab similitudine ferventis aquae, quod in fretum s⟨a⟩epe concurrrat ⟨a⟩estus atque effervescat; ISID. 13.18.2: fretum autem appellatum quod ibi semper mare ferveat . . . nam freta dicta Varro ait quasi fervida, id est ferventia, et motum fervoris habentia; SERV. A. 1.607: proprie fretum est mare naturaliter mobile, ab undarum fervore nominatum (sim. in Serv. Auct. A. 1.557, and see Maltby for more sources).

Cerda (1608) 252, Bartelink (1965) 97, Mynors (1990) on 327.

**G. 1.328–33:**

ipse pater media nimborum in nocte corusca
*fulmina* molitur dextra, quo maxima motu
terra tremit, fugere ferae et mortalia corda
per gentis humilis stravit pavor; ille flagranti
aut Atho aut Rhodopen aut *alta Ceraunia telo*
deicit

Line 332 is modeled on Theoc. 7.77: ἢ Ἄθω ἢ Ῥοδόπαν ἢ Καύκασον ἐσχατόωντα. Vergil translates the first half of the line precisely but then (perhaps following Cinna; see below) substitutes *Ceraunia* for Theocritus' Καύκασον. The words *fulmina* in 329 and *telo* (= *fulmine*) next to *Ceraunia* in 332 allude to the etymology of *Ceraunia* from κεραυνός, which is given by Servius here, and treated explicitly at Apoll. Rhod. 4.518–21 (with signpost and wordplay at ends of consecutive lines—see intro. 2.6 and 9):

οἱ δ' ἐν ὄρεσσιν
ἐνναίουσιν ἅπερ τε Κεραύνια κικλήσκονται
ἐκ τόθεν ἐξότε τούσγε Διὸς Κρονίδαο κεραυνοί
νῆσον ἐς ἀντιπέραιαν ἀπέτραπον ὁρμηθῆναι.

Thomas notes that the words *alta Ceraunia* translate the name Acroceraunia (*alta* = ἄκρος; note Servius' phrase *propter altitudinem nominati*), which occurs in no extant text earlier than the *Georgics,* and first occurs in Horace C. 1.3.20. Horace's propempticon to Vergil, Nisbet and Hubbard note, seems to owe much to Cinna's propempticon to Pollio, which mentioned the nearby island of Corcyra, so, Thomas suggests, Cinna may have mentioned Acroceraunia. Thomas notes further that since Theoc. 7.77 (see above) is from a propempticon, Vergil may have "conflated not only two favored poets, but the propemptica of two favored poets."

McKeown, citing Vergil, suggests that "in characterizing *Ceraunia* as *violenta* at [*Am.*] 2.11.19, Ovid is alluding to the derivation of that name from κεραυνός" (for Ovid cf. intro. 2.14).

For etymologizing with conflation of translated models see also G. 1.137–38 and perhaps A. 8.425.

For plays on ακρ-, *altus, arduus* see on **A. 3.270–71** *Neritos ardua.* For wordplay with *fulmina* see on A. 6.842–43 *geminos, duo* ***fulmina belli, / Scipiadas.***

SERV. A. 3.506: Ceraunia sunt montes Epiri, a crebris fulminibus propter altitudinem nominati; unde Horatius (C. 1.3.20) expressius dixit "Acroceraunia" propter altitudinem et fulminum iactus (sim. on G. 1.332); ISID. 14.8.12: Ceraunii sunt montes Epiri, a crebris dicti fulminibus. Graece enim fulmen κεραυνός dicitur.

Cerda (1608) 253, Bartelink (1965) 46, O'Hara (1990b), Nisbet (1990) 261, McKeown (1987) 47, Thomas (1988) on 332 and (1986) 194–95, Paschalis (1995) on Hor. C. 1.3.

**G. 1.337:** quos ignis caelo Cyllenius *erret* in orbis

Servius, Bartelink and Thomas note the gloss here: Cyllenius is the planet Mercury, and *erret* alludes to the etymology of *planeta* or πλανήτης from πλάνη, "wandering."

See on **A. 4.211** for Vergil's elaborate use of this etymology in the *Aeneid.*

SERV.: bene "erret"; nam planetae vocantur ἀπὸ τῆς πλάνης, id est ab errore; CIC. *ND* 2.20.51: maxume vero sunt admirabiles motus earum quinque stellarum quae falso vocantur errantes. nihil enim erran quod in omni aeternitate conservant progressus et regressus reliquosque motus constantis et ratos (more sources in Maltby s.v. planeta).

Bartelink (1965) 88, Thomas (1988) on 337.

**G. 1.353?:** menstrua luna

Perhaps an allusion to the derivation of *menstrua* or *mensis* from μήνη.

SERV. 353: MENSTRVA LVNA unde et μήνη dicitur; VARRO *LL* 6.10: mensis a lunae motu dictus, dum ab sole profecto rursus redit ad eum. luna quod Graece olim dicta μήνη, unde illorum μῆνες, ab eo nostri (more sources in Maltby); differently CIC. *ND* 2.28.69: novem lunae cursibus, qui quia mensa spatia conficiunt menses nominantur.

**G. 1.356–57?:** continuo ventis *surgentibus* aut *freta* ponti / incipiunt *agitata tumescere* et aridus altis

De la Cerda suggests further allusion (as at G. 1.326–27) to the derivation *fretum ab undarum fervore.*

Cerda (1608) 259.

**G. 1.364:** atque *altam* supra volat *ardea* nubem

Servius connects the name for the heron, *ardea,* with *arduus,* because the bird is thought to fly higher when storms approach; *altam* here may allude to that etymology. Elsewhere Servius connects the name with *arduus* κατ' ἀντίφρασιν, because, he says, the bird does not fly high.

For other plays on *arduus* or *altus* see on **A. 3.270–71** *Neritos ardua.* Cf. esp. **A. 7.411–12** *locus* ***Ardea*** *quondam / dictus avis, et nunc* ***magnum*** *manet* ***Ardea*** *nomen.*

SERV.: ardea dicta quasi ardua: quae cum altius volaverit, significat tempestatem; SERV. A. 7.412: sciendum tamen ardeam κατ' ἀντίφρασιν dictam, quod brevitate pennarum altius non volat: Lucanus (5.553) "quodque ausa volare ardea sublimis pennae confisa natanti"; ISID. 12.7.21 (quoted on A. 7.411–12).

Bartelink (1965) 102, Ahl (1985) 265 n. 29.

**G. 1.373:** *aeriae* fugere grues

Wordplay or soundplay: Farrell notes that *aeriae,* "flying aloft," is used where one model at *Il.* 3.7 has ἠέριαι, "early morning"; he notes that the word was of interest to Apoll. Rhod. as well. For other such "mistranslations" see intro. 2.1a.

Farrell (1991) 221–23, citing Conington (1963) ad loc.

**G. 1.402–3:** solis et occasum servans de culmine summo / nequiquam *seros* exercet *noctua cantus.*

Vergil probably glosses the name of the *noctua,* which Varro and others derive, unsurprisingly, from its singing at night; see on **A. 12.862–64,** where he probably suppresses and glosses the name, in verses that recall these.

**G. 1.404–9:**

apparet liquido sublimis in aere Nisus,<br>
et pro purpureo poenas dat Scylla capillo:

quacumque illa levem fugiens *secat* aethera pennis,
ecce inimicus atrox magno stridore per auras
insequitur Nisus; qua se fert Nisus ad auras,
illa levem fugiens raptim *secat* aethera pennis.

Thomas: Vergil "glosses the (omitted) name of the bird: the *ciris,* which once cut (κείρω) her father's lock, now 'cuts' the air with her wings." He notes Ovid's more explicit etymologizing of the name Ciris (for Ovid cf. intro. 2.14), and the repetition of 406–9 at *Ciris* 538–41, which may point to a common model in Gallus or elsewhere.

Nisbet suggests a further (suppressed) pun here between Nisus and *nisus.*

For Vergil's glosses on the name of the other Scylla, see on **A. 3.432.** For suppression see intro. 2.7.

OVID *Met.* 8.150–51: plumis in avem mutata vocatur / Ciris et a tonso est hoc nomen adepta capillo; [VERG.] *Ciris* 488: facti de nomine Ciris; possibly a lost gloss in CALLIM. fr. 113.4: Κ]εῖριν. . . ; cf. also on **A. 3.432** for the *Hecale.*

Thomas (1988) on 404–9 and on 406–9, Nisbet (1990) 261, O'Hara (1996).

## G. 1.427–35:

luna revertentis cum primum colligit ignis,
si nigrum obscuro comprenderit aera cornu,
*ma*ximus agricolis pelagoque parabitur imber;
at si *virgineum* suffuderit ore ruborem,
*ve*ntus erit: vento semper rubet aurea Phoebe.
sin ortu quarto (namque is *certissimus auctor*)
*pu*ra neque obtunsis per caelum cornibus ibit,
totus et ille dies et qui nascentur ab illo
exactum ad mensem pluvia ventisque carebunt

Brown argues that these lines present Vergil's name in a kind of acrostic: the first two letters of 429, 431, and 433 are *ma, ve,* and *pu,* spelling out, in reverse order, the first two letters of each element of the name Publius Vergilius Maro.

This is less improbable than it may at first seem, because of other features of the lines. Vergil is adapting a section of Aratus that includes, at *Phaen.* 783–87, a noteworthy acrostic (see Brown, Thomas, or Levitan). In 430, *virgineum* plays on the name *Vergilius,* and Vergil's nickname Parthenias. *Auctor* in 432 may also suggest secondarily the notion of a literary "author."

SERV. A.1 Praef.: adeo autem verecundissimus fuit, ut ex moribus cognomen acceperit; nam dictus est Parthenias (cf. too Suet. *Vita Verg.* 11).

Cf. 4.563–64: Vergilium . . . Parthenope.

Brown (1963) 103, Levitan (1978) 55–68, Fowler (1983), Thomas (1988) on 427–37, Bing (1990), Haslam (1992), Hendry (n.d.); on suggested etymologies for Vergil's name, see Suerbaum (1981) 1172, 1243–46 and 150–51; on Vergil's nickname cf. also Knight (1944) 36–37.

**G. 1.460:** et *claro* silvas cernes *Aquilone* moveri

Knight suggests wordplay in which "*claro* neatly contradicts the etymological meaning of *aquilone,* 'the black wind,' derived from *aquilus,* 'dark-colored.'" See intro. 2.3 for glosses κατ' ἀντίφρασιν.

Cf. on **A. 5.2,** ***fluctusque atros Aquilone secabat.***

Knight (1934), Bartelink (1965) 101; on Aquilo as "the Black Wind" cf. Lindsay (1928) 20.

**G. 1.462?:** quod cogitet *umidus Auster*

Knight suggests that Vergil calls "the southeast wind 'wet,' *umidus,* because its name was Auster, which he and others derive from a root meaning 'dry,' a root appearing in the English, and indeed the Greek, word 'austere.'" Bartelink finds this "extremely doubtful," since southern winds are always described as bringing rain.

LSJ derives αὐστηρός from αὔω = ξηραίνω, "dry, parch" (cf. αὖος, dry). Walde-Hofmann s.v. *auster* (p. 87) deny any connection between the wind *auster* and Greek αὖος, but this would not prevent wordplay. For wordplay on "dryness" see on **G. 1.7–8,** pinguis . . . arista. See intro. 2.3 for glosses κατ' ἀντίφρασιν.

A better approach, however, might be that of de la Cerda, which is to see in *umidus Auster* a gloss of the wind's suppressed other name *Notus* or Νότος, which Aulus Gellius quite reasonably associates with νοτίς, "moisture." For suppression see intro. 2.7, for alternate names, intro. 2.10.

AUL. Gell. 2.22.14: is (sc. ventus) Latine auster, Graece νότος nominatur, quoniam est nebulosus atque umectus; νοτίς enim Graece umor nominatur; NON. p. 50, 20 M: Austrum, qui graece Νότος dicitur, ab umore et nebula, quod νότος graece umor latine interpretatione dicatur ac sit is ventus sudoris effector; cf. ISID. 13.11.6: auster ab auriendo aquas vocatus.

Cerda (1608) 273, Knight (1934) 124, (1944) 199, Bartelink (1965) 103, Weber (1991) 326 n. 15 (Knight is "probably incorrect").

**G. 1.491–92:** nec fuit indignum superis bis *sanguine* nostro / Emathiam et latos *Haemi* pinguescere campos.

Doig: "*Haemi* . . . after the mention of *sanguine* . . . could not fail to evoke the association with the Greek αἷμα, producing 'the plains of Blood.'" Thomas says that *pinguescere* implies that the soil is "rich with the blood of civil war," and helps the wordplay with *Haemus.*

Hunter suggests similar wordplay at Apoll. Rhod. 3.1090, Αἱμονίην δὴ τήνγε περικτίονες καλέουσιν (note the signpost; see intro. 2.6), on the name Αἱμονίη as "'the land of blood,' a proffered return for the blood of Prometheus which Medea has given him." Hunter refers to the αἱματόεντ' ἰχῶρα Προμηθῆος, the "bloody ichor of Prometheus." (The elaborate description of the drug Prometheion at Apoll. Rhod. 3.844–57 resembles that of the *felix malum* at G. 2.126–41, *amellus* at G. 4.271–78, and *dictamnum* at A. 12.412–17 [see on those passages].)

Doig (1965), Thomas (1988) on 492, Hunter (1989) 218.

**G. 1.500?:** hunc saltem everso *iuvenem succurrere* saeclo

The collocation *iuvenem succurrere* may allude to the derivation of *iuvenis* from *iuvare* found in Varro, as Du Quesnay suggests. Elsewhere, Vergil seems to connect *iuvare* with the name Juturna and perhaps also the name Jupiter (see on **A. 10.439–40**). At A. 12.813–14, ***Iuturnam** misero (fateor) **succurrere** fratri / suasi,* Vergil seems again to use *succurrere* to suggest a derivation from *iuvo.*

VARRO fr. 447 (*GRF* p. 367): iuvenis appellatos, eo quod rem publicam in re militari possent iuvare.

OVID *Am.* 3.6.23 (for Ovid cf. intro. 2.14): flumina debebant *iuvenes* in amore *iuvare.*

Du Quesnay (1981) 133; on Ovid, McKeown (1987) 49.

**G. 1.507:** *squalent* abductis arva *colonis*

Page: "*squalent* presents an artistic contrast with *colonus,* for *colonus* suggests *colo* and *cultus,* 'elegance,' 'neatness.'"

Page (1898) on 507.

**G. 2.4–6:** huc, pater o *Lenaee:* tuis hic omnia plena / muneribus, tibi pampineo gravidus autumno / floret ager, spumat *plenis vindemia labris*

Servius notes that Dionysus' epithet Lenaeus (= Ληναῖος) comes from ληνός, "wine vat." Vergil's *plenis vindemia labris* seems to be an etymological gloss, perhaps even a polemical one, because Servius notes and rejects Donatus' explanation, *quod mentem deleniat.*

For other wordplay involving Dionysus see on **A. 6.805**.

SERV. 4: Lenaeus autem ἀπὸ τῆς ληνοῦ dicitur, id est a lacu: nam quod Donatus dicit ab eo, quod mentem deleniat, non procedit; nec enim potest Graecum nomen Latinam etymologiam recipere (sim. on A. 4.207, Brev. Exp. G. 2.4, [Prob.] G. 2.2).

Cf. Cerda (1608) 287.

**G. 2.47–49:** sponte sua quae se tollunt in luminis oras, / infecunda quidem, sed laeta et fortia surgunt; / *quippe solo natura subest.*

Ross calls attention to Servius' connection of the word *natura* with the verb *nascor,* "to be born," and translates *quippe solo natura subest* as "for of course the power of growth lies hidden in the soil." Elsewhere he puts it, "*Natura* means 'birth,' and comes to represent the process of life. . . . Virgil will play with the etymology of *natura* more than once."

SERV. 49: quia . . . naturaliter rerum omnium mater est terra. . . . nam natura dicta est ab eo, quod nasci aliquid faciat; LACT. *Inst.* 2.8.21: naturam, quae . . . a nascendo dicitur (sim. Isid. 11.1.1).

Cf. G. 2.65–66: nascuntur et ingens / fraxinus; G. 2.178: quae sit rebus natura ferendis.

Ross (1987) 102, 19; on *natura* and *nasci* cf. also Brown (1984) xxxvii.

## G. 2.63–68:

sed truncis oleae melius, propagine vites
respondent, solido Paphiae de robore myrtus,
plantis edurae coryli. *nascuntur* et ingens
fraxinus Herculeaeque arbos umbrosa coronae,
Chaoniique patris glandes; etiam ardua palma
*nascitur* et casus abies visura marinos.

Ross argues that here too, Vergil plays on the connection between the verb *nascor* and the word *natura*. In 65, Ross argues that *nascuntur* means "are products of nature," that is, that they are born naturally, instead of being produced by man's cultivation. See Ross' whole discussion of "wild" and "cultivated" in G. 2.

(Ross endorses Mynors' text and punctuation of 65: *plantis edurae coryli. nascuntur et ingens.* Most editors place a full stop after 64 and follow the Medicean manuscript in printing *plantis et durae coryli nascuntur et ingens.*)

Cf. on **G. 2.47–49.**

Ross (1987) 101–2.

**G. 2.88:** Crustumiis Syriisque piris *gravibus*que *volemis*

*Gravibus* may be a gloss on *volemis,* for which Servius and Servius Auctus present different etymologies. Servius says *gravibus = magnis,* and that *volema* are so called because they fill the hand *(manum impleat),* Servius Auctus more specifically that they fill the palm *(volam impleant).* Servius Auctus also says that *volema* itself is a Gallic word meaning *bona et grandia.*

SERV. 88. GRAVIBUS VOLEMIS magnis: nam et volema ab eo, quod manum impleant, dicta sunt, unde et "involare" dicimus (cf. Brev. Exp. ad loc.); SERV. Auct. A. 3.233: pira volema dicuntur, eo quod volam impleant; SERV. Auct. G. 2.88: volema autem Gallica lingua bona et grandia dicuntur (both derivations in Isid. 17.6.67).

**G. 2.101–2:** non ego te, dis et mensis accepta secundis, / transierim, Rhodia, et *tumidis, bumaste, racemis.*

Thomas: "with *tumidis* ('swelling') V[ergil] provides an elegant gloss on the etymology of *bumastus,* lit. 'with huge breasts' (βου- a prefix indicating large size, from βοῦς, 'ox,' μαστός, 'breast')."

SERV. 102: BVMASTE uva in mammae bovis similitudinem (sim. Brev. Exp., [Prob.] ad loc.); PLINY *NH* 14.15: tument vero mammarum modo bumasti.

Thomas (1988) on 102, Bartelink (1965) 73, Forbiger (1873–75) 1.306.

**G. 2.112?:** litora myrtetis laetissima

A doubtful example. Isidore derives *myrtus* from *mare* and connects that etymology to two passages in Vergil.

ISID. 17.7.50: myrtus a mare dicta, eo quod magis litorea arbor sit. unde et Vergilius (G. 2.112) "litora myrtetis laetissima" et (G. 4.124) "amantes litora myrtae."

## G. 2.126–41:

*Media* fert tristis sucos tardumque saporem
*felicis mali,* quo non praesentius ullum,
pocula si quando saevae infecere *novercae,*
[miscueruntque herbas et non innoxia verba,]
auxilium venit ac membris agit atra venena.
ipsa ingens arbos faciemque simillima lauro,
et, si non alium late iactaret odorem,
laurus erat: folia haud ullis labentia ventis,
flos ad prima tenax; animas et olentia *Medi*
ora fovent illo et senibus *medicantur* anhelis.
sed neque *Medorum* silvae, ditissima terra,
nec pulcher Ganges atque auro turbidus Hermus
laudibus Italiae certent, non Bactra neque Indi
totaque turiferis Panchaia pinguis harenis.
*haec loca non tauri spirantes naribus ignem*
*invertere satis immanis dentibus hydri*

An elaborate etymological aetiology, as Ross has explained. In the first two lines, *Media* and *felicis mali* gloss the suppressed name of the citron or lemon, *medica,* which Servius supplies, along with a comment on Vergil's suppression *(eius supprimens nomen)* (for suppression see intro. 2.7). Then the reference to *novercae* gently suggests Medea, the most famous savage stepmother associated with poisons, who is said to have given their name to the Medians (as noted by [Probus] on 126, citing Varro of Atax, perhaps from his *Argonautica*). In 134–35 Vergil plays on the resemblance between the suppressed word *medica* and the words *Medi* and *medicantur:* the *medica* is medicine for the Medes. With 136 the *Laudes Italiae* begin, but the plays on *medica* continue, first with *Medorum* in 136, then with 140–41, *haec loca non tauri,* as Vergil alludes more clearly to the story of Jason and Medea. Ross notes that "Virgil's prime concern is healing, since healing provides the etymology, as . . . Servius recorded."

Ross notes that "a further gloss is provided by the attribute *felicis (mali)*. . . . If we allowed the old pun on *malum* 'apple' and *malum* 'evil,' then we have in *felicis* a gloss from the opposite" (for glosses κατ' ἀντίφρασιν see intro. 2.3).

Following Servius' note, Ross observes that the elaborate description of the *medica* here is like that of the *amellus* in G. 4.271–78 and is also the first of four major etymological aetiologies in the *Georgics,* related by style, structure, cross-references, and similar thematic suggestiveness. The others involve the *asilus* (G. 3.146–53), *hippomanes* (3.280–83), and the *amellus*. One might also compare the description of the healing herb *dictamnun* at A. 12.412–17; see there.

The treatments of both the *medica* and the *amellus* resemble, in their wealth of botanical detail, the aetiological description of the drug Prometheion, said to have been sprung from the ichor of Prometheus, which Medea gives to Jason to help him survive the fire-breathing bulls and the earth-born warriors at Apoll. Rhod. 3.844–57 (cf. intro. 1.4, where the passage is quoted in a note). Apollonius may have served as a model for both Vergilian passages, especially the description of the *medica,* which looks to Medea and the East, and is followed by the reference in 140–43 to the fire-breathing bulls and the earth-born men. Another of these four major aetiologies, as Ross explains, follows the precedent of Apollonius: see on G. 3.146–53, for Vergil's treatment of the *asilus.*

For other Vergilian wordplay on *mala* see on **A.** 7.740 *maliferae . . . Abellae.* For Vergil's following Apollonian precedent see O'Hara. For Varro of Atax cf. intro. 1.6.

medicus: SERV. 126: apud Medos nascitur quaedam arbor, ferens mala, quae medica vocantur: quam per periphrasin ostendit, eius supprimens nomen. hanc plerique citrum volunt; SERV. 134: notandum sane, uni tantum arbori incubuisse Vergilium et expressisse ubi sit, qualis sit, cuius potestatis sit, sicut in quarto (271) de herba amello: quod qui de arboribus aut herbis dicunt in omnibus exsequuntur; PLINY *NH* 5.47: Medica . . . Graeci vocant patrio nomine; ISID. 17.4.8: Medica (sc. vicia) dicta quia a medis translata est in Graeciam tempore quo eam Xerxes invasit (a bit more in Maltby).

Media: [PROB.] on 126: Pars Parthorum Media est appellata a Medo, filio Medeae et Aegei, ut existimat Varro, qui quattuor libros de Argonautis edidit (*GRF* p. 439, possibly from his *Arg.*, or from a *Chorographia*); HYG. *Fab.* 27.5: Medus . . . ex suo nomine terram Mediam cognominavit (more sources in Maltby).

Ross (1987) 113–15, O'Hara (1990b).

**G. 2.131:** ipsa *ingens* arbos faciemque simillima lauro

Mackail argued that in Vergil *ingens,* because of its similarity to words like *gens* and *ingenium,* often has a sense of " 'engendered,' sometimes tending to pass into the sense of 'native' or 'natural.' " Calling attention to Mackail's long-neglected observation, Ross notes that the adjective *ingens* in 131 would be odd if it meant "huge," for "lemon trees are hardly 'huge,' " and suggests that Vergil uses *ingens* to mean "native"; "the lemon tree is a 'native product' of Media."

Cf. PAUL.-Fest. p. 101, 26 L: ingens dicitur augendi consuetudine, ut inclamare, invocare. quia enim gens populi est magnitudo, ingentem per compositionem dicimus, quod significat valde magnum.

G. 4.20: ingens oleaster; G. 4.273: ingentem . . . silvam; A. 7.376?: tum vero infelix *ingentibus* excita *monstris;* A. 12.225: *genus* a proavis *ingens.*

Mackail (1912), Conway (1912), Ross (1987) 115, Bartelink (1965) 28–29, Keith (1991).

**G. 2.139?:** *tota*que turiferis *Pan*chaia pinguis harenis
*Tota* may gloss *Panchaia* (cf. πᾶν, all). See intro. 2.2 for single-adjective glosses. [Probus] suggests an eponymous king.

Cf. [PROB.] on 137–39: Panchaia . . . a rege Panchaeo dicitur.

VAL. Flacc. 6.119: *tota*que Riphaeo *Pan*chaia rapta triumpho; cf. HES. *Op.* 80–82: ὀνόμηνε δὲ τήνδε γυναῖκα / Πανδώρην, ὅτι πάντες Ὀλύμπια δώματ' ἔχοντες / δῶρον ἐδώρησαν.

**G. 2.173?:** salve, magna parens *frugum, Saturnia* tellus
Varro and others derived the name Saturnus from *sero, satus*. Here and elsewhere the association of Saturn and the adjective Saturnius with agriculture may allude to, or simply derive from, that etymology.
For possible allusion to a different etymology for Saturn see on **A. 5.606–8.**

VARRO *LL* 5.64: ab satu est dictus Saturnus (sim. at Macrob. 1.10.30, Isid. 8.11.30; more in Maltby); FEST. p. 432, 18–20 L: (Saturnus) in Saliaribus Sat⟨e⟩urnus nominatur, videlicet a sationibus.

G. 2.405–7: iam tum acer curas venientem extendit in annum / *rusticus,* et curvo *Saturni* dente relictam / persequitur vitem attondens fingitque putando; G. 2.538: aureus hanc vitam in terris *Saturnus* agebat.

Johnston (1980) 63–64; cf. Anderson (1958) 523 n. 10.

**G. 2.177:** quae sit *rebus* natura *ferendis*
Ross argues that Vergil again alludes to the connection between the verb *nascor* and the word *natura:* "The etymology of *natura* is indicated by *rebus ferendis.*"
Cf. on **G. 2.47–49.**

Ross (1987) 130.

**G. 2.201–2?:** et quantum longis carpent armenta diebus / exigua tantum gelidus *ros* nocte reponet
In describing the fertility of his own Mantua here, Vergil seems to allude to something Varro said in *de Re Rustica* about the region *Rosea* near his own home of Reate. Paulus also preserves a fragment of Varro connecting the name Rosea with *ros,* "dew." Vergil combines the comment on fertility from the *de Re Rustica* (where the word *ros* does not occur) with the etymology preserved by Paulus-Festus from elsewhere in Varro's works.
Cf. on A. 7.712 *Rosea rura Velini.*

SERV. 201: ut in Aeneide (7. 712) diximus, hoc dicit Varro fuisse in Rosulano agro, postquam Velinus siccatus est lacus: ubi longam perticam magnitudo superabat herbarum; SERV. A. 7.712: (citing Varro) tanta est loca secuta fertilitas, ut etiam perticae longitudinem altitudo superaret herbarum: quia etiam quantum per diem demptum esset, tantum per noctes crescebat: quod Vergilius ad suam provinciam transtulit, dicens "et quantum"; VARRO *RR* 1.7.10: Caesar Vopiscus, aedilicius causam cum ageret apud censores, campos Roseae Italiae dixit esse sumen, in quo relicta pertica postridie non appareret propter herbam; VARRO fr. 403 (= Paul.-Fest. p. 355, 5–6 L = *GRF* p. 352): Rosea in agro Reatino campus appellatur, quod in eo arva rore umida semper seruntur; PLINY *NH* 3.108: Velinos accolunt lacus, roscidis collibus.

**G. 2.207?:** aut unde *iratus* silvam devexit *arator*

Thomas: "the near jingle, reinforced by the placing of the adjective and noun at main-caesura and line-end respectively, is uncharacteristic; does V[ergil] intend some sort of gloss?" Cf. intro. 2.1 on paronomasia.

Thomas (1988) on 207; Horsfall (1991a) 216 is skeptical.

**G. 2.238–47?:**

*salsa* autem tellus et quae perhibetur *amara*
(frugibus infelix ea, nec mansuescit arando
nec Baccho genus aut pomis sua nomina servat)
tale dabit specimen. tu spisso vimine qualos
colaque prelorum fumosis deripe tectis;
huc ager ille malus dulcesque a fontibus undae
ad plenum calcentur: aqua eluctabitur omnis
scilicet et grandes ibunt per vimina guttae;
at sapor indicium faciet manifestus et ora
tristia temptantum sensu torquebit *amaro*.

This passage has the look of etymological wordplay, but I cannot claim with confidence that wordplay is actually taking place. In 238 *quae perhibetur amara* resembles the etymological signpost (see intro. 2.6) and seems to call attention to *amara* at the end of 238. The word *amarus* is also the last word in 247, so the word in a sense frames the ten-line sentence (cf. intro. 2.8a). Could this be wordplay? Thomas sees instead in *perhibetur* only a reference to the diction of predecessors—besides etymologizing, this is the other main use of such naming constructions—although "this is the first attestation of the adjective *(amarus)* to describe soil." Vergil plays on the resemblance between *amor* and *amarus* twice in the *Eclogues,* and once possibly on the connection between *amarus* and *mare,* "sea" (Isidore derives *mare* from *amarus*). Could *salsa* in 238 point to the connection between *amarus* and *mare* here as well? Thomas' note elsewhere on how Vergil "closely links farming and navigation" could be part of an explanation of these lines, but I can offer no conclusive analysis.

Cf. E. 3.109–10 *amores . . . amaros;* E. 10.4–6 *Doris (= mare) amara . . . amores.*

ISID. 13.14.1: proprie autem mare appellatum eo quod aquae eius amarae sint.

Thomas (1988) on 238; for farming and sailing see Thomas on 1.50.

**G. 2.328:** *avia* tum **resonant** *avibus* virgulta canoris

A pun or wordplay on *avia,* "pathless" and *avis,* "bird," found also in Roman rhetorical treatises. On such simple wordplay see intro. 2.1.

Thomas suggests further that "the words surrounding *resonant* . . . draw attention to its meaning."

*RHET. HER.* 4.21.29: hinc avium dulcedo ducit ad avium; QUINT. 9.3.69–70 quotes the puns in *amari iucundum est, si curetur ne quid insit amari* and *avium dulcedo* ⟨*ad*⟩ *avium ducit* and says that this kind of wordplay is *frigidum* and to be avoided. See the full quotation in a note in intro. 2.1; cf. LUCR. 2.145: *et variae volucres nemora avia pervolitantes,* where *volucres = aves.*

Snyder (1980) 65–66, 177 (on Vergil as well as Lucretius), Thomas (1988) on 328, Farrell (1991) 99–100.

## G. 2.380–83:

> non aliam ob culpam Baccho *caper* omnibus aris
> caeditur et veteres ineunt proscaenia ludi,
> praemiaque ingeniis *pagos et compita* circum
> Thesidae posuere

In 380–81, Vergil alludes to the derivation of the (here suppressed) word *tragoedia* from τράγος, "goat" (cf. 380 *caper*) and ᾠδή, "song." As Brink and others note, this theory is not found in Aristotle and is possibly "of Alexandrian provenance."

In 382, to quote Thomas, "through the gloss contained in *pagus* (Gr. κώμη, 'village'), V. alludes to the theory . . . that the word 'comedy' derives from itinerant players who left the city and performed 'around the villages' (κατὰ κώμας)." Note the resemblance between Vergil's *pagos et compita circum* and Varro's *circum pagos* (see below).

Thomas suggests that with the phrase *pagos et compita circum* Vergil "also intends a reference to the Paganalia and Compitalia, the two rustic festivals which will be the Italian settings at 385–96."

For suppression see intro. 2.7; cf. also the possible etymology of *dithyrambus* at A. 9.618, *biforem dat tibia cantum.*

Tragedy (more in Maltby): VARRO fr. 304 (*GRF* p. 320, apud Diom. *Gramm. Lat.* 1.487.11ff. K): tragoedia, ut quidam, a τράγω(ι) et ᾠ(ι)δῆ(ι) dicta est, quoniam olim actoribus tragicis τράγος id est hircus praemium cantus praeponebatur, qui Liberalibus die festo Libero patri ob hoc ipsum immolabatur, quia, ut Varro ait, depascunt vitem; cf. HOR. *Ars* 220: carmine qui *tragico* vilem certavit ob *hircum;* ISID. 8.7.5: Tragoedi dicti, quod initio canentibus praemium erat hircus, quem Graeci τράγος vocant. unde et Horatius.

Comedy (more in Maltby): ARIST. *Poet.* 1448a: οἱ Δωριεῖς . . . μὲν γὰρ κώμας τὰς περιοικίδας καλεῖν φασιν, Ἀθηναίους δὲ δήμους, ὡς κωμῳδοὺς οὐκ ἀπὸ τοῦ κωμάζειν λεχθέντας ἀλλὰ τῇ κατὰ κώμας πλάνῃ ἀτιμαζομένους ἐκ τοῦ ἄστεως; VARRO fr. 305 (*GRF* pp. 320–21, apud Diom. *Gramm. Lat.* 1.488.3ff. K): comoedia dicta ἀπὸ τῶν κωμῶν, κῶμαι enim appellantur pagi id est conventicula rusticorum; itaque iuventus Attica, ut ait Varro, *circum vicos* ire solita fuerat et quaestus sui causa hoc genus carminis pronuntiabat; ISID. 8.7.6: Comoedi appellati sive a loco, quia *circum pagos* agebant, quos Graeci κώμας vocant, sive a comisatione. Solebant enim post cibum homines ad eos audiendos venire; differently VARRO *LL* 7.89: comiter hilare ac lubenter, cuius origo Graeca κῶμος, inde comisatio latine dicta et in Graecia, ut quidam scribunt, comodia.

Paganalia: VARRO *LL* 6.24: dies Septimontium . . . feriae non populis, sed montanarum modo, ut Paganalibus, qui sunt alicuius pagi.

Compitalia: VARRO *LL* 6.25: Compitalia dies attributus Laribus vialibus: ideo ubi viae competunt tum in competis sacrificatur; D.H. 4.14.4: ἣν ἔτι καὶ καθ' ἡμᾶς ἑορτὴν ἄγοντες Ῥωμαῖοι διετέλουν . . . Κομπιτάλια προσαγορεύοντες αὐτὴν ἐπὶ τῶν στενωπῶν· κομπίτους γὰρ τοὺς στενωποὺς καλοῦσι (more in Maltby s.vv. compitum, Compitalia).

Tragedy: Bartelink (1965) 89, Brink (1971) 273–78; more on the etymology in Winkler (1990) 58–62; comedy: Bartelink (1965) 86, Shechter (1975) 377 (skeptical), Thomas (1988) on 380–83.

**G. 2.391–93:** complentur vallesque cavae saltusque profundi / et quocumque deus circum caput egit *honestum.* / ergo rite suum Baccho dicemus *honorem*

Ross: "Sacrifice . . . is the *honorem* (end of line 393) we pay to Bacchus, *caput honestum* (end of line 392)—a verbal gloss containing, it seems to me, no little irony."

For wordplay at ends of consecutive lines see intro. 2.9.

Ross (1987) 137.

**G. 2.402?:** atque in se sua per vestigia volvitur *annus*

De la Cerda suggests allusion to the etymology connecting *annus* with words for circle or ring like *anulus.*

VARRO *LL* 6.8: tempus a bruma ad brumam dum sol redit, vocatur annus, quod ut parvi circuli anuli, sic magni dicebantur circites ani, unde annus; SERV. A. 1.269: annus autem dictus quasi anus, id est, anulus, quod in se redeat ut "atque in se sua per vestigia voluitur annus" (more in Maltby).

Cerda (1608) 349.

**G. 2.438?:** *Naryciae*que picis lucos

Nisbet suggests wordplay here between *Naryciae* and *nares.*

For Ennius' wordplay on *Nar* and *nares* see on A. 7.517, *sulpurea Nar albus aqua.*

Nisbet (1990) 261.

**G. 2.441:** animosi Euri

De la Cerda and with more caution Thomas suggest possible allusion to the connection of *animus* with ἄνεμος, "wind"; see on **A. 1.56–57** for more certain examples.

Cerda (1608) 353, Thomas (1988) on 441.

**G. 2.454–57?:**

quid memorandum aeque Baccheia dona tulerunt?
Bacchus et *ad culpam causas* dedit; ille furentis
Centauros leto domuit, Rhoecumque Pholumque
et magno Hylaeum Lapithis cratere minantem.

Ross sees in these lines possible allusion to or use of Varro's etymology *vitis a vino, id a vi* (*LL* 5.37), which Ross translates as "'Vine' is derived from 'wine' and that from 'violence.'" In Vergil's phrase *ad culpam causas* and in the whole passage 397–457 he suspects an allusion to the phrase found in Serv. G. 3.297 and 458, *vitium vituperatio*.

Ross (1987) 144–45.

**G. 2.519:** venit hiems: *teritur* Sicyonia bacca *trapetis*
Varro derives *trapetus* or *trapetes,* "oil mill," from *terere,* "rub, wear down," but adds the warning, "unless it is a Greek word" (which it is).

VARRO *LL* 5.138: trapetes molae oleariae; vocant trapetes a terendo, nisi graecum est; differently Brev. Exp. 519: trapeta autem sunt saxa trahendo dicta, quibus frangitur oliva.

Bartelink (1965) 90.

**G. 2.528:** socii cratera coronant
Thomas explains that this line is "thought by some to be a mistranslation of the Homeric line κοῦροι μὲν κρατῆρας ἐπεστέψαντο ποτοῖο, 'the young men filled the bowls with wine,' *Il.* 1.470, *Od.* 1.148; if so it was doubtless deliberate, for at A. 3.525–6, V. renders both senses of ἐπεστέφομαι—'to fill' and 'to crown or wreathe' *(Tum pater Anchises magnum cratera corona / induit implevitque mero)*. Evidently he was aware of the scholiastic debate on the word subsequently reported by Eustathius and Scholia ABT on *Il.* 1.470 and by Athenaeus (1.13d-3; 15.674f.)."
For such "mistranslations" or "translation by homonym" see intro. 2.1a.

Thomas (1988) on 528, Bartelink (1965) 33, Mühmelt (1965) 49.

**G. 2.538?:** aureus hanc vitam in terris *Saturnus* agebat
For possible allusion, in this description of rustic life, to the derivation of Saturnus from *sero, satus,* see on G. 2.173.

**G. 3.1–3:** Te quoque, magna *Pales,* et te memorande canemus / *pastor* ab Amphryso, vos, silvae amnesque Lycaei. / cetera, quae vacuas tenuissent carmine mentes
In 2 *pastor ab Amphryso* evokes and then explains Apollo's epithet Nomios, as Servius notes; the epithet itself is suppressed (see intro. 2.7). Thomas notes that Vergil's source is the explanation of the name at Callim. *Hymn* 2.47–49 (note the signpost there, and also 'Αμφρυσσῷ):

> Φοῖβον καὶ Νόμιον κικλήσκομεν ἐξέτι κείνου,
> ἐξότ' ἐπ' Ἀμφρυσσῷ ζευγίτιδας ἔτρεφεν ἵππους
> ἠιθέου ὑπ' ἔρωτι κεκαυμένος Ἀδμήτοιο.

There may be polemical point to this etymologizing, because Servius explains that Nomios could also be derived from the musical word νόμοι, which Servius glosses as *lex chordarum,* "law/rule of (musical) strings." But Vergil may also allude to that etymology as well, by using *carmine* in line 3, and calling on Apollo for poetic inspiration; this would be the kind of double etymology that Porte's study of Ovid's *Fasti* has described.

(Longus, *Daphnis and Chloe* 2.35 seems to play on two senses of the word εὐνομία ["harmony" and "good husbandship"] in describing the music of the herdsman Philetas.)

Vergil also probably alludes to an etymological connection between *Pales* in 1, *pastor* in 2, and the unexpressed name *Pan,* evoked (as Servius notes) by the adjective *Lycaei* in 2. Ross earlier explained the systematic etymologizing at Tib. 2.5.25–30 linking *pasco, Palatia, Pan, Pales,* and *pastor,* and more recently has noted the etymological connection in G. 3.1–2 between Pan and pastoral.

On Pan see also on G. 1.17–18, *Pan . . . favens;* on Pales and pastoral see also G. 3.294, *nunc, veneranda Pales.*

SERV. 3.2: (Apollo) Nomius vocatur vel ἀπὸ τῆς νομῆς, id est a pascuis, vel ἀπὸ τῶν νόμων, id est a lege chordarum. SILVAE AMNESQVE LYCAEI κατ' ἐξόχην montem Arcadiae posuit, vel quia pecorosa est, vel qui Pan illic est rusticum numen; CIC. *ND* 3.23.57: quartus (Apollo) in Arcadia, quem Arcades Νόμιον appellant quod ab eo se leges ferunt accepisse.

TIB. 2.5.25–30:

> sed tunc *pascebant* herbosa *Palatia* vaccae
> et stabant humiles in Iovis arce casae.
> lacte madens illic suberat *Pan* ilicis umbrae
> et facta agresti lignea falce *Pales,*
> pendebatque vagi *pastoris* in arbore votum,
> garrula silvestri fistula sacra deo.

Thomas (1988) on 1–2, Depew (1993) 74–75 (Callim.), Ross (1975) 155–57 (Tibullus), (1987) 168 *(Georgics),* Porte (1985) 220–30, Cairns (1979) 79–81; on Longus, Gill in Reardon (1989) 316. With Tibullus' *pa-* cluster, cf. *Il.* 16.141–44 as discussed by Stanford (1939) 100 (see intro. 1.1).

**G. 3.8–9:** temptanda via est, qua me quoque possim / tollere humo *victor*que virum volitare per ora.

Wigodsky: "*Geo.* III 8–9 . . . is a clear imitation of Ennius' epigram on his own death (*Var.* 17–18): 'Nemo me lacrimis decoret nec funera fletu / flexit. Cur? Volito vivus per ora virum.' The echo of Ennius makes it clear that 'victor' in *Geo.* III 9 is a pun, suggesting a derivation from *vivere* (Ennius' 'vivus') as well as *vincere.*"

Wigodsky (1972) 75, Buchheit (1972) 99–100.

**G. 3.27?:** victorisque *arma Quirini*

The reference to "arms of Quirinus" may allude to one etymology offered for that name for Romulus, from a Sabine word for spear, *curis.*

See on **A. 6.859** *tertiaque **arma** patri suspendet capta **Quirino,*** where the reference to dedication of *spolia opima* to Quirinus is problematic.

**G. 3.34:** *stabunt* et Parii lapides, *spirantia signa*

Thomas: "*stabunt*: a gloss on the subject matter *(Parii lapides*; i.e. *statuae).*" The noun is suppressed (see intro. 2.7).

Thomas (1988) on 34.

**G. 3.146–53:**

> est lucos *Silari* circa ilicibusque virentem
> plurimus Alburnum volitans, cui nomen *asilo*
> Romanum est, oestrum Grai vertere vocantes,
> asper, acerba sonans, quo tota exterrita silvis
> diffugiunt armenta; furit mugitibus aether
> concussus silvaeque et sicci ripa Tanagri.
> hoc quondam monstro horribilis exercuit iras
> Inachiae Iuno pestem meditata iuvencae.

Thomas and Ross explain the elaborate etymological aetiology here; they should be consulted for more detail than can be given here. Vergil draws upon an Alexandrian tradition of playing with names for the gadfly and their etymologies and adds what seems to be his own derivation for the Latin name, although it may owe something to a fairly recent work of Nigidius Figulus. Aeschylus, Callimachus, and Apollonius referred to the two names (μύωψ and οἶστρος) for the gadfly, with Apollonius providing (in another passage, 1.1265–69) a suggested etymology from the root of μύκημα, "mooing." Vergil's setting (*est lucos Silari circa . . .* ) suggests a derivation of the Latin term *asilus* from the name of the river *Silarus*, comparable to his derivation at G. 4.271–78 of the name *amellus* from the river *Mella*. Vergil will evoke the word *asilus* and the tradition of glossing the name of the gadfly also at A. 12.715–17 and at G. 3.219, *pascitur in magna Sila formosa iuvenca.*

SERV. Auct. 146: Nigidius de animalibus (fr. 40, *GRF* p. 176) "asilus est musca varia, tabanus, bubus maxime nocens. hic apud Graecos prius μύωψ vocabantur, postea (a) magnitudine incommodi oestrum appellarunt." et hoc est quod ait "oestrum Grai vertere vocantes," non de latino in graecum, sed de graeco in suam linguam, quae prior fuit; SERV. 148: οἶστρος autem graecum est: latine asilus, vulgo tabanus vocatur (sim. Isid. 12.8.8); PAUL.-Fest. p. 213, 1 L: oestrum furor Graeco vocabulo; SERV. Auct. 148: Graeci . . . furiam oestrum vocant.

AESCH. *Supp.* 306–8:

> {Cho.} τί οὖν ἔτευξ' ἔτ' ἄλλο δυσπότμῳ βοᾶι;
> {Ba.} βοηλάτην μύωπα κινητήριον.

{Cho.} οἶστρον καλοῦσιν αὐτὸν οἱ Νείλου πέλας

APOLL. Rhod. 3.275–77: Τόφρα δ' Ἔρως πολιοῖο δι' ἠέρος ἷξεν ἄφαντος, / τετρηχὼς οἷόν τε νέαις ἐπὶ φορβάσιν οἶστρος / τέλλεται, ὅν τε μύωπα βοῶν κλείουσι νομῆες; 1.1265–69:

ὡς δ' ὅτε τίς τε μύωπι τετυμμένος ἔσσυτο ταῦρος
πίσεά τε προλιπὼν καὶ ἑλεσπίδας, οὐδὲ νομήων
οὐδ' ἀγέλης ὄθεται, πρήσσει δ' ὁδὸν ἄλλοτ' ἄπαυστος,
ἄλλοτε δ' ἱστάμενος καὶ ἀνὰ πλατὺν αὐχέν' ἀείρων
ἵησιν μύκημα, κακῷ βεβολημένος οἴστρῳ

CALLIM. *Hec.* fr. 301 Pf. (cf. 117 Hollis): ⟨οἶστρον⟩ / βουσόον ὅν τε μύωπα βοῶν καλέουσιν ἀμορβοί.

Thomas (1982b) 81–85, Shechter (1975) 360–62, Ross (1987) 157–63, O'Hara (1990) 78–80.

**G. 3.158:** continuoque *notas* et *nomina* gentis inurunt
Juxtaposition of apparent cognates.
Cf. **A. 3.444** fata canit foliisque *notas* et *nomina* mandat.

Bartelink (1965) 108.

**G. 3.172:** post valido nitens sub pondere *faginus axis*
Mynors and Thomas note that Vergil is virtually translating *Il.* 5.838: μέγα δ' ἔβραχε φήγινος ἄξων βριθοσύνῃ, but for the wood he instead transliterates, using *faginus,* which in Latin should be "beech," for the Homeric φήγινος, "oak." For such "mistranslations" or "translation by homonym" see intro. 2.1a. For *fagus* = φηγός, see on **E. 1.1**, where some information is provided about possible poetic precedent for the identification. For this passage, it may be important that φήγινος appears once only in Homer, and then once in the *Eclogues* and once in the *Georgics*. The adjective also appears once only in extant fragments of Callimachus (*Epig.* 34.1).

Thomas (1988) on G. 3.172, Mynors (1990) on G. 3.172–73.

## G. 3.266, 280–83:

scilicet ante omnis *furor* est insignis *equarum,*
. . . . . . . . . . . . . . . . . . . . . . . . . . . . .
hic demum, *hippomanes* vero quod nomine dicunt
pastores, lentum **destillat** ab inguine virus,
hippomanes, quod saepe malae legere novercae
miscueruntque herbas et non innoxia verba.

In 280 *vero quod nomine dicunt* is the signpost (see intro. 2.6) calling attention to the name *hippomanes,* for which Vergil suggests two different derivations. The standard etymology, glossed in poetry by Theocritus, involves the Greek words *mania,* "madness," and *hippos,* "horse"; the phrase *furor equarum,* "madness of mares," in

266 looks to this derivation. Jacobson has noticed that *distillat,* "ooze, drip down," in 281 suggests the Latin verb *manat,* "flow, run, exude," and a hybrid etymology from *mano* and *hippos.* So Vergil alludes to two etymologies, the second (to which Tibullus perhaps alludes, in the line quoted below) perhaps a playful "correction" of the first, or an alternative proposed in the open-minded style typical of Ovid's *Fasti.* Thomas comments, "this is Vergil at his most Alexandrian, subsuming and reshaping the tradition" (see his references to Aristotle, etc.).

Servius puts it a little differently: he says Vergil is trying to straighten out people who think that *hippomanes* is an herb, by telling them that it is an oozy secretion.

For the Greek-Latin hybrid etymology see on A. 12.412–17.

In a number of passages Alexandrian or Roman poets remark that "shepherds" or "herdsmen" have named something; this may be coincidence, or some or all of them may be related. Discussing the passages that treat the gadfly (see on G. 3.146ff.), Thomas suggests a distinction between functional and "poetic" terms ("Herdsmen call it μύωψ, poets, οἶστρος"). Campbell suggests such phrases are the equivalent of "called in the trade." Collart comments on references to "shepherds' names" in Varro *LL.*

COLUM. 6.27.3: libidinis exstimulatur furiis (sc. equus), unde etiam veneno inditum est nomen ἱππομανές, quod equinae cupidini similem mortalibus amorem accendit; SERV. 280: scit lectum esse apud Hesiodum, herbam esse quandam, quae hippomanes vocatur, quasi ἵππου μανία: si enim eam comederint equi, furore quatiuntur. unde nunc adiecit "vero quod nomine dicunt": nam vult illam herbam abusive hippomanes dictam, quod possint equi furere et alia quacumque ratione. re vera autem hippomanes dicit esse virus, defluens ex equarum inguinibus quo tempore feruntur amoris furore, ut sit hippomanes virus natum ἀπὸ τῆς μανίας τῆς ἵππου.

TIB. 2.4.58: *hippomanes* cupidae *stillat* ab inguine *equae;* OVID *Am.* 1.8.7–8 (for Ovid cf. intro. 2.14): scit . . . quid valeat virus amantis *equae; Med. Fac.* 38: nocens virus amantis *equae;* THEOC. 2.48–49: ἱππομανὲς . . . τῷ δ' ἔπι πᾶσαι / καὶ πῶλοι μαινόνται ἀν' ὤρεα καὶ θοαὶ ἵπποι.

"Shepherds call . . .": APOLL. Rhod. 3.276–77: οἶστρος / τέλλεται, ὅν τε μύωπα βοῶν κλείουσι νομῆες; CALLIM. *Hec.* fr. 301 Pf.: ⟨οἶστρον⟩ / βουσόον ὅν τε μύωπα βοῶν καλέουσιν ἀμορβοί; ARAT. *Phaen.* 220–21: οἱ δὲ νομῆες / πρῶτοι κεῖνο ποτὸν διεφήμισαν Ἱππουκρήνην; NIC. *Ther.* 554: τὴν ἤτοι μελίφυλλον ἐπικλείουσι βοτῆρες; EUPHOR. fr. 96.3 P: Βοιωτὸν δ' ὀνόμηνε· τὸ γὰρ καλέσαντο νομῆες; E. 9.33–34: me quoque dicunt / vatem *pastores;* G. 4.271–72: est etiam flos in pratis cui nomen amello / fecere *agricolae;* ENN. *Alex.* fr. 64 J: quapropter Parim *pastores* nunc Alexandrum vocant; cf. too VARRO *LL* 5.92: pecunia a pecu: a pastoribus enim horum vocabulorum origo (cited on E. 2.20) and 5.108 (pulmentum).

Bartelink (1965) 87, Norden (1981) on 6.440f. (p. 249), Shechter (1975) 363–65, Ross (1987) 113, 166, 212–13, Jacobson (1982) 217, Thomas (1988) ad loc., Horsfall (1991a) 216 (laconically skeptical), *EV* s.v. hippomanes (Zumbo). Much on *hippomanes* in Pease (1963) on A. 4.515 (pp. 426–29); cf. also Tupet (1976) 79–82. On "herdsman call" see Collart (1954) 235–36, Thomas (1982b), Hollis (1990) 304, Campbell (1983) 25, 102; on double names, divine and human, in Homer see Rank (1951) 113–29.

**G. 3.294:** nunc, veneranda *Pales,* magno nunc ore sonandum.

Ross: "The invocation of *veneranda Pales* points (again, as in the first line of the book, *magna Pales*) directly and etymologically to the pastoral." Vergil established the etymological connection between *Pales* and *pastor* in **G. 3.1–2.**

Ross (1987) 168.

**G. 3.304:** iam cadit extremoque *inrorat Aquarius* anno.

Thomas suggests that "*inrorat* functions as a gloss on *Aquarius* (the Water-bearer)"; he compares the gloss of Aprilis at 1.217–18.

Thomas (1988) on 303–4; Horsfall (1991a) 216 is skeptical.

**G. 3.338:** litoraque alcyonen resonant, *acalanthida dumi.*

The juxtaposition of *acalanthida* with a word for thorns seems to allude to the etymology from ἄκανθα, "thorn," mentioned by several sources (the bird is thought to have fed on thorns). A note in Pliny indicates that Callimachus may have offered a similar derivation for a plant with a similar name, although we can be certain only that he named that plant.

For wordplay involving thorns cf. on A. 1.720 *matris Acidaliae.*

SERV. 338: ut . . . apud Graecos acalanthis dicta sit ab acanthis, id est spinis, quibus pascitur (cf. Serv. G. 2.119); ISID. 12.7.74: carduelis . . . apud Graecos acalanthis dicta est, ab ἀκάνθαις, id est spinis, quibus alitur; PLINY *NH* 25.168: caput eius (sc. erigerontos) numerose dividitur lanugine, qualis est spinae . . . ; quare Callimachus (fr. 585 Pf. = *Hec.* fr. 157 Hollis) eam acanthida appellavit, alii pappam.

Cerda (1608) 437; for other wordplay involving thorns in Prop. and Ovid cf. McKeown (1989) 202 and Courtney (1969) 80–81.

**G. 3.343–48:**

omnia secum  
*armentarius* Afer agit, tectumque laremque  
*arma*que Amyclaeumque canem Cressamque pharetram;  
non secus ac patriis acer Romanus in *armis*  
iniusto sub fasce viam cum carpit, et hosti  
ante exspectatum positis stat in agmine castris.

For the perceived etymological connection between *arma* and *armenta* see on **A. 3.540** *bello armantur equi, belli haec armenta minantur.* Serv. 344 notes that *armentarius* is not strictly appropriate here; Vergil's word choice shows the desire to etymologize. The wordplay here comes at the start of consecutive lines (see intro. 2.9).

SERV. 344: ARMENTARIUS AFER abusive: nam de gregibus loquitur.

Ross (1987) 173–74.

**G. 3.382:** gens effrena virum *Riphaeo* tunditur Euro

Servius derives the name of the Riphaean (elsewhere Rhipaen) mountains from Greek ῥιφή (= ῥιπή), "rush, gust." Ross describes the appropriateness of the Scythians' "inhabiting mountains named from the wintry blasts." Apollonius of Rhodes, as Livrea notes, probably alludes to the etymology at *Arg.* 4.285–87:

> ὅς δή τοι τείως μὲν ἀπείρονα τέμνετ' ἄρουραν
> εἷς οἶος, πηγαὶ γὰρ ὑπὲρ πνοιῆς βορέαο
> Ῥιπαίοις ἐν ὄρεσσιν ἀπόπροθι μορμύρουσιν·

SERV.: Riphaei autem montes sunt Scythiae, ut diximus (1.240) a perpetuo ventorum flatu nominati: nam ῥιφὴ graece impetus et ὁρμὴ dicitur ἀπὸ τοῦ ῥίπτειν.

Cerda (1608) 445, Ross (1987) 177, Livrea (1973) ad loc.

**G. 3.406–8?:** numquam custodibus illis / *nocturnum* stabulis *furem* incursusque luporum / aut impacatos a tergo horrebis Hiberos.

*Nocturnum* may gloss *furem* here (cf. intro. 2.2 for the single-epithet gloss): Varro is quoted by Gellius as deriving *fur* from the adjective *furvus,* "black," since thieves steal at night, which is black. The derivation may seem wrong to us, as it did to Gellius, who notes the Greek cognate φώρ, but if the etymology was in Varro, Vergil's *nocturnum . . . furem* would seem to allude to it. Still, caution is needed, since a thief may be nocturnal without the help of the etymologist.

SERV. 407: fur autem a furvo dictus est, id est nigro; nam noctis utitur tempore . . . aut certe a graeco venit; nam φὼρ vocatur; VARRO fr. 131 (*GRF* p. 235 = Aul. Gell. 1.18.3): Varro . . . furem dicit ex eo dictum, quod veteres Romani furvum atrum appellaverint et fures per noctem, quae atra sit, facilius furentur; many more sources cited in *GRF* and by Maltby.

**G. 3.418?:** aut tecto adsuetus *coluber* succedere et *umbrae*

Isidore offers a derivation of *colubrum* from *colat umbras;* if this is not his invention, Vergil may be alluding to such an etymology here. See also next entry, on *Calabris* in 425.

ISID. 12.4.2: colubrum ab eo dictum, quod colat umbras, vel quod in lubricos tractus flexibus sinuosis labatur.

**G. 3.425–34:**

> est etiam ille malus *Calabris in saltibus anguis*
> squamea convolvens sublato pectore terga
> atque notis longam maculosus grandibus alvum,
> qui, dum *amnes* ulli rumpuntur *fontibus* et dum
> vere *madent udo* terrae ac *pluvialibus* Austris,
> stagna colit ripisque habitans hic piscibus atram
> improbus ingluviem ranisque loquacibus explet;
> postquam *exusta* palus terraeque *ardore* dehiscunt,

exsilit in *siccum,* et flammantia lumina torquens
saevit agris asperque siti atque exterritus aestu.

As Thomas explains (I partially paraphrase his note here), although the name of the snake is suppressed (see intro. 2.7), it is readily identifiable as the *chersydrus* described by Nicander, whose name, as Nicander's lines imply, defines its amphibious nature (369 ἐν χέρσῳ = dry land; 367 ὕδωρ, water). Lines 428–33 gloss both elements of the snake's name: 428–29 *amnes, udo, pluvialibus* = ὕδωρ; 432–33 *exusta . . . ardore, siccum* = χέρσος.

Ross describes further (simple) wordplay: "this unnamed snake is a Calabrian (*Calaber* [425]), which I suspect is an intentional play on *coluber* in the same metrical position seven lines earlier." Cf. on G. 3.418 above.

NIC. *Ther.* 359–60, 366–71:

Νῦν δ' ἄγε χερσύδροιο καὶ ἀσπίδος εἴρεο μορφάς
ἰσαίας· . . .
. . . . . . .
ὃς δ' ἤτοι τὸ πρὶν μὲν ὑπὸ βροχθώδεϊ λίμνῃ
ἄσπειστον βατράχοισι φέρει κότον· ἀλλ' ὅταν ὕδωρ
Σείριος αὐήνῃσι, τρύγῃ δ' ἐν πυθμένι λίμνης,
καὶ τόθ' ὅγ' ἐν χέρσῳ τελέθει ψαφαρός τε καὶ ἄχρους,
θάλπων ἠελίῳ βλοσυρὸν δέμας· ἐν δὲ κελεύθοις
γλώσσῃ ποιφύγδην νέμεται διψήρεας ὄγμους.

Thomas (1988) on 425–34 and on 425, Ross (1987) 178.

**G. 3.461?:** acerque Gelonus

Nisbet suggests wordplay here between Gelonus and *gelu,* "frost, cold," suggested perhaps by *acer.* Cf. intro. 2.2 for the single-epithet gloss.

Cf. the possible play at A. 3.701–2 *apparet Camerina procul campique* ***Geloi,*** / ***immanisque Gela fluvii*** *cognomine dicta.*

Nisbet (1990) 261.

**G. 3.474:** aerias Alpis

Servius says that *Alpes* is the Gallic word for "high mountains," and that *aerias* is thus a gloss *(verbum expressit ex verbo).* One might think that etymology was not required to call the Alps "high," but I know of no prose author who does so, while such phrases appear in verse in Catullus (Ellis suggested an etymological gloss), Ovid (cf. intro. 2.14), Petronius (see Connors), and Silius. It may well be that Vergil is imitating Catullus, the others Vergil.

For single-epithet glosses see intro. 2.2. For possible allusion by Vergil to "mountain" as the original meaning of the name *Alba* see on A. 9.386–88. For Vergil's several other other plays on words like *altus* and *arduus,* see on 3.271 *Neritos ardua.*

SERV. 474: AERIAS ALPES: id est Galliam. et dicendo "aerias" verbum expressit ex verbo: nam Gallorum lingua alti montes Alpes vocantur; SERV. A. 4.442: ALPINI

BOREAE flantes de Alpibus, quae Gallorum lingua alti montes vocantur; SERV. Auct. A. 10.13 says, sane omnes altitudines montium licet a Gallis Alpes vocentur, proprie tamen iuga montium Gallicorum sunt, then cites Varro's discussion of ways of crossing the Alps. Varro may well have mentioned the meaning of the word Alps (Varro fr. 379, *GRF* p. 346); similarly in COMMENT. Lucan 1.183, Isid. 14.8.18; differently PAUL.-Fest. p. 4, 8 L: Album, quod nos dicimus, a Graeco, quod est ἀλφόν, est appellatum. Sabini tamen alpum dixerunt. Unde credi potest, nomen Alpium a candore nivium vocitatum (evidence for discussion of the question by the Augustan Verrius Flaccus?).

CAT. 11.9: altas . . . Alpes; OVID *Met.* 2.226: aeriaeque Alpes; PETR. *Sat.* 122, *BC* verse 144: Alpibus aeriis; SIL. 1.117: celsae . . . Alpes, 370: Alpibus altis, 15.168: aerias Alpis.

Ogilvie (1970) on Livy 1.3.3 (p. 43; quoted on A. 8.328–32), Ellis (1878) 42, Connors (1989) 108–9, O'Hara (1996); Servius' comment is rejected by Bartelink (1965) 39 n. 5

**G. 4.20:** palmaque vestibulum aut *ingens* oleaster inumbret

Ross observes that the *oleaster*, the wild olive, "is hardly 'huge,'" and suggests that "the epithet *ingens* carries Virgilian suggestions, 'native,' and 'natural' (that is, untampered with by man) that we have seen before."

Cf. on **G. 2.131,** *ingens arbos.*

Bartelink (1965) 29, Ross (1987) 192, Mackail (1912).

**G. 4.42–48:**

saepe etiam effossis, si vera est fama, latebris
sub terra ***fovere larem,*** penitusque repertae
pumicibusque cavis exesaeque arboris antro.
tu tamen et levi rimosa *cubilia* limo
unge ***fovens*** circum, et raras superinice frondes.
neu propius tectis taxum sine, neve rubentis
ure **foco** cancros

In 43 *larem,* "home, household gods," is part of the gentle personification of the bees, but Vergil's phrase really means *fovere favum,* "they warm their honeycomb" (on the suppression of the noun *favus* cf. intro. 2.7). Paulus-Festus tells us that *favus* comes from the verb *foveo,* "to warm." So the bees "warm their place of warmth." Cf. on G. 4.55–56 *nidosque fovent,* and 4.104 *contemnuntque favos et frigida tecta relinquunt.*

Thomas sees wordplay between *focus* in 48 and *fovere* in 43 and 46; the words are connected etymologically by Varro and Ovid.

Favus: PAUL.-Fest. p. 78, 9 L: favi a fovendo.

Focus (more in Maltby): VARRO ap. Serv. Auct. ad A. 11.211 (cf. fr. 158 *GRF* p. 243): an quod focum dicat ubicumque ignis est et fovetur: unde et Varro focum dici vult; ISID. *Diff.* 307: focus vero fomes ac nutrimentum ignis; nam Varro focus ait dictus quod foveat ignem. focus ergo dictus a fotu; OVID *F.* 6.301 (for Ovid cf. intro. 2.14): focus a flammis et quod fovet omnia dictus.

Thomas (1982) 91 n. 42.

**G. 4.55–56:** hinc nescio qua dulcedine laetae / progeniem *nidosque fovent*

*Nidos* in 56 can mean "nestlings, young" (Thomas on 56: "perhaps a metonymy for *pullos*"), or it can mean "nest, hive," and so stand for *favus,* thus with further allusion to the derivation of *favus* from *foveo.*

See on **G. 4.42–46** *fovere larem.*

**G. 4.88–102:**

verum ubi ductores acie revocaveris ambo,
deterior qui visus, eum, ne prodigus obsit,
dede neci; *melior* vacua sine regnet in aula.
alter erit maculis auro squalentibus ardens—
nam duo sunt genera: hic *melior* insignis et ore
et rutilis clarus squamis; ille horridus alter
desidia latamque trahens inglorius alvum.
ut binae regum facies, ita corpora plebis:
namque aliae turpes horrent, ceu pulvere ab alto
cum venit et sicco terram spuit ore viator
aridus; elucent aliae et fulgore coruscant
ardentes auro et paribus lita corpora guttis.
haec *potior* suboles, hinc caeli tempore certo
*dulcia mella* premes, nec tantum dulcia quantum
et liquida et durum Bacchi domitura saporem.

Vergil puns on *mel,* "honey," and *melior,* "better." He uses *melior* in 90 and 92, then replaces it with *potior* in 100, right before saying that from the "better" bees one gets *dulcia mella.* Ross calls this "a pun straight from Varro."

Cf. on G. 4.271–78, *amellus.*

VARRO *RR* 3.16.18: qui ita melior, ut expediat mellario.

Ross (1987) 198–99.

**G. 4.104:** contemnuntque *favos et frigida tecta* relinquunt

Vergil again alludes to the derivation of *favus* from *foveo,* "to warm": *frigida tecta relinquunt,* "they abandon a cold place"; *contemnuntque favos,* "they abandon a warm place."

See on **G. 4.42–46,** *fovere larem.*

**G. 4.124?:** amantes litora myrtae

A doubtful example. Isidore derives *myrtus* from *mare* and connects that etymology to two passages in Vergil.

ISID. 17.7.50: myrtus a mare dicta, eo quod magis litorea arbor sit. unde et Vergilius (G. 2.112) "litora myrtetis laetissima" et "amantes litora myrtae."

**G. 4.126?:** qua *niger* umectat flaventia culta *Galaesus*

Nisbet points to the color contrasts of this line *(niger, flaventia)* and suggests an implied connection between Galaesus and Greek γάλα, "milk." *Niger* glosses the word by its opposite (for such glosses κατ' ἀντίφρασιν see intro. 2.3).

Cf. the connection possibly implied at **A. 8.657ff.** between the white-skinned Galli and γάλα, and also Theoc. 11.19 ὦ λευκὰ Γαλάτεια, and also Ovid *Met.* 13.789 *candidior folio nivei, Galatea, ligustri* (for Ovid cf. intro. 2.14).

Nisbet (1990) 261.

**G. 4.149–52:**

nunc age, naturas apibus quas Iuppiter ipse
addidit expediam, pro qua mercede *canoros*
*Curetum sonitus crepitantia*que aera secutae
Dictaeo caeli regem pavere sub antro.

Shechter: "Callimachus . . . etymologizes Κούρητες with κουρίζοντος, 'to make infant sounds' (cf. Aratus 32, 34). . . . With *canoros sonitus* and *crepitantia* Virgil explanatorily derives the name Curetum, while presupposing an association with κουρίζω. Lucretius, 2.629–39, had set forth etymologies for *Curetes,* adhering to accepted Greek beliefs about the name . . . , whether for Asian celebrants (cf. *capitum . . . cristas* 632) or Cretan warriors (cf. *vagitum . . . Creta* 634)." Lucretius' *pueri* glosses the name with reference to κοῦροι.

LUCR. 2.629–39:

hic armata manus, *Curetas* nomine Grai
quos memorant, Phrygias inter si forte catervas
ludunt in numerumque exultant sanguine laeti
terrificas capitum quatientes numine cristas,
Dictaeos referunt Curetas, qui Iovis illum
vagitum in Creta quondam occultasse feruntur,
cum *pueri* circum puerum pernice chorea
[armat et in numerum pernice chorea]
armati in numerum pulsarent aeribus aera,
ne Saturnus eum malis mandaret adeptus
aeternumque daret matri sub pectore volnus

CALLIM. *Hymn* 1.52–54: οὖλα δὲ Κούρητές σε περὶ πρύλιν ὠρχήσαντο / τεύχεα πεπλήγοντες, ἵνα Κρόνος οὔασιν ἠχήν / ἀσίδος εἰσαίοι καὶ μή σεο κουρίζοντος; ARAT. *Phaen.* 32–35: κουρίζοντα (sc. Δία) / Δίκτῳ ἐν εὐώδει, ὄρεος σχεδὸν Ἰδαίοιο / . . . / Δικταῖοι Κούρητες ὅτε Κρόνον ἐψεύδοντο (for text see on A. 12.411–19).

Shechter (1975) 370, Von Jan (1893) 80 n. 1; on Lucretius, Friedländer (1941) 21, Snyder (1980) 96.

## G. 4.219–22:

his quidam signis atque haec exempla secuti
esse apibus partem divinae mentis et haustus
aetherios dixere; *deum namque ire per omnis*
terrasque tractusque maris caelumque profundum

Norden and others have suggested that Vergil's phrase *deum namque ire per omnis* alludes to the connection seen by the Stoics and others between Δίος and the other oblique forms of the name Zeus, and διά = *per,* "through."

CHRYSIPPUS ap. Stob. *Eclog.* 1., p. 31 II W. = fr. 1062 Arn. *SVF* ii. 312: Δία δὲ αὐτὸν λέγουσιν, ὅτι πάντων ἐστὶν αἴτιος καὶ δι' αὐτὸν πάντα (see intro. 1.3); HES. *Op.* 2–3: δεῦτε Δι' ἐννέπετε . . . / ὅν τε διὰ βροτοὶ ἄνδρες ὁμῶς ἄφατοί τε φατοί τε; AESCH. *Ag.* 1485–86: ἰὼ ἰή, διαὶ Διὸς / παναιτίου πανεργέτα; cf. too PLATO *Crat.* 396 b, SCHOL. *Il.* 20.127.

Bartelink (1965) 87, Norden (1981) 17 n. 2, Rank (1951) 43–44, Feeney (1991) 9, 21 and n. 64.

**G. 4.257?:** aut illae *pedibus* conexae ad limina pendent

Servius reports a possible derivation of *apes* from the way that bees hang together by their feet *(pedibus)*. But that etymology is likely to have been simply derived from Vergil's own line, if not by Servius then by the sources *(multi)* to whom he alludes (for other possible examples of etymologies deduced by grammarians from Vergil's text cf. on **A. 1.164–65**; on bees see esp. on **G. 4.310**).

Cf. on A. 7.66 *pedibus per mutua nexis.*

SERV. 257 (sim. Isid. 12.8.1): PEDIBUS CONEXAE hinc multi apes dictas volunt, quod se pedibus invicem tenent: licet crebrior sit illa opinio, quod sine pedibus primo esse dicuntur, ut (310) "trunca pedum primo."

Maltby (1993) 264–65 (skeptical).

## G. 4.260–63:

tum sonus auditur gravior, tractimque susurrant,
frigidus *ut* quondam silvis immurmurat Auster,
*ut* mare sollicitum stridit refluentibus undis,
aestuat *ut* clausis rapidus fornacibus ignis.

Farrell notes a kind of bilingual wordplay or "translation by homonym," as *ut* . . . *ut* . . . *ut* is used to correspond to οὔτε . . . οὔτε . . . οὔτε in the Iliadic model. For similar "translation by homonym," see intro. 2.1a.

HOM. *Il.* 14.392–401:

ἐκλύσθη δὲ θάλασσα ποτὶ κλισίας τε νέας τε
᾿Αργείων· οἳ δὲ ξύνισαν μεγάλῳ ἀλαλητῷ.
οὔτε θαλάσσης κῦμα τόσον βοάᾳ ποτὶ χέρσον
ποντόθεν ὀρνύμενον πνοιῇ Βορέω ἀλεγεινῇ·
οὔτε πυρὸς τόσσός γε ποτὶ βρόμος αἰθομένοιο
οὔρεος ἐν βήσσῃς, ὅτε τ' ὤρετο καιέμεν ὕλην·
οὔτ' ἄνεμος τόσσόν γε περὶ δρυσὶν ὑψικόμοισι
ἠπύει, ὅς τε μάλιστα μέγα βρέμεται χαλεπαίνων,
ὅσση ἄρα Τρώων καὶ ᾿Αχαιῶν ἔπλετο φωνὴ
δεινὸν ἀυσάντων, ὅτ' ἐπ' ἀλλήλοισιν ὄρουσαν.

Farrell (1991) 248–49.

## G. 4.271–80:

est etiam flos in pratis cui nomen *amello*
fecere agricolae, facilis quaerentibus herba;
namque uno ingentem tollit de caespite silvam
aureus ipse, sed in foliis, quae plurima circum
funduntur, violae sublucet purpura nigrae;
saepe deum nexis ornatae torquibus arae;
asper in ore sapor; tonsis in vallibus illum
pastores et curva legunt *prope flumina Mellae.*
huius odorato radices incoque Baccho
pabulaque in foribus plenis appone canistris.

The signpost *nomen . . . fecere agricolae* (see intro. 2.6) calls attention to the name *amellus,* which "is the subject of one of the four major, related aetiologies" in the *Georgics* discussed by Ross and "is of significance both in its own context, and in its relation to the other three."

The etymology is given at the ends of the first and last lines of the sentence at 271–78, which thus frame the passage (see intro. 2.8a). The derivation of *amellus* from the river *Mella* is like that of the *asilus* from the river *Silarus* at G. 3.146–48. Ross notes that the *amellus* is presented in such a way that "it ought to be a powerful medicine against our diseases," but then 281ff. discuss a situation in which all of a beekeeper's bees have died.

Shechter discusses another etymology suggested by the passage: "If *a-* in *amellus* is taken as privative, *asper in ore sapor* furnishes an additional meaning, that is, 'not honeyed,' 'bitter to taste.' " Thomas puts it differently: "V. perhaps intends a secondary etymology: the plant cures sick bees, which presumably produce 'no honey.' "

See Ross for the *amellus* in context: compared with the *medica* (G. 2.126–41), the gadfly (3.146–56), and *hippomanes* (3.280–83), "the *amellus* alone emerges as natural, native [to Italy], and beneficial, in habitat, characteristics, and use, and as such it ought to be a powerful medicine against our diseases (*nostros casus,* 251)."

Ross notes that in 273, "*ingens . . . ,* again where vast size is clearly inappropriate . . . again must suggest 'native.' "

For *ingens* see on G. 2.131. For amellus as "without honey," cf. the play at G. 4.88–102 on *melior, potior,* and *mella*. For the phrase *nomen . . . fecere agricolae* cf. on E. 9.33–34 *me quoque dicunt / vatem pastores.*

SERV. 271: plene hanc herbam, ut etiam supra (2.127) arborem felicis mali, exsequitur: nam dicit ubi creetur, qualis sit, quid possit; 278: Mella fluvius Galliae est, iuxta quem haec herba plurima nascitur; unde et amella dicitur, sicut etiam populi habitantes iuxta Lemannum fluvium Alemanni dicuntur.

Bartelink (1965) 79, Shechter (1975) 379–81, Marouzeau (1949) 76, Ross (1987) 111–13, 211–14, Thomas (1988) on 271–72.

**G. 4.283–85:** tempus et Arcadii memoranda inventa magistri / pandere, quoque modo caesis iam saepe iuvencis / *insincerus apes* tulerit *cruor.*

Vergil refers to the creation of bees from the blood of slaughtered cattle. The description of the blood as *insincerus* may involve a punning reference to a supposed etymology of *sincerus*. Donatus explains the word by citing the phrase *mel sine cera,* "honey without wax." The *insincerus cruor* that produces the bees is, literally, foul or putrid blood, but because of its ability to produce bees Vergil may be punningly suggesting that it is "blood that is not without wax."

Ross comments that *insincerus* here is "a word both rare and odd in its context"; he implies that the word may suggest Vergil's lack of belief in the process of bougonia that he is beginning to describe. He does not suggest etymological wordplay.

Wordplay between *sincera* and *Ceres* has been suggested for the *Moretum*. Cf. too the etymologizing of *segnis* as *sine igne* implied at A. 12.521–28, and cf. on G. 4.271–80 for *amellus* as possibly "without honey."

DON. on Ter. *Eun.* I 2 97: "sincerum" purum sine fuco et simplex est, ut mel "sine cera"; ISID. 10.242: sincerus, quasi sine corruptione; cf. SERV. A. 2.374: "segnis" autem est proprie "frigidus," "sine igni," ut "securus" "sine cura," "sedulus" "sine dolo."

[VERG.] *Mor.* 41–42: subsidit *sincera* foraminibusque liquatur / emundata *Ceres.*

Ross (1987) 216; on the *Moretum* see Ross (1975a) 257–58.

**G. 4.310?:** *trunca pedum* primo, mox et stridentia pennis

Servius reports the opinion of some that bees are called *apes* because they are born "without feet" *(sine pedibus);* cf. on **G. 4.257**. Maltby correctly warns that this interpretation is likely to have been deduced from the present line (for other possible examples of etymologies deduced by grammarians from Vergil's text cf. on **A. 1.164–65**).

SERV. 4.257: quod sine pedibus primo esse dicuntur, ut (310) "trunca pedum primo."

Maltby (1993) 264–65 (skeptical); cf. Cerda (1608) 526.

**G. 4.376–77:** *manibus* liquidos dant ordine fontis / germanae, tonsisque ferunt *mantelia* villis

The word *manibus* may gloss *mantelia,* both here and at A. 1.701–2, even though the Homeric model also mentions hands.

SERV. 376: MANTELIA quibus manus tergunt; on A. 1.702: mantelia vero a tergendis manibus dicta; HOM. *Od.* 1.146: ὕδωρ ἐπὶ χεῖρας ἔχευαν.

A. 1.701–2: dant *manibus* famuli lymphas Cereremque canistris / expediunt tonsisque ferunt *mantelia* villis.

## G. 4.425–28:

iam rapidus *torrens* sitientis *Sirius* Indos
ardebat caelo et medium sol igneus orbem
hauserat, arebant herbae et cava flumina siccis
faucibus ad limum radii tepefacta coquebant

Both *torrens,* as a single-epithet gloss (see intro. 2.2), and the stress on heat in 424–27, may allude to the connection between the name *Sirius* and Greek σειριάω, "to be hot, scorching." Aratus once so glosses the name.

On names of stars see also G. 1.137–38, *Pleiadas, Hyadas.*

SCHOL. Germ. Bas. p. 95: Sirium dicunt ab ardore; HYG. *Astr.* 2.35.2: Sirion appellasse propter flammae candorem (a bit more in Maltby).

ARAT. *Phaen.* 328–32:

ἀλλα; κατ' αὐτὴν
γαστέρα κυάνεος περιτέλλεται, ἡ δέ οἱ ἄκρη
ἀστέρι βέβληται δεινῷ γένυς, ὅς ῥα μάλιστα
ὀξέα σειριάει· καί μιν καλέουσ' ἄνθρωποι
Σείριον.

On the associations of heat in these lines see Ross (1987) 225.

**G. 4.450–52?:** ad haec *vates vi* denique *multa* / ardentis oculos intorsit lumine glauco, / et graviter frendens sic fatis ora resoluit

The juxtaposition of *vates* and *vi* here may allude to the etymological connection between the words attributed by Isidore to Varro.

VARRO ap. Isid. 8.7.3 (cf. fr. 66, *GRF* p. 213): vates a vi mentis appellatos Varro auctor est (sim. Serv. A. 3.433, Schol. Bern. E. 9.34); vel a viendis carminibus, id est flectendis . . . et proinde poetae Latine vates olim . . . quod vi quadam et quasi vesania in scribendo commoverentur; vel quod modis verba conecterent, viere antiquis pro vincire ponentibus; VARRO *LL* 7.36: antiquos poetas vates appellabant a versibus viendis (more in Maltby).

**G. 4.478–80:** quos circum limus niger et deformis harundo / Cocyti tardaque palus *inamabilis* unda / alligat et novies *Styx* interfusa coercet.

Cf. on **A. 6.438–39** for the frequent association of the name Styx with Greek στυγέω, "hate," and στυγερός, "hateful," so that Vergil's *inamabilis* is thus a gloss on the name.

Bartelink (1965) 82, Henrichs (1989) 1–19, esp. 11 n. 30.

**G. 4.521?:** *nocturni*que orgia *Bacchi*

Servius Auctus notes that Bacchus is called *nocturnus* because his rites were observed at night and says that this is the origin of the cult name Nyctelius. The epithet here may (but need not) allude to the name Nyctelius. For the single-epithet gloss see intro. 2.2; for suppression see intro. 2.7.

Cf. on **A. 4.302–3** *ubi audito stimulant trieterica* ***Baccho*** */ orgia* ***nocturnus****que vocat clamore Cithaeron.*

SERV. Auct. 520: NOCTURNIQUE ORGIA quia sacra eius nocte celebrantur: ex quo Nyctelius est cognominatus (sim. on A. 4.303) (he also explains *nocturnus* as a transferred epithet: "nocturnique orgia" pro "nocturna orgia" ut "udae vocis iter" [A 7.533]).

Cerda (1608) 559.

**G. 4.563–64:** illo *Vergilium* me tempore dulcis alebat / *Parthenope* studiis florentem ignobilis oti

The proximity of the proper names *Vergilium* and *Parthenope* may allude to the pun *Vergilius/virgo* and to Vergil's nickname Parthenias. See on **G. 1.427–35**, esp. 430 *virgineum*.

# Appendix: Additional Examples at Asterisks in Catalogue

In a paper on "Interactive 'Speaking' Names in Vergil's *Aeneid*" at a British Academy conference on The Language of Latin Poetry in April 1995, available only when this book was in production, S. J. Harrison (or Roger Rees or David West, responding to the paper) suggests that names are being glossed in the following passages, in ways that should be apparent from the brief notes placed after each quotation. Asterisks appear in the catalogue where these examples belong. The end of this listing also notes a forthcoming suggestion by David Sansone.

**A. 1.498, 500:** in Eurotae ripis aut per *iuga* Cynthi . . . *Oreades* (ὄρος; cf. Paul.-Fest. 199, 1 L: *Oreades nymphae a montibus appellantur*)

**A. 1.535:** *adsurgens* . . . *Orion* (*oriri*)

**A. 3.49:** hunc *Polydorum* auri quondam *cum pondere magno* (Eustath *Il.* 16.175: Πολύδωρος διὰ τὰ ἐκ φύσεως δῶρα οὕτως ὠνομάσθη)

**A. 3.687:** *angusta* ab sede *Pelori* (κατ' ἀντίφρασιν; πέλωρος = "monstrous, huge")

**A. 6.299:** *terribili squalore Charon* (χάρις; cf. on A. 6.299)

**A. 6.870–71:** nimium vobis *Romana* propago / visa *potens* (ῥώμη, "strength, might;" suggested by Rees; cf. Maltby [1993a] 269 on Horace)

**A. 7.191:** fecit *avem Circe* (κίρκος, "hawk")

**A. 10.318:** *immanemque Gyan* (cf. 5.118 ingentemque Gyas ingenti mole Chimaeram; Mørland [1960] 105–6; Harrison [1991] on 10.318)

**A. 10.322–23:** ecce *Pharo*, *voces* dum iactat inertis, / intorquens iaculum clamantis sistit in *ore* (cf. φάρος, "throat," and Harrison [1991] ad loc.)

**A. 10.575:** interea buiigis infert se *Lucagus albis* (cf. λευκός, ἄγειν and Harrison [1991] ad loc.)

**A. 11.270:** *pulchram Calydona* (καλός)

**A. 11.557–58:** *hanc* . . . *famulam* voveo [sc. *Camillam*] (cf. Servius here and on 11.543, Varro *LL* 7.34: camilla⟨m⟩ qui glos⟨s⟩emata interpretati dixerunt administram)

**A. 11.612–13:** continuo adversis Tyrrhenus et acer *Aconteus* / conixi incurrunt *hastis* (ἀκοντιζω; cf. on 11.615–17)
**A. 11.648–49:** *Amazon* / *unum* exserta *latus* pugnae (latus = μᾶζα; suggested by West)
**A. 12.304–5:** *Alsum* / *pastorem* (ἄλσος, "(pastoral) grove," as in Theoc. 1.117)
**A. 12.827:** Romana potens (ῥώμη, as at A. 6.870–71)

In another paper, which I hope will be published soon, David Sansone notes that in **A. 5.835–36** the phrase *Nox . . . metam / contigerat* links three words whose Greek equivalents, *νύξ*, *νύσσα*, and the verb *νύσσω*, were thought by some ancient etymologists to be related.

# Bibliography

Abbreviations of the names of journals may be deciphered with the aid of the list in the front of *L'Année Philologique,* although I have simplified some of their abbreviations, in ways that should not cause confusion.


Ahern, Charles F. 1991. "Horace's Rewriting of Homer in *Carmen* 1.6." *CP* 86:301–14.

Ahl, Frederick M. 1976. *Lucan: An Introduction.* Ithaca.

———. 1982. "Amber, Avallon, and Apollo's Singing Swan." *AJP* 103:373–411.

———. 1985. *Metaformations: Soundplay and Wordplay in Ovid and Other Classical Poets.* Ithaca.

———. 1986. *Seneca: Three Tragedies.* Ithaca.

———. 1988. "Ars Est Caelare Artem (Art in Puns and Anagrams Engraved)." Pp. 17–43 in Culler (1988).

———. 1991. *Sophocles' Oedipus: Evidence and Self-Conviction.* Ithaca.

Albis, Robert V. 1995. "Jason's Prayers to Apollo in *Aetia* 1 and the *Argonautica.*" *Phoenix* 49:104–9.

Ambrose, Z. Philip. 1980. "The Etymology and Genealogy of Palinurus." *AJP* 101:449–57.

Amsler, Mark. 1989. *Etymology and Grammatical Discourse in Late Antiquity and the Early Middle Ages.* Amsterdam.

Anderson, William S. 1958. "Juno and Saturn in the *Aeneid.*" *SP* 60:519–32.

André, J. 1975. "Ovide Helléniste et Linguiste." *RPh.* 49:191–95.

Austin, R.G. 1955. *P. Vergili Maronis Aeneidos Liber Quartus.* Oxford.

———. 1964. *P. Vergili Maronis Aeneidos Liber Secundus.* Oxford.

———. 1971. *P. Vergili Maronis Aeneidos Liber Primus.* Oxford.

———. 1977. *P. Vergili Maronis Aeneidos Liber Sextus.* Oxford.

Badian, Ernst. 1988. "The Clever and the Wise: Two Roman Cognomina in Context." Pp. 6–12 in *Vir bonus discendi peritus: Studies . . . O. Skutsch,* ed. N. Horsfall. *BICS* Suppl. 51.

Bandera, Cesáreo. 1981. "Sacrificial Levels in Virgil's *Aeneid.*" *Arethusa* 14:217–39.

Barchiesi, Alessandro. 1991. "Discordant Muses." *PCPS* 37:1–21.

———. 1993. "Future Reflexive: Two Modes of Allusion and Ovid's *Heriodes.*" *HSCP* 95:333–65.

Bartelink, G.J.M. 1965. *Etymologisering bij Vergilius. Mededelingen der Kon. Neder. Akad. van Wetenschappen.* Deel 28, no. 3. Amsterdam.

Baxter, Timothy M.S. 1992. *The Cratylus: Plato's Critique of Naming.* Leiden.

Belfiore, Elizabeth. 1984. "*Ter frustra comprensa:* Embraces in the *Aeneid.*" *Phoenix* 38:19–30.
Bertoldi, Vittorio. 1936. "Problemi d'etimologia." *Zeitschrift für Romanische Philologie* 56:179–88.
Bing, Peter. 1988. *The Well-Read Muse: Present and Past in Callimachus and the Hellenistic Poets.* Göttingen.
———. 1990. "A Pun on Aratus' Name in Verse Two of the *Phaenomena?*" *HSCP* 93:281–85.
———. 1993. "Aratus and His Audiences." *MD* 31:99–109.
Bloch, R. Howard. 1983. *Etymologies and Genealogies: A Literary Anthropology of the French Middle Ages.* Chicago.
Bornmann, Fritz. 1968. *Callimachi Hymnus in Dianam.* Florence.
Bowie, A.M. 1990. "The Death of Priam: Allegory and History in the *Aeneid.*" *CQ* 40:470–81.
Boyd, Barbara W. 1983. "*Cydonea Mala:* Vergilian Word-play and Allusion." *HSCP* 87:169–74.
———. 1984. "Tarpeia's Tomb: A Note on Propertius 4.4." *AJP* 105:85–86.
Bramble, J.C. 1974. "Cui non dictus Hylas puer? Propertius 1.20." Pp. 81–93 in *Quality and Pleasure in Latin Poetry,* ed. David West and Tony Woodman. Cambridge.
Bréguet, Esther. 1956. "Virgile et les augures: A propos d'Enéide IX 324–28." *MH* 13:54–62.
Brenk, Frederick E. 1984. "*Unum pro multis caput:* Myth, History, and Symbolic Imagery in Vergil's Palinurus Incident." *Latomus* 43:776–801.
Brink, C.O. 1971. *Horace on Poetry: The "Ars Poetica."* Cambridge.
Brooks, Robert A. 1966. "*Discolor Aura:* Reflections on the Golden Bough." Pp. 142–63 in Commager (1966). Reprinted from *AJP* 74 (1953) 260–80.
Brown, Edwin L. 1963. *Numeri Vergiliani: Studies in Eclogues and Georgics.* Coll. Latomus 63. Brussels.
Brown, P. Michael. 1984. *Lucretius: De Rerum Natura I.* Bristol.
Brown, Robert D. 1990. "The Homeric Background to a Vergilian Repetition (*Aeneid* 1.744 = 3.516)." *AJP* 111:182–86.
———. 1990a. "The Structural Function of the Song of Iopas." *HSCP* 93:315–34.
Buchheit, Vinzenz. 1972. *Der Anspruch des Dichters in Vergils Georgika.* Darmstadt.
Buffière, Félix. 1956. *Les mythes d' Homère et la pensée grecque.* Paris.
Bulloch, Anthony W. 1985. *Callimachus: The Fifth Hymn.* Cambridge.
Bulloch, Anthony W., Erich S. Gruen, A.A. Long, and Andrew Stewart, eds. 1993. *Images and Ideologies: Self-Definition in the Hellenistic World.* Berkeley and Los Angeles.
Bury, J.B. 1888. "Paronomasia in Pindar." *Hermathena* 6:185–208.
Cairns, Francis. 1969. "Propertius 1.18 and Callimachus, *Acontius and Cydippe.*" *CR* 19:131–34.
———. 1973. "Catullus' *basia* Poems (5, 7, 48)." *Mnem.* 26:15–22.
———. 1979. *Tibullus: A Hellenistic Poet at Rome.* Cambridge.
———. 1984. "The Etymology of *Militia* in Roman Elegy." Pp. 211–21 in *Apophoreta Philologica Emmanueli Fernandez-Galiano a Sodalibus Oblata,* ed. Luis Gil and Rosa M. Aguilar. Madrid.

———. 1989. *Virgil's Augustan Epic*. Cambridge.

Calame, Claude. 1993. "Legendary Narration and Poetic Procedure in Callimachus' *Hymn to Apollo*." Pp. 37–55 in *Callimachus: Hellenistica Groningana*, vol. 1, ed. M.A. Harder, R.F. Regtuit, and G.C. Wakker. Groningen.

Cameron, H.D. 1970. "The Power of Words in the *Seven against Thebes*." *TAPA* 101:95–118.

Campbell, Malcolm. 1983. *Studies in the Third Book of Apollonius Rhodius' Argonautica*. Hildesheim.

Cerda, Juan Luis de la (= Ioannes Ludovicus de la). 1608. *P. Virgilii Maronis Bucolica et Georgica Argumentis, Explicationibus, et Notis Illustrata*. Frankfurt am Main.

———. 1612. *P. Virgilii Maronis Priores Sex Libri Aeneidos Argumentis, Explicationibus, et Notis Illustrati*. Lyon.

———. 1617. *P. Virgilii Maronis Posteriores Sex Libri Aeneidos Argumentis, Explicationibus, et Notis Illustrati*. Lyon.

Christmann, Eckhard. 1976. "Der Tod des Aeneas und die Pforten des Schlafes." Pp. 251–79 in *Studien zum Antiken Epos Franz Dirlmeier und Viktor Pöschl gewidmet*, ed. H. Görgemanns and E. Schmidt. Beitr. zur Klass. Phil. 62. Meisenheim.

Clark, Raymond J. 1978. *Catabasis: Vergil and the Wisdom Tradition*. Amsterdam.

Clausen, Wendell. 1970. "Catullus and Callimachus." *HSCP* 74:85–94.

———. 1976. "*Cynthius*." *AJP* 97:245–47.

———. 1977. "*Cynthius*: An Addendum." *AJP* 98:362.

———. 1987. *Virgil's "Aeneid" and the Tradition of Hellenistic Poetry*. Berkeley and Los Angeles.

———. 1994. *A Commentary on Virgil: Eclogues*. Oxford.

Clay, Diskin. 1988. "The Archaeology of the Temple to Juno in Carthage (*Aen.* 1.446–93)." *CP* 83:195–205.

Cockburn, Gordon T. 1992. "Aeneas and the Gates of Sleep: An Etymological Approach." *Phoenix* 46:362–64.

Coleman, Robert. 1977. *Vergil: Eclogues*. Cambridge.

———. 1984. Review of Williams (1979). *CR* 34:30.

Colish, Marcia L. 1985. *The Stoic Tradition from Antiquity to the Middle Ages*. Vol. 1: *Stoicism in Classical Literature*. Leiden.

Collart, Jean. 1954. *Varron Grammairien Latin*. Paris.

Commager, Steele. 1966. *Virgil: A Collection of Critical Essays*. Englewood Cliffs, N.J.

———. 1981. "Fateful Words: Some Conversations in *Aeneid* 4." *Arethusa* 14:101–14.

Conington, John. 1963. *The Works of Virgil with a Commentary*. Rev. by Henry Nettleship. Hildesheim. Reprint of 1883–84 London edition.

Connors, Catherine M. 1989. "Petronius' 'Bellum Civile' and the Poetics of Discord." Ph.D. diss., University of Michigan.

———. 1991. "Simultaneous Hunting and Herding at *Ciris* 297–300." *CQ* n.s. 41:556–59.

———. 1992. "Seeing Cypresses in Virgil." *CJ* 88:1–17.

Conte, Gian Biagio. 1986. *The Rhetoric of Imitation: Genre and Poetic Memory in Virgil and Other Latin Poets*. Ithaca.

———. 1992. "'Rhetoric of Imitation' as Rhetoric of Culture: Some New Thoughts." *Vergilius* 38:46–55.
Conway, R.S. 1912. "Note" on Mackail (1912). *CR* 26:254–55.
Courtney, Edward. 1969. "Three Poems of Propertius." *BICS* 16 (1969) 70–87.
———. 1981. "The Formation of the Text of Vergil." *BICS* 28:13–29.
———. 1993. *The Fragmentary Latin Poets*. Oxford.
Cruttwell, R.W. 1945. "Virgil, *Aeneid* IV.247: '*Atlantis Duri.*'" *CR* 59:11.
Culler, Jonathan. 1975. *Structuralist Poetics: Structuralism, Linguistics, and the Study of Literature*. Ithaca.
———, ed. 1988. *On Puns: The Foundation of Letters*. New York.
———. 1988a. "The Call of the Phoneme: Introduction." Pp. 1–16 in Culler (1988).
Curtius, Ernst Robert. 1953. *European Literature and the Latin Middle Ages*. Trans. W.R. Trask. New York.
Dahlmann, Hellfried. 1964. *Varro und die Hellenistiche Sprachtheorie*. Berlin. Reprint of 1932 edition.
Daly, James. 1982. "The Name of Philoctetes: *Philoctetes* 670–73." *AJP* 103:440–43.
Dalzell, Alexander. 1987. "Language and Atomic Theory in Lucretius." *Hermathena* 143:19–28.
Davis, Gregson. 1991. *Polyhymnia: The Rhetoric of Horatian Lyric Discourse*. Berkeley and Los Angeles.
De Lacy, Phillip. 1939. "The Epicurean Analysis of Language." *AJP* 60:85–92.
———. 1948. "Stoic Views of Poetry." *AJP*:241–71.
Della Corte, Francesco, ed. 1984–91. *Enciclopedia Virgiliana*. 6 vols. Rome.
Depew, Mary. 1993. "Mimesis and Aetiology in Callimachus' *Hymns*." Pp. 57–77 in *Callimachus: Hellenistica Groningana*, vol. 1, ed. M.A. Harder, R.F. Regtuit, and G.C. Wakker. Groningen.
Dilthey, C. 1863. *De Callimachi Cydippe*. Leipzig.
Dimock, George E., Jr. 1962. "The Name of Odysseus." Pp. 106–21 in *Homer: A Collection of Critical Essays*, ed. G. Steiner and R. Fagles. Englewood Cliffs, N.J.
———. 1989. *The Unity of the "Odyssey."* Amherst.
Dodds, E.R. 1960. *Euripides: Bacchae*. Oxford.
Doig, George. 1965. "Vergil, *Georgics*, I, 491–2." *AJP* 86:85–88.
———. 1968. "Vergil's Art and the Greek Language." *CJ* 64:1–6.
Doob, Penelope Reed. 1990. *The Idea of the Labyrinth from Classical Antiquity through the Middle Ages*. Ithaca.
Dougherty, Carol. 1991. "Linguistic Colonialism in Aeschylus' *Aetnaeae*." *GRBS* 32:119–32.
———. 1992. "When Rain Falls from the Clear Blue Sky: Riddles and Colonization Oracles." *CA* 11:28–44.
———. 1993. *The Poetics of Colonization: From City to Text in Archaic Greece*. New York.
Du Quesnay, Ian M. Le M. 1979. "From Polyphemus to Corydon: Virgil, *Eclogue* 2, and the *Idylls* of Theocritus." Pp. 35–69 and 206–21 in *Creative Imitation and Latin Literature*, ed. David West and Tony Woodman. Cambridge.
———. 1981. "Vergil's First *Eclogue*." *PLLS* 3:29–182.
Du Quesnay, Ian M. Le M., et al. 1977. "Topics in the *Aeneid*." *LCM* 2:138–40.

Duckworth, George E. 1952. *The Nature of Roman Comedy: A Study in Popular Entertainment.* Princeton.

Due, Otto Stern. 1973. "Zur Etymologisierung in der *Aeneis.*" Pp. 270–79 in *Classica et Mediaevalia Francisco Blatto Septuagenario Dedicata.* Copenhagen.

Dyck, Andrew R. 1993. "The Fragments of Heliodorus Homericus." *HSCP* 95:1–64.

Eden, P.T. 1975. *A Commentary on Virgil: Aeneid VIII. Mnem.* Supplement 35. Leiden.

Edwards, Mark W. 1960. "The Expression of Stoic Ideas in the *Aeneid.*" *Phoenix* 14:151–65.

———. 1987. *Homer: Poet of the Iliad.* Baltimore.

Egan, Rory B. 1983. "Arms and Etymology in *Aeneid* 11." *Vergilius* 29:19–26.

Ellis, Robinson. 1878. *Catulli Veronensis Liber.* 2d edition. Oxford.

Ellis, Vivien E. 1985. "The Poetic Map of Rome in Virgil Aeneid 8." M. Litt. thesis, University of Newcastle upon Tyne.

Enk, P.J. 1962. *Sexti Propertii Elegiarum Liber Secundus.* Leiden.

Erbse, Hartmut, ed. 1969–88. *Scholia Graeca in Homeri Iliadem.* 7 vols. Berlin.

Ernout, A., and A. Meillet. 1967. *Dictionnaire étymologique de la langue latine.* Paris.

Farrell, Joseph. 1988. "Lucretius, *DRN* 5.44 *insinuandum.*" *CQ* 38:179–85.

———. 1991. *Vergil's "Georgics" and the Traditions of Ancient Epic: The Art of Allusion in Literary History.* Oxford.

Feeney, D.C. 1984. "The Reconciliations of Juno." *CQ* n.s. 34:179–94.

———. 1986. "History and Revelation in Vergil's Underworld." *PCPS* 32:1–24.

———. 1986a. "'Stat magni nominis umbra': Lucan on the Greatness of Pompeius Magnus." *CQ* 36:239–43.

———. 1991. *The Gods in Epic: Poets and Critics of the Classical Tradition.* Oxford.

Finkelpearl, Ellen. 1990. "Psyche, Aeneas, and an Ass: Apuleius *Metamorphoses* 6.10–21." *TAPA* 120:333–47.

Fitzgerald, William. 1984. "Aeneas, Daedalus, and the Labyrinth." *Arethusa* 17:51–65.

Fletcher, Frank. 1961. *Virgil Aeneid VI.* Oxford.

Forbiger, A. 1873–75. *P. Virgilii Maronis Opera.* Vols. 2 and 3. 4th ed. Leipzig.

Fordyce, C.J. 1932. "Puns on Names in Greek." *CJ* 28:44–46.

———. 1932a. "Plays on Names In Greek." *CJ* 28:290.

———. 1961. *Catullus: A Commentary.* Oxford.

———. 1977. *P. Vergili Maronis Aeneidos Libri VII–VIII with a Commentary.* Ed. John D. Christie. Oxford.

Fowler, D.P. "An Acrostic in Vergil (*Aeneid* 7.601–604)?" *CQ* 33:298.

Fraenkel, Eduard. 1948. Rev. of E.K. Rand et al., *Serviani in Vergilii Carmina Commentarii.* Part I. *JRS* 39:131–43.

Fraser, P.M. 1972. *Ptolemaic Alexandria.* 3 vols. Oxford.

Frazer, J.G. 1931. *Ovid's Fasti.* Cambridge, Mass.

Frede, Michael. 1978. "Principles of Stoic Grammar." Pp. 27–75 in *The Stoics,* ed. J. Rist. Berkeley and Los Angeles.

Friedländer, Paul. 1941. "The Pattern of Sound and Atomistic Theory in Lucretius." *AJP* 62:16–34.

Funaioli, Hyginus. 1907. *Grammaticae Romanae Fragmenta.* Leipzig.

Gaisford, T., ed. 1848. *Etymologicum Magnum*. Oxford.
Gaisser, Julia Haig. 1993. *Catullus and His Renaissance Readers*. New York
Gantat, Kajetan. 1971. "Ucalegonte in Virgilio, Omero e Giovenale." *AAM* n.s. 39:1–6.
Garson, R.W. 1971. "Theocritean Elements in Virgil's *Eclogues*." *CQ* 21:188–203.
Gelzer, Thomas. 1993. "Transformations." Pp. 130–51 in Bulloch et al. (1993).
Geymonat, Mario. 1993. "Callimachus at the End of Aeneas' Narration." *HSCP* 95:323–31.
Giangrande, G. 1981. *Scripta Minora Alexandrina*. Vol. 2. Amsterdam.
Gini, Anthony. 1989. "Philosophy and Wordplay in the Epistles of Horace." Ph.D. diss., Brown University.
Goetz, G., and G. Gundermann, eds. 1888–1923. *Corpus Glossariorum Latinorum*. Leipzig.
Goldhill, Simon. 1984. *Language, Sexuality, Narrative: The "Oresteia."* Cambridge.
Gow, A.S.F. 1950. *Theocritus: Edited with a Translation and Commentary*. Cambridge.
Gow, A.S.F., and A. F. Scholfield. 1963. *Nicander: The Poems and Poetical Fragments*. Cambridge.
Gransden, K.W. 1976. *Virgil: Aeneid Book VIII*. Cambridge.
Griffith, Mark. 1983. *Aeschylus: Prometheus Bound*. Cambridge.
Griffiths, C. 1969–70. "Myricae." *PVS* 9:1–19.
Hanssen, Jens S.T. 1948. "Vergilius ἐπιθέτως λέγων: Vergilian Notes 2." *SO* 26:113–25.
Hardie, Philip R. 1986. *Virgil's Aeneid: Cosmos and Imperium*. Oxford.
———. 1987. "Ships and Ship Names in the *Aeneid*." Pp. 163–71 in *Homo Viator: Classical Essays for John Bramble*, ed. M. Whitby, Philip Hardie, and M. Whitby.
———. 1992. "Augustan Poets and the Mutability of Rome." Pp. 59–82 in *Roman Poetry and Propaganda in the Age of Augustus*, ed. Anton Powell. London.
———. 1993. *The Epic Successors of Virgil: A Study in the Dynamics of a Tradition*. Cambridge.
———. 1994. *Virgil: Aeneid Book IX*. Cambridge.
Harrison, S.J. 1990. "Dictamnum and Moly: Vergil *Aeneid* 12.411–19." *Papers of the Leeds International Latin Seminar* 6:45–47.
———. 1991. *Vergil: Aeneid 10*. Oxford.
Haslam, Michael. 1992. "Hidden Signs: Aratus *Diosemeiai* 45ff., Vergil *Georgics* 1.424ff." *HSCP* 94:199–204.
———. 1994. "The Homer Lexicon of Apollonius Sophista: I. Composition and Constituents." *CP* 89:1–45.
Haywood, Mark S. 1983. "Wordplay between ΘΕΩ/ΘΟΟΣ and ΘΕΟΣ in Homer." *PLLS* 4:215–18.
Hecht, R. 1882. "De etymologiis apud poetas Graecos obviis." Ph.D. diss., University of Konigsberg.
Heinze, Richard. 1915. *Virgils epische Technik*. 3d ed. Leipzig.
Henderson, John. 1988. "Lucan/The Word at War." Pp. 122–64 in *The Imperial Muse: Ramus Essays on Roman Literature of the Empire, to Juvenal through Ovid*, ed. A.J. Boyle. Berwick, Victoria.

Hendry, Michael. 1992. "More on Puns in the Cleopatra Ode." *Mnem.* 45:529–31.
———. N.d. "A Martial Acronym in Ennius." Forthcoming in *LCM.*
Henrichs, Albert. 1989. "Zur Perhorreszierung des Wassers der Styx bei Aischylos und Vergil." *ZPE* 78:1–29.
———. 1993. "Response" to Gelzer (1993) and Parsons (1993). Pp. 171–95 in Bulloch et al. (1993).
Henry, James. 1873–92. *Aeneidea, or Critical, Exegetical, and Aesthetical Remarks on the Aeneid.* 5 vols. Dublin.
Heubeck, Alfred, and Arie Hoekstra. 1989. *A Commentary on Homer's Odyssey.* Vol. 2, books 9–16. Oxford.
Hexter, Ralph. 1992. "Sidonian Dido." Pp. 332–84 in *Innovations of Antiquity,* ed. R. Hexter and D. Selden. New York.
Hinds, Stephen. 1985. "Booking the Return Trip: Ovid and *Tristia* 1." *PCPS* 211, n.s. 31:13–32.
———. 1987. *The Metamorphosis of Persephone: Ovid and the Self-Conscious Muse.* Cambridge.
———. N.d. *Ovid: Tristia I.* Forthcoming, Cambridge.
Hirtzel, F.A. 1900. *P. Vergili Maronis Opera.* Oxford.
Holland, Louise Adams. 1935. "Place Names and Heroes in the *Aeneid.*" *AJP* 56:202–15.
Hollis, A.S. 1990. *Callimachus: Hecale.* Oxford.
———. 1992. "Hellenistic Colouring in Virgil's *Aeneid.*" *HSCP* 94:269–85.
———. 1993. "Parthenius on the Saronic Gulf." *ZPE* 95:50–51.
Hopkinson, N. 1984. *Callimachus: Hymn to Demeter.* Cambridge.
———. 1984a. "Rhea in Callimachus' *Hymn to Zeus.*" *JHS* 104:176–77.
———. 1984b. "Callimachus' *Hymn to Zeus.*" *CQ* 34:139–48.
———. 1988. *A Hellenistic Anthology.* Cambridge.
Horsfall, Nicholas M. 1973. "Three Notes on Horace's Epodes." *Philologus* 117:12–14.
———. 1978. Rev. of R. Daut, *Imago. CR* 28:163.
———. 1981. "Virgil and the Conquest of Chaos." *Antichthon* 15:141–50.
———. 1986. Rev. of Ahl (1985). *JRS* 76:322–23.
———. 1987. "Caeculus and the Foundation of Praeneste." Pp. 49–62 in N.M. Horsfall and J.N. Bremmer (1987).
———. 1988. "Camilla, o i limiti dell'Invenzione." *Athenaeum* 66:31–51.
———. 1989. "Aeneas the Colonist." *Vergilius* 35:8–27.
———. 1990. "Virgil and the Illusory Footnote." *PLLS* 6:49–63.
———. 1991. *Virgilio: L'epopea in alambicco.* Naples.
———. 1991a. Rev. of Thomas (1988). *RFIC* 119:211–17.
———. 1991b. "Virgil and the Poetry of Explanations." *G&R* 38:203–11.
———. 1991c. "Virgil, Parthenius, and the Art of Mythological Reference." *Vergilius* 37:31–36.
Horsfall, N.M., and J.N. Bremmer. 1987. *Roman Myth and Mythography. BICS* Supplement 52. London.
Hunter, Richard L. 1986. "Apollo and the Argonauts: Two Notes on Ap. Rhod. 2, 669–719." *MH* 43:50–60.
———. 1989. *Apollonius of Rhodes: Argonautica Book III.* Cambridge.

———. 1991. "'Breast Is Best': Catullus 64.18." *CQ* n.s. 41:254–55.

Jackson, B. Darrell. 1975. *Augustine: De Dialectica*. Dordrecht.

Jacobson, Howard. 1982. "Vergil, *Georgics* 3.280–81." *MH* 39:217.

Johnson, W.R. 1976. *Darkness Visible: A Study of Vergil's "Aeneid."* Berkeley and Los Angeles.

Johnston, Patricia A. 1980. *Vergil's Agricultural Golden Age: A Study of the Georgics*. Leiden.

Johnston, S.I. 1991. "Crossroads." *ZPE* 88:217–24.

Kahn, Charles H. 1979. *The Art and Thought of Heraclitus*. Cambridge.

Kaster, Robert A. 1980. "The Grammarian's Authority." *CP* 75:216–41.

Keith, A.M. 1991. "Etymological Play on *Ingens* in Ovid, Vergil, and *Octavia*." *AJP* 112:73–76.

———. 1992. *The Play of Fictions: Studies in Ovid's "Metamorphoses" Book* 2. Ann Arbor.

Keller, Otto. 1974. *Lateinische Volksetymologie und Verwandtes*. Hildesheim. Reprinted, Leipzig ed. 1891.

Kennedy, George A. 1989. "Language and Meaning in Archaic and Classical Greece." Pp. 78–91 in *The Cambridge History of Literary Criticism*, vol. 1: Classical Criticism, ed. George A. Kennedy. Cambridge.

Kenney, E.J. 1979. "*Iudicum Transferendi:* Virgil, *Aeneid* 2.469–505 and Its Antecedents." Pp. 103–20 and 224–29 in *Creative Imitation and Latin Literature*, ed. D. West and T. Woodman. Cambridge.

———. 1983. "Virgil and the Elegiac Sensibility." *ICS* 8:44–59.

———. 1986. Introduction and notes to *Ovid, Metamorphoses*, trans. A.D. Melville. Oxford.

———. 1989. "A Prophet without Honour?" *CQ* 39:274–75.

Kerferd, G.B. 1981. *The Sophistic Movement*. Cambridge.

Kidd, I.G. 1988. *Posidonius: II: The Commentary*. 2 vols. Cambridge.

King, Joy K. 1980. "The Two Galluses of Propertius' Monobiblos." *Philologus* 124:212–14.

Kirk, G.S. 1985. *The Iliad: A Commentary*. Vol. 1, books 1–4. Cambridge.

Kleinknecht, H. 1963. "Laokoon." In *Wege zu Vergil*. Darmstadt. Reprinted, *Hermes* 79 (1944) 66–111.

Knauer, Georg Nicolaus. 1964. *Die Aeneis und Homer: Studien zur poetischen Technik Vergils mit Listen der Homerzitate in der Aeneis*. Hypomnemata 7. Göttingen.

Knight, W.F.J. 1934. "*Clarus Aquilo*." *CR* 48:124–25.

———. 1944. *Roman Vergil*. London.

Knox, Bernard M.W. 1950. "The Serpent and the Flame." *AJP* 71:379–400.

Knox, Peter E. 1986. *Ovid's "Metamorphoses" and the Traditions of Augustan Poetry*. Cambr. Philol. Soc. Suppl. Vol. 11. Cambridge.

———. 1991. Rev. of McKeown (1987) and (1989). *CP* 86 (1991) 239–48.

Koenen, Ludwig. 1983. "Die Adaptation Ägyptischer Königsideologie am Ptolemäerhof." Pp. 143–90 in *Egypt and the Hellenistic World*. Studia Hellenistica 27. Leuven.

Konstan, David. 1973. *Some Aspects of Epicurean Psychology*. Leiden.

Koster, Severin. 1983. "Die Etymologien des Properz." Pp. 47–54 in *Tessera: Sechs*

*Beiträge zur Poesie und poetischen Theorie der Antike.* Erlanger Forschungen: Reihe A Geisteswissenschaften 30 Erlangen.

Köves-Zulauf, Thomas. 1978. "Camilla." *Gymn.* 85:182–205, 408–36.

Kraggerud, Egil. 1960. "Einige Namen in der Aeneis." *SO* 36:30–39.

———. 1965. "Caeneus und der Heroinenkatalog, Aeneis VI 440 ff." *SO* 40:66–71.

———. 1992. "Which Julius Caesar? On *Aen.* 1, 286–296." *SO* 67:103–12.

Kranz, Walther. 1933. *Stasimon: Untersuchungen zu Forum und Gehalt der Griechischen Tragödie.* Berlin.

Kristol, Susan Scheinberg. 1990. *"Labor" and "Fortuna" in Vergil's "Aeneid."* New York.

Lapp, Friedrich. 1965. "De Callimachi Cyrenaei Tropis et Figuris." Ph.D. diss., University of Bonn.

Lascu, N. 1961. "Ovidio linguiste." *Studii Clasice* 3:305–11.

Lendle, Otto. 1957. *Die "Pandorasage" bei Hesiod.* Würzburg.

Levin, D.N. 1971. *Apollonius' Argonautica Re-examined. I: The Neglected First and Second Books. Mnem.* Supplement 13. Leiden.

Levitan, William. 1978. "Plexed Artistry: Three Aratean Acrostics." *Glyph* 5:55–68.

———. 1993. "Give up the Beginning? Juno's Mindful Wrath (*Aeneid* 1.37)." *LCM* 18:14–15.

Linderski, Jerzy. 1992. "Vergil and Dionysius." *Vergilius* 38:3–11.

Lindsay, W.M. 1928. "Aquilo, the Black Wind." *CR* 42:20.

Livrea, Enrico. 1973. *Apollonii Rhodii Argonauticon Liber IV.* Florence.

Lloyd-Jones, Hugh. 1990. "A Hellenistic Miscellany." Pp. 231–49 in *Greek Comedy, Hellenistic Literature, Greek Religion, and Miscellanea: The Academic Papers of Sir Hugh Lloyd-Jones.* Oxford. Reprinted from *SIFC* 3d ser., 2 (1984) 52–71.

Long, Anthony A. 1992. "Stoic Readings of Homer." Pp. 41–66 in *Homer's Ancient Readers: The Hermeneutics of Greek Epic's Earliest Exegetes,* ed. R. Lamberton and J. Keaney. Princeton.

Lyne, R.O.A.M. 1987. *Further Voices in Vergil's "Aeneid."* Oxford.

———. 1989. *Words and the Poet: Characteristic Techniques of Style in Vergil's "Aeneid."* Oxford.

Maass, E., ed. 1958. *Commentarium in Aratum Reliquiae.* Berlin.

MacDowell, D.M. 1971. *Aristophanes' Wasps.* Oxford.

Mackail, J.W. 1912. "Vergil's Use of the Word *ingens.*" *CR* 26:251–54.

———. 1930. *The Aeneid: Edited with Introduction and Commentary.* Oxford.

Mackie, C.J. 1992. "Vergil's Dirae, South Italy, and Etruria." *Phoenix* 46:352–61.

Macleod, C.W. 1979. "Horace and the Sibyl (*Epode* 16.2)." *CQ* 29:220–21.

———. 1982. *Homer: Iliad Book XXIV.* Cambridge.

Malamud, Martha. 1989. *A Poetics of Transformation: Prudentius and Classical Mythology.* Ithaca.

Maltby, Robert. 1991. *A Lexicon of Ancient Latin Etymologies.* ARCA Classical and Medieval Texts, Papers, and Monographs 25. Leeds.

———. 1993. "Varro's Attitude to Latin Derivations from Greek." *PLLS* 7:47–60.

———. 1993a. "The Limits of Etymologising." *Aevum Antiquum* 6:257–75.

Marouzeau, Jules. 1940. "Virgile linguiste." Pp. 259–65 in *Mélanges de philologie et de littérature anciennes offerts à Alfred Ernout.* Paris.

———. 1949. *Quelques aspects de la formation du Latin littéraire.* Paris.

Martin, Jean, ed. 1974. *Scholia in Aratum Vetera.* Stuttgart.

McCartney, E.S. 1918–19. "Puns and Plays on Proper Names." *CJ* 14:343–58.

———. 1927. "Modifiers That Reflect the Etymology of the Word Modified, with Special Reference to Lucretius." *CP* 22:184–200.

McGushin, P. 1964. "Virgil and the Spirit of Endurance." *AJP* 85:225–53.

McKeown, J.C. 1987. *Ovid: Amores.* Vol. I: *Text and Prolegomena.* Liverpool.

———. 1989. *Ovid: Amores.* Vol. II: *A Commentary on Book One.* Leeds.

———. 1994. "Sound-Imitation: A Neglected Technique in Ovid and Other Roman Poets." Paper delivered at the 125th Annual Meeting of the American Philological Association. Atlanta.

McLennan, G.R. 1977. *Callimachus: Hymn to Zeus: Introduction and Commentary.* Rome.

Meineke, Augustus. 1964. *Analecta Alexandrina, sive Commentationes de Euphorio Chalcidensi Rhiano Cretensi Alexandro Aetolo Parthenio Nicaeno.* Hildesheim. Reprint of 1843 Berlin edition.

Merkelbach, R. 1972. "Palinurus." *ZPE* 9:83.

Mineur, W. 1984. *Callimachus, Hymn to Delos. Mnem.* Supplement 73. Leiden.

Moles, J.L. 1983. "Virgil, Pompey, and the *Histories* of Asinius Pollio." *CW* 76:287–88.

Møland, H. 1956. "Die Hyrtacide in der Aeneis." *SO* 32:69–80.

———. 1957. "Nisus, Euryalus und Andere Namen in der *Aeneis.*" *SO* 33:87–109.

———. 1960. "Zu den Namen in der Aeneis." *SO* 36:21–29.

———. 1964. "Zu Aeneis VI 601ff." *SO* 39:5–12.

———. 1965. "Zur Aeneis (IX 772; IV 236)." *SO* 40:72–74.

———. 1968. "Die Carmina des Horaz in der Aeneis." *SO* 42:102–12.

———. 1973. "Zu Einigen Stellen in der Aeneis." *SO* 48:7–23.

Morwood, J.H.W. 1985. "Aeneas and Mount Atlas." *JRS* 75:51–59.

Moskalew, Walter. 1982. *Formular Language and Poetic Design in the "Aeneid." Mnem.* Suppl. 73. Leiden.

———. 1990. "Myrmidons, Dolopes, and Danaans: Wordplay in *Aeneid* 2." *CQ* 40:275–79.

Mühmelt, M. 1965. *Griechische Grammatik in der Vergilerklärung. Zetemata* Heft 37. Munich.

Murgia, Charles E. 1967. "Critical Notes on the Text of Servius' Commentary on *Aeneid* III–V." *HSCP* 72:311–50.

———. 1987. "The Servian Commentary on *Aeneid* 3 Revisited." *HSCP* 72:303–31.

Murrin, Michael. 1980. *The Allegorical Epic: Essays in Its Rise and Decline.* Chicago.

Mustard, Wilfred P. 1892. *The Etymologies in the Servian Commentary to Vergil.* Colorado Springs.

Myers, K. Sara. 1992. "The Lizard and the Owl: An Etymological Pair in Ovid, *Metamorphoses* Book 5." *AJP* 113:63–68.

———. 1994. "*Ultimus ardor:* Pomona and Vertumnus in Ovid's *Met.* 14.623–771." *CJ* 89:225–50.

———. 1994a. *Ovid's Causes: Cosmogony and Aetiology in the "Metamorphoses."* Ann Arbor.

Mynors, R.A.B. 1972. *P. Vergili Maronis Opera.* 2d ed. Oxford.

———. 1990. *Virgil: Georgics: Edited with a Commentary.* Oxford.

Nadeau, Y. 1982. "Caesaries Berenices (or, the Hair of the God)." *Latomus* 41:101–3.

Nagy, Gregory. 1979. *The Best of the Achaeans.* Baltimore.

Nisbet, R.G.M. 1990. Rev. of Thomas (1988). *CR* 40:260–63.

Nisbet, R.G.M., and Margaret Hubbard. 1970. *A Commentary on Horace: Odes, Book 1.* Oxford.

Norden Eduard. 1915. *Ennius und Vergilius: Kriegsbilder aus Roms grosser Zeit.* Leipzig/Berlin.

———. 1966. "Vergils Aeneis im Lichte ihrer Zeit." In *Kleine Schriften.* Berlin. Reprinted from *NJb* 7 (1901) 249–82, 313–34.

———. 1981. *P. Vergilius Maro Aeneis Buch VI.* 7th ed. Stuttgart.

Ogilvie, R.M. 1970. *A Commentary on Livy Books 1–5.* Oxford.

O'Hara, James J. 1990. *Death and the Optimistic Prophecy in Vergil's "Aeneid."* Princeton.

———. 1990a. "The Significance of Vergil's *Acidalia mater,* and *Venus Erycina* in Catullus and Ovid." *HSCP* 93:335–42.

———. 1990b. "Etymological Wordplay in Apollonius of Rhodes, *Aeneid* 3, and *Georgics* 1." *Phoenix* 44:370–76.

———. 1990c. "Homer, Hesiod, Apollonius, and *Neritos ardua* at *Aeneid* 3.271." *Vergilius* 36:31–34.

———. 1992. "Naming the Stars at *Georgics* 1.127–28 and *Fasti* 5.163–82." *AJP* 113:47–61.

———. 1993. "A Neglected Conjecture at *Aeneid* 12.882." *RhM* 36:371–74.

———. 1993a. "Medicine for the Madness of Dido and Gallus: Tentative Suggestions on *Aeneid* 4." *Vergilius* 39:12–24.

———. 1994. Rev. of E. Courtney, *The Fragmentary Latin Poets. CP* 89:384–91.

———. 1994a. "They Might Be Giants: Inconsistency and Indeterminacy in Vergil's War in Italy." In *Studies in Roman Epic,* ed. H. Roisman and J. Roisman, *Colby Quarterly* 30:206–32.

———. 1994b. "Temporal Distortions, 'Fatal' Ambiguity, and *Iulius Caesar* at *Aeneid* 1.286–96." *SO* 69:72–82.

———. 1996. "Vergil's Best Reader? Ovidian Commentary on Vergilian Etymological Wordplay." Forthcoming in *CJ* 91.

———. N.d. "An Unconvincing Etymological Argument about Aeneas and the Gates of Sleep." Forthcoming in *Phoenix.*

Olson, S. Douglas. 1992. "Names and Naming in Aristophanic Comedy." *CQ* 42:304–19.

Page, T.E. 1894. *The Aeneid of Vergil: Books I–VI.* London.

———. 1900. *The Aeneid of Vergil: Books VII–XII.* London.

Paratore, Ettore. 1978–83. *Virgilio: Eneide.* 6 vols. Milan.

———. 1965. *P. Vergili Maronis Bucolica et Georgica.* London. Reprinted, London ed. 1898.

Parsons, Peter. 1993. "Identities in Diversity." Pp. 152–70 in Bulloch et al. (1993).

Paschalis, Michael. 1995. "Names and Death in Horace's *Odes.*" *CW* 88:181–90.

Paskiewicz, T.M. 1988. "Aetia in the Second Book of Apollonius' *Argonautica.*" *ICS* 13:57–61.

Patterson, Annabel. 1990. "Intention." Pp. 135–46 in *Critical Terms for Literary Study*, ed. Frank Lentricchia and Thomas McLaughlin. Chicago.
Pease, A.S. 1935. *Publi Vergili Maronis Aeneidos Liber Quartus*. Cambridge, Mass.
———. 1963. *M. Tulli Ciceronis De Divinatione*. 2 vols. Darmstadt. Reprinted, Illinois ed. 1920–23.
———. 1979. *M. Tulli Ciceronis De Natura Deorum*. 2 vols. New York. Reprinted, Cambridge, Mass. ed. 1958.
Peradotto, John J. 1969. "Cledonomancy in the *Oresteia*." *AJP* 90:1–21.
———. 1990. *Man in the Middle Voice: Name and Narration in the "Odyssey."* Princeton.
Petersmann, H. 1987. "Demeter in Dodona und Thrakien: Ein Nachtrag." *WS* 100:5–12.
Petrini, Mark J. N.d. *The Child and the Hero: Coming of Age in Catullus and Vergil*. Forthcoming, Ann Arbor.
Pfaffel, Wilhelm. 1981. *Quartus gradus etymologiae: Untersuchungen zur Etymologie Varros in "de Lingua Latina."* Beiträge zur Klassichen Philologie Heft 131. Königstein.
Pfeiffer, Rudolf. 1949–53. *Callimachus*. 2 vols. Oxford.
———. 1968. *History of Classical Scholarship: From the Beginnings to the End of the Hellenistic Age*. Oxford.
Platnauer, M. 1938. *Euripides: Iphigenia in Tauris*. Oxford.
Pollmann, K. 1993. "Etymologie, Allegorese und Epische Struktur: Zu den Toren der Träume bei Homer und Vergil." *Philologus* 137:232–51.
Porte, Danielle. 1985. *L'étiologie religieuse dans les "Fastes" d'Ovide*. Paris.
Porter, James I. 1992. "Hermeneutic Lines and Circles: Aristarchus and Crates on the Exegesis of Homer." Pp. 67–114 in *Homer's Ancient Readers: The Hermeneutics of Greek Epic's Earliest Exegetes*, ed. R. Lamberton and J. Keaney. Princeton.
Putnam, Michael C.J. 1965. "The Riddle of Damoetas (Virgil, Ecl. 3, 104–105)." *Mnem*. 18:150–54.
———. 1985. "Possessiveness, Sexuality, and Heroism in the *Aeneid*." *Vergilius* 31:1–21.
———. 1986. *Artifices of Eternity: Horace's Fourth Book of Odes*. Ithaca.
———. 1990. "Virgil's Lapiths." *CQ* 40:562–66.
———. 1993. "The Language of Horace *Odes* 1.24." *CW* 88:123–35.
———. 1994. "Structure and Design in Horace *Odes* 1.17." *CW* 87: 357–75.
Quandt, Kenneth. 1981. "Some Puns in Aristotle." *TAPA* 111:179–96.
Quincey, J.H. 1963. "Etymologica." *RhM* 106:142–48.
Rank, Louis P. 1951. *Etymologiseering en Verwante Verschijnselen bij Homerus*. Assen.
Raven, D. 1975. "A Note on Vergil, Aen. IV 9–14." *AC* 18:147–48.
Rawson, Elizabeth. 1978. "The Identity Problems of Q. Cornificius." *CQ* 28:188–201.
———. 1985. *Intellectual Life in the Late Roman Republic*. Baltimore.
Reardon, B.P. 1989. *Collected Ancient Greek Novels*. Berkeley and Los Angeles.
Reckford, Kenneth. 1966. "Horace, Odes 1.34: An Interpretation." *Studies in Philology* 63:524–25.
Redfern, Walter. 1984. *Puns*. New York.

Rehm, Bernhard. 1932. *Das geographische Bild des alten Italiens in Vergils Aeneis. Philologus* Suppl. Band 24, Heft 2. Leipzig.

Reitzenstein, Richard. 1909. "Etymologika." *RE* v. 6 col. 807–817.

Renehan, R. 1987. "Curae Callimacheae." Rev. of Hopkinson (1984) and Bulloch (1985). *CP* 82:240–54.

Renkagos, A. 1992. "Homerische Wörter bei Kallimachos." *ZPE* 94:21–47.

Ribbeck, Otto. 1966. *P. Vergili Maronis Opera.* Hildesheim. Reprinted, Leipzig ed. 1894–95.

Richardson, L.J.D. 1942. "Direct Citation of Ennius in Vergil." *CQ* 36:40–42.

Richardson, N.J. 1974. *The Homeric Hymn to Demeter.* Oxford.

———. 1975. "Homeric Professors in the Age of the Sophists." *PCPS* 21:65–81.

Robinson, D.E. 1969. "Topics in Sophocles' *Philoctetes.*" *CQ* 19:34–56.

Roessel, David. 1990. "The Significance of the Name Cerinthus in the Poems of Sulpicia." *TAPA* 120:243–50.

Roscher, W.H. 1884–1937. *Ausführliches Lexicon der griechischen und römischen Mythologie.* Leipzig.

Rosen, Ralph M., and Joseph Farrell. 1986. "Acontius, Milanion, and Gallus: Vergil *Ecl.* 10.52–61." *TAPA* 116:241–54.

Rosenstock, Bruce. 1992. "Fathers and Sons: Irony in the *Cratylus.*" *Arethusa* 25:385–417.

Ross, David O., Jr. 1973. "*Uriosque apertos:* A Catullan Gloss." *Mnem.* 26:60–62.

———. 1975. *Backgrounds to Augustan Poetry: Gallus, Elegy, and Rome.* Cambridge.

———. 1975a. "The *Culex* and *Moretum* as Post-Augustan Literary Parodies." *HSCP* 79:235–63.

———. 1987. *Virgil's Elements: Physics and Poetry in the "Georgics."* Princeton.

Rusten, Jeffrey S. 1982. *Dionysius Scytobrachion.* Opladen.

Saunders, Catharine. 1940. "Sources of the Names of Trojans and Latins in Vergil's *Aeneid.*" *TAPA* 71:537–55.

Savage, J.J.H. 1925. "The Scholia in the Virgil of Tours Bernensis 165." *HSCP* 36:91–164.

———. 1925a. "Notes of Some Unpublished Scholia in a Paris Manuscript of Vergil." *TAPA* 56:229–41.

———. 1958. "The Art of the Third *Eclogue* of Vergil (55–111)." *TAPA* 89:142–58.

Schibli, Hermann S. 1990. *Pherekydes of Syros.* Oxford.

Schlunk, Robin. 1974. *The Homeric Scholia and the Aeneid.* Ann Arbor.

Schmid, Wilhelm. 1934. *Geschichte der Griechische Literatur.* Teil 1, Band 2. Munich.

*Scholia Bernensia ad Vergili Bucolica atque Georgica,* ed. H. Hagen. 1967. Hildesheim. Reprinted, Leipzig ed. 1867.

Scott, Kenneth. 1941. "The Sidus Iulium and the Apotheosis of Caesar." *CP* 36:257–72.

Segal, Charles P. 1982. *Dionysiac Poetics and Euripides' "Bacchae."* Princeton.

———. 1986. *Pindar's Mythmaking: The Fourth Pythian Ode.* Princeton.

Servius. 1881–84. *Commentarii in Vergilii Carmina.* Ed. G. Thilo and H. Hagen. 2 vols. Leipzig.

———. 1946. *Serviani in Vergilii Carmina Commentarii.* Ed. E.K. Rand et al. Vol 2. Lancaster.

———. 1965. *Serviani in Vergilii Carmina Commentarii.* Ed. A.F. Stocke, A.H. Travis et al. Vol. 3. Oxford.

Shackleton Bailey, David R. 1956. *Propertiana.* Cambridge.

Shechter, Stanley. 1975. "The *Aition* and Virgil's *Georgics.*" *TAPA* 105:346–91.

Sider, David. 1988. "Vergil's *Aeneid* and Hesiod's *Theogony.*" *Vergilius* 34:15–24.

Skulsky, Susan. 1985. "*Invitus, regina . . .* : Aeneas and the Love of Rome." *AJP* 106:447–55.

Skutsch, Otto. 1968. "De Fulminum Appellatione Scipionibus Indita." Pp.145–50 in *Studia Enniana.* London.

———. 1972. "Readings and Interpretations in the *Annals.*" Pp. 3–37 in *Ennius.* Entretiens sur l'antiquité class. 17. Geneva.

———. 1985. *The Annals of Quintus Ennius.* Oxford.

Slater, Niall. 1990. *Reading Petronius.* Baltimore and London.

Snyder, Jane. 1980. *Puns and Poetry in Lucretius' de Rerum Natura.* Amsterdam.

Soubiran, Jean. 1972. *Céceron: Aratea, Fragments Poétiques.* Paris.

Springer, Carl. 1983–84. "Aratus and the Cups of Menalcas: A Note on *Eclogue* 3.42." *CJ* 79:131–34.

Stanford, W.B. 1939. *Ambiguity in Greek Literature: Studies in Theory and Practice.* Oxford.

———. 1965. *The Odyssey of Homer.* 2 vols. London.

Stanley, Keith. 1963. "Rome, Ἔρως, and the Versus Romae." *GRBS* 4:237–49.

Stanton, G.R. 1971. "*Cunctando Restituit Rem:* The Tradition about Fabius." *Antichthon* 5:49–56.

Starobinski, Jean. 1979. *Words upon Words: The Anagrams of Ferdinand de Saussure,* trans. Olivia Emmet. New Haven.

Suerbaum, Werner. 1981. "Von der Vita Vergiliana über die Accessus Vergiliani zum Zauberer Virgilius." *ANRW* II 31.2:1156–1262.

Tatum, James. 1984. "Allusion and Interpretation in *Aeneid* 6.40–476." *AJP* 105:8–14.

Taylor, Daniel J. 1974. *Declinatio: A Study of the Linguistic Theory of Marcus Terentius Varro.* Amsterdam.

Theodoridis, Christos. 1976. *Die Fragmente des Grammatikers Philoxenos.* Berlin.

Thomas, Richard F. 1979. "Theocritus, Calvus, and *Eclogue* 6." *CP* 74:337–39.

———. 1982. *Lands and Peoples in Roman Poetry: The Ethnographical Tradition.* Camb. Phil. Soc. Suppl. vol. 7.

———. 1982a. "Catullus and the Polemics of Poetic Reference." *AJP* 103:144–54.

———. 1982b. "Gadflies (Virg. *Geo.* 3.146–48)." *HSCP* 86:81–85.

———. 1986. "Virgil's *Georgics* and the Art of Reference." *HCSP* 90:171–98.

———. 1988. *Virgil: Georgics.* 2 vols. Cambridge.

———. 1988a. "Tree Violation and Ambivalence in Virgil." *TAPA* 118:261–73.

———. 1988b. "Vergil's 'White Bird' and the Alexandrian Reference (*G.* 2.319–20)." *CP* 83:214–17.

———. 1992. Rev. of Harrison (1991). *Vergilius* 38:134–44.

Thornton, Agathe. 1976. *The Living Universe: Gods and Men in Vergil's Aeneid. Mnem.* Suppl. 46. Leiden.

Tissol, Garth. 1992. "An Allusion to Callimachus' *Aetia* in Virgil's *Aeneid* 11." *HSCP* 94:263–68.

Toll, Katharine. 1989. "What's Love Got to Do with It? The Invocation to Erato, and Patriotism in the *Aeneid*." *QUCC* 33:107–18.

Toohey, Peter. 1984. "Politics, Prejudice, and Trojan Genealogies: Varro, Hyginus, and Horace." *Arethusa* 17:5–28.

Tracy, H.L. 1963. "Seven Homecomings." *Vergilius* 9:28–31.

Tupet, Anne-Marie. 1976. *La magie dans la póesie latine.* Paris.

Van Sickle, John. 1978. *The Design of Virgil's Bucolics.* Rome.

Verducci, Florence. 1984. "On the Sequence of Gallus' Epigrams." *QUCC* 16:119–36.

Vernant, Jean-Pierre. 1981. "Ambiguity and Reversal: On the Enigmatic Structure of *Oedipus Rex*." In J.-P. Vernant and P. Vidal-Naquet, *Myth and Tragedy in Ancient Greece,* trans. Janet Lloyd. Atlantic Highlands, N.J.

Vine, Brent. 1986. "An Umbrian-Latin Correspondence." *HSCP* 90:111–27.

von Arnim, J., ed. 1921–24. *Stoicorum Veterum Fragmenta.* 4 vols. Leipzig.

von Duhn, M. 1957. "Die Gleichnisse in den Allectoszenen des 7. Buches von Vergils Aeneis." *Gymnasium* 64:59–83.

Von Jan (= de Ian), F. 1893. "De Callimacho Homeri Interprete." Ph.D. diss., University of Strassburg.

Wagenvoort, H.W. 1956. *Studies in Roman Literature, Culture, and Religion.* Leiden.

Walde, A., and J.B. Hofmann. 1930–56. *Lateinisches etymologisches Wörterbuch.* Heidelberg.

Wallach, Barbara Price. 1976. *Lucretius and the Diatribe against the Fear of Death: De Rerum Natura III 830–1094.* Lyon.

Waszink, J.H. 1963. "*Agmina Furiarum.*" *Harvard Theological Review* 56:7–11.

Weber, Clifford. 1987. "Metrical *Imitatio* in the Proem to the *Aeneid*." *HSCP* 91:261–71.

———. 1990. "Some Double Entendres in Ovid and Vergil." *CP* 85:209–14.

———. 1991. "Dodona Reneges: A Neglected Oxymoron in *Georgics* 1.149." *CP* 86:323–27.

———. N.d. "Roscius and the 'Roscida Dea.'" Manuscript.

Webster, T.B.L. 1970. *Sophocles: Philoctetes.* Cambridge.

Wellesley, Kenneth. 1968. "Virgil's Araxes." *CP* 63:139–41.

West, David. 1969. "Multiple-Correspondence Similes in the *Aeneid*." *JRS* 59:40–49.

West, M.L. 1966. *Hesiod: Theogony: Edited with Prolegomena and Commentary.* Oxford.

Wheeler, Stephen M. 1993. "Lost Voices: Vergil, *Aeneid* 12.718–19." *CQ* 43:451–54.

White, Heather. 1987. *Studies in the Poetry of Nicander.* Amsterdam.

White, Peter. 1988. "Julius Caesar in Augustan Rome." *Phoenix* 42:334–56

Wigodsky, Michael. 1972. *Vergil and Early Latin Poetry. Hermes* Einzelschr. 24. Wiesbaden.

Wilamowitz, Ulrich von. 1924. *Die hellenistiche Dichtung.* 2 vols. Berlin.

Williams, Frederick. 1978. *Callimachus: Hymn to Apollo.* Oxford.

Williams, Gareth. 1991. "Vocal Variations and Narrative Complexity in Ovid's Vestalia: *Fasti* 6.249–468." *Ramus* 20:183–204.

Williams, Gordon. 1968. *Tradition and Originality in Roman Poetry.* Oxford.

Williams, R.D. 1960. *P. Vergili Maronis Liber Quintus.* Oxford.

———. 1962. *P. Vergili Maronis Liber Tertius.* Oxford.

———. 1973. *The Aeneid of Vergil.* 2 vols. Basingstoke.

———. 1979. *Virgil: The Eclogues and Georgics.* New York.

Wilson, John R. 1968. "The Etymology in Euripides, *Troades,* 13–14." *AJP* 89:66–71.

Winkler, John J. 1990. "The Ephebes' Song: *Tragoidia* and *polis.*" Pp. 20–62 in *Nothing to Do with Dionysus? Athenian Drama in Its Social Context,* ed. John J. Winkler and Froma I. Zeitlin. Princeton.

Wiseman, T.P. 1974. "Legendary Genealogies in Late Republican Rome." *G&R* 21:153–64.

———. 1979. *Clio's Cosmetics: Three Studies in Greco-Roman Literature.* Leicester.

Wölfflin, E. 1887. "Das Wortspiel im Lateinischen." *Sitzungsberichte der kön. bayer. Akad. der Wissenschaften* (philos.-philol. und histor. Classe) 2:187–208.

Woodhead, William D. 1928. *Etymologizing in Greek Literature from Homer to Philo Judaeus.* Toronto.

Wright, John. 1974. *Dancing in Chains: The Stylistic Unity of the Comoedia Palliata.* Rome.

Zanker, G. 1987. *Realism in Alexandrian Poetry: A Literature and Its Audience.* London.

Zanker, Paul. 1988. *The Power of Images in the Age of Augustus.* Ann Arbor.

Zeitlin, Froma I. 1982. *Under the Sign of the Shield: Semiotics and Aeschylus' "Seven against Thebes."* Rome.

———. 1985. "The Power of Aphrodite: Eros and the Boundaries of the Self in the *Hippolytos.*" Pp. 52–11 and 189–208 in *Directions in Euripidean Criticism,* ed. Peter Burian. Durham, N.C.

Zetzel, James E.G. 1983. "Recreating the Canon: Augustan Poetry and the Alexandrian Past." *Critical Inquiry* 10:83–105.

———. 1988. Rev. of Wiseman, *Catullus and His World. CP* 83:80–85.

———. 1989. "ROMANE, MEMENTO: Justice and Judgement in *Aeneid* 6." *TAPA* 119:263–84.

# General Index

This index tries to avoid duplicating information found in the introduction's features lists, the index of words glossed, or my extensive cross-references. The introduction is more thoroughly indexed; references to the catalogue suggest that an author is not merely cited there, but at least briefly discussed. References in bold are to the main discussion of a topic, with further cross-references provided there. Romans are listed by nomen except for those with much more familiar cognomina (Varro, Cicero, Gallus).

# Index of Words Glossed

This index covers both the Vergilian examples from the catalogue and the Vergilian and non-Vergilian examples in the introduction; it includes doubtful examples, but does not include those merely listed in a footnote. Greek names, and where possible other Greek words, are assimilated to Roman forms. The remaining Greek words are listed at the end.

**Greek words**

# General Index for New Introduction and Examples

# Index of Words Glossed in New Introduction and Examples